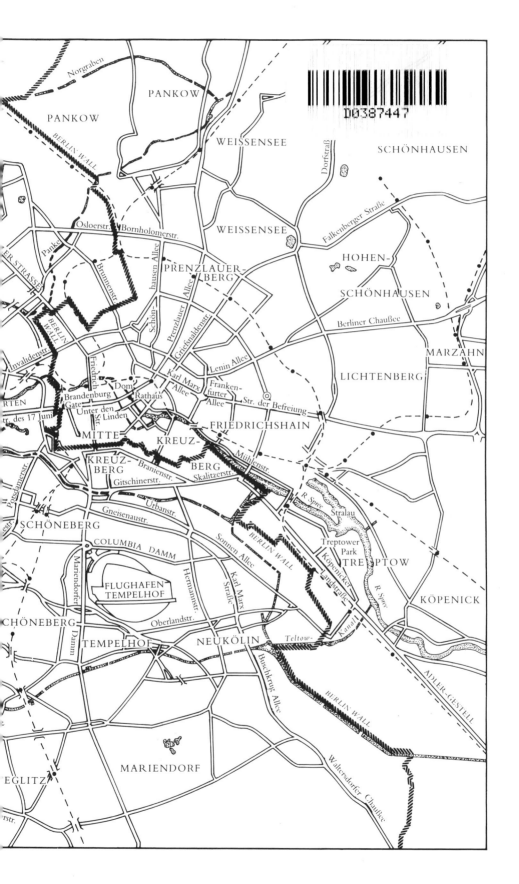

BERLIN

BERLIN

GILES MACDONOGH

ST. MARTIN'S PRESS ❧ NEW YORK

Library of Congress Cataloging-in-Publication Data

MacDonogh, Giles.
  Berlin / Giles MacDonogh.
    p. cm.
  Includes bibliographical references and index.
  ISBN 0-312-18537-5
  1. Berlin (Germany)—History. 2. Political culture—Germany—
Berlin. 3. Berlin (Germany)—Intellectual life. 4. Jews—
Germany—Social life and customs. 5. Architecture—Germany—
Berlin. 6. Berlin (Germany)—Social life and customs.
I. Title.
DD860.M22   1998   98-16068
943'.155—dc21   CIP

First published in Great Britain by Sinclair-Stevenson, an imprint of
Reed International Books Ltd

First U.S. Edition: August 1998

10 9 8 7 6 5 4 3 2 1

For Candida Brazil

Wem gelingt es? – Trübe Frage,
Der das Schicksal sich vermummt,
Wenn am unglückseligsten Tage
Blutend alles Volk verstummt.
Doch erfrischet neue Lieder,
Steht nicht länger tief gebeugt:
Denn der Boden zeugt sie wieder,
Wie von je er sie gezeugt.

Faust, II, iii, Schattiger Hain

Contents

List of Illustrations

Photographs marked with an asterisk are by the author.

Preface

The twentieth of June 1991 was post-war Berlin's day of destiny. I had an appointment that afternoon to see a well-known authority on the history of Prussia in his office in the Tiergarten. I had come to discuss the past, but our conversation drifted on to the present. That night the Bundestag was to vote on whether the capital of the reunited Germany should remain in Bonn, or migrate to Berlin, where it had been until 1945. He thought the issue cut and dried: Bonn would remain the centre of the administration; it was 'the classic split between the Catholic south and west and the Protestant north and east. Only, since the war and the changes to the German border, there were more people in the south than there were in the north-east.'

When I got back to my room I switched on the television. Deputies were coming forward to explain their reasons for voting for one or other city. Most of those I saw had opted for the former Prussian capital, but I took the professor's word for it that Bonn, the old Prussian university city in the Rhineland, would win the day. I switched off and went to Dahlem, where I was to dine with an old friend.

It was a relaxed evening, unruffled by the commotion in Bonn. Only briefly did our conversation turn to the vote. She, too, thought Bonn was a foregone conclusion. I left early to catch the *U-Bahn*. When I got out at a station in Berlin's West End, I stopped at a pub in the Brandenburger-straße for a nightcap. The atmosphere was calm. There was no hint of premature celebration; the usual bleary-eyed north Germans were staring into their beers and glasses of schnapps.

They seemed indifferent to the fate of their city. I went to bed.

The next day I took a taxi to my morning appointment. I asked the cabby who had won. 'Berlin!' he said. I stopped the car and bought the *Extrablatt* of the *Berliner Morgenpost*, which newspaper vendors were eagerly touting through the streets. So it was true: Berlin had ended a bare few months of insignificance. At least until October 1990 it had been the capital city of the socialist East German state. Now it was much more: the metropolis of a united Germany.

Berlin was entering its ninth life. Throughout the seven and a half centuries since the first settlers took up residence on the River Spree and chased those *Urberliner*, the Slavic Wends, into their lakeside fishing villages, Berlin had always been of more than local importance. Until 1443 it was a significant *Handelsstadt*, or trading centre, in what was contemptuously referred to as the 'sandpit of the Holy Roman Empire'. Then the Hohenzollern prince and Elector of Brandenburg, Frederick Irontooth, decided to make Berlin his *Residenz*, the centre of his court. Berlin grew in importance as, first, Brandenburg's electors and, later, Prussia's kings assumed an ever greater role in the balance of power in central Europe. The Great Elector created Brandenburg-Prussia's first standing army. His grandson, the 'Soldier-King' Frederick William I, and his great-grandson, Frederick the Great, greatly added to the military character of the upstart state. The electors and kings cut short their visits to the capital, concentrating their courts on Potsdam, while Berlin filled up with soldiers and their families. The *Garnisonstadt* or garrison town was Berlin's third incarnation.

Until industry took off in Berlin in the second quarter of the nineteenth century, the general impression Prussia's capital wrought on travellers was of a city dominated by soldiers, with a moral profile to match. Berlin was still comparatively small until heavy industry caused the fourth metamorphosis: the Prussian capital was now a *Großstadt*.

Daily arrivals of fresh blood from the provinces assured Berlin of a rapid development in the mid-century, but the biggest factor in its nineteenth-century growth was the unification of Germany during the Franco-Prussian War. As Prussia had been the motive force, Prussia's capital had the undisputed right to be the new imperial metropolis. Such cities were novel in central Europe. With the exception of Vienna, Germany was a network of small towns with few pretensions to the cosmopolitan style of a Paris, London or Rome. Berlin now joined the club of *Weltstädte*. When William II became the third Hohenzollern Kaiser, he proceeded to tear much of his capital down in the hope of creating something more in keeping with his own imperial visions and the showy trappings of the new Reich.

That dream was dispelled by defeat in the First World War. The Kaiser fled, but Berlin remained the capital of the Weimar Republic. With the departure of the royal family, the city's artistic life came to the fore. Many of the cultural movements now associated with Weimar, however, had their origins in the years immediately prior to the war. The moral degeneration occasioned by revolution, inflation and political chaos added its own allure to the German capital, and one which attracted significant numbers of foreigners to the city for the first time. Then Wall Street crashed, German democracy collapsed and the National Socialists came to power. The Nazis put an end to the cosmopolitan pretensions of the *Weltstadt*; small-town prudes with Messianic visions, they wanted a return to the doughty values of the German lower-middle classes. In some things, however, Hitler resembled the last Kaiser. He, too, believed his capital unworthy of his majesty. He, too, set about remodelling it and replacing it with something more in keeping with his megalomaniac *Weltanschauung*.

After Hitler's war, the capital of the West German state moved to a small town on the Rhine. The western sectors of the city were preserved at great cost to provide both a foothold in the east and an ideological message to its inhabitants. This eighth incarnation of Berlin resembled none of the others, especially after the student revolution of 1968 removed the chiefly *petit bourgeois* image the city had taken on in the immediate post-war years. It was a cranky, exceptional place, favoured, and chiefly populated, by drop-outs and radicals who had converged on the city from other parts of Germany. The throbbing night-life of Kreuzberg and Charlottenburg, and the political radicalism of Schöneberg, were maintained by American, British and French arms.

More *Berlinisch* by far was the regime in the east. Here the German Democratic Republic (DDR) built its ministries in Lichtenberg and Pankow, and blended something of the priggish austerity of Nazism with the stripped-down values they had inherited from the Prussian rulers. Behind them stood the full force of the Soviet army, which, from its gigantic headquarters in Karlshorst, made sure there was no stepping out of line. Both the few remaining monuments and the light veneer of Prussian *Obrigkeit*, or authority, lent East Berlin a traditional feel, whereas the western sectors were little more than a historical bubble. There, too, vandalism was practised on a scarcely imaginable scale in the interests of defusing *Angst* over the country's troubled history, but there was more to destroy in East Berlin, and less money available for the sort of whole-scale slate-wiping that was carried out under Western eyes in the American, British and French sectors.

In the past six years every effort has been made to pull the two halves of the city together. All is in flux. Berlin is the biggest building site in Europe. At the time of writing, the first constructions in the new Potsdamer, Leipziger and Pariser Plätze are taking shape. Mitte, or the centre of Berlin, is largely under wraps, with bemused tourists dodging diggers and cranes to catch a glimpse of the remaining monuments. For the time being it remains a provincial place which lacks the infrastructure of a great capital. It may be 'wacky' in the west, but it is not sophisticated, and, despite the disappearance of the Wall and the emergence of life in the Scheunenviertel and the Prenzlauerberg, east Berlin has yet to shake off the dowdiness of its socialist years. In 1999 the government is due to arrive, bringing with it 12,000 civil servants and their families. The general view is that this alone will shake the city out of its doldrums, and inject it with some of the vitality which it last saw in the Weimar years.

Modern Berlin is wildly self-obsessed. Go into any bookshop in the capital and you will find entire bookcases dedicated to the history of the city. Much of it is ephemeral and anecdotal. For a scholarly approach the starting point is the two-volume *Geschichte Berlins* edited by Wolfgang Ribbe (Munich, 1987). Nothing of the sort exists in English. The earlier history of the city has been largely ignored, possibly because Prussia and Germany's capital excited very little interest from Britons before 1914. Events have proved more exciting since then: the revolution; Weimar Berlin with its clubs, cabarets and sexual licence; and the Third Reich, when the main organs responsible for the implementation of the Final Solution were scattered over the capital. The fall of Berlin in 1945, the Airlift and the Wall have also drawn ink, but the result has been to present an unbalanced view of the city, as some great mire of blood, lacking normality and daily life.

It has been my intention to present a broader picture without ridding the book of Weimar, the Third Reich or the *Rosinenbomber* of the Airlift, but I have endeavoured to show that Berlin's history is more than the drug addicts of 1920s Charlottenburg, or the mean-minded Nazis of 1930s Steglitz. Berlin is also the retired First World War colonel in Lichterfelde, Germany's Camberley; or the 1950s academic in Dahlem, Berlin's Hampstead. In the nineteenth or early twentieth century Pankow was a borough inhabited by prosperous shopkeepers; socialist toolmakers lived in Friedrichshain; communist factory workers had their stronghold in Wedding. Berlin was and is a city of villages, each with a different character and political complexion. Even in such troubled times as the Third Reich when communists were being rounded up and shipped off to concentration camps in Oranienburg, Sachsenhausen or Ravensbrück, there were parts of the city where *razzie*, street violence and political murder were unknown. People got on with their lives. They worked the system as best they could. This is as true of the Nazi years as it was of the DDR time. Brecht surely had the Berliner in mind when he wrote: 'Erst kommt das Fressen, dann kommt die Moral' ('Grub up, then morality'). Berlin marches on its stomach.

I have not written a narrative account. It would be scarcely possible to cover in one volume all aspects of the city's history in any detail. Instead I have explored themes relating to politics, society and the arts and I apologise in advance for the necessary lacunae. I have also dedicated space to food and drink. This is because the subject interests me. I believe that diet and leisure activities are important indicators to how people lived their lives. The critic who was dismayed to come across eight references to food in my book *Prussia* will be appalled to find a whole chapter here.

It deserves a book in its own right. Indeed, so do all the themes I have treated in these pages. I shall be satisfied, however, if I manage to convey something of the colour of this great city and the variety of life that has been lived there in the past seven and a half centuries.

Giles MacDonogh
London, 1996

Acknowledgements

Getting to know a city and its history would be a thankless task without friends, and to my Berlin circle I owe the greatest debt of gratitude – above all, to those who lodged me, wined me and dined me. I couldn't want for two better friends than Stuart Pigott and Ursula Heinzelmann. They put their spare room in Wedding at my disposal, collected relevant cuttings from the local press, and together with Ursula's brother, Markus Müller, showed me many unfamiliar faces of the city. Clarita and Urs Müller-Plantenberg also put me up in their flat in Friedenau and proved an endless source of knowledge of the student movement in the sixties, and of political and academic life in the city ever since. Clarita von Trott zu Solz was not only her usual, hospitable self, she provided an invaluable service by bringing together Will Dambisch and Karl Henssel to talk to me about their experiences of life in the Third Reich. I am also grateful to Dickie Bielenberg and Britta Düysen, Gottfried Graf von Bismarck, Thomas Blake, and the genial hotelier Alain Bolle, who kept me amused on the many occasions I spent under his roof. Arnulf Conradi and Elizabeth Ruge of the Berlin Verlag offered many valuable suggestions; Judy Dempsey and Frederick Stüdemann of the *Financial Times* both taught me a lot, and allowed me to use their office on occasion. I also learned from Andrew Gimson of the *Daily Telegraph*, Roland, Mary and Marina Richter of the restaurant Borchardt, Danielle Sauter of the hotel Brandenburger Hof, Denis Staunton of the *Observer*, Barbara Strang of the Aufbau Verlag, Jost and Ulrike von Trott zu Solz, Asta Wegener of the Schultheiß Brewery in Kreuzberg and Franz Prinz zu Sayn Wittgenstein.

At home in London Angela Bielenberg and Inga Haag both deserve lavish praise for their help and encouragement. Through Lord and Lady Gowrie's hospitality at their house in Wales I was able to have several long talks about Berlin in the twenties with Tisa Gräfin von der Schulenburg. I owe thanks to Max Wilkinson, Paul Betts and Jill James at the *Financial Times* for allowing me to try out one or two Berlin ideas in print. More credits are due to those who helped with a book, a word or a reference: Richard Bassett, Hugh Lawson-Tancred, Terence MacCarthy, my sister Katharine MacDonogh, Colonel Sebastian and Elisabeth Roberts, Catherine Sackville-West and Christopher Moorsom.

In Vienna Gabrielle Urabl allowed me to take over her flat to write the initial outline of the book and Uwe Kohl and Günter Farnleitner of the restaurant Zu den drei Husaren provided me with further details of the life of the extraordinary restaurateur Otto Horcher.

The entire manuscript was read by my friends Candida Brazil and Angela Bielenberg, by Mark Frankland and Michael Ratcliffe, as well as by my agent Peter Robinson. At Sinclair-Stevenson I am grateful to Penelope Hoare and Roger Cazalet for their kindness, interest and patience. Again Douglas Matthews has kindly consented to compile the index.

Once again my thanks to the staff of the Staatsbibliothek and the other institutions of the Stiftung Preußischer Kulturbesitz in Berlin, the German Historical Institute, the Goethe Institute and the British Library in London.

Chronology

1230	Foundation of the twin town of Berlin-Cölln.
1237	Cölln first named in an official document.
1244	First mention of Berlin.
1442	Frederick 'Irontooth' Hohenzollern subdues the town. Work begins on the Schloss.
1486	Berlin becomes the capital of Brandenburg.
1630	As a result of the Thirty Years War the population decreases to 6,000.
1685	Edict of Potsdam. Influx of French Huguenots to Berlin.
1701	Elector Frederick becomes first King *in* Prussia and seeks to turn his capital into a city worthy of the new monarchy.
1709	The satellite towns of Friedrichswerder, Dorotheenstadt and Friedrichstadt incorporated into Berlin.
1713	Accession of the 'Soldier-King' Frederick William I. End of the beautification of Berlin. Schlüter leaves for St Petersburg.
1740	Frederick the Great comes to the throne.
1742	Construction of the Forum Friderizianum.
1743	Opening of the new Opera House.
1757	Berlin sacked by the Austrians.
1760	Berlin sacked by the Russians.
1786	Death of Frederick the Great. Berlin has 147,000 inhabitants. Accession of Frederick William II.
1788–1791	Construction of the Brandenburg Gate.
1795	Frederick William III accedes.

1806	Defeat of the Prussian army at Jena. Berlin occupied by the French.
1810	Foundation of Berlin University.
1813	Berlin liberated by the Russians. Napoleon defeated at Leipzig.
1818–1821	New Schauspielhaus built to designs by Karl Friedrich Schinkel.
1824–1828	Schinkel builds the Altes Museum.
1830	Rioting greets news of the French Revolution. Pre-March (*Vormärz*) period in Berlin.
1840	Accession of Frederick William IV.
1848	Berlin Revolution.
1861	Accession of William I. Berlin has just under 500,000 inhabitants.
1870	Franco-Prussian War.
1871	Berlin becomes capital of the Second German Reich. Vast population expansion.
1888	Accession of Kaiser William II.
1918–1919	Revolution in Berlin. The Kaiser abdicates. The Weimar Republic is declared.
1920	Kapp *Putsch* from the right. Creation of Groß-Berlin.
1933	Hitler comes to power.
1940	First British air attacks on Berlin.
1943	Beginning of the 'Battle of Berlin' with the November raids.
1945	End of the 'Battle of Berlin' in March. 50,000 dead and over 25,000 square kilometres destroyed. April arrival of the Red Army. British, American and French troops arrive in July. Division of the city into four military sectors.
1948–1949	Berlin Airlift.
1953	After Stalin's death, Revolution of 17 June in East Berlin.
1957	Khrushchev threatens to invade Berlin's western sectors.

1961	Construction of the Berlin Wall, dividing the city into two. The western sectors no longer accessible from the Russian sector. Arrival of Turkish *Gastarbeiter* to replace East Germans in the western sectors.
1967	Death of Benno Ohnesorg sparks off period of student rioting.
1968	Student revolution.
1980	Christian Democratic Union takes over West Berlin government. Growth of 'alternative' politics.
1989	On 9 November the Wall is pierced.
1990	On 3 October Germany is reunited.
1991	On 20 June Berlin is chosen as Germany's capital.
1999	The Bundestag due to arrive in Berlin.

Introduction

Berlin, the Inextinguishable City

On the western edge of Berlin lies the Havel. The river flows down from Oranienburg to Potsdam, regularly breaking out into deep, blue lakes: the Templiner See is to the south of the city, then comes the Wannsee of sinister memory, the Tegeler See by the main airport and the still rural Heiligensee to the north. The Havel is Berlin's border, not its river; that is the Spree, which rises in the Upper Lausitz on the present Polish–Saxon frontier. The Spree joins Berlin in the east, feeding the Grosser Müggelsee with its pleasure boats and bathing huts. There are one or two relatively picturesque flourishes left around Köpenick and Treptow, but once it hits the city centre the Spree is a modest affair. At times it is hard to tell it apart from Berlin's many canals. It forms the northern limit to the Tiergarten, then winds through the western industrial belt before joining the Havel below the Citadel in Spandau.

Few cities have a greater potential than Berlin. Few make so little of their natural attractions. The Havel lakes are the prettiest in Berlin, but they are far from being the only ones on offer. Swimmers and the city's many nudists are well aware that an expanse of water is never far away: the Halensee and the Lietzensee in Charlottenburg, and the Teufelssee out in the Grunewald woods; the Neuer See in the Tiergarten; or the Weisse See and Malchower See on the far side of the now vanished Wall. Indeed, East Berlin had its own version of the Havel lakes in the Müggelsee, the Dahme and the Langer See in the vast Berliner Stadtforst.

Despite the undeniable charm of its lakes, pine forests

and occasional outcrops of low, undulating hills, few foreign literary tourists have left accounts of Berlin and the Mark Brandenburg. What descriptions there are were generally written by Prussians. Germans from the south and west mock the region as the 'flat land'. True, it rises to no great height. To the east of the city there is a range of hills which is known, one assumes ironically, as the *märkische Schweiz* or 'Switzerland of the Mark'. This was the scene of one of the last pitched battles of the Second World War, when the remains of Hitler's *Wehrmacht* fought to protect the capital from the Red Army. Even today farmers still pull a rusty weapon or a mangled skeleton out of the sandy soil.

Berlin itself lies on the plain. The only relief in the centre of the city are the hills of Kreuzberg in the south and Prenzlauerberg to the east. Before Kreuzberg was consumed by Berlin in the last century its rural charm made it popular for Sunday picnics. Berlin's best wines (the best of a bad lot) grew and still grow on the south-facing slopes of the hill. Prenzlauerberg never had the same reputation. Only in the later years of the DDR did the hill become the home of a restless student element who created something of their own, rather tame, Bohemia, in the pubs and cafés of the *quartier*.

Berlin's only prominent range of hills is the Müggelberge in the south-east. Throughout the history of the city it has proved a useful look-out for approaching enemies and dignitaries. During the Seven Years War Berliners realised they had been abandoned to their fate when Austrian cavalry was seen on the Müggelberge.

Pine, birch and beech forests are the final element in Berlin's physical make-up. From the time when the three western sectors became an island in a hostile, Soviet sea, the huge tracts of woodland in Grunewald, Wannsee, Spandau and Tegel assumed an added importance as the city's 'lungs'.[1] Short of travelling to West Germany, these clumps of greenery were the nearest thing to nature the West Berliner knew. In the eastern sectors the pressures were different. Circumscribed in virtually everything else, citizens of the DDR were none the less welcome to the forests: either those north of the Müggelsee or farther afield in the Mark.

Berlin was born between these woods and the water. Unlike London or Paris it was never a Roman town, although its roots are ancient enough. There is evidence of settlements as early as 4000 BC. Some of these early Berliners, at least, appear to have been cannibals. Germanic tribes were certainly present in Britz in the third century BC as recent digs have shown. These were very probably the Semnones who lived between the Elbe and the Oder and who, according to Tacitus, were a Suebian tribe like the Langobardi or Lombards. With their allies the Cherusci, the Semnones annihilated Publius Quinctilius Varus's three-legion force in Westphalia in AD 9. Seven years later they were instrumental in checking Germanicus's advance to the Elbe, thereby ensuring that East Elbian Germany never became a Roman colony.[2]

The fate of the Semnones and their settlements is unclear. There were still pockets of Germans in the area in the fifth and early sixth centuries, but evidence of their existence then begins to peter out. It is possible that there was a hiatus between the departure of the Germans for the west and the arrival of the Slavs from across the Oder, or that the two races managed to coexist for a time. This happened in Spandau. One thing is certain: German dialects made way for Slavic ones, and it was the Slavs who gave us the name *Berlin*.

Despite the continued presence of the animal on the city's coat of arms, despite the persistent maintenance of a colony of three brown *Wappentiere* in a specially constructed cage or *Zwinger* outside the Märkisches Museum, the name Berlin has nothing whatsoever to do with bears. The word derives

from the Slavic *Brl*, which means a marsh or a damp place.★
The myth that the city's name has something to do with
animals, or indeed Albert 'the Bear', the first of the Christian
Askanian princes to establish a bridgehead on the right bank
of the Elbe, is of great antiquity. Already in the thirteenth
century the inhabitants of the town had begun to associate
the Slavic *Berelin* with the Germanic diminutive *Bärlein*, or
'little bear'.³ It was an indication that the Slavs had ceased
to count for much in the newly established German colony.†

Slavic tribes had the run of the place for a good four
centuries before they heard any more from the Germans.
The Stodoranen or Heveller established villages throughout
the area now known as Berlin. Relics have been found in
Marzahn in the eastern suburbs, but the Slavs were chiefly
attracted by the strong points: islands in the Havel or the
Spree such as Spandau and Köpenick, both of which were
Wendish fortresses long before the Germans turned their
minds to defending or embellishing them.

The Heveller Wends established dynastic links with other
Slavic territories in central Europe. In 906 or 907 a Heveller
princess, Drahomira, married Prince Vratislav of Bohemia.
She was the mother of Good King Wenceslas, the Bohemian
national saint. At roughly the same time the Heveller Wends
had their first problems with the Germans. The Saxon King
Henry the Fowler and his son, the Emperor Otto I, sacked
the characteristic round Wendish fortress of Spandau: an
earthwork crowned with wooden palisades.⁵ Otto had
received the title of Holy Roman Emperor from Pope John

★ The writer Kurt Tucholsky must have been aware of this ety-
mology when he dismissed the city as a 'swamp'. See Fritz
Raddatz, *Tucholsky Ein Pseudonym*, Hamburg 1989.
† Zeisig: 'A bear? . . . Really little shepherdess? Probably a play
on Berlin's coat of arms! This bear has only recently begun to
growl, because he has got tired of lying on his back, and wants
to go off and taste some honey.' Ad. Brennglas (Adolf
Glassbrenner.)⁴

XII. In return Otto sought to extend the cause of Christianity beyond the Elbe, founding the bishoprics of Havelberg and Brandenburg from the new Metropolitan See of Magdeburg, which was created to convert the East Elbian Slavs.

The Wends accepted neither military nor Christian colonisation. The Prussian writer Theodor Fontane tells the story of the Obotriten Prince Mistiwoi who had already converted to Christianity and served on Otto's side at the Battle of Basantello. After the fight Mistiwoi heard himself referred to as a 'Wendish dog' by one of the German princes. Too late the Germans realised their mistake: Mistiwoi deserted them and proved impervious to their embassies. He later sent word that 'the day would come when the dogs bite'. He renounced his new faith and told the Germans: 'Now watch out, Mistiwoi the dog is coming to bark and will bark so loud that he will strike terror into the whole of Saxony.' In 983 the Wendish prince defeated the Saxons on the River Tanger, ridding the Mark of its German colonists for a further 150 years. Fontane remarked, 'This was done by Mistiwoi the dog.'[6]

It was Albert the Bear who repaired the damage caused by this early outburst of German racialism. The Askanian prince worked his way into the confidence of the Wendish prince Pribislav, who recognised him as his successor. This did not prevent Prince Jaxa of Köpenick from rising up against the German interloper in 1150. It took another seven years before Albert established total control over the Mark Brandenburg.

Albert the Bear created an important precedent among rulers of Brandenburg: he despatched emissaries to find settlers for his new land. For the most part they came from lower Germany, from Holland and Flanders. The towns of the Altmark across the Elbe from Magdeburg were the first to be stocked with this new blood. At this time Berlin was no more important than Stendal and Salzwedel, and considerably less so than the new cathedral cities of Havelberg and Brandenburg. Between the main centres German colonists founded their own villages in a different form from the original Wendish *Kietze*, often fishing villages tucked into the corners of the lakes. The new Brandenburgers settled in *Angerdörfer* with a communal meadow between two rows of farmhouses and, at the centre of it all, a stone-built church and cemetery. Some of these *Angers* are still clearly visible on the outskirts of modern Berlin, in Mariendorf or Marienfelde, for example, both established by the Templars. Particularly pretty is Heiligensee on the shores of the lake.[7]

People have lived in what is now called Berlin since prehistoric times, but it is impossible to deny the upstart status of the city. There was no Roman grid to guide the hands of its mediaeval builders; nor was there an important religious foundation set up in the early Middle Ages. The early history of Berlin is less significant not only than that of the very many Roman settlements in southern and western Europe but also of the many cathedral cities which have their roots deep in the Dark Ages. The first mention of the twin town of Berlin-Cölln occurs in a document dated 1237 which also names the first real Berliner: 'Symeon plebanus de Colonia', or Father Simeon of Cölln. Seven years later we hear more of Simeon, who has become 'dominus Symeon de Berlin prepositus', or Provost of Berlin, across the Spree. Finally, in 1247, the same clergyman is cited as 'Symeon prepositus de Colonia juxta Berlin', rectifying the earlier mistake.[8]

The twin town must have been fairly well established by Simeon's time, as Berlin was recognised as a *civitas* in 1251 and Cölln a decade later. There is no satisfactory answer to the question why the German inhabitants of this important crossing on the Spree should have wished to form themselves into two separate camps rather than establishing a single town. One which has been suggested is that it was easy to protect the towns that way.[9] Whatever the case it seems certain that the Wends did not join them in either, but remained in their own *Kietze*, on the south bank of the Spree.

Before the Hohenzollerns arrived in the early years of the fifteenth century and changed the shape of the town with their massive *Schloß*, Cölln was the smaller of the two segments, squashed into the lower end of an island in one of the Spree's many oxbow kinks. At its centre was the Petrikirche, or church of St Peter, and its own *Rathaus*, or town hall, looking out on the fish-market. The only other important institution in mediaeval Cölln was the Dominican Friary, the church of which was later to serve as Berlin's cathedral.[10]

Surrounded by its own walls, Cölln was connected to Berlin on the north side of the river by the Mühlendamm. Berlin was by far the larger town. The counterpart to Cölln's Petrikirche was the Nikolaikirche, the oldest church in the twin town, begun around 1230.[11] By 1270 or 1280 the town had grown to such an extent that a second parish church was required: the Marienkirche behind the new market. A further religious institution was provided by the Franciscans, who built their friary up against the town walls.* Berlin now enjoyed the privilege of three markets, while the main arteries, the Spandauer and Oderberger-Straßen, teemed with merchants dealing with their counterparts in the mediaeval trading centres of Stettin, Oderberg, Spandau, Hamburg, Meißen and Halle.

The first three Berlin churches were built of stone. The Franciscans used red brick from their kilns in Kreuzberg following the practice introduced by the Cistercians at their monasteries in Chorin and Lehnin. The same material was used for the Hohes Haus, the earliest administrative building in Berlin, parts of which survived until they were carried

---

* The Petrikirche has gone, but the Marienkirche and Nikolaikirche have been restored. The Franciscan Friary survives as a substantial ruin near the Alexanderplatz.

off in a typically *Berlinisch* act of philistinism in 1931. For the time being brick was reserved for important constructions. Houses were half-timbered with wattle-and-daub infilling: a method of construction which survived as late as the nineteenth century in Berlin, and which is occasionally revealed on dilapidated houses in the east where the stucco coating has fallen off.

Berlin was still just one of several important towns in the Mark. Its chief rival was Spandau, which had the advantage of a secure fortress where the Berliners could house the Margrave on his progresses. They were anxious to woo him away from Spandau, and this may have been the pretext for the first recorded visit by a margrave to Berlin in 1280. He came in the company of the Bishop of Brandenburg and with an escort of fifty-seven noblemen from the Mark.[12]

The Margrave was received by his *Schultheiß*, the mediaeval functionary who represented him in Berlin. Berlin's first *Schultheiß*, Marsilius, is named in 1247. He laid down the law: a craftsman who murdered his wife at the time was punished simply with a small fine; a coppersmith who abused municipal authority was beheaded.[13] At the beginning of the fourteenth century Berlin received its first town council, consisting of twelve Berliners and half a dozen citizens from Cölln, reflecting the comparative sizes of the two towns. The two town halls were built at this time. In front of the Berlin *Rathaus* the citizens erected a larger-than-life statue of Roland, in imitation of the people of Brandenburg. Roland symbolised the judicial independence of the town.[14]

Berlin was still not the capital of the Margravate, or indeed of the Electorate, as the Mark Brandenburg became in 1415 with the arrival of the first Hohenzollern, Frederick, Burgrave of Nuremberg. Brandenburg itself was out of the question; as a bishopric it was an imperial city and therefore could not become a *Residenz*. At first the question hardly applied. Like the earlier margraves, the Hohenzollern electors lived elsewhere, in the more civilised west. The first elector to live permanently in Brandenburg was the fourth of the Hohenzollerns, John Cicero, who succeeded his father, Albert Achilles, in 1486.[15] The electors continued to reside much of the time in their palace in Tangermünde in the Altmark during their visits to the east. Berlin was undeniably an increasingly important town but, even during the reign of Albert Achilles' son Joachim, the *Bürgermeister* of Berlin and Cölln ranked behind those of the old and new towns in Brandenburg, and the mayor of Stendal too.[16]

In 1432 the twin towns finally pooled their resources. A communal *Rathaus* had been built on the long bridge over the Spree as early as 1342, but it took nearly a century more before the two towns could agree on a joint mayor and free the surrounding meadows from the constraints of divided grazing rights. Real progress towards achieving *Residenz* status only came about by dint of the first rebellion against Hohenzollern rule in 1442. This pushed the elector into starting work on a fortified *Burg* which would keep the population in check. This was to become the great Berlin Schloss, the most powerful symbol of Hohenzollern rule in the city until 1918; indeed, the city's greatest monument, until it was dynamited in 1950.

I

Ich bin ein Berliner

I

The establishment of a royal *Burg* in Cölln was just what
the twin-town's merchants desired. Berlin had received the
equivalent of a royal warrant: now more people would take
this small trading town in the 'sandpit of the Holy Roman
Empire' seriously. By a twist of fate Berlin had achieved its
new status among the towns of Brandenburg precisely
because of the need to tame its unruly, independent spirit.
Whatever the cause, the results may not be doubted: the
decision by the Swabian Hohenzollerns to build a fortress
cum palace on the Spree was the true source of Berlin's
greatness. If Berlin was created by the Hohenzollerns,
however, the Berliner was not. The true Berliner in fact and
fiction did not fully evolve until much later; probably not
before the second quarter of the nineteenth century.

In 1889, the Prussian novelist and writer Theodor Fontane
wrestled with the historical development of the Berliner in
his essay 'Die Märker und die Berliner und wie sich das
Berlinertum entwickelte'★ ('The people of Berlin and the
Mark, and How the Berliner Evolved').[1] Fontane's conclusions were coloured by the contemporary hero-worship
for Frederick the Great and he chose to see the creation of
a huge garrison following the Seven Years War as the real
seed-time of the Berlin soul. There is a grain of truth in

★ First published in the *Deutsches Wochenblatt*. No. 47, 21 Nov.
1889, pp. 560–564.

this: the presence of so many troops from all over Branden-burg-Prussia, not to mention soldiers of fortune from elsewhere, was the *fond de sauce* for the Berlin melting pot in the nineteenth century. Fontane, however, went too far, and saw the Berliner to some extent imbued with Frederick's own character and wit: almost an illegitimate child of the monarch.

While Berlin remained small there was precious little dif-ference between the town-dweller and the *Märker* in the surrounding villages. It is possible that the Berliner's character owes something to the Slavic Wends, but as a rule, once the colonists arrived from the eleventh century onwards, the Wends retired to their own settlements on the periphery. Their legacy is to be seen in so many originally Slavic village names and in words such as *Werder* (an island or strip of land projecting into a lake or river) or *Kietz*. Evidence of intermarriage is thin on the ground. Wendish women appeared in Berlin as nannies and wet-nurses and they were a familiar sight, pushing prams in the years before the Second World War, dressed in their native *Tracht*: a blouse crossed over the breasts under a spencer, apron and black stockings. On their heads they tied their scarves like nuns' cowls.*

The Germanic towns and villages of the Mark were popu-lated by a cocktail of Lower Germans from the Rhine, Flanders, Westphalia and the Harz Mountains, as well as a few from the Thüringer Forest in Middle Germany. They brought with them the dialects associated with *Plattdeutsch*.[2] *Platt* is the collective term for the rather harder-sounding German spoken north of the Benrath Line,† and character-

---

* See Heinrich Zille's cartoon *Der Abschied der Amme* (The depar-ture of the nanny). '*Wenn Sie wollen, gnädige Frau, komme ich det nächste Jahr wieder.*' ('If you want, ma'am, I can come back next year.')
† Benrath is now a suburb of Düsseldorf.

ised by words such as *ick, det, maken, eten, grot* and *Zit.*★[3]
Originally the language spoken in Berlin and Brandenburg
would have sounded very little different from that still used
in Mecklenburg and other parts of north Germany. At the
end of the Middle Ages, however, the speech of the Berliners
underwent an important change. The growth of trade with
Saxony in general, and Leipzig in particular, led to a gradual
adoption of Meißen German: 'In Berlin the merchants found
their old *Plattdeutsch* unusable.'[4] Like the Brandenburgers, the
Saxons softened the hard German 'g',† but other distortions
linked to current *Berlinisch* such as 'ee' for 'ei' or 'oo' for
'au' were innovations brought up from the south.

An element of the population which made its first appearance under the patronage of the Hohenzollerns, and which
with time was to become a significant constituent in this
ever people-hungry city, were the Swabians of south-west
Germany. In the early years of the sixteenth century the
Elector Joachim Nestor summoned Abbot Trittenheim from
Sponheim to Berlin. The abbot produced one of the first
descriptions of the Berliners: 'The inhabitants are good
people, but too coarse and unschooled; they have a higher
regard for feasting and drinking than they have for knowledge. They consider drinking to excess a vice, but there are
many among them who do it for all that; and the newcomers
from Franconia and Swabia, as I have often had cause to
observe, are more given over to drunkenness than the
natives.'[5]

★ 'I', 'the', 'make', 'eat', 'big', 'time'.
† e.g. *Ne jut jebratne Jans ist ne jute Jottes.* (A well-roasted goose is
a gift of God.)

II

When a city has been so completely devastated as Berlin was in the Second World War and by its subsequent division into military sectors, it is often hard to visualise the past. At times it seems that all trace has been lost, and the recent past is as remote as the shattered remains of ancient Athens, or Rome. In one area, however, Berlin still presents an impressive testimony to its history, and that is in its numerous cemeteries.

In the old Stadtmitte, in an area of semi-wasteland which has yet to be included in some scheme for major redevelopment, is the Französischer Friedhof, or French Cemetery. It is a favourite place of pilgrimage for the many devotees of the novelist Theodor Fontane. Indeed, clearly the old women who come daily to tend the graves of the dead assume that any strange face is a Fontane fan, and direct him straight away to the writer's modest headstone.

The most striking monument is by the Liesenstraße gate, which was formerly up against the Berlin Wall. It is inscribed to members of the French colony who fell during the Wars of Unification: Prusso-Danish, Austro-Prussian and Franco-Prussian. The participation of members of the colony in the last of these is particularly poignant when it is recalled to what extent the French colony had retained its French culture. Part of the monument is even written in French.[6]

The presence of a sizeable number of Frenchmen among Berlin's population was a result of the far-sighted policy of the Great Elector Frederick William I. The hospitality of the Prussian prince was founded on the need to restock his underpopulated lands. His first great opportunity occurred in 1685 when King Louis XIV of France chose to revoke the Edict of Nantes, under which French Protestants had enjoyed a measure of tolerance since 1598. Frederick William countered with the Edict of Potsdam, which encouraged the Huguenots to take up residence in his realm, which was still reeling from the effects of the German civil war. In 1647 more than 100 villages were deserted and the total population of the electorate had fallen from 330,000 to 190,000.[7]

Berlin was still a small town and had little to offer a refugee with sophisticated tastes. At the end of the seventeenth century there were some 35,000 inhabitants, making it the sixth or seventh biggest in the Empire, on a level with Frankfurt, Königsberg and Nuremberg, but behind Dresden, Cologne, Danzig, Hamburg or Vienna.[8] Berlin's remoteness and absence of allure influenced the choice of those who settled there. Huguenot intellectuals, for example, went where there were academies and universities for them, not to mention presses to publish their books.[9] Those who came to Brandenburg tended to be from certain parts of France: Lorraine in particular, followed by the Languedoc, Champagne and Brie, and Sedan.[10] Fontane's family, for example, was Gascon on his father's side, while his mother's people came from the Cévennes.[11]

By the turn of the century there were nearly 6,000 Huguenots in Berlin, representing between a third and a fifth of the city's population.[12] The colony was still expanding: in 1724 the figure had grown to 8,496. Huguenots occupied many of the more important jobs: there were 54 civil servants, 25 doctors, 82 merchants and 52 goldsmiths. Their presence also revolutionised Berlin's awareness of taste: there were 47 French wig-makers, 27 gardeners and 18 inn-keepers.[13] In their smallholdings to the west of the city they planted vegetables which they had enjoyed in France. It was the Huguenots who introduced the Berliners to asparagus, artichokes and broccoli.[14]

Frederick William, Prussia and the city of Berlin did everything possible to make the new arrivals feel at home. On 25 November 1685 a 'refugee commission' headed by a French Protestant pastor was set up to examine the Huguenots and see how best they could be accommodated. They were provided with money and lodging. When Louis XIV overran the principality of Orange (which should have fallen to Brandenburg-Prussia on the death of the last prince), another 600 French-speaking refugees descended on Brandenburg. Naturally, the lion's share of these went to Berlin. They tended to be a cut above the Huguenots of the first wave: officers, lawyers and members of the local *noblesse de robe*. Some of the latter were snapped up by the civil service. The rest went into the army, where some 15–20 per cent of the officer corps was French in the early years of the eighteenth century.[15]

Since 1672 the French had had their own pastor who was allowed to preach in the chapel of the Schloss. In 1699 their extended numbers meant finding a larger space and they were granted use of the Margrave of Brandenburg-Schwedt's stables on the Gendarmenmarkt. This was later transformed into a copy of the great Huguenot temple at Charenton, near Paris, by Louis Cayard and Abraham Quesnays. In the 1780s both the French church and its German neighbour were embellished with domed towers by another member of the colony, the architect Karl von Gontard.*[16]

The Huguenot immigrants chose to settle in the new suburbs to the west of the mediaeval town, chiefly in the Friedrichstadt south of the Linden. They also established their own colony on the north bank of the Spree, in the so-called Kleine Tiergarten. They called the land 'Moabit'. This was once believed to be a corruption of the French *terre maudite*, or 'cursed land', but the truth is the reverse: it is a reference to the Prophet Isaiah XV, 5 – 'My heart shall cry out for Moab. His fugitives shall flee unto Zoah.'[17] It was an allusion to the land to which the Israelites escaped after the flight out of Egypt.[18] The Huguenots were quick to use the site for a little French hospitality. One of the first to try his hand was one 'Petit Martin' in the present Beusselstraße. The Berliners promptly translated his name into their own dialect as 'Martinicken' and Martin's inn later became the

---

* The churches have been sensitively restored since the war.

site of the Martinickenfelde. Even by Frederick the Great's time the origins of the name had been lost. A contemporary wrote: 'In good German "Martinichen" means a hare . . . But this silly name for the suburb should be changed. The "Rhubarb district" is more appropriate.'[19]

The Rhubarb had much to do with Berlin's growing military vocation: it was thought to be good for sick horses. Le Petit Martin was soon joined by other French innkeepers. One Menardié opened a house and garden which soon became a favourite destination for Berliners seeking a little Sunday excursion with the promise of decent food and drink.[20] These *Budiker* (from the French *boutiquier*) created a fashion in eighteenth-century Berlin which was to continue well into the nineteenth. Bourgeois and workers alike used their Sundays to head for the more countrified areas around the city and spend the day at an inn.

In the first years of the eighteenth century Moabit contained no more than ten houses, surrounded by plots of peas, beans, lettuces, soup greens and melons. Then in 1716 refugees from Orange convinced King Frederick William I that they could rival the Lyons silk industry if mulberry trees were planted in the area. The idea appealed to the thrifty monarch: 'Here you must plant mulberry trees in the wilderness.' The scheme was no more of a success than that sponsored by James I of England a hundred years earlier, which had had a similar goal. Brandenburg's sandy soils were not ideal for mulberry trees, even if a few hardy ones managed to stay alive until the 1840s.★[21]

The French colony was a noticeable element in Berlin society for a century or so, and through one or two of its institutions, such as the church and the Collège Royale (the later Französische Gymnasium), it is still represented today. The Huguenot women, naturally, had the reputation for

---

★ In 1718 the silk manufacturer Jean Belchier Fayé designed a park on the site of the present Schloß Bellevue.

being more elegant than their German counterparts,[22] and their reluctance to marry outside their own community made them instantly visible to visitors to Berlin. In 1770 one such wrote (with a degree of exaggeration), 'You are really pretty well in the middle of Paris here; almost always is it safer to address a stranger in French, rather than German.'[23] In 1783 members of the colony created the Mittwochgesellschaft (the Wednesday Society), which was to survive into the darkest days of the Second World War. Its last members included the surgeon Sauerbruch, ambassador Ulrich von Hassell, General Ludwig Beck and many others associated with the 20 July Plot to kill Hitler.

Not only was Berlin stamped with French style, the language of the Berliner was expanded to include a wide variety of French words. Some of these are even used today.[24] After three centuries of distortion in the mouths of East Germans, many of these words look like the results of a game of Chinese whispers: *quincaillerie*, for example, has become *Kinkerlitzchen*; *cislaveng* is a corruption of *ainsi cela vient*; *Feez* is *fête*; *Cheese* is *chaise*; *Deez*, *tête*; *dusemang*, *doucement*; *Lamäng*, *la main*; *Bredullje*, *bredouille*; and *Eau de Mief*, *parfum*. The most popular French word of all is *Boulette*, the meatball which might still be the Berliner's favourite food. Peter Schlobinski has traced no fewer than twenty-four Berlin slang words to describe it.[25]

After the French Revolution of 1789 there were a few more refugees from France. The most famous of these was Louis Charles Adelaide de Chamisso, a young nobleman from Champagne who was to swop his French identity for a Prussian one and, as Adelbert von Chamisso, become the creator of the shadowless fictional character, Peter Schlemihl. Chamisso plugged the numerous gaps in his education by a belated schooling at the Französische Gymnasium[26] and, much later still, Berlin University. One of Chamisso's closest friends was another noble *émigré*, Louis de La Foye. Later

Chamisso formed the literary 'Nordsternbund' with La Foye, Julius Hitzig and the Huguenot Franz Theremin.[27]

Prussia was not to remain the safe-haven it had appeared to Chamisso's parents at the time of the Terror. Defeat at Jena and Auerstedt led to the occupation of Berlin by French troops. After the arrival of Napoleon Bonaparte in the city, the head of the Huguenot colony, the theologian Jean-Pierre Erman, was summoned to see the self-proclaimed emperor. Erman rejected several generous offers made to him by the Corsican. 'We have become Prussians', he said, 'and we wish to remain so.'[28] But if Erman refused, the merchant Paul Antoine Jordan agreed to command the new civil guard[29] – an unwise move, perhaps, at a time when patriotism and hatred of the French were two sides of the same coin.

Defeat and occupation by the French also prompted wide-ranging reforms in the Prussian state. The privileged position of the French colony was abolished and responsibility for their spiritual needs placed with the new Kultusministerium (the equivalent of Ministry for Education, the Arts and the Church). The decision caused great excitement among the Huguenots in the Friedrichstadt and the government backtracked to some degree by offering them a few more jobs in the reformed administration. This was the time of escalating German national consciousness. Even while the Francophile King Frederick the Great had been on the throne there had been a move to promote the German language over the French.

As early as 1787 there had been a call for a German dictionary based on that produced by the Académie Française. Once the French army was garrisoned in Berlin the hotter heads were calling for the replacement of such French words as *madame* by *Ehrenfrau* or *edle Frau*. In 1812 the rabid nationalist Ernst Moritz Arndt penned the following blood-curdling lines:

Wir wollen heute Mann für Mann
Mit Blut das Eisen röten,
Mit Henkerblut, Franzosenblut –
O süßer Tag der Rache!
Das klingelt allen Deutsche gut,
Das ist die große Sache![30]

(There's not a man who doesn't now
Want fresh blood to stain his steel,
Some hangman's blood, some Frenchman's blood –
Oh revenge, how sweetly you sing!
To every German that sounds good,
That is the important thing!)

'Never had the Berliners so bombastically proclaimed their hatred of the French.'[31]

The wiser members of the colony read the writing on the wall. The question was whether or not they could still afford to maintain the French language in their church and day-to-day affairs. In 1813 or 1814 the Pastor David-Louis Théremin released a pamphlet proposing to abolish the use of French in church services. The eradication of French, he suggested, would be a proof of loyalty to the Prussian crown. Théremin's arguments were not supported by the entirety of the colony. Another pastor, Jean Henry, replied in print to defend the use of French,[32] but it was none the less clear that after a century and a quarter in Berlin most of the Huguenots now thought as Prussians. By the time the Franco-Prussian War broke out in 1870 there was no more question of divided loyalties. By 1870 French had been reduced to an occasional, formal language of religious observation, like Latin in the Tridentine Mass, or Coptic.

III

Unlike the post-war regimes in Poland and Czechoslovakia which sought to conceal the evidence of German history in their land by bulldozing graveyards, the socialist Sozialistische Einheitspartei Deutschlands (SED) in East Berlin destroyed few tombs. Not so their predecessors, the Nazis. In 1943 they cleared away the oldest Jewish cemetery in the city in the Große Hamburger Straße. The graves had dated back to the foundation of the cemetery in 1672. Other Jewish graveyards have survived, notably those on the Prenzlauer-berg, which opened in 1827 once the Große Hamburger Straße site had become too cramped,* and the vast, over-grown cemetery in Weißensee – 'the largest and most important in Europe' – which opened in 1880. It is particu-larly moving to see how many of the Jews buried there died for Kaiser and country in the First World War.

The oldest Jewish grave in Greater Berlin is more ancient than any of these. It predates the first Frenchman by four hundred years: there is a Jewish headstone in Spandau from 1244. It is fair to deduce from this that the Jews had been present in Spandau for some time: at least since the end of the twelfth century.[33] The very important role played by Jews in the history of the city of Berlin has led two recent writers to state that the ' . . . exodus of Berliners of Jewish descent did more to damage the city than the obliteration of its buildings in the Blitz'.[34]

This is a gross, if understandable, exaggeration. Berlin was possible without the Jews, but it would have been a very different place, and one with far less sophistication or culture. Jews already represented an important element in the medi-

---

* Here are the tombs of the singer Sophie Loewe (1876), the painter Max Liebermann (1935), the merchant David Friedländer (1834), the composer Giacomo Meyerbeer (1864), Bismarck's banker, Gerson von Bleichröder (1893), the publisher Leopold Ullstein (1899) and James Simon (1932).

aeval town. They lived apart from the Gentiles, the poor Jews often lodging in huts belonging to the richer members of the colony. In the first half of the fourteenth century they excited the wrath of the closed order of *Knochenhauer* (butchers) by selling off the organs of slaughtered animals which their religion forbade them to eat. The town council, or *Magistrat*, responded in 1343 by imposing a tax on Jews who chose to slaughter their own beasts.[35]

The Jews were banished from Berlin and Brandenburg in 1572.[36] True to form, it was the Great Elector who brought them back a century later. A few *Hofjuden*, or court Jews, were allowed to defy the ban at first because they were seen to be useful to the state, principally as bankers. The Königsberg coiner Aaron Israel was the first to be officially granted the right to settle in Berlin. In 1671 Frederick William extended permission to fifty Jewish bankers from Vienna. For the time being they were only permitted to settle in Berlin, rather than courtly Cölln, Friedrichswerder, Friedrichstadt or Dorotheenstadt.[37]

Berlin must have proved attractive to them, for despite these petty restrictions their numbers rapidly increased. In 1688 there were already forty Jewish families living in the old town. By 1700 this had risen to 117. Fourteen years later they were given leave to establish their own synagogue by King Frederick William I. The Soldier-King was in two minds about the Jews. To his son he wrote that they were 'scarecrows for a country . . . and ruin Christians. I beg of you give them no more letters of protection* even if they pay heavily for them . . .' He later admitted his difficulty in loving his neighbour, 'especially the Jews', and on one occasion is said to have laid about a Jew with a cane who was cowering in his presence: 'You should love me! Love me, not be frightened of me. Love me!' he growled.[39] Yet

---

* *Schutzjuden*. In the 1770s Jews had to pay as much as 1,000 Talers for limited protection under the law.[38]

during Frederick William's reign not only did the legal status of Berlin's Jews greatly improve, numbers also increased in proportion.[40]

Frederick the Great was less choleric than his father, but his attitude to the Berlin Jews was not radically different. When he came to the throne there were 3,000 or so in Berlin.[41] Frederick was happy to keep them well away from the capital, in the east. Those who settled in Berlin had to carry out his bidding, like, for example, including china from his new Königliche Porzellan-Manufaktur among their stocks.[42] He also leased the Berlin Mint to the Jews Herz Moses Gumperts and Moses Fränkel in 1754, and Veitel Ephraim in 1758. On Frederick's orders the Prussian thaler was devalued, with ever more copper and brass and less and less silver going into a coin.[43] The Berliners somewhat unfairly blamed Ephraim for this chicanery. Referring to the new coins they rhymed:

> Außen schön und innen schlimm.
> Außen Friedrich, innen Ephraim.[44]

> (Nice outside but bad within.
> Outside Frederick, inside Ephraim.)

This raillery is unlikely to have troubled Ephraim too much: he was literally laughing all the way to the bank. In 1762 the architect Friedrich Wilhelm Diterichs started work on his palace on the Mühlendamm, a lovely rococo building which was soon baptised 'prettiest corner in Berlin': a reference to its site.★[45]

Frederick the Great had seen uses for the Jews as far as trade with the east was concerned and in the course of his

---

★ It owes its salvation to a National Socialist road-widening scheme. The Ephraim Palais was taken down in 1935 and therefore missed the Blitz. It was re-erected, more or less on its old site, in 1985–1987.

reign Prussia became increasingly eastern in its outlook, as a result of the conquest of Silesia and the First Polish Partition. He was none the less anxious to keep the numbers of Jews in the capital down. In that he was unsuccessful. By the end of his reign there were already 4,500 of them in Berlin. It was the dawn of intellectual emancipation for the Prussian Jews even if full civil rights came later. During the reign of his great-nephew, Frederick William III, Jewish women in particular, such as Rahel Levin and Henriette Herz, became highly influential through the pull of their salons. Berlin society teemed with enlightened ideas. As far as the Jews were concerned the most influential text was Gotthold Ephraim Lessing's *Nathan der Weise* (Nathan the Wise), a dramatic poem inspired by the writer's friend Moses Mendelssohn.

The example of Moses Mendelssohn and his descendants must have been an inspiration to countless poor German Jews in the course of the nineteenth century. Moses followed his rabbi, David Fränkel, up to Berlin in 1743 and in the next four decades (he died in the same year as Frederick the Great) proceeded not only to amass a considerable fortune but to gain a reputation as one of the foremost philosophic minds of his time. Moses wrote a large body of work in Hebrew as well as the immensely popular *Phädon*. As far as winning acceptance for Berlin's Jews, however, his most important work was *Jerusalem oder Über die religiöse Macht und Judentum* (Jerusalem or on Religious Might and the Jews) of 1783, in which he demonstrated that it was possible to be both a good Jew and a modern European.[46]

Moses' arguments did not prevent virtually all his progeny from converting to Christianity. His eldest daughter, Dorothea, married Friedrich Schlegel (after the banker Simon Veit) and eventually followed his path to Rome. His son Abraham is chiefly remembered for his self-effacing description of himself as the man who had spent the first half of his life as the son of a genius and the second half as the father of another, Felix Mendelssohn-Bartholdy. Abraham had all his children baptised in 1816, a gesture which considerably enhanced the repertory of nineteenth-century church music (see below, pp. 398–99). Abraham's younger brother Joseph founded the Mendelssohn bank, which existed as late as 1939. One of Felix's children, Paul Mendelssohn-Bartholdy, was the creator of AGFA.[47]

Felix Mendelssohn died wretchedly young, at the age of thirty-eight. His son Paul was just thirty-nine when he died in 1880, but he had lived long enough to see a complete change in the nature of Berlin's Jewry (even if he was no longer, religiously speaking, a Jew). There were now many more places of worship. The first had been opened in the presence of Frederick the Great's mother, Sophie-Charlotte. The Oranienburger Straße synagogue, the burnt-out shell of which was such a poignant reminder of the *Reichskristallnacht* to visitors to East Berlin,* was not begun until 1859. It was only the second in Berlin, but another ten were built before Hitler's *Machtergreifung* in January 1933.[48]

In Moabit, the Levetzowstraße synagogue opened in 1912, the second of five constructed in the first years of the century. There were already in the area 2,512 Jews, led by the liberal Rabbi Julius Lewkowitz, who published *Judentum und die moderne Weltanschauung* (Judaism and Modern Ideology) in 1909. He was murdered by the Nazis in 1943.[49] By 1933 Kreuzberg had two synagogues and a population of more than 6,000 Jews. Both synagogues were pulled down in 1938.[50] Despite the increasing number of places of worship, for many Jews the period between 1880 and 1933 represented the chance to assume an increasingly German identity and a more relaxed attitude to their religious obligations. The physician and novelist Alfred Döblin, for example, was far

---

* Restoration was begun before the 'change' in 1988. It reopened in 1995.

from being an observant Jew. In October 1922 he made light of the recent annual blow-out:

> They are over, the last few weeks with the Jewish holidays. It was the well-loved blend of fasting and lavish feasting. Such festivities are hazardous in the bird world; among geese and chickens there must be an exceptional amount of anti-Semitism.[51]

Döblin was also aware that Berlin Jewry was changing. During his brief career as a theatre critic for the *Prager Tagblatt* he had been to review a play at the Jüdisches Künstlertheater. It was in Yiddish, a language which the Stettin-born Döblin could not understand. He was sceptical about the play's capacity to make a profit:

> The people who understand this mishmash of languages, Yiddish – which is a sort of naturally developed Esperanto – live on the Alexanderplatz and have no money.[52]

Döblin had put his finger on the new problem for Jewish assimilation: the arrival of floods of Jews from the Russian Empire in the wake of the pogroms. In 1900 there were 41,000 of these in Prussia; and in 1914, 78,000. In Berlin they already formed 30 per cent of the Jewish population. As a result of the turmoil of the First World War their numbers shot up to 160,000 in Prussia, with 44,000 of them in Berlin in 1925.[53] Speaking little or no German and dressed in the unsophisticated garb of their eastern villages, they were bound to excite the hatred of narrow-minded elements in Berlin.

They were the same Jews whom Franz Biberkopf encountered in the Sophienstraße in Döblin's best-known novel *Berlin Alexanderplatz*. Biberkopf has just been released from Tegel prison. A stranger takes pity on him: 'It was a Jew with a red beard, a little man wearing an overcoat, a black velour hat on his head and a stick in his hand.'[54] Biberkopf had stumbled into the world of Berlin's *Ostjuden* with their comical German who had taken hold of the old Jewish *quartier* around the Scheunenviertel during the time that Biberkopf had been locked away in prison. The richer, suaver Berlin Jews had long since moved out to the west. Smart Wilmersdorf was now the most Jewish *Bezirk* in Berlin with 14 per cent. Mitte came second with nearly ten per cent, followed by Charlottenburg and Schöneberg with between seven and eight.[55]

If most Berlin Jews were involved in trade, industry or crafts, there were also many who lived on their incomes or in the professions. In 1933 there were 3,160 Jews in public office and 73.5 per cent of all Berlin lawyers were Jews.[56] All that was before the Nazis came to power. In June 1933 there were 160,564 Jews in Berlin; in May 1939, 75,344. At the end of the war there were about 1,400.*[57] In Spandau, where the Jews had first breathed the famous Berlin air, there were 725 when the Nazis came to power; 205 in 1939; and just 81 in 1945.[58]

IV

On 18 January 1701 the Elector Frederick III of Brandenburg crowned himself King *in* Prussia in the *Schloß* in Königsberg. *In* Prussia, because his Baltic duchy lay outside the Holy Roman Empire, and the Holy Roman Emperor took a dim view of having kings on his own beat. Frederick was a monarch with a singularly *un*-Prussian idea of magnificence. Like William II nearly two centuries later, he wanted his capital to be a splendid reflection of his own new status. Not only did he line the Linden with palatial buildings, but whole new streets of the Friedrichstadt sprang up to accommodate

---

* The number had risen to 7,274 on 1 November 1946.

his court. His son was another kettle of fish altogether. When Frederick William I came to the throne in 1713 he put a stop to most of his father's grandiose schemes. Berlin lost its chance to become a great show-place of the baroque.

On one issue, however, the two kings saw eye to eye. They both believed in the necessity of attracting immigrants to their country, but Frederick William's thrifty approach to kingship actually aggravated the situation. The shrinking size of the court after 1713 meant that former courtiers sold off their houses and retired to their estates. Nor were sales easy, as few people in Frederick William's Berlin had sufficient income to buy the property. In the smart new Friedrichstadt, building came to a halt. In 1721 Berlin counted 583 unconstructed sites. 'The capital needed people who could fill its oversized frame.'[59]

With its tally of Huguenots and Viennese Jews Berlin had already shown itself a haven for those fleeing religious persecution. In 1732 it was the turn of 2,000 Bohemian Protestants.[60] To complicate matters, half were Lutherans and the other half Calvinists. A good number of them settled in southern Friedrichstadt, where they lived in great poverty[61] as textile workers. Here was their own church, the Bethlemskirche on the Mauerstraße, with its circular plan, one of the sights of Berlin until it was shattered by bombs during an Allied raid in 1943.* Others went to 'Böhmisch' Rixdorf (in the present Neukölln in the south of the city), or to the 'Böhmeberg' in Schöneberg.[62] The Rixdorf Bohemians had originally settled in the Friedrichstraße, but in 1737 the King, swayed by their Pastor Liberda, granted them land of their own where they could build to their own specifications. One or two of their houses have survived.[63] Until 1873 'Deutsch' and 'Böhmisch' Rixdorf had separate magistrates.[64]

Other Slavs besides Wends and Bohemians made their way to Berlin. There has always been a smattering of Poles. In

---

* The ruins were not demolished until the 1960s.

the past most of these would have come from the Polish-speaking parts of Prussia: the Grand Duchy of Posen (Great Poland) and West Prussia. Franz Biberkopf's first girl in Döblin's *Berlin-Alexanderplatz*, the plump Lina,[65] was presumably one of these. Now the Polish border is just 60 kilometres to the east, Berlin is overrun with Polish prostitutes who line the Kurfürstendamm on Friday and Saturday nights. In the first half of the nineteenth century, however, Poles came to Berlin for more respectable reasons. During his spell at Berlin University Heine observed them at close quarters:

> You see immediately from their faces that there is no
> shopkeeper's soul hiding beneath their moustaches.
> A good many of these Sarmates could show the sons
> of Hermann and Thusnelda a thing or two about
> amiability and aristocratic behaviour.[66]

The reputation of the University of Berlin drew more than just Poles. Russians too availed themselves of its famous faculties. Russians didn't arrive in bulk, however, until after the Revolution. When that happened Berlin became the favoured place of exile; even more than Sofia, Prague or Paris. One reason for this was unfinished business: there were still 700,000 Russian prisoners-of-war in Germany at the beginning of 1919. This gave rise to the first official discussions between the German government and the new Soviet state. As in 1994, when a good many Soviet soldiers chose to stay in Germany rather than go home, many of the Russian officers could see no future for them in the new USSR.[67]

An accurate figure for the number of Russians in Berlin in the early twenties is hard to come by. Estimates range wildly between 50,000 and 300,000.[68] They had six newspapers, ranging from the rabidly pro-Soviet to the fiercely monarchistic; political parties of every complexion; six banks, 87 Russian-language publishing houses; twenty bookshops;

plus schools and refugee organisations.[69] Alfred Döblin was mystified by their comings and goings:

> Tens of thousands, if not a hundred thousand, Russians must live in Berlin. They are *émigrés*. Refugees from the turmoil in their great land. I don't know the individual details of why they have fled, but the fear of impoverishment can't have played an insignificant role. It can't be said that the refugee Russians have found a place in Berlin's proletariat. For certain they are well-dressed bourgeois who prefer to hang about the west end and go to balls. Finally they have their own Russian cabaret in the 'Blaue Vogel'. Now the Russian theatre in Moscow has paid them a visit, they can attend performances and pay their monstrous [ticket] prices; the majority of educated Berliners would seek in vain for tickets to these performances: everything has sold out, and the prices are fantastic.[70]

The Russians had their own itineraries in Berlin. Some – Vladimir Nabokov, for example – were able to carry on their lives almost wholly oblivious of the Berliners around them.[71] They lived in 'Charlottengrad', in the network of streets bounded by the Tauentzienstraße, the Kantstraße and the Kurfürstendamm. Besides the 'Blaue Vogel' they frequented the 'Haus der Künste' in the Café Leon on the Nollendorfplatz, the Café Landgraf and the Prager Diele.[72] Just as today the more cultured members of Berlin's Russian colony while away their time in the Café Hegel on the Savignyplatz. Ironically, perhaps, the Kantstraße has become the centre of Berlin's thriving Russian mafia, which has been held responsible for a great deal of robbery and murder since the Wall came down.

The colourful life of the *émigré* community of the twenties proved short-lived. When inflation came, Berlin was far less tempting than Paris: there were no more bears left to speculate on. The Russians were still numerous, however, but less stylish. They stopped staying at the expensive Adlon hotel and rented rooms in Berlin's gloomy back courtyards.[73] Communal life centred on their little church in the Nachodstraße in Schöneberg[74] which carried on dispensing absolution until it was bombed out in the war. The most dogged and the most Aryan of them clung to German skirts throughout the thirties and forties, hoping against hope for the collapse of the Soviet Union. The launch of Operation Barbarossa against Russia in the summer of 1941 gave them cause for reflection:

> As one can imagine, great excitement reigned in the
> Nachodstraße. They were firmly convinced that
> the Germans would free Russia from Bolshevik
> tyranny. The peasants would give back the land, the
> Holy Orthodox Church would be restored to its rights
> and the exiles would return home. In a way they
> were already packing their bags.[75]

But it took a little longer, and the death of the Soviet system, rather than regathering the disparate elements of the Russian diaspora, set off a new flood of *émigrés* to the west. Once again many of these stopped in Berlin.

V

Despite National Socialist attempts to effect the contrary, Berlin has always been full of immigrants. Today Turks make up a sizeable element in the population. They are mostly to be found in Kreuzberg and Schöneberg, and to some degree in former working-class areas of West Berlin, such as Wedding. They came in the sixties. They replaced the East Berliners who had done the menial jobs up to then, but who were now prevented from working in West Berlin by the Wall. At the beginning of the decade there were just 225 of them. There were 39,000 by 1970; making one Kreuzberger in five a Turk.[76] Like the Russian *émigrés* of the later twenties and thirties, they keep themselves to themselves. The accidental death of a Kurdish militant woman in police custody in the summer of 1995 gave rise to a massive demonstration on the streets of the city, which served to remind Berliners that a fair number of them were not Turks at all, but Kurds.

The Turks' most distant Berlin ancestors were the courtiers, or *Kammertürken*, Hassan and Ali. In 1704 the court architect, Eosander von Göthe, built them both houses in the Schloßstraße in Charlottenburg. Both Turks had been brought back from the victory at Ofen in 1688,* to become a decorative feature of the Brandenburg-Prussian court. Ali was personally brought back by the leader of Brandenburg's expeditionary force, Hans Albrecht von Barfus. In 1692 he was convinced of the necessity of baptism.[77] One doubts that any such treatment was meted out to Achmet Effendi, the Turkish envoy who rented the Palais Verzenobre in 1763,[78] but that was in Frederick the Great's time and the ruler was already threatening the inhabitants of the capital with a mosque to prove how tolerant he was in religious matters.

Ali, Hassan and Achmet Effendi provided a rare touch of exoticism in the Prussian capital in the seventeenth and eighteenth centuries. A hundred years later 'moors' were to be had in exchange for coin in Berlin's brothels. In the 1840s there were two of them, and a mulatto living at number 36, Königsmauer. One of the moors ended her days in the Charité Hospital, presumably riddled with syphilis. The other, we are informed, was

> . . . a very merry and amusing creature who had no inkling of the lowly position in which she found

---

* Ofen is the German name for Buda (i.e., the part of Budapest lying on the right bank of the Danube). During the battle the name gave rise to a pun: 'Je näher dem Ofen, je größer die Hitze.' ('The nearer you are to [the] Ofen [oven], the hotter it gets.')

herself. She sang, screamed and skipped around the whole day long, was always good-natured and endeavoured to use her forces to keep her white colleagues in a good mood. She was so fat and ugly that it was actually difficult for her to pursue her trade as a prostitute and she succeeded above all as a result of her rarity value.

The mulatto was the offspring of a white sailor and a slave woman from Guadeloupe. She had arrived in Berlin after occupying similar positions in Paris and Hamburg.*[79]

In general, however, it would not be possible to make out that Berlin possessed the exotic, racially variegated character of port-cities such as Hamburg before this century. Most of the foreigners in Berlin were far less noticeable arrivals from the German-speaking world. Prussia's acquisition of the Swiss canton of Neuchâtel (or *Neuenburg*) in 1707 brought numbers of Swiss to the capital. There was a Swiss Guard in the Brandenburg-Prussian army and a Berner, Robert Scipio Lentulus, decided the Battle of Zorndorf in the Seven Years War. Probably the most famous Swiss in Berlin's history was the *Konditor* Johann Josty who founded the café of that name in the first years of the nineteenth century. Where others went out of fashion, Josty always contrived to remain somehow chic; possibly because its owners always had the sense to relocate the business to whatever part of Berlin was 'in' at any given time: from the Königstraße it went to the Schloßfreiheit, from the Schloßfreiheit to the Potsdamerplatz, from the Potsdamerplatz to the Kurfürstendamm, until it was finally burned out in November 1943.[80]

Apart from a few hundred Swiss, Berlin contained colonies of Walloons and Germans from the Palatinate.[81] As the city took on the character of a *Weltstadt* naturally other foreigners

---

* Coincidentally very similar in background and profession to 'Prinzessin Tebab', Hendrik Höfgen's lover in Klaus Mann's 1936 novel *Mephisto*.

came to see what the fuss was about, or to escape from unpleasantness at home. The latter was the case with the numerous German-speaking Bohemians, Hungarians and Romanians who came to Berlin when nationalist regimes and nation states were established after the First World War. These 'Austronaten' contributed greatly to the literary life of the city in the twenties.*[82]

Before the interwar years Berlin rarely if ever figured on the itineraries of Anglo-Saxon tourists. There is a rather ill-defined English *milord* and his lady in David Kalisch's farce *Berlin bei Nacht* (Berlin by Night) of 1849 who find everything 'sehr pluastisch', but in general it is fair to say that the only other Englishmen around would have been there on business or attached to the Embassy. One assumes that the former, but not the latter, made up the bulk of the British subjects interned in the race-track of Ruhleben in Charlottenburg during the First World War. The location was far from ideal: 'In that camp men of education, men in delicate health, were compelled to sleep and live six in a box-stall, or so closely that the beds touched each other in the haylofts, the outside walls of which were only four feet high.'[83]

It was the job of the American ambassador, James Gerard, to check on the correct handling of these British civilians. The commander of the camp was a kind-hearted old Junker called Graf Schwerin. The inmates were represented by a cinema-owner named Powell. The prisoners were allowed what now seems a remarkable amount of liberty within the walls of the race-track. The poorer ones were paid to cook and clean for the others, clubs were formed and the better-educated organised courses for the others. There were even performances of *Cinderella* and *The Mikado* in 1916 and 1917. It is all very different from accounts of how Britons were treated in the Second World War. In a now famous passage

* The name refers to the fact that they were formerly Austrian subjects.

in her book *The Past is Myself*, Christabel Bielenberg chanced
on a group of British and Irish soldiers who, despite the
strictures of the Geneva Convention, had been put to work
on the railway line in Klein Machnow, on the way to
Potsdam.[84] This was a rare sighting in either war. In general
POWs were kept away from the towns.

Ambassador Gerard also had dealings with a small, but
vociferously pro-German, group of American expatriates in
Berlin. There were reasons for certain Americans to be sympathetic, after all. A great many of them had only recently
emigrated to the United States and they were still thoroughly
imbued with German culture. One who particularly tried
Gerard was Maurice Somborn, who liked to make
impromptu speeches in beer halls attacking the president of
the United States.

> The American newspapers stated that I called a servant
> and had him thrown out of the Embassy. This
> statement is not entirely true. I selfishly kept that
> pleasure for myself.[85]

Later the Americans formed themselves into a 'League of
Truth' under the lead of a dentist. Their work was to tell
the German people that Woodrow Wilson and his policies
did not represent the true voice of America.

Beyond gradually emptying the city of its Jewish population, the early years of the Third Reich did not greatly
alter the ingredients of the Berlin stew; except, of course,
that first Bavarians and, later, Austrians took over some of
the functions of the civil service, particularly when it came
to policing and security. The Jews did not totally disappear
from view until 1943 (see below, pp. 434–5), by which time
Berlin had filled up with foreign workers: Poles, French,
Scandinavians, Balts, Ukrainians and Russians. In November
1944 the journalist Ursula von Kardorff ran into a huge

group of foreign workers taking refuge in the Friedrichstraße station:

> ... it is how I imagine Shanghai. Quaint, tattered forms in padded jackets with the high cheekbones of Slavs, between them flaxen-haired Danes and Norwegians, sexily got-up French women, Poles with looks of hatred in their eyes, pale, shivering Italians – a mishmash of peoples which can never have been seen in a German city before. Nearly all of them are foreigners, you scarcely hear a word of German. Most of them are forced labourers in munitions factories. Despite all that they don't give the impression of being in low spirits. Many of them are loud and jolly, they laugh, sing, swop, trade and live according to their own laws.[86]

As the war came to a end, Berliners began to make up to the foreign workers in the hope that they might speak up for them once the Allies arrived. As one woman put it, 'because we are going to take the blame for what happened to the Jews and Poles, and they are going to pay us back in kind'.[87] It proved an accurate enough prediction, only she had not reckoned on the fury of the Red Army, which was not likely to listen to special pleading from anybody.

VI

Berlin was the capital of Prussia, and from the time of the Great Elector onwards Prussia was best known for its army. The sight of men in uniform struck visitors before 1918 and again from 1933. Frederick William, the Great Elector, installed his bodyguard in the vicinity of the Schloss in 1658: 1,500 men with 400 wives and 500 children. As there were no barracks buildings yet, each and every one of them had to find lodgings in the small city. Later, under the Soldier-

King, Frederick William I, new houses in the Friedrichstadt were built with roomy mansards for the soldiers. Despite the homeliness of these arrangements, the presence of so many squaddies gave Berlin increasingly the appearance of an armed camp.[88]

The Soldier-King further altered the picture of his capital by more than doubling the size of the army in the course of his reign. The Ritterakademie, where noble children had received the rudiments of education, was closed down, and its buildings turned into a factory where cloth was worked into Prussian-blue uniforms.[89] In 1721 soldiers amounted to 12,000 in a population of just 53,355, or more than one in five. By 1735 their numbers had gone up to 16,000 by the garrisoning in the city of two more infantry regiments together with the Zieten Hussars. All had to be lodged with the citizens of Berlin.[90]

The Soldier-King's huge army was deemed inadequate by his son and successor. By the time of his death Frederick the Great had 190,000 troops under arms. The Austrian army may have been a third as much again, but Prussia had twice as many in proportion to its population.[91] Once again a large number of these soldiers were garrisoned in Berlin and Potsdam. Potsdam was well adapted for the use of soldiers. There were barracks buildings and a stately garrison church, with its austere lines one of the most characteristic pieces of architecture constructed in the Soldier-King's time. After the Seven Years War, Frederick created a proper garrison in Berlin complete with its own church[92] in order to house a military force which was to grow to 40,000 by the time of his death.[93] And it was not only Berlin proper which was clogged up with masses of soldiers; the royal palaces of Charlottenburg and Niederschönhausen required guards and the fortress of Spandau needed to be protected. In the mid-eighteenth century there were 4,484 civilians in Spandau (including 263 in fortress detention). The military presence amounted to 1,207 men, 416 women, 561 children and 22 servants.[94]

After Frederick's death, his nephew and great-nephew allowed the garrison levels to drop to under a sixth or a seventh of the total population.[95] By 1805, a year before Prussia was defeated at the battles of Jena and Auerstedt, the garrison numbers had fallen to 11,449, of which only 3,500 were actually soldiers.[96] The totals are possibly indicative of Frederick William III's innate pacifism and reluctance to get involved in the wars raging all over Europe.

Frederick William's lack of preparation and the antiquated tactics of the Prussian army led to a new expansion in the size of the garrison in Berlin; this time, though, they were not Prussian, but French troops. Tallies fluctuated between 12,000 and 30,000 in the months following the disaster. Even a year later there were still 10,000 of them. In Friedrich Nicolai's old house in Cölln there were twenty-two people and twelve horses to feed. Minister von Redern was putting up a general, a colonel, sixteen men and forty-one horses. Graf Dönhoff assessed his personal expenses during the French occupation at 30,000 thalers.[97]

When peace returned, barracks buildings went up all over the city. Berlin was now the biggest garrison in Germany. Kreuzberg had a particularly martial flavour. Soldiers had always drilled at the Rondell (Belle-Allianceplatz) and before 1913, when it was gradually transformed into an airport, the Tempelhofer Field was used for parading the colours. The events of 1848 worried the military authorities and prompted a further spate of barracks building on the then outskirts of Berlin. In 1850–1853 the architect Wilhelm Drewitz built the fortress-like edifice on the Mehringdamm* for the First Dragoon Guards. By 1900 Kreuzberg was home to five out of the thirteen regiments of the Berlin garrison.

It was inevitable that such a huge concentration of soldiers

---

* This has survived.

should begin to influence the *moeurs* of the Berliners, and possibly their way of thinking too. As much as 60 per cent of Frederick the Great's army had been made up of foreigners, German and non-German. These soldiers of fortune naturally had an attitude to life widely different from that of those poor Prussians who had been conscripted into the army by their king.[98]

More than the presence of the army, however, the factor which chiefly contributed to the formation of the Berlin character was the rapid industrialisation of the city in the second quarter of the nineteenth century. Before 1825 the city was still a *Residenzstadt*; life revolved around the royal palace and the institutions of the Prussian monarchy. In the 1830s and 1840s heavy industry took off in Berlin and floods of workers arrived from Silesia, Brandenburg and elsewhere in Germany in order to find work in the factories.

This was *Vormärz*: the period between Waterloo (or 'Belle-Alliance', as it was known to Prussians) and the 1848 Revolution. Berliners had been slow to present an image of themselves. After 1830 their first literary genre emerged in the *Posse*, or farce. The greatest *farceur* of the period was David Kalisch. Kalisch was born in Breslau in 1820. It was not until 1846 that he settled in Berlin after a two-year period in Paris and Strasbourg. Here he began to frequent Hippels Weinstube and rub shoulders with the likes of the philosophers Max Stirner and the brothers Bruno and Edgar Bauer. His first *Possen* were produced that same year. During the May days of the 1848 revolution Kalisch published the first issue of his radical newspaper *Kladderadatsch*.[99]

In plays such as *Berlin wie es lacht und weint* (Berlin as It Laughs and Cries) and *Berlin bei Nacht*, Kalisch gently taunts the reactionary Prussian state. One curious feature of all of Kalisch's farces is the presence of crooked Jews, typified by the brokers Zwickauer and Zittauer. Kalisch was a Jew himself and one assumes these typecast money-grubbers were supplied to pander to the anti-Semitic leanings of the Berlin populace.

Because Kalisch himself had travelled beyond the Rhine and seen the glories of Paris, he had more perspective than most when it came to describing Berlin's provincial air. In *Einmalhunderttausend Taler* (One Hundred Thousand thalers) of 1847, the fop Stullmüller returns from a trip to Paris, like the anti-hero of an English Restoration comedy, with a smattering of French words and fashions.

> *Zittauer*: 'Surely you could scarcely compare Berlin to Paris?'
> *Stullmüller* (with a refined smile): 'Berlin? Weak, very weak, compared with Paris, a market town, a village, a hole, a clod. Why, the place de la Concorde is bigger than the whole of Berlin, ha ha! Berlin is not a city – Linden are not proper trees. You should see the Champs-Elysées, now that's really something. The Tiergarten – pitiful, nothing special at all. The Jardin des Plantes – ah! That would make me happy, 50 elephants, 100 hyenas, 1,000 orang-utans and – bears, bears, bears – as far as the eye can see. Oh!

Kalisch can mock the pretensions of Berlin, but another stock in trade is the gormless provincial who arrives in the big city like a goose to be plucked. In *Berlin bei Nacht*, Dietrich Fischer comes up to Berlin to redeem his profligate nephew Heinrich. Almost at once an artful anarchist manages to filch his cigar with the justification that 'property is theft'. In his efforts to find Heinrich he falls foul of the police:

> No, that is too much! Really too much! To try to arrest me, an old man, on the public highway! Oh Berlin, so this is the face you wear by night! What must you be like in daytime![100]

★ ★ ★

The army was a transient element in Berlin's population. Some stayed after their period with the colours, others went home. The aspiring workers who left their homes in east and central Germany from the mid-thirties onwards were different. They tended to mingle into the never-ending flow of arrivals who had quit their provinces for good. This massive influx meant that the native Berliner became a rare bird indeed. The writer Kurt Tucholsky, writing to Marcel Belvianes in 1929, expressed the commonly held view that Berlin was a Silesian city. Referring to himself, he writes: 'The chap was born in Berlin in 1890 (most Berliners come from Breslau).'[101]

This was certainly true of some of the more famous Berliners of the nineteenth and early twentieth centuries. Adolph Menzel, for example, was born in Breslau in 1815. Another painter, Hans Baluschek, whose canvases and prints depict the Berlin worker at the turn of the century and the first three decades of the twentieth, was another Breslauer who came to Berlin with his family, aged six.[102] Later in life he made a light-hearted sketch of the Friedrichstraße complete with a sign showing the way to Breslau. On the literary side, writer and actor Karl von Holtei and the writers Gustav Freytag and Gerhart Hauptmann were all Silesians.

Within the fifty years from 1800 to 1850, the nature of the Berliner had changed utterly. When Freiherr Adolf von Lützow made a brief halt in Berlin in 1813, in the course of his 'wild and daring pursuit' of the French, the born Berliner surveyed the population with contempt; possibly this had been affected by the years of occupation:

> Incidentally, Berlin is a dreadful hive of petty
> bureaucrats. Everyone apes the court. I shan't wholly
> write off the education and intelligence of the
> Berliner, [but] there is something lacking, they have
> all sunk into dilettantism, outward show and snobbery.

Great luxury reigns. A father would rather see his
children beg than deny his guests champagne. Women
never cease to need new fripperies and don't give a
thought to the fact that one day their children will be
reduced to rags.[103]

Goethe had been attracted by the sharper side of Berliners
when he described them as 'a saucy brand of humanity';[104]
to his friend Carl Friedrich Zelter he wrote, 'Describe it as
crudely as you can, that fits you Berliners best.'[105] Zelter, for
his own part, was not unaware of the special nature of his
fellow citizens. Writing to Goethe in June 1819 he pointed
out

That Berlin is a rather individual place is rarely
acknowledged, but it is none the less just as true as
it is for the good. This is no complaint against
strangers, who for the most part are happy to come
and also like to prolong their stay . . . The king himself
feels a stranger here [yet] he can't stay away from us.
Frederick the Great wanted to make something out of
Potsdam, both he and his forefathers had done
enough for Berlin, the Berlin Prussian is a hardy beast
who lives according to his own laws . . .[106]

Goethe and Zelter indicate that something of the Berlin
character was identifiable before the city burst its bounds
with the influx of easterners. Hebbel, too, thought he could
spot a Berliner at close quarters. In 1854 he ran into a
parvenu Berlin jeweller taking the waters at Marienbad:

A farcical character who reminded me of [E. T. A.]
Hoffmann's Peter Schönfeld and who proved that the
most fantastic creations of our novelists, *even if they are
not derived from the real world, they can at least be modelled
on Berlin.*★[107]

★ Hebbel's italics. The barber Schönfeld appears in Hoffmann's
Die Elixiere des Teufels. The novel was conceived in Leipzig.

But it is hard to believe that this individual character of the Berliner was not greatly stretched, if not radically altered, by first industrialisation and secondly the lure of the new imperial capital the city became in 1871. In that year the police reported 133,700 people applying for residence, most of them 16 to 30-year-olds. Some of these left again, but at least 50,000 of them stayed on.[108]

By the turn of the century the old incumbents were beginning to decry these newly wrought Berliners. The ill-fated Weimar foreign minister, Walther Rathenau, referred to the city as 'Parvenupolis . . . the parvenu among capital cities and the capital of parvenus'.[109] He was not wrong. A modern commentator points out that Berlin at the time was overwhelmingly made up of 'homines novi': the Berliner was a typical big-city product, one who believes more in performance than privilege and thinks the future carries more weight than a man's origins. The new Berliner was a self-made man such as Kommerzienrat Treibel in Fontane's *Frau Jenny Treibel* of 1892.[110] It is this quasi-total break with the city's past which leads so many writers to draw comparisons with North American cities, notably New York; it was the precise reason why the old Prussian nobility hated the city so much, and why they came no closer than Potsdam unless the court was there, they had a new dress to buy or a daughter to marry.

The Berlin masses were increasingly polarised from a political point of view: a real proletariat mechanised with demonic Prussian efficacy. Their only hope was the overthrow of the regime which held them down through the infamous three-tier electoral system. It took Germany's defeat in the First World War to bring this about. The sheer nihilism of the Berlin's *hoi polloi* appalled the novelist Heinrich Mann in 1906. He wrote to a friend:

> Since I came to Berlin I live under the weight of this slavish mass without ideals. The old, misanthropic

mentality of the Prussian NCO has been welded on
to the mechanised enormity of the capital city and
the result is the decline of human dignity on all
fronts . . . In the stations, in the sweating cafés, I
sometimes have the feeling that if a detachment of
policemen were to appear suddenly and butcher ten
or twenty units [sic] from the crowd – the others
wouldn't either miss their trains as a result or let their
coffees get cold.[111]

The *Weltstadt* Berlin shocked Mann, but for many other
Germans it had a lethal attraction: 30,000 of them arrived
each day at those very same stations in which Mann had
imagined the police wielding their sabres.[112] Arthur Eloesser
was born on the Prenzlauerberg in 1870, the son of a small-
time Jewish businessman who had migrated from Ortelsburg
in East Prussia.[113] Eloesser grew up in a city in rapid transition.
By the time he had finished his studies at the University
certain 'streets of his youth' were already unrecognisable. As
a successful journalist and *littérateur* he moved to the 'new'
west in the years before the First World War, where he
penned, among other things, nostalgic articles for the
Voßische Zeitung on the good, old Berlin.

In Eloesser's childhood, Berlin was still a horse-drawn city.
The *Mietshaus* where the family lived in the Prenzlauerstraße
had stabling at the back and reeked suitably of horses. A
short walk brought young Arthur out into the fields, where
he and his friends could romp around in the haystacks bor-
dering sandy pastures: 'without exaggeration, we were in the
middle of the Mark'.[114] By the turn of the century, Berlin
had become the bland, mechanised place of Mann's description. Even the dialect had become a rarity. The Silesians,
Brandenburgers and East Prussians concealed their individual
origins: 'People don't speak *Berlinisch*, but they don't speak
any other dialect either; no one allows himself to be an
exception from the general colourlessness and odourless-

ness.'[115] Another notable feature of the new citizens was their ignorance of the past.

> For the 'old Berliner' who moved to Friedenau from
> Breslau ten years ago, I should actually let it be
> known that the *Stadtbahn* wasn't always there, that it
> doesn't date from the time of the Wends either.[116]

A new Berliner was being gradually formed, one which exhibited only a few of the characteristics of the old. *Pace* Eloesser, the language had not disappeared. Evelyn Blücher, an English Catholic woman who had married a descendant of that 'Marshal Vorwärts' who defeated Napoleon at Waterloo, passed the First World War in the Esplanade Hotel in the Tiergarten surrounded by a coterie of fellow nobles. She found Berlin speech 'abrupt and slangy'[117] and compared it unfavourably to Bavarian (which she confessed she didn't understand). Albert Albinus, the refined victim (one could hardly call him the hero) of Vladimir Nabokov's novel *Laughter in the Dark* of 1933, was excited by the same 'vulgar garrulity' and coarse Berlin slang which so offended Fürstin Blücher when he heard it in the mouth of his tormenter, Margot Peters.[118]

Margot was Albinus's undoing. Many shared Fürstin Blücher's distaste when it came to the vulgar habits of the Berlin mob. Alfred Döblin came from Stettin in Pomerania, Berlin's seaport, and as such could pass for a Berliner just as well as any Breslauer. He was none the less repelled by the coarse behaviour of theatre-goers in the twenties. In the bars and foyers 'they stuff their cheeks full of food, slobber and stare at one another. They all have plenty to occupy their hands at the buffet; only when the bell rings do they get up, wipe their mouths and leave, sucking their teeth all the way to the auditorium. Then the play begins.'[119] Döblin's nightmare was just beginning: chocolates and sweets were now unwrapped and the papers noisily scrunched up during the play. A later visit yielded no improvement in the situation:

> Even before the beginning of the performance they
> were sucking pralinés right and left; in the intervals
> a crowd of people stood there; a gaggle of common
> faces, laughing, gossiping and shouting, their dewlaps
> stuffed with ham rolls: beer glasses in their hands . . .
> Art! Artistic achievements! God save the artist from
> coming into contact with his 'fans'.[120]

★ ★ ★

The Second World War wrought new changes in the Berliner. Many died either in the fighting or in the bombing; some were evacuated; others fled the Russians. With the Airlift, the uprising of 1953 and Khrushchev's sabre-rattling in 1957, many Berliners gave up the struggle. Their places were taken by refugees from the parts of Germany east of the Oder-Neiße Line, which had been ceded to Poland and the Soviet Union. In the western zones young people in particular took advantage of the open-handedness of the regime towards those who wanted to come and fill the void. There was no military service for Berliners and the city was showered with subsidies. The result was, at least as far as the west was concerned, that the *Urberliner* (i.e., those who had been there since before the war) became an endangered species. Much of what was considered *Berlinisch* after 1945 was merely an expression of the unique political role performed by the divided city. West Berlin had lost touch with its roots.

2

Berlin Itineraries

I

Our century has been one of brutal purges: political, social, racial and, indeed, historical. Rewriting the history of central Europe has amounted to nothing short of an industry since the war, especially in the old communist block: east of the Elbe, history was a weapon until 1989, and to some extent it still is.

If the history books needed to be rewritten, monuments also needed to be realigned, moved, rededicated, put into storage, or, indeed, pulled down when and if they didn't fit in with the ruling orthodoxy. It was a form of political correctness *avant la lettre*, and, in many instances, a thousand times more pernicious. In its simplest form it meant taking down an eagle or a swastika or cleaning a tomb of an inscription: 'Für Führer und Vaterland gestorben' ('Died for the Führer and the Fatherland'). In Poland it has meant setting up Catholic-style onion domes on top of old Lutheran churches, or bulldozing cemeteries filled with German graves so that later inhabitants can happily deny the fact that Germans had ever lived there. When it came to the major monuments – public buildings, *Schlößer* and manor houses – many of these were destroyed in the Russian advance. Of those that survived, a percentage were pulled down or simply fell down. Only when the Party, the police or the army could find a suitable use for a building did it survive.

Naturally many buildings in Berlin were politically sensitive when it came to the new SED regime in the east. None more so than the Schloss. Its detonation in 1950 rid the socialists of an embarrassing reminder of Hohenzollern power and magnificence. For five hundred years it had been the symbol of their political ambitions on the one side, and their authority on the other. The Schloss was a paradox: it was built specifically to subdue the independent spirit of the Berliner, but as a guarantee of Hohenzollern residence it underlined the status of Berlin. While the Schloss was there, so were the princes; and the princes brought work, money and status.

The Berlin Burg, or fortress, as it was originally known, was begun in 1443 following the revolt or *Unwillen* (see below, p. 409). Towards the Spree the building wore a forbidding face, with its copper-covered towers. One of these, the *grüner Hut*, or 'green hat', together with a small number of late mediaeval rooms, survived until the building was dynamited after the war. Towards the town of Cölln, however, the Elector modified the design to allow for an open courtyard in the form of a *cour d'honneur*. The Elector had evidently forgiven his subjects and built a *Schloß* instead of the promised *Burg*. This less austere aspect once again underlined Berlin's transformation from a trading community to a royal residence.[1]

With those one or two exceptions, Frederick Irontooth's building survived for only a century. The Elector Joachim II, the first of the Hohenzollern rulers to make Berlin his one real home, had the mediaeval palace taken down and replaced by something more suited to contemporary tastes. His architects were Konrad Krebs, a Saxon who had designed Schloß Hartenfels in Torgau, and Caspar Theiß, another Saxon who finished off the work after Krebs' death in 1540. Theiß also designed hunting lodges at Köpenick* and Gru-

---

* The present Schloss Köpenick was constructed by Rutger van Langervelts and Nering between 1677 and 1693.

newald, connecting the latter with Berlin by laying out a new road, the Kurfürstendamm.[2]

An anonymous painting of 1685 in the Märkisches Museum shows the Schloss from the banks of the Spree, much as Theiß left it, modified only by Nering's one-storey arcade. The decoration is chiefly made up of high Renaissance gables, which cover not only the side wings, but also the top of the *grüner Hut*. In the *cour d'honneur* Krebs and Theiß made the centrepiece a complicated spiral staircase based on the one built at Blois by King Francis I of France. The Blois-style staircase was swept away in the changes made by Andreas Schlüter, but one part of the Krebs and Theiß alterations survived until 1945: the Erasmus Chapel. South of the Schloss a collegiate church staffed by eight canons had been built in 1465, but the elector needed a chapel of his own.[3]

The chapel was dedicated to St Erasmus or Elmo and served as a showplace for the relics of the same Syrian bishop, who gave his name to 'St Elmo's fire'. Here Theiß designed a superb late Gothic vault of sinewy, interlaced ribs. Renaissance motifs and coats of arms figured in the divisions between the transverse arches: a mixture of styles readily comprehensible to anyone from the British Isles, where the transition to full-throated Renaissance architecture was a long drawn-out affair. The need for a private chapel must have been partially dictated by Joachim's reluctance to go over to the Lutheran religion which had captivated most of his subjects in Berlin. In the eighteenth century the chapel was divided in two.[4]

The next architect to be involved in the development of the Schloss was the Florentine, Rocco Guerrini, or Rochus von Lynar, to give him the name he adopted as a Prussian nobleman, who had been responsible for the new design of the citadel in Spandau. Lynar designed the 'Duchess's Wing' on the Spree side of the palace with its pepper-pot towers and Dutch gables and the 'Apothecaries' Wing', a rather more informal range of buildings which the last Kaiser, with his customary combination of zeal and philistinism, had shortened to create his Kaiser-Wilhelm bridge and avenue. It was a piece of grandfather-worship which reduced the tally of interesting old Berlin monuments at a stroke. Lynar also built half the range that separated the two courtyards of the palace, the 'Kanzleibau', or Chancellery, a curious seven-storey building divided half-way up by an overhang.[5]

Damage in the Thirty Years War gave the Great Elector an excuse to remodel the Berlin Schloss. He had visited his capital for the first time as elector in 1643 and found to his dismay that the palace could provide him with no animal fodder, beer, butter or wax. Worse still, there was no wine for his majesty.[6] The decision to rebuild provided work for the city population but materials had to be brought in from as far away as Hamburg, an inconvenience which may have inspired Frederick William to build the canal that bore his name.* The new rooms built during the Great Elector's time were swept away by his successors. The one substantial piece of work which survived (until 1950) was the 'Alabaster Hall' next to Lynar's Kanzleibau; its squat form making it an uncomfortable partner for the lofty Chancellery. It was designed by Johann Gregor Memhardt, who also laid out the Lustgarten, or royal pleasure garden, to the north.[8]

As far as the abiding exterior image of the Schloss was concerned, the real creator of Berlin's greatest monument was the Great Elector's son, the hunchbacked Elector Frederick III, later first King in Prussia. Initially he continued the piecemeal reconstruction of his father's time using the architects Michel Matthias Smids and Johann Arnold Nering. Nering worked with Jean de Bodt on the new Arsenal and was responsible for the royal stables across the way from the Schloss to the south.[9] Nering's work was also visible on

* When it was finished in 1669 ships could travel all the way from Hamburg to Silesia via Berlin.[7]

the Spree wing, between the Duchess's House and the Apothecaries' Wing.

The real incentive to build something splendid came with Frederick's grasping after a royal crown. Not only his capital, but also his palace, had to be a perfect mirror image of his own pretensions. His chief collaborator in this was the Danzig-born architect and sculptor Andreas Schlüter, whose ideas had a magnificence which echoed Frederick's own. It is an indication of how far Schlüter was prepared to go that he designed the famous Amber Room which German soldiers stole from Catherine the Great's palace in Tsarskoe Selo during the Second World War. It had originally been destined for Berlin but was still incomplete when Frederick died. His austere son wanted nothing to do with it and in 1716 he gave it to Peter the Great as a present in exchange for fifty-five of the giant soldiers, or *lange Kerls*, he valued so highly.[10]

Schlüter was not the only architect then working at the Prussian court who envisaged a beautiful baroque conception for the Schloss: Jean-Baptiste Broebes, a member of Frederick's newfangled Academy of the Arts, laid plans in 1701 to double the size of the Schloss by adding a central square, a military hospital and a new cathedral to replace the Dominican church, which, being Gothic, was now unfashionable.[11] The scheme is reminiscent of the position of the church of Santa Agnese in the Piazza Navona in Rome. It was a period for grandiose palace projects: the Louvre and Whitehall came only partly to fruition; then there were the Escorial lookalikes: the unfinished Klosterneuburg in Austria and Mafra in Portugal.

In 1704 Schlüter built a wonderful baroque mint tower between the Arsenal and the Schloss, but he did not understand how to lay the foundations for the building and two years later the tower had to be dismantled. Frederick's construction mania was already stretching the patience of the thrifty Brandenburgers. Charlottenburg was being financed by a stamp tax; Köpenick was paid for by postal charges. In 1698 Frederick was reduced to taxing the luxuries he loved so dearly with his wig and carriage tax. Architects who couldn't do their measurements properly had become increasingly difficult to justify. Schlüter's dismissal had a wider significance for the architectural history of Berlin. With his departure Berlin's first golden age came to an end.[12]

Schlüter introduced the full armoury of baroque theatre in his designs for the Schloßplatz and Lustgarten frontages, as well as the triumphal façade on the Kleiner Schloßhof, or second courtyard, of the palace: a unified composition with projecting sections with attached giant columns and grandiose stairways leading to the most palatial rooms. Naturally the triumphal arch was a favourite motif when Schlüter collaborated with his king's ambitions. It is used much more sparingly in the work after Schlüter's departure.[13] The change in direction this represented also involved scrapping plans to demolish the Kanzleibau and the Alabastersaal which obscured the effect of Schlüter's magnificent design for the inner courtyard. Schlüter's great stairway was possibly his most notable achievement. As a sculptor he understood how to arrange the smallest detail of the rich decoration and free-standing figures.

Schlüter's work was carried on by two lesser talents, the Swede Johann Friedrich Eosander von Göthe and Martin Heinrich Böhme, who had the thankless task of bringing the work to completion for Frederick's frugal son, Frederick William I. Eosander duplicated Schlüter's work on the Lustgarten façade and built the large-scale triumphal arch facing the Schloßfreiheit. Böhme unified the exterior, repeating Schlüter's Schloßplatz portico and keeping the rest very much in harmony. Gone, however, were the projects for monumental rooms such as Schlüter's Rittersaal (knights' hall) and Schwarze-Adler Saal (Black Eagle Hall). Magnificent interior arrangements would have to skip a generation.

Frederick's baroque city was the centre of his absolute

state. Sadly, he was unable to emulate fully that other *nouveau royal*, the King of Saxony, whose capital, Dresden, far exceeded Berlin in splendour. Frederick simply did not have that sort of money. He none the less abolished the last of the city's privileges and sent the cult of kingship out on to the streets of the new *quartier* of Friedrichstadt. The names of the main avenues were dedicated to the glory of his house: Friedrichstraße, Charlottenstraße, Wilhelmstraße and Markgrafenstraße.[14] Frederick the Great dismissed his grandfather's court as 'one of the most luxurious in Europe . . .'[15] He was not wrong. It was certainly the most spendthrift in Germany. In 1711 and 1712 Frederick I employed 55 noblemen at court and six doctors. The court orchestra was composed of 36 musicians, plus a further 24 trumpeters and two timpanists.[16] Antonio Cambiola, the court castrato, was paid the princely stipend of 500 Talers.

Frederick William I stopped the expenditure at once, going so far as to cut the feed to the horses in the royal stables. The building continued, presumably because it had to be finished, but it is hard to imagine that Frederick William had any enthusiasm for the project. Unlike most of his forefathers and successors he left no new rooms. In the substantial tracts which were finished in the first three years of his reign there was no gilding; the rooms were covered with a few coats of whitewash and that was that.[17]

Frederick the Great was born in the Berlin Schloss, but it was not high up on the list of his favourites. He preferred Potsdam and, if he were forced to come any nearer to Berlin, Charlottenburg. To tidy up the Schloßplatz he had the Dom, the former Dominican church, pulled down and a rather weak new cathedral set up in the Lustgarten on the other side of the palace. He confined his improvements to the Schloss to the interior. In 1745 he had a suite prepared for his own use. This included the *Schreibkammer*, or study, which managed to survive the destructive zeal of Kaiser William II. The room was circular with a shallow dome: a nostalgic allusion to his study in one of the towers at Rheinsberg in the Mark, where he had enjoyed a relatively carefree youth. Among his favourite palm motifs and rococo *boiseries* he hung up the Antoine Pesne portrait of Barbarina Campanini, the Venetian dancer who won fame and fortune by being the token woman in the old misanthropist's life.[18]

It was to the Schloss that Frederick reluctantly returned after the final campaign of the Seven Years War. Graf Ahasverus Lehndorff committed the scene to his diary, including the king's curmudgeonly treatment of his court, family and wife:

> *30 March 1760.* The whole city has been on its feet since eight. The city guilds are doing their best to make this as splendid as possible.
>
> Before 3 p.m. there is a new alarm every quarter of an hour: the king is before the gates. This goes on until 7 p.m., when we finally receive the report that he won't arrive before nine. I have never experienced such dejection. All these poor citizens, for whom no effort would have been too much to properly honour their lord, absent these seven years, are inconsolable.

The windows closed and 50,000 Berliners disappeared from the streets. Only the burghers remained.

At nine, 3,000 people reassembled according to rank before the Schloss. There was still no sign of the king. Then came the news that he had deviated from the planned route and that he had secretly entered the palace. He had been in his apartments for fifteen minutes. 'It was destined to be a day of disappointments in every respect', noted Lehndorff. Half an hour later Frederick appeared. He embraced both his surviving brothers and thanked the Dutch consul for his heroic behaviour during the occupation. The Danish consul, who had acted cravenly, he ignored. Then he returned to his rooms. Later he reappeared and led the company in to dinner. His only words to his wife were: 'Madam, you have got fatter!'[19]

Frederick William II took more interest in the Schloss than his uncle had done. It was he who discovered the Silesian architect Carl Gotthard Langhans and brought him from Breslau to Berlin. As well as building the Marmorpalais in Potsdam and the Brandenburg Gate in Berlin, Langhans was responsible for a suite of rooms at the Schloss. The new guardroom, or *Pfeilersaal*, was the most sumptuous of these with its marble Ionic columns and its elliptical ceiling. After forty years of Frederick's mania for rococo *putti* Berlin was longing for a new style. Langhans introduced a sober, Anglo-Saxon brand of neo-classicism. The *Parolesaal* was designed by Friedrich Wilhelm von Erdmannsdorf, who had been working with the Prince of Anhalt-Dessau at Schloss Wörlitz. Once again the room owed more to the Brothers Adam than any German precedent.[20]

The very modest King Frederick William III eschewed luxury and preferred to live in the Kronprinzen-Palais on Unter den Linden. His son, the later Frederick William IV, however, was an amateur architect of talent and a patron of Berlin's greatest architect, Karl Friedrich Schinkel. In 1825, the then crown prince made some sketches for converting Frederick the Great's old quarters into his own apartment and entrusted them to Schinkel. The best of these rooms, in a sober, Greek-revival style, were the tea-room and the Sternsalon (or star salon, from the stellar motif on the ceiling). Both fell victim to William II before the century was out.[21]

A born romantic, a believer in the divine right of kings, Frederick William promised an aesthetic regimen. When he came to the throne in 1840 Prussian liberals had high hopes for the new monarch. Bettina von Arnim witnessed the Berlin ceremony from the steps of Schinkel's Altes Museum, behind the city's notables in their specially constructed box.[22] The king spoke from a construction tacked on to the side of the Schloss richly hung with gold and purple, into which his throne had been installed.* He told the orders what he expected from their homage: 'Do you wish to help me and support me . . . to reveal ever more splendidly the qualities which Prussia with its fourteen million has delivered to the world?' Bettina commented, 'They were words that one had never before read or heard from a Prussian king.'[23]

For the first time since 1716, changes were made to the exterior of the Schloss. In 1845–1853, Frederick William had the architects Friedrich August Stüler and Albert Dietrich Schadow build a dome over Eosander von Göthe's portal on the Schloßfreiheit. The design was adapted from one by Schinkel, who had died in 1841.[24] The dome was tall enough to become a notable feature in Berlin's skyline. In Fontane's novella *L'Adultera* of 1882 the party gazes back towards the city centre from the river at Stralau: 'Look, Melanie', says van der Straaten. 'The dome of the Schloss. Doesn't it look like Santa Maria Saluta?' ' "Saluté," corrected Melanie, placing the accent on the last syllable.'[25]

The creation of the new dome was a pretext for some new interior arrangements. Under it Frederick William had Stüler design a new court chapel with seating for 700 worshippers. The octagonal room under the dome was in a contemporary *Rundbogensstil*, drawing on Florentine Renaissance forms with a profusion of marble and historical portraiture. Next door Stüler converted Frederick William I's ballroom into the new Weißer Saal. Frederick William IV's last changes were to introduce the first terrace on the Lustgarten side of the Schloss.[26]

Frederick William had a stroke in 1857, and was no longer capable of carrying out his duties as Prussia's ruler. His brother William stepped in as regent and in 1861 took over from the childless aesthete who had earned only opprobrium

---

* In the KPM vase made to celebrate the occasion, the awnings over the royal throne are red.

for himself by his attempts to steer Prussia safely through the revolutions of 1848. William was far from being a pacifist (neither Frederick William III nor his eldest son, Frederick William IV, had much time for the Prussian arts of war), but in one thing he took after his father: he was simple and sober and shunned luxury. After taking over from his brother in 1858 he continued to live in his own palace on Unter den Linden, a former residence of the Margraves of Schwedt, cousins of Prussia's rulers, which had been refitted by Schinkel and Carl Ferdinand Langhans.[27] It was here that his devotees or *Schwärmer* came to observe him at his desk in the years after the Wars of Unification. When the guards came down the Linden he would rise to accept their salute. At this moment the crowd would break into spontaneous applause.[28] The scene is captured in an 1887 watercolour by Franz Skarbina.[29]

William was the first Hohenzollern Kaiser. His son ruled for too short a period to have much influence on Prussia's destiny or its architecture. Not so his grandson, Kaiser William II. As far as the Schloss was concerned, the Kaiser continued his great-uncle's comparatively harmless policy of surrounding the building with terraces. He had the Apothecaries' Wing shortened for his new Kaiser Wilhelm Straße and in the Großer Schloßhof he rebuilt a section of Eosander von Göthe's work, ruining the proportions of the fenestration in the process.[30] The Kaiser's effect on the interior of the palace was even more damaging. Apart from filling his own quarters with the usual clutter of late nineteenth-century *Gemütlichkeit*, William ripped out some of the best interiors and transformed Stüler's Weißer Saal by adding a giant order and elaborate screens and staircases.[31] It was here on 4 August 1914 that he assembled the members of the German Reichstag and informed them, to their immense joy, 'I recognise no more political parties, only Germans.'[32]

The Kaiser had been pulling his palace apart right up to the beginning of the war. In 1914 he had asked his favourite

(and truly second-rate) architect Ernst von Ihne* to alter
Eosander's picture gallery. The Kaiser also had the tiny garden
rearranged to his taste. It was here that Ambassador Gerard
had his interview with him after the outbreak of war.

> I drove in a motor into the courtyard of the Palace,
> and was there escorted to a door which opened on
> a flight of steps leading to a little garden, about fifty
> yards square, directly on the embankment of the
> River Spree, which flows past the Royal Palace . . .
> I found the Emperor seated at a green iron table,
> under a large, canvas garden umbrella. Telegraph
> forms were scattered on the table in front of him, and
> basking in the gravel were two small dachshunds.[33]

The war cost the Kaiser his throne and his Schloss. The
building played its role in the creation of the Republic when
Karl Liebknecht made a dramatic gesture calculated to make
him popular with the crowd, described by Fürstin Blücher:

> Out of the great gateway a rider dashed on horseback,
> waving likewise a red flag, and at the same moment
> one of the windows opened on to a balcony in front
> of the castle, and on the same spot where four and a
> half years ago the Kaiser made his great appeal to the
> enthusiastic people, Liebknecht appeared, shouting
> to the masses that they were now freed from the
> bondages of the past and that a new era of liberty
> was opening out before them. History repeats, or
> rather mimics herself [sic], in a somewhat tasteless
> way at times.[34]

Unlike Evelyn Blücher, the aesthete and diplomat Harry Graf
Kessler's curiosity got the better of him and he made his way
up to the Schloss. It had been occupied by revolutionaries,
who had caused a good deal of damage: 'Lights burned
brightly but desultorily in one or another part of the Palace;

---

* Ihne had been ennobled in 1906.

everything was quiet. Patrols all around; they challenged and let me through. In front of the Imperial Stables a good deal of splintered masonry. A sentry told me that "young rascals" were still hidden in the Palace and Stables. There are secret passages through which they disappear and reappear.' Kessler slowly made his way home. It had been 'one of the most memorable and dreadful days in German history'.[35]

The liberal Kessler was able to win the revolutionaries' trust. On 28 December he visited the Schloss to inspect the damage.

> A grenade landed in the Hall of Pillars and, tearing to shreds a Skarbina painting, pierced the rear wall. The private apartments of the Emperor and Empress, especially the dressing-rooms, have been pretty badly looted. With a single exception, the Empress's wardrobes have been emptied and deep inroads made into those belonging to the Emperor . . . It seems difficult to say how far the sailors have been responsible for the pillage. But these private apartments, the furniture, the articles of everyday use, and what remains of the Emperor's and Empress's mementoes and *objets d'art* are so insipid and tasteless, so philistine, that it is difficult to feel much indignation against the pilferers. Only astonishment that the wretched, timid, unimaginative creatures who liked this trash, and frittered away their lives in this precious palatial haven, amidst lackeys and sycophants, could ever make any impact on history. Out of this atmosphere was born the World War, or as much of the guilt for it as falls on the Emperor. In this rubbishy, trivial, unreal microcosm, furnished with nothing but false values which deceived him and others, he made his judgements, plans and decisions. Morbid taste and a pathologically excitable character in charge of an all too well-oiled machine of state. Now the symbols of his futile animating spirit lie strewn around here in the shape of doltish odds and ends.[36]

Once the revolution had been quelled and the mutinous soldiers and sailors dismissed, the new Weimar Republic had the Schloss patched up and turned into a museum. There lived on in the vast building a few old courtiers such as Eberhard von Schweinitz, the son of Bismarck's ambassador to St Petersburg. In the course of a visit to his friend Adam von Trott, the British historian A. L. Rowse was given the chance to look round the old royal apartments.

> I well recall the Kaiser's study: the telephone cords
> looking as if they had just been cut, the big desk
> made of timbers from Nelson's *Victory*, the books, half
> German and half English, half Lutheran theology, half
> contemporary history and biography. I still recall
> among them Churchill's biography of his father, Lord
> Randolph, and Bishop Boyd Carpenter on prayer.
> Behind the doors everywhere, I was surprised to see,
> were stacked pictures of the *Allerhöchste* in peacock
> attitudes, eagles in his helmet, flunkeys bowing before
> him . . .[37]

Rowse saw only what the Kaiser had left behind. In the summer of 1919 the Weimar authorities had allowed the ex-Kaiser to take away around eighty wagonloads of property to the seat of his exile, the manor house at Doorn in Holland. In the rooms of his Berlin palace appeared a museum of the decorative arts, a museum composed of the royal apartments, and, more curious by far, a PE museum devoted to physical jerks. Various academic bodies had their headquarters in the Schloss. The number of remaining residents varied during the Weimar years, from a dozen to thirty.[38] The huge building was clearly an embarrassment to the *petit bourgeois* who made up the bulk of Nazi bigwigs (although it seems a surprise that Göring didn't make a grab for it). It remained largely empty and underused until it was gutted by fire in February 1945.[39]

After the end of the war parts of the building were patched

up and used for exhibitions. Many recall the show devoted to the future of Berlin planning which opened in the Weißer Saal in August 1946. Few remember that other exhibitions followed: modern French art, objects from the city's collections and finally, in March 1948, the Schloss honoured the men of the 1848 Revolution. This was to be its final role. The man chiefly responsible for the demolition of the substantial ruins of Berlin's greatest historic monument was the Party Secretary Walter Ulbricht. Various motives have been ascribed to him, including Saxon resentment towards Prussia and revenge for the former's successive invasions.[40] The city's new architectural supremo, Hans Scharoun, wanted funds for the palace's restoration as early as 1946. These were opposed by the communist Mayor of Friedrichshain, Heinrich Starck, who expressed the view that the Schloss was the symbol of 'period which is no longer acceptable to us'.[41] Ulbricht's opinion, advanced in the course of the 3rd Party Conference, did not hinge on the need to remove the monuments to Prussian militarism. He wanted to see the centre of the city used for 'a huge square where we can demonstrate . . . both the readiness of our people for struggle and for recreation'.[42]

Despite last-minute attempts to save small sections of the Schloss and rebuild them in the Monbijou Park across the river,★ the demolition was begun on 6 September 1950 with the destruction of the Apothecaries' Wing. All in all it took just three months to destroy the work of five centuries. Eosander's triumphal portal was the last to go. It crumbled into dust just before the old year came to an end, on 30 December 1950.[43]

★ Scharoun pleaded with Otto Grotewohl for the preservation of the Schlüter courtyard as a memorial to the wartime destruction.

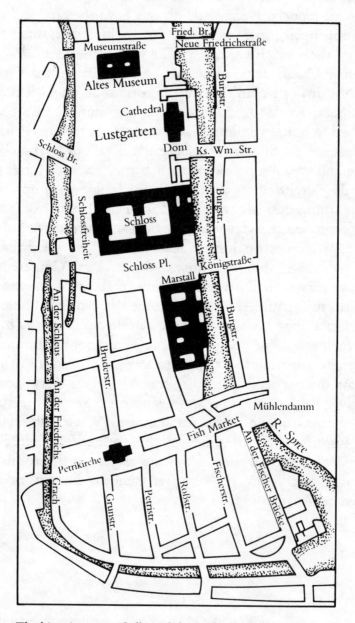

The historic centre: Cölln and the Schloss

II

From the desolate exercise yard created by Ulbricht after he had the Schloss blown up it is almost impossible to get an impression of how the area originally looked. With its back towards Friedrichswerder was originally the Schloßfreiheit: 'a row of massive, mostly tall houses' was how the topographer Nicolai described them in 1769. The Schloßfreiheit was neither in Cölln nor Berlin, but depended directly on the Royal Palace, which absolved residents of the need to pay certain civic levies – hence the name.[44] The terrace contained a number of hotels and cafés, including Josty. Old photographs show a pleasant *alt-Berliner* jumble of shops and pubs. In the early 1890s the Kaiser had it all torn down to put up another monument in the cultus of his ancestors: Reinhold Begas's statue of Kaiser William I. The equestrian group was surrounded on three sides by a colonnade by Ihne in a fashionable neo-baroque style.

Before Unter den Linden was laid out, the Lustgarten, to the north of the Schloss, was the city's fashionable promenade. Originally it extended as far as the tip of Cölln, but its site was always too circumscribed to make it a proper park like the Tiergarten. The landscape gardener Peter Lenné transformed the Tiergarten at the precise moment when the Prussian kings were turning the northern tip of the Lustgarten into the 'Museum Island', leaving just a small patch of garden between the Schloss and Schinkel's Altes Museum. The Nazis expressed their perverse understanding of the word 'pleasure'* by ripping up the trees and bushes and transforming the compact space into a parade-ground.

South of the Schloss was the Marstall, or royal stables. The surviving building is partially the work of Smids and Memhardt, but needless to say the ubiquitous Ihne – the Kaiser's Schinkel – had a go at it too. Berliners loved to mock its pompous statuary. One of the figures described Prometheus chained to his rock, his liver being very slowly pecked out by an eagle: 'Ach, der arme Adler; alle Dage Leber!' ('Poor old eagle; never gets a break from liver!')[45]

Until Frederick the Great's time Berlin's 'Cathedral' (an English-style national church with bishops was not established until 1817) lay between the Schloss and the Marstall. Frederick had the church rebuilt on the Lustgarten to a design by himself and his friend 'Apollodore', Georg Wenzeslaus von Knobelsdorff, and had Johann Boumann the Elder carry it out. This building was substantially altered by Schinkel between 1816 and 1821,[46] but, perhaps due to the restrictions imposed by the earlier building, it was not one of his happiest compositions: a dome set on a tall drum was squashed between two pepper-pots above an Ionic portico *in antis*. the poet Heinrich Heine found the pepper-pots 'ridiculous', comparing them to bird cages.[47] Schinkel's cathedral may not have been a great work, but it hardly deserved its replacement. In 1867, the then Crown Prince (later Kaiser Frederick) organised a competition for a cathedral worthy of Prussia and Germany's new status in the world. Plans were not drawn up until 1885, when Julius Raschdorff's design was adopted; so the awfulness of the building cannot be entirely ascribed to the influence of William II.

Work didn't begin until 1893, however, and continued

---

* Lustgarten means 'pleasure garden'.

until 1905. During this time the Kaiser had plenty of opportunities to interfere with the minutiae of the design,[48] coating the walls with as much gold and marble as he indecently could. The Kaiser's style doubtless suited the needs of his subjects in the swaggering new Reich. A pamphlet dated 1903 expressed the *nouveau riche* mood of the time:

> The acquisition and handling of sandstone, basalt, granite and marble presents absolutely no problem today; even getting it from the quarries of Sweden and Norway is no more difficult than extracting it from the Alps, Sudeten Mountains, the Main or the Elbe; and money plays such a paltry role in our country nowadays that it is no longer acceptable to build without these lovely stones. Nothing is too colossal, nothing too expensive.[49]

The Cathedral is a powerful symbol of Berlin's history: a small mediaeval building demolished on the orders of the Great King; a rococo church built by a free-thinker; a neo-classical replacement erected at a time when the city really was 'Athens on the Spree', and finally the expression of the Kaiser's vulgar optimism shattered by bombs in just retribution for the horrors perpetrated by a bunch of Godless Nazis. Of the handful of Berlin buildings restored by the old DDR, this was surely the least deserving.

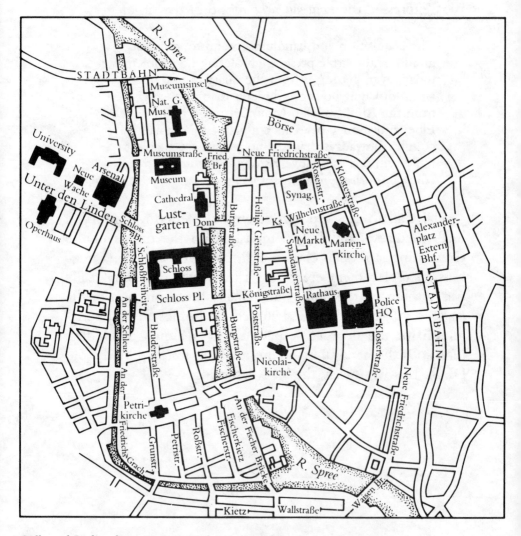

Cölln and Berlin: the twin town in the nineteenth century

III

Mediaeval Berlin was a small town by European standards. Even its stews were modest in scale. There was the Krögel, which was pulled down by the Nazis, and the Fischerstraße in Cölln. In his sub-Dickensian *Die Chronik der Sperlingsgasse* of 1878, Wilhelm Raabe tries to evoke this picturesque Berlin of the past, focusing on a crumbly chunk around the Sophienstraße: 'Here are the dark and smoky counters of the old and self-important merchant houses; this is the proper realm of cellar and attic dwellings.'[50] The attics were no longer the province of the Berlin garrison. Since the city had filled up with barracks, these *Dachstuben* had become the homes of artists and writers. The mania for civic improvement rid Berlin not only of its Sperlingsgassen, but also of most of its old palaces. With *Gründungsfieber*, or 'foundation fever', a building mania gripped the city after the creation of the new Reich. The character of the old *Residenz* was its first victim.[51]

A few churches remained. The Nikolaikirche was still a late Gothic building. Until 1878, however, the left-hand tower finished in a gable. When the DDR decided to rebuild the flattened church in the eighties, they restored this embellishment from the post-1871 *Gründerzeit*. As Berlin-Cölln's first Christian temple, it deserved to be restored. Over the centuries it had been served by some fiery preachers, such as the Pastor Heinzelmann, who in 1660 had defied the 'Blasphemy Edict'[52] which ensured tolerance in Brandenburg-Prussia (at least for different Protestant sects) by shouting from his pulpit: 'So we damn Papists, Calvinists and the *Helmstedtler** too with one word: whoever is not a Lutheran is cursed.' The Great Elector had him banished for this outrage. In more recent history the father of the Nazi martyr Horst Wessel was a preacher at the Nikolaikirche.[53]

The Petrikirche in Cölln fared even less well. It was rebuilt in 1717[54] but later the shops abutting the church caught fire and set the whole building ablaze. The nineteenth-century edifice which took its place fell victim to the war and the DDR's lack of sentiment in these matters. The Marienkirche on the Neue Markt slipped through the net. It was singed by the Great Fire of Berlin in 1380 and in 1661 the tower was struck by lightning. As it smoked and flamed it was feared that the blaze would spread to the body of the church. The old General Otto Christoph von Sparr, however, knew exactly what to do: he brought in cannon and had the crown of the spire shot down.† In 1789 Langhans built the present spire to replace a baroque construction put up by Smids.[55]

The most important Gothic building in pre-war Berlin was the Klosterkirche in the Klosterstraße. After the Reformation in the Mark Brandenburg the conventual buildings of the old Franciscan Friary became the school Zum grauen Kloster. The school retained considerable amounts of Gothic work, and the old chapel was a pure example of the red-brick architecture of Kloster Chorin in the Mark. It was sadly burned out in the Blitz and only the outside walls have been retained on the edge of the empty, multi-carriage motorways of the Alexanderplatz. The DDR naturally had no time for the private school where the sculptor Schadow,

---

* Followers of Georg Calixt 1586–1651, a liberal theologian at the University of Helmstedt.
† Sparr's fine tomb is still in the church.

Schinkel, the theologian Schleiermacher, Bismarck and the nationalist Jahn had been put through their paces. After the war it was relocated to Grunewald in the American Zone.[56]

The Klosterstraße was once Berlin's best street. You get an impression of this from three of Eduard Gaertner's depictions of the subject: a pencil drawing, a watercolour and an oil.[57] Here are the town palaces of the Creuzsch and Podewils families and the Parochialkirche, which was begun by Nering and eventually received the peal of bells destined for Schlüter's ill-fated Mint tower.[58] In his oil painting of 1830 Gaertner sets out to show the artistic importance of the Klosterstraße, which at the time contained Christian Wilhelm Beuth's Craft Institute and the house of the sculptor Christian Daniel Rauch. In the foreground Beuth is to be seen talking to Schinkel, while on the right-hand side of the canvas Rauch is going into his palatial residence. In the centre of the tableau, Gaertner, hat in hand, is talking to the mounted figure of the painter Franz Krüger.[59]

Philipp Gerlach had finished off the Parochialkirche with an allusion to Santa Agnese in Rome,[60] but despite these high baroque flourishes Gerlach was to be best remembered for the sober style of Frederick William I. His progression was typically Prussian: the son of a soldier, he was born in Spandau and practised his profession of architecture under the cover of military rank. His best-known building was the Garnisonkirche in Potsdam, another victim of post-war communist ideology. Less well known was the garrison church he built in Berlin, but then that didn't last as long: it was burned down and rebuilt in 1908.[61] A more typical representation of Gerlach's style was the Kammergericht in Kreuzberg: doing a good job despite a shortage of money and the bad habits of a king prone to massacring an architect's plans in the interests of economy.[62]

Another architect of the later Prussian baroque was Johann Friedrich Grael who designed the Sophienkirche in the

Sophienstraße, as well as the tower of the Heiliggeistkirche in Potsdam.* The tower owed something to Schlüter's Münzturm. It has been described as the last incarnation of Berlin baroque.[63]

IV

It is customary to say that, with Frederick the Great's accession in 1740, Prussia passed from Sparta to Athens. Frederick William, however, merely amassed an army and the money to feed it; it was his son who used it, again and again and again. Certainly, the style of building changed overnight, from the stripped-down baroque of Frederick William (whose favourite residence was the almost primitive tower house at Königs Wusterhausen) to the ever-so-slightly kitsch rococo of Frederick the Great (whose favourite residence was Sanssouci).

In his less martial moments, Frederick the Great genuinely turned his mind to the beautification of Berlin. The destruction of the mediaeval Cathedral was done to double the size of the Schloßplatz. On the Opernplatz and the Gendarmenmarkt, Frederick created two monumental spaces to show off the rococo beauties of Knobelsdorff. During Frederick's time the weight of Berlin was shifted westwards, into the fine new quarters laid out in his grandfather's time.[64]

One of Frederick's greatest innovations was to build a Catholic church in his new Forum. Sankt Hedwig's was the first for two centuries. Frederick liked the outward show of tolerance, but his more private utterances about Catholicism are not so broad-minded.[65] In theory, St Hedwig's was there to serve the king's new Silesian subjects. It was a bold design partially sketched out by the king himself – who then passed on his ideas to Knobelsdorff, who in turn had Johann

---

* Demolished in 1974!

Boumann the Elder construct the king's round church, based on the Pantheon in Rome.[66]

Frederick was not anxious to spend too much money on a Catholic church, and for many years it lay open to the sky. It remained unfinished for a decade, until, encouraged by Frederick's friend Algarotti, Cardinal Quirini stepped in to provide the necessary funds to complete it. The Vatican had realised the rarity value of Frederick's gesture: a (nominally) Calvinist monarch sanctioning the construction of a Catholic church in his capital. Quirini none the less extracted a *quid pro quo*: that his name should stand beside the King of Prussia's on the façade. Despite the appalling damage done to the Church of St Hedwig during the crude restoration of the thirties, during the Blitz and the even cruder rebuilding by the culture boffins of the DDR, the inscriptions still tell the tale: in the middle is written simply 'Hedwig', the protectress of Berlin; to the right, 'Federici regio clementiae monumentum'; and to the left, 'A.M. Quirinus S.R.E. card. suo aere perfecit'.[67]

When large numbers of Catholics arrived in Berlin a century after St Hedwig's was built, they didn't tend to settle on the Linden. They made their homes in the poorer, eastern districts and St Hedwig's was patronised by the rich. Fürstin Blücher shows us that Berlin boasted its very own Catholic Mafia in the early years of this century:

Sunday, August 9, 1914. Today we went to Mass at 11 o'clock at the Hedwig Kirche, which is a fashionable place for smart Berlin, where it is accustomed to congregate on the steps every Sunday to gossip over the news. I could not help comparing it with my last remembrances in February just six months ago. Then everyone had a laugh or joke on his lips. We were all dressed in our best, discussing the last Court Ball, or the latest scandal, criticizing and abusing our neighbours, and bent on enjoying life to the full. Now the women were sad and quiet, with none of

the vivacious sparkle of other days; they only
welcomed us with a pressure of the hand, tears often
pouring down their faces. There were the
Hohenlohes, the Reischachs, the Ratibors, the
Sierstorpffs . . .[68]

In the Second World War St Hedwig's had a rather more
serious vocation than to muster Berlin's resident Silesian
princes, dukes and counts. As the city's Catholic cathedral it
was the seat of its bishop, Konrad Graf von Preysing, one of
the bolder prelates, whose sermons showed he had no truck
with Nazi doctrines of race, and who maintained contacts
with the Opposition through his meetings with Helmuth
James von Moltke.[69] St Hedwig's was also the church of
Berlin's Second World War Catholic martyr: Dean, and now
the Blessed, Bernhard Lichtenberg. After the Reichskristallnacht he instituted daily prayers for the Jews and inmates
of the concentration camps. In October 1942 his protest
against the killing of mental patients led to his arrest. He
died in the course of being transported to Dachau in November 1943.[70]

There is a monument to Lichtenberg in the crypt of St
Hedwig's, under the ugly modern church which was built
within the old walls. The original interior had been ripped
out ten years before the war. This time it was the Church
and not the destructive Nazis who appear to have been to
blame.[71]

The other two sides of the open-ended Forum Friderici-
anum were the Opera House and the Royal Library, or
'Kommode', as the Berliners dubbed it from its resemblance
to a chest of drawers. It took its design from a drawing by
Fischer von Erlach, which had been originally intended
for Vienna's Hofburg. Boumann put up the building in
1774–1784, by when its curvacious baroque must have
seemed curiously dated. The Austrian architect's ideas for
Vienna's Kohlmarkt were not realised until shortly before

the First World War.[72] The king was impatient to see his
new opera house rise on the Linden. He thought it could
be built in two months, but it took two years, finally opening
in 1743. Very little of the fabric dates from the time of
Knobelsdorff's building. Langhans modernised it in 1788 and
it was burned out in 1843 and rebuilt by his son Karl Ferdinand. In the Second World War it was destroyed not once
but twice, but such was the Berliners' devotion to music
that it was rebuilt and put back into service.* The final
reconstruction took place in the fifties.[73]

By then it had long since ceased to be the 'Royal'
Opera and become the 'State' or Linden Opera. After 1933
it was a fief of Hermann Göring, who, among his many
other titles, held that of Minister President of Prussia. Apart
from making full use of the ex-royal box, Göring used the
building for his parties. Klaus Mann in his novel *Mephisto*, a
fairly vicious attack on his former brother-in-law, the actor
and director Gustav Gründgens, imagines the scene of the
Minister President's forty-third birthday party:

> The well-groomed crowd milled around the extensive
> foyers, corridors and vestibules. Corks popped in the
> boxes, the parapets of which were hung with gorgeous
> draperies; there was dancing in the stalls from which
> the rows of seats had been taken away. The orchestra
> took its seats on the whole expanse of the empty stage.
> It was vast enough to handle a symphony by Richard
> Strauss at the very least.† However, it was playing a
> cheeky medley of military marches and that jazz music
> which, though it was frowned upon for its niggerish
> indecency in the Reich, its grandees couldn't do
> without on their birthdays.[74]

* How unlike the Londoners. Covent Garden was turned into a
dance hall for the duration of the war.
† Strauss wasn't noted for symphonic composition, but he did not
go into exile in 1933, which made him hateful to Mann.

On the Opernplatz (now Bebelplatz), Göring's rival for Hitler's affections, the Propaganda Minister and Gauleiter for Berlin, Joseph Goebbels, ordered the burning of the books he had placed on the Nazi 'index'. On 10 May 1933, St Hedwig's, the Kommode (where, among others, Lenin had once swotted) and the University were witnesses to a giant bonfire stoked up by members of the Nazi student unions. Dancing like dervishes, the students shouted: 'Burn Heinrich Mann, burn Stefan Zweig, burn Erich Kästner, burn Karl Marx, burn Sigmund Freud.' They even burned Heine, who had been prophetic enough to say: 'There, where they burn books, they will also burn people.'

All in all, 20,000 books were destroyed on the Opernplatz on 10 May.[75] After the war a subterranean monument was placed on the square representing a row of empty library shelves. By 1995 the glass had become so scratched that it was impossible to make out what it was about.[76]

Little had changed in the Opernplatz since it was part of Heine's own itinerary in his student days. Even now, with the buildings restored or reconstructed, it is still recognisable as Frederick the Great's creation. Less so the Linden, which Frederick intended as a new *via triumphalis* to replace the Königstraße in old Berlin.[77] As a promenade the avenue had taken the place of the Lustgarten once successive kings had chosen to stow their clutter in the latter: stock exchanges, cathedrals and museums. Heine wondered, a little tongue in cheek, whether he was standing on the very same spot where Gotthold Ephraim Lessing had stood.

> . . . under these trees was the favourite promenade of so many great men who have lived in Berlin . . . But isn't it splendid now? It has just gone twelve and the *beau monde* is on the move. The elegant brigade is pushing itself up and down the Linden. Do you see the dandy wearing twelve multicoloured waistcoats? Can you hear the profound observations he lisps into his donna's ear? Can you smell the exquisite pomades

and essences in which he has drenched himself? He is
studying you through his lorgnette, smiling and
curling his hair. But look at the lovely ladies! What
figures! They bring me out in verse!

Ja, Freund, hier unter den Linden
Kannst du dein Herz erbaun,
Hier kannst du beisammen finden
Die allerschönsten Fraun.

Sie blühn so hold und minnig
In farbigem Seidengewand;
Ein Dichter hat sie sinnig
Wandelnde Blumen genannt.

Welch schöne Federhüte!
Welch schöne Türkenschals!
Welch schöne Wangenblüte!
Welch schöner Schwanenhals![78]

(Yes, friend, here under the linden trees
You can delight your senses,
Here you may find in twos and threes
The loveliest ladies.

They reek of sweetness and charm
In colourful silk costumes;
A brooding poet called them
A flock of *ambulent blooms*.

A lovely feather hat, what!
A cute Turkish shawl, what!
Beautiful rosy cheeks, what!
A superb swan neck, what!)

It was the golden age of the Linden, from the death of
Frederick the Great to the end of Berlin as a simple *Residenz*.
Once the city became a mighty metropolis complete with
slums and factory smokestacks, elegant society moved west
and found other itineraries and promenades. At the turn of

the century Arthur Eloesser found the avenue quite dead on a Sunday morning.

> ... barren, empty, jilted and widowed in proud loneliness. In its wide sweep from the Brandenburg Gate there was hardly a *flâneur* to be seen, still less a poet, and despite its historical dignity there have been poetical relationships. E. T. A. Hoffmann experienced nocturnal visions here, while the oil lamps flickered, and Heine met beautiful children who were forbidden to greet him publicly.[79]

As Eloesser put it succinctly: 'The extremities of the city have become so monstrously swollen that the insides are suffering from a shortage of blood.'[80] He was right, too, about Hoffmann, who had seen ghosts at number 9, next door to the once famous *Konditorei* Fuchs.

> Imagine a fine but cramped building; a low, four-bay, two-storey house; the first floor only just rising above its neighbour's ground-floor window, its roof in need of repair, windows partly patched up with paper, unpainted walls attesting to the property's complete dilapidation. Think how exceptional such a house must seem in its tasteful, magnificent and luxurious surroundings.[81]

Hoffmann's deserted house was an oddity in the Linden in the years after Waterloo. Demand for a small flat was so great that the houses were 'like beehives'.[82] Here were the best hotels, the richest citizens and the foreign legations, while under the eaves teemed 'the writing class'.[83]

The Nazis renumbered the street in 1937 and felled the linden to lay a new *U-Bahn* tunnel. The Cassandras muttered: 'Now the linden will bloom no more ... Soon it will be all over for Berlin.' Hoffmann's little seventeenth- or eighteenth-century house had long gone anyhow, as the Kaiser and Hitler put their seals on a megalomaniac Linden, conceived on another scale altogether. This was where the grand hotels were, until they became truly grand, and moved south or west: Zur goldene Sonne, the Hôtel de Petersburg, the Hôtel de Russie, the Hôtel de Rome, to which the first Kaiser, the modest, abstemious William, went over for his weekly bath; the Hôtel du Nord, Memhardts, the Victoria and the Bristol. Only part of the Carlton remains. Since the 'change' it has become a bank. Together with the ruins of the Amalienpalais (which had been the Russian Embassy from 1840), the Bristol was swept aside to make room for the extraordinary post-war Soviet mission, which hogged the top spot on the Linden until foundations were laid to put back the British, French and American embassies in 1995. The post-war French and Italian embassies took over the site of the Hôtel de Rome.

With the Schloss gone the Linden has lost its point. The traveller entered Berlin from the west, passing under the Brandenburg Gate. The procession of luxurious hotels, palaces and cafés and shops was just preparation for the royal palace, which presented its façade obliquely to the avenue. Even before the war wrought its havoc, many buildings which had played a key role in Prusso-German history had made way for the Kaiser's hollow pomp. The old Akademie der Künste had been set up in the royal stables on the north side of the street, giving rise to the jocular description for its uses: *mules et muses*. Here the philosopher Johann Gottlieb Fichte delivered his famous speeches to the German nation during the French occupation. The building, in a version designed for it by Schinkel, was pulled down for Ihne's characterless Royal Library, the eastern half of the current Staatsbibliothek. The University was formerly the town palace of Prince Henry, Frederick the Great's more lavish brother. It was spared.

Hero worship of Prussia's great king drew many eighteenth-century travellers, who were often struck by the appearance of the country in general and Berlin in particular.

One of these was Boswell, who came in the summer of 1764 with the hope of getting an introduction to Frederick, but sadly failed:

> The houses are handsome and the streets wide, long
> and straight. The palace is grand. The palaces of some
> of the royal family are very genteel. The Opera House
> is an elegant building, with this inscript: 'Fridericus
> Rex Apolloni et Musis'.
>   At night we sauntered in a sweet walk under a grove
> of chestnut trees by the side of a beautiful canal . . .

The Scotsman had clearly never seen a linden. Later Boswell decided that Berlin was 'the finest city I have ever seen. It is situated in a beautiful place, and like London has its river.'[84]

The DDR restored or rebuilt the eastern end of the Linden, although they were prone to take liberties with the original appearances of the buildings. All the inscriptions disappeared from the University, including the proud legend over the door: 'Fridericus Guilermus III Rex Universitatis Literariae 1809'. The Prinzessinnen-Palais, the work of the same Heinrich Gentz who designed some of the loveliest rooms in the *Residenzschloß* in Weimar, was put back together in 1963 using bits of the original building, and turned into a café-cum-restaurant in the DDR's own brand of baroque. Worse was the fate of the remains of the Niederländische Palais, which had once been the residence of the Dutch royal family. It was flattened in the sixties and replaced by a copy of the old Gouverneurshaus in the Rathausstraße, which had in turn been pulled down for road widening.[85] The interior of the DDR's former state guesthouse, the Kronprinzenpalais, will doubtless soon spawn studies of the regime's curious affection for a modernised baroque which seemed to have been inspired more by a high-class brothel than any palatial model.[86]

If the modern Linden has any charm to offer it is in

the Kastanienwäldchen, which lies between Schinkel's Alte Wache, the University, the classical Singakademie, the Zeughaus and the Palais am Festungsgraben. The Alte Wache is Schinkel's best remaining building in Berlin, and the Singakademie somehow continues to reflect something of the *bonhomie* of its creator, Zelter. The Festungsgraben palace used to house the offices of Johannes Popitz, who continued as Prussian Minister of Finance after the state's other ministries had been closed down in the interests of the Nazi concept of *Gleichschaltung*, or 'bringing into line'. Popitz was one of the most powerful minds on the right wing of the opposition to Hitler. He struck on the *risqué* idea that it was possible to do a deal with Himmler to destroy Hitler's state from within. Himmler kept his options open at first, but after the failure of the plot on 20 July 1944 Popitz was arrested and suffered gravely for having got so close to compromising the chief of the SS. Still Himmler preserved his life until February 1945, encouraging the former minister to write drafts for a new, post-Nazi administration in his cell. It is believed that he was only hanged on Hitler's insistence.[87]

The Zeughaus or Arsenal was Berlin's second most important baroque building after the Schloss. The design probably goes back to an idea of the French architect François Blondel, and the Frenchness of the composition is emphasised by the portico on the Linden, reminiscent of Perrault's Louvre façade.[88] The work was started by Nering and continued by Schlüter after Nering's death. Once again Schlüter's lack of technical skill was demonstrated when he built an attic storey too heavy for the structure. Schlüter was left to carry out the stunning statuary and replaced by Jean de Bodt, a pupil of Blondel's who had worked in Holland and on the Stadtschloß in Potsdam.* De Bodt later left the Prussian

---

* The badly damaged (but not irreparable) building was demolished in 1968.

service and settled in Saxony, where they made him a general and where he worked on the Japanese Palace in Dresden.[89]

The Zeughaus was the scene of one of the great might-have-beens in German, and indeed world, history. On 21 March 1943, in connection with the annual 'heroes' remembrance day, Army Group C organised an exhibition of captured weapons at the Arsenal which was to be graced by the presence of the Führer himself. Army Group C's chief of staff was Henning von Tresckow, before Claus von Stauffenberg's arrival on the scene the most indefatigable opponent of Hitler in the German army. Tresckow arranged for Colonel Rudolf-Christoph Freiherr von Gersdorff to escort Hitler round the exhibition. Gersdorff had agreed to pack his clothes with explosive and detonate both himself and the Führer at some point along the way. But Hitler arrived to tell the soldiers that he had only two minutes to see the show, and Gersdorff's fuse required ten. Hitler returned to the Chancellery after his brief visit, and Gersdorff hurried into a quiet place to defuse the bomb.[90] Had Gersdorff only succeeded he might have brought the war to an end, and possibly prevented a second explosion: the destruction of the Schloss.

V

Berlin is a self-destructive place. There has rarely been any sentiment about the past. Successive kings and regimes have believed themselves justified in wiping the slate clean and beginning all over again. The city has been remodelled many times, but until the Nazis and the Blitz there was no metamorphosis quite as radical as that which followed Berlin's elevation to imperial capital in 1871. Berlin had a genuine need for new buildings to house the Reich's institutions: the bank, post office, patent and insurance offices and, most important of all, the Reichstag itself. A style had to be found for these constructions that would reflect Germany's new confidence and position. It was either a proud neo-baroque, or a heavy imitation of German Romanesque or Gothic models. The Austrian writer Hugo von Hofmannsthal called Berlin the 'great ape city'.[91] The most prominent display of the new historicism was the Reichstag: 'a symbol of unity, power and strength'.[92] The style expressed itself particularly well in memorial churches: the Kaiser-Wilhelm-Gedächtnis-kirche, the Kaiser-Friedrich-Gedächtniskirche, and the Kaiserin-Augusta-Gedächtniskirche; or other monuments to the new Reich such as the Gnadenkirche in the Invaliden-park or the new garrison church on the Südstern.

The Kaiser couldn't wait to pull down his old-fashioned city and put up something which he thought was the reflec-tion of himself and his dynasty. Like Hitler later, the Kaiser planned a city which would surpass the metropolises of Western Europe. If respect to a great monarch (and ancestor) made him spare the 'Forum Friderizianum' and the other civic improvements of Frederick the Great, there was no hope for the mediaeval city any more than there was for the modest scale of Schinkel, Ludwig Persius or Friedrich August Stüler.

The Kaiser wanted a most un-Prussian thing: luxury. Grand hotels should feature heavily in the new Berlin. He was particularly pleased to patronise Louis Adlon. When he proposed building the equivalent of the London or Paris Ritz on the corner of Unter den Linden and the Pariser Platz the Kaiser's enthusiasm knew no bounds. The site was occupied by Schinkel's neo-Florentine Redernpalais. William obligingly suppressed the objections voiced by his historic-monuments people: 'Thank God that old barn is finally going to be pulled down!' he said. 'It was certainly an eyesore; it ruined the whole Linden for me . . . At last my residence is going to become a modern city.'[93] In the music halls Berliners heard a new song by Viktor Holländer with words by Julius Freund. The old Graf Redern who built the palace returns to earth to see the demolition men moving in on his old home:

> Mit neuen Moden kommt die neue Zeit,
> Berlin schlüpft in ein neues Kleid . . .
> Und jetzt das Herz mir blutet, wenn ich seh'
> Fällt mein altes, herrliches Palais.
> Was Schinkel gebaut, was die Linden geziert:
> Nun wird's ein Hotel, das nur Fremde bezieh'n,
> So schwindest Du hin, Du mein altes Berlin.
>
> Es tut jetzt allen Urberlinern leid
> Um die Lokale aus der alten Zeit,
> Wo man im Dunst und Rauch behaglich aß,
> Oft sechs Mann hoch bei einem Weißbierglas . . .
> Das Orchester aus Ungarn, die Kellner aus Wien
> So schwindest Du hin, Du mein altes Berlin![94]

> (With new fashions begins the new epoque,
> Berlin slips on a brand-new frock . . .
> But yet my heart starts to bleed when I see
> The fate of that fine old masonry
> That Schinkel built and which bejewelled the Linden.
> Now it will be a hotel, where strangers move in.
> Where are you going, you, my good old Berlin.
>
> It troubles all us old Berliners so
> To see the good old pubs we used to know,
> Where you ate all snug in smoke and fug,
> Often six of you around the *Weißbier* jug . . .
> Viennese waiters and Magyar fiddlers are now in,
> Where are you going, you, my good old Berlin.)

Where indeed? What happened to the old city so loved by the painter Heinrich Zille? The Molkenmarkt, the Krögel, the Nikolaikirche, the Fischerstraße, the Gasthaus am Nußbaum, the Petristraße or the Jungfernbrücke?[95] Only the Jungfernbrücke on the Spree, with its characteristic Dutch profile, survived the wartime Armageddon, although the DDR painstakingly rebuilt the old Nikolaikirche, and placed a copy of the Gasthaus am Nußbaum nearby in their own little *Disneyviertel*. The Nazis bear as much of the blame as the Kaiser or the bombs. They ruined the Molkenmarkt for road widening. They pulled down the mediaeval bath-house and brothel quarter in the Krögel. What was left of 'good, old Berlin' was levelled by the SED after the war.

At every blow there was a muted outcry. Even during the Third Reich the papers summoned up the courage to mourn the passing of the Krögel.[96] The nineteenth-century journalist Julius Rodenberg adopted an attitude of resigned detachment to the progressive destruction of his city by the Kaiser. Writing in the 1890s he asked, 'What is old Berlin besides a few churches?' One of these, the Spittal, or Getrau-denkirche, had been swept away to make room for the *Pferdebahn* or horse-drawn tram. Rodenberg called it a 'cramped, ugly thing'. In Gaertner's painting it still has a tower. By the time F. A. Schwartz photographed it in 1868 this had already been trimmed off. The picture shows a four-bay building with a steep gable and a semicircular apse.[97]

When they did not simply demolish the monuments of older, less important eras than their own, the Nazis had a curious habit of dismantling things and putting them into store. This they did with the Ephraims Palais, the Semitic name of which must have been a great provocation for them. The scheme was excused by the need to equip the capital of the Third Reich with fast-moving avenues on which the new German *Übermensch* could show off his *Kraft-durch-Freude* car ('strength through joy', the prototype of the Volks-wagen 'beetle'), which was promised to every thrifty German household, but which none ever received. Another victim of the road-widening project was the Palais Schwerin opposite the Palais Ephraim, which the Nazis pushed back a few metres and incorporated in their new mint. Like the Palais Podewils it was the work of Jean de Bodt; unlike that building, its interiors survived the war. Some of these date from an earlier construction of the later seventeenth century.*

It was one of a number of policies which carried on seamlessly into the administration of the DDR. As we have seen, the communists were, if anything, even less sentimental about preserving Berlin's heritage than the Nazis had been, and they had the even greater advantage of starting out with what amounted to a virtual *tabula rasa*. They also shared the Nazi love of urban motorways and their desire to have one of these running along the Breite Straße led to the demolition of half the street. The Ermelerhaus used to stand opposite the early seventeenth-century Ribbeckhaus until it was pulled down and rebuilt as a tourist restaurant on the so-called 'Märkisches Ufer' in the old *Kietz*. Its baroque neighbour was ferried over from the Friedrichsgracht opposite to join a handful of old buildings in the first of the DDR's appointed architectural theme-parks.

Their second and more ambitious attempt at the genre was only completed in 1987, at a time when the DDR was liberalising, a bit, and they had begun to see the advantages of tourism. A few nineteenth-century buildings on the site were spared the pickaxe and the bulldozer, while all the other available spaces were filled with replicas of vanished Berlin monuments such as Zum Nußbaum, the mediaeval pub once frequented by Heinrich Zille.

Charting historical continuity in Berlin is hampered not only by the physical loss of buildings, but by the Continental habit of renaming streets. The Kaiser was no opponent of this practice and the Nazis, too, set up their worthies on the street corners of the capital. Since the 'change', names have also undergone a spot of revision, chiefly to restore a few streets to their original dedicatees after the massive obfuscation carried out by the DDR. The communist regime had

---

* They added some friezes from the old Mint, which had been designed by Gentz. The frieze itself is Schadow's work.

been keen to eliminate evidence of royalty, *Junkertum* and militarism from the city's past, while avoiding any bad feelings with their new allies in the east by reminding the Poles, for instance, that their post-war state was partially ensconced on old Prussian soil. Queen Sophia Dorothea metamorphosed into politician Clara Zetkin; Kaiser Franz Joseph became Bebel; Kaiser Wilhelm reappeared as Karl Liebknecht. The Königstraße was now the Rathausstraße; the Luisenplatz commemorated Robert Koch the chemist; the Markgrafenstraße, Wilhelm Külz the former Mayor of Dresden. Frederick the Great's planned noble boulevard, the Wilhelmstraße, was made over to the communist toady Otto Grotewohl.

The Artilleriestraße was a victim of its warlike mien; it was reawarded to Tucholsky. Though the Gendarmenmarkt commemorated a regiment disbanded in 1806, it none the less ceded to the Platz der Akademie. Allenstein, Bartenstein, Braunsberg, Danzig, Elbing, Elsaß (Alsace), Ermland, Gnesen, Goldap, Lothringen (Lorraine), Oliva, Pregel, Rastenburg, Thorn and Wehlau were no longer politically correct. Their places were taken by figures from the new SED Valhalla: Dimitrov, Wilhelm Pieck, John Schehr, and Hermann Matern. One square seems to sum up the fickle nature of Berlin nomenclature: once it served to honour the pre-First World War Chancellor von Bülow; the Nazis renamed it in honour of their martyr Horst Wessel; after the war it was allotted to Rosa Luxemburg, but since the 'change' her future might be in doubt. Whatever name they give it, it is unlikely to revert to either of its previous owners; nor is there much chance that it will one day receive the effigy of Erich Mielke, the former Chief of the East German Ministry of State Security or 'Stasi'. Mielke murdered a policeman here in 1931 and hot-footed off to Moscow to escape imprisonment. He must have established some sort of legal record when he was indicted for murder in 1991, sixty years and three regimes after the event.*

VI

In the twilight years of the twentieth century the site of the old twin town of Berlin-Cölln has little to offer the tourist or educated traveller. What is still good lies outside the old walls and there remain only tiny, isolated pockets, which have been robbed of their ability to tell a story by themselves: so there is the Nicolaihaus and the old deanery to the Petrikirche in Cölln's Brüderstraße. The latter has lost its church, while the former now looks out on some of the most soul-despairing stretches of *Plattenbauten* in the inner city. A similar little cluster exists on the north side of the Burgstraße in old Berlin: the parsonage of the old Garrison Church (the latter was pulled down in 1960) stands opposite a business-school which incorporates one of Berlin's least-known antiquities: the Heiliggeistkapelle, a red-brick, late thirteenth-century, hospital chapel.

After Groß, or greater, Berlin was created in 1920 'Alt-Berlin' was used to define a far larger area than the former walled towns of Berlin and Cölln. It also took in the poor districts on the left bank of the Spree, the so-called *Kietz* around the present Märkisches Museum. It was here that Jakob Fabian and his friend Stephan Labude witness a shoot-out between a Nazi and a Kozi (as Communists were called at the time) in Erich Kästner's novel *Fabian*. It was night, and the two men were walking past the monument to the liberal politician Franz Hermann Schultze-Delitsch. On the river side of the Museum . . .

. . . stony Roland peered dimly from his ivy-clad

* He was released in the spring of 1996.

corner, while, on the Spree, a steamer mourned. Up on the bridge they stood and looked out at the blind warehouse buildings and the dark river. The sky was ablaze over the Friedrichstadt.[98]

In the past the *Kietz* had had a little more bustle. This was a trading corner of Berlin where the city's dairies, mills, brick kilns, loam quarries and wood markets were to be found. The huge Inselspeicher repository was across the Inselbrücke to the north. Behind it lay the picturesque slums of the Fischerstraße. In Ernst Dronke's novel *Aus dem Volk* of 1846, he calls it a 'dirty narrow street'.

> The houses in this lane are tall and gloomy in appearance and the interiors do not belie the impression a stranger might have gained from the outside.

Photographs taken some fifty years later show that the early Communist and friend of Karl Marx may have exaggerated the street's charmlessness, but it is doubtless true that the interior arrangements of these narrow seventeenth- and eighteenth-century houses left much to be desired. That not withstanding, the jumble of pubs, shops and cheap lodgings visible from the pictures reminds us of what modern Berlin sadly lacks: an attractive old centre.[99]

Across the Jannowitzbrücke is the grim Holzmarktstraße, which eventually leads to the old Berlin riverside resort of Stralau. There is not much to see there now besides a stretch of Berlin Wall running along the Spree. In 1753 Voltaire lived here in the Belvedere. He had fled Frederick the Great's court in disgrace after the king had discovered that he had been the author of libels against the President of the Academy, Maupertuis.[100] Nearly a century later the Silesian author and actor Karl von Holtei lived here in some style:

> It was neither grand nor elegant, but it was individual and comfortable, and therefore something that is

worth its weight in gold in a great royal city. It was
also very rare in being rustic in a Berlin where
building mania was daily grubbing up more and more
of the surrounding land. It was a little, low-built
house of which we were the sole tenants and disturbed
by no other lodgers; five big rooms and five smaller
ones with a few of the latter really so small that three
of them knocked together were hardly capable of
housing my desk, books and person. Immediately
behind the house was a large patch of green with a
lovely old walnut and other trees; and beyond this
greenery the Spree, that so often mocked river, which
without being an Orinoco, to be sure, has an advantage
over many greater waterways, chiefly over the Oder
in my beloved Silesian fatherland, that even in the
hottest summer days it flows fresh and deep.[101]

The Alexanderplatz, a space thrown up accidentally by the
creation of the Great Elector's defensive wall, was intended to
be one of the great triumphs of post-war planning in East
Berlin. On the eve and in the immediate aftermath of the
'change' it presented a sorry picture: an architect-inspired
nightmare in Europe only to be compared to London's disastrous Elephant and Castle. Lying at the eastern extremity of
the old city, it was naturally the main pole of attraction
for Berliners from the poorer areas from Friedrichshain to
Köpenick. It was here that Alfred Döblin set the scene for
his big-city novel, *Berlin Alexanderplatz*, of 1929. Döblin
paints a picture which for most people, sadly, is only familiar
from pre-war photographs.

On the Alexanderplatz they are pulling up the roads
for the underground railway. You have to tread the
boards. The trams come out of the Alexanderstraße
crossing the square before disappearing down the
Münzstraße in the direction of the Rosenthal Gate.
There are streets off to the left and right. In the streets
the houses stand in solid rows. They are stuffed full of
people from cellar to attic. The shops are downstairs.

Bars, restaurants, fruit and vegetable shops, grocers and delicatessens, haulage contractors, decorators, seamstresses, brands of flour and grinders, garages and insurance companies.[102]

Pictures show the Berlin jumble: with the tower of the 'red' town hall forming the backdrop, the huge Wertheim department store performing for popular Berlin a similar function to Wertheim on the Leipziger Platz, which drew its parishioners more from the affluent west. Until the *U-Bahn* arrived during the Weimar years, the 'Alex' was (and is) served by the overground *S-Bahn*, which cut the space in half. Trains came in and out of the huge station with its parabolic roof. Here was the headquarters of the Berlin police, and a favourite gathering place for the city's lowlife.[103] Döblin's hero, Franz Biberkopf, sold newspapers and bootlaces here; a typical Berlin duality. There is even a Zille drawing of a similar hawker.[104]★

The streets right and left were notorious battlefields for gangs of Nazis and Kozis in the twenties and thirties. The nearby Jüdenstraße had, as its name would suggest, been the Jewish trading centre in the Middle Ages. Ironically, perhaps, this is where Horst Wessel spent his childhood, at numbers 51–52, a former Jewish patrician house. From here the impressionable Horst had watched his pastor father go off to war as a volunteer to join Hindenburg in the east. His patriotism was 'pretty well unquestioning'. He was rewarded by the Iron Cross, First Class.[106]

The little baroque palace of Monbijou lay beyond the mediaeval walls on the Berlin side of the Spree. It had been built by Eosander at the beginning of the eighteenth century and became the favourite palace of Frederick the Great's mother, Queen Sophia Dorothea. Latterly it had become one of the centres of the Kaiser's ancestor cultus as the

---

★ During the Second World War the Alex was the centre of the black market.[105]

Hohenzollern Museum. The family continued to own the building until it was wrecked by bombs during the war. Once again, the communists saw fit to tear down what remained of the palace. As one writer bitterly commented: 'It must be stressed that the last traces of the biggest and most important buildings, those which most effectively gave the city its character, in east and west, finally disappeared only after 1945.'[107]

Beyond Monbijou was the disreputable Scheunenviertel, one of the few parts of the inner city to retain something of its original appearance today. Many poor Jews lived in or off the Große Hamburger and the Sophienstraßen among the prostitutes and it was only natural that their impressive new synagogue should be set up on the Oranienburger Straße, which was the main artery of the *quartier*. The Oranienburger Gate was dubbed the 'Latin Quarter' of Berlin, as this was where most of the poorer students lived, within easy reach of the Linden and the University. Eloesser describes a 'hideous intermediary zone' between the two, rendered all the more sinister by the presence of so many pawnbrokers.[108]

The other magnet for Berlin students was the Charité Hospital, until 1945 the city's principal medical academy. The Charité began life as a plague hospital, placed at a suitable distance from the city. As it transpired, the danger of such an epidemic was not great, and in 1726 the site was already being used as a garrison hospital. A year later civilians were also admitted. Although the Charité ceased to be used as a military hospital, it maintained its association with the army through the Pepinière, Brandenburg-Prussia's academy for military medicine until the creation of a separate Kaiser-Wilhelm-Akademie for military medicine in 1903.[109]

The Charité continued to exercise the dual functions conceived for it by Frederick William I. It was to be the institute responsible for training military physicians (and after 1897 ordinary doctors) and *the* hospital for the poor. The Soldier-King himself saw to it that food brought illegally into the city was delivered up to the Charité to help feed the patients. The association with the poor meant that a number of the inmates reflected the nature of Berlin's *bas fonds*. Venereal disease and lunacy were specialities from the start.[110] At the end of the eighteenth century the hospital received new buildings, but for the main its functions remained the same. A new cabinet order of 6 July 1835, for example, required the hospital to treat all cases of venereally infected prostitutes who were not deemed the responsibility of the prisons, as well as lunatics and military pensioners.[111]

The neo-classical buildings of the old Charité have now gone. The earliest surviving clinic is the Pockenkrankenhaus, or smallpox hospital, of 1836. Between 1897 and 1916 most of the older buildings were taken down and replaced by red-brick Gothic buildings more suited to contemporary taste. The visual integrity was not too greatly upset during the Second World War (which suggests that Allied bombing crews could avoid sensitive targets if they wanted to), but in 1975 the DDR built a high-rise block to demonstrate the modernity of their medical treatment.[112] Naturally the party *Bonzen* had the first call on its wards and private rooms, followed by the regime's pampered athletes. After the 'change' it was discovered they had also enjoyed privileged access to blood and spare parts.

To the east of the Charité, beyond the Rosenthaler Gate was Voigtland, from the 1830s onwards the city's most notorious slums. Dronke described it as 'a great number of pitiful huts spreading right and left from the Hamburger Gate . . . In the middle of the miserable slums of this area stand a few large houses, seven in all, in which 2,500 people are to be found in 400 rooms.'[113] The tenements had been built by private speculators. Each one of these 'stinking lairs' was administered by an inspector, whose job it was to keep order and collect the rents. The 'small and regular' rooms were shared by sixteen people, two families in all, who maintained their privacy by hanging a screen diagonally across the room.[114]

The army was never very far away in Prussia. The Chausseestraße, which went up towards Wedding in the north, had always had a slightly military feel to it, probably due to the Invalidenhaus nearby. Only two low, uncared-for wings survive of the three courtyards that once made up Prussia's equivalent of Les Invalides or Chelsea Hospital. By the mid-century industrialisation in nearby Moabit had added another, equally well-regimented element to the feel of this corner of the old city. In Fontane's *Stine* of 1890, the novelist sets the scene of *louche* goings-on in this lower-middle-class area of Berlin, a district growing increasingly shabby as a result of the factories to the west.

> Things looked very much as usual in the Invalidenstraße: the horse-drawn trams rang their bells, and the machine workers were heading off for their midday break and anyone who had really wanted to winkle out something remarkable would have looked no further than the first-floor windows of number 98e. Despite the fact it was neither Easter nor Whitsun – it was not even Saturday – they were being cleaned with something approaching gusto.[115]

In the same novella Fontane conceded that the area was 'rich in cemeteries' (he is himself buried not far off). Nowadays the dead offer the highlights of a district which has lost most of the appeal it had in Fontane's day. In the Chausseestraße is Berlin's most distinguished necropolis; housing, among lesser luminaries, the artists Chodowiecki, Krüger, Schadow, Rauch, Schinkel and Stüler; the actor Ludwig Devrient; the political scientist Ancillon; the industrialist Borsig; the printer Litfaß, inventor of the advertising columns; Hufeland the physician; the philosophers Fichte and Hegel; the composer Eisler; and the writers Hitzig,

Heinrich Mann, Johannes R. Becher, Arnold Zweig and Bert Brecht.

To be buried in the Chausseestraße Cemetery was to be honoured by the DDR. Those who had fallen foul of their version of history could not hope to have their tombs maintained. A few of Germany's black sheep are still to be found in the Invalidenfriedhof. Attempts were made to destroy this dangerously militaristic and substantially noble cemetery in the course of the DDR's four decades, but its position on the border between the western and eastern sectors made it a sort of no-man's-land, out of bounds to impressionable citizens. Here is the creator of the Prussian General Staff, Scharnhorst, his tomb by Schinkel shorn of its reliefs by the sculptor Christian Friedrich Tieck. The monument to War Minister von Boyen is, appropriately perhaps, riddled with machine-gun bullet holes. The unfortunate army chief Werner von Fritsch is also here, despite the fact that he seems to have intentionally had himself shot before Warsaw in 1939 to atone for the disgrace brought on his name by Göring and Hitler, who trumped up charges of homosexuality against him. Another suicide whose tomb has survived is Göring's friend and First World War air ace, Ernst Udet. Many of the other tombs were swept away to make room for the Berlin Wall.[116]

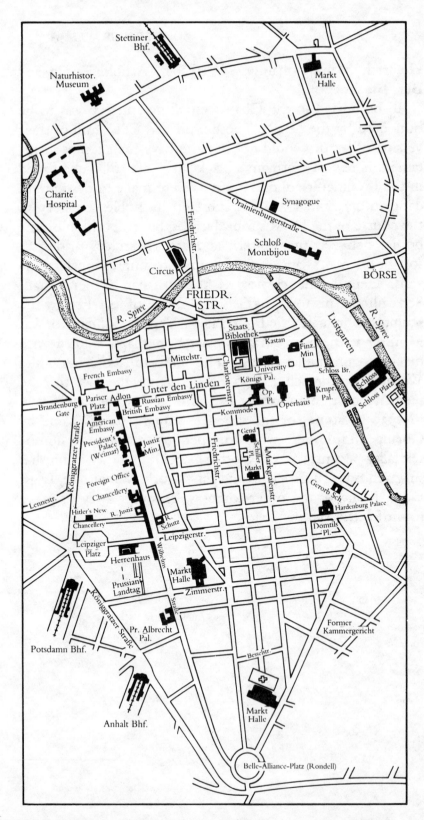

The administrative centre in 1939

VII

Berlin has spread eastwards, but fashionable Berlin has nearly always gone west. It started with Friedrichswerder, the Fried-richstadt and the Dorotheenstadt. After the death of Frederick William III's beloved Queen Louise in 1810, the old Köpenicker Vorstadt was renamed the 'Luisenstadt'. In the west between the Charité and the Spree, her widower endowed a new *quartier*: the Friedrich-Wilhelmstadt. Now, in the west at least, Berlin had filled up all the nooks and crannies within the 1734 wall circuit.[117]

The shape of Friedrichswerder had been dictated by the mid-seventeenth-century defences, but it had shown the citizens of Berlin a way out of their cramped quarters. It remained a thin strip of land with no distinct character of its own until Schinkel replaced the baroque church in the Werderschen Markt with the present 'Tudor' building in the 1820s. Schinkel had prepared two designs, one 'antique', the other Gothic. The Crown Prince had set his heart on a Gothic building, and so it was to be.[118]

The new church appealed greatly to Gaertner, who painted a set of panoramas from its high roof. These were intended for inclusion in a 'diorama', an early precursor of 'virtual reality' where pictures were brought to life with special effects. The completed set show the church at the completion of Schinkel's last finial. Various characters the artist had espied from his perch have been brought up on to the roof, including the natural scientist Alexander von Humboldt. Gaertner himself is represented, clutching his sketchbook.[119] The panorama presents a wonderful glimpse of *Spree-Athen* at its purest point: the observer's eye travels from the Hedwigskirche to the Kommode, from Prince Henry's Palace and the Zeughaus on the Linden to Schinkel's Altes Museum and Dom in the Lustgarten. Behind the Schloßfreiheit is the Marienkirche and the Schloss itself; then after the as yet single spire of the Nikolaikirche, a stretch of flat Märkisch landscape appears behind the square towers of the church. To the right the Friedrichstadt stretches away to the French and German churches and Schinkel's new Schauspielhaus, set firmly between the two.[120]

In the left-hand corner of the second set is the other great building of Friedrichswerder: the Bauakademie, or architectural school. At the time of Gaertner's painting only the outside walls of the school had been finished and these are partly clad in wooden scaffolding. The design was heavily influenced by Schinkel's trip to England in 1826, when he took considerable interest in the industrial buildings he saw in Manchester. In this work Schinkel freed himself from historical forms in the main design, limiting decoration to the sculptural details he worked out with Friedrich Tieck and August Kiß. The Bauakademie was repaired after the Second World War, but the DDR's foreign office selected the site for their new building, and the demolition men were sent in. In the summer of 1995, bulldozers moved in on the now defunct Foreign Office building. At the time of writing there is a strong chance that Schinkel's building will be re-erected in its place.[121]

When the Great Elector's son extended building into the Friedrich and Dorotheenstädte there was a hint that Berlin was to have its own noble quarter like the new West End of London, which developed after the Great Fire, or the Faubourg Saint-Germain in Paris, but by no means all

Brandenburg-Prussia's noble families took the opportunity to avail themselves of the building plots. The curious Krosigk'sches Haus in the Wallstraße, with its three superimposed orders, is evidence of this,[122] as are the various palaces which remained inside the walls of the twin-town.

In the Wilhelmstraße Frederick the Great had hoped to see a noble avenue on the same lines as the Herrengasse in Vienna.[123] The first town palaces, such as the Schwerin and Schulenburg, the later Reichspräsidentenpalais and Reichskanzlei, had been built in his father's time. They were both fine old eighteenth-century buildings, but in their last years they were hardly treated with respect. Hitler gave the Presidential Palace to his Foreign Minister, Ribbentrop, who promptly pulled it down. The Schulenburg Palais had been badly mauled by Bismarck, who had ripped out its insides long before Hitler and the bombing destroyed its outward appearance.

Across the road was another Schinkel building, the palace of Prince Leopold. In 1933 this became the new Ministry of Propaganda, and Goebbels moved in. Like that self-proclaimed 'Renaissance man', Hermann Göring, Goebbels was not wholly insensitive to beauty. When Germany's cities were picked off one by one by the RAF and the USAAF, he occasionally permitted himself a moment of sorrow in the pages of his diary.[124] He sniffed around his new demesne: 'a beautiful building by the great architect Schinkel, but so old-fashioned we shall have to have it adapted to our requirements'. The outside remained unchanged for the time being, but all the interiors were pulled out: 'I simply take a few bricklayers from the SA and have the stucco and wainscoting knocked off during the night; newspapers and documents as old as the hills are taken down off the shelves, where they have lain musty and dusty for years, and are flung downstairs pell-mell. Only clouds of dust attest to the bygone splendours of bureaucracy!'[125]

Nazis also took over the loveliest of the old palaces on the

Wilhelmstraße, the Prinz-Albrecht-Palais, the former Palais Verzenobre. In 1830 Prince Albert had commissioned Schinkel to remodel the interior. Many of his rooms were altered in the 1860s, but the stairwell and banqueting rooms remained as the great architect had left them. In 1941 Heydrich made some alterations to the rooms. In November 1944 it was burned out by bombs. The Americans had it blown up in 1949.*[126]

The Prinz-Albrecht-Palais had been part of the complex of buildings that made up the SS chiefs Himmler and Heydrich's headquarters: Gestapo, SS and *Reichssicherheitshauptamt* (Centre for Reich Security). On the other side of the terrain, in the former art school, men and women had been tortured to death in the cells. The American attitude was understandable, but it is none the less hard to think of the dynamiting of another of Berlin's most magnificent buildings without a sense of loss. Looking at the waste land which has taken its place today, few would maintain that the public has been in any way served by its destruction. They lack even the physical evidence of the façade.

It could have been restored as a museum or *Mahnmal* to those who suffered. The art historian Johannes Sievers went over the site in 1945:

> Up above the rubble of the Great Stairway, on the
> western wall, it is possible to make out various pieces
> of almost untouched decorative detail; the wall
> paintings in both of the great reception rooms on the
> first floor were also partially visible, a sign that the fire
> had been to some extent kept under control . . . It is
> certain too that the outside of the palace, which was
> so important architecturally, had not been damaged
> at all by fire or bullet holes. What a consolation to see
> the intact keystones still in place; even the decorative
> work along the roof parapet and the vast majority of

* It was owned by the Hohenzollerns throughout. They sold the site in 1961.

> Schinkel's iron vases which lined the entrance ramp
> were still there ... Despite this, in May 1949, instead
> of standing before a ruined, but still noble and
> impressive palace with a beautiful forecourt fronted by
> a distinguished row of columns, you stood before a
> formless mound of rubble.[127]

Few of the Prussian nobility responded to Frederick the Great's call to make something out of the Wilhelmstraße either. Not many had the incomes of their equivalents in Western Europe or in the Habsburg lands, and with Frederick's wars there were other things to think about. In the nineteenth century the Wilhelmstraße became the centre of Prussian, and later German, government. The street still had a noble cachet, however. The modest-sounding 'Wohnhaus Borsig' (Borsig 'residence') was here, a *savonnette à vilain* for a *nouveau riche* family in the form of an Italianate *palazzo*. Next door at number 70 was the Pleß palace, built in the Chambord style. The Berliners called it the 'Schornsteinfegerakademie', or chimney-sweeps' academy, mocking its many chimneys.[128]

The focal point of the Friedrichstadt was the Gendarmenmarkt. Frederick the Great had the two churches crowned with elegant towers and drove the Markgrafenstraße up to the Opernplatz to link his two best bits of urban renewal. In the first years of the nineteenth century Langhans filled the space between the churches with his Schauspielhaus. This burned down in 1817, destroying, among other things, Schinkel's set designs for E. T. A. Hoffmann's opera *Undine*. It was Schinkel who designed its successor in 1818. Like the churches, this was restored after war damage.

Despite the grandeur of the setting, the Gendarmenmarkt was a real market filled with the particularly coarse-tongued market women, or 'Hökerinnen', who were one of the satirist Glaßbrenner's stock in trades. After 1815 there was a period of peace in Prussia's warlike history, something which made the army sensitive. A lieutenant who wants to buy fruit from one of the market women is hit in a sensitive spot: 'He's a fine, proud fellow, the Lieutenant! Such a pity he hasn't got a penny. He's got a sword as long as a cow's tail, but so far he wouldn't so much as hurt a fly with it.'[129]

In another part of the market a passing actor excites the men to reflect on life in the theatre.

> Do you see, there's that actor again I told you about yesterday. God! It must be wonderful being an actor like that. How finely he's dressed, the elegant gentleman, and how well things are going for him; look, with every step another pose, each one finer than the last. What does a lad like that lack! He lives in the lap of luxury! In the mornings he goes to the wine house, afternoons he eats himself sick at an ordinary,* after that he has a little siesta for three and a half hours; then in the evening he treads the boards, and speaks the lines which have been written for him, and shakes his hands and feet. Today he's a courtier [*Hofmann*], tomorrow a bootblack, the day after a lawyer, and the next a thug . . .[130]

The drunken habits of his actor, and the use of the unusual word *Hofmann*, would seem to allude to Ludwig Devrient and his friend E. T. A. Hoffmann. Hoffmann lived on the corner of the Mohrenstraße and the Gendarmenmarkt,† almost within spitting distance of Lutter und Wegner, the wine house in which he and Devrient passed their Dionysiac nights. In the last months of his life, Hoffmann wrote a little satire on his sick self, describing his lodgings and the bustle of the Gendarmenmarkt below. In *Des Vetters Eckfenster* the narrator is a fictional cousin of Hoffmann's who comes to

---

* The German contains an untranslatable pun: 'ißt er sich an de Tabeldodt halb dodt . . .'

† Hoffmann's house was pulled down at the beginning of this century. Its replacement survives, complete with a portrait roundel of the writer.

pay a call. It is market day, but as the cousin approaches his door he can see Hoffmann at his corner window wearing his red cap and the dressing-gown he acquired in his days as a civil servant in Warsaw. He is smoking his Sunday pipe filled with Turkish tobacco.[131]

From his window Hoffmann makes the cousin observe the crowd below: 'The entire market looked like one mass of people, thickly packed together, so that it seemed that if one were to toss an apple into the crowd it would never hit the ground.'[132] Hoffmann is not impressed with his cousin's reticence. He hands him a telescope so that he can observe the different characters going about their shopping: a French woman, with a yellow cloth tied round her head like a turban, fingers a goose with professional fingers. Hoffmann's cousin thinks her a 'left-over' from the last war 'who had managed to feather her own nest'. Hoffmann himself takes the opportunity to expound on his theory of drinks. Certain drinks are for the philistine and the mean-spirited: beer and coffee in particular. Two old market sellers attract his attention: 'With each cup of coffee they must mutter a slander as fat as your fist.'[133]

The invalid Hoffmann finds an entire microcosm of Berlin society in the market below. It is not just composed of servants and the city poor. The daughters of high-ranking civil servants, for example, are sent out to the market to learn the practicalities of shopping before their betrothal.[134] Hoffmann had developed a keen interest in a flower girl who took every opportunity to plunge her pretty head in a book. It occurred to him that it might have been one of his, which, indeed, it turned out to be. When Hoffmann enquired about the book, the flower girl recounted the tale in detail. Hoffmann glowed with authorial pride: 'Here, my sweet angel, here stands the creator of the book which has given you so much pleasure, here in flesh and blood.' But it transpired that the poor girl had no conception of authorship and believed that books grew from God's bounty, like mushrooms. She asked him finally whether he had penned all the books at the travelling library. Hoffmann rushed away with his carnations, his vanity chastened.[135]

The Wilhelmstraße was the street of government; the Friedrichstraße was the commercial street, where Berliners went to shop. Naturally that also meant cafés and cheap hotels, which found their clientele in the travellers who alighted at the main-line station north of the Linden. The most famous of the cafés was Bauer, which formed the corner of Unter den Linden and the southern stretch of the Friedrichstraße. Bauer was a huge building, with seating on two floors. Inside, thin Ionic columns supported a gallery and the walls were covered with murals *à l'antique*. It was a respectable place, good for families and young officers entertaining their people from out of town. In a light-hearted mood, Anton von Werner painted the artist Adolf Menzel there, sketching in the corner with a *Weißbier* and a schnapps at his elbow.[136]

Even in the 1880s the cafés were open all night.[137] The mixture to be found in a café such as the National in the Friedrichstraße is exploited by Carl Zuckmayer in his play *Der Hauptmann von Köpenick* of 1931. There is the usual bevy of officers lounging around, but in the corner the cobbler Voigt and his ex-cellmate 'Kalle' are sharing their experiences of the previous night. Voigt has slept on a variety of station benches. Naturally, for a provincial this side of Berlin could be alarming. Diederich Hessling, the central figure in Heinrich Mann's novel *Der Untertan* of 1918, arrives in Berlin to study at the University. He rents himself a room in the Tieckstraße across the Spree because he is frightened of straying too far from the Friedrichstraße.

> Now he had only to walk down in a straight line and he couldn't miss the University. When he had nothing else on he went there twice a day. In between he cried a lot from homesickness. He wrote a letter

to his father and mother and thanked them for his happy childhood. He rarely left the house without anxiety. Whenever he did so he got frightened that he'd spend his allowance before the month was out. And he was constantly grabbing at his pocket to see if it was still there.[138]

With time the tentacle spread south to the Leipziger Platz when the new branch of Wertheim opened there in 1904. Wertheim's first big shop started up in the Rosenthaler Straße of Kreuzberg in 1885, dealing exclusively in textiles. In 1890 another branch opened in the Oranienstraße, followed by the first proper 'department store' in the Moritzplatz. Here began Alfred Messel's involvement with the company,[139] and he started work on the Leipziger Platz building in 1897. Messel broke the mould in Berlin architecture: if the detail was historical, for the first time glass exceeded stone or brick.[140]

The Wertheims were Jews from Stralsund in Pomerania. Georg Wertheim married the daughter of I. A. Gilka, the Berlin distiller who made the most popular brand of Kümmel drunk in the city.[141] 'A proper Berliner', wrote Fontane, 'needs only three things: a *Weiße* [beer], a Gilka, and leaks.'[142] The business suffered from the Nazi boycott of Jewish shops and was 'Aryanised' as 'AWAG' (Allgemeine Warenhaus AG – or the General Department Store Ltd) in 1937. Georg Wertheim had the good fortune to die in his eighty-third year, in December 1939, and miss the deportations.[143]

Hessling's digs in the Tieckstraße lay beyond the Dorotheenstadt, as the area north of the Linden was known, where the building of a properly planned suburb had begun in 1676.[144] An impressive little palace which went back to the beginnings of the *Vorstadt* was the *Landhaus*, or garden house, of the Gräfin Kamecke, designed by Schlüter in 1711,[145] with its exuberantly baroque central *corps de logis* and one-storey wings. It was later turned over to the 'Royal

York' freemasonic lodge. It was destroyed in the war. The best remaining buildings in this section of the town are on the Kupfergraben, including the house where Max Reinhardt lived until his emigration in 1933. It is attributed to Boumann the younger and Knobelsdorff.[146]

On 19 October 1820 Zelter wrote to Goethe about his new house in the Dorotheenstadt. It was in the Georgenstraße, on the site of the railway station.

> I have a special house with a courtyard and garden
> where I live all alone. There is a pretty promenade
> by the Spree where most of the traffic from the Havel
> and the Oder passes silently, but vividly, by. The main
> building on the Friedrichstraße is 35 windows wide,
> and is inhabited by a great many of my acquaintances;
> the big garden lies between the two buildings where
> we might have a few get-togethers on winter
> evenings. Whether great use can be made of it remains
> to be seen . . .[147]

Frederick I unified the different districts, or *Vorstädte*, of Berlin at the same time as he abolished the last of the city's privileges. One further royal borough was established across the Spree as the Friedrich Wilhelmstadt. Frederick William III was not the Maecenas his father was. Frederick William II was almost as generous in the favours he distributed to his architects as he was with his mistresses. It was he who brought Langhans up to Berlin from Breslau, Erdmannsdorf from Dessau, Friedrich Gilly from Stettin, and retrieved Schadow from self-imposed exile in Rome.[148] His son's little *quartier* has survived in many instances between the Charité and the river. The houses are simple Biedermeyer blocks, visible in the Schumann-, Marien- and Luisenstraße. In the latter, number 18 was the Palais Bülow, which was turned into the 'Möwe' artists' club by the communists.[149]

Berlin's reception room was the 'Quarré' or Pariser Platz on the eastern side of the Brandenburg Gate. Before the railway station in the Friedrichstraße was equipped with a special waiting-room for princely guests, high-ranking visitors were met at the gate. The practice was scrapped in 1912. It was not popular with the mayor, who rued the fact

> that the city's envoy should be obliged to wait on the
> Pariser Platz in the flimsiest clothing and headwear,
> in all weathers, until the court coach arrived from the
> station; that a welcome should be delivered and
> perhaps a few verses read out from a pretty mouth or
> a bouquet offered up at the coach door; and that he
> should have to wait after it was all over in a graceful
> pose, head inclined, until the party had driven on.[150]

It was not only visiting princes who rode under Schadow's quadriga and through Langhans' neo-classical gate. In December 1793 Frederick William II christened the Gate after his return from the (hardly victorious) Champagne campaign. His soldiers were greeted with the new anthem, *Heil Dir in Siegerkranz*.* Frederick William set the precedent of using the Gate for victory marches. On 30 January 1933 it was defiled by the SA, drunk with power, and not a little alcohol too. President Hindenburg is said to have complimented the Chief of the General Staff on the turn-out of his troops, 'How well they are marching.' Then, observing the shambling SA men behind, he added: 'And what a lot of prisoners they seem to have taken!'[151]

After 1945 the role of the Gate changed. It became the symbol of the divided city, rather than a monument to Prusso-German arms. They even tampered with Schadow's quadriga in the interests of political correctness, robbing Victoria of her iron cross. The painter Lovis Corinth thought the statue, 'after the Great Elector on the Lange Brücke, the most accomplished work of art the capital possesses'.[152]

---

* 'Hail to Thee in the Victor's Laurels', sung to the tune of 'God Save the Queen'.

Once through the Gate you were in Berlin. Max Liebermann used to direct guests to his patrician mansion on the western side of the Pariser Platz by saying: 'When you come into Berlin, first on the left.' Pre-war photographs show the Liebermann residence with a glass canopy on top, which was presumably his studio. He too witnessed the torch-lit procession of 30 January 1933. In a much quoted passage he expressed his disgust in pure *Berlinisch*: 'Ick kann gar nich so ville fressen, wie ich kotzen möchte' ('I really couldn't eat as much as I would like to throw up'). As a Jew he lost his position in the Academy, but died peacefully in 1935. His wife, aged eighty-two, hurled herself from the window of the same building in 1943 when the police came to deport her.[153]

The *Viereck* (or 'Square') was renamed the Pariser Platz after Prussian troops entered the French capital in 1814. Even in Nicolai's time it was important that the first houses in Berlin should make an impression on the visitor.[154] This was Berlin's best address. Over the years it numbered the mathematician Maupertuis, the dramatist Kotzebue, the jurist Savigny, the thespian Iffland and the writer Achim von Arnim among its residents. In the nineteenth century the original scale was lost. The first to change the tone was Schinkel's Redern'sche Palais, dwarfed in its turn by its successor, the Adlon Hotel. Next door, on the south side of the square, was the Arnim palace, which was later turned over to the Akademie der Künste. In 1937 Albert Speer grabbed it for himself, but his presence was a great boon to hotel guests, who could avail themselves of his 'bomb-proof' air-raid shelter. The next building to the west was the 'feudal' Casino-Gesellschaft, a gentleman's club. This was given to the chief of forced labour, Todt, in the gradual Nazification of the square.

In the south-western corner was the neo-baroque American Embassy. Either side of the Gate were Italianate buildings, partly occupied by offices. On the north side were

Liebermann's house and studio. They were constructed in 1859. In the north-west corner lived Fritz von Friedländer-Fuld, the richest man in Germany after the Kaiser. Naturally his house did not remain in Jewish hands, and was taken over by Todt after 1939. The French Embassy next door was by Stüler. On the northern side of the Linden, opposite the Adlon was the massive headquarters of the Deutsche Länderbank of 1923.

The Russians and their stooges in the DDR cleared away the ruins of the Pariser Platz, including the Arnim'sche Palais, which might have been preserved, and turned it into a great windy space that had the advantage of being easy to patrol. In 1995, the City of Berlin unveiled plans for rebuilding the square in an unsatisfying compromise between replica and modernism. Muted classicism was decreed for the Adlon, and to some extent the buildings either side of the Gate. The American and French Embassies were to reproduce their earlier façades. Only the British round the corner in the old Strousberg palace in the Wilhelmstraße had refused to play ball, preferring to integrate their design into the fabric of the new Adlon. By the summer of that year a huge hole in the ground betokened work in progress.[155] A year later the form of the Adlon was recognisable behind the scaffolding.

VIII

All die Lachenden Dörfer, ich zähle sie kaum:
Linow, Lindow,
Rhinow, Glindow,
Beetz und Gatow,
Dreetz und Flatow,
Bamme, Damme, Kriele, Krielow,
Pelzow, Retzow, Ferch am Schwilow,
Zachow, Wachow, und Groß Bähnitz [sic],
Marquadt-Ütz an Wublitz-Schlänitz,
Senzke, Lenzke und Marzahne,

Lietzow, Tietzow und Reckahne,
Und zum Schluß in dem leuchenden Kranz
Ketzin, Ketzür und Vehlefanz.★[156]

Like London, Berlin grew to swallow up the villages and
hamlets which surrounded it, so that even now you may still
come across a modest mediaeval church plumb in the middle
of some otherwise drab stretch of suburbia. Berlin's expansion
was more rapid than London's. Between 1867 and 1914 it was
second only to Budapest in Europe.[157] The transformation
was total. A landscape by Menzel in the Ephraim Palace
shows Wilmersdorf in 1853. It is an entirely bucolic scene
depicting fields and a distant church. By the turn of the
century all this was gone. Wilmersdorf had become a
network of *Mietshäuser*.

Despite gallant attempts to impose a plan on Berlin, the
speculators managed to get their own way. In many places
the result was a shambles. In Nabokov's short story *The
Leonardo* of 1933 the novelist writes of a ' . . . dark and
desolate part of Berlin . . . On the right were vacant lots
from which a few hastily silhouetted houses had turned their
backs away.' The wartime destruction added to this gap-
toothed image of the city: unkempt and unloved.[158]

For Prussian-born writers like Fontane the old villages
squashed between the pine forests and the hidden lakes had
enormous charm. Others were unimpressed – the French
writer Stendhal, for instance, who thought 'the sand turns
the outskirts of the city into a desert . . . I have no idea who
thought of planting a town in the middle of this sand.'[159]
Ernst Dronke, whose negative attitude to the city was to
land him with a two-year prison sentence,†[160] described his

---

★ 'All the laughing villages, I can hardly count . . . And at last in
the glittering crown . . .' Not all Fontane's villages are in Groß
Berlin.
† The former communist died in Liverpool, having spent the
second half of his life as a representative for a copper mine.

journey up from Anhalt. The fields were '... monotonous, uninterrupted ... huge, gloomy seas of sand in the middle of which Berlin lies like an oasis'. From the window of his compartment he saw '... no inviting farmyard, no jolly fields', just potatoes and heather. He expanded the analogy to encompass the city itself: 'the image of unfruitful criticism in the soil of which all the hotbed and greenhouse flowers of the poets and painters can neither flourish nor develop on their own'.[161]

Most travellers were struck by the newness of Berlin; by its extraordinary propensity to digest itself every generation or so and spit out a radically altered, often gimcrack version of its former self. In 1829 a born Berliner, Alexander von Humboldt, wrote to his brother Wilhelm in the course of a journey from Königsberg to Riga. He fantasised about creating a second Berlin on the Baltic:

> If Schinkel could have a few brick churches thrown up, if we could have a Monday Club, a circle of art-loving young Jewish ladies and an Academy in these sandy steppes, then we'd be short of nothing to build a new Berlin.[162]

Berlin's growth was spectacular. In 1680, shortly after the disastrous Thirty Years War, the city's population was under 10,000. By 1700 it had nearly tripled. In 1800 it had already reached 172,000 souls.[163] When Frederick the Great ascended the throne of Prussia in 1740, there were just 5,400 houses. When he died in 1786 Berlin counted 6,888 houses on the streets, and a further 3,355 courtyard houses.[164]

In the year following the revolution of 1848 the by now industrial city numbered 412,000; at the onset of the Second Reich, 826,000. Six years later, in 1877, it had topped the million mark. In 1905 it had doubled that figure. The growth began to slacken off from 1912, but it should be borne in mind that we are talking here of the old city limits, before the creation of the new Groß-Berlin, or 'Greater Berlin', in 1920. By that time the conurbation already contained seven large towns: Charlottenburg, Neukölln, Schöneberg, Lichtenberg, Wilmersdorf, Steglitz and Spandau.

After Greater Berlin was created, the pressure on the old hub abated. In 1925 the population of Alt-Berlin had dropped below a million.[165] Many of these lived in the poky back courtyards of the infamous *Mietskasernen*, 'barracks-dwellings'. Some of these have survived on the Gerichtstraße and the Müllerstraße in Wedding. There were anything up to a dozen courtyards stretching back from the (comparatively) respectable façade. The problem was that Berlin could not build fast enough to cope with the incomers. The city was (and is) desperately short of housing.[166] By 1918 nearly 40 per cent of all Berliners were living in one-room flats. Infant mortality was exceedingly high. In 1905 it was 19.5 per cent for the whole city. In the poorest area, Wedding, it was 40 per cent. Heinrich Zille spoke from experience when he uttered his famous line: 'One can beat a man to death with his home just as effectively as with an axe.'[167]

Berlin's progress after 1871 can only be compared to the North American cities'.[168] It was in the period between then and the foundation of the Weimar Republic that the last of Berlin's villages merged with the urban sprawl. Both Spandau and Charlottenburg had populations in the region of 20,000 when the Empire was founded. By 1919 the latter had shot to 322,000. Steglitz and Wilmersdorf had been under 2,000; now the one was over 83,000 and the other a little under 140,000. Simple villages such as Dahlem had shot from 105 inhabitants to 6,244. Friedenau, which had not previously existed, now boasted 43,833 citizens; Grunewald had leapt from 32 to 6,448. Wannsee and Zehlendorf owed a modest sixfold expansion to the fact that they were constructing villas for the rich. Köpenick also maintained a 600 per cent rise. Only one village remained: little Gatow, between

Potsdam and Spandau, and even here there had been an increase by a third, from 399 to 609 inhabitants.[169]

Naturally there had been attempts to impose a little Prussian order on this swelling monster. Not for nothing was it the royal aesthete Frederick William IV who first mooted the idea of creating some splendid avenues on the Paris model.[170] Peter Joseph Lenné was the natural choice to carry out the work. Born in Bonn in 1789, he had studied landscape gardening in Paris and Vienna and been to England in 1822 to experience London's squares at first hand. Lenné recreated the park at Sanssouci in Potsdam and during the years 1833 to 1840 turned Berlin's Tiergarten into a landscape park on an English picturesque model.[171]

The basis for Lenné's plan was the laying out of a city ring road of the sort only introduced *after* 1853 by the Paris *Préfet* Haussmann and after 1858 in Vienna. Indeed, Lenné actually entered the competition to build Vienna's famous Ringstraße. The plan for Berlin, which was first aired in 1844, involved a series of avenues that linked square or circular spaces. All Lenné was able to achieve, however, were the first stages of the development in northern Kreuzberg.[172]

The project obtained limited support from Frederick William's philistine brother William. By that stage Lenné had retired to Potsdam and it was James Hobrecht, the son of an East Prussian landowner and the brother of a future *Oberbürgermeister* (lord mayor) of Berlin, who now took over the baton. From 1859 to 1861 Hobrecht worked on a scheme to continue Lenné's work. Alas he too was bedevilled by the power of vested interest and was only able to extend Lenné's avenues into Schöneberg. The streets now commemorated the generals of the War of Liberation, while the squares and circuses were named after the battles: Gneisenau Straße, Yorck Straße, Bülow Straße, Kleist Straße, Tauentzien Straße and the Hardenberg Straße to honour a politician with a leading role; then the Wartenberg Platz, Dennewitz Platz, Nollendorf Platz and Wittenberg Platz. The Stein Platz doesn't observe the rules: it celebrates the reforming minister vom Stein.[173]

The grandest square of all was to be the Wahlstatt Platz, a tribute to Blücher. It was to have a 'magnificent park' which would form the southern end of a projected avenue that was to cross Berlin from north to south. The plan was blocked by the railway companies, who had previously opposed the Lenné plan because its implementation would have required the termini to be brought back behind the new boulevards, rather than sitting squat in the centre of town. In the north the railways similarly disrupted attempts to create avenues to mirror those in Kreuzberg and Schöneberg. Here it was the Lehrter and Hamburger stations which wouldn't budge and destroyed the chance of establishing Berlin's 'belt road'.[174]

The Hobrecht Plan was not just limited to the creation of fine avenues. It was far more wide-ranging than that. Lenné had also envisaged blocks of flats as part of his scheme for Kreuzberg. Both Lenné and Hobrecht had expressed a certain amount of idealism here, as one writer has pointed out. Originally '*Mietskaserne*' had a positive sense and was similar to Le Corbusier's idea of a 'machine pour vivre':[175]

> ... the good flats on the street frontage would be occupied by the well-off, the others would be inhabited by the poor. [This would impose] social controls and integration and hinder the creation of slum areas.[176]

The first *Mietshäuser*, or blocks of flats, were built on a human scale on two or three floors, with a side wing to lodge the horses and shops. With the population explosion occasioned by Berlin's elevation to the new imperial capital, however, builders began piling on extra floors and building more and more courtyards.

Behind the neo-classical façades on the street, where
often the landlord inhabited the *piano nobile* and
where there was often to be found a distiller, cobbler
or coal-merchant down in the basement, there were
bare side wings and courtyard buildings filling the
entire depth of the block; as many as five passages
strung the dark courtyards together.[177]

Hobrecht had worked out his *Mietshäuser* to the last detail.
His ambition was to lodge up to four million people in these
blocks. The buildings were to be 120 to 150 metres wide
and 75 metres deep, with more elaborate designs for market-
places or squares. He sought above all to avoid what he knew
of London, where the poor lived in their own ghettos away
from the civilising influence of the middle classes. The best
flats would be on the first floor with rents as high as 500
thalers. The ground and second floors would pay 200. The
third floor would be divided into two flats, each paying 150;
the fourth into three, each paying 100. The cellar and the
flats in the courtyard would pay just fifty.[178]

Hobrecht's idea was to make the *Mietshaus* a stabilising
element in society; to excite in the working class a desire to
emulate their 'betters'. In his plan of things, a good neigh-
bourly feeling would grow up: 'here a bowl of soup, there a
piece of clothing . . .' Children from the basement of the
Mietskaserne set off across the same hallway on their way to
the free school as the children of businessmen and civil
servants on their way to the *Gymnasium*, or grammar
school.[179]

Hobrecht wanted to see an end to the infamous *Keller-
wohnungen*, particularly dark, basement dwellings, which
were 'good only for barrels, potatoes and vegetables [*sic*], not
for people'. He wanted more 'light and air'. Hobrecht's
schemes were defeated by capital; his measurements revised
in order to secure the greatest profits.[180] The minimum size
of the courtyards, for example, was fixed at a paltry 5.34

square metres: just enough room to manoeuvre a fire engine. By 1900 a travesty of Hobrecht's ideal had grown up in the densely populated parts of the capital. In Kreuzberg there were buildings with factories on five floors with a lift connecting the different levels. This was the *Kreuzberger Mischung* or 'Kreuzberg mix': a building which combined offices, workshops, small-scale factories and flats. Some of these have survived to this day in the northern reaches of the Luisenstadt.[181]

In 1893 a commission looking into work and health reported that blocks of flats erected by one Paul Haberkern afforded residents less space than inmates in the Plötzensee Prison. Hobrecht's socially inspiring ideals had survived only in a handful of streets, although it is true to say that before the war the social composition of many blocks of flats in Berlin varied considerably from the street frontage to the courtyards; only the integration promised by Hobrecht was simply not the rule.[182]

IX

From the first the twin-town of Berlin-Cölln was bounded by walls. By the beginning of the fourteenth century they enclosed 47 hectares of Berlin and 23 of Cölln.[183] Outside the walls Berliners kept their market gardens, vineyards and orchards. Potatoes were as yet unknown; their promotion by Frederick the Great was fiercely resisted by conservative farmers.[184] For the time being cabbages covered the bulk of the land. In 1565 Berlin possessed 55 vineyards on steep sites and a further 19 on flat land; a hop garden; and 120 orchards and vegetable gardens. Cölln had a total of 22 vineyards and 116 orchards and vegetable gardens.[185] The extent of Berlin's arable land meant that a quarter of all its citizens could tend their own crops, leading to a very high degree of self-sufficiency. Common lands were also available for the grazing of horses, oxen, pigs and geese. There were five sheep farms providing ewes' milk and seventeen dairy farms selling cows' milk.[186]

Berlin changed its shape in the seventeenth century as the need arose to erect something a little stronger to resist Swedish and Imperial armies of the Thirty Years War. In fact Berlin suffered less than many other German cities, less even than Frankfurt an der Oder and considerably less than the archbishop's see, Magdeburg. Magdeburg's impregnability had led it to be dubbed 'the Virgin', until it was raped by Tilly's armies. The Elector George William was King Gustavus Adolphus of Sweden's brother-in-law, a connection which doubtless ensured better treatment for the town while the Swedish star was in the ascendant. The Statthalter, Adam Graf zu Schwarzenberg, none the less had a series of new defences thrown up around the town, but these did nothing to prevent Berlin from being singed in 1641, when Cölln's suburbs were destroyed by ravaging armies.[187]

The Thirty Years War and its aftermath were a grim time for Berlin. It lost its *Residenz* status when the court fled to Königsberg on the Baltic, and its prowess as a trading centre received a considerable blow when the merchant houses of Weiler, Engel and Essenbrücher were forced to close around 1639. Plague hit the town five times between 1626 and 1638, and an epidemic in 1631 claimed more than 2,000 lives.[188]

For once Berlin was shrinking. Schwarzenberg had much of the suburbs destroyed in order to make Berlin easier to defend. In 1640, the year of George William's death, Berlin had declined to a town of just 1,197 households. During the course of the war its population had dwindled from 10,000 to 7,000; it was in desperate need of new blood to recapture its old *élan*.[189]

Schwarzenberg's wall was short-lived. It was replaced by a rather more solid affair, built by Johann Gregor Memhardt in 1658, which enclosed Friedrichswerder, across the water from Cölln, as well as the original mediaeval twin-town.[190]

This served the double purpose of keeping out the elector's enemies and taxing his subjects through the so-called 'excise wall'.[191] This was itself replaced by a far more wide-ranging wall in 1730, which was intended to separate Berlin from its 'neighbouring townlets' of Charlottenburg, Köpenick and Spandau, as well as fifty church-possessing satellite villages. There is still a chunk of Berlin's mediaeval wall in the Waisen-straße in Mitte, but there is nothing left of either the Schwarzenberg or the Memhardt walls. Friedrich Nicolai reported that they were already down by 1769, but for a minute stretch on the Weidendamm.[192] It is none the less possible to trace much of the circuit today if you follow the Wall-, Niederwall- and Oberwallstraßen, and the Kupfer-graben. The Alexanderplatz was built in a bastion, as was the Hausvogteiplatz, which even reproduces its trapezoid form.

The wall of 1730 took in the town's recent spread. In the west it skirted the Rondell (later, Belle-Alliance; even later, Mehringplatz), the Achteck (later, Leipziger Platz) and the Quarré (Pariser Platz). North of the Spree it encompassed the Spandauer and Königs Vordstädte and the Stralauer Vor-stadt to the east. South of the Spree it took in much of the chiefly still arable Köpenicker Vorstadt.[193]

In 1802 the wall was further stretched to include newly built-up bits of Berlin. In the west, it had been but a wooden palisade. Now the whole circuit was replaced by a stone construction 4.2 metres high. The most radical changes were in the north and east. The Charité Hospital now came within its bounds as well as the sprawl that had grown up along the river bank to Stralau.[194] The wall was not only intended to be a more efficient way of collecting taxes, it also had a singularly Prussian vocation of retaining would-be deserters. Every hundred metres a sentry was posted and the population of the surrounding villages was alerted to each flight by a discharge of cannon shot. Any poor soldier caught was forced to run the gauntlet on the Rondell; beaten with iron rods by his comrades.

The city wall was now 17 kilometres long, while Berlin counted 13.5 square kilometres, about the size of the Tiergarten *Bezirk* today. The only built-up area that remained unenclosed was the shanty town in the Rosenthaler Vorstadt, which was full of poor Saxons from Neu-Voigtland.[195] The wall had few pretensions to beauty. There were just three monumental gates, the Brandenburger, still the best-known symbol of the city, the Oranienburger, with its martial dressings capping two small archways, and the Hamburger Gate, with its twin pyramids. The latter has disappeared, but the Oranienburger Tor still exists. The Borsig family had it removed to their estate at Groß Behnitz west of Spandau. The Russians burned the *Schloß* to the ground, but they were considerate enough to spare Berlin's penultimate gateway.[196]

Two more victims of the Russians' destructive ardour were Schinkel's Greek Doric lodges on the Leipziger Platz, which were designed in 1823. They were badly damaged in the war and eventually cleared away along with the other reparable ruins in both the Leipziger and the Potsdamer Plätze to make the border crossing between the Russian and American sectors easier to patrol. The last time the wall circuit was improved was in 1840. Twenty years later the whole lot was ripped down with the exception of a very unimpressive clump of masonry which stands in the middle of the Stresemannstraße in Kreuzberg.[197]

These days there isn't that much more of Berlin's most famous wall left, the one put up on 13 August 1961. The construction of the shoddy concrete division was only made possible by Khrushchev's decision to hand over responsibility for security within the Soviet sector to Ulbricht and the SED. Literally overnight, Berlin changed its very nature. Up until then East Berliners had worked in the west and had access to western culture. They attended theatres, concerts and cinemas and they were able to study at the Free University. The erection of the Wall marked a half-way point in the history of the DDR. From now on the state would wholly align itself with its Communist Bloc neighbours. It has been called an admission of failure on the part of Ulbricht and the SED, but there was sound economic reasoning behind it. East Germans had been fleeing at a rate of 20,000 a month. After the Wall went up, between 1961 and 1988 this total went down to roughly the same amount per annum, thereby stabilising the East German economy. It rid West Berlin of its cheap, German labour force and brought in the *Gastarbeiter*: Turks and Portuguese; it meant the death of scores of East Germans who chanced their luck with an ill-planned dash; and it covered the eastern half of the city with a permanent cloud of cultural deprivation, which is only now beginning to disperse.[198]

X

Sunday was always a great day all over the Christian world and Berlin was no exception. Once the business of worship was over and done with, workers in their finery spouted in droves from the city gates and sped towards Moabit, Stralau or Kreuzberg. The better-heeled Berliner generally contented himself with the Tiergarten, which Frederick the Great had enclosed, and Frederick William III had landscaped. The park was strewn with cafés and dance halls, and here a little fresh air could be drunk in, along with a *Weiße* or two, or a bottle of wine.

It was obviously a good place for chance encounters. It was here that E. T. A. Hoffmann met Christoph Willibald von Gluck, or, rather, his ghost. The composer had died twenty-one years before the meeting, which took place during the French Occupation.

> Late autumn in Berlin generally offers a few fine days.
> The sun steps warmly out from behind the clouds,
> and the damp quickly evaporates in the luke-warm air
> which scurries through the streets. When this
> happens you will see a long line, a multicoloured
> medley proceeding down the Linden towards the
> Tiergarten: dandies, stout citizens with their ladies and
> the little ones in their Sunday best, pastors, Jewish
> women, young men doing their pupillage in lawyers'

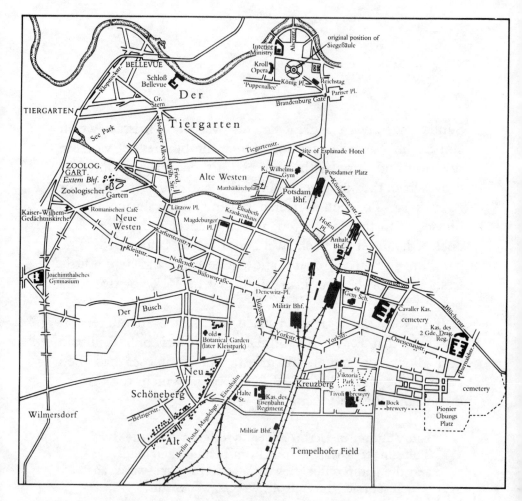

The old and the new West in the second half of the
nineteenth century

chambers, *filles de joie*, professors, milliners, dancers, officers and the like. Soon all the seats at Klaus and Weber are occupied; the carrot-coffee is on the boil and the dandies are putting a match to their cigars.[199]

A group of musicians strikes up a cacophonous din which wrenches Hoffmann from his dream-world. Sitting at the same table is another man who finds the music hard to take. This is Gluck. Hoffmann fills his glass with burgundy. Gluck naturally responds differently to a rendering of the overture from *Iphigenia in Aulis*; he begins to conduct from an imaginary keyboard. They go inside, and, Hoffmann being Hoffmann, they empty a bottle.

Frederick the Great's act of generosity towards the people of his capital had rapidly transformed the nature of the park. Only seven years later, in 1752, the three royal princes gave an informal party in the Tiergarten. The servants had clearly been banned for the occasion. 'We did the cooking ourselves', writes Lehndorff. 'That is no easy matter, but there was much merry-making for all that. The Prince of Prussia thought he was making a fricassee, but ended up with a soup.'[200]

The first 'refreshments tent' opened in 1745. With time these temporary tents, or *Zelte*, were replaced by more solid structures, but they retained the name.[201] Even today, when no trace survives of the *Zelte* whatsoever, there is still an alley in the Tiergarten called 'In den Zelte'. It was the *cafétier* Johann Gottfried Winguth who transformed the old Tiergarten hunting lodge into a fashionable café in 1803, naturally giving it the name 'Zum ewigen Zelte' (The Eternal Tent). Winguth's café spawned a number of imitations. By 1830 Berliners could choose from his Hofjäger, Teichmann's Blumengarten, Elysium, or Kempers Hof.[202]

Lenné's transformation of the Tiergarten into an English landscape garden rang the knell for the park's old, fun-loving days. Now it became a big city park. It had and has its hidden corners, though, such as the goldfish pond where Jehovah's Witnesses held their clandestine meetings during the Third Reich, when their sect was suppressed. That collector of old Berlin, Julius Rodenberg, also found a pleasantly informal side to the Tiergarten on his rambles. Where the railway bridge crossed the Landwehrkanal he saw 'two men standing upright in high fishing boots tossing out baskets and pulling them out so that the blackish water dribbled from them. They were catching eels . . .'[203] The park's sandy soil also provides Berliners with wild mushrooms.*

From 1871 the Tiergarten filled up with the clutter of empire. The first to arrive was the Siegessäule. The design was by a pupil of Schinkel, Heinrich Strack. He made his initial sketches in 1864, but the Prussian habit of winning wars meant that the column was not finished until 1873, when it was crowned by a figure of Victory by Friedrich Drake. The Berliners thought it looked funny and christened it the 'Siegesspargel', or 'Victory Asparagus'. Naturally, the Nazis were not happy to leave it as it was. They moved it to its present site on the Siegesallee and heightened it by a further 6.5 metres. After the Second World War it was defaced by the French.[204]

With time the winged Victory was given some company. She was joined by other imperial worthies such as Bismarck (by Reinhold Begas), Moltke and the War Minister Roon. The most controversial pieces of statuary in the new imperial theme-park were the Kaiser's ancestors, who were lined up along the Siegesallee. The Berliners had their name for this too, and very soon everyone referred to the avenue as the 'Puppenallee', or 'Dolls' Alley'.

The Kaiser called it his 'Ahnenallee', or avenue of ancestors. He flicked through the histories and came up with

---

* Since Chernobyl they have become wary of eating them. The author once found a large cep within a few hundred metres of the Brandenburg Gate.

thirty-two kings and electors of Prussia and Brandenburg, each to be flanked by their familiars: a brace of generals was the ideal, but if none were to hand, then ministers or overmighty clerics would do.[205] For the princes, the Kaiser dipped into his personal pocket to the tune of 30,000 gold marks and provided marble brought in specially from Carrara.[206] The sculptors were given the brief to glorify his lineage. His own favourite, Begas, got several commissions; elsewhere the Kaiser used the patronage as a stick to beat any sculptor guilty of modernity: *Rinnsteinkunst*, or 'gutter art', he called it. He had a particular aversion to Gustav Eberlein, who had offended him with a realistic Adam and Eve cycle, with the protagonists *au naturel*.[207]

Some mocked; others howled in fury. Everyone had an opinion on the Puppenallee. As a child, Walter Benjamin rather liked it. He stared at the minions, 'and I was filled with the certainty that my parents were not so far removed from the present powers in the land as these worthies were from their ancestors . . .'[208] Lovis Corinth was still incensed years later. It was 'a disgrace to German art'.[209] Others thought it a huge joke. In 1903, the magazine *Jugend* produced a montage of the Puppenallee where all the Hohenzollerns had been replaced by bottles of Odol mouthwash.[210] The Kaiser encouraged the provinces to copy, or put up an effigy of William 'the Great' (as he called his grandfather) at the very least. In *Der Untertan*, Heinrich Mann has one of the Puppenallee sculptors come to the town to do just that: he 'had been accorded the distinction of creating a fine likeness of the Margrave Hatto the Mighty, together with his most important contemporaries, the Monk Tassilo, who could drink a hundred litres of beer in a day, and the knight Klitzenzitz, who emancipated the slaves of Berlin, and who was hanged for his pains'.[211]

Even the Nazis took a dim view of the Puppenallee and moved the sculptural depiction of the Hohenzollerns' rise to a less prominent part of the park.[212] The Allies were even more brutal after 1945, and had the effigies unceremoniously swept away. Besides the column, the Siegesallee was left with just one monument to feats of arms: not German, but Soviet. As the group lay in the British sector, it served a useful purpose to the Russians, who had to be allowed to cross British lines to guard it.

The Tiergarten has its own *Schloß*, Bellevue, the Berlin seat of the President of the Federal Republic. Bellevue had originally been Knobelsdorff's house and farm. After the architect's death it had been sold to a Kommerzienrat Schneider. In 1785 the land was bought by Prince Ferdinand of Prussia, who commissioned Michael Philipp Daniel Boumann to build him a summer palace.[213] After the death of the 'Prussian Alcibiades', Louis Ferdinand, at a skirmish near Saalfeld, four days before the double defeat at Jena and Auerstedt, it passed to Ferdinand's second son, Prince Augustus. If for nothing else, Augustus should be remembered as the man who fired the otherwise frigid heart of Juliette Récamier, who was driven to the point of suicide by her love.[214] Schloß Bellevue used to contain a bust of the great beauty, presumably a present from the woman herself. A similar terracotta was in the possession of her cousin and admirer, the judge and gastronomic writer Anselme Brillat-Savarin.[215]

Schloß Bellevue was underused until our own time. Charles X of France lived in it for a while in 1830, after his flight from the July Revolution. The Kaiser used it as a school for his children. It also doubled as a large garden while the Kaiser was in residence in Berlin, as the little Spree-side patio was too small for the royal children to run round in. Under instruction from their uncle Henry, the boys had built an earthwork which they called their fort. At Easter there was an egg-hunt in the garden; ' . . . the Kaiser didn't disdain to participate in person'.[216]

In 1928 Bellevue was acquired by the state. The Nazis turned it first into a Museum for German Ethnology, edified by an exhibition entitled 'German Man, German Land'.[217] After 1938 it became the state guesthouse. The first guest was Prince Paul of Jugoslavia in June 1939. In 1940 Molotov stayed there on his fraught visit to his National Socialist allies. The last guest was the Grand Mufti of Jerusalem, whom the Nazis were cultivating for his ability to help raise a legion of Bosnian Moslems for the SS.[218]

In its original position, the Siegessäule was on the Königs-platz, in between the Kroll Opera House and the Palais Raczynski, a pedimented late classical building with three bay wings connected by arcades. The Raczynskis kept their famous art collection there. The palace fell to the sledge-hammers, making way for the new Reichstag building designed by the Rhinelander Paul Wallot in the elaborate neo-baroque idiom of the day. The original 1872 competi-tion had been restricted to German applicants. Work did not start on Wallot's design until 1884, and the final inscription over the door 'Dem Deutschen Volke' (For the German People) was only unveiled in 1916.[219] The old Kaiser laid the first stone on a particularly cussed June day. Photographs show the crowds cowering under their un. rellas. It was no good augury.[220] As the building pushed its way up on to the Berlin skyline, increasing numbers of voices were heard in criticism. Wallot's style was south German. Here: once again, was a repudiation of the Schinkel school which had set the tone in Berlin for two whole generations.[221]

The city architect Ludwig Hoffmann thought it looked like a 'first-class hearse', while the ill-fated Weimar Foreign Minister Walther Rathenau dismissed it as 'sickly-sweet macaroon and marzipan taste'. Harry Kessler likened it to a 'badly copied Augsburg chest'. The astonishing thing is that the new Kaiser agreed with him: 'the pinnacle of bad taste', he called it.[222] To a large extent this was because he had failed to get his own way. He had wanted to dictate to his own architects and sculptors, Begas in particular, and Begas continued to pour scorn on Wallot. The Kaiser preferred

German Romanesque, but above all he didn't like the idea of the Reichstag: 'the imperial monkey house' was his soubriquet for the institution.[223]★

It continued to be an unloved institution even after the Kaiser had gone off to sulk in Dutch Doorn. Neither the extreme left nor the far right had any time for it. The left laid siege to it in January 1920, leaving more than 30 dead and 400 wounded on the steps.[225] On 24 June 1922 Walther Rathenau was murdered by right-wing extremists. On the 27th his body lay in state in the Chamber. The building he had rightly condemned as hideous had been cheered up for the occasion.

> Enormous palms flanked the coffin at its four corners. The speaker's rostrum was shrouded in black, as was the Government Bench, beneath magnificent wreaths with ribbons in the Republican colours, black-red-gold. The galleries, draped with crepe, were decorated with banks of blue and pink hydrangeas. Long crepe veils hung from the ceiling's arc-lights, which were turned on. The galleries, like the Chamber itself, were packed. There was not one empty seat, not even among the nationalists. The focal point was the coffin, draped with a huge flag in the national colours. At its feet there lay two immense wreaths, of red and white flowers . . .

> . . . The orchestra, out of sight in the vestibule behind the coffin, played the *Egmont* overture . . . Then the music played Siegfried's Funeral March from *Götterdämmerung*. This undoubtedly brought the ceremony inside the Chamber to its highest pitch of emotion. In the circumstances the effect was overwhelming. Many of those around me wept. The historic significance of this death echoed from the music in the hearts of of those present.

★ Wallot was obliged to bring down the height of the dome because it exceeded that of both the Cathedral and the Schloss.[224]

The coffin was carried through the lobby to the
entrance stairway. At the foot of the steps stood a
Reichswehr company, in field-grey uniform, steel-
helmeted. The drums rolled and the resonant tones of
a funeral march rose muffled into the air, strangely like
distant thunder. The coffin, wrapped in the national
colours, was laid on the hearse, which was swathed in
red roses. Slowly, to the accompaniment of drum-
beats, the cortège set off. In spite of the rain, or
perhaps because of this grey gossamer appropriate to
the muffled roll of the drums, the impression made
upon the spectators was almost even more intense
than it had been in the Chamber. Lassalle's dream of
passing through the Brandenburger Tor as President
of a Republic of Germany was today fulfilled by the
Jew Rathenau because of his martyrdom in the
service of the German people.[226]

Eleven years later, on 27 February 1933, the French
ambassador was dining with high-ranking Nazis when he
noticed something was happening to the Reichstag: 'The
glass dome was quite red, looking as if they had lit a Bengal
light underneath it.'[227] A young Dutch Communist, Marinus
van der Lubbe, actually managed to set fire to the building,
gutting the Chamber in the process. It should come as no
surprise that the Nazis were not unduly upset about the
destruction of this democratic institution, a fact that has led
many to suppose that Göring and his henchmen set fire to
the Reichstag themselves.[228] The debate is bound to continue
for years, as to whether it was humanly possible for one lone
man, not greatly endowed with intelligence, to set a huge
and well-guarded building ablaze, or whether it was indeed
the Nazis who committed the arson, having both the motive
and the means to carry it out. One aesthetic argument is
advanced which would tend to back the stronger evidence
that van der Lubbe perpetrated the crime: Hitler was fond
of the Reichstag building. He even clashed with Speer to
have it retained in the final rebuilding of Berlin. Didn't

Wallot's design owe much to the Paris Opera? And wasn't the architect Charles Garnier's lavish conception Hitler's favourite building?[229]

Sessions of the now emasculated assembly then passed to the Kroll-Oper on the far side of the Königsplatz. It was increasingly just a rubber stamp for Nazi laws; after the removal of most of the democratic parties the majority of the members appeared in black or brown uniforms. General Alexander von Falkenhausen, who came to Berlin to watch eleven of his comrades in arms being invested with marshals' batons after the Fall of France, was reminded of a Bologna sausage: 'half pork and half donkey'.[230]

Josef Kroll was a discovery of Frederick William IV. They met in Breslau and Kroll must have impressed on the king the need for a festive 'winter garden' in the capital. Land was granted Kroll on the west side of the former exercise yard beyond the Brandenburg Gate. From the first the project was on a massive scale: thirteen halls, fourteen large rooms and a tunnel. There was space for 5,000 Berliners.[231] The architects were Persius, Carl Ferdinand Langhans the Younger and Eduard Knoblauch. Berliners took the Kroll *établissement* to their bosoms. Kalisch set the final scene of his *Berlin bei Nacht* of 1849 at a rout *chez* Kroll. Kroll had died the year before, and there is some suggestion that the running of the institution passed to Wilhelm Stieber, the criminal police-chief.[232] Whatever the truth, Kroll had refused to entertain the democrats of 1848 who had gone to the 'tents' to clamour for a constitution.[233]

In 1851 the place caught fire and was totally destroyed. It was rebuilt bigger and better. From 1848 it had served as a second opera house to the city and at least two of Albert Lortzing's operas received their first performances there, including his most famous, *Undine*. As time went on, Kroll's musical role got the upper hand. The house was rebuilt again from 1895 to 1898 as the Neue Königlichen Oper. Kroll's reputation for innovation persisted. Under Jacob Karl Engel's direction Berliners heard the first concert performance of Wagner's *Tannhäuser* there.[234]

The Kaiser planned to pull the Kroll-Oper down and build afresh, but the project had to be shelved in 1914. The opera house enjoyed its greatest fame in the twenties and thirties under the direction of Otto Klemperer. Here the Nazi prudes were scandalised by the sight of a soprano in her bath in Paul Hindemith's *Neues vom Tage* on 8 June 1929. Darius Milhaud's *Le pauvre matelot* also received its first performance there in September the same year, and Leoš Janáček's *House of the Dead* was performed in May 1931.[235]

Klemperer did the wise thing and fled in 1933. The Nazis took over the stage and hung a huge swastika over the auditorium. In Dresden, a distant cousin, Viktor Klemperer, noted: 'The Kroll-Oper is now the Reichstag. It is in character. Power is in the hands of the choir, the minor players, the *claque* and the chorus.'[236] One of the new assembly's first acts was to debate the Enabling Law, which allowed the Nazis to treat their enemies how they liked. In a last brave gesture ninety-four socialist deputies rejected the bill. The Reichstag met eighteen times at the Kroll-Oper over the next nine years. The formula was always the same: Göring, as President, greeted the members; there was a moment of silence for the Nazi martyrs; Hitler spoke: Göring thanked the Führer; laws were rubber-stamped; the Horst-Wessel Lied was sung. Then they all went home.[237]

The last session of this farcical assembly took place on 26 April 1942. The building had already begun to revert to its more pleasant functions. Their own house wrecked, the Staatsoper performed *Tannhäuser* there on 1 October 1941. Later that month it was the turn of the earlier *Rienzi*. On 20 December Herbert von Karajan conducted the first performance of Orff's *Carmina Burana* at the Kroll-Oper.

The Gestapo were developing an interest in opera too. Like other totalitarian regimes, they were worried by the public's reaction to liberal sentiments expressed in the libretti.*[238] The Berlin audience at the Kroll-Oper were a little too strident in their enthusiasm for the baritone Heinrich Schlusnus when he made his plea for liberty as Posa in Verdi's *Don Carlos*; but that was nothing to the applause received by Franz Völker as Florestan in Beethoven's *Fidelio* when he sang 'Wahrheit wagt ich kühn zu sagen, und die Ketten sind mein Lohn' ('I bravely dared to tell the truth and was rewarded with chains') at the beginning of act II. The cheering continued for minutes. At the premier of Umberto Giordano's *Andrea Chenier*, another baritone, Willi Domgraf-Faßbaender, sang the line 'Nicht hier ist das Vaterland, wo man die Dichter mordet' ('This isn't my country, where writers are murdered'). He was just singing his role, but that didn't stop the Gestapo from interrogating him for seven hours.[241]

After the war the Tiergarten formed part of the British sector. Like the other occupying powers they were anxious to rid Berlin of not only its Nazi monuments (except when they were useful), but also anything which smacked of 'militarism' or 'Prussianism'. The gutted General Staff Building didn't stand a chance. The 'Moltke Palais' was on the Königsplatz, and it was here that the great general lived after the victories of the Franco-Prussian War. Moltke was a highly cultured, well-read officer, who claimed after the end of the fight that he wanted no more than to 'watch a tree grow'.[242] He had his chance now. In a letter he wrote: 'The furnishing of the house proceeds slowly. The balcony is ready and rather lovely with its view over the Tiergarten which is greener than ever before.'[243] The real powerhouse of the Prussian

---

* The French Revolution provides numerous examples. In the Terror Corneille's *Cinna* could not be performed because of the line 'Le pire des états, c'est l'état populaire', while the same author's *Horace* was banned due to the appearance of the King of Rome in the last act.[239] In Bordeaux 200 middle-class traders were arrested after a cry of 'Vive le Roi!' during a performance of Calderón's *La vida es sueño*.[240]

army was round the corner on the Moltke Brücke. During the Third Reich it fell to Himmler, giving the British a further incentive to destroy it.*

XI

There was another clutch of countrified inns on the southern side of the Tiergarten. From 1790 onwards this was known as the Tiergartenviertel, and was chiefly inhabited by rich Berlin citizens. As early as 1764 Boswell enjoyed 'cherry wine' at Corsica's Garden in the Tiergarten.[245] The maps show houses set in large gardens, and the occasional orchard or vegetable plot added a more rustic feel to it all. From 1831 the strip received the name of the 'Tiergartenstraße'. By then there were a couple of dozen large dwellings, many more summer houses and more than half a dozen inns.[246] The latter were immensely popular with the bourgeoisie on their Sunday jaunts. On a site somewhere between the present Staatsbibliothek and the Philharmonie was the Richardsche Kaffeegarten, which changed its name to Kempers Hof after 1820. Even more distinguished was Tarone, not the shop on the Linden,[247] but the 'wine garden' in the Tiergarten. In 1830, Klaus Heinzelmann converted the Italian garden into 'Elysium', Berlin's biggest *Vergnügungslokal* (or house of pleasure) until the advent of Kroll's Wintergarten in 1843. There were splendid rooms for entertaining and concerts, a bath-house as well as kit more often associated with the fun-fair.[248]

The inns and pleasure gardens progressively gave way to villas. A second street, the Bellevue Straße, opened up to the west of the old Potsdam road. Here and in the Tiergartenstraße the best Berlin architects of their time, Stüler, Persius,

---

* The Alsenviertel which had occupied the bend in the Spree above the Reichstag had been bombed flat in November 1943.[244]

Knoblauch and Friedrich Hitzig, built large houses in the style bequeathed to the city by Schinkel. The new area was settled by university teachers, artists, bankers, politicians and industrialists. The brothers Grimm, for example, settled at Lennéstraße 8, after Frederick William IV rescued them from Göttingen, where they had been sacked for their liberal views. The socialist leader Ferdinand Lassalle lived at Bellevue Straße 13 from 1859. Karl Marx was (briefly) here in 1861. In 1875 Adolf Menzel took up residence at Sigismundstraße 3.[249]

The progress made by the 'Geheimratsviertel', or 'Privy Councillors' District', was astonishingly rapid: by the time it was absorbed into the city limits of Berlin it was already considered one of the best addresses, if not *the* best. The development was accelerated by the arrival of Prussia's first railway line, to Potsdam, in 1838. The new terminus was built in the Potsdamer Platz, creating a hub for this collection of leafy villas. In the second half of the century the old *cabarets* ceded their places to new streets such as the Friedrich Wilhelmstraße and the Kaiserin-Augusta-Straße with their towering *Mietshäuser*.

The 'alte Westen' was chiefly associated with villas. Walter Benjamin grew up in one, complete with 'porch on columns, frieze and architrave'. His childhood passed under 'caryatids and atlantes, *putti* and Pomonas'.[250] The Bellevue Straße was a natural place to find a well-heeled young officer like Botho von Rienäcker in Fontane's *Irrungen, Wirrungen* (Aberrations). Here, too, lived Harry Graf Kessler, in a flat where he kept a Seurat and sculpture by his friend Maillol. One evening he had the British ambassador over with a few old nobles and a Rothschild.

> D'Abernon displayed enormous interest in, and a surprisingly expert knowledge of, Maillol and my large Seurat. His verdict on Maillol's *Crouching Woman* was that it was the finest piece of modern sculpture he

knows. He kept on going back to it and inspecting it
from all sides.

The library, dining-room and study once more
seemed to make a deep impression on everyone.
With these exquisite women moving though them,
they really did look festive and artistic.[251]

After Berlin became capital of Germany, embassies
installed themselves in the villas of the alte Westen and the
Berlin rich moved further out. This was the stamping-ground
of Bella Fromm, the Jewish social editor of the *Voßische
Zeitung* in the thirties. As the Nazi grip tightened around
the throat of Berlin's high society, the embassies were just
about the only places where Berliners could be sure of a
decent thrash. Bella Fromm went to one at the Turkish
Embassy that turned out to be a sad sign of the times.

> Outside, the Tiergarten was wrapped in fog. The old
> Renaissance [*sic*] Palace glowed in dazzling light. The
> mighty gates were flung open. An endless stream of
> cars flowed in. A cordon of perfectly trained servants
> in green uniforms, the golden half-moon on [a] red
> background adorning their collars, took care of the
> wraps and coats of the arriving guests. The General,
> in full regalia, the highest order of the Turkish
> republic pinned on his uniform, stood side by side
> with Princess Emineh, [the] beautiful daughter of the
> former Turkish Minister Abas Halim Pasha. The
> Princess was exquisite in a silver-grey gown coiling
> around her feet in a long train and glittered in the
> thousandfold fire of her gorgeous diamonds.[252]

The splendour of the occasion, however, was marred by
the presence of many members of the new 'brown elite',
including the SA leaders Röhm, Gehrt and Ernst. At 11.30,
the creator of the Weimar army, Colonel General Hans von
Seeckt, tried to have the boors removed.

The 'gentlemen' protested. With their loot of several dozen bottles of the sparkling liquid, they had settled down in a little boudoir. Group Leader Karl Ernst, comfortably stretched on a pink silk sofa, had planted his boots on a damask stool. He roared for more champagne.

A diversion was created by the arrival of the Nazi 'philosopher' Alfred Rosenberg in white tie and tails. 'Look at the Baltic pig. The sissy hasn't even got the guts to drink!' exclaimed Röhm. Ernst had better things to do: he 'was busy rocking a Brown Shirt on his knees'.[253]

Almost all of these Tiergarten villas were wiped out by the war. Of the representative buildings of the area only seventeen of a total of 529 have been maintained. One of the best is the Von der Heydt Villa, a late neo-classical building with a four-column portico which now houses the Stiftung Preußischer Kulturbesitz (the Prussian Cultural Foundation). From 1874 to 1890 it was the home of Chinese Consulate.[254] During the Third Reich it became the fief of Hitler's Chancellery Chief, Lammers.[255] Missie Vassiltchikov's friend Maria von Gersdorff operated an opposition salon from her villa despite the destruction all around her. Her nerves only cracked in 1945, when she was told that her husband Heinz had been killed in the Battle for Berlin. He hadn't; but she committed suicide.[256]

A scant handful of buildings has survived from the Nazis' new diplomatic quarter. With West Berlin's much reduced role on the diplomatic circuit, the new embassies have begun to look rather pale embodiments of their former grand design. Of the big Fascist buildings on the Tiergartenstraße, the Japanese tinkered with theirs in the eighties, pulling down large tracts. The Italian Embassy appears to be partly ruinous. The saddest of all is the Estonian Consulate in the Hildebrandtstraße. Although people appear to live in it, the building has been blackened by fire and there are heaps of rubble strewn around the forecourt. As it stands it is a heart-jerking reminder of what post-war Berlin must have looked like.

The social centre of the alte Westen was the Matthäikirchplatz. Although Stüler's red- and yellow-brick church still stands, there is nothing left of the old square to give an impression of the bustle that once belonged here. The one-time Hohenzollern pretender, Prince Louis Ferdinand, 'Lulu', of Prussia, had a four-room flat on the Matthäikirchstraße, which served not only him, but also his rakish father, the Crown Prince. 'My father simply loves my flat,' he told Bella Fromm. 'Recently, I was tactless enough to return from a little trip ahead of schedule. I must say I found myself an intruder in my own apartment!'[257]

The Nazis had other plans for the square, which meant clearing the elegant officers and society beauties out of the church, which served for their Sunday devotions.[258] Here Speer built his massive Reichsverkehrsbüro, which was still only partly finished when Berlin had to button up for the Blitz. The church was to be demolished to make way for a circus along the proposed North–South Axis, but the war saved it. In the sixties the blackened ruins of Speer's building were cleared away for the new Staatsbibliothek and National Gallery, the latter an unexecuted design by Mies van der Rohe which had originally been intended for the Bacardi Rum Company in Havana.[259] It was integrated in Hans Scharoun's 'Kulturforum', which proposed to use the vacuum created by Speer and the Anglo-Americans to create a cultural centre valid for both East *and* West Berlin. On the east side of the square Scharoun built his own, faceless Staatsbibliothek. His Philharmonie was a more successful design, owing something to Berlin's Expressionist architects of the twenties. Other buildings have followed, in the more restrained idioms of the seventies, eighties and nineties.

Until recently it has been hard for anyone standing in the middle of the Potsdamer Platz to conceive of this wasteland as the equivalent of London's Piccadilly Circus or New York's Times Square. Apart from the dogged inhabitants of the old Weinhaus Huth, the only signs of life here came from the rabbits.[260] Since the end of 1994, big holes have been dug in the sandy soil, and huge iron-mesh rafts laid to support the tall buildings promised before the turn of the century. Potsdamer Platz is due to make a come-back. Yet, the process has not been without its heartaches. One victim of the scheme has been the last vestiges of the last of Berlin's grand, Wilhelmine hotels, the Esplanade, once the jewel of the old Bellevue Straße promenade (see below, pp. 297–300). The Japanese electronic giant Sony had promised to rebuild the façade, but ultimately reneged, claiming the costs were too high. They have taken away a couple of the best rooms and plan to install them in some incongruous futuristic development away from their original site.[261]

Whether the ambitious plans for the area will be able to breathe any life into these old bones remains to be seen.[262] There is no doubt about the importance of the pre-war Potsdamer Platz. In his *Besuch vom Land* (Country Cousins), Erich Kästner satirised the confused provincial faced with the teeming masses on the square.

> Sie stehen verstört am Potsdamer Platz,
> Und finden Berlin zu laut.
> Die Nacht glüht auf in Kilowatts,
> Ein Fräulein sagt heiser: 'Komm mit, mein Schatz!'
> Und zeigt entsetzlich viel Haut.
>
> Sie wissen vor Staunen nicht aus und nicht ein.
> Sie stehen und wundern sich bloß.
> Die Bahnen rasseln. Die Autos schrein.
> Sie möchten am liebsten zu Hause sein.
> Und finden Berlin zu groß.
>
> Es klingt, als ob die Großstadt stöhnt,
> Weil irgendwer sie schilt.
> Die Häuser funkeln. Die U-Bahn dröhnt.

Sie sind das alles so gar nicht gewöhnt.
Und finden Berlin zu wild.

Sie machen vor Angst die Beine krumm,
Und machen alles verkehrt.
Sie lächeln bestürzt. Und sie warten dumm.
Und stehn auf dem Potsdamer Platz herum,
Bis man sie überfährt.[263]

(They look appalled at the Potsdamer Platz,
And complain about the din.
The night's a blaze of kilowatts,
A girl who brays hoarsely: 'Come up, *mein Schatz!'*
Shows an awful lot of skin.

Astonished they dither and scratch at their heads.
In amazement they stand, aghast.
The rails they rattle, the cars they dread.
They'd much prefer to be home in their bed.
And find Berlin is too vast.

It sounds as if the city groans
To hear a muttered curse.
The buildings twinkle, the *U-Bahn* moans.
An odd sensation creeps into their bones.
And they find Berlin gets worse.

With legs like jelly from worry and fear,
Beside themselves with bother,
They smile all perplexed while they dumbly leer,
And about the Potsdamer Platz they veer,
Until they get run over.)

The Potsdamer Platz had become so terribly clogged up by traffic in the years just before the First World War that the Police President, von Jagow, banished the flower-sellers from the pavements.

No more shall pedestrians be halted in their rapid
motion, no more by the breadth of a basket, which

the poor seller may no longer set down, no more by
their cheering cries . . . no more will the characterful
steam of benzine vie with the scent of lilac and violets
and snowdrops.[264]

For Eloesser, flowers were the salvation of the ugly Potsdamer Platz. As students he and his friends had sat in the
Café Josty, day and night, to see if there was a particular
light that lent something to the jumbled lines of the square.
Not even Schinkel's Grecian gate lodges were able to pull it
together. Only flowers could conceal the disharmony of the
Potsdamer Bahnhof.[265]

For others it had a big-city charm. By 1916, when George
Grosz sketched a solitary drinker at Josty, the social life was
going out of the square, heading west. Josty had decamped
from the Schloßfreiheit. By 1930 it had decamped again,
permanently seeking out the fashionable world which had
appreciated its pastries and hot chocolate.[266] There was also
the Weinhaus Rheingold and the Schultheiß restaurant
where Menzel drank, and which later ceded its place to the
Columbus Haus. The Weinhaus Huth is an extraordinary
survival. The present building dates from 1912; it replaced
an earlier incarnation that sat behind a garden forecourt with
a glazed veranda. But the old Huth, which had been good
enough for Fontane's *Effi Briest*, was not smart enough for
the Kaiser's flashy new Berlin. The new building rapidly
mustered a faithful clientele in its first floor dining-room –
an incongruous mix, by all reports: Adenauer, the conductor
Furtwängler, Himmler and Röhm.[267]

The Potsdamer Platz was wrecked on the night of 7 September 1941. Josty, Rheingold, the Siechen-Bier-Palast, the
Konditorei Telschow, all were gone, but besides the Weinhaus
Huth there were some substantial relics. After 1945 there
were cinemas on the border here with the Russian sector.
Ossis could pay *Ostmarks* to watch Hollywood films, on
production of valid papers. The Voxhaus Cinema was a stable

ruin, with the West Berlin police using the upper floors as a look-out post. It was finally blown up in 1973, 'a late victim of the Berlin passion for pulling things down'.[268] In 1948 there was still a restaurant on the square; the number 74 bus still stopped by the Weinhaus Huth. The architect Erich Mendelsohn's *avant-garde* Columbus Haus was set on fire by the insurgents of 17 June 1953 because the East Berlin *Vopos* (police) had a post there. 'The last bit of life was extinguished by the construction of the Wall.'[269]

XII

With the Second Reich, the alte Westen was joined by a new neighbour, the 'neue' Westen, which joined the old at the Zoo. Possibly the denizens of the neue Westen were not as rich as the villa-haunting Berliners of the alte Westen, but they were rarely poor. As Walter Benjamin summed it up:

> In my childhood I was a prisoner of the old and new West Ends. My clan lived in these two areas in an attitude that was a mixture of determination and self-esteem which made it feel like a ghetto . . . In this *quartier* I was shut in. I knew no other. The rich children of my age group saw the poor only as beggars.[270]

As the gateway to the new West End, the Berlin Zoo assumed an importance that similar institutions in other Europeans cities have never enjoyed: the Zoo was a part of all well-off Berliners' lives. The project to create a Berlin zoo went back to 1841, the sponsors being Lenné, the zoologist Martin Hinrich Lichtenstein (who became the Zoo's first director), Alexander von Humboldt and a Herr von Ladenberg. Frederick William IV supported the project, donating animals from his menagerie on the Pfaueninsel as well as part of the site of the old royal pheasantry in the Tiergarten.[271]

The Zoo opened in 1844. Two years later it was visited by Dronke. He was not impressed.

> A few apes, who spend their time courting one
> another around a great big tree, two bears, a few
> strange birds and otherwise a lot of animals over the
> cages of which is written 'Indigenous to this region'.
> The most pitiful menagerie of a peripatetic market-
> crier from a provincial fair is better than this public
> institution.[272]

By the mid-seventies, when Fontane set his *Irrungen, Wirrungen*, in the neue Westen, the Zoo had become more sophisticated. Botho von Rienäcker's lover Lene lives in a market garden on the site of the Kaiser-Wilhelm-Gedächtniskirche. When they go for a walk at twilight the moon is standing over the Elephant House, casting a silver light that makes the building look 'more fantastic than ever'.[273]

Soon after, the Zoo made the fortunes of Lorenz Adlon. Prince William, the later Kaiser, was a fan of the Zoo, and never went without stopping to eat at Adlon's restaurant there. William encouraged his brother officers to follow suit. When Adlon sought permission to create Berlin's most luxurious hotel, he received the blessing of the Kaiser.[274]

The Zoo had become another favourite for Sunday excursions. In *Der Untertan* ('The Subject') Hessling goes with his Berlin lover, Agnes, and her family. They take coffee and then look at their favourite animals: 'But the animals smell so dreadful,' says Agnes.[275] The Zoo also made an impression on the infant Benjamin. He loved the beasts in their elaborate cages: the hippopotamus, which lived in its pagoda 'like a magic priest'. As a child he also noted the potential for flirting offered by the Zoo. On Sundays a military band played in the middle of the 'sandpit of the gnus and zebras, the bare trees and crevices where the condors and vultures nested, the stinking wolves' enclosure and the rutting grounds for pelicans and herons. The calls and cries of these animals mingled with the noise of the trumpets and drums.'[276] The animals affected more than just courting couples. Bertolt Brecht visited the Zoo during his first months in Berlin and found the feeding of the anthropoid apes 'sensational'.[277]

The child hero of Wolfdietrich Schnurre's novel *Als Vaters Bart noch rot war* also admired the monkeys. It was the Depression and the boys were hungry: 'We visited the apes as often as not; most of the time we pinched their peanuts when no one was looking; the apes had enough to eat, they certainly had a lot more than we did.'[278] The boy also enjoyed the Zoo's position in the centre of the new town.

> Grey slowly took the colour from the twilight. You could hear the S-Bahn across the way on the overhead rails and the seals chuckling; a peacock squawked in the distance and on the marble bust of the first director a blackbird perched with a worm in its beak. It smelled of spring, big cats and benzine . . .[279]

The Zoo had gone from strength to strength during the Wilhelmine years. Up went ever more fanciful cages for elephants, antelopes and zebras. When the Second World War visited Berlin it all came crashing down. The first bombs fell on the Zoo as early as 8 September 1941. On 22 November 1943, the British killed nearly seven hundred animals. The bombers returned two days later. The Director called it a vision from Dante's *Inferno*.[280] Katharina Heinroth, who worked at the Zoo, reported the Moorish antelope house burnt out with seven elephants buried under slabs of concrete. Two 'splendid giraffes' had been killed as well as two apes and fifteen smaller monkeys. The next raids hit the crocodiles. Lutz Heck found a giant catfish gasping for life on dry land and pushed it back into the water. The furious ardour of the mambas had been dampened by the extreme cold, and they could be taken back to temporary cages. The dead elephants posed problems in proportion to their size: they were hard to get rid of, and they soon began to stink.[281]

There were hidden benefits, however, in this time of shortage:

> We had meat coming out of our ears. Many of the edible animals which had fallen victim to the air raid ended up in the pot. Particularly tasty were the crocodiles' tails; cooked tender in big containers, they tasted like fat chicken. The dead deer, buffalo and antelopes provided hundreds of meals for man and beast alike. Later on bear ham and bear sausage were a particular delicacy.[282]

Rumours spread throughout Berlin. Lions were said to be roaming the ruins of the Gedächtniskirche. The young Russian *émigré* princess Missie Vassiltchikov reported crocodiles being shot as they clambered into the Spree.[283] Ursula von Kardorff speculated on whether a tiger would pop up in the West End at any minute.[284] The Berlin wags had a field day. It was recounted that one had indeed escaped, and had sought solace at Josty's. The animal had gobbled up a piece of *Bienenstich* pastry, turned on its back and died. The jokers attributed the mythical tiger's death to the quality of the cake-making. Josty's owners are said to have sued.[285]

When the Russians reached the city they shot the last gorilla. No one knows quite why. All but one of the elephants were dead. One solitary hippopotamus was swimming slowly round its blood-red pool. 'The famous Pongo, the biggest gorilla in Europe, lay dead on the cement floor of its cage . . . The last elephant, Siam, had been driven to insanity by the bombing and was endlessly trumpeting his terror. Frightened apes chased about the ruins and a few exotic birds flew from tree to tree trying to escape from the acrid, black smoke clouds.'[286]

Botho and Lene's paradise garden in *Irrungen, Wirrungen* gave way to the definition of Wilhelmine architecture in all its gaudiest colours: the Kaiser-Wilhelm-Gedächtniskirche. Not for nothing did the name of William's grandfather take the place of the more usual saints in the dedication. Once again, Berliners showed no inclination to accept the canonisation of the man they had dubbed 'der Kartätschenprinz' in his allegedly trigger-happy days during the 1848 Revolution. The style of the church was to be German Romanesque in its most massive form. The design was by Franz Schwechten – like Wallot, a Rhinelander who had previously shown his mettle in the Anhalter Bahnof. Schwechten was also responsible for the rest of the square, which he built in the same idiom: hence the 'Romanische' Café.[287]

On 23 November 1943 the Gedächtniskirche was blown sky-high. It was like 'a burning torch. For the first time it looked like a Romanesque building.'[288] Understandably, perhaps, the decision was taken not to reconstruct after the war. The ruined tower was retained and attached to a fluorescent blue hat-box designed by Egon Eiermann in the late fifties. The result is an all too powerful metaphor for old West Berlin: the flashiness and gimcrackery of the sixties erected on the ashes of Wilhelmine pomposity.

The Augusta-Viktoriaplatz was to be the knee-joint that connected the old Kurfürstenstraße with the new Kurfürstendamm.* Both Bismarck and the old Kaiser had a hand in its creation. Bismarck had the Champs-Elysées in Paris in mind as a model. He had doubtless admired the street from his time as ambassador to France in 1862. More recently he had had a chance to see the avenue ever more lined with the palatial buildings of the Second Empire.[289] The 53-metre width of the Kurfürstendamm, however, was dictated by the Emperor, not his Chancellor.[290] It was to take Berliners from the centre all the way to Halensee with its water-lily-covered

* *Damm* is a north German word for a main street.

lake. Building was slow. There were even a few gaps in the terraces in 1914, but the avenue had found increasing popularity with the new nobility of wealth. In 1905 the industrialist Ernst Borsig, the physician Robert Koch, the actress Tilla Durieux and the great violinist Joseph Joachim all lived on the Kurfürstendamm.[291]

The large number of rich Jews who lived on the avenue made the Nazis increasingly anxious to use the street for political demonstrations. One of their number was shot by an irate Republican there as early as 1925. After that, SA gangs prowled the classier establishments looking for men and women with Jewish features and lashing out at them. On 10 November 1938 it was a 'sea of glass'.[292] Five years later it was the turn of the buildings themselves, although when the diplomat Gogo von Nostitz travelled along it in July 1944 he was impressed to see how the rubble had been cleared away and the tarmac glinted in the hot sun.[293]

A few months later it was all but over. On 7 February 1945, Erich Kästner noticed that they were beginning to fortify the Ku'damm against the impending arrival of *Iwan*. Tank traps had been installed at the junction of the Wilmersdorferstraße and the avenue itself:

> Tank traps? They have dragged along a lot of clapped-out vans and broken-down cars and dumped them at the crossing and thrown a lot of old iron and crumpled tin. Do they really believe that they can hold back Russian tanks for a minute with such a heap of rubbish and junk?[294]

The expansion of the new Berlin West End was a common theme for artists at the turn of the century. The new Nollendorfplatz in Schöneberg inspired very different approaches from the painters Franz Skarbina, Max Beckmann and Ernst Ludwig Kirchner.[295] The Expressionist painter Ludwig Meidner also painted an *Angst*-filled representation of a newly laid street in Wilmersdorf. Skarbina's painting of 1885 is a particularly interesting piece of evidence for the transformation that was taking place all over the west. The backs of the fine new *Mietshäuser* are visible across a wintry landscape of flat fields. In the centre of the watercolour there is a half-timbered farmhouse. A peasant woman is carrying her shopping home to the south-western suburbs.[296]

By the time Beckmann and Kirchner got round to painting the Nollendorfplatz twenty-five years later, the setting was entirely urban. Beckmann's painting of 1911, for example, shows us a picture of the square which is surprisingly recognisable to our eyes.[297] The conversion of so much unprofitable farm land into expensive, sought-after property made many fortunes for the inhabitants of the former villages. In Schöneberg they were christened the 'Millionenbauern', and some of their ostentatious villas can still be seen in the Hauptstraße. In Wilmersdorf they joked about the 'milkmaids' being good matches for members of the old nobility on their uppers.[298] This was the area for some of Berlin's very finest *Mietshäuser* in the Kurfürstenviertel and the Bayrisches Viertel in Schöneberg and around the Rüdesheimer Platz in Wilmersdorf.[299]

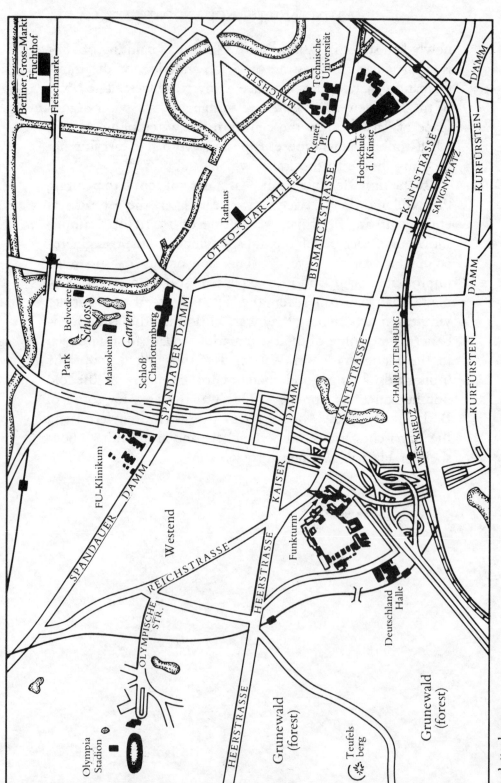

Charlottenburg

XIII

When Fontane's Botho von Rienäcker and his silly wife, Käthe, look out from their capacious balcony in the Land-grafenstraße, Käthe is curious to know what the village is that lies beyond the 'Zoologischen'. Botho, who knew perfectly well, replies that he believes it is Wilmersdorf.[300] Wilmersdorf had grown up as a hamlet on the way to Charlottenburg. Until the Charlottenburger Chaussee was cut through the Tiergarten to the north, the main road to Charlottenburg was the Lietzenburger Straße, as the original name of Charlottenburg had been Lützenburg or Lietzenburg.[301]

It was no more than a hamlet then, midway between Spandau and Berlin, smaller even than the (pretty insignificant) villages of Wilmersdorf and Schöneberg.[302] The change of name was apt. Charlottenburg was created for the second wife of Elector Frederick III (later Frederick I of Prussia), Sophia Charlotte of Hanover. The cultured princess craved her own residence. She was given the baroque Schloß Caputh, south of Potsdam, but that was too far from the court. The Elector bought the land in Lützow for her, together with a small *Schloß* to provide her with a summer residence for the months from March to November.[303]

After the death of the Queen in 1705, suggestions were canvassed for new names for the now royal borough of Lietzenburg: Königinburg was one; the Queen's friend, the philosopher Leibniz, proposed Sophienburg. Charlottenburg was the name that stuck. The village now became a fully fledged town. The court equerry's house became the first town hall, and courtiers milled through the streets called the Schloß – and Berlinerstraßen. A separate village church was built to rid the court chapel of *hoi polloi*. A charter of rights followed in 1721.[304]

The original twelve-bay building was constructed by Nering between 1695 and 1699.[305] That was the palace Queen Sophia Charlotte knew. It was modified, after her death, by Eosander, who added the wings, tower and chapel, turning Charlottenburg into a Berlin version of the Habsburg summer residence at Schönbrunn near Vienna. The compactness of the design was slightly marred by the new Knobelsdorff wing executed for Frederick the Great which reproduced the thin Eosander wing on the western side. Langhans added the theatre, and the lovely belvedere in the park. Heinrich Gentz contributed the first full-throated neo-classicism to Charlottenburg with his mausoleum of 1810–1812. The last substantial work on the collection was that of Schinkel, whose Neuer Pavillon was intended as a retreat for Frederick William III after his morganatic second marriage to Augusta von Harrach in 1824.*[306]

Frederick William I disliked his mother's palace and had plans to remove the royal status from Charlottenburg and turn it back into a village. It was the same old see-saw: Frederick William hated the luxury of his parents; Frederick the Great had no intention of abiding by his father's austere regimen. After Frederick William's death in Potsdam, Frederick the Great left the bedside and went directly to Charlottenburg in his first incarnation as king. Alterations to the huge palace were commissioned almost immediately:

---

* The design was based on the Villa Reale del Chiatamone in Naples, where the king had lodged in 1822.

there was to be a new suite of public rooms and a 'golden gallery', which explains itself.[307]

Frederick's homosexual brother Henry was married in Charlottenburg to Wilhelmina of Hesse-Cassel on 25 June 1752. It was a chance for Frederick to show off his new gallery, and a 'terrifying crowd' gathered outside the palace to get a glimpse of the proceedings. The ceremony was a long drawn-out one. On the 26th there was a big lunch for the couple, followed by an opera and a ball. The next day an intermezzo and another ball. The next day there was a great dinner, then the court 'returned to the city'.[308] Presumably such a long-winded process served to postpone the inevitable moment of truth.

Frederick William II was the son of another brother, Augustus William. He was no ascetic either. He had the gardener Johann August Eyserbeck come up from Schloß Wörlitz in Dessau to pull up the baroque parterres and *bosquets* of Simeon Godeau and turn the park into a more contemporary English landscape. It was here at Charlottenburg that Frederick William concluded his extraordinary series of marriages *de la main gauche*: Julie von Voß (Gräfin Ingenheim), Sophie Juliane Gräfin Dönhoff (Gräfin Brandenburg) and Wilhelmine Enke (Madame Ritz or Gräfin Lichtenau). Unlike the other two, 'die Enke' was not of noble birth, but the daughter of a trumpeter in the court band. History and Frederick William's successors have been unkind to her. She was banished and even briefly imprisoned after her lover's death.[309]

When the third Frederick William died in 1840, Charlottenburg had a paltry 7,000 inhabitants. This figure had doubled by 1865 and quadrupled by 1880.[310] Until that time the character of the town was still chiefly bourgeois. In 1848 the revolutionaries had dismissed it as a 'reactionary haven'.[311] Three years earlier Glaßbrenner had written about the character of the Charlottenburger in connection with the drivers who parked their coaches before the Brandenburg

Gate to ferry customers across the Tiergarten to Charlottenburg.

> It has a wide street with countless inns and public gardens, a palace theatre, a police station and plenty of gendarmes. You might say that people come here to breathe freely – they are not allowed to smoke – and to look at the way one another is dressed. They amuse themselves thus until the sun goes down and then drive back to the city whose goddess of victory receives all homecomers with her back turned.

> The Charlottenburgers are, without wishing to get too close to the street Arabs, unquestionably the coarsest category of Berlin plebeians. Unlike the [Berlin] layabouts, not one ray of warmth shines through their spiritual and physical filthiness, but they are the complete register and personification of nastiness, drunkenness and the vices of gambling and flashiness. These are the virtues that daily absorb them and their pale faces and dead eyes are the most graphic indication of their worthlessness.[312]

Things were already changing. By 1860 Charlottenburg had outgrown its town hall. The next year came the gas works and the beginning of industrialisation: on 15 December of that year for the first time Charlottenburg radiated the light from 150 gas lanterns. The rich came too: Bismarck's banker, Gerson Bleichröder, built himself a country house on the 'Knie' (now the Ernst Reuter-Platz). It was still in a purely Schinkelesque idiom with its two-storey Doric portico, swags and upper floor set behind a frieze.[313] But the writing was now on the wall. In 1866 the factory owner Albert Werckmeister and five other entrepreneurs (including Heinrich Quistorp and the architect Martin Gropius) created the Baugesellschaft Westend (West End Building Company). They sought to construct a new, elegant district on a London model, beyond the Schloss, on the heights of Grunewald.[314]

Around the Schloss, Charlottenburg's character was unimpeachable: new barracks buildings opposite the palace, built to Stüler's designs in the 1870s, brought more officers into the neighbourhood.[315] The Kaiserin-Augusta-Gymnasium was also founded here for the children of orphaned officers.[316] It didn't impress the writer Ernst Wiechert, however:

> I went to the school and presented myself to the headmaster. The school was the Kaiserin-Augusta-Gymnasium in Charlottenburg, a grey, unloved barn of a place with a Latin inscription over the doors. I often reflected later that these would have been better replaced by Goethe's verse
>
> Opfer fallen hier,
> weder Lamm noch Stier,
> aber Menschenopfer unerhört.[317]
>
> (This place here it kills
> Not lambs nor bulls,
> But human sacrifices in droves.)

There was another side to this shiny coin. Charlottenburg was becoming increasingly working-class. The Wallstraße (the present Zillestraße) was known as 'Little Wedding'. Nearly half the inhabitants lived in the dark, back court-yards.[318] The present name of the street is excusable. This was the world which inspired the artist: a world of *Mietskasernen* where workers' families lived together in one room without the benefits of electricity or sunlight. As often as not they were forced to bring in 'Schlafburschen' – rent out a bed to a young worker in order to earn a little extra cash. After 1918 the Wallstraße became one of the Berlin strongholds of the Communist Party.[319]

As such, it became the target for SA gangs in the course

of the twenties: 'Die Rote Front schlägt sie zu Brei!/SA marschiert. Achtung die Straße frei.' ('Beat the Red Front to pulp!/The SA is on the march. Watch out, keep off the streets.') The Nazi share of the vote in Charlottenburg was growing steadily. By 1930 it was 18.46. By July 1932 it had risen to just under a third, slipping back to under 30 per cent in November.[320]

In the east, Charlottenburg stretched out a hand to Wilmersdorf and the Tiergarten. The Kantstraße provided the axis for a new area with the Savignyplatz at its centre. Here were some of Berlin's smartest *Mietshäuser*, a surprising number of which survived the destruction of the war. It was arty, literary and Jewish. The Jewish colony centred on their synagogue in the Fasanenstraße.[321] The gaps between Charlottenburg and Spandau filled up after the First World War: Hans Poelzig's Haus des Rundfunks, or Broadcasting House, of 1931 was constructed by the new exhibition halls with their Funkturm, a scaled-down Eiffel Tower.[322]

Beyond the exhibition halls, the Heerstraße ran all the way to Spandau. In January 1926 Kessler was invited by Pauline and Richard Strauss to join them for dinner at a friend's house ' . . . on the Heerstraße, near the Stadium where until recently there was nothing but pine-woods. Apparently, though, this part is being transformed into a smart western suburb for those who have cars.'[323] The Nazis rebuilt the Stadium, bigger and better, for the 1936 Olympics. A year later, on 27 September 1937, Hitler greeted Mussolini on the Heerstraße and the bands struck up *Giovinezza* in the Italian's honour. A leaflet was passed through the crowds: 'Two butchers meet in Berlin: the murderer of the German people greets the executioner of the Italian.'[324] After the war the Heerstraße from the Theodor-Heuß-Platz (the former Reichspräsidenten-Platz and Adolf Hitler-Platz) was taken over by the British army, who had their officers' club in Marlborough House on the square and whose brigadier lived in a prefectorial position at the beginning of the avenue. The more menial officers generally lived in the leafier streets behind.[325]

XIV

The 'English Model' was much sought after in providing the richer Berliners with large houses and wide-ranging gardens. Grunewald on the edges of Wilmersdorf was a virtual *tabula rasa* of 234 hectares acquired by the Kurfürstendamm Gesellschaft group in 1889. Away in the woods was Kurfürst Joachim's old hunting lodge and the profusion of greenery and relative distance from the city centre made it rapidly into a ghetto for the affluent Berliners.[326] It was here that one of the leading intellectuals of Wilhelmine and Weimar Berlin, Werner Sombart, lived. Sombart was something of an exception for Grunewald. Despite German respect for professors as a group, money alone was generally the only way in to this exclusive world.

As Sombart's son Nicolaus has written, although Grunewald developed at the peak of Wilhelmine pomposity it was always the opposite pole to the Reichstag and the Dom.

> It would be wrong to call it a collection of villas. In Grunewald the *haute bourgeoisie* built themselves country mansions set in gardens like great parks; unlike Paris and London, Berlin characteristically had no experience of the town palace. Even the nobility, with a few exceptions, owned no *hôtels particuliers*, but stayed at a hotel when they left their properties in the country to go to the court or sit in the *Herrenhaus*. The avenues are so wide here because they were used for morning rides . . . What looks like a grand house today was once a stables or an outbuilding.[327]

It was a self-contained world. The journalist Maximilian Harden lived out his last years in a *Gartenhaus* in the Werner-straße. He was lucky to die in a Swiss bed in 1927. The Nazis had already marked his card.[328] Another Jewish intellectual who lived in Grunewald was the theatre critic Alfred Kerr, who shunned the denizens of the 'Romanischen' and had his permanent table, or *Stammtisch*, at the Gartenkonditorei in Grunewald. He corrected his copy on the number 76 tram on his way up to town.[329]

The Jews were steadily hounded out of Grunewald between 1933 and 1938. As money was rarely an object, most had the good sense to sell up and emigrate before it was too late. Sombart describes the changes their departure wrought on the neighbourhood:

> During the Third Reich Grunewald was an apolitical enclave which got quieter as the years passed. In the front gardens of the great villas, the number of estate agents' 'For Sale' boards proliferated. On bright, warm summer evenings – particularly lovely in Grunewald – we sat with friends over a bowl of fruit cup. *Sotto voce* discussions possibly tackled Gustav Gründgens' last production, an exhibition at the Akademie der Künste, or a new book such as Ernst Jünger's *Marmorklippen*★ . . . We never spoke about politics. We lived on an island, completely divorced from our time.[330]

As the Jews moved out, the new elite moved in: Nazis and fellow travellers. Hendrik Höfgen, Klaus Mann's parody of the Prussian Staatsrat† and theatre *Intendant* Gustav Gründgens, also takes advantage of the falling prices and wide availability of Grunewald property to buy himself a house:

> He bought it for a relatively paltry sum from a Jewish

★ *Auf den Marmorklippen* (On the Marble Cliffs) was first published in 1939. It was considered particularly daring.
† An honorary Privy Councillor.

banker who had moved to London. He called it
'Hendrik Hall' . . . The servants wore black livery with
silver braid; only little Böck was allowed to be a mite
negligé. Most of the time he appeared in a grubby, blue
and white striped jacket, or occasionally in a brown
SA uniform.[331]

For most inhabitants of the crowded, dowdy city, Grune-
wald was an unbelievable place. In Kästner's *Fabian* of 1931,
Labude's parents own a villa posing as a Greek temple there.
Fabian himself thought such expenditure silly.

> What he really couldn't understand was how, plunged
> into such luxury, one could ever rid oneself of the
> feeling that one was merely visiting.*[332]

★   ★   ★

Dahlem continues the theme, though the houses tend to be
smaller. Also the presence before the war of the Kaiser-
Wilhelms-Gesellschaft, and, after it, the Free University, have
given this leafy suburb a slightly more acerbic, academic feel,
which leads one inmate to describe it as 'Berlin's
Hampstead'.[333] Dahlem was a mediaeval village which grew
up around the church. It possesses the rare distinction in
Berlin of having preserved its manor house opposite the
eighteenth-century *Dorfkrug*, or village inn. The present
manor was built in the more secure times following the
Great Elector's victory over the Swedes at Fehrbellin in
1675,[334] although it retains a vaulted chapel from its late
mediaeval incarnation.[335] It has had a chequered history,
having been passed like a parcel through the hands of various
Märkisch noble families such as the Pfühls and the Podewils.
In 1804 it was bought by the future Chancellor, Carl Fried-

---

* Since the war much of Berlin's diplomatic life has moved to
Grunewald. Not for nothing has Karl Lagerfeld's new palace hotel
been housed in the old Villa Pannwitz.

rich von Beyme, who built a schnapps distillery nearby. In 1841 his daughter sold the manor to the state.[336]

There is still a little farm behind the manor, and much of Dahlem was farmland until this century. The fields were eventually covered with plush new villas by famous Berlin architects such as Peter Behrens, Hermann Muthesius and Walter Gropius – who built the rustic Haus Sommerfeld and a rather more modernistic house, Am Erlenbusch. In 1895 there were just 153 people living in Dahlem. In 1910 that figure had already advanced to 3,099. Only four years later there were 5,500.[337] Some of the villas were as grand as anything in Grunewald, mirroring the huge wealth which had been mopped up in speculation since the foundation of the Second Reich. Nicolaus Sombart recalls the villa of his childhood friend Karl:

> The Meißen cups in which a serving girl dressed in
> an apron and a lace bonnet brought us coffee, the
> wide, comfortable sofas in the drawing-room with
> their down-filled bolsters, the exquisite leather
> bindings in the library, and the magnificent flower
> arrangements everywhere.[338]

What made life so attractive in the new western suburbs was not only the chance to escape from Berlin's poor, in their cluttered slums in the old city centre, but also the proximity of the Grunewald and the lakes and forests of Wannsee and Potsdam – the subject matter for so many ravishing canvases by the landscape painter Walter Leistikow. Before the name of Wannsee became associated with the shadowy conference on the progress of the Final Solution, the implications were rather more joyful. The suburb had been famed for its large villas, like the one inhabited by the painter Max Liebermann, and it was in Wannsee that the first Berlin lake resort was created in 1924.[339]

The western suburbs of Berlin, strung out in a chain along

the lakes leading down to Potsdam, were a magnet to the new rich who grew up after the foundation of the German Empire. Naturally there were many Jews among them. One area which was almost exclusively Jewish before 1933 was Schwanenwerder, just a few hundred metres away from the Wannsee beach resort. It is a little island attached to the mainland by a bridge. As visitors crossed to Schwanenwerder they were greeted by a single Corinthian column carrying a small segment of architrave. It bore the legend: 'This stone from the banks of the Seine, planted here in German soil, warns you, passer-by, how quickly luck can change.' The column had been brought back by soldiers after the Franco-Prussian War. It was a fragment from the Tuileries Palace, which had been burned down by revolutionary Communards in 1871. Since the war the inscription has disappeared. It was probably removed by the Americans in deference to their French allies.[340]

Schwanenwerder was highly exclusive. It had been uninhabited until the 1880s. Before that the only structure was a wooden tower and viewing platform. Then a petrol-lamp manufacturer called Friedrich Wilhelm Wessel built Schwanenhof. It was followed by 'Das Schloß' for W. Lohse. The Jewish settlers arrived next. At the turn of the century came Haus Blumberg, started for Richard Blumberg and completed for the banker Adolph Salomonsohn. Next was Haus Israel for the department store proprietor Berthold Israel, Haus Mosler and Haus Waltrud. After the First World War came the Villa Brückmann, Haus Schlitter, for the banker of that name, Schloß Monheim (the 'Bonbon Schloß') and Haus Guggenheim.[341]

Haus Israel was the home of Wilfrid Israel, the model for Gustav Landauer in Christopher Isherwood's *Goodbye to Berlin*, the general manager of the family business until he finally sold out in 1939. The Israel shop was able to carry on projecting its provocative name on to Berlin's night sky because the owners possessed joint German and British nationality. Israel's mother, Amy, also insisted that only English be spoken at her dining-table: 'German is for servants,' she maintained.[342]

After 1933 the Jews were gradually replaced by a sinister collection of Nazi *Bonzen*. Hitler's doctor, Morell, took over the Solmssen villa. Lammers added to his portfolio of properties with the Haus Blumberg; Speer replaced Goldschmidt-Rothschild; the Nazi Women's League leader, Gertrud Scholz-Klink, opened an ideologically correct finishing school in the Villa Brückmann with courses in 'cleaning, sewing, cooking, and infant welfare and household management';[343] there was even talk of a house for Hitler. The most important of all the Nazis, however, was Goebbels, who grabbed Haus Schlitter.

It was the scene of his many peccadilloes; the many opportunities which now offered themselves to enjoy the fruits and flowers of power. Not far away lived the actor Gustav Fröhlich with the Czech starlet Lida Baarova. The Minister for Propaganda showed a keen interest in the cinema and was eager to promote talented young actresses. With Lida Baarova, however, it went further than usual. Fröhlich even made so bold as to slap the minister's face. Magda Goebbels quit the family nest and the whole sordid affair was brought before Hitler himself. On 16 August 1938 Hitler told his Berlin Gauleiter that he must drop Lida. 'Die Jugend ist zu Ende' ('Youth has come to an end'), wrote Goebbels in his diary.[344]★

But for royal favour the Pfaueninsel might well have become an exclusive *Villenkolonie* (garden suburb) like Schwanenwerder. Originally Kaninchenwerder, it was once covered with rabbits. Then came a glass works to exploit the fine sand of the Mark. The first small *Schloß* was built in

---

★ To the astonishment of later commentators Lida Baarova seems to have genuinely loved Goebbels, and confessed to still loving him at the end of her long life.[345]

1794, when the homely love of Frederick William III and his Queen Louise lifted the island from obscurity. Now the whole space was clad in a rather twee interpretation of a fashionable English garden and the *Schloß* was remodelled to look like a romantic ruin. In 1797 the peacocks arrived and the name of the island changed in their honour. The royal menagerie followed: apes, kangaroos and llamas. They remained there until the foundation of the *Zoologischen* in the 1840s.[346]

The Pfaueninsel was filling up. There was a dairy and a big dipper. In 1824 Schinkel added a guesthouse in the style of a Danzig patrician's mansion. When Frederick William IV came to the throne, however, the Hohenzollerns lost interest in the Pfaueninsel and it became more and more the haunt of lovesick couples, *à l'insu de Frédéric-Guillaume et la reine Louise*. The Nazis put a stop to all that. They destroyed the *montagnes russes* or big dipper, but not for ideological reasons, it was because Goebbels wanted to throw a gigantic party to celebrate the end of the Olympic Games in 1936:

> As it had rained during the day, he had sent off planes
> in all directions to look for new material. Trees were
> turned into luminous candelabra. The Reichswehr
> Pioneer Corps threw up a bridge of boats to link the
> island with the land and soldiers mounted a guard of
> honour, presenting their oars to the guests, who were
> shown to their places by a swarm of young girls dressed
> as Renaissance pages. At midnight there was a
> splendid firework display that reminded everyone of
> an artillery barrage.[347]

Despite the shame of having come second to the Americans, the Olympics meant party-time in the Nazi Reich. Ribbentrop gave a huge sparkling soirée at his Dahlem villa, and Göring asked the foreign guests to the garden of his ministry, where he had built a whole eighteenth-century village in miniature.

Potsdam was near, and it was natural that the royal family should snap up land on the right bank of the Havel. Even after the abolition of the monarchy in 1919 many of the princes lived in Potsdam, and 'Auwi' (August-Wilhelm), the Nazi Hohenzollern, had a villa in Wannsee, where, according to his sister, he entertained a cultured and cosmopolitan circle of friends which included many Jews. Auwi was the most obviously bookish Hohenzollern of his generation, and the least soldierly; his enlistment in the SA remains largely unexplained, even today.[348]

Prince Frederick Charles of Prussia belonged to a less controversial generation of Hohenzollerns. He took over the estate at Neu-Zehlendorf in 1859 which was renamed Düppel in 1865 to celebrate the Prussian victory over the Danes. In Berlin he lived in his palace on the Wilhelmsplatz, Goebbels' later Propaganda Ministry. Here at 'Dreilinden' the prince ran a model estate. Part of the land was sold off for the creation of yet another *Villenkolonie*, while the rest paid its own way with forestry and a schnapps distillery.[349] The Hohenzollerns sold the estate in 1927 and during the Third Reich it became a riding school for the SA. Perhaps for this reason no one seems to have lamented its demolition in 1954.[350]

Prince Frederick Charles was a great friend of the writer and *Borussolog* Fontane, who lived in nearby Potsdam and formed a part of his circle at Dreilinden. He was evidently a Hohenzollern in the tradition of the hospitable Prince Henry. As Fontane reminds us, keeping an open house in this way was fairly exceptional both in the Mark or Berlin.[351] Of course the guests were generally connected with the army in some way. Prince Charles received them on the steps of his chalet-style house (it was no *Schloß*). In a reception room, Prince Charles offered visitors a Swedish *Smörgåsbord* and his liqueur 'ABC': Allasch,* Benedictine and Chartreuse. At

---

* A type of Kümmel.

table a curious subtlety was observed: one might discuss the 'questions of the day', but politics remained taboo.[352]

Between Prince Frederick Charles and his relatives in Potsdam lay Nowawes, one of the few blights on the generally smart image of Berlin's western residential areas. For as long as it survived (it was eventually submerged into the burgeoning town of Babelsberg), Nowawes was a weavers' colony of great notoriety. It was founded by Frederick the Great for Bohemian weavers after the Seven Years War. A few of the simple, one-storey dwellings survive in an adapted form around the eighteenth-century church. In the 1840s, when cottage industries of this sort were being phased out in favour of heavy industry, the weavers reputedly turned to theft, plundering the local fields and occasionally venturing into nearby Potsdam to pick a pocket or two. The communist Dronke, who was remarkably frank about the bad behaviour of the weavers, none the less claimed mitigation: they had been cruelly treated by a member of the Mendelssohn family who owned both the land and the looms. It transpired that one of his supply ships had failed to materialise with the raw cotton and he had consequently laid the weavers off. Having no other source of income, they had turned to plunder.[353]

The palatial feel of the western approaches to Berlin reappears at Glienicke. Today the name is chiefly associated with the modern bridge, which replaced that blown up in the last days of the war by the Hitler youth squads who died in droves to protect Berlin from the Red Army. The bridge was reserved entirely for 'inter-allied' traffic. Even then the transfer of spies was only a smallish part of its vocation. In February 1962 the U2 pilot Gary Powers walked one way to freedom while Rudolf Abel walked the other. In June 1985 twenty-three agents were exchanged for just four easterners. Nine months later Anatoly Scharansky was bought for a similarly one-sided bargain.[354]

There has been a bridge here connecting Berlin with

Potsdam since 1660. The third on the site was a 565-foot construction by Schinkel which disappeared in 1905 when the iron bridge was built. Schinkel was also responsible for the present appearance of Schloß Klein-Glienicke, which was built on the site of a royal hunting lodge, and orchard, and one of Berlin's many vineyards. The pretext to create something impressive overlooking the Havel here came when Chancellor Hardenberg acquired the land in 1814. Lenné did the garden and Schinkel started work on the house. Schinkel's work was continued under the new owner of Klein-Glienicke, Prince Charles of Prussia (the brother of King Frederick William IV and Kaiser William I). It is one of Schinkel's greatest ventures into the picturesque. Even so it narrowly escaped being replaced by a monomaniac entrance arch to Berlin conceived by Albert Speer.[355]

In June 1841 the future Chief of the General Staff, Helmuth von Moltke, stayed at Klein-Glienicke after his secondment to the Turkish army. A soldier with wide-ranging interests outside his chosen *métier*, Moltke was entranced by the beauty of the little world created by Lenné and Schinkel. He wrote to his wife, 'Mariechen':

> I wish I could give you a tour of this lovely park. As far as the eye can see the lawn is of the freshest green and the hills are crowned with the most beautiful deciduous trees. The river and lakes weave their blue band through a landscape in which are strewn mansions and villas, gardens and vineyards. Gliniker [*sic*] is surely one of the loveliest parks in Germany. It is unbelievable how much headway art has been able to make in this ungrateful soil. A steam engine labours night and morning to pump water up to the sandy heights and to create lush meadows where otherwise only weeds would grow. A mighty waterfall thunders from the cliffs . . . and tumbles fifty feet into the Havel from a terrain where level-headed Mother Nature would never have considered having a bucketful of water flowing, because the barren sand would have

instantly drunk it up. Forty-foot trees were uprooted
from spots where they might have stood these forty
years. In order to continue this mighty image huge
blocks of stone have been cast about which geologists
will one day tell us . . . came from Westphalia via
Hamburg and Bremen. The mosses covering the stones
come from Norway, the sloop on the water from
England. Pretty fountains leap thirty feet into the air
and marble figures stand and scrutinise one another
through the thicket of flowering lemon trees.

My window gives out on to a wonderful court. From
a grass carpet like green velvet rises a delicate fountain
and all around there is a veranda which is thickly
clothed in passionflowers and aristolochia.*
I am already looking forward to showing you all
these lovely things.[356]

The Crown Prince, later Frederick William IV, had a hand
in the building of Klein-Glienicke too. There are extant
drawings in his hand for the little Jägerhof, with further
sketches by Schinkel. The design was finally executed by
Persius.[357]

In June 1922 Alfred Döblin joked with his readers in the
Prager Tagblatt: 'I've quit the east . . . and I have flown to
the paradise of the west. Beyond the Kurfürstendamm, the
centre of snobbery. This unbearably helpless magnificence,
this fear-filled vacuum of men cursed with riches. Zehlendorf! Even beyond the splendours of the botanical gardens.'[358]
Possibly it was this *Angst* which led so many of Döblin's
psychoanalytical colleagues to live in Zehlendorf. There must
have been fine pickings for them among the neurotic rich.[359]
Even Einstein had a house not far off, on the lake above
Caputh. Zehlendorf was not just rich men's villas, however,
it was also the breeding ground for different architecturally
distinguished social projects.

* Dutchman's pipe.

The most famous of these was Onkel Toms Hütte. The name had little or nothing to do with 'Uncle Tom's Cabin'. The Tom in question was Fritz *Thom*as, the owner of an up-market inn, originally called the Wirtshaus am Riemeister. The first settlements on the site were started in 1922. In 1926 Bruno Taut and his colleagues began mapping out Onkel Toms Hütte proper. The estate always had a comfortable but left-wing feel to it. As a 'red fort' it began to attract attention from the SA almost as soon as mortar was applied to bricks, but with 2,200 houses in all, their leaders thought an all-out attack 'virtually pointless'.[360] The artisans living on the land thought so too. As one told a Nazi, 'Don't talk such rubbish. If that happens we'll just press the button and there will be a general strike.'[361]

The left never did get the chance to repeat their great moment when they defeated the right-wing Kapp *Putsch* of 1920 with a well-planned general stoppage, not in Onkel Toms Hütte or anywhere else. But the estate was none the less the centre of a remarkable amount of resistance activity during the Hitler years. One group that was active here was the Rote Stoßtrupp, or 'Red Raiding Party', which ran its own dissident paper until some copies were discovered at a post office in November 1933 and the press was traced from the postmark. The leader of the Rote Stoßtrupp, Rudolf Küstermeier, was only liberated from Bergen-Belsen when the British arrived at the camp in 1945.[362]

Another group that held meetings in Onkel Toms Hütte was Neu-Beginnen. Most of the members of the group emigrated during the thirties. At Fischtal 8 lived Julius Leber, the former socialist deputy, whose arrest during negotiations with communists in July 1944 pushed Stauffenberg and his group to go ahead with the Plot. Onkel Toms Hütte was the scene of regular meetings between Leber and other old socialists such as Adolf Reichwein, Theodor Haubach and Carlo Mierendorff. Mierendorff was killed during a bombing raid on Leipzig; the others were all executed. Also hanged was the former civil servant Ernst von Harnack, another resident of Onkel Toms Hütte, who was unwise enough to protest against Leber's arrest.[363]

Away on the Nikolassee lived another prominent victim of the regime. Jochen Klepper was the son of a Silesian clergyman. Having decided against following in his father's footsteps, Klepper became a journalist and wrote a historical novel, *Der Vater*, about the life of the Soldier-King, Frederick William I. The book was a little plea for the simplicity and decency of the old Prussia, before its corruption by imperial ambitions. As such, there was an implied criticism of Nazism too, but it was not something the Nazis really noticed: Frederick William was one of their heroes. The book sold well. The first copy was bought by the Kaiser's second wife, Hermine. It had a wide following in the officer corps. Hitler received a copy for his birthday. It even won praise from the Nazi daily, the *Völkische Beobachter*. Klepper was mildly perplexed by the reaction of the authorities: 'Heavens, the "Father's" regime is a criticism, not a glorification of the present one. This Old Testament king cannot be made into a forerunner to National Socialism.'[364]

For the Nazis there was just one thing wrong with Klepper and his book: he was married to a Jewish woman, Johanna Gerstel, and lived with her and her two Jewish daughters by a previous marriage. He was able to get one of them out of Germany to England, but his attempts to find a refuge for Renate in Sweden failed. In December 1942 all three committed suicide in Nikolassee.[365]

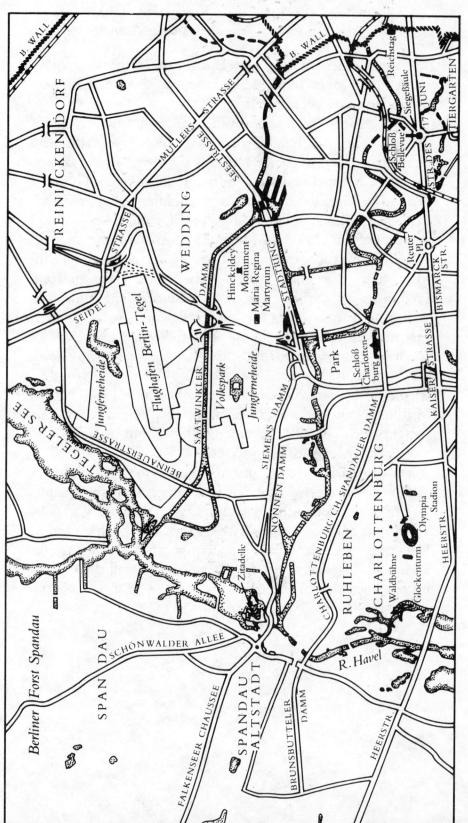

North-west Berlin in 1989

XV

The north-west of Berlin was once the promised land of the expatriate Huguenots. There was common land and, where the Humboldthafen is now, another of Berlin's vineyards. The rustic ideal persisted into the last years of Berlin's *Residenzstadt* incarnation. Moabit was the most popular destination for Sunday trippers – if Glaßbrenner is to be believed, generally armed with a bottle of schnapps or three.

> Tailors' boys and cobblers' boys, pewterers and
> locksmiths, brushmakers, linen and woollen weavers,
> and tinkers, basket-weavers and market-criers,
> shoeshine boys and house boys; in short, everyone
> who has legs to stir, and pennies to drown, spills out
> of the Wasser Gate, Potsdamer Gate or
> Brandenburger Gate . . .[366]

Writing in 1848, Glaßbrenner preferred to pretend that the factories had not yet arrived to spoil the idyll of Berlin's common man. Moabit was still 'the little land of tiny oaks, of green meadows, sandy paths and countless taverns!'[367] After a constructive Sunday of schnapps and *Weißbier* swilling, they trooped back across the sand to their dwellings. 'The half-cut with a bottle in their hands occasionally squawking "hurrahs"! The paralytic are guided back by their friends. There is singing, screaming and endless laughter.'[368]

In fact the rural charms of Moabit were waning fast. In 1839 the old powder-mill had been replaced by a barracks for the Uhlan Guards. Six years later the locomotive builders Borsig quit their premises by the Oranienburger Gate and moved to Moabit. By that time there were already 8,000 inhabitants. In 1862 the area was deemed urban enough to be incorporated into Berlin. Its first councillor was Albert Borsig. The character of the new district was increasingly working-class and unruly. In 1910 the population vented their displeasure at poor living conditions in a series of riots called the 'Moabiter Unruhen'.[369]

Industrialisation was rapidly to swamp the entirety of Berlin's north-west, from Moabit to Spandau. As we have seen, Spandau was once a town with the same value as, if not more significance than, Berlin itself. Nationalist, and above all National Socialist, historians were ever keen to prove that the town was a pure German colony and had never been a Wendish *Kietz*.[370] The Slavs, however, appeared to have fortified their settlement before the arrival of the first Askanian in 1157 and Spandau is now believed to have been the far-eastern stronghold of the Heveller tribe, the capital of which was Brandenburg.[371]

The still-extant Juliusturm, or keep, in the citadel is thought to be of 'German' rather than Slavic origin, and the discernible grid-plan is also typical of 'colonial' German cities of the period. By 1239 Benedictine nuns had founded the 'most important convent in the Brandenburg Mark'.[372] It acted as a 'collection centre' for the unmarried daughters of the nobility, exercising thereby a powerful formative influence on female education in its time. A century later the town was surrounded by ragstone and brick walls to a height of up to nine metres. The convent disappeared in 1639; the walls, between 1880 and 1887.[373]

Spandau expanded rapidly in the twelfth and thirteenth

centuries.[374] By 1386 there were already 169 houses; in 1564 270 big houses and 170 small ones. There was the attraction of royalty. Until 1555 the widows of Brandenburg's electors lived in the fortress. Possibly the old fort was of Slavic origin; certainly it was unlikely to have measured up to Renaissance standards of comfort. In 1560 it was pulled down and two Italian engineers, Francesco Chiaramella da Gandino and Rocco Guerrini, who was later ennobled as Rochus Graf zu Lynar, were commissioned to provide a replacement more in keeping with its time.

The town of Spandau declined after the Thirty Years War. Only in 1790 did its population rise to something approaching sixteenth-century numbers.[375] The mediaeval past was traceable only in a few modest merchant houses in the old town, although the Café zum Franziskaner continued to commemorate the long-departed friars.[376] A survey conducted in 1910 showed that 85 per cent of the population were on low incomes, and just 0.6 per cent could be classified as rich.[377] By that time Spandau had expanded to include the villages in its periphery, such as Ruhleben, once the site of a *Lustschloß* belonging to Frederick I. Ruhleben was also the love nest of Sir Lionel Sackville-West, who installed his mistress, and later wife, the gypsy dancer Pepita da Oliva, in her own villa: 'Pepitas-Ruh'. The then British Consul General had the seventeenth-century house converted for her use. Later it became a restaurant. British soldiers occupied the house after the war and it was pulled down in 1954.[378]

As its name would imply, Gesundbrunnen began life as a spa, and a respectable one too. Nicolai found the area 'rather pleasant'[379] with its bath-houses on the Panke River. Later, when Berlin lost its power to attract spa-goers, the old bath-houses were turned into dance halls. One of Schinkel's best neo-classical suburban churches was built in Gesundbrunnen, and even in the closing years of the century Diederich Hessling could move up to Gesundbrunnen, to escape from the social pressures of living in the immediate vicinity of the University.[380]

Gesundbrunnen became part of Wedding, which was roped into Berlin in 1861. Even now, long after the working-class feel of Wedding has been weathered away (it is now more Turkish than proletarian), the *Bezirk* excites a certain superciliousness in the smarter areas to the west. 'Red Wedding' has not been forgotten. In the eighteenth century Wedding was populated chiefly by Saxons.[381] It was the industrialisation of nearby Moabit from the 1840s, as well as the arrival of the enormous AEG electrical company in the 1890s, that succeeded in turning Wedding into a working-class ghetto. A handful of surviving *Mietskasernen* on the Gerichts- and the Müllerstraße still testify to life as it used to be lived in these tenements.

When Fontane visited Wedding in 1860 it had yet to show any signs of declining into a slum. What he resented was rather its lack of character.

> The houses are mostly well-built; there are no signs
> of bad management or decay. There are no holes in
> the roofs and no stuck-on bits of paper deprive the
> window-panes of their rights and functions.[382]

Everywhere Fontane discovered those fundamental Prussian qualities: order, cleanliness, hard work, thrift and sober-mindedness. What Wedding lacked, 'in a frightening way, was any sense of the picturesque'. 'They don't want any swallows on the window-sills – they attract insects; they don't want any ivy around the house – it damages the brickwork; they don't want any pretty trees in the courts and gardens – they bring damp and keep out the light . . .'[383]

Within a generation this image of Spartan self-help, of puritanical workers in a mechanised society, had been altered by the rise of a powerful socialist movement. Wedding had been politicised. After the First World War the socialists of

Wedding graduated to Independent Socialists to Communists. The area became increasingly truculent as the years
went on. Thwarted in love, Jakob Fabian wanders disconso-
lately up to Wedding, past the police barracks on the
Chausseestraße, where he notices the shining headlamps of
the green patrol cars through the gates. On the Weddingplatz
he runs into a fully-fledged riot:

> Mounted policemen waited behind the cordon for the
> order to attack. Uniformed proletarians in their
> chinstraps waited for proletarians in mufti. The
> workers were not far off; their songs got louder and
> louder. The police took one step forward. A metre
> separated man from man. The songs gave way to a
> furious bellowing. Without being able to see the
> preliminaries, one got the idea from the ever-
> mounting noise that the workers and the police were
> about to clash. A minute later the screams confirmed
> the supposition. The two sides had met and the police
> had struck out . . . A shot was heard in the distance.
> Window-panes shattered. Horses galloped . . . Stones
> flew. A constable was stabbed. The police raised their
> truncheons and charged. Three coaches brought
> reinforcements; the men jumped down from the slow-
> moving vehicles. The workers took flight, coming to
> a halt again at the extremities of the square and its
> connecting streets.[384]

★ ★ ★

The ever-growing network of canals ringing the city were
another source of work for Berlin's proletarians, as were the
Westhafen docks. In the 1840s the canal builders were known
as 'Rehberger' after the range of hills on the borders of
Wedding, Charlottenburg and Reinickendorf. Their outdoor
life was considered better than that of most Berlin workers,
and gave rise to a mocking rhyme:

Ein scheenes Leben führen wir,
Ein Leben voller Freide:
Der Dag verjeht bei Schnaps und Bier,
Und Abends denn erholen wir
Uns in die Jungfernheide.[385]

(We lead a lovely life up here,
A life that is wild and gay.
The days spin round to schnapps and beer,
At night we rest, oh, somewhere near,
On the Jungfernheide, say.)

With time too, Borsig outgrew its Moabit works and moved up to Tegel, where from 1898 its works tower rose up over a once rural backwater chiefly associated with the *Schloß* that Schinkel had rebuilt for Wilhelm von Humboldt in the 1820s.

The other famous Reinickendorf institution was the lunatic asylum in Dalldorf (now the Karl-Bonhoeffer-Klinik). Berliners enjoyed a joke at the expense of the inmates of one of Germany's largest psychiatric hospitals: 'It must be holiday time at Dalldorf if they've let you out!'; 'He belongs in Dalldorf!' 'He must have escaped from Dalldorf!' The jokes clearly became too much for the normal residents of the suburb and it changed its name to Wittenau.[386]

Before it became the stamping-ground for high-ranking party officials under the DDR, Pankow was a respectable, if not particularly fashionable, area with some large houses and villas. After 1945 diplomats accredited to the East German state tended to find flats and lodgings there too. The communist leader Wilhelm Pieck himself grabbed Schloß Niederschönhausen as his palace, once the home of Frederick the Great's unfortunate queen. Subsequent party leaders did not share Pieck's taste for luxury. In 1959 the baroque palace by Eosander von Göthe and Nering was turned into a state guesthouse.

It is hard to see the history beneath the kilometres of grey,

The Royal Residence in 1870.

The demolition of its ideologically incorrect ruins in 1950.

The Schloss seen from Unter den Linden, *c.* 1885.

The replica of the Schloss erected in 1993, photographed shortly before the mock-up was taken down in the summer of 1994.

Commerce: the Friedrichstraße, an anarchic jumble of architectural styles.

The Arts:
the Klosterstraße in Eduard Gaertner's oil painting of 1830 (p. 69).

E. T. A. Hoffmann's tomb
in Kreuzberg (p. 176).

One of the dead 1848 revolutionaries in Friedrichshain.

Left: The tomb of the Adlons: Huguenots in the French Cemetery.
Right: A tomb in the Jewish graveyard in Weißensee: 'He died for
Kaiser and Fatherland'.

Humboldthain in the north of the city.
The ruins have been landscaped, but the turrets remain.

The last vestiges of Friedrichshain, where many of
Berlin's greatest treasures perished in the mysterious blaze of 1945 (p. 218).

Gaertner's two panoramas of Berlin of 1834 show the city at its
architectural high point. *Top*: towards the Linden – St Hedwig's, the
Royal Library, the University, the Arsenal, Schinkel's Museum and
Cathedral, and the Schloss. *Bottom*: the Schloss, the Nikolaikirche,
Schinkel's Bauakademie, and, to the right of the towers, the French and
German churches with Schinkel's theatre building between the two.

The former Italian embassy, part of Hitler's monumental new diplomatic *quartier*, now partially ruinous; it is still used as a Consulate.

The remains of the Esplanade Hotel before work began in 1995 on the new Potsdamer Platz development (p. 297).

All that remained of Hitler's Bunker in 1995. Tomatoes grow on the sandy mounds. The Esplanade is in the distance.

concrete *Plattenbau* now. These densely populated tracts of East Berlin are some of the bleakest townscapes in Europe: Weißensee, for example, must have changed a lot since King Frederick William III was spotted here on 23 December 1809 returning from his undignified flight to Königsberg and Memel. The Berliners were overjoyed to see their king again after three years' absence. He entered his city through the Bernauer Gate and along the old Bernauer Straße. In his honour both were renamed: the Königstor and the Königsstraße. In 1945 the Russians came this way too. Both the working-class districts of Weißensee and Lichtenberg yielded without a fight.[387]

XVI

The east's lack of character was largely politically engineered. So was the lively, party-going nature of West Berlin. West Berlin's formal centre was in the Kurfürstendamm, with its cinemas and theatres, and in the seemingly infinite number of restaurants dotted about Wilmersdorf and Charlottenburg. Until 1989, however, West Berlin had an informal hub in Kreuzberg, with its artistic and academic population living cheek by jowl with the mainstay of the city's large Turkish colony.

In the Silhouette restaurant in the Grand Hotel on the Friedrichstraße, the wine list offers red and white wine from Kreuzberg, at 50 marks a bottle. The vineyards are said to be on the south side of the hill. They must be very small: it is possible to climb to the top of Viktoria Park without even noticing them. However, wine-making was an important part of Kreuzberg's original vocation. The Franciscans made bricks on their land in Tempelhof, while the Order of Saint John planted vines on Kreuzberg hill.[388] The existence of the vineyards, like the Tivoli brewery later, exercised a pull on Berliners which cannot be explained simply by the charm of the verdant hill and the sight of open country to the south. The name 'vineyard' seems to have been synonymous with 'country tavern'.[389]

The present 'Kreuzberg' is confusing. It was created in 1920 by sticking together parts of the Friedrichstadt, the Luisenstadt, Kreuzberg itself and the Tempelhofer Vorstadt.[390] There was not much building in the real Kreuzberg before the nineteenth century. Then, with so many barracks planted on the city's doorstep, Kreuzberg had an obviously military stamp. The regimental associations representing the reservists and veterans tended to choose Kreuzberg too. The biggest was the First Dragoon Guards, with around four hundred members, which met in Habel's brewery in the Bergmannstraße, where they were serenaded by the trumpeter 'Handsome Hermann' Baartz, the composer of more than two dozen marches, as well as waltzes and *Lieder*.[391]

Obermusikmeister Baartz was on the approved list. Others were placed on an index as a result of their politics. The landlady of the 'Kaiser-Wilhelm-Garten', for example, was not allowed to receive soldiers in her pub, because she had entertained members of the Social Democratic Party. She was also banned from using the Kaiser's name for her pub.[392] She would have missed out on the soldiers in their colourful uniforms on Sundays. The Dragoon Guards wore horsehair bushes on their helmets and gathered for a festive parade followed by a lavish meal in the barracks. In the evening there was a ball to which local girls and wives were invited.[393]

Kreuzberg still possesses many nineteenth-century *Mietshäuser*. The best of these are Riehmers Hofgarten bounded by the Yorck Hagelberger- and Großbeerenstraßen. Riehmers Hofgarten serves as a useful reminder today of just what the more grandiose *Mietshaus* could look like. The complex took almost twenty years to build, the final lick of paint being applied just before the turn of the century. The flats were not the largest – they ranged from three to seven rooms – but the scale of the exterior, with its massive balconies supported by neo-baroque atlantes, was intended to give a palatial appearance in the same way as one of John Nash's terraces in London's Regent's Park. The speculators wanted officers to live in the flats. They seem to have succeeded: in 1906 there was a 'Hoheit', Oberleutnant Prinz Schleswig-Holstein-Glücksberg, living there.[394]

The Viktoria Park behind Riehmers Hofgarten only became a park in the 1890s.[395] It provided a proper, formal setting for Schinkel's iron monument to the Wars of Liberation: the cross which gives the area its name (in the eighteenth century Kreuzberg was called Götzens Weinberg) towers over the park, and the Schultheiß 'Tivoli' Brewery below. Sacked from his job, Jakob Fabian comes up here to reflect on his past and future. In Kreuzberg he had spent the worst of the inflation winter buried in an unheated room, wrapped in an overcoat, preparing a lecture on Schiller's moral-aesthetic system. He notes an ambiguous signpost and 'a giant tree trunk. The bark had been pinched by a thousand vertical wrinkles. Even trees had worries.'[396]

Down below Kreuzberg was a network of railway lines leading to the Anhalter, Potsdamer and Görlitzer stations, as well as the overhead S-Bahn line where trains rattled past drawing-rooms in the *Beletagen*, or first floors, of elegant *Mietshäuser*. The poet, and later DDR Minister of Culture, Johannes R. Becher must have had Kreuzberg in mind when he wrote the lines:

> Mit Lichtreklame übergrell geschminkt,
> Schluchtartige Straßen zwischen Lärmfassaden,
> Und von der Stadtbahnbrücke quillt ein Schwaden
> Von Rauch herab, der uns verrußt und stinkt . . .[397]

> (Gaudily made up with their neon blink,
> Cavernous boulevards between strident house-fronts,
> And from the S-Bahn bridges some clumps
> Of smoke rise that putrify us and stink.)

There is, none the less, plenty of green in Kreuzberg. Much is provided by the cemeteries that were built at the southern tip of the Friedrichstadt, and fell to Kreuzberg at its creation in the twenties. During the closing skirmishes of the Second World War there must have been a bit of fighting among the headstones. Chamisso, Mendelssohn, the historians Treitschke and Mommsen, Schleiermacher and Menzel were pelted with machine-gun bullets. The Nazis hadn't had time to clear away the traces of poor Mendelssohn from his Berlin resting place, unlike the civic authorities in Leipzig, who had used the absence of the mayor, Goerdeler, in Scandinavia to demolish his statue before the Gewandhaus. Mendelssohn's body had been brought up from Leipzig on the night train, to be buried in the Dreifaltigkeitskirchhof. His sister had died just a few months before and he had recorded his grief in his F-Minor string quartet. Also in the Friedhof vor dem Halleschen Tor lies Baudelaire's 'divin Hoffmann',[398] shorn of the 'Amadeus' he adopted as his third Christian name in honour of Mozart:

E. T. W. Hoffmann
geb. Königsberg in Preussen
den 24 Januar 1776
gest. Berlin. den 25 Juni 1822
Kammer Gerichts Rath
ausgezeichnet
im Amte
als Dichter
als Tonkünstler
als Maler.*

Parts of neighbouring Neukölln remained fairly villagey. In Nicolai's day there had been large dwellings with gardens. In Rixdorf the Bohemians lived in houses with

---

* E. T. W. Hoffmann b. Königsberg in Prussia 24 January 1776 d. Berlin 25 June 1822. Judge on the Bench of the Kammer Gericht. Distinguished in office, as a writer, as a musician, as a painter.

exposed, half-timbered gable-ends.[399] It was also popular for Sunday excursions. As late as 1889 the music halls sang:

> Auf den Sonntag freu' ick mir
> Ja dann jeht es raus zu ihr,
> Feste mit verjnüjtem Sinn
> Pferdebus nach Rixdorf hin.[400]
>
> (Come Sunday, I have my fun
> Then I visit my loved one,
> Content, and with no great fuss
> In Rixdorf, on the horse bus.)

Britz has its old *Schloß* and manor house, and the minister Graf Herzberg lies buried under his sword and three-cornered hat in the church. In Buckow it is still possible to determine the form of the mediaeval *Dorfanger* beneath the modern accretions.

If some Sunday trippers made their way to Rixdorf, many more took their paths along the river to Stralau. Even in the ailing last days of the DDR, though a power station had been planted in Rummelsburg to terminate the view and the marshalling-yards of Ostkreuz had sprawled south of their confines towards Treptow, there was still a little holiday feeling left. At least in Treptower Park, opposite the patched-up mediaeval tower of Stralau Church. At the Zenner's inn on the water's edge (once a pure Langhans building), a band of musicians struck up 'It's very daring, the Continental!' while DDR-accredited portrait artists wandered between the tables with sketch-books at the ready, eagerly touting for business.

On the far side of the Spree, Stralau is a sorry place. There are a few grim pubs, but little or nothing that might recall the great days of the 'Stralauer Fischzug' (the Stralau Catch).

> No day is more remarkable, no day is more hotly longed for than 24 August. Already at the break of

dawn the streets are full of life. Big and small, young
and old, rich and poor, elegant and dowdy – each
and every one of them has something to get ready for
the afternoon. Hawkers and market girls hurry to
the Stralow [sic] Gate to give themselves the time to set
up their stalls; dandies rush down to the pawnshops,
where they pledge watches and rings in order to take
part in today's merry festival; cabbies bring their
bone-shakers out on to the streets; boatsmen decorate
their canoes and punts; housewives run down to the
shops to procure the solid and liquid needs of the
stomach – yes, even the hackney-cab drivers put on
a bit more speed than usual.[401]

Some Berliners took to the boats and enjoyed a day on
the water. Others settled down in one of the village's many
pubs and drank themselves silly. If Glaßbrenner is to be
believed, the day generally ended up with a few choice
punch-ups.[402] David Kalisch set the third act of his farce
Einmalhunderttausend Taler! in a Stralau pub. The dandy
Stullmüller has fallen on hard times and has had to marry a
wealthy servant girl who has inherited a pub. Now they run
the place together. There is a view of both Treptow and
Berlin and a small sign tells guests of the availability of
'genuine Bavarian lager'. Other notices tell the customers to
pay on the nail and the knives and forks are chained to the
tables. Yet the stage instruction reads: 'Everything as picturesque as possible'.[403]

Stralau was effectively preserved until 1920, at which time
it was brought under the umbrella of Groß-Berlin. By then
Friedrichshain to the north was already a grim working-class
area grouped around the old Schlesischer Station. In the
twenties it was fashionable for smart families to adopt workers
in the Berlin stews. Young Erika von Hornstein remembered
trips to Friedrichshain in the company of her mother:

My eyes sought out a single splash of colour in the
street scene. Dead grey had consumed it all.

Mietskasernen, stark façades, never before had I seen
such naked hideousness. The courtyards I was walking
through were holes into which daylight seeped from
above, one after the other. [We passed] through a
narrow stairwell, stiff with filth, over cemented steps
from floor to floor to the top of the house.

Not all the unemployed workers were prepared to co-
operate with the noble do-gooders. 'I want work not alms.
I want to look after my family myself. Give me work, I don't
care what sort.' In another flat they met a mother big with
child. When they collided with the eldest daughter she, too,
seemed to have reached the same degree of pregnancy: 'I
suspected that the producer of both these unborn children
was the man in the bed.' The Hornsteins eventually adopted
a family in Wedding and brought them their old clothes.
The Kuppkes now received regular visits: ' "Our baroness is
here!" the Kuppke children would cry, running out to my
mother and leaping up at her.'[404] During the Third Reich
the inhabitants of Friedrichshain had to put up with the
indignity of having the borough's name changed to 'Horst-
Wessel'. It was done to punish them for their earlier commit-
ment to Communism.

Renaming Friedrichshain was another linguistic purge; a
further instance of Berlin's attitude to its past. Examine the
rows of books in any contemporary Berlin bookshop and
you will know that Berliners long to find tangible evidence
of what the city was once like. Yet there was a time, not
fifty years ago, when the truth was too hot to handle.

3
Berlin Life

I

In one respect, Berlin was unlike other cities: its society was only seasonally dominated by the nobility; and it was a short season at that. Traditionally the Junkers converged on Berlin for the carnival which began before Christmas and lasted throughout January.[1] In his Prussian way, Goethe's friend Zelter thought it a waste of time and money which brought the people little joy.[2] It was a concentrated season of operas, grand and lesser balls, concerts, blow-outs 'and a few important bankruptcies'.[3] In the second half of the nineteenth century it was replaced by a more formal 'season', but by the turn of the century this had degenerated into less than a handful of stultifyingly boring balls in which the Kaiser endeavoured to stamp out any foreign dances that might have become fashionable in the course of the year.[4] The French-born princess Marie Radziwiłł thought the royal pair frightened of Berlin, 'an enormous town decorated in the worst possible taste and incredibly high houses. These are now only banks and hotels. Quite American without a Court or any royal carriages, only motor-cars which now and again announce by peculiar tunes that a Prince is in the street.'[5]

While Berlin was just a small *Residenz*, things were a little livelier. The pages of Graf Lehndorff, for example, reveal a number of Prussian nobles trying vainly to inject a little French *ton* into the eighteenth-century city. In the case of a Frau von Bismarck, this seems to have failed miserably. The diarist thought her the 'most ridiculous woman in Berlin. She has quite extraordinary manners which would reduce even the most earnest stoic to laughter. The supper resembled Boileau's banquet.* For all that I enjoyed myself beyond measure.'[6]

Elsewhere Lehndorff's fellow nobles seemed to have only the most rustic comprehension of the duties incumbent on their stations. In May 1752 'a dispute grew up between Baron Schmeiß and Colonel Grumbkow, one of the Field Marshal's sons. Schmeiß, a quite despicable character, refused Grumbkow's challenge, after the other had beaten him black-and-blue. But one day he found his moment when Grumbkow and his sister, Gräfin Sparr, were sitting in a carriage; he threw himself from his horse, and came to beat Grumbkow with a whip; he then promptly disappeared from the city.'[7]

As a student in Berlin at the beginning of Berlin's industrial incarnation, Dronke found the nobility little in evidence. 'The only class [sic] in which the nobility is still represented is the officer corps.'[8] They surfaced occasionally in a few smart restaurants and *Konditoreien*. Their apartments were to be found on the Linden, or on the stretch of the Wilhem-straße closest to it. 'You see how small this world is when it can be contained in one and a half streets.'[9] Half a century later the Prussian nobility had mostly abdicated their flats in favour of the new palace hotels mentioned by Princess Rad-ziwiłł. In Fontane's *Der Stechlin*, for example, the old Dubslav von Stechlin prefers to stay in a hotel for his son's wedding, as 'staying with children is always awkward'.[10]

As Dronke discovered, except in the ultra-rapid flowering of the Berlin season, the leadership of society passed to the embassies and the diplomats stationed in them. In the pre-March days the leader was the British ambassador, the Earl of Westmorland, whose circle included not only members of

---

* *Le Repas ridicule, Satire III*, of 1665.

the Prussian ruling house, but also some of the city's more distinguished painters. The Sardinian Legate Count Rossi had the advantage of his wife, the famous soprano Henriette Sontag (born Gertrud Walburga), who not only sang the soprano part in the first performance of Beethoven's Ninth Symphony but created the title role in Weber's *Euryanthe*. Her relationship with the flamboyant, cosmopolitan Fürst Pückler can have been no drawback either. Not even for her husband.[11]

The situation had not changed a century later.[12] What few noble palaces the city possessed were divided up into flats or had been sold off as ministries. Fürstin Blücher waited until the end of the First World War, living in the Esplanade, until an apartment became available in the family's town palace.[13] Other Silesian magnate families such as the Princes Pleß or the Henckel von Donnersmarcks occasionally gave grand balls in their residences 'but preferred to stay at the Adlon, Bristol or Excelsior, because it was more comfortable'.[14]

For many members of Berlin's *haute bourgeoisie*, a visit to one of the top embassies was their one real contact with palatial living. Through his mother's salon, and his father's status as one of the grand old men of Berlin's academic world, Nicolaus Sombart was a regular guest at the embassies of the main powers, from his childhood onwards. He recalls festive occasions at the French Embassy on the Pariser Platz when Stüler's great staircase was covered by a red carpet and lined with flunkeys – a metre apart – dressed in powdered wigs, pumps with buckles, blue frock-coats, red vests and white breeches.[15] The Italians had yet to decamp to their Hitlerian palace on the Tiergarten and were still in a converted villa nearby. Sombart was shown round by the Ambassador's wife. The linchpin was a huge gymnasium, filled with every imaginable form of sporting equipment.[16]

The best insight into this diplomatic world, however, comes from the pages of Bella Fromm's diaries. During the

Weimar Republic, when the Soviet Union was playing a shadowy role protecting and encouraging German Communist leaders, the Embassy received with all the pomp and magnificence of its predecessors. Indeed, nothing much had changed: the building, the former palace of Princess Amalie, the huge logs in the grate, the white marble staircase, or the softest Smyrna carpets.

> The Russians entertain on a great scale. Caviar is flown from Moscow, heavy wines from the Crimea. The hosts and their staff shower the guests with their attention . . . [but] the Russians withhold themselves personally from the abundant food and rich drinks, which seem there for the guests only . . .
>
> At dinner parties, eighty guests are usually seated at two long tables in the rococo room with the marble walls and the heavy gold decorations. Precious damask, covering the table, stresses the deep glow of red roses, the hostess's favourite flower. The heavy wine is poured into costly crystal cups, all relics of the former Imperial Ambassador's household. The only modern objects are the multicoloured plates and dishes, a product of present Russia.[17]

The British inhabited the town palace of the railway speculator Bethel Henry Strousberg at 70 Wilhelmstrasse, between the Adlon and the Reichspräsidentenpalais. The interiors had been modified to suit the tastes of its occupants, but from Strousberg's time the 'two-storey marble hall in which fountains splash with refreshing coolness' remained.[18] At the Egyptian Legation, Bella Fromm attended a soirée for four hundred to celebrate the king's coronation day. An Egyptian lady danced. The papal nuncio diplomatically turned his head to the wall to scrutinise an enormous picture of King Fuad, 'which is dazzlingly illuminated on festive occasions'.[19]

Once the Nazis achieved power such diplomatic gatherings became a safety-valve for the oppressed members of Berlin's smart set, but not even the accredited diplomats were entirely immune from the blundering ministrations of Nazi thugs. Bella Fromm discovered this to her horror when she gave one of her own regular parties for members of the diplomatic corps. It was March 1933, and gangs of lawless SA men roamed the streets, setting upon anything and everyone which, in their sensitive souls, they found offensive or provocative. Foreigners loomed large in this category, and Frau Fromm had a number of foreigners round to her house that night: chiefly ambassadors and attachés. She also had a few Germans: the wife of Otto Meißner, the chief of Hitler's cabinet, who had played a significant role in the downfall of Prime Minister Brüning, and Herbert Mumm von Schwarzenstein, a member of the champagne family who was Vice-Chief of Protocol at the Foreign Office. He was later to be shot in the back of the head by the SS on wasteland by the Lehrter Straße Prison in a last act of spite while the Russians mounted their assault on the city.[20]

A tragi-comic scene ensued. The SA men prepared to storm the house which they knew to belong to 'non-Aryans', because, as they put it, neighbours had seen 'spies driving up'. When a police captain turned up with orders to search the house, Frau Fromm was forced to call the Chief of Protocol and explain that they were on the brink of a serious 'diplomatic incident'. The Secretary of State at the Foreign Office, von Bülow, informed Vice-Chancellor von Papen. Papen went to Hitler. Meißner told Frau Fromm to be patient. The next caller was Papen: 'Frau Bella, fifteen mounted police are on their way out to you with orders to shoot; tell the crowd.'[21]

The SA men were amusing themselves by tearing the flags off the diplomats' cars in the forecourt. This led to scuffles with the chauffeurs, which were interrupted by the arrival of more Nazis, this time sent to defuse the situation. A Gruppenführer Schäfer was then obliged to half-throttle one of the ruffians in order to get him to return the stolen flags. Three of the Gruppenführer's men were left behind as security. Later that evening Frau Fromm ran into the omniscient Louis Adlon, who commended the Jewish woman on her heroic stand.[22]

In wartime the surviving foreign embassies and legations assumed a new significance for those lucky enough to have an introduction to diplomatic circles: they were the only places left where one could be almost guaranteed of decent food and drink. Not all the foreigners who remained in Berlin throughout the Hitler years were diplomats. There were others, like the strange André Germain, who remained because of their admiration for features of the new system. Germain is severely mocked in Klaus Mann's *Mephisto* as Pierre Larue. Nicolaus Sombart has rather more affectionate memories of him as a little man who rented a *Schloß* near Berlin and filled it with blond beasts from the SS, peacocks in black uniforms, eating and drinking at the Frenchman's expense.[23]

II

If Berlin lacked the noble cachet of Paris, Madrid, Rome or London, it had its businessmen, who kept the machine oiled, bringing in the cash to finance its civic pride. Berlin's activities as a *Handelsstadt*, or trade centre, had ebbed away after the Middle Ages and the Thirty Years War, but a stock exchange was established in a horseshoe-shaped building in the Lustgarten in 1738. The dealing room was decorated with shells and puzzle-mirrors.[24] In the 1840s the stock exchange migrated to a fine new neo-classical building on the Berlin bank of the Spree. Here the intrepid policeman Stieber uncovered an early instance of insider trading in the autumn of 1854. A telegraph operator was leaking details of foreign deals before the market opened.[25]

This was take-off time for Berlin and Prussia. There was no planning as such, but 'economic and social rank growth'. A need for greater profitability led to the transformation of Berlin's artisan businesses into large industrial concerns. Berlin became an industrial city. Wages improved in the factories of the industrialists Egells, Wöhlert and Borsig. Berlin's first new bank was formed: the Hansemannsche Disconto-Bank.[26] Hansemann's son Ferdinand went on to found the 'Hakata', an extreme right-wing league for the depolonisation of Poland.[27]

As early as 1808 one third of Berlin's thirty banks were Jewish-owned. Naturally the Jews also played a hefty role in the creation of a proper chamber of commerce in 1850.[28] The Jews ran the department stores which began to appear at the end of the century: Wertheim, Hermann Tietz, Nathan Israel. When Alfred Döblin's father's business failed and he fled to the United States, Döblin's elder brother was apprenticed at Nathan Israel's Spandauerstraße premises.[29]

Berlin also contained huge numbers of civil servants, who were needed (or so it was supposed) to ensure the smooth running of the Prussian state. In 1786 Nicolai had already put their number at 3,433.[30] With the introduction of the *Städteordnung* of 1808 a proper system of local government was introduced in Berlin. Stein, the great reformer, intended to bring more bright men of bourgeois extraction into the business of administration. Berlin was to have its first mayor in Leopold von Gerlach, a member of the *new* nobility. From the first the office was seen as a bourgeois fief. Only two other noblemen were mayors of Berlin before Richard von Weizsäcker took over the town hall in Schöneberg in 1981.[31]

All attempts to inject a revolutionary spirit into the growing proletariat had to reckon with a stifling political apathy which was to some extent based on the many benefits that existed for artisans or members of the lower middle class. When Goethe sent the former builder Zelter a trainee carpenter, Zelter knew exactly what to do with him. He packed him off to the carpenters' hostel, where 'he will be entered first of all in the journeymen books and for sickness and death benefits'.[32]

A relatively easy life among the middle classes led to the prevalence of 'Weißbier philistinism'. Lortzing's *Weißbierlied* was the song of an impotent generation. The radical poet Ferdinand Freiligrath also summed up apathetic Berlin *Bürger*:

> Du sollst verdammte Freiheit mir
> Die Ruhe fürder nicht gefährden!
> Lisette, noch ein Gläschen Bier!
> Ich will ein guter Bürger werden.[33]

> (Damn you, freedom! You will not queer
> My pitch with talk of revolution!
> Lisette, another glass of beer!
> I will be an upright citizen.)

Like Glaßbrenner's Herr Buffey, they discussed political developments over a glass of beer and a pipe of tobacco in the *Weißbierkneipe*, and, as Dronke observed, arrived at a sort of conclusion, which in no way advanced them towards the goal of political freedom or responsibility.[34] Things had not changed much by 1924 when Zille drew a scene of men drinking *Weißbier* together. A 'broadminded' worker speaks: 'Bei mir jibts det janze Jahr bloß zwee Feiertage! Det is Kaisersjeburtstag und der erste Mai.' ('For me there are just two moments for celebration in the whole Year! And those are the Kaiser's birthday and the first of May.')[35]

Of course there were other places where the middle-class or even upper-class Berliner could meet his or her peers that were not quite as earthy as the *Weißbierkneipe*. At the turn of the eighteenth and nineteenth centuries, Berlin had its famous salons, where women, chiefly Jewish women, entertained a mixture of noblemen and intellectuals. Henriette Herz was the daughter of a leading Berlin doctor. At the age of twelve she was married to another doctor, Marcus Herz, who had been Kant's best pupil in Königsberg. From 1784 onwards, the Herz household received its guests on two separate levels: the early romantics went to Henriette, and the philosophers to Marcus. Chamisso joined the set rather late, but his initiation into Henriette's circle was vital to his development. It was here that he met both the scholar and statesman Wilhelm von Humboldt and Fichte.[36]

'He who has seen neither the Gendarmenmarkt nor Madame Herz', Berliners used to say, 'has not seen Berlin.' Intellectual qualities counted for more than beauty in those rare days. Neither Henriette's portrait by Georg Friedrich Adolf Schöne in the Märkisches Museum nor the well-known representations of Rahel Levin depict good-looking women. Henriette Herz must have been well-off during her husband's lifetime (he died forty-four years before her, in 1803). At the end of her life Henriette Herz received a pension from Frederick William IV, but Rahel Levin did not even have money to recommend her.[37] Yet she mustered an equally glittering circle in her attic lodgings: Prince Louis Ferdinand 'the Prussian Alcibiades', killed by the French, the feudal-revivalist Friedrich Ludwig von der Marwitz, Schleiermacher (who converted Henriette to Christianity), Schlegel (who married the third great female Jewish intellect of the day, Moses' daughter Dorothea), Wilhelm von Humboldt, and finally the man Rahel married, Varnhagen von Ense. In her humble apartment the Berlin Goethe cult also flowered.

Hannah Arendt saw the Jewish salon as a historical accident, 'a chance constellation in a period of social transition'.[38] Even at its peak, before it was destroyed by the upsurge of narrow-minded nationalism occasioned by Bonaparte's roughshod ride over German dignities, the Jewish salon remained *outside* society, something for which convention had yet to dictate rules. Salons, where such things existed in the later years of the century, were run by Gentiles. Frau von Lebbin, for example, looked after the 'grey eminence' of the German Foreign Office, Friedrich von Holstein. Others were Gräfin Schlippenbach and the Freifrau von Spitzemberg, the sister of the Liebenberger Axel von Varnbüler.[39] Philipp zu Eulenburg's Schloß Liebenberg was also a salon of sorts, filled with the Kaiser's arty, chiefly homosexual friends.[40]

After the foundation of the new Reich in 1871, Gräfin Schleinitz ran an artistic salon, where liberal opinions were expressed that were said to have annoyed Bismarck. Bismarck responded by telling the countess to discontinue her receptions.[41] The catty Polish princess Katharina Radziwiłł, who had little good to say of anyone in Berlin, thought Gräfin Schleinitz 'the best-educated [and] most intelligent woman in Berlin'.[42] She defied Bismarck's orders, but made her soirées smaller and less noticeable all the same. Katharina Radziwiłł believed she had just one fault: she was a great enthusiast for the music of Richard Wagner, and initiated the Wagner cult in Berlin.[43] The Polish princess saw Wagner as the musical equivalent of Bismarck for whom power and noise were the only divinities.[44] There is no doubting the respect Wagner had for Frau von Schleinitz. He praised her 'untiring efforts' and called her his 'most excellent benefactress', in letters to King Ludwig of Bavaria.[45]

Princess Radziwiłł reserved her full fury for the remaining women of Berlin. Sex was apparently not considered a big issue: 'one satisfies the needs of love with the same calm as one does one's appetite'.[46] If she was right, there was precious little else to occupy their minds. 'In general, the upper-class Berlin woman does not read, does not work and busies herself with nothing. She spends her time gossiping, dressing and undressing, and looking for people to help her with all three.'[47]

Between the wars Nicolaus Sombart's Romanian mother maintained a salon in Grunewald, and her son insists that women have been wrong to abandon such institutions, where they might fully exercise their power in the most feminine way. People came to tea, as cocktail parties had yet to reach Berlin, and there were occasional dinners with culinary specialities.[48] Regulars included the artist Emil Orlik, the economist Jens Jessen and the right-wing jurist Carl Schmitt. There were a great many Chinamen and the philosopher Graf Hermann Keyserling came calling for 'champagne and beautiful women'. After 1933 there were fewer and fewer Jews.[49] In recent years Sombart himself has tried to revive this all but disappeared Berlin institution in his home.

One of the last Berliners to run a salon, albeit an accidental one, was the Freifrau Maria von Gersdorff in her Tiergarten villa. Many of her regulars were also her tenants: Prince Vassiltchikov and his daughter Missie; and the tennis-ace Gottfried von Cramm; others dropped round from their offices at lunchtime or on leave from the front, including anti-Nazi conspirators such as Adam von Trott, Paul Metternich, Gottfried and Otto von Bismarck. Successive air raids managed to gut the upper floors, but the Gersdorffs merely moved down into the basement and the entertaining continued while Berlin burned. In the spring of 1944 the house was patched up and looked 'like an oasis' with its peach blossoms and hyacinths among the ruins of the old diplomatic quarter.[50] After July that year Maria Gersdorff's small world was slimmed down even more, as many of its members perished on Nazi gibbets.

Even in that apocalyptic war social divisions were somehow preserved. Reading Missie Vassiltchikov's diaries, it seems quite astonishing now that on 22 July 1944 this young Russian princess could flit from the Adlon (where she was meeting Fürstin Loremarie Schönburg) to the house of Freifrau Aga Fürstenberg for tea on the lawn with Tony Saurma von der Jeltsch and Graf Georg zu Pappenheim. The pathos becomes all the greater when Adam von Trott, a leading civilian member of the conspiracy, appears, looking like death.[51] Even 1944 was another age – one where divisions of rank and class could be maintained by armies of servants. One source estimates their number in Berlin at 30,000 in the thirties. Even in the house of a leading academic there was a '*Mamsell*', to look after the children, a housekeeper and his wife, an upstairs maid and a French governess. On important occasions when the family was giving a dinner party a butler was brought in from one of the other big houses in the neighbourhood.[52]

The Second World War seems to have made Berlin more aristocratic than it had ever been, except in small and insignificant enclaves. Berlin's life was generally typified by the *Milljöh*: the milieu of the Berlin worker, whose life was the special study of Heinrich Zille. Zille's demands were not high; 'he treasured a good glass of beer, in summer above all a Berliner *Weiße*, and a powerful schnapps'.[53] Later in life he was told he was diabetic and had to forgo the beer. After that he stuck to schnapps. By then Zille can't have been poor, yet he lived in the same flat. As he put it, 'I have risen enough – to the fourth floor!' After he died the popular singer Claire Waldoff paid tribute to him by adding *Das Lied vom Vater Zille* to her repertoire: 'Das war sein Milljöh,' she croaked.*[54]

Zille's subject-matter was Berlin's increasingly brutalised urban proletariat. There was something quintessentially Prussian about the way the poor were regimented in their factories and billeted in stark *Mietskasernen*, but Berlin's working classes knew how to return the favour. In the years following economic take-off in the 1840s and 1850s they became supremely well organised, and a constant thorn in the sides of their less responsible employers. In 1906, Eduard Bernstein was able to write that 'in absolute figures and from every city in the world, today Berlin has the strongest contingent of politically and syndically organised workers'.[55]

---

* The sound of her voice was described by a contemporary as 'a throat oiled with dust'.

Bernstein expressed the prejudices of his time and of his dialectical ideology: Berlin's workers were not worth talking about until they began to manifest some sort of political consciousness in the pre-March days. For his story he wanted factories with smoke-stacks and diabolical capitalists to run them. For Bernstein the kernel of the new Berlin lay around the old Oranienburger Tor, where the first industrial work-shops of Borsig, Egells and Wöhlert were to be found. His romantic vision was no less than that of the painter Carl Eduard Biermann, who painted Borsig's works in 1847 under billows of smoke; or Carl Blechen, who was able to transform an iron mill in Eberswalde into a scene of Constable-like lyricism.[56] Gaertner, too, painted the Borsig works once they moved to Moabit, but it is not one of his most inspired watercolours.[57] It might not be too far-fetched to suggest that this romanticism persisted into the DDR years, with their insistence on gracing every decent landscape with a factory or a power-station.

The trade-union movement started in Berlin with English prototypes. The *Handwerkervereine* were based on the mechanics' institutes, 'training grounds for growing revolutionaries'.[58] The inspiration came from the printer Behrends and the 'Rütli', a group of poets, journalists and artists who were in regular contact with the neo-Hegelian 'Freie' intellectuals who met at Hippels Weinstube in the Friedrichstraße.[59]

Radical ideas were disseminated by a series of short-lived journals which had to fight tooth and claw to survive under the publishing restrictions imposed by the Prussian state. The *Berliner Monatschrift* lasted just one issue, despite being published in Mannheim. Bruno Bauer, one of the 'Freie', was able to keep his *Allgemeine Literaturzeitung* afloat for a year, while in Leipzig F. W. Held produced regular issues of *Die Lokomotive*. Engels contributed to *Der Volksvertreter*. G. Julius's *Die Zeitungshalle* was filled with short stories and sketches which Bernstein dismissed as 'weepy, sentimental stuff'.[60]

The iron fist of the Prussian authorities led to plenty of Boy's Own-style conspiracy which came up against the eagle eye of Police Commissioner Stieber. At the trial of the communist Christian Friedrich Mentel and the cobbler Karl Joseph Hätzel, the court learned that Berlin had been divided up into four revolutionary sections: 'spring', 'dawn', 'morning star' and 'forwards': nomenclature that must have inspired G. K. Chesterton in his novel *The Man Who Was Thursday*. The plotters met in Herter's pub in the Leipziger-straße or Bechers in the Alte Jacobstraße, where they were arrested in December 1846. An apprentice tailor and an apprentice carpenter were released immediately. At their trial the two revolutionaries expressed their aim of bringing about gradual revolution through the teaching of workers about their rights to a free press and trade unions. Despite all that was said about the severity of Prussian law they were released at the end of their trial having been deemed to have served their sentences while in police custody.[61]

The golden days of 1848 were soon over and the police once more in control of the streets of Berlin. The assassination attempt on Frederick William IV on 22 May 1850 gave the Commissioner Hinckeldey the chance to renege on the promises made to the workers about their right to assemble. The police closed down both the artisans' 'Gutenbergbund' (which called for a free press) and the 'Verein der Arbeiter', as well as the paper *Verbrüderung*.[62] The workers' new health insurance organisation was accepted until March 1853, when another plot (Bernstein says it was the work of an *agent provocateur*) allowed the police to go for the throat of the nascent proletarian bodies of the Prussian capital.

It took the determination and brains of Ferdinand Lassalle to create a workers' organisation that actually stuck. Lassalle had met Marx in the Rhineland and taken part in the 1848 revolution there. In 1857 he returned to Berlin to publish a dissertation on Heraklites. Writing to Marx in June 1859, he showed himself little inspired by the revolutionary mettle of the Berliners, whom he found to be still imbued with monarchical sentiments and in the 'train of the dim *petit-bourgeois* democrats'.[63] This downtrodden state lasted into the sixties: the Berlin branch of the Allgemeine deutsche Arbeiterverein had just 200 members in 1863. The following year it had dwindled to thirty-five. On 22 November 1863 the first assembly was held in a common-or-garden dance hall on the Elsässerstraße (Wilhelm Pieckstraße). Like Lenin later, the intellectual Lassalle failed to sway his audience and the meeting was broken up by the police. When the speaker was arrested for high treason, some of those present even applauded.

Lassalle's arrest had nothing to do with the speech made at the dance hall, but was occasioned by a passage in his book *An die Arbeiter Berlins* (To Berlin's Workers). His trial began on 12 April 1864 before the Staatsgerichthof, which had a special jurisdiction in political matters (comparisons with the Nazi Volksgerichthof spring to mind, but Lassalle was acquitted, which was not the rule at Freisler's court). Lassalle had already entered into secret negotiations with Bismarck to win concessions for his movement in return for lending the Chancellor support against the bourgeois parties. The architect of German parliamentary socialism died the same year as his acquittal, as a result of a duel over a woman, in Geneva.[64]

Berlin's working class had indeed undergone a major change. In the 1840s there was little structure either to the work place or to workers' organisations. In 1845 6,000 Berliners were in receipt of alms. Particularly onerous was the 'quiet time' when workers were laid off by their factories and workshops. A female silver-polisher, for example, worked for only four months a year; a male roofer, just six. Men generally had to reckon with two months' forced holiday; women four. Dronke insists that anything under five

Silbergroschen fell below a living wage. A wagoner received two, and a basket-weaver got five. The highest-paid females were laundresses; the lowest, barmaids and cigar-rollers. A skilled craftsman such as a draughtsman, jeweller or copper-smith could earn up to 40 *Silbergroschen*. Among the worst paid were servant girls. If they possessed the keys to the house where they were in service they could supplement their wages through prostitution. Dronke insists that many were reduced to theft or fraud.[65]

Dronke worked his experience of Berlin's stews into his fiction too. In *Aus dem Volk* he describes the lodgings of a poor seamstress in the Fischerkietz. On the first floor (the *Beletage*) lived the shopkeeper; up one came the minor func-tionary, scribe or copyist; on the third floor more doubtful, underworld characters; while our heroine lives even closer to the Gods: 'The stairs became steep, and some of the individual steps were missing. And behind some of the steps the backing was missing, so that the staircase looked like a ladder.'[66] Marie, ensconced in her attic, presents a picture of the last stage of human misery. Her work earns her six *Silbergroschen*, on which she must feed an entire family.[67]

Dronke found some of the detail for his picture of the Berlin poor in Bettina von Arnim's *Dies Buch gehört dem König* (This Book is for the King) of 1843. Like many others, Bettina had high hopes of the new monarch and for his widely appreciated love of his people. Bettina von Arnim herself gleaned her information from a Swiss doctor who had visited the slums of Voigtland outside the Oranienburger Gate. It was an entirely unregulated sweatshop with workers lying in bed knitting stockings although they themselves had no such thing; not even a shirt on their backs.[68] The children went naked, deriving what warmth they could from one another or shivering on the straw that served as a bed. Four families shared a room in the tenement blocks, with a brace of screens ensuring the bare modicum of privacy. Where the sheet-screens met was a bed where any invalid inmate could be looked after by the collectivity.[69]

Just by the Hamburger Tor, Bettina's Swiss visited one of the city's cellar dwellings and discovered a carpenter with a bad leg. He had injured himself building Schinkel's Bauakademie. His compensation amounted to a mere fifteen *Silbergroschen*. He broke down his expenses: with six and a half thalers a month he had to pay two for his rent; three and a half to procure enough potatoes to feed his family (his daughter sat through the interview peeling potatoes); and a thaler for wood. Other cellars revealed destitute weavers, ruined by a slump which had caused a revolt in Prussian Silesia. In another he found a man who considered himself well enough off to alternate his diet between potatoes and porridge.[70]

Bettina produced an impassioned plea for the Voigtländer:

> Voigtländer, bejammere nicht dein eignes Geschick.
> Beklage nur die, die kein Mitleid fühlen mit dir.[71]

> (Voigtländer, bewail not your fate.
> Rue only those who can have no pity for thee.)

Her reflections on the duties of nobility bear a similarity to certain Pietistic conservatives of the time, such as Ludwig von Gerlach and Adolf von Thadden-Trieglaff.[72] 'The nobility should ennoble you', she wrote to the slum-dwellers; 'instead of landscape gardens filled with temples, grottoes and dancing springs [they should build] parks for the homeless, and their summer pleasure, the English cottage, they should turn into a German cabin in which German poverty might be relieved; the English lawn can be turned into fields for potatoes and bread. As a man of magnanimity, how could [a nobleman] resist?'[73]

Once big factories such as Borsig opened up in 1837–1838, conditions for these unskilled sweatshop workers began to improve. A toolmaker now received a weekly salary of 36–39 marks, while a tailor got only 12–15 and a weaver 7.50–12.[74] Borsig's locomotive works had became so successful with the beginnings of the railway boom in Prussia that, after a mere ten years on its Oranienburger Tor site, it was obliged to up sticks and move to Moabit, where the architect Johann Heinrich Strack built a fine set of buildings and a villa for the Borsigs.★[75] Johann Friedrich August Borsig was yet another Berliner from Breslau. He came to the capital at the age of nineteen and trained at Beuth's Königliches Gewerbe Institut before working as an engineer at Egell's Neue Berliner Eisengießerei. By 1837 he had already acquired the necessary land for his Borsig Werke in the Chausseestraße. He had begun to specialise in repairing the first imported locomotives on the Berlin–Potsdam line, 'thereby learning the strengths and weaknesses of the imported rolling stock'.[76]

Work was not restricted to trains. Borsig built the moorish pumphouse for Sanssouci in Potsdam, with its minaret, and the ironwork frames for the domes of both Schinkel's Nicolaikirche in Potsdam and Stüler's completion of the Berlin Schloss. Real wealth, however, came from railway engines. By the time he moved his works to Moabit, Borsig had already completed 119, 109 of them for Prussia. By 1854 that figure had risen to 500 and August Borsig had been honoured by the King, who made him a *Geheime Kommerzienrat* shortly before his death. The business was taken over by his son Albert.

In 1858 the firm celebrated its thousandth locomotive. The train was baptised 'Borussia' the 'Jubiläumslokomotive'. Borsig's 2,800 workers paraded with the engine all the way

---

★ It was decorated with wall paintings by Paul Meyerheim depicting the history of the locomotive. The last traces of the Villa Borsig disappeared after the end of World War II. The paintings are now in the Märkishes Museum.

to the Stettiner Bahnhof. The festive atmosphere briefly returned to Moabit with flags and gates of honour everywhere. A colossal bust of August Borsig was also unveiled. There was dancing and all manner of popular entertainments in the streets.

Albert Borsig died in 1878 and the business was inherited by his three sons, all minors. The third generation, a hard one for Borsig, proved the need to adapt in the face of competition. The economic depression at the end of the 1870s led to the nationalisation of the Prussian railway network. In 1874 181 locomotives were built, but in 1878 that number had dwindled to seventy-six.[77] In 1898 they moved to Tegel in the far north of Berlin with a new product range. The Borsigs themselves were now Prussian nobles with an estate at Groß Behnitz near Nauern, where groups of the oppositional Kreisauer Kreis met during the Second World War to discuss plans for the future non-Nazi Germany.[78] It is perhaps significant that the family, by now aristocratic, had washed their hands of the business. They sold out to Rheinmetal in 1933.[79]

By 1856 Borsig was exporting locomotives to England and Berlin was well on the way to becoming the biggest industrial town on the European continent. Electronics were a speciality, earning the city the nickname of 'Elektropolis'. Siemens was founded in 1847 and in 1866 electrodynamism was discovered there. In 1883 Walter Rathenau's father, Emil, started the AEG. Osram was another giant Berlin electrical concern. After iron and electrical works came the chemical industry. Schering began life in 1851. In 1873 came the Aktiengesellschaft für Anilinfabrikation, or AGFA.[80]

The British were still involved in some of the projects. Berlin's lighting was assured by Imperial Continental Gas, who built the gasometer in the Fichtestraße in Kreuzberg.[81] Also in Kreuzberg, Frau Jenny Treibel's politically ambitious husband has his textile factory in Fontane's novel of that name. Moabit and all points north, however, was still the area most densely covered by heavy industry. When Borsig left for Tegel, new factories were opened: Ludwig Loewe, which made machine tools, weapons and munitions, and AEG. The Westhafen, between Wedding and Charlottenburg, was the second-biggest inland port in Europe. It was also the scene of one of the last senseless acts of the senseless war. The harbour was defended by an Austrian SS detachment who proved worthy of the great faith Goebbels had placed in them as 'the last great reserve'. They blew up the Föhrer Brücke over the Schiffahrtskanal and the Putlitz Brücke over the railway lines. While they fought tooth and claw, the Russians were already dividing up stocks of potatoes and handing them out to the people in the goods station in Moabit. The Viennese SS men, however, would let no one approach the building. When women, children and old men went to them to ask for flour 'or a tin of marmalade at the very least', the SS shot into the crowd, killing a woman and her two children.[82]

Such scenes recalled the savagery of Berlin strikes in their heyday The working-class movement had its first successes in 1868. A strike at Borsig was called after a foreman by the name of Krall slapped a worker's face. Max Hirsch of the union demanded the dismissal of Krall. By the new year he was gone. The same year the carpenters went on strike for more money and fewer hours. Clara Zetkin, bringing news of the Russian Revolution in 1905, seems to have set off the 'Moabiter Unrest'. August Bebel led a series of demonstrations against the Prussian three-tier voting system which was heavily loaded in favour of the rich. He came up against the strong arm of the Police President Traugott von Jagow: 'The streets are there to serve traffic alone. Arms will be used to crush any resistance to state authority. I warn all those seeking to intervene.'[83]

The unrest turned to rioting when the police brought in strike-breakers to replace 141 workers at a coal merchant's. On 23 September the police stepped in after the workers began pelting the coal transports with stones. Only a hundred policemen faced a crowd of some 3,000, but by using their swords they managed to wound a large number of workers. As the riots continued, the police responded by closing the bars in the Beusselkietz. The workers directed their wrath at the landlords, beating up Oskar Rippberger, of the Patzenhofer Ausschank in the Beusselstraße, and demolishing the Helmkneipe. The Jews were also targeted: the stores of the Preuß Brothers and the offices of the fashion goods manufacturer Moses Raba in the Beusselstraße.[84]

The police became more and more savage in their attempts to gain the upper hand. As they closed the Beusselstraße no one was safe from their sabre strokes. The correspondent of the London *Daily News* was attacked, and a car containing four more investigative British journalists. The Reuters man was badly cut on the hand. Jagow informed German journalists in a light-hearted way, 'You might impress on your English colleagues that this accident should not be taken too tragically. They were, after all, wounds sustained on the field of battle.' Moabit continued to be live wire. In January 1918, when the army leadership was claiming that it was being 'stabbed in the back' by industrial unrest at home, a policeman was killed when metal-workers went on strike.[85]

A strike in time, it should not be forgotten, saved the infant Weimar Republic during the Kapp *Putsch*. This one great example of the strike as a political instrument was never satisfactorily repeated. There was no strike to resist the *Preußenschlag* of 20 July 1932, when the lawful Prussian government was scrapped. Nor was there any resistance to the Nazi *Machtergreifung*. On 14 February 1922 Döblin faced a major Berlin strike with sympathetic resignation. 'I am writing in an antediluvian manner', he told readers of the *Prager Tagblatt*; 'two candles stand before me. They are flickering away, producing a strange but not disagreeable light.' The railways had been out for three days; the electrical workers, twenty hours. There were no *Droschken* or cars on the roads. There was no domestic water, and around the fountains there were little pockets of women gathering water in pails. Döblin was on strike too: '... I am not rebelling. Heavy fighting has broken out between the workers and powerful industrial interests. I shan't go to the theatre this evening.'[86]

III

Slang is a common feature of the world's great cities; indeed, the possession of a private language, intentionally unintelligible to outsiders, is something of a *sine qua non*. London has its cockney; Paris, *Parigot*; Vienna, *Wienerisch*; the farmers of the Latium are at a loss to understand the language of the Roman; the denizens of New York State can rarely keep up with the new coinings minted in North America's largest city. Berlin developed a dialect of its own remarkably early on in its history, through the need to trade with more important cities in Saxony, but slang came later. It comes as no surprise that Berlin slang was first written down in the 1820s and 1830s: the precise time when industrialisation brought it to maturity.*

Even now the badge of the Berliner is the soft 'g'. In the 1840s, travellers arriving at the customs posts before the walls of the city would be asked, 'Ham se Jerste, Jrieß, Jraupen, Jrütze oder sonst wat zu verzollen?' ('Have you any barley, semolina, pearl barley, groats or anything else to declare?') Simple Berliners in the past had problems returning to the hard 'g' when they wanted to speak *Hochdeutsch*. Frederick the Great, who spoke French when he could, had only the vaguest notion of correct German. He is also believed to

---

* The first play in the Berlin dialect was Julius von Voß's *Der Stralauer Fischzug* of 1821.

have said that he was going out with the 'Gäger auf die Gacht' (for 'Jäger auf die Jagd' – hunters hunting).[87]

Another hallmark of the true Berliner was his inability to differentiate between the accusative and the dative. This was a legacy of *Plattdeutsch*, where no such sophistications occurred:

> Wat macht dat mir und mich für Müh!
> Up Plattdütsch segg ick slankweg mi!
>
> (Such a lot of fuss over *mir* and *mich*!
> In *Plattdeutsch* we just say me!)

The confusion over the correct use of *mich* and *mir* led Berliners to create a usage which was all their own. *Mich* was used whenever they wanted to put on airs of refinement, or give the impression of a higher education. One reliable observer stated that he knew Berliners who used *mir* during the week, and *mich* on Sundays. NCOs added to the debate, telling their recruits, 'When you are on parade you say *mich* always. When you are off duty you can say *mir* as much as you please.' Berlin children got round the term by reverting to a *Plattdeutsch* all-purpose *ma*: 'Jib ma Jeld' ('Give me money'); 'Laß ma doch in Ruhe!' ('Leave me alone!')[88]

Berlin slang had its inventive side. From *Wurst* came *Wurscht*, a term to denote both the sausage and indifference: *det is' mir Wurscht* ('I don't care'). Bismarck himself is supposed to have developed the word further into an abstract noun meaning indifference: *Wurstigkeit*. Eloesser remembers his schoolfriends rounding on excessive supposition with the phrase 'Wenn meine Tante vier Räder hätte, so wäre sie ein Omnibus' ('If my aunt had four wheels she'd be an omnibus'), a variation on the rather coarser French phrase: 'Si ma tante en avait elle serait mon oncle'.[89]

It was Adolf Glaßbrenner, or 'Brennglas', as he called himself, who first established the respectability of Berlin's language in his sketches *Berlin wie es ist – und trinkt* (The Real Berlin, and *How* It Drinks!).* Glaßbrenner was born in Berlin in 1810 and trained as a journalist. At some stage he came into contact with the work of Louis Sébastien Mercier and his *Tableau de Paris*, which had been inspired, in turn, by the low-life cravings of Rétif de La Bretonne. The title of Glaßbrenner's series was taken from a much more worthy piece of writing: C. von Kertbeny's *Berlin wie es ist* of 1831. Glaßbrenner, however, had a rather different idea. He wanted to amuse his readers with a group of stock characters such as the 'Eckensteher' (layabout) Nante, a 'Guckkästner', a farcical magic-lantern man, various serving wenches and fishwives and his most famous creation, the 'Weißbierphilister' (beer-swilling philistine), Herr Buffey.[90]

In Glaßbrenner's writings, each of these characters is imparted with his or her own brand of *Berlinisch* representing the variations existing between the worker, the *petit bourgeois* and so forth; he is not always accurate, as modern researchers have striven to demonstrate[91]: 'gs' were never softened on words like *fragen* and *sagen*. Glaßbrenner none the less manages to bring out the humour of Berlin slang, the self-mockery which highlighted both the city's provincialism, in the broad, European sense, and its lack of obvious cultural sophistication. Foreign words in particular were subjected to witty transformation: *guillotine*, for example, becomes *Julejottdiene*; *philosophie*, *Viehlosophie*; the German borrowing *kultiviert*, *coltiviert*; or *boulevard*, which is turned into *Bullewarze* at the hands of Glaßbrenner's Berliners.[92]

Naturally there are poorly concealed messages galore in Glaßbrenner's writings. He was a political liberal in the *Vormärz* period who agitated to see the promises made by Frederick William III in 1815 become reality. He wanted

---

* This title is untranslatable. It puns on the third person singular of the verb to eat, *ißt*, which is indistinguishable in sound from the third person singular of the verb to be, *ist*.

Prussia transformed into something more like Britain: a constitutional monarchy where citizens would no longer be hounded by an over-zealous police force. In almost all Glaßbrenner's sketches and plays there is a liberal who is there to put the country to rights. In *Herr Buffey auf der Berlin-Leipziger-Eisenbahn* it is Dr Zeisig: Zeisig is a perceptive observer when it comes to Berlin too:

> Berlin has expanded too quickly and is not capable of filling out its form. It strikes me like a man who has shot up and who doesn't know where to stop. Every day it is more like Paris and London all wrapped up together, yet the German philistine still oozes out of its buttonholes. It possesses the seeds of greatness, of the highest capabilities, yet it is unable to control itself, to round itself off . . .

Zeisig turns his attention from the city to the citizens:

> The Berliner can often touch a raw nerve through his sarcasm and ambition, but he is fundamentally open and honest and he is always willing and capable of coming together and being German, or, in the further sense, cosmopolitan.[93]

In *Nante Nantino, der letzte Sonnenbruder*, the layabout Nante has a more earthy interpretation of the nature of his city:

> Berlin has seven elements. The tea element, which is to be found in the novels of Frau von Paalzow* and even elsewhere; the white-beer element, office life and philistinism; the vinegar element, philosophy; the blood element, the better writers; the ink element, furious writing, education without intellect or talent;

* Henrietta von Paalzow (1788–1847), historical novelist and author of *Godwie Castle, aus den Papieren der Herzogin von Nottingham*, 1836.

the milk element, gentle Berlin womenfolk; and
finally the spirit element: me![94]

Nante and his idle friends begin their days deep in schnapps
and end them in torrents of quaint abuse (*Schafskopp!*
(Muttonhead!), *Theekessel!* (Teapot!) and punch-ups. Nante
finds his female companions among the hawker-women,
servants, fishwives and market-sellers whose *Platt* even Glaßbrenner feels the need to footnote.

Buffey, Nante's *petit bourgeois* counterpart, first appeared in
the sketch *Die Schnapsläden* of 1835. Elsewhere he is
described as 'a proper Berlin citizen of modest education,
but one with a good head for all that'.[95] Buffey and his
cronies flash French words around as much as possible to
impress others with their sophistication. 'Sau Terne' wine
developes a porky note in their mouths; why say *Flasche*
when you can use *Putelje* for bottle; in matters of the heart
it is smarter to be *Schalu* than plain German *eifersüchtig*.
Glaßbrenner represents a blend of humour and social com-
mentary that remained a tradition in Berlin at least until the
Third Reich. Grosz was the most extreme example. Not for
nothing was Theodor Hosemann the author of the frontis-
pieces of many of Glaßbrenner's writings. Hosemann was
Zille's teacher. Without Zille there would have been no
Grosz.

The repartee of the Berlin street urchin is his *Schnauze*: a
good-humoured rudeness which often takes visitors by surprise. Ernst Dronke was quite taken aback by the manners
of *hoi polloi*: 'Berlin street Arabs are the cheekiest and most
badly brought-up in all Germany.'[96] He had fared no better
with the fishwives. They ' . . . often sink into the most
flawless coarseness and crudity and I advise no man to crack
a joke with these women'.[97]

The style naturally had its devotees, most of whom were
Berliners. Much of it is funny, but difficult to render into
English. The Berlin humour has a pronounced macabre side

to it: large shoes are *Kindersärge*, children's coffins; a hat, a *Lausekaserne*, or barracks for lice; a bed, a *Flohkiste*, or flea-chest. The poverty of the workers and the very modest salaries of officials are reflected in expressions such as *Beamtenlachs* (civil servants' salmon) for a herring. Mild racialism is expressed in the pet name for the bus which runs between the Kurfürstendamm and the Opera: the *Palastina-Expresszug*, or Palestine Express. For similar reasons the fast train to Zehlendorf and Wannsee was called the 'Jerusalem Train'.[98]

Many of the favourite expressions referred to food and drink. The white beer of the Berliners with its dash of syrup became a 'dolled-up Laura'; the classic Berlin snack of herring and fried potatoes, a submarine with hand-grenades; oysters, horses' eyes in aspic. Like Fontane, some commentators believed that Frederick the Great initiated this brand of humour. His was certainly wry. Once he received a petition from two officials' wives who wanted to know which of them had precedence at court. 'The most idiotic goes first,' was his laconic reply.[99]

Prussia's misunderstood monarch Frederick William IV was another king with a celebrated sense of humour. During his reign, *Berlinisch* became presentable at court.[100] He enjoyed a joke, and recounted the latest Berlin gags to his brother-in-law, the Czar. Once again the style was down-to-earth; a sausage manufacturer who has sent him some of his best creations was rewarded with a silver snuff box in the shape of a sausage. Herr von Nagler, a senior postmaster, arrived at court covered in medals, only to be greeted by his king with the quip 'My God! What bronze foundry have you sprung from?'[101] But if Frederick William was not embarrassed to utter something of the same direct language of the ordinary Berliners, his most senior general and, later, field marshal, Friedrich Heinrich Ernst Graf von Wrangel, was positively coarse. Once when he was mounting the staircase to the marble hall of the Schloss in the company of one of the princesses, he let fly a noisy fart. The princess was outraged: 'But, Excellency, nothing like this has ever happened to me!' Wrangel replied in his raw *Berlinisch*: 'Ach, ick dachte det wär' *mir* passiert' ('Oh, but I thought it had happened to *me*').[102]

It was Frederick William IV who instituted the civil chapter of the order *pour le mérite*, a gesture which demonstrated both the king's love of the arts and his disinclination towards the traditional pursuits of the Hohenzollerns. One of the first to receive the order was the sculptor Gottfried Schadow, the possessor of another celebrated sense of humour. Schadow showed himself little impressed by this token from the king:

'But, Your Majesty, what would I want with medals?'

'But, my dear Schadow . . .'

'Jut, jut, jut, I'll take it, but on one condition, Your Majesty: that when I die, my son Wilhelm must get it.'

And this, according to Fontane, is precisely what happened.[103]

The neo-classical sculptor Schadow must have found it difficult to reconcile his sense of humour with the formalism of his compositions. But there is plenty of *Berolinismus* in his sketches and etchings: Schiller with his big nose; or the patriotic philosopher Fichte cutting a somewhat ridiculous image with his heavy sabre. *Publikum auf der Kunstausstellung* ('The public at an art exhibition') is another example of Schadow's satirical skill, doubtless derived from the English caricaturists. The best of all is the *Déjeuner à la fourchette* of 1813, where a group of mangy French soldiers are cooking their lunch: puppies impaled on bayonets over a campfire. Others are roasting rats suspended from their carbines by their tails, while two elegant soldiers are hacking up a horse. Another appears to be eating his map.[104]

Not since Schlüter had Berlin played host to a sculptor of Schadow's talent, but when he died aged eighty-six in 1850 his fame had already been eclipsed by Christian Daniel Rauch. As he himself put it, his fame 'went up in smoke

[German *Rauch*]'. Schadow seems to have initiated a characteristic strain of Berlin artists notable for their earthy good humour. Adolf Menzel was another; so was Max Liebermann. The most famous of all, of course, was Heinrich Zille.

Liebermann had joined in the chorus of disgust that went up at the laying out of the 'Puppen-Allee', where the Kaiser sought to glorify his race with a collection of white marble statues stretching out to the crack of doom. 'Ick koof mir noch 'ne Schneebrille' ('I'll buy myself another pair of snow goggles'), said Liebermann.[105] Zille went one better and actually posed as a model for the sculptor August Kraus, who had been commissioned to do the Ritter Plotho. The similarity of Plotho to Zille gave rise to a persistent rumour that Zille was an illegitimate Hohenzollern. The Berliners naturally had a field day when it came to jokes about the statuary, a game which had been rendered all the more delightful by the high-seriousness with which the Kaiser had undertaken the project, going so far as to pose for Joseph Uphues' portrait of Frederick the Great. The citizens called it the 'knick-knack alley', the 'cadaver alley' or the 'sea of Marmora' (*Marmor* is marble in German). The Elector Otto 'the Idle' Wittelsbach caused great mirth. Berliners recounted that he slept on a park bench at night. A Munich paper took offence at this slight directed at their ruling house, insisting that the 'dumb expression' on the Elector's face was nothing less than Prussian perfidy. 'If Otto had really looked so brainless, it can only have been as a result of his long sojourn in north Germany.'[106]

Zille was actually a Saxon, but then there was never any accepted geographical limitation to the term 'Berliner' any more than there is for the Parisian. Long residence is deemed enough.[107] The Zille family decamped to Berlin when the boy was nine. They lived in a shabby flat near the Schlesische Bahnhof, known as the 'Catholic Station' because the trains shunted off towards Silesia and Poland. Zille studied at the Academy under Hosemann (who had been a pupil of

Schadow's), but he became an industrial lithographer, and didn't sell his first picture until he was forty-seven. Later the buyer returned and demanded his 37 RMs back.[108]

Of all the artists who have portrayed the Berliners it is Zille who has done so with the greatest affection. He delighted in their coarseness and vulgarity, their fondness for the gaudiest colours and fabrics. Every now and then in the few really working-class districts of Berlin, or on the *U-Bahn* travelling south from Wedding, a visitor to the city falls upon a group of Zille characters. They wear multicoloured shell-suits these days, but they are unquestionably the same people; a living testament to an astonishing continuity against all odds.

Zille actually subsidised his subjects, giving away almost all his money to the poor.[109] Every Berlin beggar seemed to know the way to his door in Charlottenburg. Zille's son remembered the usual sob-stories:

'If you don't give me something, Meister Zille, I'll hang myself in front of your door.'

'*Na*, then just wait here a bit. I'll go off and fetch the rope.'[110]

One picture seems to typify Zille's love of the Berlin worker. A poor woman is sitting on a park bench: 'So, ick setze mir'n bisken. Det mein Olle mal wat uff die Bank hat!' ('I'll just sit down here for a mo'. Then my old man will also have something in the bank!' *Bank* also translates as 'on the bench'.)

The nationalist bigot Friedrich Ludwig Jahn was keen to adapt the language of young Berliners as he put his boys through their paces up on the Hasenheide in 1811. Jahn was a teacher at the Graue Kloster. Together with his friend Friedrich Friesen from the Plamann Institute, he encouraged boys to use their free afternoons and holidays to work out on the heath between Kreuzberg and what later was to become Neukölln. After their drill and physical jerks the boys were given a spartan snack of bread and water, or occasionally potatoes with salt and a sip of beer. Berlin was still occupied by the French and the object of the exercise was not only to toughen up German manhood, but also to encourage the boys to hate the Gauls and all they stood for. Like Goebbels later, Jahn was also keen on purging the language of its French words: *Deutsch* was weedy, *Teutsch* was brave; 'Wälschen ist Fälschen' ('to speak foreign languages is to speak false'). In 1815 a society for the German language was set up to this end. French words were deemed particularly suspect: *Protokoll* was replaced by *Berichtbuch*, *Honorar* by *Ehrengeld*, *Redakteure* had to make way for *Druckordner*. Blücher made a mockery of the whole movement when he visited Jahn's *gymnopaedes* on the Hasenheide and greeted the new Spartans with a cheery '*Messieurs!*' and enquired after their 'Fatiguen'.

Jahn's equivalent in the Third Reich was Dr Goebbels, who, by excising so many non-German words from the language, rendered it so much the poorer, and hastened its descent into the ugly *Beamtendeutsch* or 'civil-servicespeak' of our own time. Goebbels' effect on German is not our concern: his purgings were not limited to *Berlinisch*, which had, of course, always been peppered with foreign words. *Berlinisch* was always a humorous language and, although there was less to joke about in the Nazi years, humour was not outlawed; it afforded Berliners the chance to debunk the high-mindedness of the self-righteous thugs and prudes who were running the country. Even before the Nazis came to power, the Reichstag sessions in which the Nazis and the Kozis had sought to sing proceedings to a standstill, with successive bursts of the *Horst-Wessel-Lied* and the *International*, had led the wags to dub the assembly 'the most expensive choral society in the world'.[111] During the war the jokes reflected a stubborn refusal to be taken in by Goebbels' propaganda machine: 'What is the difference between Germany and Russia?' they asked. 'It's colder in Russia.' Children altered the words of the *Horst-Wessel-Lied*:

Die Preise hoch, die Läden fast geschlossen,
Der Hunger naht dem deutschen Volk sich
  Schritt und Schritt,
Doch hungern nur die Volksgenossen,
Die Reichen hungern nur im Geiste mit!

(With prices up, our shops are in the doldrums,
Famine nears the German people with deadly stealth,
But only the poor comrades feel the symptoms,
In spirit only suffer those with wealth!)

To the hit-song *Es geht alles vorüber* new words were set:

Es geht alles vorüber, es geht alles vorbei,
Erst geht Hitler kopfüber und dann die Partei.[112]

(It's all nearly over, time is galloping by,
The old Party's over, but first, the head guy.)

Even in those times the Berliner's spirit was hard to repress, despite the machinery the state had at its disposal. One man remembers travelling on the bus to Adolf Hitler-Platz (the former Reichspräsidentenplatz, now Theodor Heuß-Platz) towards the end of the war. As the bus swung into the square the conductor shouted: 'Adolf Hitler platzt!' ('Adolf Hitler is going up in smoke!') At first he thought he had misheard. He took the same bus the next day and the conductor's words were exactly the same. 'He could have been hauled before the People's Court for far less.'[113]

The increasingly daring utterances of Berliners, Communists and others, were signs that the city was preparing itself to shake off the Nazi spectre. Slang was an important act of self-assertion. By the Second World War the kit was complete; the Berliner had been moulded from the different regional and national groups who had made their homes within its grey walls. Wartime destruction and the four-power occupation after 1945 meant that many fled. The true Berliner has become something of a collector's item.

IV

Berlin has always included a substantial criminal element, with two possible exceptions: during the Third Reich the police had a tendency to shoot criminals 'trying to escape' from concentration camps, which discouraged crime to some extent; and during the period of the divided city. In the DDR half of Berlin draconian punishments made crime unattractive to all but the state. In the west the problems of getting out of the city with the loot or escaping the scene of the crime made most potential criminals think twice. The IRA failed to act against the British garrison in Berlin for this precise reason.[114] Since the reunification Berlin has returned to normality. The days of trust are over.

Early Berlin's most famous reprobate was Hans Kohlhase, who became the hero of Heinrich von Kleist's novella *Michael Kohlhaas*, about a sixteenth-century horse-dealer who is robbed by an overmighty Saxon Junker and takes his just retribution a mite too far: he puts Leipzig to the torch. As he refuses to see reason he is later executed on orders of the Margrave of Brandenburg. The real Kohlhase was a merchant in Cölln who sold herrings and honey. As he crossed the border into Saxony the Junker Günther von Zaschwitz purloined his best horses. When he got the horses back on his return to Brandenburg one promptly turned up its hoofs. Kohlhase demanded satisfaction from Zaschwitz. When by 1534 he had received no such thing, he threw down the gauntlet, declaring war not only on the Junker von Zaschwitz, but the whole of Saxony.[115]

As in Kleist's story, Kohlhase had nothing more to lose, and his honour to regain. Zaschwitz and the Saxons, he declared, he would 'lame in hand and foot, also rob, put to the flame, and abduct and hold prisoner until such time as Günther von Zaschwitz makes good the damages...' Kohlhase's vengeance was indeed terrible, as in Kleist's account. Luther, called in to mediate, could do nothing to control him. The Kurfürsten Joachim I and Joachim II of Brandenburg stood by. Relations were not good with the court in Dresden. Kohlhase, however, overstepped the mark. He attacked a silver transport in Stolp (now Kohlhasenbrück on the Griebnitzsee), thereby touching the Elector in his most sensitive place. The Elector had Kohlhase lured to Berlin, where he was broken on the wheel.[116]

As Berlin metamorphosed into an industrial *Großstadt*, crime began to be associated with the conditions of the working class. Dronke recorded around 1,000 people arrested and taken to the Stadtvogtei in 1845: 97 cases of theft; eight of fraud; one of sexual delinquency; 150 of loitering; 183 of vagrancy; 60 of begging; and 500 of pure poverty.[117] There was a tendency to exaggerate the mitigating circumstances surrounding petty crime, even in those days. Berlin's most famous rogue, Wilhelm Voigt, doubtless had a rough deal in life, but he was no spring lamb. His feat, as an ageing, unemployed cobbler, was to dress up as a Prussian officer and rob the town hall in Köpenick. The ensuing court case made a laughing-stock of Prussia, which was shown as a country where the military could behave according to whim.[118]

Since the days of the Soldier-King it had been respectable to wear uniform in Prussia. The blue *Waffenrock* was the badge of the old warrior, and one of the few tangible rewards for having served in the colours. After the First World War many of the returning soldiers were slow to change into mufti. In the revolutionary days following defeat there were a number of *Köpenickiaden* perpetrated by men in uniform.[119]

Eighty years before, Police Commissioner Stieber was, by his own account, the scourge of Berlin's criminal confraternity. He was particularly vigilant when it came to his king, whom he believed he had rescued in the dark days of 1848 when a crowd had approached him on his horse. It turned out to be a double, but Stieber was rewarded with the job of chief of the criminal police. When a monolingual

Greek defrauded Frederick William IV to the tune of 5,000 *thalers* for a forged ancient Greek manuscript, Stieber managed to find a half-blind, half-deaf magician and fire-eater aged eighty to interview the culprit. When Stieber had got what he wanted from him he had the Greek locked up in a dark cell.[120]

Crime reached its apogee in Berlin the *Weltstadt*. The *Ringvereine* went back to the body-building days of the 1890s. Working-class men in the building trade met to box and formed themselves into gangs. After a while these turned into protection rackets, with the *Ringvereine* increasingly a law unto themselves. They had their own season, with balls at which the crooks donned white tie and tails. Famous criminal lawyers came as their guests on these occasions, and were not frightened to be associated with these gangland figures. In January 1929 open warfare broke out between two gangs and the largely impotent police put one leader, 'Muskel-Adolf', on trial. The case proved a farce. The Nazis were far more successful in dealing with the thugs, who in many ways resembled their own wild SA members. They banned the *Ringvereine* and arrested their leaders.[121]

The twenties were the golden age of Berlin crime. With inflation and the uncertainties that followed defeat there were plenty of opportunities for sharp practice of all sorts. In Max Klante Berlin had its Robert Maxwell, whose fortunes swelled like an enormous bubble and burst, ruining thousands. Russians were prominent in the confidence-trick business, chiefly speculating in currency.[122] Karl Friedrich Bernotat was a crook of the Raffles type, apparently a gent. Like so many of the underworld stars of the twenties, he was shot 'trying to escape', when the Nazis came to power. A similar end awaited the Saß brothers, safe-crackers, whose apartment still stands, Birkenstraße 57, four flights up at the back. The police found it hard to make their case against the Saß brothers stick after a spectacular bank job where they had dug a tunnel from a local cemetery. The brothers celebrated their release with a slap-up dinner at Horchers.[123] The Nazis had less respect for the niceties of law. The Saß brothers fled to Denmark, even going so far as to pretend to be communists in order to avoid deportation to Germany once they were apprehended by the Danish police. The Danes handed them over.

The most famous crooks of Weimar Berlin were the Sklarek brothers. The Sklareks were Jews from the Russian part of Poland, with offices in the Kommandantenstraße by the Spittelmarkt. In 1926 they bought from the city the Kleider Vertriebs Gesellschaft (KVG), a clothing company which supplied the city's hospitals, police force and fire-brigade. The *Bürgermeister*, Böß, told the councils that from now on they were to get all their requirements from the Sklareks.[124]

The Sklareks themselves began to live well. They had a villa in the Ahornalle in Westend and a hunting lodge in Mecklenburg; big names came to their parties.[125] They became a prominent feature at the races, horses from their stables competing in the Derby, Union and St Leger.[126] In 1928, Leo Sklarek's horse won the German Derby.[127]

The dream came to an end in September 1929 when the Sklareks were arrested for receiving stolen goods. As they sat in police custody, the police uncovered a massive credit scandal implicating a number of highly placed civic officials. Berlin became 'Sklarekstadt'. The most important name brought up in the investigation was Böß, who had accepted a fur jacket for his wife from the Sklareks. Böß wanted to pay for the jacket and repeatedly asked for a bill. When it finally arrived it was for the paltry sum of 375 marks (the jacket was worth 4,950 marks). Although Böß was clearly ill-informed as to the real prices of such luxuries, he knew that the sum was too little. He sent the Sklareks a further 1,000 marks in order to buy a picture for the city, a canvas by the Expressionist painter Max Pechstein.[128] Böß had had no idea that he was digging his own professional grave. Other city politicians were less naïve. The communists Gäbel and Degner, who could offer the Sklareks lucrative contracts in schools and hospitals, received their kickbacks in special bank accounts, and drove around Berlin in flashy cars which were presents from the textile traders.

Böß was in America when the scandal broke. He was on a goodwill tour, drumming up support for Germany over the Reparations issue. He failed to understand the gravity of the situation. In Germany the press was baying for his blood. In the cabarets a new version of *Schöner Gigolo* was all the rage:

> Bürgermeister Böß, Bürgermeister Böß,
> Denkst Du noch der Zeiten,
> Wo Du einst in Amt,
> Gingst in Seid und Samt,
> Könntest Deutschlands Hauptstadt leiten?
> Stellung ist passé,
> Sklarek sagt ade,
> Schöner Pelz, Du gingst in Fransen!
> Und nun zahlen wir zum Hohn,
> Dir 'ne riesige Pension.
> Geh' und schnür den Ranzen![129]

> (Bürgermeister Böß, Bürgermeister Böß,
> Ever think of the time when
> Once you had some loot,
> Wore a silken suit,
> Ruled the city like a king, then.
> Now you've scarce a dime.
> Sklarek's doing time.
> Lovely fur you're wearing thin now.
> And we pay out to our shame,
> A huge pension all the same.
> Go, and keep your head down!)

Böß continued his tour, failing to reappear in Germany to answer the accusations levelled at him by the boulevard press. On his return he was appalled to see the crowds waiting for him with fists clenched and to hear cries of 'Trafficker!', 'Crook!', 'Rogue!', 'Scum!', 'Jew-lover!', 'Beat him to death!' When he reached Berlin he was suspended awaiting disciplinary proceedings. He was sent to court, but there was no evidence to convict him of corruption. Later the Nazis tried him again, but again the case fell through. Böß had to pay a month's wages in fines and was forced into retirement. He died in 1946.[130]

Not only individuals steal things; states do too. In the Seven Years War the Austrians had been content to break as much as they could find. Napoleon's armies were out for plunder. Dominique Denon was the Göring of his day. As the general inspector of Napoleon's museums he seized on 116 paintings, 32 antique statues, 74 antique busts, 10 bas-reliefs, 183 bronzes, 538 carved stones, 7,262 medallions and coins, 22 West Indian curiosities which had been brought back from the Antilles by Alexander von Humboldt, 25 ivories and 23 pieces of amber. The cache filled two ships. They also lifted Schadow's Quadriga from the Brandenburg Gate. Napoleon himself quietly pocketed Frederick the Great's sword.[131]

From their arrival in Berlin in April 1945 to May 1946, the Russians managed to effect 'the most gigantic abduction of cultural property in history'.[132] A total of over two and a half million works of art, books and archives disappeared into the Soviet Union, most of them never to re-emerge. It was a well-planned operation which involved a close co-operation between the military and the Russian museums. Its origins went back to the time of the German invasion of Soviet Russia in 1941, when the Nazi authorities had sanc-tioned the theft and destruction of large numbers of Russian works of art. A special museum was designed but never built; in scale it dwarfed by far Hitler's megalomaniac ideas for his own art gallery in the new Reich's capital in Linz.[133]

Berlin was ill-prepared. Some of the city's collections had been lodged elsewhere, away from the bombs. In some cases these were found by the Anglo-Americans, who, eventually, gave them back to the West German state.[134] In theory Schliemann's famous hoard of gold from Mycenae should have left the city, but the curator in charge, Dr Wilhelm Unverzagt, decided not to risk it, and housed it in the Flakturm Zoo instead. Much of the rest was placed in the great air-raid shelter tower in Friedrichshain, the Reichsbank, the Preußische Staatsbank, and the Mint. In the latter, large quantities of KPM porcelain were destroyed when the British scored a direct hit on the building on the night of 10–11 March 1945.[135]

Much was damaged or destroyed in the fighting as the Red Army took the city. The tower in Friedrichshain was hit by artillery shells; what was left in the Mint, undamaged after the British bomb, was shattered when Russian soldiers lobbed grenades into the vaults. In hand-to-hand fighting in the Schloss, the Erasmuskapelle and the circular study of Frederick the Great were ruined.[136] The worst tragedy occurred after the fighting was over, when a fire broke out in the Friedrichshain Tower and destroyed 400 priceless canvases including works by Rubens and Donatello, 50 Italian Renaissance sculptures and some of the most famous paintings by Menzel. It is believed that his Sanssouci *Tafelrunde* perished in the blaze. The Russians later blamed the Germans for the fire, but it is just as likely that it was caused by clumsy Soviet soldiers.[137] Other objects were simply wantonly destroyed, such as the Wilhelm von Humboldt archives, and the ancient weaponry in the Zeughaus.

There is still speculation about the Friedrichshain fire. Some believe that a part of the collection was saved. One work by Dierick Bouts, which had been in the tower, was found hanging in a shady antique shop just after the war. Other objects unconnected with Friedrichshain mysteriously reappeared too. For example, the Kadolzburg Altar from the Erasmuskapelle was found in a village in East Germany. The

Russians who were stealing it had simply dropped it and an old lady had taken it into her house.[138]

The robbery was accorded top priority and soldiers were released from their usual activities to ensure that the bulk of the art works were shipped out before the Western Allies made their entry into the city. The Pergamon Altar was stolen from under the noses of the British. It was in the Flakturm Zoo, which was in the British sector, but the Russians managed to distract the British military for long enough to get the precious stones out and off to Moscow.[139] The Altar eventually returned to Berlin as a gesture of goodwill towards the SED, but most of the rest remains. At the time of writing, both sides have drawn up lists of works missing from pre-war collections, but the chances of seeing a wholesale redelivery of Berlin's collections remain slim.

As the Russians were busy packing up the contents of Berlin's museums, the city enjoyed its first important court case of the post-Nazi years. Helene Schwärzel had been apprehended by the policeman 'Jean Blomé' in a house on the Wittenauer Damm in Tegel. She was the East Prussian woman who had recognised and denounced Carl Goerdeler in Marienwerder. The former Mayor of Leipzig had fled following the 20 July plot and the Nazis had put a bounty of a million marks on his head. Helene Schwärzel had spent very little of the money, placing most of it in the bank, where it was promptly devalued at the end of the war. Her arrest prompted an orgy of self-righteous hypocrisy.

Helene turned out to be a pitiful ageing spinster who had formerly been in awe of the politician she had once or twice spotted with his family in the East Prussian seaside resort of Rauschen. *Der Morgen* described her as 'mouse-like' once it had spent its fury on the 'millionaire' and her Judas bounty. Her one friend from home, Elizabeth B., couldn't wait to denounce her as she had Goerdeler. Indeed, there was little about the trial when it came before the court in Moabit that was not fishy. 'Blomé' turned out to be Hans Blume, who had been employed by the police after he had said that he was a former Communist party member who had done time in a concentration camp, and who had been in the force before 1933. The real Hans Blume was a former pimp who had been sent to Buchenwald for fraud, and who had acted as a spy for the camp guards while he was there. In the meantime the poor woman was going mad, and seeing visions of the hanged Carl Goerdeler in her cell.[140]

The Allies kept their distance, only moving in to break Helene's sentence when it was imposed. In 1946 each occupying power acted by its own laws within its own sectors. The French ran Tegel. When Proclamation No. 3 was brought into power on 30 October 1945, it reiterated the judicial principle *nullum crimen sine lege*, something notably (but perhaps understandably) absent from the proceedings at Nuremberg. Helene Schwärzel's case opened on 14 November 1946. Sixty places were allotted to the press for the show trial.[141]

Morality has never been Berlin's strong suit either. Not for nothing, perhaps, did Casanova consider making the city his permanent residence. The great lover arrived in the summer of 1764 and stopped at the hotel 'Stadt Paris'. He had better luck than Boswell, who was there at precisely the same time, and met Frederick the Great twice. Frederick considered appointing Casanova to the staff of his new Académie des nobles and entrusting the education of Prussian youth to the hyperactive Italian. Casanova was, however, discouraged when he witnessed the king bawling out an instructor because a cadet in his charge had failed to empty his chamber-pot.[142]

The Austrian author Johann Friedel sent up contemporary Berlin morals in his scurrilous book, *Briefe über die Galanterien von Berlin*, although this may have been mere revenge for a Prussian account of the loose mores of the Viennese. There is, none the less, a certain consensus on this matter. Boswell, for example, consoled himself for his failure to meet the king by leaping on a soldier's wife who had come to sell him chocolate. The fact that she was pregnant didn't deter him for one moment: 'To bed directly. In a moment – over... I sent her off. Bless me, have I committed adultery? Stay, a soldier's wife is no wife.' In 1772 the British consul expressed his disgust when he said: 'Berlin is a city which boasts neither honest man nor chaste woman.'[143]

From Dronke's account there had been no change by the 1840s. After the briefest acquaintance, girls from the middle class and *petite bourgeoisie* tended to move in with their lovers. Dronke calls them *grisettes*, after the French prototype. The lucky ones graduated to the position of 'kept woman'. Dronke was not overly impressed by the *Berlinerin* anyway: '... not particularly pretty, most of them have feet too big'. He thought them frivolous and too fond of life. Their husbands, however, were immune from jealousy. If Dronke was correct, such emotions would hardly have done them much good anyway.[144]

He probably was. 'It was no longer striking', he wrote, to see the poorest girls on the arms of the leaders of society.[145] He was virtually describing the plot of Fontane's novel *Stine* of 1890, where the Stine of the title becomes the sickly Graf Waldemar's mistress. When Waldemar gets it into his head to marry his *grisette* his relations gang up on him to prevent the match. Like much of Fontane, it prefigures E. M. Forster's 'Only connect'.[146] Dronke's fiction was not on the same level. In *Aus dem Volk* the *grisette* Alwine has recently become the lover of the Baron von Herzberg: '... he comforts all my moods, he buys me everything I want. He takes me everywhere, accompanies me to the theatre and once a week to a get-together of his friends where we drink champagne and eat wonderful things.'[147]

While Alwine's poor seamstress friend, Marie, drinks her frugal glass of milk, Alwine lies all morning on her *chaise longue*, reading a novel. Here she is visited by Marie's friend Paul, a worker who is really a baron, but who never finds out the truth. 'Would you like a cup of chocolate?' she asks him. 'Or would you prefer a liqueur? Or a glass of anisette?'[148] Elsewhere Dronke tells us that champagne was more in vogue.[149] Girls didn't become *grisettes* for the money, but simply from a desire to enjoy their lives while they had the chance. Often they began their careers as young as thirteen or fourteen, and as soon as the first lover was out of sight they made off with another.[150]

Stieber naturally also knew a thing or two about the *louche* side of Berlin life. When one Charlotte von Hagen came to see him to complain about the infidelities of her husband, Herr von Oven, the Police Commissioner agreed to help her find the information necessary for the divorce courts. This was the Hinckeldey era, when the police were to some degree at war with the upper classes. Stieber was possibly keen to help Frau von Hagen for that reason. When the police sleuth started working on the case, he discovered that Oven was making frequent calls on a Frau von T. and that other guests were 'very young girls', who left deep in the night. From these facts Stieber deduced the house was being used for immoral purposes.[151]

Stieber waited for his moment. One night a large number of upper-class men turned up together with a similar quantity of girls. Plain-clothes men surrounded the house. Stieber rang the bell. 'Without a care, gaily warbling, her complete nakedness only unsatisfactorily covered by a kimono, Frau von T. opened the door with a candle in her hand.' She expected a late arrival, 'but suddenly there stood before her dreaded myrmidons of the police'. As she stepped back in horror, in walked Stieber and his men. 'Here sat or lay lost in the most shameless play, and "clothed" only in black masks, several high-ranking civil servants in close embrace with the equally undressed girls. With wild cries they ran this way and that . . .' Two men even managed to leap out of the window in their 'Adam suits', only to be apprehended by Stieber's men as they landed.[152]

Stieber was not interested in this bare fry. He wanted
Oven. He promised not to arrest the men and allowed them
to dress. Then the bell rang. 'Tilly' (the *Madame*) went to
answer it: it was Oven. Charlotte von Hagen obtained her
decree, and Stieber acquired valuable information on the
aristocratic brothel-keepers of Berlin. One other thing he
discovered (which seems slightly far-fetched) was that many
of the girls, by dint of their frequent close contact with
high-ranking civil servants and 'Gelehrten', had managed to
acquire an impressive education: the whores spoke Latin in
nineteenth-century Berlin. They could 'roll off a verse of
Virgil or Horace and master an entire index of judicial or
military terminology, and I found to my horror that they
were utterly made for espionage'.[153]

Stieber displayed little hypocrisy as far as prostitution was
concerned, in that he seems to have been a typical Berliner.
He even made a special study of the subject which he published in the 1840s,[154] complete with a bibiography of
important 'scientific' books on the subject. The chief inspiration, however, seems to have been Parent-Duchâtelet's *Sur
la Prostitution dans la ville de Paris*. Stieber's book is enriched
by a healthy dollop of national prejudice: in London, where
brothels were illegal, there were '90,000' prostitutes, and
'nowhere was it more horrible, revolting and bestial'. Vienna
was, of course, the most whore-infested city in the German-
speaking world; the larger half of the female population,
Stieber contended, was on the game. His source for this,
however, seems far from trustworthy: *Die Galanterien Wiens
auf eine Reise gesammelt und in Briefen geschildert von einem
Berliner* was almost certainly as worthless as the similar-
sounding book on Berlin (see above, p. 220). On other
German cities Stieber was both better informed and more
objective: Hamburg's sailors created an obvious demand;
there were just three brothels in Prussian Königsberg. There
must be a great many more in the Russian city of Kaliningrad
which now occupies the site.[155]

Stieber undertakes a small history of prostitution in Berlin, which must be to some extent speculative, given that, by his own admission, there were no police records kept before 1790. Pimping was severely punished in the Middle Ages. One Jesmann who put his wife and daughter out to work in 1390 was burned at the stake. In the seventeenth century marital infidelity merited draconian punishments such as hanging in cages and beating, yet *maisons closes* existed from the earliest times. The robber-baron Dietrich von Quitzow was allowed to choose from pictures of the city's whores in 1410, who apparently resided in a house maintained for that purpose and which paid the state for the privilege. The denizens of such broad-minded institutions had to go veiled in the fifteenth and sixteenth centuries. In 1580 the public executioner beat a drum to drive out bad whores from their lodgings in the 'Hurengasse' (the present Rosenstraße by the Hackescher Markt).[156]

Prostitution naturally blossomed during the Thirty Years War and with the installation of Berlin's first permanent garrison by the Great Elector. The number of prostitutes had become so large by 1690 that they were rounded up and put into the prison and workhouse in Spandau. Eight years later the Elector shut down the *maisons closes* in the Dorotheen-stadt, but such measures were doomed to failure in a city where so many inhabitants were squaddies. In 1717 a report decided that most of the prostitutes were actually the children of members of the garrison. In 1780 Berlin contained a hundred whore-houses, with an average staff of eight. Visitors could choose between three categories. Sailors from Hamburg and Amsterdam, it transpired, preferred the *bourgeoise* image; ordinary artisans, painted ladies.[157]

Another ruse was the bath-house in the Krögel. This was the favourite resort of the richer and grander Berliner, who went to share a bath with the woman of his choice. Berlin's first *Bordell Reglement* operated from 1700 to 1792. It was strikingly liberal. Article 1 recognised the brothel as 'a necessary evil'. Whores had to register for the quarter with the commissioner, who limited their numbers. New applicants would only find a position when one fell vacant. In order to preserve the customers' health (the document uses the quaint term 'Schwärmer', or 'enthusiast') prostitutes were required to submit to an examination by a *chirurgus forensis* for which they paid the fixed sum of two *Groschen*. No whore was allowed to work when ill. If a customer was infected with a venereal disease the brothel-keeper was obliged to pay for his treatment. If the whore was deemed incurable she was transferred to the Charité.[158]

The problem of venereal disease continued to obsess the far-sighted Berlin authorities. The new *Reglement*, of 1792, introduced a *Huren-Heilungs-Kasse* (Treatment Fund for Whores), to which prostitutes paid a small part of their earnings as insurance against treatment for disease. The new code was based on a report by Police Director von Eisenstadt. Eisenstadt reiterated the official view that brothels were 'sadly a necessary evil', particularly for the young, who were not yet in a position to marry but whose 'reproductive instinct rages most powerfully'. The new code, however, came down hard on anyone found guilty of leading women astray: a year in prison for the first offence; beating (*Staubbesen*), two years' imprisonment and expulsion from Berlin for the second. Any diseased whore who carried on her business was also threatened with three months behind bars as well as paying the costs of treatment for her victims.[159]

The 1792 rules added substantially to the existing body of law. No prostitute could be kept in a brothel without her permission, even if she were in debt to the management; there was to be no dragging of customers in from the streets by 'signs and signals'; there were to be no 'intoxicating drinks' served; they had to close their doors at midnight; the code was to be distributed to each working whore along with information on venereal disease; no brothels were allowed on the main thoroughfares; street-walkers (*Winkelhuren*) were not permitted.[160]

Berlin then numbered some 150,000 inhabitants. Registered prostitutes fluctuated between 311 and 249, according to monthly figures; in 1795 they were portioned out into fifty-four brothels. The best of these were in the Friedrichstadt. Most of the girls came from the smaller Prussian towns and cities: Stettin, Frankfurt an der Oder, Potsdam, Magdeburg, Neustadt, Havelberg and Prenzlau. This modest, state-approved and controlled vice ring was upset by the arrival of the French in 1806. Not only did numbers of prostitutes increase, but so did the incidence of venereal disease. General Wrede was moved to complain that all his troops were infected with syphilis; a subsequent examination revealed 200 cases, of which twenty were declared incurable.[161]

With the French in residence, attempts to keep whores off the streets proved vain. Girls as young as twelve or thirteen were offering themselves to the French army of occupation, and even French officers began to complain that their men were debilitated by syphilis. The city authorities were moved to round up 490 street-walkers. Twelve per cent were infected. In the Prussian infantry a further 142 cases of syphilis were discovered. The epidemic began to influence the way the city fathers looked at prostitution. The new council decided that it was no longer a necessary evil but a '*Schandfleck*', or disgrace to the state. In 1809 Graf Dohna suggested that all brothels (including the one remaining first-class establishment, Bernhardt's, at Friedrichstraße 64) should be relocated to distant parts of the city, or the crummier parts of Cölln such as the Petristraße, the Friedrichsgracht or the Krausenstraße in the southern Friedrichstadt. No further licences were to be granted, in the hope that Berlin's brothel life would be stamped out before too long.[162]

The moral climate of Berlin was changing. The king was no longer the over-sexed Frederick William II, but his prudish, *bourgeois* son, Frederick William III. In 1828 the inhabitants of the Petristraße complained to the police about the brothels and asked to have them removed. In 1839 all thirty-three remaining institutions were shifted behind the Königsmauer by the Alexanderplatz. The number of establishments declined, but the tally of inmates increased. The problem with putting all the rotten eggs in one basket was that the Königsmauer became a red-light quarter. A local pastor described what it was like to officiate at a christening in the area:

> A christening or marriage in this circle is a veritable red-letter day. The pimps and whores turn up in magnificent coaches, wearing the most sumptuous costumes and with numerous attendants . . . The church fills up with all this depraved riff-raff . . . Hundreds of harlots and pimps whose serving girls hem in the pastor, laughing impishly at the reverent expression of the latter and openly mocking the lower church dignitaries . . . In this way, amid screams and shouts, mockery and derision, is the holy ceremony carried out.[163]

If Frederick William III had little time for the seedier side of his capital, the theocratic Frederick William IV had less. Moreover Berlin was undergoing a profound change to its nature with its transformation from a homely residence to a buzzing, smoky industrial town complete with armies of migrant workers who may have had to wait a while before they were joined by their wives; and who lacked friends or contacts in their new city. In April 1844, the Ministry of the Interior decided to abolish the brothels. Now brothel-keepers lost their rights to keep their houses open on the third infraction. There would be no new concessions. It was hoped that within a few years the evil would disappear. At the end of the year continued impatience with the situation led the government to decree immediate closure. The advantage of such institutions was 'illusory'; in official circles it was held to be a sophism to say that it protected society from greater evil.[164] The ban had little or no effect. It merely removed the modicum of legal protection offered to prostitute and client during the time when the trade had been tolerated.

The law was only enforced two years later, and then it turned out to be a wasted effort: the trade had moved on to the pavements or the new-wave dance halls modelled on the Kroll, where the whores were 'younger and prettier' and whence they could be taken off to some more discreet place for the night. Stieber thought much of the change had been perpetrated by the ease of railway travel: in 1835 only 1,500 single women had beached up in the city; in 1845 the figure was 5,824. Writing in 1846, he estimated the number of prostitutes at between 10,000 and 12,000. (His critic Zimmermann put the figure nearer 15,000.) In 1842 1,192 had been arrested. They seemed to function at certain times of the year: the warmer months in particular. In the late 1830s, the Charité was treating an average of 1,362 cases of syphilis a year. There was also an increasing incidence of part-time prostitution among servant girls and piece-workers.[165]

Stieber was aware of the changes going on around him. He saw three terrible enemies: the proletariat, crime and prostitution – 'The unnourished proletariat turns to crime, the lustful prole is the victim of prostitution.' Dronke was another of his enemies, but they saw eye to eye on this issue. He estimated that one *Berlinerin* in eight or nine between the ages of seventeen and forty-five was on the game; and there were as many as 5,000 amateurs, servant girls and the like. One in six children was born out of wedlock.[166] Stieber had a few theories about how women became prostitutes. The better sort, he thought, were poor provincials who were lured up to town, impregnated and abandoned. The second class was composed of nymphomaniacs, who tended to be found more in the upper echelons of society. The third sort were the daughters of sailors, bargees, executioners, criminals and textile workers, not forgetting the offspring of the harlots themselves.[167] Unlike his contemporary Zimmermann, he was not prepared to blame poverty and the increasingly brutal behaviour of Berlin's capitalists for the growth of prostitution.

Stieber exhibits a remarkable knowledge of the stars of the contemporary scene; all these Berthas, Lieses, Carolines, Emilies and Jettes who had transmogrified into Sidonies, Camillas, Thusneldas, Amalies, Huldas, Amandas, Auroras, Floras, Nanettes, Veronikas and Augustas. They had their *noms de guerre* too: the Chimneysweep (a swarthy shoplifter), the Forest Devil (also dark-skinned), Matchstick Marie (specialised in cavalry officers), Margräfin Camilla (the prettiest and most talented of the lot who made lots of money from her base in the Markgrafenstraße), the Polish Countess (impersonated a Polish noblewoman to extort money), Catholic Church Marie (plied her trade on the steps of St Hedwig's), Jewish Bertha, Hermine the Bean Queen, the Ship's Captain (rolling gait), Scots Mary (tartan coat), the Stockpot (huge head), Moth-Head (pock-marked face), Mousse Claire (was once daubed in *Pflaumenmus*, or plum jam), the Daughter of the Regiment, Godforsaken Rosalie (committed incest with father), the Bed of Nails or the Dappled Wolf, Lock-Luise (lived on the canal), Parrot Nose, Gherkin Barrel, and the Ox.[168]

To a woman, they were all addicted to strong drink, although a glass of Bavarian beer, then at the beginning of its popularity, doesn't seem to have gone amiss. One, the 'Droschkenpferd' (Hansom Horse), could put away twenty-four pints of it to no ill effect. Others put away three bottles of champagne of an evening. It was a good sign that they drank. If they had syphilis it would not have been allowed. Although their street clothes were often soiled and torn, they wore clean underwear and washed their bodies as often as possible. Stieber was of the opinion that Berlin women were not overly zealous about washing, and that foreign whores were both 'cleaner and nicer'.[169]

Some of his theories sound strange today. He claimed that prostitutes rapidly became less fertile than other women, tending to miscarry their children in their sixth or seventh months, if they had the misfortune to become pregnant. Constant sexual intercourse had a tendency to displace their wombs and slacken their sexual organs. They also smelled bad. One of them he singled out for her smell: 'Schweine-kreuz Minne' (Pig's Groin Minnie). In general, brothel whores developed 'a repulsive and penetrating odour'. Not only that, their bodies yellowed from excessive make-up and their hair fell out from continued use of the curling tongs. Syphilis added to their counter-allure: it gave them bad breath and seeping sexual organs.[170]

Dance halls were the new thing. The Wegener'sche Tabagie in the Französiche Straße, the Römersaal in the Münzstraße, the Letz'schen Anlagen (later Villa Bella) by the Oranienburger Tor, the Friedrichstädtische Halle in the Krausenstraße, the Gräbert'sche Lokal in the Waldemarstraße, and the Krüger'sche Colosseum in the Jakobstraße. The latter was the best-appointed that Berlin had known up till then, but sadly it burned down. Krüger himself was a jailbird. The Villa Bella was expensive to get into, but once you had passed the portals you found something of the Berlin mix: students, artists, lawyers, superannuated rakes, shop assistants, hairdressers, elegantly turned-out thugs and pickpockets. It opened between seven and eight in the evening but there was no life before ten. At midnight the music stopped to allow customers to eat, or sit down with one of the available whores. Stieber advised eating *à la carte* as it generally proved expensive to buy drinks for the girls. Dancing started up again after the break and continued to three or four in the morning.[171]

He gives us the prices too. An evening would cost seven thalers, five *Silbergroschen*, including two thalers for the prosti-tute. Similar establishments were the Colosseum in the Commandantenhaus and Kroll's Wintergarten. Such places were both dangerous and costly. For those on a tighter budget there were the *Absteigedirnen*, whores who worked in the small *hôtels garnis*, serving gentlemen who were nervous of being caught in a *louche* bar. The *Absteigedirnen* dressed as respectable women to please officers and elderly civil servants.[172] Stieber none the less thought it advisable to warn his readers of the danger of frequenting the grimmer parts of Berlin where the *Absteigequartiere* were located. Clients were frequently robbed, if not presented with a dose of syphilis.[173]

In the new and burgeoning *Weltstadt*, numerous prostitutes operated from quite ordinary bars, the number of which had increased beyond measure in the preceding decade. These were the bottle-shops beloved of Glaßbrenner, where it was possible to sit or stand over a glass of crude schnapps, the *Konditoreien* or the newfangled *Bierstuben* with their inevitable Bavarian-style beer. 'They appear and disappear almost as quickly as they are created. Bavarian *Bierstuben* have existed in their present great number only in the past few years, in particular since the time that one has begun to brew so-called Bavarian beer here in Berlin and to sell it for the knock-down price of 18 *Pfennige* a pint.'[174]

Such places yielded only the slimmest pickings for the whores who worked them. The schnapps-shops attracted only the 'coarsest, commonest and most insignificant class' of people, few of whom had enough money to pay. An innovation in these places, especially the so-called Bavarian pubs, was the use of young girls as waitresses to attract men in. In the old-fashioned *Konditoreien*, such as Stehely, Hildebrand and Spargnapani, men served the tables. Stieber doesn't want to suggest that the use of waitresses necessarily implied immorality, but in some of the lowlier *Konditoreien* where it was the case there was a 'dark back room', specially arranged for venereal transactions.[175]

In the Bavarian *Bierstuben* young girls took away your glasses and had them refilled; this they did as unpaid work, simply in order to acquire the right to use the premises for picking up clients. Nor did wine necessarily ennoble in this case. There was one place the policeman particularly singled out for its awfulness where, working the tables, there were two waitresses who were 'almost without equal in their scandalousness and nastiness'. The older of the two showed evidence of secondary syphilis from her rasping voice, and was generally drunk too. The younger appeared innocent by comparison, but this was obviously not the case. The bar stayed open until one or two with a guitar player to entertain customers. Anyone who entered late at night would have believed that he had come into 'Bacchus's cave'. The wine had nothing to recommend it. For a thaler you received a bottle of 'acidic red drink beside which a bottle of the nastiest Grünberger from the deeply shaded part of the valley would have tasted like manna itself'.[176]*

Berlin's street-walkers favoured the Friedrichstadt and one or two other choice spots such as the Schloßplatz, the Alexanderplatz, the Lust- and Tiergarten. The technique was to stare at a man passing in the street, stop and look back at him. If he seemed interested, the prostitute hummed an obscene song and brandished a bunch of keys. The job of policing this network, says Stieber, had become increasingly onerous. One raid on a *Kellerwohnung* in the Büschingplatz revealed a tall, tired woman in rags and a fat man with a beard lying in soiled straw. There were two daughters of fourteen and twelve. The first was fully operational, the second was learning the trade. The police investigation revealed that the woman was the former mistress of a count, who was related to a princely house. The eldest daughter was his. He had chased her away, but sent money for the

---

* Grünberg in Silesia, now Zielona Góra in Poland. 'From time immemorial Grünberger wine had a reputation for being acid.' The sharp wines of the Saale Valley were thought to be 'sweeter than sugar' in comparison. The most drinkable Grünberger was, apparently, the sparkling *Sekt*.[177]

upkeep of his child. The count had died, and the fat man had moved in. Now both daughters were being put to work.[178]

It wasn't going to get better, it got worse, as Berlin swelled up from *Großstadt* to *Weltstadt*. Naturally every economic crisis sent more women out on to the streets as factories closed and workers were laid off. The classic case was Weimar. Like Hoffmann before him, Erich Kästner dispels the illusory romance surrounding a view of Berlin by night.

> You're deluding yourself [Jakob Fabian tells Cornelia Battenberg]; the moonlight and the scent of flowers, the stillness and the small-town kiss under the porch, they are all illusions. Over there on the square is a café where Chinamen sit with Berlin whores; only Chinamen. Just up there is a pub where perfumed homosexual lads are dancing with elegant thespians and smart Englishmen, letting them know their skills and prices, and in the end everything is paid for by a dyed-blonde old woman who is allowed to tag along for that reason. On the corner on the right is a hotel inhabited wholly by Japanese. Next to it is a restaurant where Russian or Hungarian Jews scrounge off one another or clout one another round the ears. In a neighbouring street is a lodging house where under-aged schoolgirls sell their bodies to supplement their pocket-money. A year ago there was a poorly-hushed-up scandal when an old boy went into one of the rooms bent on pleasure, to find a stark-naked sixteen-year-old girl, which was nothing less than he wanted, only it turned out to be his daughter, which he hadn't expected at all . . . Inasmuch as this huge city is built of stone, not much has changed, but in the eyes of its inhabitants it has long looked more like a lunatic asylum. Crime resides in the east, crooks in the centre, poverty in the north and vice in the west, and decadence in every direction you care to name.[179]

It was a side of Berlin that made the Nazis wince with

provincial priggery. Where possible they stamped it out. During the war prostitution was placed largely beyond the reach of the ordinary civilian population. One contemporary described prostitution as a 'dying profession. I have heard that there are a couple of suitable establishments, one in the Kanonierstraße near the Wilhelmstraße and another in the Giesebrechtstraße in the west. The latter is apparently run by the Foreign Office to serve the needs of subordinate diplomatic guests, principally Japanese. It is also possible to pick people up in the street if one makes a big effort, but a big effort is needed.'[180] The Foreign Office brothel was presumably the place where Adam von Trott and his colleague Alexander Werth used to leave the Indian nationalist Subhas Bose to indulge his patrician longings among the harlots.[181]

A similar prudery affected East, but not West, Berlin after the war. Brothels were tolerated once again and the old system of medical checks reinstated. Today the Kurfürstenstraße, the Lietzenburgerstraße and a particularly notorious stretch of the Straße des 17 Juni (the old Siegesallee) are the centres of the trade; but there are pockets everywhere, including a particularly blatant brothel on the chic Savignyplatz. Since the fall of the Iron Curtain prices have been undercut by 'away-day' Polish women who travel the short distance from the Oder to earn extra strong currency. They tend to line the Kurfürstendamm at the weekends.[182] There are an estimated 5,000 prostitutes in Berlin today. Half of these are believed to be non-Germans, chiefly Thais and Eastern Europeans.[183]

The Berliner's earthy attitude to sex in general, together with an irrepressible German inclination to narcissism, has led to frequent outbreaks of nudism in the city's history. They had their early version of *Health and Efficiency* in *Der Lichtfreund*, 'an illustrated weekly for natural body culture'. In Rixdorf there was the headquarters of the 'Deutsche Luftbadegesellschaft', while in Wünsdorf nudists congregated around an old gravel pit which had been filled with water for their use.[184] Such matters must have placed the Nazis in a quandary. The worship of the Aryan body was certainly ideologically correct but free-love was *mal vu*. In 1933 pornography was banned by the regime, but devotees of naked bodies could get round it by buying 'body-beautiful' magazines such as *Glaube und Schönheit* (Beauty and Belief), *Der Tanz* (The Dance) and *Moderne Photographie*. As one contemporary wrote, 'The sales figures must be fantastic.'[185]

Another long Berlin tradition which the Nazis tried vainly to suppress was homosexuality. In May 1815 Zelter informed Goethe with some regret that the city was about to lose one of its best comedians, who had been sentenced by the courts to fortress detention and banishment because 'he had been teaching boys Greek'.[186] Stieber linked the practice to onanism, which he saw as one of the growing evils of his day. Onanism was not limited to men. In the past decades it had spread like wildfire through Berlin's female population too. Stieber believed that 60 per cent of young Berliners were given to masturbation.

> There are entire educational institutions which are
> blighted by this vice. It is certainly no myth that, in
> the lower classes of certain *Gymnasiums*, whole rows
> of schoolchildren freely and openly give themselves
> over to this vice during religious instruction, and there
> are numerous girls' schools in Berlin, indeed some
> of the best of them, where the pupils have always
> classed onanism among their favourite activities.[187]

It will come as no surprise that Stieber also saw homosexuality as a danger to public morals, and one which had been on the increase in the first decades of the nineteenth century. The policeman tells us that the city contains a number of 'assembly points' where 'paedophiles' (he leaves the word coyly and appropriately in Greek) gather. These were the Kastanien-Wäldchen behind the Neue Wache on the Linden (now partly covered by the extensions to the Humboldt University), and the carp pond in the Tiergarten. Being Prussia, most of the male prostitutes were moonlighting soldiers. A male brothel had recently been unearthed by the police and its denizens thrown into prison. The problem was that incarceration encouraged onanism. There was clearly no end to this vicious circle.[188]

Homosexuality was illegal under Article 175 of the Prussian Code. Offenders were known as 'Hundertfünfundsiebziger'. At the beginning of the twentieth century there were already Berliners in public positions who thought the law silly or unnecessarily severe. One of these was Police Commissioner Hans von Tresckow, who led the investigations into the numerous homosexual scandals touching on the Court in general and the circle of the Kaiser's friend Fürst Philipp zu Eulenburg in particular.[189] In the course of his work, Tresckow plunged into the works of Krafft-Ebing and the Berlin 'Sexologist' Magnus Hirschfeld. With so much vice about, it is possibly not surprising that Berlin should have led the way in this field. It is hard to think of someone like Hirschfeld achieving such prominence in Edwardian London.

Magnus Hirschfeld kept his surgery on the Berliner Straße (now Otto Suhr Allee) in Charlottenburg. In 1897 he founded a 'Wissenschaftlich-humanitäre Komitee' with a view to revising the law on homosexuality. The year before he had published under a pseudonym: *Sappho und Sokrates – Oder: wie erklärt sich die Liebe der Männer und Frauen zu Personen des eigenen Geschlechts* (Sappho and Socrates – or: What form the love of men and women takes towards persons of their own sex). The male homosexual he called the 'Uranier', the female 'Urninde'.* The book was published by the specialist house of Max Spohr in Leipzig as part of Hirschfeld's campaign to abolish Article 175.[190]

---

* Female homosexuals were not covered by Article 175.

Hirschfeld enlisted the support of the Westphalian lawyer Edmund Oberg to aid him in raising a petition to help scrap Article 175. It was signed by (among others) the jurist Franz von Liszt, Krafft-Ebing, the politician August Bebel, the poet Richard Dehmel, Max Liebermann, and the writers Detlev von Lilienkron, Rilke, Schnitzler and Ernst von Wolzogen. The final document contained around a thousand signatures. It stated that the law merely served to encourage male prostitution and blackmail, and that it should be reduced to an act protecting minors or punishing cases of male rape. In short, not unlike Article 218 of the present *Grundgesetz*.[191]

Despite the striking incidence of homosexuality at court, the petition was unlikely to have appealed to the Kaiser much, but Hirschfeld carried on his activities undeterred. Through Max Spohr again, he published a *Jahrbuch für Zwischenstufen unter besonderer Berücksichtigung der Homosexualität* (Yearbook for Intermediary Sexuality with Special Reference to Homosexuality), which contained accounts of prosecutions for homosexuality★ as well as an extensive bibliography. He followed it up in 1902 with *Was soll das Volk vom Dritten Geschlecht wissen?* ('What Should People Know about the Third Sex?') Over the next two years 3,000 questionnaires were issued to students at the Technische Hochschule in Charlottenburg, asking for intimate details of sexuality. Of these 1,696 were returned proving that 94 per cent of scientifically inclined students were nominally heterosexual, or at least wanted Hirschfeld to believe as much.[192]

Influenced perhaps by the scandals emanating from the Schloss, Hirschfeld next endeavoured to find out whether there was a greater preponderance of homosexuality in certain classes of society. This led him to collect information from 5,721 metal-workers. Presumably few of them admitted homosexuality, for Hirschfeld pronounced: 'Homosexuality

---

★ To prosecute, the police needed to catch homosexuals *in flagrante delicto*, otherwise the offence was impossible to prove.

is more widespread in the upper classes of the population than it is in the lower classes of the people.' The authorities began to get annoyed with Hirschfeld and his researches. In 1904 he was fined 200 marks for immoral writings. He retreated into his venereal-disease practice, which seems to have kept him occupied: every second waitress in Charlottenburg had VD.[193]

Hirschfeld's research flowered during the Weimar period when he ran his *Institut für Sexualwissenschaft*. As Yvan Goll observed,

> ... at that time perversion was high fashion in Berlin. Moral nihilism and physical despair had reached new heights: to escape them the most sensitive souls fled into the pastures of lechery and illusion. Sodom and Gomorrah resurfaced in Berlin. People publicly announced that they enjoyed taking drugs, mystical hoodoo was lauded; despite Article 175* people flaunted their homosexuality or lesbianism. And because everything German must have a cause and effect, an entry in a catalogue and a reason for existing, they called that liberty; living life to the full, the great frenzy, divine ecstasy.[194]

After 1933 the pendulum swung the other way. Hirschfeld figured on a Nazi hitlist. He fled to Nice, where he died in 1935. The SA vented their moral indignation by wrecking his surgery and publicly burning his books.

V

'The most miserable police blackguard of our century' was how Engels described Wilhelm Stieber;[195] Wilhelm Liebknecht called him a 'scoundrel'[196] for his cold-hearted

---

* See above, p. 236.

attempts to stamp out Socialism and Communism, root and branch. Stieber, however, had the occasional *mauvais quart d'heure*. In April 1860 he was made the scapegoat for the illiberal regimen of Frederick William IV. His house was searched, his papers confiscated and he himself thrown into the Stadtvogteigefängnis. The boot was fairly and squarely on the other foot. Stieber was now plunged into

> a dim dungeon, in which in my former life I had had
> many a malefactor incarcerated, that contained
> nothing but a hard bench, a stinking dung-bucket,
> cockroaches and mice. I threw myself down on a
> sack of rotten straw, my eyes melancholically fixed on
> a pot filled with water.

There was naturally great jubilation in the neighbouring lock-ups from the crooks Stieber had helped to catch. Stieber shouted at them: 'Just wait until I get out, I shall personally deal with you scoundrels!' The policeman claims that silenced them.[197]

Desperate to prove his innocence of the charges, Stieber escaped. The newspapers splashed the headlines 'Director disappears from custody!' 'The Police are hunting Stieber down!' 'Warning: Stieber carries a gun!' The story becomes even more wonderful when we learn that Stieber makes for the house of Tilly von T., the woman whose orgy he broke up in order to procure Charlotte von Hagen's divorce. The police raid the house, but Tilly conceals the policeman in her bed by lying across him so that he felt the 'weight of Frau von T's hot limbs . . . My head was pressed to her swelling breast like a helpless child, and like a spent swimmer my arms clung to her body, which quivered with fear . . .'[198]

It was still open season on Stieber in the press. He was accused of abuse of power; of false imprisonment; and bending the law. A message from his enemy Oberstaatsanwalt Schwack appeared asking people to come forward and say what they knew about Stieber's activities. There were plenty of applicants. One called Luger ('liar' – *nomen est omen*) told the lawyer that Stieber had used a whip on him. Stieber was eventually able not only to prove his innocence but to have both Schwack and the Minister of Justice, Simons, sacked. He renewed his fight against Berlin's villains. 'To make my victory complete, I turned my revenge to Berlin's criminals who had so willingly blackened my character with their vile lies, and it was all the more agreeable for the fact that I was serving the common weal at the same time.' Stieber had lost none of his artfulness. Knowing that crooks needed to get rid of the goods they had stolen, he set up as a fence. A wave of arrests followed which decimated the underworld: 'The biggest trawl of crooks in the history of the Berlin force'.[199]

If Stieber is to be believed, which sometimes takes a considerable effort of will, he was a trusted friend of the Police President Carl Ludwig von Hinckeldey. Hinckeldey had been responsible for reforming the police after 1848. He created the paramilitary *Schutzmannschaft* filling its ranks with former officers and NCOs. He was head of the security police or *Sicherheitspolizei* too, and there was a plan to bump him up into a prefectorial position embracing the whole of Berlin, a sort of Prussian version of the Paris *Préfet* Haussmann.[200] He was chiefly famous for his 'democrat hunting' after 1848. The press was bridled, any suspect taken immediately into custody without respect to social status (which proved his downfall), his spies were unleashed in all public places, houses were searched, papers confiscated. No one was immune, not even the prominent right-wing von Gerlach family.[201]

His principal duty was to protect the king and his family. He uncovered a plot to kill Frederick William in his bath by stabbing him through the plug-hole,[202] but he failed to prevent Maximilian Sefeloge firing at the king at point-blank range in the Postsdamer Bahnhof.[203] Despite his ugly zeal,

Hinckeldey was immensely popular with the middle classes. He specifically came down as hard as he could on a noble caste which believed itself endowed with special privileges; the army too. Varhagen called it 'open war'. On the night of 23–24 June 1855, Hinckeldey and his men raided an illegal gambling session at the Hotel du Nord on Unter den Linden. The gamblers were chiefly members of the Jockey Club plus a few who sat in the Herrenhaus, or Prussian House of Lords, such as Hans von Rochow-Plessow. The military was furious. Officers refused to show their passes to the police, and at a ball for five hundred given by Hinckeldey not one officer turned up.[204]

Hinckeldey had confiscated the money on the table, some of which belonged to Rochow-Plessow. At a fraught interview in Hinckeldey's house, the Junker accused the policeman of being a nark and a thief. Hinckeldey then called Rochow-Plessow a 'state criminal because he had infringed a royal command'.[205] A duel followed. Stieber claimed that he witnessed this together with Hinckeldey's second, a Freiherr von Münchhausen. Other accounts make no mention of him, and his own version of the story is suspicious in that he has the duel take place in a cemetery ('Dead man found in graveyard') complete with the morning sun casting its ghostly light on the buckled headstones.[206] In reality the duel was fought on the Jungfernheide in north Berlin. Even today a small cross marks the spot where the Berlin middle classes' hero fell. The short-sighted Hinckeldey[207] had known all along that First Lieutenant von Rochow-Plessow was a crack shot.[208]

Hinckeldey's death polarised the Berlin middle and upper classes: the *Bürgerstand* and the Herrenhaus. Around 100,000 Berliners are said to have filed past Hinckeldey's coffin.[209] Rochow-Plessow served a nine-month sentence, but his record in no way prevented him from becoming Vice-President of the Prussian Herrenhaus in 1888. Stieber says that Hinckeldey had entrusted him with the key to his desk, and the task of destroying certain files should he fall in the duel. Stieber found a few packets of love-letters and some reports on the disreputable activities of the high and mighty.[210]

Police spies were a leitmotif of Berlin life from the pre-March days, when Minister Eichhorn, the ubiquitous squirrel who infiltrates Engels' sketch of the *Freie* at Hippels, adopted the system from Austria and Metternich.[211] *Vigilanten* were former jail-birds who undertook to work for the police in return for remission. Hinckeldey had his own security force which employed a network of sneaks, and so it went on. Even the Weimar police had their Department 1A: Political Police, which later became the bare bones for Himmler's Gestapo.[212]

Department 1A had been housed in Berlin's Police Head-quarters on the Alexanderplatz. In April 1933 Göring appointed the young Oberregierungsrat Rudolf Diels to head it. Diels was a bright young adventurer not overly taxed by moral scruples. At Marburg University he had been 'a member of a prominent *Korps* where he set a record for beer consumption. Even then he had a powerful reputation as a womaniser, but what impressed all the stalwart beer-swilling students the most was the quality of his bite: he was prone to crowning a bacchanal by chewing the beer glasses.'[213] One day Diels would find himself incarcerated in the very same cells he had once so ably administered.

The 'Gestapa' (Geheime Staatspolizeamt) was the name given to the compound of buildings where the new secret police, or Gestapo (Geheime Staatspolizei), had their organis-ational headquarters: the old Prinz Albrechtspalais, the School and Museum of Industrial Arts and Crafts, and the Hotel Prinz Albrecht. Here they were joined by the SS and its intelligence service, the Sicherheitsdienst (or SD). At the beginning, the Gestapo's 3,900 employees worked only in the two-thirds of Germany which were Prussia. The Gestapo was reasonably honest about its functions and its location in northern Kreuzberg until 1938, when Prinz

Albrechtstraße 8 was listed in the telephone directory as the address of Kriminal Assistent Kleidorfer. In 1943 the residents were Hausmeister (porter) Kunke and 'Gogolla W., Pol Gefäng. Hauptmstr.' (i.e., Senior Political Prison Warder Gogolla). Before he joined the service, Obersturmbahnführer (his rather more impressive SS rank) Gogolla was a master butcher.[214]

Just a year after creating the Gestapo, Diels was replaced by Himmler. Diels had always exerted some small power over Göring, presumably because he had had access to information that might have embarrassed the Minister President, but he could do nothing to defend himself from the austere Himmler. Himmler used the art school's old lecture rooms to teach his *Lebensphilosophie* to his largely Bavarian staff, which for a time included another *Obersturmbahnführer*, Eichmann, with his 30-man staff, until they found new quarters in the Kurfürstenstraße. There were other changes that heralded Himmler's arrival: busts of Hitler and Göring appeared in the foyer and the canteen, and nineteen cells were built into the cellars and another seventeen on the corridors.[215]

The three hundred or so men and women who worked in the Prinz Albrechtstraße had jobs ranging from the mundane day-to-day work of police administration to operating the Gestapo's torture chambers. The initial interrogation of suspects was done here, in the old studios under the mansard roof. Torture was not the rule, although it became more often the case as time went on. Certainly many of the men of 20 July 1944 were badly beaten and subjected to some quite mediaeval treatments.* Day-to-day life for those in the Prinz Albrechtstraße could achieve a sort of quiet normality: there was a small library; books, papers and tobacco could be purchased; prisoners were allowed to write letters and receive occasional visits.[216] For most, the Prinz

---

* Diels had laid down a few rules: a maximum of 25 strokes with a cane, but no one seems to have listened to him.

Albrechtstraße was just a short period of interrogation before being despatched to a concentration camp. On 24 April 1945 the SS shot most of the remaining prisoners among the ruins. When the Russians liberated the building on 1 May, they found just six alive in the basement cells.[217]

Justice had not always been so rough. Prussia was once proud of its reputation as a *Rechtstaat* ruled by law. Its 1794 legal code was the envy of Europe. Berlin's earliest court was the Kammergericht, which was originally housed in the Schloss. In 1538 it was transferred to new buildings on the Schlossplatz, but the Elector kept an eye on proceedings from behind a glass door. With the troubles that arose from John Sigismund's decision to become a Calvinist, the Elector threatened to remove both the court and the Kammergericht from Berlin, stressing that the two institutions were indivisable. During the Thirty Years War it briefly operated from Bernau to the east.[218]

The Kammergericht moved several more times before it found a permanent home. Its old premises were given to the Joachimstaler Gymnasium in 1655 and it moved to a new site near the Cathedral. With the rebuilding of the Schloss, it was allotted the old palace of Statthalter Schwarzenberg in the Brüderstraße, a move which finally ruptured a three-century-old tradition of having the Kammergericht a part of the Electoral furniture. In 1643 the Great Elector presented the Kammergericht with a painting by Lucas Cranach the Elder of King Cambyses of Persia skinning a judge who had been found to have arrived at an incorrect verdict. The Elector was making a point: the gift was made after a disagreement with the Vice-Chancellor of the court, Andreas Kohl. When, in 1815, someone recalled the existence of this valuable painting, and suggested it might be the moment now to return it to the royal collections, it was nowhere to be found. It had last been seen in the court secretariat, totally neglected.[219]

In 1733 the Kammergericht moved to the Collegienhaus

at the southern end of the Friedrichstadt by the Rondell. The Soldier-King laid down typically penny-pinching instructions to the architect, Philipp Gerlach, which may account for the simplicity of its design.★ Here Frederick the Great's judges rejected the suit of the Miller Arnold of Kreis Züllichau, who claimed he could not pay his rent because the *Landrat* had diverted his water to dig a carp pond. Frederick felt they had failed in their duty and reached the wrong conclusion (just as his father had when a court martial had recommended leniency for Frederick's friend and co-fugitive Katte). He had the judges sentenced to nine months' fortress detention rather than skinning them, but in all probability they had reached the correct conclusions as far as the law was concerned.[221]

The most famous judge ever to sit on the Kammergericht bench was surely E. T. A. Hoffmann, who, after ten years in musical and literary limbo in Bamberg, Dresden and Leipzig, returned to his first profession of law in 1816. He sat on the Instructionssenat and the Criminalsenat under President von Trützschler. Elsewhere in the building was his old friend from Warsaw days, the *Criminalrat* Julius Hitzig. Hoffmann had finally made it back to Berlin at the end of October 1814 and worked as an assistant in the office of Minister of Justice von Kircheisen. At that time his eyes were firmly on the Schauspielhaus, but he was to be disappointed when Graf Brühl got the job he coveted and succeeded the director, Iffland. On 1 March 1816 Hoffmann went back to law.[222]

There is an old image of Hoffman as a reluctant jurist, collecting his salary to allow himself the peace of mind to write prose and music, and to tope, late into the night, with his bosom friend Devrient. Ernst Wichert, another literary

---

★ 'Gut in ordre, sollen alles anschaffen und die Fundemente dieses Jahr legen, und zukommen Jahr will ich sagen wie viell ich disponiren kann oder nit.'[220]

judge from Königsberg in Prussia, tried to examine Hoffmann's rulings to gain a picture of the writer as a jurist.[223] He found most of them decorated with marginal drawings, chiefly representing little devils emerging from ink-pots.[224] He concluded that most of his work had been in the field of *cassation*, or legal revision and appeal.

The picture of the half-hearted judge is no longer sustainable. Hoffmann's six years on the Bench were an important period in Prussian law, and the writer made his own contribution. Trützschler himself was the first to admit that Hoffmann played an important role in the deliberations of the criminal division of the Kammergericht. Writing to the Minister in January 1819, he expressed his admiration for his 'striking talent, his astuteness and the precision of his work which Your Excellency knows well, just as much as the thoroughness he demonstrates like the pleasant stuff with which he seeks to clothe the most abstract matter'.[225] Trützschler was careful to show the Minister that Hoffmann's extra-curricular activities in no way prevented him from carrying out his work for the court: 'The writing which he does during his hours of idleness and leisure does no harm to his efficiency, and the rich strain of fantasy, which tends towards the comic, contrasts in a remarkable way with the cold reflection, with the high seriousness, with which he goes about his work as a judge.'[226] The 'leisure time', Trützschler mentions, may have been a little more prolonged than the court desired. Two years before, the President had alluded to Hoffmann's frequent absences through illness.[227]

In the case of the murderer Schmolling, Hoffmann examined the notion of whether a homicide might be committed by a man in a state of momentary passion, who was not clinically mad. Naturally this was the sort of case in which the writer Hoffmann would have felt most at home. The Schallenberger case was perhaps the most important one for Hoffmann the judge. Samuel Schallenberger was a coiner in the Canton of Neuchâtel in Switzerland. Before 1806,

Neuchâtel had been included in the extensive portfolio of Prussian lands, but after the Battle of Jena it was handed to Bonaparte's Marshal Berthier, who became briefly its duke. During the French interregnum, Schallenberger was apprehended and sentenced to death. In 1814 the duchy was returned to Prussia. Schallenberger was still on 'death row.' When the case was brought before Frederick William III he refused to agree to the execution before his own criminal bench had examined it. The judge chosen to draw up the report was Hoffmann.[228]

Hoffmann's recommendation that Schallenberger's sentence be commuted to imprisonment was based on the fact that his confession had been extracted under the threat of torture. Torture had been abolished in Prussia by Frederick the Great (it was revived by Adolf Hitler), and the news that the Neuchâtel was still using physical pain to extract confessions caused uproar in the Prussian capital. As a result of Hoffmann's report, the Prussian Chancellor Hardenberg pushed the king to express his personal displeasure at the continuing use of torture in Neuchâtel, and order its abolition.[229] The principality was not actually subject to Prussian law (which complicated matters), but the king was free to command as its prince.

Hoffmann was on much more slippery ground when it came to the Mühlenfels case. Ludwig von Mühlenfels was a radical lawyer who fell foul of the reactionary Prussian state after 1815. Hoffmann and his colleagues on the criminal bench were required to support the government's attempts to stamp out radical demagogy in the years following the Treaty of Vienna. While Hoffmann had no time for boorish bigots like Jahn, his heart was not in the persecution of democrats either. He reminded his superiors that Prussia was still a *Rechtstaat*, and that there had to exist a genuine suspicion that a crime had been committed before anyone could be imprisoned. In the meantime, in his writings Hoffmann expressed his mockery of the whole paranoia when it came to the demagogues, and his no less sharp observations when it came to the silliness of some of the radicals. Heavy-handed police measures are poked fun at in *Klein Zaches*, while in *Kater Murr* Hoffmann sends up the liberal student Burschen- schaften when the cats get together to sing *Gaudeamus igitur* and drink herring bile on the rooftops.[230]

It was an even-handed approach and the authorities held fire until Hoffmann's tale *Meister Floh* was in proof: then they moved swiftly into action. Heine was in Berlin at the time and dwelled on the situation in his letters. It was certainly no secret in Berlin that the novel contained a good many 'political jibes',[231] something which made the city's literary public all the more anxious to read it. In the meantime, however, Police-Director von Kamptz, ridiculed in the novel as the idiot Hofrat Knarrpanti, had sent word to Frankfurt to impound the pages.[232] As Heine correctly reported, the fifth chapter made fun of the activities of the anti-demagogue commission on which Hoffmann himself sat. The novel would only appear in a censored form. Meanwhile Hoffmann, whom Heine 'greatly loved and honoured', had taken to his bed.[233] When Heine did get hold of the book he was disappointed to find no trace of the promised scene.[234]

Hoffmann was actually in deep water. Kamptz wanted blood. Disciplinary action was taking place when the writer died at the tender age of forty-six in 1822. He was accused of being an unsuitable judge by the powerful cabal mustered against him. There was even talk of banishing him to Inster- burg in East Prussia, where his own father had vegetated as a lawyer on Prussia's far eastern border. The novel itself was not published in its original form until long after Heine's death, not until 1908 in fact.[235]

With Hitzig a fellow member of the bench, the Kammer- gericht must have been tolerant of eccentricity until Kamptz laid his hands around Hoffmann's throat. Julius Hitzig was not only the most important criminal judge in Berlin, but a member of the Serapionsbrüder and the translator of Cer-

vantes and Camoëns. An Assessor von Winterfeld was an
enthusiastic member of Zelter's Singakademie, and later
forsook the law to become Professor of Music at Berlin
University.[236] The court itself was reformed in 1849 when it
became Prussia's Ober-Appellationssenat, or highest appeal
court. In 1913 it moved into new buildings in the Kleistpark
in Schöneberg, and the old buildings were turned over first
to the Church, before finally becoming a museum.[237]

The Kammergericht was not the only court building in
Berlin to witness the conflict of authoritarian government
and the requirements of an independent judiciary. The court
building in the Witzlebenstraße in Charlottenburg was once
the Reichsmilitärgericht, or military court. It was here that
the revolutionary Liebknecht was sentenced to four years'
imprisonment in 1916 for agitating against the war. He was
let out by Philipp Scheidemann in October 1918 and murdered three months later. During the Weimar Republic it
became a commercial law court, but reverted to military use
under the Nazis. Here Colonel-General von Fritsch had to
defend his honour against trumped-up charges of homosexuality, which were engineered to have him removed from
the headship of the Army to make way for Corporal Hitler.
The pro-Russian Rote Kapelle group was tried here and
most of those forty-six arrested were executed. In April 1944
General von Seydlitz-Kurzbach, who had set up the Freies
Deutschland committee in captivity in Russia, was tried *in
absentia*.[238]

The most notoriously unjust court in the history of Prussia
or Germany was the Volksgerichthof which was established
in April 1934 after the acquittal of the Communists Dimitrov
and Torgler at their trial for burning the Reichstag. No such
slip-ups were to occur again. Indeed, as one of the men of
20 July was to discover, the niceties of law were never
properly observed in the court: at his trial a copy of the
Prussian legal code was nowhere to be found.[239] From
the first only the president and one assistant judge had to be

professional lawyers. The remaining three magistrates were brought in from the SA, SS, or, in the case of treason, the Wehrmacht. Defence lawyers, where assigned, were rarely allowed access to the prosecution documents.[240]

The Bench was composed of a president (Roland Freisler), a vice-president, two *Senatspräsidenten*, five elected judges and 95 honorary judges. The regime brought them no lack of work: in 1934 they tried 94 cases of treason. The following year 210 sentences were meted out. By 1940 this figure had all but doubled. Two years later it was a staggering 1,033. In 1944 it had doubled once again, to 2,087 sentences out of a total of 4,380 cases. The trials were necessarily short. As Goebbels had said, recalling a famous line of Fouquier-Tinville, 'Don't bother yourself about the law; just decide that the man has to go.' The number of death sentences was estimated to be as high as 32,600, but there are documents proving only 12,891 (12,212 of these between 1940 and 1944). Plötzensee Prison was the scene of 1,785 of these. The 20 July trials did not all take place in the building on the Bellevuestraße. Some happened in the Kammergericht building, and latterly in Potsdam, after all other suitable Berlin locations had been gutted. In 1968 one of the court's judges, Kammergerichtsrat Rehse, was tried for his role at the Volksgerichthof, and acquitted. It was a judgement typical of the earlier years of the Bundesrepublik, where Freisler's widow was to receive a pension long before the widows of the men who rose up to kill Hitler and were butchered on his authority.[241]

Berlin's biggest criminal court was the Kriminalgericht in Moabit. The huge neo-baroque building was constructed between 1902 and 1906 in the Turmstraße. It united the Stadtvogtei and Hausvogtei courts which dated from mediaeval times and which had been progressively merged into three *Landgerichte*. One of the first sensational cases to be heard in its courtrooms was the murder trial of Gotthilf Heinze, a pimp, and his prostitute wife, which lifted the lid on the moral 'quagmire' of Berlin's 'Latin quarter' around the Oranienburger Tor and the *demi-monde* which inhabited it. Particularly galling to some was the fact that Heinze's two counsels drank *Sekt* in the courtroom.[242] A few years later the same courts were the scene of the trials of Philipp Eulenburg and his friends which revealed the extent to which the Kaiser's immediate entourage was inclined to homosexuality.

As far as the law and the courts were concerned, Weimar was far from being the liberal society some might assume. The trial of the murderers of Karl Liebknecht and Rosa Luxemburg was a sham, which pointed the finger directly at the government which had seen fit to remove the revolutionary menace by the crudest and most desperate means imaginable. The perpetrators were tried by court martial and all but two of the accused were acquitted. The Hussar Runge and Oberleutnant a. D. (*ausser Dienst* – i.e., retired) Kurt von Vogel received derisory sentences and were amnestied a few months later.[243]

Weimar was by no means an open society, and in many respects it continued the illiberal ways of the Kaiser's time. One of those who stretched its patience beyond endurance was the painter George Grosz. The basic Prussian legal code was still more or less in place, and Grosz had to reckon with articles such as 166, 184 and 185, which had their origins in another time altogether. His first tussle with the law came in 1921 on the publication of the folder *Gott mit uns*, which presented the army in an unflattering way. The *Reichswehr* proved they had been libelled and Grosz and his publisher, Herzfelde, had to pay large fines.[244] Similarly, a doll dressed as a soldier at the famous Dada exhibition of 1920 brought the Dadaists before the Bench.

The collection *Ecce Homo* was the next to get Grosz into trouble with the law. It was executed by the painter between 1915 and 1922 and published again by Herzfelde. The court believed the series infringed Article 184 of the code book. They spent much time on a picture of *Rudi S* which described a man with his penis hanging out, a ball and chain on his foot and a paintbrush in his hand holding a woman's boot. A copy of Dühren's *Sadismus und Masochismus* lies on the floor. They concluded, one assumes correctly, that the man had been masturbating with the paintbrush. They deliberated on just what the public might be allowed to see: pubic hair, naked women with their legs apart, penises etc., and decided that the folder was indeed pornographic. Grosz was fined 500 goldmarks in Moabit, and the folder was banned.[245] Canetti none the less received one when he visited Grosz in his studio with Herzfelde, and was thrilled with the gift.[246]

Between 1928 and 1931 Grosz and Herzfelde fought their biggest battle of all with the Prussian courts over certain drawings in the collection *Hintergrund* (Background). The one that was thought to be the most offensive was *Maul halten und weiter dienen* (Keep your mouth shut and carry on serving), which portrayed Christ on the cross wearing a gas mask. In December 1928 a local court in Charlottenburg had ordered the destruction of the plate. This judgement was crushed, much to everyone's surprise, by Judge Julius Siegert in Moabit. In his astonishment, Alfred Kerr pronounced, 'There are still judges in Berlin.' The liberal verdict was suppressed, however, by the Reichsgericht (or supreme court) in Leipzig, which once again ordered the destruction of the plate.[247]

Blasphemy was still a highly sensitive issue and one which seemed to upset judges more and more in the last years of the Republic. Tucholsky's *Song of the English Choirboy* was indicted under the same statute, and at various times both Kurt Weill and the writer Walter Hasenklever had their hands slapped for blasphemy. Just as with the case against the journalist Carl von Ossietzky for libelling the armed forces, Weimar's courts continued to uphold the values of the 'moral majority' by means of a largely unaltered legal code.[248]

It was the old problem with Weimar: the bourgeoisie was not with it, many disliked it and willed its downfall. The men who became judges were almost without exception those who preferred the sparkle of the Kaiser's days, or looked forward to the rather more draconian law-and-order policies of an Adolf Hitler. On 19 April 1927 Tucholsky summed up the situation with remarkable prescience in *Die Weltbühne*:

> . . . it might be noted that the present sort is as good as gold compared with those who will be passing judgement in 1940. This politically excited *petite bourgeoisie* which today is rioting in university lecture halls is far more frigid and heartless than the desiccated old gentlemen we struggle against. With the older generation there was still very often a streak of liberalism; a dash of claret-coloured goodwill to be found; a modicum of humour, to which you might occasionally appeal; the cold, glazed fish-eyes of the post-war *Freikorpsstudent* cast these more joyful aspects aside: when these young men put on their gowns for the first time our children will experience something new: they lack any sense of justice.[249]

Tucholsky was not wrong. The Nazis rolled the three Moabiter jurisdictions into a special court to deal with the enemies of the Third Reich, where, among others, they tried the Catholic martyr Bernhard Lichtenberg. It didn't take much to feel the heavy hand of National Socialist justice: 'Hitler can lick my arse': sentenced to six months; 'Goebbels is a Jew': sentenced to three months; 'Rotfront an allen Ecken, Adolf Hitler soll verrecken!' (Red Front on every corner, Adolf Hitler should keel over!): nine months; 'Ley has raped BDM★ girls': seven months; 'We must shoot Hitler and Göring': one year; 'Colonel-General Fritsch was shot in the back': ten months; 'The government has started extermi-

★ Bund deutscher Mädel – the female counterpart of the Hitler Youth.

nating races': six months; 'Himmler sei ein Arsch mit Ohren' (literally 'an arse with ears' – a silly bugger): five months.[250]

Prison had not always been such a grim prospect. Spandau was a fairly jolly place for the disgraced judges in the Miller Arnold case. They were lodged in the Citadel, which had served a dual role as a fortress to protect Berlin's north-western approaches and a penitentiary for state prisoners. Before the seventeenth century prisoners had been confined to the Juliusturm in conditions that were notorious throughout Brandenburg, but high-ranking state prisoners in the eighteenth century could live a decent sort of life, as is borne out by the journals of Councillor Neumann.

Neumann got very rapidly into the swing of things. He took a lively interest in an Italian spy, who had been incarcerated for twenty years, and who had given his bedder a daughter. Now the daughter was eighteen, and she too was reduced to 'whoring' for the prisoner. Neumann could see this continuing 'into the third and fourth generation'. The prisoner was presumably Giovanni Renazzi, who was apprehended during the Seven Years War on the initiative of the marquis d'Argens.[251]

When a pretty girl came in with a dish of roast venison, gherkins and preserved meats 'various prisoners complained a good deal that they could not enjoy the girl in the same way as the leg of venison'. Neumann and his colleagues did not want for good food and drink. A few days later friends from Berlin brought wine, cakes, sausages, ham, roast hare, a saddle and haunch of venison and a carp. Friedrich Nicolai provided a ham pasty together with two tubs of mustard for the judges. Amid considerable amounts of lavatorial ribaldry a young officer gaoled for desertion had his pet poodle killed and a bobble-hat made from its pelt.

Neumann was intrigued by the motions of Judge Busch and his exaggerated metabolism. Obsessiveness was not confined to his visits to the *chaise percée*, it involved a manic cleaning of his ears, cutting of finger- and toenails. His teeth he cleaned with his little fingers because the others were 'too swollen'. 'He washes his hands every day, but not his face, because, in his view of things, that is the barber's business.' The litany of the judge's disgusting behaviour ends with his nose- and tooth-picking.[252]

Matters got better and then worsened again. One day they were issued with packets of butter and were eating Spandau crayfish the size of crabs. The next day a consignment of similar crustaceans was scoffed by the maid. Busch found diversion in a dog called Emire, which he took off to bed with him. Rather more distracting were the pleasures provided by *Hof-Fiskal* Schlecker, who found the judges a willing local girl whom they took it in turns to occupy.[253]

Thirty years earlier, in 1750, Graf Lehndorff had visited the prison in the company of Prince Augustus William and the Princess of Schwedt. 'We looked over the entire fortress and among others we met a Frau von Martinfeld, who had had herself incarcerated with her husband: an extraordinary occurrence in this day and age, when marital devotion is not particularly strong.'[254] Three years later he found that Spandau was not always one long party: 'Among the large number of unfortunate fellows here there is an unknown man in the prison whom no one may see or address. The commandant alone knows who he is. He has neither chair nor bed; it is believed he is someone of standing.'[255]

Spandau was for state prisoners. Lesser fry went into the Stadtvogtei on the Molkenmarkt, a sixteenth-century building tacked on to the police headquarters. In 1791 the police moved out, allowing the prisoners the run of the whole building. Wagner's friend Heinrich Laube did time there, as did Glaßbrenner, who was another of the radical composer's Berlin set.[256] Dronke described the cells as 'narrow, gloomy holes' containing anything up to ten inmates: 'the new arrival is best advised to tread carefully while he looks for a place, lest he step on a human body, which will then direct its full fury at him'. One bucket served the needs of all prisoners in the cell. The last arrival had the plum job of emptying it. Money helped secure less-cluttered cells.[257]

The better-born prisoners were generally confined to the more comfortable Hausvogtei anyway. When a new prison was built in Moabit in 1881, neither of the two old central Berlin prisons was needed any more. The Hausvogtei was pulled down in 1891.[258] Moabit was built on the fashionable 'panopticon' system advocated by the English philosopher Jeremy Bentham. The star-shaped arrangement of cell blocks meant that the warders could survey the prisoners from a central post. Moabit was equipped with a punishment block in the cellars, and high-security cells on the first floor for important prisoners. In the attics there was room for any large bag brought in after a police *razzia*. Women were accommodated in two blocks placed either side of the central court-house. There was a hospital block which also contained twelve special cells to confine those 'for whom it is not desired that they should consort with the ordinary prisoners', i.e., persons from the upper classes.[259]

The Zitadelle in Spandau gradually ceased to be used as a fortress prison. From 1878 to 1898, important prisoners were housed in a new building in Spandau's Wilhelmstadt, which occupied the land to the south of the Altstadt, on the left bank of the Havel. In 1920 this became a civil prison. In 1933 the Nazis used it for some of the thousands of Communists they rounded up after the Reichstag fire. One of these was Alfred Kerr's friend, the Bohemian journalist Egon Erwin Kisch. He described the horrors he endured in his cell:

> We heard screams of 'Help! Help!' People were being beaten bloody. It touched us to the quick, but we had no more nerve to heed this cry from the unknown, we had heard too much about the fate of our

comrades who had been arrested by SA and the
Auxiliary Police and who had been bestially
mistreated.[260]

After the war Spandau Prison was given a new role: to
look after the top Nazi *Bonzen* who had escaped the gibbet at
Nuremberg: Neurath, Baldur von Schirach, Dönitz, Raeder,
Funk, Heß and Speer. The latter described his arrival in his
secret prison diary:

> One last sharp turn and [the bus] came to a stop. Still
> handcuffed to our soldiers, we got out. Behind us,
> at the same moment, the gate closed in a mediaeval-
> looking entrance. A number of Allied military men
> were posted about. A command rang out in English:
> 'Take off those handcuffs. None of that here.' With a
> certain solemnity, the American guard shook hands
> with me in parting.
> Inside the building we were shown a wooden bench
> to sit on. We were wearing our own clothing, which
> had been returned to us for this trip, for the first time
> since the trial. Now, one by one we filed into a room
> where we exchanged these clothes for long blue
> convict's trousers, a tattered convict's jacket, a coarse
> shirt, and a convict's cap. The shoes are canvas, with
> a thick wooden sole. We are being issued the clothing
> of convicts from concentration camps; the officials
> make a point of telling us this. I was fifth in line.
> After that I passed through an iron door that clanged
> loudly behind me . . . In the cell block I was assigned
> to one of the many empty cells. One of us began to
> work off his nervousness. A guard immediately
> snapped at him.[261]

And so they remained, like seven little pigs, in this case
waiting to go home. The world's most expensive convicts.
Speer began to reflect on his career, on how he might have
been a 'second Schinkel', which was possibly a rather over-

inflated view of his architectural mastery, but so many compliments must have gone to his head.

> *26 July 1947.* After an absence of two years, I am back
> in Berlin, the city I love, the city to which I was
> going to devote my life work. I imagined the return
> rather differently. By this year, 1947, many of my
> buildings were scheduled for completion. The Great
> Hall, its basic structure finished, was to have
> dominated the silhouette of Berlin, and the long grand
> boulevard leading to Hitler's palatial complex was to
> be traced out. For the first time I realise that none of
> that will ever be built.[262]

They all got out, bar Heß, who, it is said, committed suicide at the age of ninety-three in 1987. Some have very plausibly maintained that there was something fishy about his death, and that he may have been murdered by the British Secret Service to prevent him from telling the world that he offered the British a reasonable peace in 1941.[263] With the last of the prisoners out of the way, the Allies had the neo-Romanesque prison torn down to prevent it from becoming a place of pilgrimage for Nazis.[264] As it lay at the centre of the British barracks complex in Spandau the British thought up a suitably profane use for the site: they built a new officers' mess there.[265]

Speer may have groused, but his lot fared rather better than their victims. The Berlin prison which saw the largest amount of blood-letting under the Third Reich was Plötzensee, one of the new-style maximum security prisons built in the second half of the last century along with Moabit and Tegel.[266] Pastor Harald Poelchau left a moving account of 'death row' in the prison, the inmates of which became his flock for almost the whole of the Third Reich. Poelchau arrived in 'die Plötze' on 1 April 1933 as one of three pastors whose job it was to minister to each of the three cell blocks of 500 to 600 prisoners. That summer came the first droves of political prisoners from the KPD and the SPD. Poelchau was supposed to give them religious instruction. Later his role was changed and he began to minister to those condemned to death.[267]

By 1945 Poelchau had worked in virtually all the maximum security prisons in the Berlin area: Tegel, Plötzensee, Moabit and Brandenburg-Görden, another prison with an overactive death chamber after 1933. In his twelve years of service he witnessed around a thousand executions. His first came on 17 April 1933. He was an ordinary criminal, a man who had tried to rob the BVG, or Berlin transport authority: he was reconciled to death, a man who was 'immature, rather primitive, stocky, short and powerful'. Poelchau had unsuccessfully tried to get out of watching the last moments of the robber. He arrived in the chamber after another man was beheaded. 'With horror I observed the fresh blood on the stone floor.' When it came to his parishioner he couldn't watch: the man was stripped to the waist and thrown to the ground, where his head was pushed down on a block. He was beheaded. 'I was overcome by a feeling of terrible sickness.'[268]

Poelchau was to learn the hard way. He went to calm the boy's mother and was all but mauled by a huge mastiff. Later he learned to avoid this situation by having the bereaved come to him. The first political prisoner to be executed was a communist, Richard Hüttig, who was accused of killing a member of the SA. In all probability he had been shot by his own men.[269]

By now Poelchau was beginning to know his fellow workers in the prison service: the three main executioners. Reichhardt was from Munich, Reindel from Magdeburg and Röttger lived in the Waldstraße in Berlin-Moabit. Röttger put on airs and graces, making himself out to be a man of a superior sort. 'In general executioners were trained butchers. Their assistants were butchers' boys, who normally stepped into their masters' shoes once their positions fell vacant.'[270]

It was a well-paid job. The executioner got 300 Reichsmark; each of his assistants, 50RMs. Röttger did twice as many executions as his two colleagues. Reindel and Reichhardt divided up the work at Plötzensee between the two of them. The latter arrived in his own car with between four and six assistants. Later there was too great a demand to leave the whole business in the hands of three men. New men appeared: Köster, Ulitzka, Weiß, Hehr and Roselieb.[271]

In the early days of the Third Reich those who fell foul of the regime were generally beheaded. 'The executioner's tool was a huge, heavy axe with an especially broad blade. Beheadings took place in the open, in front of the cell block where the condemned men were housed.'[272] This quaint, old method was discontinued by the end of 1933 when Hitler (Poelchau says it was Hitler himself) ordered twenty guillotine kits, which were assembled in Tegel Prison by the inmates themselves. Victims were brought in naked to the waist. 'Executioner, do your bidding!' shouted the court official. At this point the black curtain was drawn back and the prisoner had his first view of the guillotine. Poelchau recalls his first experience of the new method, seeing the head in a willow-basket: 'there was a monstrous loss of blood'. The prisoner's clogs had flown into the air as the blade had hit the back of his neck. The executioner then turned to the State Prosecutor: 'Herr Oberstaatsanwalt, the sentence has been carried out.' The axeman enjoyed the right to the hair in the case of a woman being beheaded. The gold teeth were also removed.[273]

In this sad catalogue of Nazi blood-lust Poelchau also tells us of the shootings, which generally took place on the Jungfernheide nearby. Although there was thought to be some sort of social superiority about being shot, the pastor could not see the advantage: 'None of the other methods of execution required such long drawn-out preparations.' Prisoners were assembled in the early morning; they were allowed to wear uniform, but without insignia of rank. They were loaded into a Black Maria with the pastor. As they were bound, Poelchau put cigarettes into their mouths and removed and replaced them on the short journey to the Jungfernheide. They were shot one by one, one of the guard giving the *coup de grâce*. By the time the last man was tied to the post and faced the two rows of pickets, 'He had died a thousand deaths before the bullet hit him.'[274]

Poelchau's account makes gruesome reading. He was, by all reports, a profoundly good, devout man who played a small role on the fringes of the Opposition's Kreisau Circle. After 20 July it was Poelchau above all who was able to report the last thoughts and wishes of so many brave men and women who passed through Hitler's claws. He sat with them on their last nights. At first he was able to offer them whatever they liked as a last meal. With rationing this became increasingly difficult and the compassionate measure was scrapped. Roast meat gave way to bread and sausage. Coffee and beer were 'tolerated'. The pastor supplemented this with tobacco and set down the prisoner's last letter.[275]

As the war progressed and defeat became obvious to all but the most deluded figures at the top, the prisons filled up with more and more enemies of the regime. Plötzensee was hit by Allied bombs. In September 1943 five Frenchmen managed to escape through the wreckage. One was later caught and betrayed the others in order to secure his own freedom. All five were hanged. The prison authorities grew worried that others would try their ploy and decided to deal swiftly with the 400 who were then on death row. Many of them were members of the Czech opposition. On the night of 7 September the mass killing began:

> It was a cold night. Every now and then an explosion lit up the dark sky. The spotlight beams danced about above us. The men were brought up one behind the other in several files. They stood there, practically

unaware of what was about to happen to them. Then they realised.[276]

The mass slaughter was interrupted by another raid and the men were led back to their cells. 'Then the murder began again.' They were all hanged, eight at a time on meathooks. The guillotine had been hit by a bomb in December 1942.[277]

Poelchau was never obliged to witness the hangings, which took place in a special room now preserved as a monument to the many men and women who died there. Quite a number of them were the natural choice to lead a future, non-Nazi Germany. The men who underwent hanging were not any worse treated than the others at first. The prison doctor assured Poelchau that they lost consciousness quickly, although the method was not as fast or efficient as the guillotine had been. After 20 July 1944 the method was changed. There is a widespread myth that cheesewire was used. That is not true, but the executioners had instructions to use thin cord, which slowly strangled the victims, rather than breaking their necks.

The authorities must have felt increasingly sensitive about the pace of slaughter in the prisons, or that Poelchau was in cahoots with some of the opponents to the regime, for they tried to keep him away from the first batch of men executed after the show trial of 8 August 1944. He was able to approach the men. The court authorities had gone to some length to make the last moments of these brave men as unpleasant as possible:

> To humiliate the superior officers they had dressed
> them all in striped jackets and convict's trousers. I can
> still see Field Marshal von Witzleben before me, who
> had to make an effort to hold up his overlarge trousers
> with his manacled hands.[278]

The former military governor of Berlin, General Paul von Hase, was worried about his wife and children. Like so many of them, he died a convinced Christian. Christianity had provided the perfect contrast and antidote to the inhumanity of Nazism.

4

Berlin Bacchanalia

Before 1943, at least, there were plenty of ways of enjoying the good things in life. Since the Second World War decent restaurants have been rather thin on the ground, and Berlin lags behind several West German cities when it comes to good food. The situation today is that the top tables are rather quiet and hidden from view. The Grand Slam in Grunewald – for some people Berlin's best – is hidden away in the clubhouse of the old Rot-Weiß tennis club, and diners have to make their way through a gallery of portraits of the city's most famous tennis stars, such as Gottfried von Cramm, before they reach their table. Another top restaurant is concealed within the walls of Berlin's freemasonic lodge, which cannot be a great lure to God-fearing Catholics.

What these establishments have in common with Berlin restaurants before the war is high prices. Their discretion, however, is something new: Berlin used to be jam-packed with huge, vulgar eating-houses. Discretion crept in during the war, when decent things could only be obtained on the black market. In February 1945, for example, the writer Erich Kästner (who was by now banned from writing) was able to make an excursion to an unnamed spot on the Havel where he tucked into unimaginable things: butter, coffee, cognac, white rolls, sausage, champagne, still wine and roast pork.[1] At precisely the same time another Berliner remembers quite appalling scenes during the raids which only then devastated the heart of the city: Silesian refugees were caught on the burning tarmac left by the British bombers and slowly perished in the flames.

With difficulty she was able to make her way up the Wilhelmstraße to the still miraculously surviving Adlon Hotel, where she washed and changed and put the gruelling scenes she had witnessed behind her. It was the cocktail hour, and Herbert von Karajan and his then wife came up for Hungarian salami and *barack pálinka*. Later they ate together in the dining-room downstairs. Frau von Karajan opened her handbag and passed the waiter some delicacy in a tin: 'That is just for the *Herr Kapellmeister* and myself.' A few minutes later Louis Adlon appeared with a bottle of wine and presented it to the couple so obviously excluded from the contents of the Karajans' tin: 'That is for the Colonel and yourself,' he said.[2]

In wartime even quite modest treats took on the appearance of luxuries. By that time Goebbels had closed down virtually all bars and restaurants in the interests of his 'total war'; only the Adlon and a few other places remained open for high-ranking officers, senior party members and diplomats. It was the end of a long tradition. Nicolai was able to produce a comprehensive list of Berlin's best inns in the mid-eighteenth century. They were the Stadt Paris and the König von Engelland in the Brüderstraße and the König von Portugal in the Burgstraße.[3] That Nicolai should have named the König von Portugal was no accident. It was a family business which had been patronised by the Soldier-King in its time. Frau Nicolai had made him his favourite dish of green cabbage and ham and Herr Nicolai had been rewarded with a miniature of the king, which the landlord wore in his buttonhole.[4]

Accommodation was best at the Stadt Paris, where a four-room apartment was available. A bottle of ordinary Cahors, made most probably by relatives of members of Berlin's French colony, cost 8 *Groschen*. By contrast, Haut Brion was 12 *Groschen* and burgundy 22 *Groschen*. Rhine wine was priced at anything between 20 *Groschen* and a thaler (a thaler being 24 *Groschen*). The most expensive drink cited by Nicolai is champagne, which sold for a thaler and a half.[5]

The *agréments* of the city had been greatly enhanced by the arrival of the Huguenots eighty-five years before. Foreign names were the rule when it came to places to eat and drink. Nicolai recommends the *Speisehäuser* (literally, 'eating-houses') Charrier and Bianchi, and the wine houses Lamartinière and Joyeur. Tarroni was already established in the Tiergarten.[6] More exclusive was courtly Charlottenburg, where eighteenth-century intellectuals sought to create a 'society without laws' over champagne and Pfalz wine in taverns such as the Tiergartenmühle, the Muscowsche Gastwirtschaft, the Hippodrom am Knie and the Türkische Zelt.[7]

While the smarter Berliners went to the Tiergarten or Charlottenburg, the artisans crossed the Spree to Moabit. On Sundays there was dancing at Eisert, with steps imported from Paris. The growing industrial proletariat from the Beusselkietz added an earthier element to Moabit's more famous pubs: the Kronenbrauerei, Moabiter Gesellschaftshaus and Moabiter Bürgersäle.[8] Smoking was another incentive to quit Berlin's walls: until 1848 it was not permitted in pubs in the city. The *Tabagie*, or smoker's inn, was consequently associated with liberalism. Not for nothing was Glaßbrenner's Herr Buffey meant to be the owner of such an establishment. The first *Tabagie* was the Tivoli garden in Kreuzberg on the site of the present (but doomed) Schultheiß brewery. It opened as the Hopfsche Bockbierbrauerei in 1838, complete with its own pub. There were several such brew-pubs in Kreuzberg: Habel, Gratweil, Kelsch and the Union in nearby Rixdorf.[9]

Even more down to earth were the pubs in the Landsberger Allee, which was also famed for its brewery pubs. Rodenberg compared (tongue in cheek, no doubt) the Böhmische Brauhaus with its tall chimney to the tower of the Alhambra in Granada. Patzenhofer had its first premises here. There was also a string of *Weißbier* pubs with the familiar sign 'Hier können Familien Kaffee kochen' ('Here families may brew coffee'). This is familiar now from Hans Baluschek's painting of 1895, which shows a group of working-class women *en plein air* stirring their coffee in tall white jugs. There are *Schnecken*, like Chelsea buns, to eat with it.[10] The pubs aimed at the family trade. As in Bavaria you could bring in your own food, or radishes could be bought; or hot sausages straight from the cauldron. While the men drank, played cards, and occasionally punched one another, the women did their sewing over the coffee cups.[11]

One adopted Berliner who had a highly elaborate theory about the nature of drinking was E. T. A. Hoffmann. At its best, wine had the power to open doors to a higher world of imagination and revelation.[12] In *Die drei Freunde*, the friends meet on a Whit Monday in Weber's 'Tent' in the Tiergarten. It was presumably a holiday, as Alexander was only able to get a riverside table with the greatest difficulty. Under the influence, Marzell compares Bellevue Palace to a Roman villa, but later the magic wears off: 'Bellevue became Bellevue again, the lightning conductor reverted to being a lightning conductor and Weber's 'Tent' went back to being an ordinary pub.'[13]

Wine was capable of lifting man on to a higher plane; beer was not. In the *Abenteuer der Silvesternacht*, Hoffmann takes the time to ridicule the Berlin beer-drinker, the ancestor of the *Weißbier* philistine of the pre-March days, through his literary persona, the conductor Kreisler. It is New Year's Eve and Kreisler is out for a walk. He crosses the little Opernbrücke, by the Opera House, continues from Friedrichswerder to Cölln over the Spree and passes the Schloss, then turns in over the Schleusenbrücke, walking up towards the Jägerstraße past the old Mint. There he is struck by the cold and begins to lust after a 'proper slug of some strong drink'.[14]

From Tiermann's premises a crowd of fashionable Berli-

ners is emerging, talking of oysters and 'Elfer' wine.★
Tiermann is evidently closing. Kreisler-Hoffmann goes next
door into a gloomy *Bierkeller*. The new fashion is rum. The
landlady is reprimanding her husband: 'You must get in some
rum, and some anchovies.' The landlord is suspicious of
such innovations: 'Once I went upstairs above the shop at
Tiermann's next door, where there are all those lovely pictures. There was a lively crowd in the room and a tiny, pale
little fellow was carrying a dish filled with the weirdest
multicoloured things: yellow, red, blue and green, all mixed
up together. They called it an Italian salad: God forbid!'[17]
He has clearly chanced on Hoffmann himself, entertaining
his friends.

The landlord has no rum, but he can produce beer from
Mannheim, Fredersdorf, Neuwald and Stettin. A man comes
in and orders a bottle of Stettin beer and a pipe of good
tobacco. 'I found myself in a world of such sublime philistinism that the Devil himself would have shown his respect
and left me in peace.' Spikher, the little old man in question,
calls the beer 'wine of the north', compounding the sin of
philistinism in Kreisler-Hoffmann's eyes. Fortunately he is
distracted from this unedifying sight by the arrival of Peter
Schlemihl, Chamisso's shadowless creation, with a collection

★ Hoffmann is referring to the 1811 'Elfer' or 'Comet' vintage
(Elf = eleven; Eilfer = comet). The wines were particular favourites
of his. At the end of his life his publishers added a case of
Rüdesheimer Hinterhäuser 'Eilfer' to his royalties.[15] Goethe was
a fellow enthusiast:

Setze mir nicht, du Grobian,
Mir den Krug so derb vor die Nase!
Wer mir Wein bringt, sehe mich freundlich an,
Sonst trübt sich der Eilfer im Glase.[16]

(Don't slam the thing down, you thug:
Can't you perform any act with class?
He must come in friendship who brings the jug,
Or he'll spoil the comet in the glass.)

of rare plants under his arm befitting a character invented by a man who was as distinguished a botanist as he was an author. Kreisler-Hoffmann recognises him too late: only after he has stridden over the top of the towers in the Gendarmenmarkt in his seven-league boots.[18]

Hoffmann disapproved of beer and beer-drinkers, which was possibly just as well: beer in Berlin was a mixed blessing anyway. At its origins, Berlin beer, like *Weißbier* later, was a cottage industry. The early electors allowed taverns to brew every two weeks or so to satisfy customers in their *Auschänke*. Few found it in their hearts to praise the results. Better beer was to be had from Bernau to the east, and Werder to the west. In 1630, when there were already 143 brew-houses in the city, a story was told about an attempt to make beer up to Bernau standards within the walls of Berlin. Malted barley, yeast, water and the brewers' boys were all brought in from Bernau, but when the results were put before a panel of tasters it was declared to be nothing more than the usual Berlin beer.[19]★

Beers from the periphery had a marginally better reputation: Potsdam and Köpenick, for example, where the beer was made from wheat, or Zerbst in Anhalt, where the

---

★ Zerbsten, Kross'ner und Ruppiner,
Breihan auch von Halberstadt,
Dachstein, Kottbusser, Berliner,
Was man sonst für tränken hat,
Alles sind zwar gute Säfte;
Doch Bernauer gibt mehr Kräfte.
    Diesem müssen alle weichen
    Und vor ihm die Segel streichen.[20]

(Zerbsten, Kross'ner and Ruppiner,
Halberstädter Breihan too,
Dachstein, Kottbusser, Berliner,
Or whatever beer they give you,
They all can make some decent swill;
But Bernau alone tops the bill.
    Bernau beer is the prince of ales
    Before it men must strike their sails.)

beer had good keeping qualities. Tangermünde and Halberstadt also had their admirers. The latter presumably derived
something from the purity of the water in the Harz Mountains. The number of beers imported from elsewhere rose
steadily in the eighteenth century. In 1711 there were fifty-
one; the following year, seventy-three. They came from
Bremen, England, Stockholm and Bohemia.[21] Werder was
later more famous for its cherries, and as the destination for
working-class excursions once Moabit had turned into an
industrial slum and the railway had offered the opportunity
to spend Sunday farther afield.* What tends to be forgotten
is that it used to be well known for its yellow and reddish
brown beer too. Like so many local brews it disappeared
under the onslaught of Bavarian and Bohemian beers from
the 1840s onwards, having first been relegated to the kitchen
and the nursery, damned with the epiphet 'nourishing' to
early extinction.[22]

Such beers were adequate for most Berliners, but visitors
to the city often felt they had tasted better. When young
Julius Levy (the founder of the *Deutsche Rundschau*, Julius
Rodenberg) arrived as a student in Berlin from Kassel in
1853, he was appalled by the thin beer. In those days decent
beer was available from just two or three places in the whole
city. *Weißbier*, that traditional Berlin brew of malted barley,
wheat and hops, was notoriously acidic; but in the first half
of the nineteenth century, at least, Berliners lapped it up.[23]
In Otto Scholz's *Posse, Eine Berliner Grisette*, there is a *Berliner
Weißbierlied*, which was set to music by Lortzing. It expresses
the sort of smug philistinism which would have shored up the
malign views of E. T. A. Hoffmann:

> Trinke Weißbier, liebe Jugend,
> Höre achtsam mein Gebot,
> Dann erreicht da jene Tugend,

* See Claire Waldoff's song *Die Radpartie* (Helmut Markiewicz).

Die dem guten Bürger not.
Hätten doch nur die Franzosen
Dies Getränk gekostet schon,
Wär keen Unglück zugestoßen,
Käm gar keen Revolution.

Sitzt man nach des Tages Hitze,
Schmachtet so'ne Weiße an,
Er ist erst der Mensch was nütze,
Wenn er einen Zug getan:
Mögen Völker revoltieren
Mag die Welt zu Grunde geh'n,
Das soll mich nicht sehr genieren,
Schmeckt die Weiße doch so schön.[24]

(Stick to *Weißbier*, all of you,
Listen carefully and take heed,
Then you'll muster all the virtue
That a good citizen needs.
If the French had only waited –
Sampled of this wheaten broth –
Would their fury have abated,
No revolution and no wrath.

The parching sun's gone down at last,
Man pants for *Weiße* beer.
After he's accomplished his tasks,
All he needs is this good cheer.
Let the people rise in anger.
Let the world succumb to flood.
There should never be a danger,
While the *Weißbier* tastes so good.)

Berliner *Weiße* was already threatened when these lines were written. It was Georg Leonard Hopf, a cooper from the Pfalz, who first introduced bottom-fermented, Bavarian-style lager-beer to Berlin in 1827. From now on more and more *Kneipen* would hang out a sign advertising 'Echt Bairisches Bier' (real Bavarian beer), in most cases when it was anything but. The Bavarian-style beer none the less made an unrelenting progress as the century wore on, pushing aside the local styles, be they bitter, brown or white.[25] After Bavarian beer, the next fashion was for 'Pilsner'-style beers from Bohemia. In Fontane's *Der Stechlin* of 1898, the wedding guests argue over where they are to go to spend the rest of the evening:

> 'Siechen, naturally.'
> 'Oh, Siechen. Siechen is for Philistines.'
> 'All right; then let's go to Schwere Wagner.'
> 'That's even more ghastly. I want Weihenstephan.'
> 'And I demand Pilsner.'[26]*

The diminishing price of bottled beer had already had the beneficial effect of weaning Berliners off schnapps. Developments in refrigeration by the Munich scientist Carl Linde (*von* Linde from 1897) made 'lager' beer that much easier to produce. By 1900 Berlin had become the most important brewing city on the Continent with 108 breweries. Of these, 77 were producing bottom-fermented lagers. Gustav Stresemann, later Chancellor of the Weimar Republic and himself the son of a *Weißbier* brewer, lamented the change in Berlin *moeurs* the shift to lager had brought about:

> What a difference between the old Berlin *Weißbier* pub
> and the famous beer palaces created by Aschinger in
> the last few years! In the one, almost venerable citizens
> installed at a simple table united behind their great
> globular glasses, either reading the newspaper or
> conversing peacefully or complacently. In the other, an
> eternal toing and froing, hustle and bustle, individuals
> scarcely giving themselves enough time to find a seat,

---

* Siechen was a famous beer palace on the Potsdamer Platz, Schwere Wagner was known for its 'heavy' Bavarian beers – hence the name. Weihenstephan was and is the former Benedictine monastery in Freising in Bavaria where Munich's Technische Hochschule has its brewing faculty. The brewery is now owned by the Bavarian state.

but standing up, eating one of the obligatory rolls or
tossing down a measure of proper beer with an eye
on the clock, then rushing off after a few minutes to
make room for others who, just like themselves, want
the chance to enjoy a little something without making
a dent in their schedules.[27]

Stresemann was referring to the Aschinger *Bierquellen*
which were springing up all over Berlin. The chain was
founded by the brothers Carl and August Aschinger from
Württemberg in 1882, with the first opening in the Neue
Roßstraße in the old *Kietz*. They were the fast-food special-
ists of the day. Customers in a hurry could swallow their pea
soup with bacon at the bar, and scoff unlimited numbers of
white rolls, or *Schrippen*. By the First World War Aschinger
had become the greatest 'gastronomic imperium' in Berlin.[28]
Those who had a little more time on their hands, like Elias
Canetti and his friend Isaac Babel, could enjoy the mirror
glass, paper napkins, beer mugs and cutlets in aspic; they
could also admire, at least, the waitresses in their white and
blue uniforms.[29]

In Yvan Goll's *Sodome et Berlin*, Odemar has a vision of
Aschinger, 'with their strings of sausages, their mountains
of golden herrings, their sacks full of mayonnaise and their
billows of whipped cream'. As Döblin put it, 'Anyone who
has no paunch can acquire one here and stretch it as far as
he wants.'[30] By 1930 there were twenty-three outlets with
snack bars in the inner city, as well as fifteen *Konditoreien* and
a further eight orthodox restaurants. Aschinger also owned
the famous Weinhaus Rheingold on the Potsdamer Platz.[31]
It was a revolution in drinking style which had come with
Berlin's elevation to the imperial capital. In 1895 the *Berliner
illustrierte Zeitung* was able to write: 'The beer palaces of the
Munich beer kings Pschorr,* Sedlmayer, etc., are a sign of

---

* Pschorr's elaborate Berlin headquarters in the Friedrichstraße
contrived to survive the Blitz; one of the few buildings in the
street that did.[32]

the new Berlin . . . through them Berliners have experienced the concept of comfortable drinking for the first time.'[33]

Local firms soon began to copy the Bavarian-type beers which had captured the imaginations of Berliners. One of the better known was 'Patzenhofer' from Spandau.[34] The one company really to steal a march on the Bavarians, however, was Schultheiß,[35] which eventually took over the Tivoli site behind the Kreuzberg. The Tivoli gardens had opened in 1829, eight years after the founding of Schinkel's cast-iron monument to the Wars of Liberation that crowns the hill. In 1842 the restaurateur Roth turned the little park into a beer garden. The brewery came fifteen years later, built to plans by Peter Lenné. Schultheiß acquired it in 1891.

The future was in beer. Glaßbrenner's Berliner had been addicted to schnapps, a drink which took the edge off the disagreeable side effects of rapid industrialisation. In the 1840s Berlin had over thirty distilleries and every fourth house sold hard alcohol. The result had been the decline of brewing skill. The 'Bavarian' beer which made its appearance from the 1840s onwards reversed the process. It had considerable advantages over the local *Weiße*: it contained less carbon dioxide and was easy to pump, and digest. Its accessibility made beer popular again and hastened the appearance of both beer palaces and beer gardens all over the city. By 1871 the Tivoli Brewery was the biggest in Berlin. Twenty years later Schultheiß was the biggest in Germany.[36]★

If the production of high-quality, cleanly fermented beer rang the knell for Berlin's brewing traditions, it is easy to imagine that it encountered little or no resistance from the local wine lobby. In the eighteenth century wine came from all sorts of unlikely places, such as Potsdam (Sanssouci was

---

★ Schultheiß celebrated its centenary in 1943 at a special party at the Opera House. Lip-service was paid to the regime then in power.[37]

built on the former vineyard when a new one was laid out on the far side of the Obeliskstraße), Werder, Spandau, Frankfurt an der Oder, Küstrin, Lebus and Oderberg.[38] Berlin's most famous vineyard was Götzens Weinberg, 'Kreuzberg'. The vineyards had been at least partially pulled up in 1813 in order to create a defensive position against the French. Possibly some were replanted, for the Staatliche Weingarten existed until 1870, when it was sold to the Tivoli Brewery to give them room for further expansion.[39]

Even as early as the 1890s Julius Rodenberg found it hard to believe that all these 'Weinberge' dotted about Berlin actually produced wine. Nicolai had written that Field Marshal Derfflinger's vines had been blighted by frost in 1740: 'What amazes me', writes Rodenberg, 'is that they had not frozen earlier.'[40] According to Franz Lederer, there were still vines in Berlin in the 1890s, at the time when Rodenberg was writing. He had tasted the wine, which he declared to be 'rather acidic'. He produces a Berlin expression for the wine: 'You must pour it through your stockings; it will close up the holes.'[41] It is a rather tamer version of a coarse epithet formerly used by the Viennese to describe the wines of the Brünn Road, which were also said to be intolerably acidic: a 'Hemdzieher', they called them.

II

Fondness for rough spirits among the Berlin working class was recognised as a social problem by the late nineteenth century when the Verein gegen den Mißbrauch geistiger Getränke ('Association to counter the Abuse of Spirits') was formed. In 1892 there were 9,200 recognised alcohol addicts in Berlin. Between 1879 and 1882 2,194 were hospitalised and forty died. In 1875 it was thought that the following percentages of inmates at Plötzensee Prison were there for alcohol-related crimes: 70 per cent of those resisting arrest,

66 per cent of those convicted for immorality, 55 per cent of those caught disturbing the peace, and 51 per cent of those guilty of wounding.[42] Even today every newspaper stall and *U-Bahn* kiosk stocks a wide display of *Schnäpse* that red-faced Berliners buy with no apparent shame when most people would be expecting nothing stronger than coffee.

The ancestor of the Berlin café was the *Konditorei*. The best known in Heine's day was Josty, but it failed to impress the poet. People were crammed into a room decorated like a pub, where they slurped at cream and licked their fingers.[43] Tiermann (where Hoffmann had spoken of oysters and comet-wine) made the best sweets, but there was too much butter in the cooking.[44] Jagor was not without its faults, including tough meat. Fuchs on the Linden was lavish in its décor, but, as Heine so cogently objects, 'I don't eat mirrors or silk hangings, and when I want something to please the *eyes* I go to Spontini's *Cortez* or his *Olympia*.'[45]

By the 1840s the *Konditoreien* had assumed a political importance for the citizens of Berlin, who lived under the constant and oppressive gaze of the minister Eichhorn and his spies. The better *Konditorei* could be assumed to stock a selection of non-Prussian papers from which one could glean a little uncensored news of what was going on in the world 'between doses of *Spitzkuchen* and java'.[46] Different *Konditoreien* became associated with different party-political allegiances and social classes. One man who set out to study the phenomenon was Karl Marx's friend Dronke. Kranzler, which has survived into our own day as the most uninteresting café in Berlin, was, according to Dronke, not much better then. Here, where officers and dandies met over ices and hot chocolate (the only available drink), 'the conversation touches on nothing besides horses, dogs and dancing girls'.[47]

By common consent the most important *Konditorei* was Stehely. Mozart had used it during his visit to Berlin in 1790 and Hoffmann had also apparently sought inspiration there.

Being on the Gendarmenmarkt, it was certainly convenient, if nothing else.[48]★ Stehely's character altered at different times of the day. In the morning in came the senior civil servants to leaf through the newspapers over a glass of Madeira or Málaga. The next to arrive were the actors and dancers from the nearby Schauspielhaus, who naturally made a good deal of noise. They were followed by members of the officer corps. When they left at three or four, their places were taken by university teachers. Their departure signalled the arrival of the writers and radicals who gathered in Stehely's famous red room. These were accompanied by teams of Eichhorn's spies who pretended to read the newspapers while they mopped up as much of the conversation as they could. When the radicals left, the evenings became calm. Stehely's plush seats were occupied by a few old gentlemen on their own.[50]

When Berlin became an imperial city, the *Konditorei* crept back into its old skin. The artists and radicals left and it was once more occupied by stout Berliners and provincials desiring coffee and cream cakes. The big city café took over on the Linden, the Potsdamer Platz and the Kurfürstendamm, as they gradually filled up with buildings. The Romanischen Café has now been replaced by the horrid Europa Centre, so that anyone wishing to imagine the famous institution at its height must look at photographs and film footage, or Willi Jaeckel's evocative picture in the Bröhan Museum. It derived its name from Schwechten's design: it had been built as part of the Kaiser-Wilhelms-Gedächtniskirche scheme, and to play the stylistic game it was modelled in the Romanesque idiom.[51]

The Romanischen's success was built on the failure of the old Café des Westens which opened its compact premises in

---

★ Stehely does not figure on Hoffmann's playful map of the Gendarmenmarkt and its neighbouring streets which he drew in 1815, but possibly he had yet to discover it properly.[49]

1895 on the corner of the Kurfürstendamm and the Joachimstalerstraße. It was owned by Ernst Pauly and rapidly gathered up the young talents working in Berlin at the time: the journalist Paul Lindau, the writers Wedekind, Peter Hille and the playwright Carl Sternheim.[52] It was soon dubbed the 'Café Größenwahn' ('Café Megalomania') by its regulars. One of these was the chemist-turned-writer ¶rich Mühsam, who having abandoned his pharmacy on the Weddingplatz moved to Moabit and joined in the all-night sessions at the 'artists' table in the Café des Westens. Pauly got greedy as a result of his success. Returning from a long period in Munich, Mühsam found his café had changed: the artists' table had been moved to a new niche, an innovation which had driven most of the revolutionary artists elsewhere. The marble table at which the academic sculptor Begas had sketched had been placed under glass. Worse: a bust of William II had been set up over the telephone box.[53]

Mühsam didn't like the new-style café and joined the search for a better place to meet his friends. The Café des Westens was in the meantime colonised by aesthetes with the works of Oscar Wilde or Stefan George tucked under their arms.[54]* At the Café Monopol in the Friedrichstraße he ran into Reinhardt and his troupe, but the Bohemians left the Monopol after the landlord refused to grant them the concession of their own 'artists' table'. The next stop was the Café Savoy, but a new colour scheme ran counter to their tastes and they moved on again. Their last stop before installing their court at the Romanischen was the Café Sezession.[55]

The Café des Westens became the 'alte Café', the 'old place'. It was still used by some. The Austrian journalist Vicki Baum was sitting in the café in the first days of the First World War, celebrating her husband's appointment to

---

* What they made of the bust of William II and Begas's table, Mühsam doesn't say.

a new job in journalism, when the waiter brought in a blackboard with the latest news scrawled across it: 'The Russians are nineteen kilometres from Berlin. In the course of its advance, the enemy has poisoned all springs and reservoirs. Beware! Drink no water! Maintain order!' It was further evidence that no rumour was too silly to be believed.[56] The hunt for spies led to tragic occurrences in many instances.[57]

Vicki Baum's continued patronage of the old place may have had something to do with her recent arrival from Austria. Anybody who was anybody had graduated to the Romanischen. That applied to the waiter, 'Red' Richard, too. The Romanischen took over the functions of protest against the pomp and posturing of the Wilhelmine Age. 'Every sip of coffee that they drank here, either for cash or on credit, was a demonstration against the stucco-façades of the Kurfürstendamm, against the damask hangings and silver-services in the flats, and above all against a world of luxury, which many began to appreciate only when it was no longer there.'[58]

In those pre-war days Else Lasker-Schüler was one of the most prominent denizens of the Romanischen, with its two groundfloor saloons known as the 'pools' for swimmers and non-swimmers.* The poetess from Wuppertal had already digested two husbands, including the editor of *Der Sturm*, Herwath Walden. She ennobled her fellow Bohemians with outrageous titles. She was 'Jussuf Prince of Thebes'; Richard Dehmel, the 'King of the Forest': Peter Hille, 'St Peter'; the satirist Karl Kraus – an occasional visitor to Berlin from Vienna – 'the Cardinal'; and the poet and physician Gottfried Benn, the 'Young King Giselher'.[59]

Other regular members of her court were the elegant scrounger John Höxter and the painters: Max Slevogt, who

---

* The sense is of participation and non-participation. Kästner's Jakob Fabian dies – literally – because he cannot swim.

was also famed for his talents as a raconteur; Leo von König, one of several to paint the Romanischen and its *Stammgäster*; and Emil Orlik, who sat in the non-swimmers' pool, where he found it easier to pick up young women. The porter, Nietz, had the job of making sure that these famous artists and poets were not unduly pestered by their fans.[60]

Not everyone chose to get involved with the tribes of self-important Bohemians like Else Lasker-Schüler (Graf Harry Kessler thought her a 'beastly person' and tried his best to ignore her until Theodor Däubler thrust her at him in an 'elephantine way') and her friends.[61] Pirandello worked in the café, but no one knew where. Upstairs, on the gallery, people came in for a quiet game of chess in the company of their *Kiebitzer*.[62] After the war, at least, the clientele was quite a hotchpotch: old-fashioned nobles, owners of large estates, impoverished officers, soldiers who had fought the last-ditch campaign in the Baltic, and communists, all jumbled together.[63]

The success of the Romanischen was unexpected. One writer called it 'an anachronism, an architectural monstrosity . . . the coffee was bad, the cakes stale, and the hard-boiled eggs expensive'.[64] Its popularity was dictated by the new *Weltstadt*'s need for artistic institutions on a Parisian model, come what may, and its size meant that it could be broad church. Pauly opened a new Café des Westens at Kurfürstendamm 26, in the hope of bringing back his old clientele, but they stayed put. Easy credit terms were naturally an advantage. Most of the 'Möchtegern Literaten' (what today in New York would probably be called 'wannabe' writers) managed to wangle their drinks 'auf Pump', or on tick. Another trick was 'Nassauerei', which meant subsisting on the same cup of coffee for as long as humanly possible. Those who abused the patience of the landlord, Herr Fiering, a man variously seen as an amateur philosopher or a sufferer from piles, were presented with an '*Ausweis*', or passport. 'You are requested to leave our establishment upon payment for your drink, and never again to set foot here. Failure to comply with this request will render the offender liable for prosecution for breach of the peace.'[65]

Receipt of an *Ausweis* was taken seriously: it meant that journalists were denied contact with editors who might be persuaded to offer commissions. From 1910, for example, Herwath Walden was to be found here surrounded by his discoveries: Benn and Döblin, and the painters Kokoschka, Kirchner and Marc.[66] The *Ausweis* meant not only the loss of credit, but also the end of free newspapers, a boon to journalists needing to plagiarise a story. Like in the best Viennese cafés even today, hour after hour could be frittered away in the Romanischen. When the café finally shut down in the early hours, the last customers sat up in the waiting-room of the Zoo Station, passing a single ticket from person to person under the table.[67] Not for nothing did one poor recipient of an *Ausweis* shoot himself.[68]

Naturally, the Romanischen thrived in the Weimar years. It wasn't long before the precocious Augsburger Bert Brecht made his first appearance in the pool for a meeting with the poet Klabund. In those years when so many patrons went out looking for undiscovered artistic talent, the Romanischen was an important place on the map for men like Elias Canetti, who had been taken up by the Herzfelde brothers but was otherwise unknown as a writer.[69] The artists' table continued until the death of the painter Slevogt in 1932.[70] A few months later the Gestapo had their own *Stammtisch* at the café, where they sat with their leather coats and German shepherd dogs, looking for signs of artistic life to stamp out.[71] It was no longer the time for artistic expression, but the Berlin wits, copying the Nazi love of superlatives, christened the public lavatory on the corner of the Joachimstalerstraße the 'greatest convenience of all time'.[72] The Romanischen in its heyday summed up everything they had resented most in their *petit bourgeois* rancour. At least one of the men of 20 July went to his death after a dressing-down from Freisler who insisted that his poor tortured body recalled the 'pitiful state' of the spineless intellectuals of the Romanischen Café.[73] By the time he had uttered those words, however, the café was a gutless ruin.

There were a few more Berlin cafés that maintained their artistic cachet during the years prior to the First World War or Weimar days. The Russian café in the Nürnberger Straße was considered to be an annexe of the Romanischen.[74] The Austrian journalist Joseph Roth haunted the Konditorei Schneider along with the philosopher Ludwig Marcuse and the actress Jenny Jugo. The attraction for Schneider seems to have been at least partly to do with its two pretty waitresses, one of whom became Marcuse's bride.[75] The editors from the two great houses of Ullstein and Mosse met at the Café Jädicke in the Kochstraße in Kreuzberg, famous for its *Baumkuchen*.[76]

The Potsdamer Platz was the alternative centre of café life to the Kurfürstendamm. In the Haus Vaterland was the Café Piccadilly, which seated 2,500. The Crown Prince and Crown Princess Cecilie came to the opening, and the Berliners rhymed: 'Der Willi und die Cilli, die jehn in't Piccadilly!' During the First World War the name was changed to Café Vaterland. The Haus Vaterland was taken over in 1927 by Kempinski, who turned the whole thing into a theme-park: 'A stroll through Kempinski is like going on a world tour . . . You docked in Spain first, where you were lured in among the barrels of a proper *bodega* and drank excellent sherry. You proceeded to Greece, unless you had stopped off to try the juice of the Sicilian grape in the *Osteria*. Suddenly the customer found himself in the quiet [confines] of a Moorish palace . . . the Golden Horn on the horizon and Constantinople with its mosques and minarets, and Turkish hookahs on Turkish tables. Original Turkish coffee was served from Turkish copper pots along with proper Turkish *raki*. The waiters wore fezzes on their heads. And when that was not quite oriental enough, one had only to wait a moment and then the beautiful women of the Orient began to dance for you.' In another section there was a background of the Vienna hills where south German and Austrian tastes were catered for: chicken in breadcrumbs, *Palatschinken, Geselchtes*,★ Bavarian *Weißwurst* and beer.[77]

More homely was the room that represented a Rhineland landscape complete with orchards in blossom and looming castles. The revellers sat in a genuine boat which took up the whole length of the brasserie with its 'thousands' of diners.

> One thousand identical German heads: one thousand huge heads, pink and translucent like bowls of tallow, pink or bald, firmly implanted on thick necks or triple chins. The faces were as hairless as the crowns, washed out by beer: the mouths alone formed a vast hole into which blond beer disappeared and out of which blasted the thunderous notes of the 'Wacht am Rhein'.
>
> All Germany was there to celebrate the launch of the beer 'Triumpfator': Herr Wotan was there, in the gold-rimmed spectacles of a chemistry professor; Herr Faffner, a senior employee on the railways; Herr Siegfried, who sold cigars and cigarettes in Moabit – ancestral heroes, stout contemporaries.[78]

The Kempinksis were Jews and Haus Vaterland was sequestered in 1937 and reallotted to Aschinger. The shell of the building finally disappeared after the uprising of 17 June 1953. The war years favoured a more intimate scale. At the Goldene Hufeisen, racially fumigated Berlin flocked to see the city's one remaining Negress. The St-Pauli Bar was run by a woman who had lost two husbands in the fighting. She might have found a third at the dance hall of Walterchen der Seelentröster ('Little Walter the Soul Consoler') which functioned as a marriage market. Die neue Welt was a huge

★ Sweet pancakes and salted and smoked meat from the mountains.

beerhall in Neukölln. Much livelier was the X-Bar where pre-war delicacies could be obtained as well as illegal Scotch.[79]

III

The rich Berliner could also offload his money in the city's restaurants. The first of these to achieve any distinction was Borchardt. Friedrich Wilhelm Borchardt was born in Labes in Pomerania in 1826. After serving in the Prussian army, he opened his restaurant and delicatessen in the Französische Straße in the Friedrichstadt. It was clearly an ambitious project from the first. The building at number 48 was a neo-Florentine *palazzo*. In just eight years Borchardt received his first royal warrant. A contemporary print entitled *Vor dem Delikatessen* describes the Lucullan nature of the new enterprise: officers are leaving the premises, while a cluster of beggars and street musicians is pressed up against the window-pane, drooling over the delicacies on show.[80]

In 1875 Friedrich Wilhelm was made a *Kommerzienrat*. The favour shown to him by the Hohenzollerns up at the palace gave the cue to the diplomatic missions in the new German capital. More and more of them ordered the food for their receptions ready-made from Borchardt. Catering was an important part of the restaurant from the beginning: as Germany grew in stature, so did Borchardt. They cooked for the Congress of Berlin in 1878; for the last session of the Council of State before Bismarck's fall in 1890; and for the opening of the Kiel Canal when 1,050 meals of eleven courses each and six different wines were served in 55 minutes flat.[81]

Borchardt was the scene of Friedrich von Holstein's little gatherings, where the Foreign Office official endeavoured to shape Europe's foreign policy from the lunch table. An idea which would have been delicious to French gastronomic writers such as Grimod de La Reynière and Brillat-Savarin. It is not certain, however, that his famous *Schnitzel* was created at Borchardt. These days it is little more than a veal escalope topped with a soft-boiled egg. The original was rather more elaborate: a veal *chop* topped with a lightly poached egg and garnished with mushrooms, caviar, lobster and salmon.[82]

The Junker was prone to worship his ruling house, and Borchardt was naturally popular among the provincial nobility. Things began to change after William II ascended the throne in 1888 and the restaurant hung his portrait in the Red Saloon. Possibly the Junkers didn't like the flashier style of the new ruler, or perhaps the food had gone off; whatever the explanation, they began to look elsewhere. Theodor Fontane records the moment in his novella *Irrungen, Wirrungen* of 1887, when Rienäcker's uncle takes him to Hiller, rather than Borchardt, which had been his choice up till then. In another of Fontane's books, *Stine* of 1890, die Pittelkow is anxious to learn whether the dinner has arrived from Borchardt to feed her elderly, aristocratic guests.[83]

Business was good enough for Borchardt's sons to expand in 1899, when a new wine-and-food shop was built next door at number 47. With the population moving west and new restaurants being founded to cater for it, Borchardt became increasingly a standby for the court and the embassies. It was still Berlin's luxury delicatessen: Fauchon and Hediard rolled into one. Even Joachim Ringelnatz alludes to the quality of Borchardt's food in his *Silvester bei den Kannibalen* (New Year's Eve with the Cannibals):

> Nur dem Häuptling wird eine steinalte Frau
> Zubereitet als Karpfen blau.
> Riecht beinah wie Borchardt-Küche, Berlin,
> Nur mehr nach Kokosfett und Palmin.[84]

(An old dowager was cooked up for the chief

Boiled like *carpe au bleu: sur le vif.*
It smelled like cooking from Borchardt in Berlin,
Save the coconut oil she was stewed in.)

By now Borchardt was the *pompier* among Berlin's eating-houses. Under the Third Reich it was 'Aryanised'. As it continued to be frequented by the diplomatic missions (the few that there were once the war began), Göring's *Forschungsamt* installed listening devices in the *chambres separées*. According to one source Borchardt had become little more than a high-class brothel. Part of the restaurant, however, was still operating normally on 1 August 1944, when Ursula von Kardorff had lunch there between two interrogations at Gestapo headquarters. Whatever Borchardt's main *raison d'être* at the time, its stoves ceased to function when number 48 was hit by a bomb.[85] After the war, the SED licensed a restaurant at number 47 called *Lukullus*, which despite the promise of its name is unlikely to have lived up to its pretensions. Later the premises were used as a storeroom, a discotheque, and finally, ignominy upon ignominy, Borchardt became a canteen. The story, however, has a happy ending: in 1991 the German state sold number 47 to Roland Mary and Marina Richter, who reopened an imitation of Paris's Coupole in the old delicatessen. It has proved a remarkable tale of regeneration.

Almost as extraordinary has been the history of another of Berlin's great gastronomic institutions, Horchers. Gustav Horcher opened his restaurant in 1905 in the Luther (now Martin Luther) Straße in the neue Westen. Its progress was slow at first, but it was mentioned in the 1923 English-language edition of Baedeker, though without the distinguishing star accorded to such restaurants as Borchardt. By the time the 1936 German edition appeared, however, Horchers had taken a leap into the firmament of Berlin's top tables. Baedeker described the food as 'excellent', and it was now star-rated. Behind Horchers rise was the portly

Hermann Göring – among other things, Minister-President of Prussia. Göring arrived in Berlin at the end of 1927. Money was short, and a seat in the Reichstag was a practical necessity. When Hitler agreed to his candidature, it was to Horchers that the former air-ace went to celebrate. Gustav Horcher had been wise enough to extend credit to Göring, who was to reward the restaurateur with his loyalty to the end. In July 1934, 'General' Göring (as he now was) held a dinner at Horchers to thank his staff for their help in the Night of the Long Knives, when a hundred or so of Hitler's opponents had been slaughtered. The party ate crab.

Once the war started, Göring did not abandon Gustav Horcher. The Field Marshal and head of the *Luftwaffe* had the cooks and waiters exempted from military service and tripled the petrol ration for the restaurant's vehicles. When Gustav's son Otto uncovered a hoard of 70,000 bottles of port, Göring ensured that the wine was acquired for the air force, but only after creaming off 10,000 bottles for Horcher and a few cases for himself. Horcher's position in Germany was incontestable. As Georg von Studnitz wrote in the autumn of 1943, 'As the favourite chef of Hermann Göring, Horcher has risen to become the foremost restaurateur of the Third Reich.' It was not just his fame which spread throughout mainland Europe; Horcher was opening branches all over the place. As the *Wehrmacht* marched into the different countries of the Continent, Horcher went too. He took over Zu den drei Husaren in Vienna from the three hussars Graf Paly Pàlffy, Peter Pàlffy and Baron Sonjok in 1938; then he acquired Maxim in Paris. He also opened up in Oslo and Belgrade. Before the war he had also owned a restaurant in London's Mayfair.

Other Nazi *Bonzen* were prone to entertain at Horchers. In its small, leather-hung dining-room Heinrich Himmler and Joachim von Ribbentrop entertained the Duke of Windsor. It was also the favourite restaurant of Admiral Canaris, the chief of the military intelligence, or *Abwehr*.

The Horchers themselves were not believed to be Nazis; their approach was broad church. Many of the anti-Nazi *frondeurs* ate there too, lured in by the quality of the food.[86] The British journalist Ian Colvin had known the restaurant before the war. He attested to its quality. With rationing in force, and all available supplies going to the army, food was 'brought in from Denmark, and his French wines were bought with occupation francs at controlled prices'. With the danger of bombing in the Lutherstraße ever greater, Horchers moved to Wannsee to a 'sand ridge above the lake'.

After Stalingrad Goebbels included Horchers in the restaurants to be closed in the austerity measures announcing 'total war'. The old rivalry between the propaganda chief and Göring had in no way slackened off. The Marshal was not amused. In the course of a forty-five-minute telephone conversation he told Berlin's Gauleiter: 'If you close Horchers today, I shall open it tomorrow as a Luftwaffe club!' Goebbels responded with the old Nazi trick of a 'spontaneous demonstration', in the course of which one of the restaurant's windows was broken. When his thugs returned the next day bent on further damage, however, they found the restaurant picketed by *Luftwaffe* sentries.

With Göring's help, Horchers limped on for a few months more, but after the massive raids of November 1943 Gustav and Otto must have decided there was little future for them. Diners arriving in search of good food and old-world charm in January 1944 found the doors shut. By that time Horchers had opened a new branch in one of the few unoccupied capital cities in Europe: Madrid. It is still there, run by Gustav Horcher's grandson, another Gustav, who was only three when his family left Germany. Naturally, Horchers in Madrid proved a magnet to the large Nazi colony which collected there after the war. One British journalist recalls seeing the Nazi daredevil Otto Skorzeny holding court there, at a time when he boasted about being in charge of the

Odessa organisation, which allowed SS men to escape the justice of the courts.[87]

With a few notable exceptions (Borchardt is one), restaurant life began when Berlin became a *Weltstadt* in 1871, and pretty well ceased, at least as far as decent restaurants were concerned, when Berlin gave up the ghost with 'total war'. West Berlin never had more than a handful of restaurants worthy of the name, and one of the more striking aspects since reunification has been the slowness of new restaurateurs to take the temperature of the water.[88] The first establishment to acquire a smart cachet was Lutter und Wegner on the Charlottenstraße.[89] That this simple *Weinhaus* managed to achieve such fame in the years following the Battle of Waterloo was entirely due to two of its regulars: E. T. A. Hoffmann and the actor Ludwig Devrient.

The friends' consumption of champagne would have been a boon to any landlord, but they were not always as enthusiastic about settling up as they were about cracking a bottle. In the course of their revels, Hoffmann and Devrient managed to invent the German word *Sekt*, meaning a champagne-style sparkling wine. Devrient was in the habit of stumbling down the stairs of Lutter und Wegner bellowing Falstaff's cry 'Gib mir ein Glas *Sekt*, Schurke.' ('Give me a cup of sack, rogue.')* The servants knew he wanted champagne and not sherry and soon the corrupt word caught on.[90] Both men returned to Berlin in 1815. Between then and Hoffmann's early death in 1822 their drinking bouts had become one of the sights of the city. Once when J. C. Lutter was unwise enough to present them with a bill they promptly migrated to Schonert in the Mohrenstraße. Lutter followed them to the new bar and tore up the bill before their eyes. When Hoffmann died at the age of forty-six, Lutter was his principal creditor. Once again he tore up the bill.[91]

Devrient died in December 1832, his gaze fixed on a

---

* Henry IV, Part 1, ii, 4.

portrait of his old friend Hoffmann, but the tavern continued to reap the rewards it had earned from its two most famous customers. Dronke's view was characteristically jaundiced. He thought the *Weinhaus* owed its fame less 'to the quality of its wines than the long and faithful frequentation of the great actor Ludwig Devrient and the celebrated author of *Kater Murr*, E. T. A. Hoffmann'. The portraits of these two 'so powerful yet attractive men' still hung on the wall of the front room of the tavern.[92]

Towards the end of the century Lutter und Wegner had become distinctly touristy. Literary travellers made sure they paid a visit to the cellar where the *Serapionsbrüder*, Hoffmann, Chamisso, Hitzig, Contessa and La Motte Fouqué, had swopped anecdotes. The portraits of Hoffmann and Devrient were still there, the latter, Rodenberg thought, 'the greatest performer of the century'. They had been joined by the character actor Theodor Döring. A legend had been pinned up beside him: 'Indifference to champagne is hypocrisy; don't be cold when it comes on ice.'[93]

Naturally Fontane set a scene in Lutter und Wegner. The Poggenpuhls ate there with their rich, military uncle, and all but Therese had sole. The General dribbled lemon juice on the batter of his fish and, after taking a bite, exclaimed: 'Berlin is really becoming a *Weltstadt*, but what is perhaps more important, it is becoming a port. They are already talking about this big harbour, I think somewhere near Tegel – and I can certainly say that this sole tastes as if we already had our harbour, or as if we were sitting in Wilken's Keller in Hamburg.'[94]

Lutter und Wegner must have already been pretty touristy, and real atmosphere rarely survives such onslaughts. The cellar restaurant had certainly lost its cachet by the time the Nazis came to power. In 1937 the building was heightened by a storey. In 1943 or 1944, the Charlottenstraße site was once more shorn of its upper floors. After the war Lutter und Wegner functioned for a while, and photographs show people taking lunch outside the building with its famous cellar door. Somewhere along the line, however, the cellar was ruined and with the SED in power in Berlin Mitte a new Lutter und Wegner was started in Charlottenburg. In the meantime the portraits appear to have been lost.* At the time of writing there are plans to open a new Lutter und Wegner on the original site under the Four Seasons Hotel. It will be managed by Borchardt next door.[95]

In the Weimar years no self-respecting *Literat* would have been seen dead at Lutter und Wegner. When Elias Canetti came to Berlin for the first time in the summer of 1928, the *in* place was Schlichter: 'Schlichter ist schlichter als Horcher'[96] ('Schlichter is simpler than Horcher') ran the line. It was here that he first met Bert Brecht, looking like a pawnbroker.

Intellectual and theatrical Berlin flocked to Schlichter. 'It was a colourful picture, but without the gaiety of the theatre.' Canetti was put off by Brecht's materialism and proletarian dress: 'He had a lean and hungry look; his cap made him appear lopsided.' He looked old for his thirty years, and contributed little to the conversation.[97] Despite the 'simplicity' of the menu, some maintained you ate better at Schlichter than at Horcher next door. The *hors-d'oeuvres* were famed, along with the Baden wines in the cellar.[98]

At the cellar-restaurant Niquet near the Stock Exchange, the speciality was steak and gherkins: simplicity indeed. Those wanting French food were recommended to try the Eden Hotel.[99] Eating in hotels had become something of a Berlin tradition since the advent of the great palace buildings before the turn of the century.[100] The Excelsior had its Thomasbraukeller, which the Berliners called the 'Bathtub'. People went there for ham in beer batter, roast chicken or pork knuckles.[101]

On a level with Schlichter was Schwaneckes Gaststätte in

---

* They still decorate bottles of Lutter und Wegner Sekt, which is a trade mark of the firm Henkell.

the Rankestraße. Here you might have seen George Grosz
eating with the publishers Kiepenheuer or Rowohlt. Joseph
Roth ate there nightly. Other prominent customers were
Sinclair Lewis and Thomas Wolfe, who enjoyed the Fran-
conian wines, *Châteaubriand* and goose giblets.[102] Here
Canetti met Isaac Babel and was intimidated by the collection
of thespians, painters, critics, top journalists and Maecenases
who were around him. Babel saved the day by suggesting
that they should go to Aschinger together, thus initiating a
regular meeting of minds over the pea soup.[103]

In the early twenties Berlin could offer a number of
Russian establishments: bars and cabarets. With so many
white Russians about they could enjoy the experience of
having their *borscht* ladled out by a real grand duke. One
of the most atmospheric was Tary-Bary in the Nürnberger
Straße, where Russians in smocks sang to the balalaika. At
Mjedewjed you could eat caviar, smoked sturgeon, and blinis
with *keta* and soured cream at Easter. Alaverdi offered Cauca-
sian Cossacks in long *kolpaki* on high heels doing sword-
dances, who presented customers with *chaklik* (kebabs)
flamed on daggers.[104]

Restaurant life took a tumble in the Third Reich, but in
wartime the situation not unnaturally got worse. At first
rationing was not applied to restaurants, however, and one
could be assured of getting enough to eat simply by going
out. As the war intensified coupons were required in all but
a few luxury establishments such as Horchers. Unless you
were a Nazi bigwig, you needed to know the porter or the
waiters to get a table.[105] By the fifth year of the war the food
offered in these few surviving places was scarcely appetising.
Konrad Warner remembered a particular lunch in a pub.
First he had to wait half an hour because the room had filled
up immediately after twelve noon.

> After a while came the soup. The bowl was pushed
> grumpily in my direction, cheap cutlery lay

alongside. After a long pause came the main course, for which I had yielded up 100 gms worth of coupons. Loss in the form of bones and shrinkage must be reckoned at 30 gms, but what in reality lay on my plate seemed to fall a long way short of 70 gms. Potatoes and green cabbage came with it: two or three blackened potatoes and two or three spoonfuls of cabbage. 'Might I have a few more potatoes?' I asked the waiter. 'You have to bring your own!' was his reply.[106]

On 30 November 1944, Matthias Menzel went on a similar mission: finding food. Gruban-Souchay had opened at five and sold out an hour later. Die Klause had nothing more to offer than thin beer. The Kindl had sold out of coupon-free stew. Stöckler had food but no seat. Finally he went to the Eden, where he was presented with a curious green drink.[107] Earlier that year Ursula von Kardorff had had a pleasant surprise walking down the Bayreuther Straße in the alte Westen to find the one surviving building contained the Newa Grill, 'a luxury establishment with polite waiters, *hors-d'oeuvres*, fried fish and lots to drink'.[108] Despite the similarity in the name, it presumably had nothing to do with the Hotel Newa, which a former British officer fondly remembers finding just across the border in the Russian Sector just after the war and where 'caviar and vodka flowed like water'. By the sixties he was unhappy to discover that 'supplies were far less abundant'.[109]

IV

From the 1870s onwards hotels provided an alternative to eating in a restaurant, and they have remained a solution even today.[110] It was not always the case. Sebastian Hensel, the founder of the Kaiserhof, maintained that 'Berlin's hotels were the mockery of the travelling world'.[111] The new palatial hotels came quickly to Germany's new capital, however, after the foundation of the Second Empire. In 1875 the Kaiserhof opened its doors: 'the bourgeois alternative to the imperial palace, but more modern and more comfortable'.[112] The Kaiserhof came with central heating, bathrooms, electric light, telephones and lifts. There was a Viennese-style café★ and an American bar. From 1930, the Kaiserhof dropped the royalist pose adopted by the city's other grand hotels and became Hitler's Berlin headquarters.[114]

In the summer of 1932 bored Oxford undergraduates found themselves at a loose end standing outside the Kaiserhof. 'Hitler must have a dull life; let us drop in on him,' they decided. They had no illusions as to the dangers surrounding the man and his movement, but foresaw an interesting experience for all that. Hitler was, however, too busy to see them, but it was made clear that they might make an appointment to meet him at some later date. In the meantime they were 'cordially entertained'. One of the men was Adam von Trott zu Solz, who was later to be executed for his part in the conspiracy to kill Hitler of 20 July 1944. 'It would have been Trott's first encounter with the man he later sought to kill.'[115]

The trend towards ever more palatial hotels continued with the Central by the Friedrichstraße station of 1880 and the Bristol in Unter den Linden. As a result of the Kaiser's dogged determination to rid Berlin of Schinkel's Palais Redern, the Adlon Hotel opened in 1907 with a staggering 140 baths for 400 beds. Adlon had been able to rid himself of any bad smells which might have clung to him from his days in the Zoo: he was seen as a new-style hotelier who 'in no way resembled the portly old-Berlin landlord with his greasy apron; he was a society master of ceremonies protected by both the Kaiser and the Crown Prince, a representative

---

★ The Viennese coffee-house was even seen to be a necessary part of the kit when the new Grand opened in East Berlin in 1987.[113]

of the modernity of imperial Germany and the cultural leadership of Berlin within it'.[116]

The Kaiser positively gloated over his new hotel, to the degree that he must have considered pulling down the Schloss to give himself the chance to build something with the same number of creature comforts. There were a million bottles in the cellar and Escoffier was briefly in charge of the kitchens. Not only did foreign heads of state such as the Czar or Edward VII prefer it to the Schloss, so did Caruso, whose appearances in Berlin were just about the only thing capable of upstaging the trial of the Kaiser's friend Fürst Eulenburg in Moabit.[117] Pierre Laval slipped away from the Adlon with a porter to enjoy a plate of *Sauerkraut*, and the Nazis' great bugbear, the Jewish Vice-Police Chief Bernhard Weiß, spent his last night in Germany there before his flight to England.[118]

Given that the Adlon only existed in its original form for thirty-nine years, it is remarkable how much actually happened there. Smart Berliners went to hear the music of the Dajos Béla Orchestra, especially once the musicians had been joined by the lyrical *Kopfstimme* of the tenor Richard Tauber. Tauber's song *Schöner Gigolo* was actually composed in the ballroom of the Adlon. It touchingly describes the plight of a generation of young officers who went to war in 1914 only to return to find their world had been eclipsed in their absence: these *Eintänzer* were also present in the Adlon. Literally: 'Man zahlt und Du mußt tanzen'[119] ('If someone pays you have to dance').

It had certainly built a huge cachet for itself by the late twenties. In *Sodome et Berlin* Odemar moves into the Adlon with his Jewish lover, Nora Finkelstein. They rent a luxurious apartment: 'Pointing to the bed, the porter told them that in that historic place already d'Annunzio had slept with La

Duse, the Princess of Saxony with Torelli,* Mata Hari and Fürst Hohenlohe, Graf [sic] Eulenburg and William II and countless other celebrated couples of the twentieth century.'[120]

In 1937 the Nazis felled the trees outside the hotel to facilitate the building of a new U-Bahn line. Cassandra-like voices echoed through the corridors: 'Nun blühen die Linden nicht mehr . . . Nun ist es auch mit Berlin vorbei' ('Now the linden will bloom no more . . . Soon it will all be over for Berlin'). The hotel assumed a new life in the war. A few nights under its roof was seen as a prize for anyone in the higher echelons of public service[121] and, of course, the kitchens were still among the city's best. Göring's *Forschungsamt* had bugged the public rooms and telephones here too, but the quietly dignified Louis Adlon knew how to steer his non-Nazi guests away from the sensitive positions and cushions were used in the bedrooms to cover the telephones.[122] Missie Vassiltchikov stayed there on the night of 10 July 1944, just ten days before the attempt to overthrow Hitler. 'Adam Trott and I dined there together. We spoke English to the head waiter, who was delighted to show how well he still remembers it. Our neighbours began to stare. Adam then took me for a drive during which, without going into particulars, we discussed the coming events, which, he told me, are now imminent.'[123]

It would be hard to imagine a couple speaking German in London's Ritz at a similar date in the last war. Some of the conspirators used the Adlon on the night itself; Dr Wilhelm Melchers, who had been initiated into the plan by Trott, saw the former ambassador Ulrich von Hassell there at dinner. Like Trott he was hanged after the wide-sweeping *razzia* that followed the failure of the *coup*.[124] The hotel survived until the cessation of hostilities, but mysteriously

---

* Tutor to the children of the Crown Princess of Saxony, a former Princess of Tuscany. The couple eloped.

burned to the ground in the first days of peace. It is presumed that the Russians were responsible.

A pastiche of the Adlon is currently being rebuilt on its original site on the Pariser Platz. As the foundations were laid there, the last vestiges of the Esplanade were swept away to make way for a new road through the modernistic Potsdamer Platz redevelopment.[125] Building work on the Esplanade started the year after the Adlon opened. It was constructed by a consortium of German noblemen, and from the first enjoyed more cachet among the aristocracy than the Adlon, which was much more the haunt of heads of state, diplomats and film stars. The architect of the Esplanade, Otto Rehnig, was instructed to build a hotel of considerable luxury. The original premises, which replaced a row of houses in the Bellevuestraße, boasted 400 bedrooms and 102 baths, as well as a restaurant run by Escoffier's Carlton-Ritz group of London. The Esplanade was enlarged in 1911–1912. Now came the palm court and the winter garden and a 1,600-square-metre dining-room complete with a fountain and lashings of Pavonazza marble. The 'princes' rooms' looked out on to the Bellevuestraße. An innovation were the 'Swedish rooms': modern-style bed-sits with connecting bathrooms.[126]

The English Catholic woman Evelyn Fürstin Blücher lived at the Esplanade for much of the First World War. There was no absence of high society in its public rooms. Officers came to the hotel during their leave to take tea in the palm court. Fürstin Blücher reflected in December 1915 that, had the 'enemy' been able to see how many there were there, 'they might think it a good moment for a fresh offensive'.[127] A month later, in January 1916, she gave vent to her vision of the hotel, and its position in Berlin society:

> It represents exactly what it was intended to be, a
> centre or gathering-place for the great world of
> Berlin in time of peace: royalties, statesmen, diplomats,

officers and high officials, and last but not least, the great financiers who are supposed to hold the wires of the affairs of the world in their two hands. At present it is a sort of caravanserai for all the homeless exiles of position and influence who have been driven away from house to house by the great tidal wave of the war.

All people of any repute passing though Berlin take up their abode here, princes and nobles, and impecunious millionaires, who somewhere or other possess the accumulated treasures of an Aladdin, but who for the time being exist here on the reputation of these treasures, which seem to have disappeared just as mysteriously as they did in the *Arabian Nights*.

All the heroes of the war meet their wives and friends here, very much astonished to find themselves suddenly grown famous overnight. American diplomats prepared for instant flight, should the scales of peace and war suddenly weigh down on the wrong side; American princesses and duchesses of characteristic lightheartedness, some married morganatically but carrying off their position with a high hand, bring a fresh, breezy and appropriate tone with them, which gives a touch of comedy to the general tragedy of human life at present.[128]

It was an international set: English were Fürstinnen Blücher, Münster and Pleß, and the Freifrau von Roeder; American were Princess Braganza (a former Miss Stewart), Fürstin Isenburg, the Herzogin von Croy (the daughter of the American Ambassador Leishman), Gräfin Götzen, Gräfin Seherr-Thoß, Freifrau von Rath, Freifrau von Barchfeld (the morganatic wife of the later Chancellor Max von Hesse). There was a French Fürstin Biron and a smattering of Poles and Russians. When the Herrenhaus was in session the ladies were joined by a glittering array of *Fürsten*, who then had permission to quit their positions at the front: Pleß, Salm, Münster, Löwenstein, Lynar, Braganza, Fürstenberg, Lippe, and Taxis.[129]

With a star-studded cast in so many glittering rooms, naturally the Berlin proletariat smelled privilege among the high-living. In May 1916 they tried to storm the hotel, imagining that the residents were receiving higher bread rations than the mere mortals who lived elsewhere.[130] In February 1917 a number of the staff went on strike after their ration tickets were appropriated for the use of the guests.[131]

The Second World War was no less turbulent at the Esplanade. The Nazis took a dim view of the building. In Speer's scheme of things it was to be knocked down and replaced by a more useful institution: a barracks.[132] The snobbery of the staff was an advantage for the noble plotters of 20 July 1944. Fritz Dietlof von der Schulenburg, for example, used the offices of the firm Nonn, whose employees had installed themselves in the building to copy documents and fly-sheets for the Resistance movement.[133] On 11 July 1944, Schulenburg met fellow conspirators Ulrich Wilhelm Schwerin von Schwanenfeld, Ewald Heinrich von Kleist and the brothers Ludwig and Kunrat von Hammerstein-Equord for coffee in the Esplanade to explain the progress of the plot so far. Stauffenberg had failed to explode the bomb on the first attempt at Berchtesgaden, 'because Himmler wasn't there'.[134]

After the failure of the plot, Fritz Dietlof's wife, Charlotte von der Schulenburg, stayed at the Esplanade on 9 August while her husband was put on trial for his life at the Volksgerichtshof. She was denied access to the courtroom. While she waited impotently in her bedroom, her sister-in-law, Tisa von der Schulenburg, tried vainly to get some sense out of the Gestapo in the Prinz Albrechtstraße.[135] The building had been shattered by bombs and she had the greatest difficulty locating a porter. When she did, he laughed in her face: 'There's no one here any more. Everything has been evacuated. Get out of the city. What do you want?' When she mentioned her maiden name, his tone changed. 'Disappear!'

he said, in a tone which was not unfriendly, but certainly insistent.[136]

The raids of February 1945 which killed the monstrous President of the Volksgerichtshof, Roland Freisler, also put paid to 90 per cent of the Esplanade. Some of the public rooms were spared, however, and rebuilding began in 1949, when the Esplanade once again began to function as a hotel. Ten years later it closed again: it was stuck in a dead end of West Berlin, right up against the Wall in an area that had been torched during the uprising of 17 June 1953.[137] In its last incarnation there was a bar in one of the remaining neo-baroque rooms of the Esplanade, and the building was hired out for pop concerts. As such, the hotel makes an appearance in Wim Wenders' 1987 film, *Himmel über Berlin*.[138]

Between 1896 and 1913 Berlin hotels accommodated 1.4 million overnight guests. Of these 262,000 were non-Germans: 17 per cent from Austria–Hungary, 11 per cent from America, 6 per cent from Britain and a mighty 36 per cent from Russia. After 1917, Berlin became a place of exile for middle- and upper-class Russians; when their money ran out, they were no longer welcome. By that stage the Excelsior was Berlin's biggest hotel.[139] It stood on the Königrätzerstraße, later the Stresemannstraße, at number 78. The original hotel was put up in 1906 with 188 rooms and a paltry 44 baths and a *Bierkeller*. It was then called Wendels Hotel Schweizerhof after its owner Hermann Wendel. In 1907 it was transformed into the Excelsior with restaurants, a hairdressing salon and a *Konditorei*. At the front of the building, opposite the Anhalter Bahnhof, there were modern suites with bedrooms, living-rooms and bathrooms. It was expanded again in 1912.[140]

By that stage the hotel had been taken over by Kurt Elschner and the Kaiser and his wife had begun to take a keen interest in the project. The Kaiser was interested in creating a proper metropolis to replace his outworn capital, and the Kaiserin, knowing his tastes, intervened to have

Elschner made a *Geheime Kommerzienrat*. A 'Russian-Roman' bath was installed and telephones and radios graced most of the rooms. An underground tunnel connected the building with the Anhalter Bahnhof.[141]

Even for today's jaded palates the Excelsior was a magnificent conception. The bath-house was vaguely Expressionist: 'Under a glass and marble ceiling, visitors splashed in pools made of faience covered in greenish enamel, [these were] surrounded by fountains which leaped from enamelled bronze and glass. Under the palms people laboured to revive their nerves in different-coloured rooms specially designed for that purpose.'[142] The Herrenbar was the favourite meeting-place of lobby correspondents, who could also drop into the wine restaurant or the hotel library with its stock of 7,000 books. The Excelsior even had its own newspaper, which appeared every afternoon except on public holidays. The Sunday edition sported columns allegedly written by the film stars Lilian Harvey and Willy Fritsch. Elschner boasted: 'In my house you can eat without fuss, sleep, drink, read, work, hold conferences, shop, bank money, dance and enjoy yourself. In a word, you can be happy without having to go out.'[143] Vicki Baum took up the idea when she worked in the hotel for a few days in order to glean ideas for her book *Menschen im Hotel*. This was later filmed as *Grand Hotel* with Greta Garbo and Joan Crawford.[144]

The Kaiser had called the grand hotels into being, and, with the exception of the Kaiserhof, they returned the favour by being staunchly monarchist institutions. Elschner took a dim view of the Nazis, and refused to have them in his hotel. In 1933 the Nazis, in an attempt to ruin him, issued a *Parteiverbot* forbidding members to use the hotel. Elschner finally cracked and allowed them to destroy some stained glass with Jewish themes. The hotel was infiltrated. The Indian nationalist Subhas Bose stayed there for a while during the war, but left after a contretemps with a Nazi *Kellner* who refused to call him 'Excellenz' as he required.[145] The

Excelsior was badly damaged by bombs in 1945. It was demolished in 1954, and the tunnel under the street to the now redundant Anhalter Bahnhof was walled up.[146]

At the Potsdamerplatz the best hotel was the Fürstenhof, built at much the same time as the others, 1906–1907.[147] The only grand hotel in the west, however, was the Eden in the Budapesterstraße, the street where many of the top chains have established their flagship hotels since the war. It was built in a neo-baroque style by Moritz Ernst Lesser in 1912. With two hundred beds, it was the first to offer guests a roof garden with views over the Zoo and the Tiergarten.[148] In January 1919 it achieved an unwelcome notoriety as the starting point for the calvary of the revolutionaries Karl Liebknecht and Rosa Luxemburg. When the papers printed a highly favourable and rather inaccurate report of the killings, the hotel's director read it out to the staff so that none of them would gainsay it. One of the soldiers involved in the shootings even showed off a shoe belonging to Rosa Luxemburg in the kitchens of the hotel.[149]

Like the Adlon, the Eden had its tea-dances where smartly turned-out men earned tips for dancing with women. The film director Billy Wilder did this as a young man up from Vienna in the twenties. In 1933 he left for Hollywood. A refit in 1928 made the Eden more attractive to foreign guests: it was Hemingway's Berlin favourite. Its kitchens, too, were meant to be among the best in Berlin.[150] Hotels showed a remarkable ability to patch themselves up and reopen for business in those days. The façade was destroyed in the Blitz, and Berliners arriving for lunch in April 1944 entered through the service door. Despite the severity of the damage, Missie Vassiltchikov got a table easily and had an extraordinary meal, 'consisting of radishes with butter and delicious venison *Schnitzels* (unrationed). We first had cocktails, then several wines, then champagne, topping it off with a bottle of . . . brandy. We had not eaten so well in months.'[151]

Eating at hotels and restaurants was (and is) a popular

leisure activity of Berliners. For the most part, filling stomachs could be adequately performed in the centre of town or in the fashionable west end. Only on Sundays did Berliners go farther afield and eat and drink in a beer garden or café in the woods. There are survivals of these out to the west: in Grunewald is the Forsthaus Paulsborn, and opposite the romantic Pfaueninsel, the Wirtshaus zur Pfaueninsel, with similar establishments at Moorlake and Nikolskoe nearby. Another weekend treat was racing at Ruhleben, or later at Hoppegarten, Karlshorst and Mariendorf. Another possibility in summer was an excursion to one of Berlin's beaches.

Berlin's many lakes from early on marked the city out as a bather's paradise. As a craze, swimming was first associated with the 'health and efficiency' mentality of the modern Sparta: Prussia. Not for nothing was Berlin's first swimming bath created in 1811, at a time when the man Hoffmann called a 'famous master of the hop, skip and jump',[152] Friedrich Ludwig 'Turnvater' Jahn, was beginning to make his mark. In 1817 General Pfuel founded the military baths in Plötzensee. Teaching the squaddies to swim paid off in the Prusso-Danish War of 1864 when the Prussian army showed an early mastery of the technique of amphibious landing. Berlin's first riverside baths opened in 1855.[153]

As Berlin grew, swimming became a vital part of escaping from the grimmer sides of urban life. The evil Margot Peters remembers it well in Nabokov's *Laughter in the Dark*:

> . . . they all used to go out on suburban sprees — she, Otto, and these sun-tanned youths. They taught her to swim and grabbed at her bare thighs under the water. Kurt had an anchor tattooed on his forearm and a dragon on his chest. They sprawled on the bank and pelted one another with clammy, velvety sand. They slapped her on her wet bathing pants as soon as she lay down flat. How jolly it all was, the merry crowd, litter of paper everywhere, and muscular,

fair-haired Kaspar on the edge of the lake shaking
his arms as though he were quaking, and roaring: 'The
water is wet, wet!' When swimming, he held his
mouth under water and trumpeted like a seal. And
when he came out, the first thing he did was to
comb back his hair and carefully put on his cap. She
remembered how they played ball; and then she lay
down and they covered her with sand, leaving only
her face bare, and made a cross of pebbles on top.[154]

It was a scene that appealed mightily to Zille, whose *Rund
um's Freibad* was published in 1926. It gave him plenty of
scope for his special cocktail of homeliness, sentimentality,
scatophilia and eroticism.[155] The *Freibäder* on the river were
becoming increasingly insanitary and it was hardly relaxing
to have to do battle with tugs and other items of river traffic.
The Wannsee site – on a steep slope opposite the suburb, by
the path through the Grunewald to the Schwanenwerder
peninsula – was ideal. There was sand, clean water and plenty
of pines to shade swimmers from the sun.[156]

The original premises was a collection of wooden thatched
huts. These burned down in 1927 and were rebuilt by Martin
Wagner and Richard Ermisch in 1929 to 1930 in a modernistic idiom.[157] It required decisive action to prevent Berliners
from continuing their practices from the less formal establishments. There were no lavatories at first, and dogs swam with
their masters in the water. Visitors brought their *Stullen*, or
rolls, with them and discarded the greasy papers on the sand.
The wags called Wannssee 'Klein-Heringsdorf' after the
popular Baltic resort.[158]

Expanses of bare flesh still had the power to shock. At the
beginning, at least, there were more spectators than swimmers, and, for that reason, vastly more men than women in
the water. A debate raged over the definition of a decent
swimming costume. The Freibäderverein advocated bathing
suits in the old imperial colours of black, white and mustard.
Zille added his sixpence with an *Antwort auf die Kleiderordnung*

(answer to the clothing regulations). The police had the last word: there were to be no more briefs. Men had to wear costumes that stretched from the upper thigh to the waist. Women were required to conceal their shoulders, breasts, bellies and legs above the knee. Berliners baptised the regulations the 'Zwickerlerlaß', or gusset edict. In 1935 another law limited freedom on Berlin's beaches: 'Juden ist das Baden und der Zutritt verboten' ('Access and swimming forbidden to Jews'). The sign was temporarily removed for the duration of the Olympic Games.[159]

V

A big city like Berlin needed its markets. As late as the eighteenth century there were whole tracts of land within the walls where sheep and cows grazed. Dairy farms were a common feature. The Berliners were great meat-eaters, and there is no indication, in the eighteenth century at least, that they went hungry.[160] In 1774 the slaughterhouses despatched 11,777 oxen and cows, 35,837 calves, 64,837 lambs and 24,730 sheep.[161] There is no mention of pigs, possibly because every household had one and the killing of it was not considered worth recording, possibly because eighteenth-century Berliners were not as fond of pork as they are now.

Ham was certainly eaten. It was imported, naturally enough, from Westphalia. From Pomerania came fat geese, while smoked goose flesh came from Riga. From Archangel, which was even farther away, came salmon, while Hamburg was the source for smoked ox tongue.[162] The police controlled the weight of loaves of bread; any found to be too light were confiscated and given to the poor or the hospitals.[163] The gestures was typical of the Prussian state: the police meddled in everything, for good or for bad. A century later they saw to it that the abattoirs conformed to health guidelines. There were 800 of them in 1875, but with the construction of the central slaughterhouse in the Thaerstraße in 1881 there was no more private slaughter permitted. In 1883 the central market halls in the Alexanderplatz were set up, and the old *laissez-faire* rapidly came to an end when the police closed down the majority of the weekly street markets.[164]

Döblin discourses at length on the Berlin abattoirs in *Berlin Alexanderplatz*. The Thaerstraße premises covered 47.88 hectares of land. On this space was thrown together the paddocks, slaughterhouses and wholesale meat market for Berlin. It was policed by two members of the city *Magistrat*, a member of the local council, eleven city councillors and three representatives of the people. The abattoirs employed 258 administrators, including vets and assistant vets, inspectors and assistant inspectors, clerks, and sundry other workers.[165] Then came the animals: 'examples of breeds of sheep, pig and ox from East Prussia, Pomerania, Brandenburg and West Prussia'.

> That is light, dear piggy, that is earth. Grope about, you are allowed to explore for a few minutes more, they are not working by the book, just go on rummaging about. You are going to be slaughtered. You arrived. You can see the abattoirs and the one reserved for pigs. There are rundown places, but yours is the latest model. It is well lit, built in red brick; from the outside you might take it for a workshop, a factory or an assembly line.[166]

The mechanisation of Berlin's food chain meant it was an early convert to mass distribution. The success story here was that of Carl Bolle, who opened a dairy in Moabit in 1881, and sold heat-treated milk processed according to Louis Pasteur's strictures. Bolle's horse-drawn carts became a feature of city life, and the dairy owner was rewarded with the *Rote Adler* order, third-class, and the title of *Geheime Kommerzienrat*. After 1914 he opened his first self-service restaurants.

These days the dairy aspect of Bolle has disappeared from view. Bolle is now a chain of small- to medium-sized super-markets principally in west Berlin.

Another prominent Berlin food firm was Carl Kühne, with its mustard and vinegar and bottles of Spreewald gherkins. After the war Kühne's successors found it hard to put their hands on these old Berlin staples, when the arable land lay outside the western sectors, and the firm went elsewhere. Berlin food has few highlights, but one local product that excited Goethe was the *Teltower Rübe*, a vegetable which tastes a little like a cross between a small turnip and a parsnip, and which was traditionally grown in the fields of Teltow, south-east of Potsdam.[167]

Goethe knew the *Rübe* from Zelter, who seems to have introduced the poet to this Berlin 'delicacy', in January 1805.

> Half a bushel of Märkisch *Rüben** are coming by
> separate post. I wanted to send you a whole bushel,
> but my wife was against it, arguing that they might be
> blighted by a heavy frost, and we could always send
> the other half later. The *Rüben* didn't want to travel
> on their own, so a healthy pike is accompanying them;
> its liver should inspire you to write a new poem.[168]

Goethe received the consignment: '*Rübchen* and fish arrived safely, the first beautifully dry, the second properly frozen'.[169]

Berlin's many lakes had their advantages in that respect: there was no absence of pike or zander. Pike, worked into *Klößchen* or dumplings like French *quenelles*, had long been a stock in trade of the Berlin cook. Visitors to Frederick William I's court ate them in veal stock, and the king's son Frederick the Great expressed a fondness for them.[170] In October 1807 Zelter was sending Goethe more *Rüben*. The poet was hooked, and enthused over his gift in a letter dated 16 December that same year.[171] In December 1816 Zelter

---

* The correspondents use both *Rüben* and the diminutive *Rübchen*.

deviated from the general nature of his present-giving by despatching a zander to Weimar.[172] The roots came too in December 1818. Goethe replied in January: 'The *Rübchen*, of the finest sort, came at the best possible time, and today they are lying alongside the fish, giving us the opportunity for an amicable meal.'[173] Four days later the warm-hearted Zelter was sending his friend more provisions (was Weimar so poorly provided?): ' . . . a little barrel of caviar from Königsberg in Prussia is making its way to you in Weimar. If you feel the urge, your household might sing a funeral march as you bury the black stuff at your table.'[174]

Caviar was hardly a regular part of the Berliner's diet, except possibly after 1945, when tins were smuggled to the west in the luggage of enterprising Russian soldiers. Even then it was Hamburg and not Berlin which lay at the centre of the trade. In a smart household such as Sombart's the menu followed classic neo-French lines: soup in cups, a fish dish (salmon trout or pike in aspic), a roast or poultry ('stuffed turkey was a house speciality'), cheese and a pudding. After the meal Mocha was served. The appearance of Bucks' Fizz at midnight was a signal for guests to go home.[175]

In the twenties it was fashionable to slum it after smart balls and eat the Berliner staple, *Erbsensuppe* (pea soup), from a stall.[176] This was much more the thing: hearty soups and stews, blood- and liver-sausage, pork knuckles with *Sauerkraut* and pease pudding, *Kartoffelpuffer* or potato cakes, etc. In more recent times the *Currywurst* has been adopted from the Ruhr. The curry is not an integral part of the sausage, rather the sausage is buried under a thick paste of tomato ketchup and dusted with curry powder.

Even this disgusting conception would have sounded positively Lucullan to a wartime Berliner. When Berlin had been a small town surrounded by fields and pastures there had been no problem with subsistence. The Excise Wall was not intended to let Berlin starve. When there was a dearth of corn or meat, prices were lowered accordingly. Foodstuffs were not seen in the same light as luxuries were under the spendthrift Elector and, later, first King, Frederick, who taxed carriages and wigs.[177] In his palace in Charlottenburg there is a picture of his granddaughter Amalie with close-cropped hair. She is showing support for the continuation of the wig tax.

Berlin didn't starve until the First World War, when the British blockade reduced much of Germany to near-famine level.[178] Bread rationing was introduced in 1915, and later that year coupons were issued for flour and potatoes. In 1916 rationing was extended to fat, sugar and meat. Later, with the frosts, came the 'Turnip Winter'. A huge police presence was required to prevent the theft of stocks from the harbours, although free food was already being handed out to the needy – albeit not enough: by the autumn of 1917 there was insufficient milk for children and the sick. Coffee had long ceased to be 'Ersatz', it was now 'Ersatzersatz'.[179]

In 1917 Fürstin Blücher was reduced to eating the kangaroos from the menagerie on her husband's Silesian estate (no great hardship), but she was kind enough to admit that other Berliners were worse off: ' . . . the population have now a portion of 1lb [of potatoes] per head per week, and even these are bad'.[180] A 'war bread' was baked from rye and potato flour. Butter became increasingly rare, along with coal. Milk was distributed to children only on presentation of a medical prescription. Even today there survives a folk memory of that terrible winter and a bitterness towards those who perpetrated the shortages.[181]

Fear that this situation might be repeated in the second war played no small part in Berliners' unenthusiastic reaction to the news of its outbreak. For Berliners, a regime that put guns before butter was hardly to be trusted. The Nazis were aware of the attitude of inhabitants in their capital. In the first war thousands had died from hunger and related causes.[182] The misery was one of the chief causes of the revolution that brought down the Hohenzollerns. Goebbels knew that he had to keep Berlin supplied. At first there was a measure of success, but later, despite Germany's access to the foodstuffs of virtually the entire European continent, Berliners went hungry. When their bellies rumbled, they grumbled about the regime.

There were very soon shortages of beer and spirits, coffee and bread, meat, dumplings and vegetables. 'Ersatz' and 'Ersatzersatz' reappeared. A pound of real, 'Bohnen' coffee shot up in price from 20 to 500RMs. Wartime Berliners must have had cause to thank and curse the memory of the Great Frederick: very soon they were subsisting on little more than potatoes. Potatoes were planted in every available space: bombed-out houses became potato plots; even window-boxes were planted.[183] Some food could be cadged off foreign workers, notably the French, who received the most interesting food parcels from their nearest and dearest. In February 1944, Ursula von Kardorff was tucking into a meal with her friend Bärchen that was composed of several rare treats: white bread (from Bärchen herself), proper coffee and *foie gras* eaten out of the tin. The last two had been kindly donated by French forced workers.[184]

The only other places where half-way decent food could be obtained were the larger hotels and restaurants which were maintained for important officials and foreign diplomats. Missie Vassiltchikov was galled by an orgiastic spectacle she witnessed at the Preußischer Hof in March 1944: 'They had just killed a pig and everyone gorged on its insides. I stuck staunchly to cheese.'[185] Even more extraordinary were the meals of Helmuth James von Moltke on death row in Tegel Prison:

> After I had connected an immersion heater in my cell to make tea, Puppi [Sarre] sent for a hotplate and whole meals, e.g., splendid risottos, were cooked on that. But ham and sausage and bacon from me to go

with the potatoes, all played a role, and on Sundays
we supplied the entire . . . watch with tea or coffee.[186]

By the fifth year of the war there were long queues for a
handful of vegetables or potatoes.[187] The milk had become
so thin through progressive adulteration that it looked more
blue than white.[188] Foul-smelling fish dishes were served up
in canteens. Nominally 'cod', it came with mustard gravy:
the whole thing 'stank like an open rubbish bin on a Monday
morning'.[189] A dead horse was a great boon. The journalist
Margret Boveri was able to turn her share of the lung into
a delicious *Lungenblutwurst.*[190]

On the last New Year's Eve of the war the Goebbels family
had goose. It was apparently rather tough. Only with the
greatest effort was it possible to chop off a mouthful without
sending a hunk of meat into a neighbour's lap. The table
had lapsed into silence as all the diners sought ways of getting
some of the precious flesh into their mouths. 'The guests
said nothing in order not to offend their hostess; our hostess
kept mum so as not to hurt the donor of the goose, Gauleiter
Hanke, and he was probably living in hope that only he had
been served such a tough piece.'

Finally Goebbels himself broke the silence: 'Tell me, my
love,' he asked his wife, 'is your goose-leg as unbelievably
tough as mine?' Everyone breathed a sigh of relief and the
conversation turned to the degree of toughness. Hanke
sought a clever way out: 'It was a good sign for the state of
German provisions that in the sixth year of a war a goose
could grow so old.'[191]

With the end of the conflict life took a good while to
pick up. In both the winters of 1946–1947 and 1948–1949,
thousands of Berliners died of starvation. Even with the
Airlift, supplies were feeble and the black market operated
with a vengeance. The aeroplanes that brought in the precious supplies were called *Rosinenbomber* (raisin bombers).
One Berliner affectionately remembers the taste of a par-

ticular dried milk and potato mixture called 'Pom'. He and his sister used to spoon it out of the packet: 'It tasted delicious.'[192]

5
City of Order

I

Berlin has its own, special sort of room, a space notorious throughout Germany. The *Berliner Zimmer* links the apartment on the street frontage of the *Mietshaus* with the rooms that lead off at right angles. Its particular features are vastness and gloominess: generally just one little window on to the courtyard was deemed enough to allow in some streaks of day.

Engels was not slow to see the Berlin room as a metaphor for a whole society: ' . . . I find the *Berliner Zimmer* quite overpowering. In the rest of the world this realm of darkness and stuffiness would be wholly impossible. It is where Berlin's philistinism feels itself most at ease.'[1] The room was the conception of a nineteenth-century architect, busy arranging the city in ordered squares; *pace* Engels, it was not called into being by the needs of the Berlin *bourgeoisie*, many of whom were at a loss to know what to do with it. Erika von Hornstein first encountered the *Berliner Zimmer* when her family moved up to Berlin from Potsdam. They found a flat in an *art nouveau* house built at the turn of the century. 'On every floor there was one of those famous Berlin rooms with a window on to the courtyard; this long, dusky corridor-room leading to the back part of the flat; like everyone else, we turned it into a dining-room.'[2]

In recent years the darkness of the Berlin room has made it an ideal place to park a television set, especially for those back-street *Pensionen* which are often the only hotel rooms available in a city that has only recently seen any boom in tourism. Erich Mühsam actually managed to rent one in the Augsburgerstraße, a huge space, which he had no problem dividing into two when the time came to bring in a second person to help pay the rent.[3] The only real drawback to the Berlin room was the lack of windows and light. Those people living on the back courtyards or in the cellar dwellings were infinitely worse off. In the latter, light made only the rarest of appearances when it broke through the iron gratings at pavement level. There may have been daylight in the attics, but that was the only advantage to a poor worker such as Dronke's Marie:

> Two chairs; a table, at which our tenant sits; a chest
> of drawers; a tiny dressing-table, and the bed; these
> form the entire furniture. The bed is covered by a
> clean counterpane . . . There is nowhere to hang
> clothes. Behind the bed, next to the oil jar is a pair of
> little shoes; the water jug, a plate and a few cooking
> pots have found a place on the chest of drawers, under
> the little mirror. We should also indicate that there
> is a frugal flame burning in the little iron oven beside
> the coal scuttle which is also used for cooking.[4]

E. T. A. Hoffmann was not a rich man, he was a Prussian civil servant; *on travaillait pour le roi de Prusse*, they said: it was more for love than money. His little sketch of his new flat on the corner of the Tauben and Charlottenstraßen shows a modest dwelling with antechamber; *Prunkzimmer*, or main room; his wife's room; a study for the master; a communal bedroom for himself and Frau Hoffmann; a *cabines* (*sic*) and kitchen. The whole site was so cramped that Hoffmann was reduced to hanging out of the window whenever he needed a smoke (a practice adopted in Warsaw). He includes a puffing self-portrait in the drawing.[5]

The painter Adolph Menzel was fascinated by the small objects of everyday life. In one fine canvas he painted his duvet. There is a certain homeliness about the Berliner. Where grand rooms existed, they were only to be used on special occasions. As a boy Nicolaus Sombart never went into the grander rooms of his parents' Grunewald villa, and his father's study only with express permission. Everyone had his or her domain: the kitchen belonged to the cook, and he was utterly convinced that his father had never set a foot in it. On the other hand only he had the right to fetch wine up from the cellar.[6]

Sombart knew a tribe of Caprivis, a nephew of the 'liberal' Chancellor and his family who lived in a tiny house in somewhere like Lichterfelde. In common with a substantial part of the old Prussian nobility, they were as poor as church mice. The rooms were too narrow and there was nowhere to sit among the Biedermeyer furniture which the mother had brought into the nest, and the father's desk. In that *gute Stube* was the family's one object of pride: a portrait of the Chancellor Graf Leo von Caprivi by Lenbach. The order broke down once you moved beyond the cluttered drawing-room: 'You could hardly use the stairs; they were entirely stuffed up with chests and boxes, skis and bicycles.'[7]

The house none the less had its own atmosphere, that of a caste that had been shunted aside by a new age where it felt irrelevant and uncomfortable. The consolation was champagne.

> The great warlords spoke of him [Hitler] only as 'the Corporal' – and that was also true of the divisional commanders . . . in whose drawing-rooms feudal manners were the norm: they had coats of arms on their staff cars and every night on the mess table there was champagne. When it was necessary an adjutant was sent from the Ukraine, right across Europe to France in order to get hold of the right stuff. National Socialism was split from German nationalism by a total, almost schizophrenic division. The gulf between patriotism and Hitler-hatred was even more

striking to me. The French and the Russians were
opponents, the enemy was the SS; especially hated was
the presumption that it was an army all of its own.
They spoke at length about the horrible regime behind
the lines in Poland. It was seen as a purely criminal
organisation. Its motto 'Loyalty is the badge of honour'
was turned into 'Complicity is the badge of loyalty'.
Every word spoken in this house could have brought
its utterer before the Volksgerichthof. But when it came
to their cavalry breakthoughs and encirclements, they
were proud.[8]

As with everything else, the most noticeable characteristic
of the Berlin room was its simplicity and lack of grandeur.
The Berlin interior is not to be compared to Paris or Vienna.
There is a hefty dollop of Prussian sobriety, or *Nüchternheit*,
in it. With certain exceptions (William II was the most
notable, a trait probably inherited from his father) the Prussian thought flashiness appropriate only to parade-uniforms.
Elias Canetti had come to Berlin from Vienna, where he
had adopted Karl Kraus as his guru. Now he was taken up
by Wieland Herzfelde, who lent him his flat at Kurfürstendamm 76. Canetti was helping Herzfelde with his biography
of Upton Sinclair, an American writer much in vogue then,
while he enjoyed the simple attic flat with its bedroom and
study with a 'fine, round table'.[9]

One of Canetti's great disappointments was Brecht, whose
materialism and passion for all things American troubled the
purity of his Krausian vision. He had been trained to reject
all forms of banality; to commune only with the spiritually
worthwhile. Brecht seemed constantly to be slapping himself
on the back. In 1931 Brecht surveyed his own bedroom
which revealed a man less wedded to materialism than
Canetti imagined:

In my little bedroom I have two tables: a small one
and a big one, an old wooden bed, which is no longer

than I am, although a little broader, if not as wide as other beds; two low Norman-style chairs with straw seats; two Chinese bedside rugs; and a big wooden manuscript cupboard with canvas panels. On top of that I have a film projector, a projection lamp, an electric fire and a plaster cast of my face. In two fitted cupboards are my clothes, linen and shoes. As far as linen is concerned I have X* shirts, and enough sheets to change the bed X* times, seven suits, eight shirts. There is a light on the ceiling, and another on my bedside table. I like most of the things in my room, but as a whole it makes me ashamed to have so much.[10]

Another whom Canetti admired, but of whom he saw too little during his stay, was Gottfried Benn who was growing increasingly frustrated by the left, and felt that better things might come from the sub-Nietzschean *Lebensphilosophie* offered by the Nazis. He was to be bitterly disappointed. They admired his writings not a jot, and stopped him from publishing. When he retreated into the army medical corps, they had him thrown out, arguing that his mother (who was of Huguenot descent) had been a Jew. They even tried their damnedest to stop him from practising medicine. Benn's wife was killed in the last moments of the war, and when the conflict finished he discovered that none of his former literary friends who had gone into exile was prepared to give him the time of day. He became a bitter old man in an uncongenial Berlin. He, too, surveyed his room in an idle moment:

I use just one room for my practice and my writing. On this desk (73 × 135 cms) there are fat bundles of letters (which I never answer), sent-in manuscripts (which I never read), newspapers, books, samples of new drugs, rubber-stamps for prescriptions, three ball-

* Figures missing.

point pens, two ashtrays and a telephone. There is really no room to write there, and yet I manage it by pushing back the clumps with the help of my elbows. Here I scribble in my terrible handwriting, which I can't even read myself, until I am satisfied enough to use the typewriter which sits on the microscope table.

The room is on the ground floor and gives out on to the courtyard. I can see a rabbit hutch with a white rabbit (it belongs to the porter's wife), washing lines which are generally hung with clothes, then hortensias, which I often used to write about, because they carried on blooming until November. The end of the view is the rear elevation of the dilapidated house opposite: grey, with peeling stucco. The room and the desk have amazed many a learned man.

Since 1945 certain things have developed here. They are always prepared intellectually at another table I use in the evening: down at my local (two hours every evening), a pub where I have my own seat to read, reflect, listen to the wireless, and restudy the letters of the three people with whom I am still in contact.[11]

Those who grew tired of the stuffiness of the Berlin room could always make for the Tiergarten, or to the new 'lungs' created with the civic improvements of the nineteenth century. In 1871–1873, Berlin was offered the Humboldthain in Wedding and the Treptower Park in the east for its diversion. The former was laid out in 1869 to celebrate the centenary of Alexander von Humboldt. Like the Tiergarten it was the site of a huge concrete bunker during the war, which was partially dynamited afterwards. Somewhere (no one seems to know the precise location) there is another one of Berlin's elusive, or optimistic, vineyards clinging to its slopes.[12]

II

A sense of order was maintained by an admirably efficient system of transport, something which has returned to the city since the change. Now the B2 line carries human traffic swiftly from east to west, the sense of rift between one half of Berlin and the other has greatly diminished.[13] Buses, even night buses, move with a rapidity unknown to London and the energy-conscious *Magistrat* has now reintroduced the tram,[14] a tradition in the city that goes back to the *Pferdebahn*, or first horse-drawn bus to be pulled along fixed rails.

Roads especially maintained to promote the fast movement of troops meant that the travelling Berliner could always get from one Prussian town to another. In the late seventeenth century there was already a post coach from Königsberg to Cleves – from one end of Brandenburg-Prussia to the other – which crossed Berlin. That ran every day; then twice a week there were services to Dresden and Leipzig, Breslau and Hamburg.[15] The coach travelled at about five kilometres an hour.[16] Proper metalled roads came later. A shortage of stone in Prussia left it at a disadvantage over other, more southerly German states: the road turned to sand in summer, to mud in winter.[17] By 1808, there were already nineteen routes catered for from Berlin, including Leipzig, Hamburg, Breslau, Königsberg, Warsaw, Paderborn and Wesel.[18]

The situation was naturally revolutionised by the train. The first railway line of all, that between Berlin and Potsdam, was planned in 1834 and opened four years later. Obviously, the link was seen primarily as a way for high-ranking officials and members of the court to get from the royal residences in Potsdam to the seat of the administration in Berlin. Unlike other lines, the Berlin–Potsdam railway certainly did not lead to progressive industrialisation along its path.[19] It did, however, provide the focal point for the new Potsdamer

Platz, which would grow to become the hub of the *alte Westen*.

The only one of the Berlin railway termini to survive the war and post-war destruction was the Hamburger Bahnhof, which had already been closed to traffic anyhow. It has recently been transformed into a branch of the modern wing of the National Gallery. It was built in a pure *Rundbogenstil* between 1845 and 1847, by the architect Friedrich Neuhaus.[20] The Lehrter Bahnhof served Hanover; the Stettiner Bahnhof (predictably), Berlin's main sea-port, Stettin; the Görlitzer Bahnhof was used for traffic to and from Silesia and Poland. Fragments existed as late as 1976.[21]

Berlin always lacked a central terminus before 1945. In the DDR there was a 'Berlin Hauptbahnhof', but in reality it was no such thing. Many of the important trains departed from Berlin-Lichtenberg, the old Schlesischer-Bahnhof. The Stettiner Bahnhoff had to change its name to the Nordbahnhof after the surprising decision to grant the Poles the German city of Stettin, on the west bank of the Oder. In West Berlin the Zoo Station was the nearest thing to a central station, although Charlottenburg had a certain cachet from the fact that it was the British military terminus.

If any station achieved a status above the others it was the Anhalter Bahnhof in the Friedrichstadt. It must have been partly to do with the name, which sounded comic to Berliners. On the one hand trains served the state of Anhalt to the south, one of Prussia's permanent allies among the German *Kleinstaaterei*, and that was logic enough for calling it the Anhalt Station; on the other, *anhalten* means to stop or halt. The infant Walter Benjamin, for example, was always intrigued to hear that his holidays would start from the Anhalter Bahnhof: 'because of its name the mother of all stations, where the locomotives came home, and the trains had to stop'.[22]

The Anhalt line was Berlin's second. In 1838 the first tracks had been laid on the Berlin–Jüterbog–Dessau–Köthen line. Three years later the original neo-classical railway station was constructed. By 1875 it had grown too small and work was begun on a new building designed by Franz Schwechten (who designed the Romanischen). The economic crisis of the late seventies brought this to a standstill. It wasn't finished until 1882. Three years earlier the *Deutsche Bauzeitung* had gloated in new imperial style that 'the new station hall was ten metres wider than Unter den Linden. Only British or American constructions could show similar proportions.'[23] Special links to the Excelsior Hotel were another point in the station's favour: the tunnel under the Königgrätzerstraße, with lifts taking you right up into the hotel lobby.

The Anhalter Bahnhof became the main station for important arrivals and departures. Visiting royalty came here and some less distinguished figures in recent German history used the platforms to drive home a political message. Joseph Goebbels, for example, who arrived here as Gauleiter in 1926 after the banning of the Nazi party. 'Trotz Verbot,' he shouted, 'nicht tot': 'Despite the ban, alive to a man'. Once Goebbels had had his way and the Nazis were in power, the station became the 'Tränengleis', the 'platform of tears'. Trains left for Trieste and Marseilles to take Berlin's Jewish population to safety in the thirties. On 2 September 1936 a special *Palastinazug* was laid on to take 650 Jews to Trieste and Palestine. The light of hope went out when the war started. Special trains picked up Jews from the stations at Putlitzstraße, Grunewald and Anhalterstraße and took them to the Anhalter Bahnhof before despatching them to Theresienstadt and the extermination camps in the east.[24]

The Anhalter Bahnhof was also the last sight of Berlin for many German Gentiles. On 1 August 1943 Gauleiter Goebbels allowed old-age pensioners, women and children to quit the city, which was under threat from the Allied bombing campaign. Over the next few months 700,000 availed themselves of the opportunity. The station went on functioning throughout. The curious and the desperate who came to gawp at the 'Reichstrümmerstadt' ('City of Imperial Ruins') after May 1945 also came into the Anhalter Bahnhof. The roof had been badly damaged, and the Americans responded by blowing it up in 1948. Four years later the trains stopped running. The Anhalter Bahnhof was in the American Zone, and trains could not cross Russian territory to get to it. In 1959 the *Oberbürgermeister*, Kressmann, took the decision to blow up the rest of the station, which was done in four stages between 1960 and 1965. In 1973 the miserable shattered vestige of the station's portico was 'listed' in a rather tardy and singularly fruitless gesture. Nothing had or has taken its place: it is a puny fragment of the rather more impressive ruin that was there before.

By the time Berlin became the imperial capital of Germany the city had nine railway termini, linked at street level by a one-track *Verbindungsbahn*, or connecting line. Over the next six years this was turned into a two-track ring line.[25] There was a growing understanding that a distinction should be made between long-distance traffic and that of the new suburbs developing in the south-west. Between 1875 and 1882 the viaduct was built that still links Charlottenburg with the Schlesischer (now Lichtenberg) Bahnhof. This created the stations at the Zoologischen, the Friedrichstraße and the Alexanderplatz. In 1874 the prosperous hamlets on the way to Potsdam got their own railway in the Wannsee Bahn.[26]

'Bankers' trains' now took prosperous suburbanites into their offices on the Linden from Zehlendorf and Wannsee. In 1913 the first 'Schnell' or S-Bahn trains began to avoid the Potsdamer Bahnhof and bring their cargo right into the city. In 1929 it had reached Krumme Lanke in the far west. In 1910 trains ran down to Dahlem past underground stations with impressive historical designs: the Gothic vaulted Heidelberg Platz, the neo-Greek Rüdesheimer Platz, or the Hohenzollerndamm with its eagles and images of Burg

Hohenzollern in Swabia. In a moment of concern for the appearance of his city, William II decided to remove the trains from the streets where they ran until 1902 and force them underground: the *U-Bahn* was born. To avoid desecrating the Linden, a tunnel was dug between the Neue Wache and the Opera for the new line in 1916.[27]

The alternative to tunnels was an overhead line. The first company to propose this solution to the city's transport problems was Siemens in 1880, which suggested a line of pillars stretching from the Hallesche Tor to Wedding via the Friedrich- and Chausseestraßen. The Siemens scheme was eventually used to build a line linking the stations in the south of the city from the Warschauerstraße to the Zoo via the Dreieck. The first section was built between 1896 and 1902. The Dreieck (or triangle) housed another branch, which ran down to the Potsdamerplatz, and later to the Spittelmarkt. The handsome stations on this route, the Bülowstraße in particular, are some of Berlin's best preserved monuments to the *Jugendstil*.[28] The overall design was by Heinrich Schwieger, but other architects were involved on the designs for individual stations: Möhring, Grenander and Messel.

New York was the model. The line opened with the minister taking a special journey on the line on 15 February 1902. The new overhead railway was considered rather smart, and its prices reflected this. Most of Berlin's poor preferred to use cheaper means of transport, which included the *S-Bahn*. Alternatively they took the bus or tram, cycled or walked. Their reticence can't have been helped by the accident that occurred at Gleisdreieck in 1908, when two trains collided and one was sent hurtling down on to the street. Sixteen people died instantly and five more later. The disaster inspired some lines by the Expressionist poet Jakob van Hoddis:

Der Sturm ist da, die wilden Meere hupfen
An Land, um dicke Dämme zu zerdrücken.
Die meisten Menschen haben einen Schnupfen.
Die Eisenbahnen fallen von den Brücken.[29]

(The storm has come, the sea tosses and rages,
To pound the fat dykes on the waters' edges.
Most people are snivelling with runny noses.
Locomotives are falling from the bridges.)

The accident at Gleisdreieck encouraged planners to find
safer means of transporting Berlin's workers, but it in no way
slowed down the development. Tunnels seemed to be the
answer. As Groß-Berlin had yet to be created, the initiative
was left to the individual towns that made up the conglomer-
ation. Both Schöneberg and Charlottenburg built their own
lines and it was not until the twenties that the system was
integrated with the forming of the BVG. The fact that
so many bodies were pursuing their own schemes wholly
independent of one another meant that Berlin's different
lines were often unsatisfactorily linked. Some of these clumsy
changes are still with us today: Potsdamer Platz involves a
painful switch-over from *S-* to *U-Bahn*; Steglitz is a total
nightmare.[30]

The war came at a bad moment, when Berlin's underground and overground railways were finally coming
together as a proper network. Electrification was not put
through until 1918; it was a long drawn-out process and not
completed until the thirties. In the meantime the streets were
torn up to lay the tunnels, a process which Alfred Döblin
found quite exciting:

> If you turn into the Leipziger Straße in the southern
> Friedrichstadt, you will see a mighty and impressive
> spectacle. The underground railway, which goes from
> the north to the south of Berlin, is about to be
> covered. A heavy concrete roof will be attached, the
> cables laid, and the new street will stretch out over

lines sunk beneath the earth. The sight can't fail to
stir anyone who lives through these times: these
indestructible cement blocks, the awe-inspiring iron
girders, right and left, embedded in the soil. A
concrete and metal tube a kilometre long lies in the
mass of sand and earth; on thin wires, directed by
current, every minute carriages full of people will be
sent this way and that through the tunnel. When you
look from the Leipziger Straße into the
Friedrichstraße, you get the feeling that the ground
might yield up a dinosaur, that an ichthyosaurus will
soon be dug out; they are already looking for its ribs,
its infinitely long back; they are already staring into its
black and empty breast cage.[31]

Groß-Berlin was a great help as far as bringing together
the separate strands was concerned. In 1926 prices were
standardised. A year later monthly passes were introduced for
use on trains, trams and buses as well. In 1929 the BVG was
created to administer the whole system. The Nazis had plans
to rationalise it yet further. The broad lines were to be drawn
by the shipping canal and the Landwehr Canal, the Anhalter
Bahnhof and the streets right and left of it, and the new
underground railway linking the Nord- and Süd-Bahnhöfe.
The *U-Bahn* in particular altered its character in wartime.[32]
Pace Döblin, the concrete ceiling over the new lines was not
indestructible, but that didn't prevent people from seeking
refuge from the bombs in the stations. One man complained
about the stench: 'the sweat of hard-working bodies' which
received monthly 'a stick of soap the size of a matchbox. It
is getting nastier and nastier. In summer it is suffocating.'[33]
In general, behaviour in the U-Bahn was good. Any
trouble in the dimly lit trains brought shouts of 'I'll denounce
you, young man!'* Or: 'My lover is a big cheese in the
Party! He'll have words to say to you!'[34] There was, however,
a spectacular series of brutal murders which took place on

* In Berlin all men are 'young' men.

the *S-Bahn* line to Lichtenberg and beyond. The murderer was one Paul Ogorow from East Prussia, a party member who worked on the railways and knew where to catch and drag his prey. After smashing their heads in with a blunt instrument he then had sexual intercourse with the corpses. He was caught and executed.[35]

The overground line has always allowed Berliners the chance to peer into the *Beletagen* of the finer *Mietshäuser* of Kreuzberg. In May 1941 the *Berliner Lokalanzeiger* reported a 'fairy-tale garden idyll amid the prosaic life of the big city'. On a rooftop at line level, a post office had planted a cherry tree which was in full bloom.[36] With the big raids that began in November 1943, no one looked for idylls in Berlin, above all on the *S-* or the *U-Bahn*, where travellers took their lives in their hands. Nor were the tunnels safe. In the last days of the war literally hundreds who had taken refuge in the tunnel of the North–South line died when the SS decided to flood it to hold up the Russian advance.[37]

Tempelhof had been the site of some of Berlin's first attempts at manned flight, and the earliest airport buildings dated from 1924–1927. From 1936 to 1941 Ernst Sagebiel built the Nazis a spanking-new airport there as part of their monumental plans for redeveloping Berlin.[38] It was in Tempelhof that Hitler arrived, pale, haggard and unshaven, on 30 June 1934 on the 'Night of the Long Knives'. Gisevius was at the airport. He described his garb as 'dark on dark': brown shirt, black tie, dark-brown leather coat, and long black army boots. His henchmen were there to meet him. It was a scene charged with menace, but the sinister feeling was shattered by a gaggle of Berlin workers who were repairing a roof. From their midst came a cry of 'Bravo, Adolf!'

> Now it has to be said that it was quite out of the
> question to call Hitler by his Christian name. You
> could call Göring Hermann or Goebbels Jupp; Hitler,

however, wasn't even referred to as Hitler, but 'the Führer'. You didn't take such liberties with divinities and their children but maintained an attitude of respect; and then in this atmosphere of oppressive solemnity of all times, somebody dared, instead of standing to attention, lifting his arm and crying out *Heil* at the very least, in a completely matey, down-to-earth manner, to call the Führer old Adolf!

Naturally Hitler and his toadies pretended not to hear, but the Berliner was not deflected from his *Schnauze*, and as the Führer's car drove away from the airport there could be heard again: 'Bravo, Adolf!'

When the war got rough after 1941 it became increasingly difficult to use Tempelhof and flights took off and landed from more distant airfields. Gatow was one of the nearest; there was a flying school there, and later it became the airport for the British sector, the equivalent of the French strip at Tegel and Tempelhof itself, which belonged to the Americans. Gatow was the first port of call for the extraordinary visit made by Robert Ritter von Greim and the female test pilot Hanna Reitsch on 26 April 1945.

Hitler was furious with Göring, because his air-chief had had the gall to suggest that he might have problems administering what remained of Germany from his bunker. He had summoned Greim to Berlin to promote him to Field Marshal and give him Göring's job. He then sacked Göring and sent orders to have him imprisoned. Greim and Hanna Reitsch left Rechlin with an escort of forty fighters, many of which failed to make it to Gatow. From Gatow Greim and Hanna Reitsch flew a plane at tree-top level and landed on the East–West Axis. While they were in the air Russian bullets tore holes in the bottom of the plane and shattered Greim's foot. Hanna Reitsch had to take over the controls. Once they landed they were able to commandeer a car and make their way to the Führer's bunker.

They found a ranting, lachrymose Hitler, still beside

himself with fury over Göring's treachery, and doubtless giving the jealous Goebbels tremendous pleasure as a result. Greim might have been informed of his new status by telegram; now he was obliged to remain in the bunker until his foot was well enough to walk on. For three days they were able to lap up Hitler's fantasies about General Wenck, and how relief was at hand. From Rechlin it was reported that Berlin was now effectively closed to air traffic, that Greim and Hanna Reitsch were there for good.

Finally Greim was well enough to leave, and although they expressed a desire to stay to the bitter end Hitler dismissed them. They made their way back to the plane and succeeded in putting enough space between themselves and the Russians to escape their bullets. 'Explosions tossed the plane to and fro like a feather, till they had climbed to a height of 20,000 feet, and, looking down, could see Berlin like a sea of flame beneath them.'[40]

Just over three years later there were more air-traffic problems over Berlin when at the beginning of July 1948 the Russians cut off all communications with West Berlin with the exception of military convoys. The official pretext was to prevent the entry of West German money into their zone after they had initiated their first currency reform.[41] In reality they were making a bid to seize control of the whole city by starving it out.

The man of the hour was the American commander Lucius Clay, who decided to bring in essential supplies by air. 'Operation Vittles' was made possible by a constant stream of type C-47 Dakotas. The planes had only a three-ton capacity, which made it difficult to meet the 12,000 tons per day that were deemed necessary to feed the population. At the beginning the Allies came nowhere near that figure, and they never succeeded in bringing in more than 8,000 tons. Many Berliners died of cold and hunger that winter, which was second only to the murderous winter of 1946–1947.

The size of the operation made it vital to open another

airport in Berlin, and Tegel was made ready in just three months. The Russian gesture had a 'boomerang effect',[42] in that it drove West Berliners into the hands of the Western Allies and for the first time instituted a bond between the conquerors and the conquered. The Russian blockade proved a massive propaganda failure. Traffic was resumed on the night of 11–12 May 1949.

III

One way of imposing order on a potentially turbulent populace was through religion. In the late Middle Ages Berlin became an increasingly important religious centre, but it could not rival the regional See of Brandenburg. Lutheranism swept up the old trade routes from Saxony, but not all the Brandenburgers were enthusiastic about dropping the relationship with Rome. The Elector Joachim was inclined to remain a Catholic, but in 1521 the citizens showed their own hand when neither the council nor the guilds, nor the schoolboys, took part in the traditional Corpus Christi procession. Joachim's wife, Kurfürstin Elisabeth, secretly took communion of the two sorts: bread *and* wine. When Joachim remonstrated with her she fled to Protestant Saxony. Joachim was obliged to heed the will of his subjects and appoint a Protestant to preach at the Petrikirche. Philipp Melanchthon made three visits to Berlin at this time to encourage the growing number of Berliners who were embracing Luther's church. In 1539 even the Bishop of Brandenburg succumbed.[43]

It was not a violent Reformation, far less so than in England or Scotland. There was no iconoclasm and the Berlin churches had to wait until the early seventeenth century before their Catholic trappings were removed.[44] There was a far greater commotion when in 1613 the Elector John Sigismund decided to become a Calvinist and abandon the principle established in Germany at the time of the religious wars: *cuius regio eius religio* (the prince's religion decides that of his subjects; see below, pp. 409–410). There were riots then, but half a century later, in 1662, the Calvanist Great Elector felt strong enough to override his subjects' Lutheranism and ban them from studying at the University of Wittenberg. Preacher Heinzelmann at the Nikolaikirche offended against John Sigismund's tolerant Blasphemy Edict when he railed against Calvinists from his pulpit. He was banished. So too was one of Brandenburg's first poets of note, Heinzelmann's friend the Deacon Paul Gerhart. In 1666 the Great Elector had him sacked too.[45]

With the Great Elector and his son, Frederick I, came the beginnings of the new heterodoxy. On the Gendarmenmarkt not only was there a church for the French, but the other side of the square had a building where Lutherans and Calvinists assembled under the same roof. There wasn't much in it for Catholics. They were not included in the Edict of Potsdam. Only Frederick the Great granted them equal rights and churches of their own, a move surely regretted by later Prussian rulers.

A homely religious fundamentalism began to grip Berliners from the late seventeenth century onwards. Again it was an import from Saxony. Philipp Jakob Spener introduced Pietism to the capital of Brandenburg when he came from Dresden to preach at the Nikolaikirche in 1691. In general, however, eighteenth-century Berlin was not rocked by religious controversy: the kings dictated the style. Frederick William I was pious; Frederick the Great a deist; Frederick William II was a libertine, and his son reacted against his father, running into trouble with his many Catholic subjects when he moved against their liberties. For the court in Frederick the Great's day, religious observance seems to have been a round of formal attendance, going to the better churches and listening to the fashionable pastors. In February 1753, Lehndorff attended a sermon delivered by a Pastor

Sack: 'He is the most famous preacher of the day. He doesn't get my support; he doesn't speak clearly, and he says little in a great torrent of words. His great gift is that he knows how to win the women over.'[46]

Pietism came into its own in the nineteenth century. Dronke saw it as part of the great machinery of repression which blocked the progress of free thought. What use was Pietism when people could be wounded on the open street, and when 'Russian tyranny' would soon be introduced?[47] Pietism depended on conversion. Its adepts were often members of the Junker nobility who visited the houses of the poor to guide them to the light. Dronke thought them very suspicious: they held no meetings and published no accounts. No one called them to order. One day a servant girl came into his room with a radiant expression on her face, bearing one of their tracts – 'a blessing from an unknown, finely dressed man ... There are some lovely things in it about the tortures of hell, God's punishment and Heaven's salvation, so that on the one hand it make your hair stand on end and, on the other, your mouth water.'[48]

The Pietists of the 1840s and 1850s set out to evangelise the urban poor, but the task was far too great for them. An Adolf Stöcker later tried to bring Berlin's Christians to order with a crusade against the Jews (see below, pp. 430–431). At first Kaiser William II was wholly on Stöcker's side, but he soon abandoned his protégé and concentrated on filling his burgeoning city with neo-Gothic churches instead. Frederick William III and Frederick William IV had had the same thought on a more modest scale, and architects such as Schinkel, Stüler and Persius to carry out the designs. Modesty was not the last Kaiser's strong suit, nor that of his architects.

The last great religious movements to capture the imagination of the Berliners were the Nazi-inspired 'Deutsche Christen' and its opposition counterpart, the 'Pfarrernotbund' or Pastors' Emergency League. The Deutsche Christen fired their first salvo in Berlin's Marienkirche on 3 February

1933 when Pastor Joachim Hassenfelde hailed the anti-
Christian new German Chancellor as an emissary of God:
'Christ makes history calling forth men. Whenever our
German people have suffered he has given us men who
appear before the people with a wonderful mission, who
know something of God's mysteries . . .'[49] Hitler's speeches
were carefully groomed by the failed priest Goebbels, who
knew how to excite the subcutaneous Messianism of the
Germans.[50] Hassenfelde went on to attempt a synthesis of
Nazism and Evangelicism. The 'Glaubensbewegung Deut-
sche Christen' had won approximately half the votes in the
Church elections in 1932. Hitler was wooing the Protestant
Church, which had felt abandoned during Weimar. Most
Protestant clerics had leaned to the far right-wing DNVP. It
was all part of his game to put the Conservatives at ease, like
the brief flirtation with the former Kaiser and his family.[51]
On 1 February 1933 Hitler spoke of the role of Christian
morality as the kernel of the nation and the body politic; of
Christianity as the 'basis of our whole family morality'.
On 10 February he even finished a speech with the word
'Amen'.[52]

The Church hierarchy was suspicious. The authorities
refused to allow two Nazi thugs (now hailed as martyrs by
the regime) to be buried in the cathedral: it was reserved for
royalty; but Bishop Otto Dibelius was taken in by the *Tag
von Potsdam* and its call for order in the land. He later realised
that it was all a sham, and went over to the opposition. The
split in the Church was accelerated when, in April that year,
the Deutsche Christen voted to ban pastors who were not
of the Aryan race. The Pfarrernotbund was created directly
as a result, and Pastor Martin Niemöller of Dahlem
emerged as its most dynamic spokesman.

The faith of the Deutsche Christen was expressed in
massive show weddings, where the grooms turned up in
brown shirts and swastika arm bands. On 29 June fifty couples
were married in this way at the tennis courts in Wilmersdorf.

Hassenfelde honoured the newly-weds with a sermon in the Kaiser-Wilhelms-Gedächtniskirche. He took his text from the Epistle to the Romans: 'Everyone is subject to the authority above him.' Most of the male members of the congregation were dressed in brown shirts. Hassenfelde's theology did not impress the incumbent, Gerhard Jacobi. He countered with Matthew 21, 13: 'My house should be for prayer, but you turn it into a den of thieves.'[53]

Jacobi was making a brave gesture. The regime had already begun to imprison opposition clergy. In Dahlem their names were read from the pulpit, and the congregation bidden to pray for them. Hindenburg, too, made a rare decision to utter some muted criticism of the regime he had called into being, and many Berlin Christians derived some consolation from the Reichspräsident's words. Marriages in brown shirts turned to mass christenings of Brown Shirts' offspring before the year was out. On 13 October the Pfarrernotbund met in Zelter's Singakademie. Karl Barth called for an uncompromising fight against the Deutsche Christen: 'What do you have to do? Grow strong by what the Reformation has to teach us today. You must resist, in the name of the true Church against the false Evangelical Church which takes the form of this movement.'[54]

There were even hotter heads than Hassenfelde's. 'Gau-Obmann' (the Nazi version of the old Lutheran super-intendent) Krause spoke out against the 'heathen spirit of Jesus' on 13 November. He called for the banning of the Old Testament and the 'scapegoat and inferiority theology of the Rabbi Paul . . . When we National Socialists are ashamed to buy a tie from a Jew, then we should also be thoroughly ashamed to accept something which speaks to our inner souls which comes from the very heart of the Jewish religion.' Krause's speech was badly received. Many conservative Protestants realised that they were dealing with a lunatic, heretical fringe. A week later the six thousand or so members of the Pfarrernotbund read their own declaration from the pulpits of their churches. They were not going to be 'dumb dogs' but represent the truth in the face of the falsification of the Gospels.[55]

The debate raged until the end of the year. On 19 December the Reichs Bishop Müller struck a blow by having all 700,000 members of Evangelische Jugend (Evangelical Youth) conscripted into the Hitler Youth. The city's Catholics were spared a similar outrage. Berlin's Catholic population was far smaller and the Zentrum, their political party, had almost doubled its votes in March 1933. As part of the Nazi Concordat signed with the Church, Catholics were allowed to opt out of the Hitler Jugend.

The Deutsche Christen may have lost a large amount of its support, but there was to be no amnesty for the Pfarrernotbund. In January 1934 the Gestapo searched Niemöller's parsonage in Dahlem and had the cleric dismissed from his cure. A month later the former *U-Boot* officer was forced into retirement. In May the opposition Church met for the 'Confessing Synod' in Barmen in the suburbs of Wüppertal. The result was a decision to reject any attempt to force an oath of loyalty to the regime on their members. The second conference of the Bekennende Kirche, or 'Confessing Church', took place in Dahlem that October, with a third taking place there in March 1935. The Nazi Church had sinned against the 1st Commandment in enciting members to worship the false gods of 'blood, race, folklore, honour, and freedom of idol worship'. 'Such worship of craven images has nothing to do with Christianity. It is anti-Christian.'[56]

The Nazis moved in for the kill. There were 500 arrests. At one time 700 members of the Bekennende Kirche were in prison. The regime was none the less forced to backtrack a little. A solution was suggested by Minister Kerrl which was acceptable to the more conservative elements in the Bekennende Kirche. The 'Dahlemite' wing continued to oppose the Nazis and their policies, however, and its popularity made it hard to suppress. The numbers of Berliners wanting to hear the pastors rose steadily. The little mediaeval church was too small. Services were held in the Jesus-Christus Kirche nearby or in the parish hall.[57]

Niemöller preached his last sermon in Dahlem on 27 June 1937. On 1 July the Gestapo broke up a meeting at his home and placed all present under house arrest while another search was instituted. After eight hours the others were free to go, but Niemöller was thrown into Moabit gaol.[58] On 4 July Dibelius made a protest declaration in Dahlem and presented a petition bearing 900 names. In seven months in prison, Niemöller received 10,000 letters of support. He was later tried for 'incitement and disparagement' of leading members of the state and sent to Sachsenhausen as a 'personal prisoner of the Führer'. The Americans found him in Dachau at the end of the war.[59]

IV

Education was another method of ordering Berlin's citizens. Prussia introduced limited public education as early as 1717. The Soldier-King wanted his soldiers and NCOs to be able to read and write. It was to be a little learning only. Both Frederick William and his son Frederick the Great were aware that educating the peasantry might give them ideas above their station. The existence of free-schools in no way inhibited the use of child labour, especially in the cities, where the infant population was harder to survey. Dronke, for example, informs us that the modern chimney had got too small for adult sweeps, and that only children would fit: 'You see whole troupes of this little black brood milling through the streets.'[60]

Schools teaching humanities came into existence with the Reformation. Before then, schooling was in the hands of the Church. After 1540 only one Church school, the Nikolaischule, remained. In 1574 the school Zum grauen Kloster was set up in the old conventual buildings of the Franciscan friary by the present Alexanderplatz, with its staff of schoolmasters, *Bakkalaurei* and *Kantors* (who originally acted as choirmasters).[61] The school drew 600 pupils from throughout the Mark. Nothing to rival it was created before 1650, when the Joachimsthalsche Gymnasium was founded as the second great institution of Berlin humanism.[62] It had originally been set up in Neu-Eberswalde but was destroyed in the Thirty Years War. The Great Elector allowed it to function in the royal Schloss until it found a permanent home on the Lange Brücke in 1690. It had 'professors' in the different faculties, like a university, and there was a theological seminary attached. The two other important schools created in the seventeenth century were the Friedrichswerdersche Gymnasium and the Collège Française.[63]

Prussian boys were ever expected to serve a while with the colours. If they came from decent families it was almost unavoidable. As the cities grew there was felt an ever greater need to offer children the chance to get out into the country, or back to nature. The Wandervogel did just this. It was founded by Karl Fischer in Steglitz in 1896, and functioned in much the same way as the Boy Scouts did in Britain. First boys bivouacked in the Grunewald. Later the movement opened up to girls too. There was a lot of rambling, singing and nature-worship, most of it totally harmless.[64] It is perhaps not surprising that some commentators have wanted to find the roots of the Hitler Jugend (Hitler Youth or HJ) in the Wandervogel, but it is scarcely just. The Wandervogel had nothing to do with military training or indoctrination. Indeed, Hitler had no time for it; he had it abolished as soon as he came to power.

Like all the organs of the Nazi state, the HJ and its female counterpart, the BDM, had their main office in Berlin. In this case Speer's building in the Heerstraße has survived, where so many monuments to the Prussian past have not. It was even restored to its original design in 1958. The HJ's first leader was the half-American, Berlin-born Baldur von Schirach, who was later to share Spandau prison with Speer and five other Nazi *Bonzen*. Schirach went on to become Gauleiter of Vienna; the nobleman was replaced in May 1940 by the proletarian Artur Axmann, who went on to lose an arm in the Barbarossa campaign in Russia.

As the Russians converged on Berlin less than four years later, Axmann sent some 600 fifteen- and sixteen-year-olds in to man the defences. They were based in the Sports Stadium, not far from Axmann's headquarters. Units were brought in from Ruhleben to witness the shooting by firing squads of their comrades who had given up the fight: 'It was our own blood, children like us, murdered because they could no longer see the point of murder and therefore sought a way out.'[65] As elsewhere where the HJ was posted in those last moments of the war, they fought furiously. The Russians took the Sports Field, but the HJ got it back. Around 2,000 boys died in the fighting.[66]

The universities of Brandenburg-Prussia – Königsberg, Frankfurt an der Oder, Halle, Breslau and Duisburg – were housed in the provinces until the defeat at Jena. The city's academic leanings were expressed in the Academy, which owed its origins to Queen Sophie Charlotte and her friend Leibniz.[67] The university came to Berlin in 1810. The shrunken state had lost in Halle its chief nursery for civil servants and jurists. The foundation is generally attributed to Wilhelm von Humboldt, but Zelter reported to Goethe that the classicist and former Halle professor Friedrich August Wolf was behind it: 'Wolf has made a plan to start a new Prussian university here instead of old Halle and to bind it where possible to the Academy of Sciences.'[68]

One of the first students (and a mature one at that) was Adelbert von Chamisso, who was unable to join in the fight between his adopted country and his motherland. The teachers impressed him, but not his fellows: 'I see only a lot of dunderheads.'[69] Chamisso was to enjoy the patronage of one of the teachers, Heinrich Lichtenstein, who guided his steps in botany, allowing Chamisso the dual career of botanist and poet. He was later the keeper of Berlin's first Botanical Garden, which was on the site of the Kleistpark in Schöneberg before it was moved to its present location in Steglitz.

The teachers continued to be the great strength of the university despite the censorship and illiberal atmosphere of Prussia in the nineteenth century. Students did not always plump for the best courses. In the winter semester of 1829 to 1830, the largest number attended the lectures of the geographer Ritter on the history of Palestine.[70] Schleiermacher's life of Jesus proved reasonably popular, attracting 251 students. The lectures on mediaeval law of the great jurist Friedrich Karl von Savigny brought in 227 attendants. Far fewer (just 137) were drawn in by Böckh's history of antiquity. The least popular of all was Hegel: his lectures on the history of philosophy were attended by a mere 116.[71]

It was doubtless the quality of the students who went to Hegel that counted. There were plenty who came to Berlin just for him: not just Marx and Engels, but the Bauer brothers, Feuerbach, Max Stirner, even Dronke. He reported on the quality of student digs at the time: the richer ones found rooms in the Friedrichstadt, the poorer ones in the *Medizinerviertel* – i.e., near the Charité Hospital, beyond the Oranienburger Tor. Some Berlin houses were entirely divided up into digs; the retired civil servants or widows who owned them lived only on their incomes from the students, whom they provided with coffee and breakfast before they left for the Linden.[72]

In the 1840s there were 1,800 students at Berlin University. Hegel had died in the cholera epidemic of 1831 (which also killed the Chief of the General Staff Gneisenau and the theorist Clausewitz), but his influence was still enough to lure in students in droves. His chair was occupied by Schelling, who had promptly declared all previous philosophy 'useless', before espousing Hegelianism himself.[73] Also protecting the great man's legacy was Philipp Konrad Marheineke, the liberal theologian who used his influence to retain the remaining Hegelians such as Bruno Bauer and Karl Nauwerck, until Eichhorn stepped in to stop the latter from lecturing. On the right was the Halle theologian Müller, a pietist. Leopold von Ranke was the leading light in the history department.[74]

Even with so much talent about, Dronke saw the University as a curate's egg. There reigned a certain freedom in its lecture rooms, but it was also the easel on to which the state pinned different ideas of statecraft. He compared these to so many potted plants. 'On the top shelf were the colourful blooms of oriental bondage and Muhammadan belief in predestination; these received plenty of manure. Those of the lower shelves for reason and free democratic development were given hard, dry earth, where they were left to wilt so that their places could be used for other things.'[75]

Dronke proved prophetic. After the 1848 Revolution ten of the philosophy teachers were sacked, and the other faculties roughly pruned. Student numbers dropped, but it was still huge by contemporary English standards. Throughout the 1850s numbers fluctuated between 2,000 and 2,300 students. After the Austro-Prussian war of 1866 they rose to over 3,000. The Treitschke era was not far off, when the Saxon general's son would demonstrate that the Prussian army was the only solid foundation for a united Germany. It is significant that the University attracted far fewer foreigners after 1848. Before the Revolution there were 150 of them. Afterwards just twenty-nine.[76]

In one area Kaiser William II proved himself a modernist. The Technische Hochschule had been founded in the first Kaiser's time. Five years later, in 1884, a new building came alongside on its Charlottenburg site. In 1899, William granted the fledgling institution *Promotionsrecht*, allowing it to grant doctorates and making it effectively the equivalent of the more traditional universities. The 'Friedrich-Wilhelms' University on the Linden was growing fast: numbers rose to 5,000 students and 350 teachers in 1896. By 1910 they had reached 10,000. To relieve some of the congestion on the Linden perhaps, Friedrich Althoft, Ministerial Director for the Universities, hit on the idea of creating a German Oxford in Dahlem. This was the Kaiser-Wilhelms-Gesellschaft, which was to bring together some of the world's great minds on the eve of the First World War.[77]

In 1908–1909 fifty hectares of the Dahlem domain were hived off as building land for new institutes for biochemistry, chemistry, physical chemistry, biology, anthropology, the Harnackhaus (named after Adolf von Harnack, who became the Society's president in 1911), cell physics and silicate research. Althoft did not live to see his ideas become a reality. The idea was taken to the Kaiser by Friedrich Schmidt (later the Kultusminister Friedrich Schmidt Ott) as a splendid way of commemorating the centenary of the university in the Linden. Details were then worked out with the new Kultusminister, August von Trott zu Solz.[78]

The KWG was a strikingly modern institution. Rather like some academic body of our own day, businessmen and 'Prussian gold barons' outnumbered dons on the steering committee. The KWG was to work very closely with industry, especially the arms industry. In its short life it none the less bred twelve Nobel Prize winners. The Institute for Physical- and Electrochemistry is a case in point. Harnack discovered the assimilated Jew and patriot Fritz Haber and put him in charge. Haber turned the place over to the war effort in due course. By the time he was given the lowly rank of captain in the Prussian army, the institute was largely dedicated to the development and manufacture of poison gas. When Otto Hahn confronted Haber with the Geneva Convention, he replied that he thought his gas would shorten the war and therefore save lives. His argument didn't prevent his wife from committing suicide when she heard that the gas had been blown back in the faces of German troops. Haber himself lived long enough to see the Nazis in power. He died across the border in Basel in 1934.[79]

Hahn worked with Lise Meitner at the Institute for Chemistry. Lise Meitner was one of many Jews, roughly a quarter of the staff, working at the KWG. As an Austrian citizen she carried on working at the Institute until 1938, when she emigrated to Sweden and told all she knew to the Nobel Institute there. More sinister was the Institute for Anthropology, where Ottmar Freiherr von Verschuer conducted his work on twins. Once the Nazis came to power he was given *carte blanche*, and more than 4,000 Berlin twins were placed on his lists. Large numbers also went through detailed examination. Elsewhere in the building Fritz Lenz had his office, where he worked on racial hygiene with a view to improving the 'collective genotype'. Down the corridor Eugen Fischer played a leading role in the forced sterilisation of up to 200,000 mental patients before 1939. Fischer publicly thanked Hitler for the Nuremberg laws, but he had his compassionate side, and allowed Kurt Gottschalk to carry on working, although he knew him to be a communist.[80]

Once the war got going, all moral or ethical scruple seems to have been cast aside – especially by Verschuer, who worked on selective breeding, collecting up embryos and organs from twins. Verschuer had supervised Mengele's doctoral dissertation in Frankfurt in his native Hesse. Now the KWG was used by Mengele to further his experiments on twins. After the war Verschuer denied all knowledge of Mengele's experiments.[81]

In the Institute for Cell Physiology the half-Jewish Otto Warburg worked on cures for cancer; he was allowed to stay in Germany, because Hitler apparently valued his work. Not so Albert Einstein at the Institute for Physics. He had left before the first reactor was built. By 1942 Heisenberg believed he could produce a uranium bomb. Ernst Telschow witnessed a talk where the scientist first used the words in the presence of the air force Field Marshal Milch: 'Heisenberg had already sat down when . . . Milch asked him: "How big does a bomb have to be to reduce a big city like London to ruins?" Heisenberg turned on his feet and Telschow thought he looked embarrassed. He demonstrated with his hands the dimensions of a small shell. "About the size of a pineapple," he said.'[82]

The KWG lasted just forty years. In 1951 it was abolished and its functions taken over by the Max Planck Gesellschaft. Berlin's scientific institutions were all sullied by their co-operation with Nazi genocidal experiments. The names of such luminaries as Rudolf Virchow and Robert Koch, whose work was devoted to the improvement of the human condition, were replaced by those made notorious by their participation in mass murder. The Reichsgesundheitsamt (the Imperial Health Department) was associated with Koch and the Berliner Physiologische Gesellschaft, which had discovered the bacilli for tuberculosis, diphtheria and typhus. After 1933 Hans Reiter decided that the Department had a new function, to research human genetics and racial hygiene. One section under Eduard Schütt concerned itself with 'racially sound, large families of German descent'; 'biological marriage guidance'; and 'biological methods of fighting venereal disease'.[83]

Robert Ritter was in charge of the Research Department for Racial Hygiene and Population Biology. Ritter it was who noted a loophole in Nazi racial law: gypsies had been categorised as Aryans because they originated in India and were nominally Christians. Ritter demonstrated that they were mongrels, their blood mixed in with 'asocial and hereditary inferior elements'. His colleague Eva Justin dedicated her doctoral dissertation to 'The destiny of foreign gypsy children and their offspring: the further influences of inferior genotypes parasitic to the German racial body'. The research bore fruit: in November 1935 mixed marriages between gypsies and Aryans were banned. On 1 March 1939 Himmler published a circular on fighting the 'gypsy plague'. Gypsies were now subject to the full force of German racial persecution: sterilisation, forced labour, and confinement in concentration camps. Ritter personally examined 2,000 gypsies before sending them off to the camps. Later on he continued his research in Buchenwald, Natzweiler and Dachau. After the examinations in Berlin-Zehlendorf, on 16 December 1942, 9,000 gypsy 'mongrels' were '*concentrated in a special gypsy camp in the Sudetenland*'. He meant Auschwitz.[84]

Of course it was not true that all medicine or all physicians were implicated in the Nazi genocide. Names such as the psychiatrist Karl Bonhoeffer (the father of Dietrich) and the surgeon Ferdinand Sauerbruch stand out. Nor were the *Bonzen* of the DDR immune from such experiments, when the lives of their politicians or the prowess of their athletes were in question. It was all a big change from the small-scale hospitals that existed in nineteenth-century Berlin, such as the Bethanien Krankenhaus in Kreuzberg, designed in a neo-Gothic style by Persius and Stüler. Fontane once worked as an apothecary in the still-extant building. In those days it was deeply aristocratic. Its superiors were all nobles until 1935: a Rantzau, a Gerlach, a Stolberg-Wernigerode, a Bethmann-Hollweg.[85]

Medical studies were as yet unencumbered with genetics and racial hygiene. Gottfried Benn – who despite his optimism for a National Socialist state thought their racial thinking nonsense – after two years at the University doing philosophy and theology to please his pastor father, studied at the Kaiser-Wilhelm-Akademie for military medicine before the First World War. It was an 'excellent academy', which had helped polish the physicians Virchow, Helmholz, Leyden and Behring. The military school was better funded than the Charité, and students could attend lectures on art and philosophy. The only condition imposed was that every student had to serve in the army for a year for every semester spent at the school.[86]

Politics wrecked the institutions of higher education from 1933 onwards. There was to be no let-up after 1945. The Friedrich-Wilhelm University fell to the Russians and their stooges. They replaced its first post-war director, Eduard Spranger, a philosopher with Opposition credentials, by a more compliant figure. The name was changed first to the University Unter den Linden, and then to the Humboldt University. Preference for places was given to members of the SED. Then in February 1947 several students were arrested for protesting against this negative discrimination. The situation was observed by the American Military Governor Lucius Clay. Seeing the need for a free university in the western zones he offered students the old buildings of the KWG in Dahlem together with whatever university institutes were now in the west. On 4 December 1948 the Free University of Berlin opened in a villa in the Bolzmannstraße in Dahlem.[87]

V

Administratively speaking, before 1920 Berlin was a mess. With the massive growth of the outlying villages into important towns in their own right, there was no effective council making policy for the whole conurbation. It was a situation that made planners wring their hands in despair and gave the architects of the new urban railway network nightmares. What was needed was a 'Greater Berlin', but this order was not to be achieved until 1920.

Until 1881 overall responsibility for the area still abided with the Regierungspräsident for Brandenburg who was based in Potsdam. That year Berlin received its own 'borough' status with a 'city committee' even if the regional president's authority was still theoretically imposable. The most powerful man in Berlin was now the Police President, a position to which Hinckeldey had aspired, but which had never come about due to his premature end. The Police President now controlled passports and residence permits, foreigners, commerce and traffic. The one exception was the fire brigade. In 1900 Charlottenburg, Schöneberg and Rixdorf were brought into his domain.[88]

Other bodies, too, exerted a large influence on public life. The state Church was run by its own *Oberconsistorium*, the schools were administered by a *Provinzialschulkollegium*, health by a *Gesundheitskollegium*. Building was in the hands of a *Ministeriell-, Militär- und Bau-Kommission*, while the Berlin garrison came under the aegis of the *Militärverwaltung*.[89]

The highest organ of civic administration was the *Magistrat*, formed by the *Oberbürgermeister* and his deputy (the *Bürgermeister*) together with thirty paid and unpaid city councillors. These formed committees together with the City Parliament. One of their chief bugbears was finance. How were they to pay for civic improvements, when the real money lay outside Berlin in Charlottenburg, Wilmersdorf, Schöneberg, Steglitz and Friedenau or in the plush villas of the suburbs in Lichterfelde, Dahlem, Grunewald, Wannsee and Nikolassee? Only the poor lived in Berlin proper. The wages were earned in Berlin, but the taxes went to beautify the satellite towns. The result of this thinking was the creation of a *Zweckverband*, or target organisation, to make a 'Groß-Berlin' of some 3,500 square kilometres, roughly twice the size of the one that came into existence in 1920, and twice the size of London.[90]

The force behind the move to create a Greater Berlin came from the new *Oberbürgermeister* Adolf Wermuth, who was elected on 1 September 1912. Even before he took up office Wermuth was shown round his new domain: the market halls, which he visited in the small hours of the morning[91] (a lunch thrown by the abattoirs which continued

late in the night); and the nerve centre of municipal power:
the council chamber of the Rote Rathaus.

> In the middle was a great big round table. This was
> where members of the *Magistrat* delivered their
> reports. When elucidation was required from plans and
> drawings. Civil Engineer Krause showed the path of
> the North–South Railway or the underground line
> from Moabit to Treptow, or the docks at the
> Westhafen, hanging the sheets up on the walls, which
> were for the most part covered with pictures of
> Hohenzollerns.[92]

The City Architect Hoffmann displayed designs for new
schools, which were approved or disapproved by Wermuth
with his *Bürgermeister* on his right and his *Syndikus* to his
left. After these weighty sessions the council retired to the
Ratskeller. 'No council, no cellar; indeed, no cellar, no
council. Even during the Revolution food emerged, as today,
victoriously from the depths.'[93]

When the chain-swinging aldermen of Berlin were not
steeping their successes in steins of beer and bumpers of
wine, they continued to colonise the outskirts of the city
for the good of its inhabitants. Here, land was acquired for
sewage disposal; there, for a park or building plot: 'one field
or bit of woodland after another, noble estates and farms
were transformed into sewage-disposal units.' The old
nobles were hit hard: Graf Redern's 4,500 hectares in Lanke
were swallowed up, as was the manor-house in Buch which
had belonged to the Roebels, and to which Fontane dedicated a chapter of his *Wanderungen.*[94] The council preserved
both *Schloß* and manor, but the former was altered after war
damage, and the latter pulled down by the DDR.[95]

Wermuth's work was interrupted by the war. The grandiose plans for a Greater Berlin as the Kaiser's imperial city
were put aside. He received foreign guests, including a delegation of Americans whom he regaled in English (he had

been German consul in Chicago): 'A friend in need is a friend indeed.'[96] For the rest, his day-to-day concerns were to do with provisions: bread, the soup kitchens (an idea of the Chancellor Bethmann-Hollweg) and the 'turnip winter', when the mortality rate rose by 300 per cent. By 1917 he believed he had mastered it. There were plenty of potatoes from the harvest that autumn and the *Oberbürgermeister* declared that hunger was *definitely not* the cause of the revolution which led to the departure of the Hohenzollerns and his abandonment of office in 1920.[97]

On 27 April 1920 all the little bits of the puzzle – Charlottenburg, Neukölln, Köpenick, Spandau – or virtually all of them, were brought together as Groß-Berlin. In their creation, however, *Bezirke* such as Kreuzberg radically altered the historical lines of the city: bits of the old *Vorstädte* such as Kreuzberg itself had been tagged on to the southern end of the Friedrichstadt and then grafted on to Tempelhof, which was gradually evolving from being the city's *champ de Mars* to its airport. Much identity was lost. Even the Mayor of Teltow, lord of the turnips (who had, in reality, nothing to fear from the encroachment of Berlin), minuted pessimistically: 'They want to create a Groß-Berlin and the days of an independent Teltow are numbered. We have lost the war and we have lost our honour. In fact with the disappearance of the borough of Teltow today we can expect no more cataclysmic events.'[98]

Even without Teltow, Groß-Berlin could claim some pretty heroic statistics. It had been welded from eight towns, fifty-nine rural councils, and twenty-seven former estates. It totalled 878 square kilometres.

To 'stone' Berlin they had added 'green' Berlin. It had leaped to thirteen times its original size and doubled its population to 3,858,000.[99] In 1929 this figure had already risen to 4.3 million.[100] Naturally the new Berlin had considerable advantages when it came to planning and provided numerous opportunities for young architects to shine. Under the city's planning officer, Martin Wagner, huge new housing projects were undertaken to relieve the slums in the city centre: the Hufeisensiedlung in Britz, the Waldsiedlung in Zehlendorf, the Weißenstadt in Reinickendorf and the Großsiedlung in Siemensstadt.[103]

Wermuth saw Groß-Berlin become a reality, then slipped away. He had been of the old school. His successor, Gustav Böß, was more of a technocrat who ruled Berlin during the high point of its history, before the Nazis put an end to its more cosmopolitan nature.[102] Neither was a Berliner, neither was Prussian: Wermuth was from Hildesheim and Böß from the little university town of Gießen. His early experience of Berlin was with the railways, and in 1910 he was put in charge of transport in Schöneberg, at a time when the town was building its own network. The problems of the *U-Bahn* took him off on a study tour to Paris, Vienna and London. London suited his needs the best: out of his journeys were born the line from Friedenau to Lankwitz and that from the Nollendorfplatz to the Brandenburger Tor.[103]

Böß was not interested, however, in designing a network just for Schöneberg; his eyes were fixed on a Groß-Berlin. The LCC in London had got private companies to build its Tube lines; Böß looked to Siemens to perform a similar role in Berlin.[104] AEG had built a line from Rixdorf in the south to Gesundbrunnen in the north, but provided no link to the *S-Bahn*. Böß was critical: the common good had been sacrificed to private interests. Pre-war Berlin was always more to the left than the right politically. When Böß succeeded Wermuth, two-thirds of the city had voted for the radical parties; the new *Oberbürgermeister* was more in keeping with the post-war mood.[105]

With the Hohenzollerns gone, the mayor assumed a far higher profile in the city. His wife was one of fifteen children from Memel. She had been brought up in poverty and understood the needs of Berliners during the Depression. For the first time the city had a 'first lady'. Böß patronised the arts (see above, p. 215). In 1924 he instituted the Rathaus-konzerte. The city took over the Charlottenburg Opera House from the Prussian government and installed Bruno Walter to direct it. A fund was established to buy paintings from deserving artists whose pictures didn't sell very well. With the money, for example, the city bought Max Lieber-mann's picture *Die Geschwister*.[106]

Böß was fiercely loyal to the Republic, which made his removal through the Sklarek scandal all the more delightful to the extremes of left and right. When the fencer Helene Mayer used the old Imperial flag at the games in Amsterdam in 1928, Böß had her invitation to the Berlin Sports Week rescinded.[107] The fateful American journey was the result of the Mayor of New York's trip to Berlin in August 1927, and was seen as part of the move towards *détente* between the two countries. Böß took the decision not to return to Germany immediately he got wind of the scandal. The absence of international telephone links meant he remained largely in the dark until he docked in Bremen.[108]

Böß's Nazi successor, Dr Lippert, was determined to have the former Mayor indicted before the courts. On 25 April 1933, the *Kripos* (the criminal police) took him off to the station at Alexanderplatz. He was interrogated at length and accused of using his office to further his tastes for luxurious living. While the police put their case together he was put into prison. His family was reduced to the indignity of begging Göring to keep him out of a concentration camp.[109]

Lippert naturally turned the city's administration upside down. In October 1933 local elections were scrapped. In 1934 Berlin received a new constitution: the Gauleiter now chose a body of forty-five councillors. The *Magistrat* was deemed to contravene Hitler's hallowed *Führerprinzip* and abolished. Julius Lippert was officially the *Kommissar* for Berlin, who was to work alongside Oberbürgermeister Hein-rich Sahm, but Sahm had no power. He was even robbed of control of the Berlin Philharmonic by Göring. When Sahm left in despair, Lippert took over his remaining functions. Meanwhile all but the most obdurate DNVP men were pushed out of the town halls in favour of Nazi *alte Kämpfer*.[110]

Lippert was to have a taste of his own medicine. He was increasingly thwarted by Hitler's pet, the Generalbauinspektor Speer. In frustration he resigned and, at the age of forty-five, joined up. He was followed by Ludwig Steeg, another pass-man.

This huge Berlin, the former capital of Prussia and the Second Reich, was to be Hitler's capital too. Hitler was anxious to fit into the norms of German history, to measure his own achievements against those of others, preferably others who had failed. If Linz was to be his German cultural centre and his bequest to the Greater German Nation, Berlin was the seat of his command. Munich might have been a more natural choice, as the birthplace of his movement and the stronghold of his power, but it had no track record, and Berlin was by far and away the greater challenge.

In one of his monomaniac ramblings in the Wolfsschanze in March 1942, Hitler put his vision for Berlin into words: 'As the capital of the world, Berlin will only stand comparison to ancient Egypt, Babylon or Rome; what is London? What is Paris by contrast?'[111] Hitler may have long kept his beady eyes on Berlin, but Berliners were slow to pick up on this Austrian with his Bavarian movement. Goebbels found the Spandauers the most prone to his charm: he thought them 'wrought from another metal to the Berliners'.[112]

That was in the time when Berlin Nazis restricted their activities almost entirely to street thuggery. A different picture was gleaned from the elections of September 1930 when Hitler's party became the second biggest in the Reichstag. In bourgeois areas such as Wilmersdorf, Zehlendorf, Steglitz, Tempelhof, Schöneberg and Charlottenburg, the Nazis won as much as 19 per cent of the votes cast. Their tally was lower in the working-class strongholds: Wedding, Kreuzberg, Neukölln, Friedrichshain, Prenzlauerberg and Weißensee. Here they averaged just 12 per cent.[113]

The Nazis' share of the vote rose, but the political character of the city's becomes clearer when one sees that nearly 70 per cent of Berliners voted against the Weimar Republic in the fateful poll of January 1933. Of these, 720,000 were in favour of the NSDAP; 800,000, however, voted for the KPD.[114] If the patterns for the election of November 1932 are compared with the two Nazi-managed polls of March 1933, Steglitz emerges as the most rabidly National Socialist *Bezirk* in Berlin: 36 per cent voted for Hitler before the *Machtergreifung* and 45.2 per cent and 48.1 per cent in the 'almost free' elections in March. The lowest poll for Hitler's NSDAP was in Wedding. In November it was 17.9 per cent, rising to 25.9 per cent and 29.9 per cent once the Communists were officially enemies of the state. Wedding was always the *Hochburg* of the Berlin *Kozis*: their tally amounted to 47 per cent in November, almost one in two votes cast. Once the persecution started they declined to 39.1 per cent and 32.5 per cent – i.e., still a little under a third for an illegal organisation. The most anti-communist borough was Zehlendorf, where the votes were 10.3 per cent, 7.9 per cent and 5.3 per cent respectively. Steglitz was only slightly higher.[115] The left and centre parties were for the chop anyhow. Hitler's cabinet contained members of the right-wing DNP and DNVP until the late thirties, but in ever more menial, less influential positions. In the Berlin boroughs members of these two parties were gradually pushed out by more dependable NSDAP *alte Kämpfer*. The only exception was Dr Meißner, the Mayor of Pankow.[116]

The Nazis had their own ways of imposing order upon Berlin. Here they had an advantage which not even Frederick the Great or the Kaiser had fully enjoyed: they could ride roughshod over all opposition. The *Führerprinzip* dispensed with the niceties of communal red tape. There were no longer any checks to projects for grandiose town planning. Only Lippert, a Nazi who had worked with Goebbels in local government, was able to operate some feeble brake as 'Kommissar'. It is significant that his status declined dramatically after Speer was named Generalbauinspektor in January 1937.[117]

Speer was Hitler's chosen stooge in transforming Berlin into the 'kernel of the Germanic race'.[118] Once more the Führer's eyes strayed across the border to the Frankish capital, Paris. He told his architect: 'Look at Paris, the most beautiful city in the world.' It was Haussmann's mid-nineteenth-century city which excited him, with its opera house and boulevards. Speer went back to the plans made by Martin Mächler between 1908 and 1920. These provided for a central axis leading to a station on the Spree in Moabit. Speer was to provide plans for a city of eight to ten million inhabitants with a north–south and an east–west axis, four concentric ring roads and four airports.[119] The central station (the project has reared its head once again since 1989) would have had the effect of invalidating the other termini. All the Nazis intended to leave was a northern station in Wedding, and a southern one in the Papestraße in Kreuzberg. These were due for completion between 1945 and 1950. Rather than the old princely waiting-room on Friedrichstraße station, the *S-Bahn* station on the Heerstraße was to be the new reception room for visiting VIPs.[120]

Hitler was as obsessed with the need for Berlin to reflect his greatness as the Kaiser had been before him. Speer's budget was vast. Plans were laid to bury the Spree at the Mühlendamn. The monumental character of the north–south axis is well known. On the Königsplatz the Reichstag (which Hitler approved) was to be dwarfed by an enormous Soldiers' Hall, reducing Wallot's building to 'a silly, decorated toy-box'.[121] Work started at the Südstern before the war. The tragic Jochen Klepper had to move from his house, as it lay in Speer's way.[122] Big holes were made in the Potsdamer- and Viktoriastraßen for the new Runde Platz where the modern Kulturforum is now. On the Königsplatz the Siegessäule and the statues were taken away, while the 'Puppen' were relocated to a more discreet avenue. Speer designed the 'candelabras' along the east–west axis. They are still there.[123]

Independent of the Nazis' more far-reaching plans for Berlin, individual projects were also conceived on a massive scale. Work began on the Reichssportfeld in 1934 under the architect Werner March. He designed the Maifeld, the world's only purpose-built polo field, where Britain defeated the German team in the Olympic Games,[124] the Olympia-turm, the Stadium and the Freilichtbühne (which is now the Waldbühne, a favourite venue for pop concerts). Like March, Ernst Sagebiel was a popular architect with the *Partei-Bonzen*. He designed Göring's Air Ministry as well as the new Tempelhof Airport which was to replace the smaller fields of Kosina and Muhlberg. The Airport is still the largest Nazi monument in Berlin, although the Ministry (Haus der Tausend Fenster – House of the Thousand Windows) is hardly modest in scale. Of the two the Airport is the more successful composition. Both were useful to the Allies after the war. They remained, where so many monuments from the Prussian past were pulled down or blown up.

Other survivals of the period are the Bendlerblock ('sanctified' because it was the scene of the denouement of the July Plot),[125] the Eiffel-Tower-like Funkturm (rebuilt by the Nazis), the Haus des deutschen Gemeindetages (the Ernst-Reuter-Haus) in Charlottenburg and the Fehrbelliner Platz. Extensive plans were drawn up to create a giant museum on the Museums Insel. The Hochschulstadt, or Student Town, by the Sports Field was actually started. At the end of the war the half-completed buildings had been turned to rubble.[126] Another victim was Speer's new Chan-cellery, where the architect had been keen to exploit the power of his medium: a 300-metre calvary took the visitor through a *cour d'honneur*, an antehall, the mosaic salon and the marble gallery, before the Führer's study was reached. The aim was to induce humility in Hitler's guests. The building was finished in just two years. Its remains were demolished after the war, and the marble reused in Mohren-straße *U-Bahn* station.[127]

Hitler and his gang literally brought the house down on their own heads. The wreck of the Thousand Year Reich was not easily forgotten. In April 1945 a Russian aircraft delivered the leading German communist *Moskowiten* to an airfield near Frankfurt an der Oder. One of Ulbricht's companions that day was Wolfgang Leonhardt. Leonhardt was astonished by his first sight of Berlin since his emigration.

> Our car slowly made its way through Friedrichsfelde
> in the direction of Lichtenberg. It was a picture of hell.
> Fires and ruins; hungry, aimless people dressed in rags.
> Leaderless soldiers who no longer seemed to
> understand what was going on around them. Members
> of the Red Army sang and rejoiced, and were often
> drunk too. Groups of women cleared out the wreckage
> under Red Army supervision. Long rows of people
> standing patiently before pumps in order to get a
> bucketful of water. They all looked terribly tired, tense
> and ragged . . . Lots of people were wearing white
> arm bands as a sign of capitulation, or red ones to
> greet the Red Army. There were a few others who
> were particularly cautious: they wore one of each,
> white and red. In the same way white and red flags
> were hung from the windows; you could see that not
> long before, they had been cut from swastikas.[128]

There was no water, gas or electricity. There was no radio, no newspapers.[129]

The destruction continued, partly along ideological lines.

> The demolition of well-preserved buildings, or those
> which had been scorched by fire after the 'collapse',

cannot be explained by planners' needs or the
requirements imposed by a representative political
system; it presumably has something to do with an
unbroken tradition of hatred towards life and history
which first surfaced with National Socialism . . .[130]

Into the great dustbin went the Great General Staff building,
the Kroll-Oper, the Philharmonie and a number of classical
villas south of the Tiergarten, all of which were in the British
sector. Zelter's house went, as did the violinist Joachim's villa.
A photograph taken in 1946 shows a rather sad Bismarck in
the middle of all this wartime and post-war destruction. He
has been removed from his plinth.[131]

Trashed too were the railway termini, with the single
exception of the Hamburger Bahnhof. *Mietshäuser* were
stripped of the decorative stucco which had been applied in
the Kaiser's time or before and simply rendered or covered
with pebble-dash, so that in many cases you are unaware of
the age of a Berlin block of flats until you have passed
through the front door. The interiors of virtually all the
churches were 'simplified' or rebuilt to the taste of unsympa-
thetic fifties or sixties artists. Hitler had been pleased about
the wartime destruction: 'We have made a start on the future,'
he said. For the post-war generation there was also a need
to remove a physical reminder of the past.[132]

The architects naturally revelled in the possibilities
occasioned by this unceasing destruction. Speer's successor
was Hans Scharoun. To do the man justice, he tried to
preserve at least a part of the Schloss, and it was in the
Weißer Saal of that building that the exhibition *Berlin plans*
was shown in 1946. Some of the ideas were simply lifted
from Speer, such as the motorway ring road, or the new
goods railway station in Schöneberg.[133] In Kreuzberg,
Scharoun created a nightmare world of urban motorways
and housing estates at the expense of the old street plan. In
the East it was worse: new Stalinist-style vistas opened up in

an idiom recognisable from all over the new Soviet empire. The only Germanic idea was to revive the *Mietshaus* behind the wedding-cake façades.

In the East too, pliant mayors carried on the traditions bequeathed by their Nazi predecessors. Only in the West were mayors capable of free or inventive thought. The greatest of these was Ernst Reuter, but Otto Suhr and the future Chancellor Willy Brandt and President Richard von Weizsäcker put their marks on the city. Weizsäcker even showed his affection for the place by settling there after his retirement.

6

Bohemian Berlin

I

While Berlin was just the sand-pit of the Holy Roman Empire creative life was confined to a few court artists, architects, jewellers, potters and painters. Before 1810 there was no university and Germany's centres of printing remained elsewhere until the eighteenth and nineteenth centuries. What little artistic foment there was before 1618 was killed off by the Thirty Years War. The Great Elector and his son, the first Prussian king, needed architects to rebuild and beautify their capital, but there was a rapid about-turn when Frederick William I inherited Prussia's shiny new throne: artists remained on sufferance, welcome only if they could do the job on the tight budget provided. Incidentally, Frederick William was also a painter: strange, tortured portraits give as good a description of his agonised soul as any ever written.

It was left to *his* son, Frederick the Great, to create a climate suitable for all the arts, and, even then, only in the years when the state was not turned topsy-turvy by war. In his time too, the purely courtly nature of art declined, so that it was possible for the first small literary circle to grow up around the printer and writer Friedrich Nicolai and his friends Gotthold Ephraim Lessing and Moses Mendelssohn. It was the first moment when writers in other parts of Germany began to look at Berlin; but whereas the city could now be sure that it had more allure than Gleim's Halbestadt, for example, it was nowhere near the equal of Weimar, with Goethe, Schiller, Wieland and Herder.[1]

If there was a pole of attraction it was Frederick himself. Both the power of Prussia and his reputation for enlightened rule recommended themselves to the young Lessing, who came up to Berlin from Leipzig in 1748 at the age of nineteen. In 1757 he and Nicolai were already editing the monthly *Bibliotek der schönen Wissenschaften und freien Künste*: a publication which went some way to uniting literary Germany – be it in Jena, Weimar, Hamburg or Zurich – behind Berlin.[2] In 1759 the journal went weekly as *Briefe, die neueste Literatur betreffend*, which was chiefly written by Lessing. It was the beginning of the German literary renaissance. Nicolai played the role of midwife, as publisher. From 1765 new talents could publish in the *Allgemeine Deutsche Bibliotek*, while reviews had their own organ in the *Rezensions-Zeitschrift*. Nicolai's labours were Herculean: 550 works in 9,000 volumes. He was also responsible for the first reliable guidebooks to Berlin and Potsdam, published in 1769 and 1786, the year of Frederick's death.[3]

Frederick himself took little interest in the literary bubble in his capital. They wrote in German, a language for which he had scant regard. He was happier with Voltaire, Maupertuis or La Mettrie. Lessing was even refused the job of Director of the Royal Library and had to look elsewhere. In 1767 he went to Hamburg and three years later to Wolfenbüttel to look after the library of the Duke of Brunswick. The seminal experience of his Berlin years was the friendship with Moses which inspired his play *Nathan der Weise* of 1779. In the play the character of Saladin, the tolerant and philosophic ruler, bears a slight resemblance to Frederick himself. 'Blood, blood alone, is a long way from making a father!' says Saladin. 'It hardly determines the paternity of an animal!'[4]

Here is the message of the Enlightenment: the difference between men, be they Arabs, Jews or Christians, is 'in colour, clothing and form'.[5] Nathan teaches them all the ways of tolerance. His wife and children were killed by Christians. 'Despise my people as much as you please,' he tells them. 'Neither you nor I chose our parents. Are we our own race? What is race? Are Christians and Jews any more Christians and Jews than they are human beings?' They are fine words which should have guided the hands of later generations of Berliners. Lessing, however, was disillusioned by his experience of 'freedom' in Frederick's 'enlightened' capital:

> It is limited simply to the liberty to attack religion in as silly a way as one pleases . . . should anyone speak up for the rights of the subject, or raise their voices against exploitation and despotism, as they do today in France and Denmark, they would soon learn which land is currently the most enslaved in Europe.[6]

The picture was less depressing than Lessing made out. Christian Wilhelm Dohm joined in the small group of prominent intellectuals calling for Jewish emancipation, and for Germany to go to the aid of Jews persecuted in French Alsace. In 1783 the Mittwochsgesellschaft was founded as a 'society for friends of the Enlightenment'. It proved hardy. In the last war it was a cell of the right-wing opposition. Not many of them survived the Nazi hangman. As for Moses' house at Spandauerstraße 68, that fell victim to the other destructive force in Berlin's history: to make way for the Kaiser's new boulevard – the Kaiser-Wilhelm-Straße.[7]

Literary circles need someone to perform the role of fly-paper on to which the volatile talents stick. In the second wave of Berlin's literary life, that role was to a large extent played by Julius Hitzig. Hitzig was the son of a rich Jewish family (the name was originally 'Itzig') who was bred for the law, and spent some time in the 'South Prussian' administration in Warsaw, where he met and befriended another Prussian civil servant, E. T. A. Hoffmann. When the French victory over Prussia at Jena brought the Prussian colony in Mazovia to an abrupt end, Hitzig went back to Berlin, where he became the close friend of Adalbert von Chamisso.[8]

Just before his death in 1805, Schiller became the first literary lion to visit Berlin. Already, in the 1790s, the Goethe cult had begun in the attic rooms of Rahel Levin.[9] The tumult occasioned by Schiller's visit affected all levels of society; a permanent crowd stationed itself outside the Hotel de Russie in Unter den Linden, where the great poet was staying. In the Schauspielhaus, Iffland (the first Franz Moor in *Die Räuber*) put on the Wallenstein plays, the *Braut von Messina* and the *Jungfrau von Orleans*. Schiller had considered settling in Berlin. After his death his widow wrote to Iffland: 'Through your influence for the first time in Berlin Schiller had enjoyed the rewarding sensation of having worked for the Nation.'[10]

Schiller had been genuinely moved. 'Berlin pleases me more than I had imagined. There exists a great personal freedom, and a lack of constraint in public life. There is plenty to offer in the way of music and drama, even if neither is quite as good as they are made out to be.' After Schiller's death Zelter commiserated with Goethe: 'The unexpected death of our dear Schiller has sent a strong shudder through us in Berlin.'[11] Iffland staged *Die Räuber* in honour of the dead man. Once again he took the role of Franz Moor.

The years of French occupation put a stop to the little literary coterie which had been created through the salons. Nationalism was the all-pervading force. Once it arrived on the scene there was an upsurge of anti-Semitism. In one instance there was a positive effect: Heinrich von Kleist's Berlin journalism in those dark years was not only to prove the first evidence of a less bridled press, but also Berlin's first experience of political journalism (while it lasted). The *Berliner Abendblätter* was closed down by the Prussian censors in 1810 when the poet overstepped the mark with his attacks on the 'foreigner' Napoleon. Hitzig was once again behind the scenes, this time as the publisher of the offending organ. In his disappointment and despair with life Kleist made a suicide pact with Henriette Vogel. They died on a slope beside the Wannsee, a hundred metres or so from the present *S-Bahn* station.[12]

Once Kleist's 'foreigner' had been soundly defeated at Waterloo, literary life could return to Berlin. Hoffmann, who had lacked the family money of a Julius Hitzig, had spent the intervening period as a conductor and theatrical director in Bamberg, Dresden and Leipzig, most of it for very little pay. Now he returned to the Prussian judiciary. Soon after, he started 'Kreisler's Musical and Poetical Club' in honour of his literary persona, the conductor Kreisler. This formed the basis of the 'Serapionsbrüder'; a gathering of writers and drinkers who met at Hitzig's hospitable house in the Friedrichstraße. Carl Wilhelm Salice-Contessa was possibly more one of the latter; writers were Hoffmann, Hitzig, Chamisso and Ernst von Pfuel. Also on the fringes of this circle were Ludwig Tieck and de La Motte Fouqué.[13]

Hoffmann drew greatly from his own experience in his stories and novellas, above all from the unrequited love he felt for Julia Mark in Bamberg. The wine-soaked evenings he spent with the Serapionsbrüder also provided material: he worked his friends into the texts of the stories he wrote in Berlin between 1819 and 1821. Chamisso's *Peter Schlemihl* made an appearance too (see above, p. 268–9) and Hoffmann and Chamisso made plans to write a novel together in the course of their bacchanals. The project came to nothing, partly because Chamisso set off around the world, and partly because Hoffmann drank himself to death.[14]

Fifty or sixty years later Hoffmann's Berlin was still recognisable, and fans like the author Ernst von Wildenbruch (the illegitimate grandson of the 'Prussian Alcibiades', Prince Louis Ferdinand) could imagine the genial writer appearing at every turn, in 'every street, restaurant, wine or coffee-house which he named in his Berlin stories and which we have preserved'.[15] By 1901, however, Wildenbruch was already calling it a lost world: much had been cleared away for the pompous new Berlin; what remained (Lutter und Wegner, for example) had been Disneyfied.

Berlin crops up again and again in his stories. In the *Baron von Bagge*, Hoffmann tells the tale of the violinist Karl Möser; there is the early story *Der Ritter Gluck*; the second 'adventure' of *Meister Floh*, where Georg falls for Dörtje Elverdink, revolves around the Linden with *Garde-Husaren* in parade uniforms;[16] or *Die drei Freunde*, in which Marzell records the jingoistic days that Hoffmann must have witnessed in 1815. Napoleon had returned to plague Europe for a further hundred days: 'As I crossed the Gendarmenmarkt, I ran into a group of volunteers marching off; it stood clearly in my mind what I had to do . . .'[17] In the same story Severin finds a revelatory bloom in the banality of the Grünstraße, an experience altogether typical of the writer: 'a mysterious carnation from which he believed he could smell the fragrance of a rose.'[18]

Lessing had not done it; and despite Nicolai's guides, nor had any member of that early circle. Heinrich von Kleist wrote masterpieces in the city, but he wrote no fiction about it. E. T. A. Hoffmann was the first great writer to put Berlin on the literary map.

Both Hebbel and Büchner worked in Berlin, but the Berlin experience failed to colour their works. By the 1840s the stultifying atmosphere of censorship had taken Berlin's literary life by the throat, as it had threatened to do to Hoffmann at the time of his death. The pressure had the effect of pushing intellectuals more in the direction of political philosophy. With Hegel and his successors at the University, Berlin became a natural port of call for just those minds which troubled the Prussian state the most.

Eichhorn and his spies kept their tabs on them, and tucked themselves into the corners of Stehely or Hippels Weinstube to observe the radicals they called 'the Free'. They took great interest in the brothers Bruno and Edgar Bauer. Both were fierce critics of religion, the former with affinities to Gibbon: the latter was even beaten up by a Christian mob and ended up impoverished and embittered in Rixdorf, coming into town once a week on a dung cart to post articles on portentous subjects to increasingly obscure magazines.[19] Then there were the two populists Ludwig Buhl and Eduard Meyen, both of whom tilted at the Crown and the long-delayed Prussian constitution; promised in 1814 but not delivered until after the Revolution of 1848. Meyen was capable of more romantic thoughts too. He even travelled to Wannsee to plant an oak on Kleist's grave, long before the present monument was set up to the poet's memory and a cramped little public garden laid out around the tomb.[20] Karl Nauwerck was the young Hegelian don and orator who was dismissed from the University and went off to run a tobacco business in Zurich, where he died in his eighties. He was the fifth of the 'Freien'; the sixth was Karl Köppen, who used Frederick the Great as a stick with which to beat the reactionaries in *Friedrich der Große und seine Wiedersacher*, which was published to mark the centenary of the king's accession in 1840.[21]

The last member of the group, Max Stirner, probably interested the Berlin police the least. He was eccentric and, through his relative lack of success, not immediately influential; even if today his reputation tends to outweigh those of his friends. Stirner's one enduring work, *Der Einzige und sein Eigenthum* (The Ego and its Own), was rediscovered by libertarian thinkers at the turn of the century, largely thanks to his first biographer, the anarchist John Henry Mackay (who, despite his Scottish name, was to all extents and purposes a German). Stirner advanced a philosophy of extreme individualism which pitched the ego against the tyranny of abstract ideas. *Egoism* becomes a kind of *reductio ad nihil*: God, humanity, patriotism, all promote themselves. They are egoists: 'Away with this business, then, when it is not entirely

My★ affair! You say that My affairs must promote *Good* at the very least? What is good or evil? I am My own affair and neither good nor evil. Neither means anything to Me.'[22] Abstractions of this sort are 'spectres' for Stirner: 'I alone am incarnate and now I take the world for what it is to Me, as Mine, as My possession: I take the blame for all of it.'[23]

Seen in one light Stirner might be advocating a full acceptance of personal responsibility for one's actions, although he would have rejected the abstraction of the idea as further tyranny: 'the state, the emperor, the Church, God, morality, order etc. are . . . thoughts or spirits which exist only for the spirit', they are not the possession of the self.[24] Stirner goes so far as to reject the humanistic notion of 'man'. 'This man is certainly no person, but an ideal, a spook.'[25] Freedom itself was an empty concept. Stirner was not afraid to attack his liberal friends in *Die Freien*; the humanistic religion of the Bauers was 'just the last metamorphosis of Christian religion'.[26] 'My might *is* My property. My might *affords* Me property. I *am* My own might and through it My property.'[27] Naturally he rejects all states as despotic, as nothing has the right to exert power over him.

The common weal was not for Stirner, and Socrates had been a fool to accept it. The freedom of the people impinged on the freedom of the ego:

> A people may not enjoy liberty except at the individual's expense. This liberty does not exist for the individual, but for the people. The freer the people, the greater the constraints imposed on the individual. At precisely the point when the people of Ancient Athens enjoyed their greatest liberty, they invented ostracism, banished atheism and poisoned their most honest philosopher.[28]

★ Stirner uses capitals for the first person.

BERLINER MORGENPOST

EXTRABLATT

Freitag, 21. Juni 1991 · Berliner Allgemeine · Zeitung der deutschen Hauptstadt · Unabhängig

Kommentar
Historische Entscheidung

Wer die gestrige Bundestagsdebatte verfolgte, mag lange und heftig geprüft haben. Daß der Bundestag das seit 40 Jahren gegebene Wort für Berlin als Hauptstadt, Regierungs- und Parlamentssitz brechen würde – es lag förmlich in der Luft. Zumal nach dem doch ziemlich schwachen Ergebnis für den von Heiner Geißler eingebrachten Kompromiß-Vorschlag, von dem man wußte, daß viele Berlin-Befürworter ihm „sicherheitshalber" erst mal ihre Stimme geben wollten.

Doch als kurz vor 22 Uhr Bundestagspräsidentin Rita Süssmuth das Ergebnis der letzten Abstimmung bekanntgab, konnten alle aufatmen, die Berlin nicht nur als nominale Hauptstadt sehen wollten. Und jubeln.

Der Beschluß der Bundestags-Mehrheit hat historische Dimension. Es kam nicht zum Wortbruch. Vor allem: Die Abgeordneten trafen die politisch einzig richtige Entscheidung. Im Blick auf das neue, geeinte Deutschland, im Blick zumal auf die Menschen im Gebiet der ehemaligen DDR. Und im Blick auf das neue, größere Europa, das künftig nicht mehr nur West-Europa sein wird. Berlin liegt im Herzen dieses neuen, freien Europa.

Eine Entscheidung gegen Berlin wäre eine eklatante Fehlentscheidung gewesen. Und böser Wortbruch, der notwendigerweise das ohnehin erschütterte Vertrauen in die Politik nur noch verstärkt hätte. Ein schwerer Glaubwürdigkeits-Verlust.

Jubel in Berlin: Parlament und Regierung kommen !

SM/AP/dpa Bonn, 21. Juni
Nach einer fast zwölfstündigen Marathon-Debatte ist gestern abend kurz vor 22 Uhr die historische Entscheidung gefallen: Bundestag und Bundesregierung kommen nach einem Beschluß des Parlaments nach Berlin.

In namentlicher Abstimmung stimmten 337 Abgeordnete für den Umzug nach Berlin, 320 für den Verbleib in Bonn. Insgesamt hatten 660 Abgeordnete abgestimmt. Zwei enthielten sich, eine Stimme war ungültig. Dies bedeutet, daß der Bundestag innerhalb von vier Jahren in Berlin arbeitsfähig sein soll. Seine volle Funktionsfähigkeit soll er spätestens in zehn Jahren erreicht haben. Bonn soll als Verwaltungszentrum erhalten bleiben. Die Bundesregierung und der Bundes...

Der Vorsitzende der CDU/CSU-Bundestagsfraktion, Alfred Dregger, erklärte, die Bundestagsentscheidung werde der großen Aufgabe gerecht, die Einheit des deutschen Volkes zu vollenden. Sie sei in Würde getroffen worden und von allen zu respektieren. Er füge aber hinzu: „Verpflichtet sind wir beiden Städten – Berlin und Bonn".

Zuvor war ein Kompromiß-Vorschlag von Heiner Geißler (CDU) abgelehnt worden, wonach der Bundestag nach Berlin ziehen und die Bundesregierung in Bonn bleiben sollte. Auch der Vorschlag des SPD-Abgeordneten Otto Schily, die Trennung von Parlament und Regierung grundsätzlich anzuerkennen, fand keine Mehrheit. Die PDS hatte zuvor ihren Antrag zurückgezogen. Parlament und Regierung sollten umgehend nach Berlin umziehen.

Die Gegner eines Umzugs nach...

wichtigen Entscheidung". Für die es ja auch gekämpft habe und die dem entsprechs, was es seit 30 Jahren als Politiker gesagt habe. Der Regierende Bürgermeister Eberhard Diepgen sagte, er fühle sich nicht als Sieger. „Dies war eine Entscheidung zur Anstellung des Hauptstadt-Begriffs. Für Berlin ist dies ein sehr glücklicher Augenblick".

Der SPD-Ehrenvorsitzende und Berlin-Befürworter Willy Brandt erklärte, „das Ergebnis spricht für sich selbst. Ich hatte eher gedacht, es würde knapp nach der anderen Seite ausgehen". Außenminister Hans-Dietrich Genscher (FDP) sagte: „Ich bin überzeugt, daß es eine richtige Entscheidung ist".

Geschafft: Berlins Regierender Eberhard Diepgen. *Foto: Weychardt*

Spontaner Jubel vergangene Nacht am Reichstagsgebäude: Mit Berlin- und Deutschlandfahnen gaben junge Leute nach Bekanntwerden der Entscheidung zugunsten Berlins ihrer Freude Ausdruck. *Foto: Bauersfeld*

„Wer A sagt, muß auch Berlin sagen"
Zitate aus dem Bundestag

„Wer A sagt, muß auch Berlin sagen." (Berlin-Befürworter Lothar de Maizière, CDU)

*

„Wenn sich zwei Städte um den Austragungsort eines Fußballspiels bewerben, kann die Konkurrenz nicht dadurch geschlichtet werden, daß die eine Mannschaft je Berlin und die andere in Bonn spielt." (Berlin-Befürworter Otto Schily, SPD)

*

„Ohne die Politik, die mit dem Namen Bonn verbunden ist, wäre ganz Deutschland entgegengesetzt worden." (Bonn-Befürworter Norbert Blüm, CDU)

*

„Deutschland braucht keine Hauptstadt für Cocktail-Empfänge." (Berlin-Befürworter Willy Brandt, SPD)

*

„Meine Frau arbeitet in Berlin. Wie läge näher, als dorthin zu ziehen!" (Bonn-Befürworter Friedbert Pflüger, CDU)

*

„Bonn ist mir wichtig. Berlin ist mir wichtiger. Aber die parlamentarische Demokratie ist mir wichtiger als Bonn und Berlin zusammen." (Bonn-Befürworter Peter Conradi, SPD)

*

„Ich möchte hier als Sachse sagen, daß es mir nicht leicht fällt, für Berlin zu stimmen." (Berlin-Befürworter Klaus Reichenbach, CDU)

*

„Was 1949 selbstverständlich war, kann 1991 durchaus falsch sein." (Bonn-Befürworter Peter Glotz, SPD)

*

„Wenn jeder hier an der Elle der Glaubwürdigkeit gemessen würde, wäre dieser Raum fast leer." (Bonn-Befürworterin Ute Titze, SPD)

Berlin becomes capital of Germany: headline from the *Berliner Morgenpost*, 21 June 1991.

The Revolution of 17 June 1953. East German workers take on Russian tanks.

Hans Baluschek's *Here families may brew coffee.*
A typical scene from a late nineteenth-century Berlin pub (p. 267).

Willi Jaeckel's *Romanisches Café.* The 'Romanischen' was
the centre of Bohemian life in the early twentieth century (p. 277).

Hoffmann and his actor friend Ludwig Devrient in 1815, commemorated by the firm of Henkell & Söhnlein. The sparkling wine is named after the old wine house of Lutter & Wegner (p. 289).

Hoffmann's playful map of his flat and the Gendarmenmarkt in 1815, pointing out its denizens and many drinking dives.

The 'Free' radicals as captured by Friedrich Engels. Max Stirner is smoking his cigar; also present are the Bauer brothers, occupying the centre stage, and Arnold Ruge, on the far right (p. 368).

Heinrich Zille poses for August Kraus as the Ritter Wendelin von Plotho. His likeness to the sculpture led to a rumour that the artist was an illegitimate Hohenzollern (p. 208).

Karl Arnold's *At the Nightclub in the Neppski Prospekt* (Nepp = 'Rip-off joint'). The caption reads: 'Please could you give a small token for the starving children in Russia?' 'No thank you, we are Russians ourselves.'

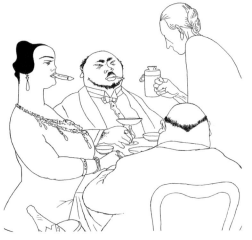

A typical
eighteenth-
century weaver's
cottage in
Nowawes
(p. 161).

The Borsig
Machine Hall as
depicted by Carl
Eduard Biermann
in 1847.

Robert Koehler's
Berlin strike scene
of 1886.

Hamburger Bahnhof, the last surviving nineteenth-century terminus, now part of the National Gallery of Art.

Prussian Eagles in the *U-Bahn* station at Hohenzollerndamm.

The Görlitzer Bahnhof in 1869.

Zille's
representation
of Berlin bathers:
'Back to Nature'
from *Rund um's
Freibad*.

Racing at
Mariendorf in
1913.

The Nollendorf-platz by Skarbina in 1885: a peasant woman makes her way home across the fields behind the *Mietshäuser*; and depicted by Beckmann in 1911. Note that in the intervening period Schöneberg has become thoroughly urban.

It wasn't quite Hobbes's state of nature. There was mutual self-interest and even the possibility of love:

> I love people too, not simply one or two, but all of
> them. I love them with the awareness of Egoism; I
> love them because love makes Me happy, I love
> because love is natural to Me, because it pleases Me.
> I accept no Commandment of Love. I sympathise with
> every fellow being, and their torments torment Me,
> their diversions divert Me too . . .[29]

It was Hegelianism arguing itself down to nothing, but it looked forward to Nietzsche. It flew in the face of both the left and the right. It struck right at the heart of Prussian orthodoxy, which placed the state as the highest good.

Stirner's influence on Berlin thought was to come more than a generation after his death when the anarchist John Henry Mackay rediscovered his works and tried to piece together his strange, solitary existence. He learned that Stirner's second wife, Marie Dähnhardt, was still alive and living in London. He crossed the Channel to talk to her but she refused to see him. Someone he saw told him that Marie had never 'loved or respected' her husband. When he finally received a letter from her she told him that Stirner had been 'too selfish to have real friends' and that he was (she wrote in English) 'very sly'.[30]

Stirner was born Johann Caspar Schmidt in Prussian Bayreuth just before the Battle of Jena finally extracted the margravate from the Hohenzollerns' collection of properties and awarded it, with the rest of Franconia, to the Bavarians. He later changed his name to Max Stirner both as a reference to his high forehead and to the stars (*Stirn*, *Stern* in German). Once again it was Hegel's reputation that lured him up to Berlin. The University had the attraction of being free of the folkloric trappings of the more ancient German institutions. Students wore ordinary street clothes and, at first at least, there was precious little of the duelling and drinking that typified other German academies. Just a few years before Stirner went up, Anselm Feuerbach had written to his father:

> ... in no other university is there such a prevailing sense of diligence, such a feeling that there is something more important than mere student life, such striving for knowledge, such peace and quiet as here. Other universities are but alehouses compared with this workhouse.[31]

Stirner matriculated at the University in October 1826. For the next two years he attended Schleiermacher on ethics and Hegel's lectures on religious philosophy and the history of philosophy. He then ex-matriculated and went to Erlangen for one semester. Later he idled away a similar term in Königsberg, but attended no lectures. Something had happened in the meantime; his scholarly resolve was broken. Mackay was unable to shed any light on the cause. In October 1832 he returned to Berlin after four years' absence and rematriculated at his *alma mater*.[32]

He showed the University authorities a 'study plan': 'major periods in the history of art', 'the mythology of the ancient Germans', 'literary history' and the 'history of Prussia'. In June 1834 he went before his examiners, not for the doctorate, which was and is the only real badge of success in Germanic education, but for the *facultas docendi*, a humble teaching certificate. It was not a sit-down exam: Stirner had six weeks to translate a gobbet of Thucydides; write a paper on education law; some translations from Horace; and another essay on Huss and the Hussites. Even then he didn't get the work done on time, blaming his poor performance on his mother's alleged insanity. Finally in April 1835, eight and a half years after his arrival, Stirner left the University with a licence to teach at secondary-school level.[33]

Stirner's life continued its downward spiral. It affords a

glimpse of Berlin's literary life of the period. He married the illegitimate daughter of his landlord who died in childbirth a few months later. He went to teach at a girls' school but gave up teaching in 1844 after five years, and never took another job.[34] He embraced a Bohemian life instead, which meant squandering a lot of time at Hippels. Hippels had already vanished by Mackay's time; number 94 Friedrichstraße had been replaced by the railway station. It was a 'tasteful and comfortable *Weinstube* of the sort still to be seen in the famous Habel on Unter den Linden'.[35]

One has the feeling that Stirner's slightly disappointing concept of a 'Union of Egoists' was based on *Die Freien*. The 'Union' was not to be compared to society. 'You are in debt to society, you are obliged to it and have social duties towards it; the Union you merely use, and may abandon without duty or fidelity when you have no more need of it.'[36] It sounds like a description of the loose bond which held together the men Mackay called 'the scattered irregulars of radicalism'. Debates at Hippels or Stehely's began in the afternoon and continued deep into the night. Most of the participants were very young. Stirner was the oldest at thirty-six, Bruno Bauer the next at just over thirty. Bauer was the star of Berlin's radical world and Stirner dedicated large amounts of his book to attacking him. He had been sacked from the University after he had published a paper alleging Hegel was an atheist. Together with his brother Edgar he bought a tobacco business (smoking was itself associated with liberalism) and used the profits to pay for the publication of his and his brother's books.[37]

None of them impressed Marx, or Engels, who drew a celebrated sketch of 'the Free' in full flight. Just after they left Berlin in 1845, they published a paper called *Die heilige Familie, oder Kritik der kritischen Kritik, gegen Bruno Bauer und Consorten* (The Holy Family, or Critique of Critical Criticism, against Bruno Bauer and his Clan), but the meetings of 'the Free' had none the less become one of the tourist attractions of Berlin. Ludwig Ruge, the brother of Arnold, the young Hegelian and later Paulskirche revolutionary, couldn't believe his eyes and ears:

> The free-thinking ascended to unimaginable levels. I saw Arnold sitting there stunned. A storm had to break out; was boiling up in him. All of a sudden he leaped to his feet and called out in a loud voice: 'You want to be free but you haven't realised that you are up to your ears in stinking filth! With such obscenities no man or nation is freed.'[38]

Ruge slammed the door and never returned. Others were made of stronger stuff. Herwegh came, and the nationalist poet Hoffmann von Fallersleben, but 'the Free' paid them little heed. They played little or no part in the 1848 Revolution. Their life went on as before: the group sat around and played cards until they were quorate. Much was written off as *Dreck* (filth): censorship and the beginnings of anti-Semitism. Hippel stood them credit. Once his patience snapped and he threw them out. They begged for thalers from passers-by in the Linden. Once a stranger took pity on them and ushered them back to the bar and paid for a night's drinking. In summer they changed their quarters and repaired to the Spandauer Bock pub, or Treptow.[39]

Stirner didn't stand out in this crowd. He sat placidly behind his silver spectacles with his whiskers, smoking a cigar. Although he called Bruno Bauer *Du*, he was not really intimate with any of them. He occasionally tossed in an observation or a witticism to show that he was listening, then returned to watching the smoke of his cigar. His relations with women were also unsuccessful. Once his first wife insouciantly or unconsciously stripped naked in the middle of the night. Stirner admitted that he couldn't touch her after that. Such inadequacy probably goes a long way to explaining the failure of his second marriage, to Marie

Dähnhardt. The couple met at the house of Friedrich Zabel, who went on to found the *National Zeitung*.

The marriage, which took place in Stirner's Berlin flat in 1843,[40] was a legend in its own time, but Mackay poured cold water on most of the more outlandish stories. It was not true that the guests had to be hauled out of the pub to attend the ceremony, but they were playing cards when the pastor arrived. Bruno Bauer and Buhl acted as witnesses: Marie, the bride, wore an old dress; and no Bible could be found. It pained 'the Free', as free-thinkers, to have to watch such a thing; but they didn't look out of the window: they looked at their feet instead. Nor was the ring taken from the curtain rail; Bruno Bauer managed to locate a brass ring in his pocket. When the cleric left they sat down to celebrate with a *Bowle*, or fruit cup.[41]

Marie Dähnhardt was a precursor of the 'liberated woman' of our own time: she smoked cigars or a pipe, played billiards and drank heroic quantities of Bavarian beer. Stirner may have been more interested in her portion, however. Her chemist father had left her 10,000 thalers. *Der Einzige und sein Eigenthum*, which came out the following year, was hardly a best-seller and Stirner began to squander her money. He started a milk-delivery business, but the milk turned sour and had to be poured down the gutter. The marriage was shortly to go the same way. It is, however, another of the enduring myths about Stirner that the marriage had never had its brighter days. Marie left for England to become a teacher, and later underwent some sort of religious conversion which made her a bigot in her old age. She wrote to him, however, soon after she left: she wanted to save him money and stay out of his hair. If and when he became successful, he was to call her back . . . 'Nothing has changed in our love, I am and remain your wife'.[42]

Stirner declined further and Marie never came back. In 1847 Hippels moved to bigger premises in the Dorotheen-gasse and finally to a building behind the Werdersche church where Hippel was arrested for debt in 1853. One wonders whether 'the Free' ever settled their slates. Stirner himself was bitten by a poisonous fly on 25 June 1856 and died in his flat on the Philippstraße in the Friedrich-Wilhelmstadt.[43]

After 1848 Berlin was bitten by the bug of realism. Wilhelm Raabe was the first to make a name for himself writing sub-Dickensian fiction around the lives of Berliners great and small. Raabe came from Brunswick and moved to Berlin in 1854. His *Chronik der Sperlingsgasse*, focusing on the lives of *petit-bourgeois* Berliners, was published two years later. He left the city in 1870 and returned to his native land, but he continued to pen 'Berlin' novels such as *Deutscher Adel* (German Nobles) of 1877, *Villa Schönow* of 1883, and *Im alten Eisen* (In Old Iron) of 1886.[44] Raabe was upstaged by Fontane, once the former chemist and journalist turned his hand to fiction late in life. Fontane's realism has a human heart; a plea for the different orders to understand one another; and a love for the better traditions of Prussia and Berlin which were being eroded by the flashy empire of William II. His best novels are *Effi Briest* of 1895, in which a misplaced adherence to an aristocratic code of behaviour manages to destroy the main protagonists of the novel; and *Der Stechlin*, which charts the changes in a Junker household caught up in the uncongenial world of the present.

Ernst von Wildenbruch represented the other face of the coin: the self-congratulatory tone of the new Reich which was administered by his Hohenzollern cousins. Fontane clearly took a dim view of him: he has the younger Poggen-puhls, and their uncle the general, pick holes in his play *Die Quitzows* over macaroni, tomatoes and beer at Lutter und Wegner. It seemed that characters from the fifteenth-century Mark were using a Berlin slang that was 'not even a century old'.[45] Wildenbruch was merely lightweight. Worse Hohenzollern worship and toadyism was provided by the

Kaiser's favourite dramatist, Josef Lauff, who was elevated to the nobility for his pains.

Hermann Sudermann was a generation younger than Fontane. His play *Die Ehre* is set in an upwardly mobile working-class family in Charlottenburg. It deals with different conceptions of honour: the natural sense of the hero, Robert Heinecke, the misguided pseudo-aristocratic ideas of the *arriviste* Mühlingks, and Graf von Trast-Saarberg, a disgraced nobleman, who left his regiment under a cloud and found fortune in the Far East. Conversation turns to Indian castes. Trast thinks things not so different to Berlin:

> There are the same castes here. They are not defined
> by dietary or marital restrictions, or rules concerning
> religious etiquette. Those are mere trifles. What makes
> them irreconcilable is sensibility: each caste has its
> own honour, its own ideas of politesse, even its own
> language.[46]

Robert has been able to rise through his own diligence and intelligence. His sister Alma, who still speaks the dialect of the slums, has found her own way up by becoming the mistress to the boss's son:

> No sun or moon peeps into a courtyard like this, and
> all around all you hear is gossip and curses . . .
> Nobody knows a thing about education . . . And dad
> scolds and mum scolds . . . And you wear your fingers
> to the bone sewing . . . And earn 50 pfennigs a day,
> which doesn't even pay for the fuel . . . And I'm
> young and pretty! And I want to have fun and wear
> pretty things, and see other worlds . . . And when it
> comes to marriage, who, for God's sake? Some pleb
> who works in the factory back there, that I couldn't
> face . . . Who drinks up his wages and then clouts
> you . . . I want a classy man, and if I can't have one
> then I don't want nothing.[47]

II

It was architecture that first drew the attention of outsiders to Berlin. There was a brief flowering under Frederick I, when Schlüter was in the city, and another under Frederick the Great. The first world-class architect to practise in Berlin was Schinkel, his importance perhaps encapsulated in the moment when Zelter entrusted a print of Schinkel's design for Graf Redern's new place in the Linden to the young Felix Mendelssohn to take to Goethe in Weimar. Goethe also took a keen interest in the progress of Schinkel's new Schauspielhaus on the Gendarmenmarkt, and Zelter acted as an intermediary between the architect and the poet. In one letter Schinkel was at pains to explain the mechanics of the new theatre to Goethe.[48]

Schinkel was a real Renaissance man: a painter of considerable talent, the author of a number of large-scale architectural fantasies including a delightfully romanticised view of Stralau at dusk. He designed the furniture and fittings for his major works of architecture, right down to the knives and forks. When, in 1816, the Prussian monarchy laid the keel of its art collection, it was Schinkel who was despatched to advise on the purchase. He designed for the theatre, which brought him into close contact with both Goethe and Hoffmann. His sets for the latter's opera *Undine* have sadly been lost. The famous designs for *Die Zauberflöte* mercifully still exist.

He benefited from the opportunities for travel that were open to him from the first. He made three journeys to Italy. The first lasted a year, from 1805 to 1806, when he met Wilhelm von Humboldt, who was then Prussian envoy to the Holy See. When Humboldt returned to Berlin he became a useful patron.[49] Schinkel visited Paris twice, and in 1826 made a journey to England and Scotland, in the course of which he learned much about industrial building. The British experience had the backing of the Crown. In this he was like Hermann Muthesius later: he travelled as a hard-working Prussian civil servant, rather than an architect in search of inspiration. He never lacked patronage from the Hohenzollerns, although it was a pity for Prussia that he died in 1841, just a year after the architecture-mad Crown Prince Frederick William ascended the throne. His ideas, however, were continued by his pupils Persius, Stüler, Arnim and Strack. It was not until after 1871 that Schinkel's influence ebbed away from Berlin architecture, to be replaced by the gaudy fussiness of the Second Reich.

Schinkel succeeded in some idioms better than in others. As a Gothic designer the decorative style he learned from Strasbourg Cathedral served him better than the English Tudor of the Friedrichswerder church. The tight neo-Greek of his early years gave way to a looser, Italian-picturesque style, in which he was probably most successful. He was highly adaptable in all he did, working from a tiny budget to a more generous one. He could shine in as mean a project as the little church in Wedding, or in one of his real masterpieces: the Altes Museum, the Neue Wache, the Schauspielhaus, or the Schloßbrücke.

In 1696 the Elector Frederick III, later King Frederick I, founded the Akademie der Künste, or the Academy of the Arts,[50] some seventy years before the Royal Academy was created in London. It seems that just four obscure artists were elected during the Soldier-King's time. Frederick's successor had little need for artists. The Parisian Antoine Pesne was made a member in 1711, and was court painter to three Prussian monarchs. Hit-and-miss that he was, Pesne stood head and shoulders above his Berlin rivals of the eighteenth century. Painters like the portraitists Joachim Martin Falbe, Anton Graff, or the engraver Daniel Chodowiecki, were no match for him. Chodowiecki's daughter Suzanne Henry and another female painter, Anna Dorothea Therbusch, represented a decent second rate, but it was not until Schadow's time that Berlin stood in the European limelight for the plastic arts at least.

The first painter of European importance to work more or less exclusively in Berlin was Adolph Menzel. Menzel represented a school of academic painting that was respectable enough to allow the Kaiser to ennoble him at the end of his long life. It was a reward for the paintings which brought the campaigns and life-style of Frederick the Great so vividly to life. Menzel, however, was better than that. His sense of light and natural aversion to studio mock-ups put him ahead of his time, as did his typically *Berlinisch* obsession with toiling workers. His picture of the Berlin iron foundry is among his most evocative and it is one which gave a lead to many modern Berlin painters – in particular, Hans Baluschek.

There was far less light-heartedness or humour in the works of Anton von Werner, who won himself the role of celebrating the glories of the Prussian and German present in a rather more strait-laced way than Menzel had seen the past. He was not entirely incapable of casting aside the pomposity of the time in his canvases. Menzel himself is depicted at the court ball: a good-natured midget surrounded by lofty Junkers and mediatised princes. It was natural that a reaction should set in by the end of the century. Lesser Ury, a painter much despised by the generation of artists who came to the fore around 1900, painted a virtually monochrome picture of the Friedrichstraße station, which was the first to tackle the reality of the new *Weltstadt*. Franz Skarbina too could turn his brush to the industrial side of Berlin with pictures like *Gleisanlage im Norden Berlins* (Railway Lines in Northern Berlin) of 1895.[51]

The cue for more radical change came as a direct result of Anton von Werner's attempts to keep the younger painters in line. As President of the Verein Berliner Künstler (Union of Berlin Artists), the Institute of Fine Arts *and* the Kunstgenossenschaft, or Art Association, he tended to side with the Kaiser. An exhibition of the works of Edvard Munch scandalised the more conservative Berlin public and Werner tried to impose certain standards on the painters belonging to his association. The drift towards modernism disappointed him. In 1895 he told his students: 'Year by year, but recently more than ever before, I find that your technique in composition and studies is so awkward that even you cannot possibly gain any pleasure from your drawings and paintings.'[52] He had the backing of his lord and master, whose views on art were as strongly held as all the others. Speaking in 1901 as he unveiled his 'Puppenallee', the Kaiser told his painters what he expected from them:

> ... when art ... as often happens today, shows us
> only misery, and shows it to us even uglier than
> misery is anyway, then art commits a sin against the
> German people. The supreme task of our cultural
> effort is to foster our ideals. If we are and want to
> remain a model for other nations, our entire people
> must share in this effort, and if culture is to fulfil its
> task completely it must reach down to the lowest
> levels of the population. That can be done only if art
> holds out its hand to raise the people up, instead of
> descending into the gutter.[53]

In a speech which strikingly recalls some of the Führer's utterances on the subject a generation later, the Kaiser declared war on *Rinnsteinkunst*, or 'gutter art'. Later the Nazis would call this *entartete Kunst*, or degenerate art, and take rather more draconian measures to stamp it out. The split between the officially tolerated and patronised world of Werner, Begas or Ihne and the new social awareness of Skarbina, Baluschek, Liebermann or Leistikow had already taken place with the creation of the Berlin Secession in 1897, the same year a similar organisation was started in Vienna. They were both modelled on the Verein bildender Künstler Münchens, founded five years earlier. Until the first years of the twentieth century Munich counted for rather more in the art world than Berlin.

The creators of the Secession were to be rapidly eclipsed by a far more modernistic movement in the form of Expressionism, which would reject at a stroke the sentimental social realism of Skarbina, Baluschek and Käthe Kollwitz, and, indeed, the dreamy *märkisch* landscapes of Leistikow, with a good deal more ferocity than had the men of 1897 who shuffled off the Werners, Begases and Menzels.[54]

Certain themes remained constant. They all derived inspiration from the turbulent sprawling city. There is a strong link between Menzel and Beckmann, between Skarbina and Kirchner, between Baluschek and Meidner. Just as a graphic tradition of observing Berlin life grew up around Schadow and was handed down to his sentimental realist pupil Hosemann – who in turn passed it on to Zille, when he too studied at the Akademie as a mature student – so too did Menzel create a tradition of observing the industrial Berlin, which he handed on to Baluschek et al., and doubtless inspired the conformist painters of the DDR in their representations of sweaty workers.

Despite the presence of the disapproving Kaiser, Berlin became the artistic capital of Germany shortly after 1900. Lovis Corinth, who had been in Munich until 1902, realised that the Bavarian capital had finally cast off the mantle it had previously worn as the new nation's *Kulturstadt*. Berlin had turned a corner:

> . . . business was booming in Berlin. The merchants were intelligent and interested in modern art. Apart from that the young [*sic* – he was forty-three] Kaiser had an aversion to everything new, so that martyrs' haloes shone around us. These were the beginnings of the Berlin Secession.[55]

A similar process was taking place in the literary world.

Berlin was to have *Rinnsteinliteratur* to match its gutter art. The first men to pull 'Bohemian Berlin' together were the Hart brothers, Heinrich and Julius, who edited the *Deutschen Monatsblätter* and the *Kritischen Waffengänge* in the late 1870s and 1880s. Mühsam described Julius Hart as 'always of the same happy "I embrace you all" temperament', who delighted in taking his guests over his flat in the Uhland-straße, pointing out the decorations by Fidus and the sculptor Metzner. Hart 'kissed men and women alike', called everyone he liked *Du*, and forbade them to use *Sie*. Heinrich had a touch more irony as far as his appraisal of himself was concerned, but was equally hospitable. 'The brothers were the most delightful cross between a brace of abbots and the keepers of a wine tavern.'[56]

The Harts had a commune on the Schlachtensee, where Berlin had its first vegetarian community in the 1890s. The *Neue Gemeinschaft*, or new community, was launched in 1900 in an idyllic spot on one of the prettiest of the Grunewald lakes. It was patronised by Mühsam and his fellow anarchist Gustav Landauer, the poet Else Lasker-Schüler, and Peter Hille, with his long hair and thick beard a sort of literary tramp, and the most noticeably Bohemian of the lot. It was the scene of plenty of parties with portentous themes: Taoism, Dionysos, spring storms, reconciliation, eternity, beauty, peace, fulfilment, death, and self-redemption.[57]

In his biography of Peter Hille, Heinrich Hart gushed about those days: 'Oh you men of the Schlachtensee! Those ambrosian, Dionysiac-Apollonian nights! They were more delightful even than the Symposia of Socratic Athens!'[58] Erich Mühsam's rather more sober account of the lives of the *Berliner Boheme* hardly tallies with this wild exaggeration, but the chemist-turned-writer gives a picture of a Berlin which was already loosening up to receive its broader, *Welt-städtische* role, where the narrow bounds of Prussian society had been burst, and where one already gleaned a foretaste of the sort of artistic freedom that is more commonly associated with the Weimar years. The Kaiser may have heartily despised all of them, but he didn't have Hitler's means and machinery to have them stamped out.

Mühsam lived through all those early years before he was called away to Munich. He sat at the *Stammtisch* at the 'Romanischen' and the Café des Westens with fellow *Literaten* Hille, Paul Scheerbart, Friedrich von Schennis, Margarete Beutler and Franziska von Reventlow; lodged with Landauer; and spent his evenings with the Harts in the Uhlandstraße where Martin Buber and Hirschfeld addressed the Bohemians. The spirit of the shambling Hille permeated the group, binding them together. There was a fashionable degree of political (if that is the word) anarchism about. Mühsam was tainted with it, as was Mackay. One of the great moments of that time was the arrival in Berlin of the French theorist Elysée Reclus.[59] The creed was to seal the fate of Landauer, who was beaten to death during the Munich revolution in 1919. Mühsam was a Jew. The Nazis needed no pretext to murder him in Oranienburg in 1934.

Mühsam compared Berlin's artistic world unfavourably with that of Paris or Munich. Paris had Montmartre, Munich, Schwabing. Berlin had grown up too quickly to allow for a comfortable and civilised artistic world to find its place there. Where such a thing did exist, it was around the Savignyplatz in Charlottenburg, spilling over into Wilmersdorf (i.e., the Uhlandstraße) and Schöneberg and having its fixed poles, such as the old Café des Westens; but the artists in this area were no more than fleas on the back of the big city hound: 'Montmartre and Schwabing are not so much geographical areas as bywords for culture; Berlin W[est] isn't really a geographical term either, but is it a cultural one . . . ?'[60]

Artistic colonies were part of the trappings of the time. Apart from the Schlachtensee, Mühsam was also involved in a 'commune' in Friedrichshagen on the Müggelsee in 1902, where he edited the magazine *Der arme Teufel* (The Poor

Devil). Part of his circle at the time was Arthur Moeller-Bruck, the racialist thinker and intellectual precursor of Nazism, who had yet to adopt his spurious Dutch noble particle. He gave himself airs for all that: 'eyeglass wedged above his cheekbone, a long grey mackintosh, a little cane with a silver handle and a light-grey top hat'. He invited the entire colony out to dinner in the Ratskeller in Friedrichshagen but at the end of it offered the management his card, rather than more conventional banknotes. It took an uncomfortable month before they could settle.[61]

In town Mühsam joined the 'Die Kommenden' group in the Nollendorf-Casino in the Kleiststraße. It was another group of young poets and artists. Margarete Beutler, the author of *Bilder aus dem Norden Berlins* (Pictures from the North of Berlin), preached 'free motherhood'; Maximilian Bern was on the look-out for 'discoveries' – 'I discovered that one!' was his line – and much resented by those who had made their own way into the open.[62] One of the great features of Berlin that carried over from the immediate pre-war days to Weimar was the presence of so many Mycaenases in search of artists to patronise: Berlin's 'Bradford millionaires', who thought the arts a *savonnette à vilain* to lend their new status a doubtful allure of nobility. They were capable of putting up with a great deal of ragging from their artistic catches in order to have them perform in their houses and flats.

The artists entertained their patrons with farces, demonstrations of rapid artistic virtuosity (of the type introduced to 1960s Britain by the Australian Rolf Harris) and singing to guitar accompanied by 'grotesque' dances. The young painters displaced the star tenors of the Opera with their performances. They arrived in their dirty street-clothes, but they didn't cost as much. An evening's entertainment was paid for by a square meal and plenty of wine, and ten or twenty marks on top.[63]

Peter Hille had his own haunts, such as the Vierzehntel-

Topp, a spirits bar on the Potsdamerplatz, or the Café Austria. From there he set out on pub crawls through the Friedrichstraße with the likes of Edvard Munch. Artistic life was still as much in the alte Westen as the neue. At the Italian Dalbelli Weinstube, the painter Max Tilke created Berlin's first cabaret called *Zum hungrigen Pegasus* (The Hungry Horse). Soon after, another was created: *Im Siebenten Himmel* (Seventh Heaven), where Mühsam met the Austrian writer Alexander Roda Roda.[64] Later Hille too had his own cabaret at Dalbelli. These institutions have now been inextricably linked to the Weimar Republic. One forgets that the famous *Blaue Engel* of the Künstlerin Fröhlich made its appearance in Heinrich Mann's novel *Professor Unrat*, published in 1905.

The circle had a great many hangers-on, as is always the case; it produced a lot of hot air, and not so much great art. One who tagged along was John Höxter, a ladies' man with sleek black hair and a fondness for drugs. He too was Jewish. In 1938 he cheated the Nazis of their prey by committing suicide. Like Mühsam his great years were those before the First World War. He sat with Else Lasker-Schüler in the Romanischen and accompanied her to the KaDeWe (as the Kaufhaus des Westens department store is invariably known), where a fight developed between the self-important poetess and a shop assistant: 'Don't you know who I am? I am the Prince of Thebes, and this [she said, pointing to her maid] is Zobeide, the head of my dancing troupe! Left, about turn, march . . .'[65]

Höxter made sure he was in on things: he had himself painted by Leo von König at the Romanischen together with the beauty Spela Albrecht. He was at the Café des Westens when Karl Kraus introduced Oskar Kokoschka to the *Berliner Boheme*. Scrounging was an established part of their existence. One day he observed Mühsam stuck for cash. A kindly Russian art-lover, Hofrat Dr von Rosenberg, stepped in to save the day and Mühsam's dignity: 'It suddenly occurs to me, I still owe you ten marks; might I possibly be allowed, now . . . ?' 'You've got it wrong,' replied the poet; 'it was twenty.'[66]

There was more continuity than is generally assumed between the 'mad, depraved, fantastic Berlin immediately after the First World War' and the wilder life on the fringes before it. Even during the war a sort of artistic foment existed. Grosz himself had been fished out of a *Lazarett* by the same Graf Harry Kessler whose beautiful Irish mother had been a favourite of the first Kaiser's,[67] but the tone then and after had to be different. It was impossible to ignore the death and suffering. Painters felt an understandable necessity to paint it: Grosz and Dix, for example, with their pictures of war-cripples, of which Dix's *Skatspieler* is one of the best known. They wanted also to expose the obscenity of the war-profiteers who had grown fat on the suffering, and the incompetent generals and senior officers who had sent soldiers to their deaths in droves; men who were even now unhappy that the war had ended and they would no longer have the chance to send another battalion over the top in the hope of securing a doubtful victory.

Grosz replaced the sentimental *Gemütlichkeit* of Zille's drawings with bile and bitter satire. Kessler was understandably fascinated by his work:

> Spent the afternoon with the painter and draughtsman George Grosz. The devotion of his art exclusively to depiction of the repulsiveness of bourgeois philistinism is, so to speak, merely the counterpart of some sort of secret ideal of beauty that he conceals as though it were a badge of shame. In his drawings he harasses with fanatical hatred the antithesis to his ideal, which he protects from public gaze like something sacred. His whole art is a campaign of extermination against what is irreconcilable with his secret 'lady love'. Instead of singing her praises like a troubadour, he does battle against her opponents with unsparing fury

like a dedicated knight. Only in his colours does he
ever let his secret ideal show through.

Kessler was a perceptive critic, but what he could not have
known at the time was that Grosz was only capable of
producing great work if he could mix his colours with bile.
When he left for America on the eve of the Third Reich
his painting went to seed, and never recovered anything of
its original verve.[68]

Long before the Nazis drove artists to it, America was the
promised land. Canetti was helping Herzfelde with Upton
Sinclair, a mediocre American writer who enjoyed a massive
vogue at the time. Grosz had adopted an Anglo-Saxon
spelling for his first name and dressed in tweeds and a bowler.
Brecht had his obsessions with advertising and fast cars. Weill
got the bug too. Canetti observed that the passion was not
based on any decent work: 'Dos Passos, Hemingway [and]
Faulkner, writers of incomparably higher rank, exerted their
influence only later on.'[69] Canetti was young and impressionable. He was star-struck by Grosz, who gave him one of the
banned *Ecce Homo* folders with its depictions of the 'dreadful
creatures of Berlin's night life'.[70] His *allumeuse* friend, Ibby
Gordon, told him that the painter was prone to get overex-
cited with women about and start talking about *Schinken*
(porking). Canetti preferred not to believe her.[71]

Canetti was naïve. The lusty Grosz is easily identifiable in
his lucidly written autobiography, *Ein kleines Ja und ein grosses
Nein*, especially when relating his early sexual awakening in
the Pomeranian garrison town of Stolp (now Polish Słupsk).
He enjoyed painting pornography too – not little watercolours, dashed off on a rainy afternoon, but great big gaudy
things; and oils too. The scales fell from Canetti's eyes when
he went to Ibby Gordon's flat-warming party, in the apartment rented for her by another indulgent Berlin would-be
patron of the arts. Grosz rapidly got drunk and leered at his

hostess: 'Schinken, Schinken, Du mein Vergnügen' ('Porking, porking, that's what I like'), he trilled.[72]

Brecht also disappointed the young Balkan. His thinking ran up against the loftier teaching of Karl Kraus. Brecht damned anything which put itself aside from or above the real world (although he and Kraus appear to have got on). Brecht loved everything American, advertisements and cars. He had a Steyr car which was his payment for writing some advertising copy; it was the object in his life that received the greatest tenderness. 'He appreciated money for what it was; it was important only *who* got it, not where it came from.'[73] He told Canetti: 'I only write for money.'[74] When Canetti heard that he had written a poem for Steyr, 'It was for me as if it had fallen from the mouth of the devil.'[75]

Two leading writers Canetti didn't manage to get to know were Döblin and Benn, the two physicians.[76] Benn was rare in deciding there was a future for him in the Third Reich. His writings had always been admired during the Weimar years, but he had earned little. Possibly he saw that with the Jews and the left-wingers out of the way, he might be elevated to the more profitable position of a national figure? He always denied it, but no one believed his protestations. Klaus Mann made him the fat poet Pelz in *Mephisto*. He put on record, however, that he had in no way toadied to the regime and didn't know why Döblin referred to him as a 'blackguard' after the war.[77]★

He was not being scrupulously honest. Like the painter Emil Nolde, he had no inkling that the little-town tyrants who had taken over would stop him and countless others from pursuing their art. He did not resign from the Academy when the Manns and the Jews were expelled. Worse, he spoke on the wireless about his faith in the new 'racial community'. When the scales fell from his eyes he slipped back into the army medical corps, but was hounded out of

★ Döblin compared him to Céline, another nerve doctor.

that. He had to receive instruction on how to be a good National Socialist doctor too, attending educational evenings on the racial problem and the dangers of miscegenation: 'Can you imagine', his instructor told him, 'putting a Daimler-Benz engine into a little Opel? It's wrong; it doesn't fit.'[78] Benn penned a bitter little quatrain:

Expressionist!

Eine Münze wird man dir nicht prägen,
wie es Griechenland für Sappho tat,
daß man dir nicht einschlägt deinen Brägen
ist in Deutschland schon Kultur-Verrat.[79]

(My friend, they will not strike a coin for you,
as in Sappho's Greece it was the case,
that they don't kill, or smash your brains in too,
is in Germany a damned disgrace.)

Benn had the choice. Neither Döblin nor his fellow Jews could say the same. The distinguished theatre critic Alfred Kerr was in bed with flu and a temperature of 39°C when the Nazis came to power. On 15 February 'The police who had remained loyal to the republic gave me the tip-off to cross the border immediately'. Kerr packed a rucksack with a few effects, and quit his beloved Grunewald villa.[80] Three and a half hours later he was over the border in Czechoslovakia. That night he celebrated his escape with a big glass of Pilsener beer. Later Göring came on the wireless to taunt him for fleeing. After all he too had had to quit his native land after the Beer-Hall *Putsch*. 'I fled vultures. Herr Göring sheep,' said Kerr.[81]

Kerr got away early. On the 27th of that month the Reichstag burned, giving the cue for a massive *razzia* in which 10,000 left-wingers would be rounded up, beaten up and locked up in the new 'wild' concentration camps. Tisa von der Schulenburg remembers helping the Jewish art historian and collector Eduard Fuchs to escape. Her first husband, Fritz Hess, took him to her studio, a shed in Schmargendorf, owned by an Italian stonemason. The next day Hess drove him to Jüterbog, a few miles south of Berlin, where he boarded the train to south Germany. He was a communist; the SA visited his house that night. They had also gone to the stonemason's yard, but the Italian (a former communist) had waved them away: 'A countess lives there.' Fuchs safely crossed into France four weeks later.[82]

The Nazis were to have their own crack-down on *Rinnsteinkunst*. In London, Kerr dashed off a little poem:

Hitlers Kunst Ukas

Was in der Kunst erlaubt ist
Und was ihr Ziel überhaupt ist,
Bestimmt ein provinzieller
Ansichtskartenmaler.

Wer nicht bei diesem Leisten bleibt
Wer etwa grüne Schatten schmiert
Und Farben-Phantasie betreibt,
Wird sterilisiert.[83]

(Hitler's Instruction to his Painters

What artists may think and see,
And what their higher aims may be,
Decides a small-town mind, a
Picture-postcard painter.

He who dares to ignore these bounds,
Whose canvases are abstract, stylised,
Or where colour fantasies abound,
Will be sterilised.)

The books were burned on the Opernplatz. The Academy was purged. Out went the Manns, Franz Werfel and Fritz von Unruh; in came Hans Grimm, the author of *Volk ohne*

Raum (Nation without Space). Ernst Jünger declined. The artists Kokoschka, Erich Mendelsohn, Pechstein, Bruno Taut, Barlach, Dix, Kirchner, Käthe Kollwitz, Liebermann, Mies van der Rohe and Schmidt-Rottluff all went. In came Speer and Breker. There was no hope for musicians such as Schönberg or Schreker; or actors, theatre people and musicians like Max Reinhardt, Elisabeth Bergner, Marlene Dietrich, Richard Tauber, Bruno Walter or Otto Klemperer.[84]

For the time being some of their works remained. Since 1919 the Kronprinzenpalais had been filled with the canvases of modern German and European painters, the special passion of the director, Professor Dr Walter Justi. Their very presence had led to furious attacks from right-wing and Nazi art historians such as Professor Dr Hans Schultze, the author of *Rasse und Stil* (Race and Style), which advocated the rejection of Gothic art because it had been influenced by the Orient.[85] The fiercest critic was the Nazi 'philosopher' Alfred Rosenberg, who vomited forth the whole vocabulary of Nazi insult against the 'half-caste art', 'bastardy', 'intellectual syphilis', 'infantilism' etc. he found in the works of Chagall, Kokoschka or Pechstein, who had been instituted as the leaders of the modern movement by 'Jewish pens'.[86]

The Kronprinzenpalais with its far-sighted policy of exhibitions had led to fury in the provincial art world. In 1927 there had been a retrospective of Munch, followed by Böcklin. In 1928 came dozens of Van Gogh canvases to Berlin. The year 1930 was the greatest of all: Klee, Leo von König, Otto Mueller, Lyonel Feininger, Maria Slavona and Lesser Ury.[87]

In February 1933 that self-proclaimed 'Renaissance man' Hermann Göring paid two visits to the gallery, during which he left Justi with few illusions about the future. At first it was the provinces which were swiftest to remove the modern works from the walls of their museums. Rosenberg dug in his heels against the Kronprinzenpalais, but it was still in Göring's parish, and Göring disliked Rosenberg. Göring none the less sacked the head of the Deutsche Kunst-gesellschaft, Fürst Schönburg-Waldenburg, and replaced him by 'Auwi' von Preußen, the Kaiser's Nazi son. Göring himself was in two minds. He had a genuine fondness for art, and was unconvinced by arguments from the hotter-headed Nazis that the museum contained only works by Jewish painters. 'It is a great deal easier,' said Göring, 'given a little time, to make a great painter into a decent National Socialist than to turn a little party member into a great painter'.[88] Encouraged, perhaps, by these words, Justi's assistant, Alois Schardt, tried to find a compromise: the basement would be turned over to the works of Friedrich and Blechen, the ground to Marées and Anselm Feuerbach and the top floor to the *Blaue Reiter* and the *Brücke* groups; plus Barlach, Feininger and Nolde.

The real drive to purge the museums came from Munich and the opening of the Haus der Deutschen Kunst from 13–15 October 1933. Rosenberg spoke, coming out with the outrageous suggestion that 'The German SA has doubt-less done more for German culture than many a university professor'.[89] In February or March 1934 Hitler visited the Kronprinzenpalais for the one and only time to see an exhi-bition of one of Heß's protégés, the artist Karl Leipold. The Führer, however, strayed into the Expressionists. He said nothing, contenting himself with some wild dismissive ges-tures. Then he went to the window overlooking the Linden and gave his views on the buildings around him, turning the monologue into an impromptu lecture on the architecture of Karl Friedrich Schinkel.[90]

Later that year Hitler spoke out at the Party Conference in Nuremberg: modern art was 'neither founded on race nor was it to be tolerated by the nation'. A year later he growled again: 'the experience of Dadaism, Cubism and Futurism and all that twaddle about objectivity[91]* will never play a

---

* *Neue Sachlichkeit*

part in the cultural rebirth of the state'.[92] Six weeks later the top floor of the Kronprinzenpalais was closed. On 5 July a strange collection of Nazi art stooges turned up to confiscate the offending paintings. They were led by an official from Rust's Kultus Ministry and included the sculptor Ziegler, Graf Baudissin and the painter Wolfgang Willrich, who specialised in warriors and blonde women. Willrich had written a book with the punchy title *Säuberung des Kunsttempels, eine kunstpolitische Kampfschrift zur Gesundung deutsche Kunst im Geiste nordischer Art* (The Cleansing of the Temple of the Arts, an Art-Political Attack Aimed at Curing German Art Invoking the Spirit of the Nordic). Another painter, called Hans Schweizer, was there too. He had changed his name to the old Norse 'Mjölnir', meaning 'hammer'.[93]

They left with 68 paintings, 33 drawings and seven sculptures. Having enjoyed their visit to the Kronprinzenpalais, they set off across Germany to do the same in the rest of the nation's cities and towns.

The actual 'degenerate art' exhibition was held in Munich, not Berlin. Poor Nolde, who had thought to offer his talents to the new regime, was one of the top scorers along with Schmidt-Rottluff, Kirchner, Beckmann, Kokoschka, Corinth, Dix, Pechstein, Franz Marc, Chagall, Kandinsky and Mondrian. Possibly Göring was not the only one of the Nazi bigwigs to have misgivings about the exhibition. Goebbels had sent Edvard Munch a telegram on his seventieth birthday. Hitler, however, wanted the exhibition with its taunting slogans brought to Berlin. Göring opposed its being set up in the Kronprinzenpalais. It opened in March 1938 in the cramped rooms of the former Japanese Embassy opposite the burned-out Reichstag. Then it went on tour to Leipzig and Düsseldorf. When the fun was over, more than 1,000 oils and nearly 4,000 watercolours were burned in the Köpenickerstraße.[94]

The technique employed on writers and artists who did stay was to break them mentally so that they fell into line with the regime. One of these was Jochen Klepper (see above, p. 165). Leaving aside his wife's race, everything he wrote was subjected to the most minute examination by the provincial-schoolmaster types who took over the Reichs-schriftumskammer. What was not politically correct could not be published. Klepper had described the small town of Helmstadt on the borders of Hanover and Brandenburg as being like Rome. The humourless Nazi censor minuted: 'Other Germans would see it quite differently.' The same critic had problems with Klepper's desire to write about loneliness.[95] In a *Volksgemeinschaft*, being on your own or wanting to be was *mal vu*.

Klepper's chief problems sprang from his refusal to divorce his Jewish wife. In September 1939 his house in Nikolassee was categorised as non-Aryan. Shortly after, a policeman appeared to remove his wireless set. Taxes went up for the Jewish members of the household and his wife was forced to pay a levy for the wrecking of Jewish shops and synagogues during the Reichskristallnacht. The one remaining daughter, Renee, had now left school, but as a full Jew there was little she was allowed to do. Eventually a fashion school for Jews only was found.[96] Klepper's diaries offer an insight into the power structure of the Third Reich: Frick, the Minister of the Interior, had no power to grant Hanni and Renee pass-ports for Sweden. The only man who did was Eichmann, and he wouldn't. Suicide was the only solution.

III

Berlin had a reputation for the quality of its stage before any artists' colony settled within its bounds. Like so much else, its origins were courtly. In Frederick the Great's time there were French pieces performed at the French comedy theatre and German ones at the Deutsche Komödie. The boxes were reserved for the nobility; the stalls were open to all.[97] It was not the period when German drama was at its greatest. By the end of the century something quite new had occurred, Germany had two of the finest dramatic writers who have ever lived and the Schauspielhaus to perform their plays. Goethe also had Zelter to fill him in on what was going on.

Although Goethe's poetry was widely admired from the 1790s, Berliners took Schiller's dramatic works more readily to their bosoms. In May 1804 the great actor Iffland performed *Wilhelm Tell*, but thought it prudent to present a copy of the text to the royal palace first, given the nature of the piece. It was not staged until July, when it was received 'with loud applause'. It was performed three times that week: 'the apple doesn't taste bad to us and the theatre promises rich pickings'.[98] *Tell's* staging showed Frederick William's Prussia to be a more liberal society than the Third Reich, which thought lines such as 'eine Grenze hat Tyrannenmacht' ('a tyrant's powers have their limits') too tempting for its subjects, and had the piece banned.[99]

Two years later Iffland put on a 'good and honest' performance of Schiller's difficult, neo-classical drama *Die Braut von Messina*. Years later Zelter also saw *Kabale und Liebe* at the Schauspielhaus, and thought he recognised the old town piper Georg in the character of the musician Miller.[100] At the same time as preparations were being made for the staging of the *Braut*, Iffland also put on Zacharias Werner's play *Weihe der Kraft* (The Consecration of Power), which scandalised Berlin by having the figure of Martin Luther on stage. At the performance on 11 June 1806 the police turned up. Zelter was of the view that Iffland had given a very creditable performance as Luther, and, indeed, had *credited* the theatre's funds by putting on such a daring piece. The Berlin garrison, shortly to ride off to face defeat at the hand of the French, was of another opinion. On 23 July they put on fancy dress and went for a summer sleigh-ride through the city. The procession staged by officers of the Regiment Gensdarmes crossed the city at 10 p.m. 'On the sledge sat Dr Luther with a huge flute and opposite him his friend Melanchthon. On the box sat Luther's wife, Katharina von Bora, with a whip which she cracked through the city, and an enormous train, ten cubits long. On horses and carrying candles sat the nuns of the Augustinian convent led by their prioress, all of them with long trains and distorted masks. In this way the procession went through the streets for hours, much to the delight of the curious public.'[101] The scene inspired Fontane's historical novel *Schach von Wuthenow* of 1882.

In October 1809 the theatre performed Goethe's *Götz von Berlichingen* twice. The loyal Zelter went both times, and reported back to the author that 'on each occasion the house was full to bursting, which it very rarely is'.[102] *Faust* had to wait until 1816 for the theatre to rehearse it for the first time. In 1820 it was performed in the new Schinkel building, the construction of which had captured Goethe's keen interest. The play was a great success.[103]

Besides the legendary Iffland, Zelter watched other great actors perform on the Berlin stage. In April 1815 he saw Hoffmann's friend Devrient for the first time as Shylock. Zelter did not dissent from his fellow Berliners' adulation. He marvelled at Devrient's mastery of 'Jewish German'. 'I have never seen anything better in this style.'[104] Devrient had encouraged the Shakespearean actor and writer Karl von Holtei as a young man when he had met him in Breslau. His wife had performed at the Berlin Hoftheater under Graf Brühl, but Holtei was slow to get a part. He arrived in Berlin in 1824, and knew the remnants of Hoffmann's circle around Hitzig. From 1828 he performed at the Königstädter Theater: 'Now my life actually began.'[105] Berlin was nothing compared with Paris, but he found it tolerably good and all the better for the music of Meyerbeer and Mendelssohn.[106]

Gradually censorship began to strangle the Berlin theatre as it had suffocated every other form of artistic endeavour in the city after Waterloo. Dronke was characteristically caustic. He quotes Hoffmann on the need for art to carry the observer on to a higher plane, which 'frees him from the pressure of daily life as one might wash the dirt from one's body, and lifts him up, so that his head, proud and free, gazes into the divine, indeed comes into direct contact with it'.[107] Contemporary theatre was unlikely to do that. The Königsstädter Theater, which was to bring entertainment to the outlying parts of town, subsisted on a diet of vaudeville, popular comedies, melodramas and *Possen*. Dronke clearly had no time for Kalisch, despite his liberal political views. By the Tiergarten there was a truly working-class theatre with wobbly walls. Families went along, each paying a *Groschen* and a half to watch some burlesque. Schnapps and beer were passed from hand to hand. It generally ended with a massive punch-up.[108]

Dronke's enemy was Frederick William IV. During his reign, the Opera was fine to look at – indeed, finer than anything else on the European mainland. The Schauspielhaus, where Goethe and Schiller had been performed, was now showing French plays again. The only talented writer was Hebbel. *Possen* were unworthy of the Berlin stage: 'Vienna, Stuttgart, Dresden, Leipzig and Hamburg, even tiny little Oldenburg, are all better, and only seven years ago the Berlin theatre was considered the best in Germany.'[109]

There was a flurry of foundations during the Empire: the Deutsches Theater in 1883, the Lessing Theater in 1888, the Freie Bühne in 1889, and the more downmarket Freie Volksbühne in 1890, where Max Reinhardt and Otto Brahm had their first great successes.[110] The Deutsches Theater was offering Strindberg, Ibsen and Hauptmann. In 1905 Reinhardt moved there and remained ensconced until the Nazis ousted him. The Schillertheater played a similar role in Charlottenburg. By 1905 Berlin had about thirty theatres. Both Richard Dehmel and Rilke settled in Berlin because of the quality of the stage.[111]

Theatre was also one of the great attractions of Berlin during the Weimar years. Poelzig's vast Große Schauspielhaus was thought to have defeated even Reinhardt, who was better off in the intimacy of the Komödie in the Kurfürstendamm. Brecht soon became the big name, but not everyone was taken in. Tucholsky sneered at the *Dreigroschenoper*: 'Now that the old English play has been a success, cleaned up with verses which are also not by Brecht, he has the cheek to bring out a score on which it is written: "Brecht, the songs from the *Dreigroschenoper*". These aren't by him either. It is more than just brazen, it is a literary lie.'[112]

An extremely hard critic was Döblin. Jeßner's productions tended to the minimal; bare boards and few props. The critic might have accepted this, but not the screeching hen-like Moor in Schiller's *Fiesko*: 'a figure from a criminal dive in Wedding'.[113] In 1921 he told his readers that the Deutsches Theater was like a polar bear which hibernated during the winter months, living off its fat: 'Older and older pieces are performed.'[114] He had time for Reinhardt at the Schauspielhaus and *Orpheus in the Underworld* and the sumptuous effects he was able to produce. Jeßner's sets never impress him, but one of Fehling's productions gets a star: 'It was much, much better, even good.'[115] Tilla Durieux was a rare bird who merited unstinting praise. In Sardou's *Fedora*, 'She was extraordinary in everything she did. In impatience, in expressing pain, revenge, love and fear.'[116] 'She is one of the very few great actresses of truly classic calibre.'[117] By the time Döblin had retired from theatre-reviewing, he had also discovered Elisabeth Bergner: 'I have met this fragile, childish, tiny little person of Japanese finesse for the third time now . . . She acts in an extraordinary way. She draws on all she's got. She speaks and sings, wonderfully modulating Strindberg's numerous banalities.'[118]

It would hardly be worth mentioning the Berlin stage under the National Socialists, although Gustav Gründgens and Emil Jannings remained on board to make sure that the less controversial of the classics were performed, and done well. Berlin theatre came to a singular flowering among the ruins after the liberation, encouraged to some degree by the armies of occupation, particularly the Russians. One Berliner remembers the first performance of the *Dreigroschen-oper* at the Hebbeltheater in Kreuzberg after the war. Berliners seemed to crawl out from holes in the ground, dressed in whatever they considered their best remaining clothes. It was an expression of liberty, the freedom to hear and see what one wanted to again.[119] Brecht naturally reaped most of the rewards for this: he came back, and to the Russian Zone.

IV

Charlottenburg was the birthplace of academic Berlin. It was also at Sophia Charlotte's court that Berlin first saw musicians of European standing. The queen liked Italian music. Her first court composer was Attilio Ariosti from Bologna. He was succeeded by Giovanni Buononcini (sometimes 'Bononcini'). Both musicians ended up in London for a while, where they taught at Händel's Royal Academy of Music.[120] She had an opera house built in Charlottenburg, and both played and directed the music. The great Arcangelo Corelli dedicated his Opus V set of sonatas and *concerti grossi* to her. She passed on her talents to her grandson, the flautist King Frederick the Great, who built the Opera House in the Linden in 1742. It opened with Karl Graun's *Cäsar und Cleopatra* with the *Kapellmeister* dressed in a red costume directing an orchestra of thirty-seven men, and a troupe of chiefly Italian singers. Frederick liked Italian music too, but his own master was Johann Joachim Quantz, and in the course of his peaceable years he brought Johann Adolf Hasse, Franz Benda and C. P. E. Bach to Berlin. His court never enjoyed the clout of the King of Saxony's in musical matters, although he was able to lure J. S. Bach up to Potsdam in 1747; Bach promptly wrote the *Musical Offering* to a theme suggested by Frederick. The famous *Brandenburg Concertos* were written for Frederick's cousin, the Margrave of Brandenburg Schwedt.

The opera was not treated with high seriousness then. Berliners did not behave as they were to in the last war, sitting through heavy works of music placidly while the bombs rained down around them. On Christmas Day 1752 Lehndorff went to the Opera, stayed for the first act only and then took himself off to supper.[121] The building was closed during the Seven Years War. In 1769, however, Berliners could enjoy the opera again on Mondays and Fridays. The performances were given at the king's own expense.[122] Where Frederick had played the flute, his nephew, the profligate Frederick William II, was a keen cellist. He managed to get Mozart to come to Berlin. The result was the 'Prussian' Quartets: K575, 589 and 590.

Court music was mostly limited to performances for a select few in Potsdam, or in the royal *Schlösser* of Berlin or Charlottenburg. With the building of the Schauspielhaus, Berlin audiences had a venue for music, especially instrumental music. Indeed, Schinkel's new building made provision for this by having a separate Konzertsaal. Operas too were performed there, including Hoffmann's *Undine*. Once again Zelter is a marvellous guide to the musical life of the capital at the time. In one of his first letters to Goethe he records a visit to a performance of Johann Friedrich Reichhardt's *Herkules Tod*. Reichhardt had composed the Funeral Music for Frederick the Great, a much underrated work. Zelter thought the unpredictable and politically radical composer had genius, and that the slow movements were both 'manly and moving'.[123]

At the Opera it was Gluck's *Alceste*, with Righini conducting, which drew in the crowds in the autumn of 1803. Goethe had met Beethoven at the Bohemian spa town of Teplitz. Berlin was still occupied by French troops in February 1813. On the 27th there was a performance of the same composer's *Egmont* based on Goethe's German nationalist play.[124] After the French forces finally vanished from the city, Zelter enjoyed Weber's music for *Epimenides*, but it was Weber's *Der Freischütz* which was the greatest opera of its time, premiered in Berlin to rapturous acclaim in 1821. *Freischütz* managed what none of Hoffmann's ten operas could do, to dent the reputation of Italian opera. Heine was in Berlin at the time and recorded that Weber had scored a signal victory over Spontini, who was the musical king of Berlin. Weber's opera was performed at the Schauspielhaus, rather than the Opera House. The bridesmaid's song 'Wir winden dir den Jungfernkranz' ('We weave you the bridal wreath') in Act III, Scene 4, immediately became the equivalent of a 'hit single'.

Heine compared the song to the novels of Walter Scott, which were currently being read by everyone in Berlin, 'from the countess to the seamstress, from the count to the messenger boy'.[125]

> Have you never heard of Weber's *Freischütz*? No?
> Unfortunate man! But at least you must have heard the
> 'Song of the bridal wreath' or the 'Bridal wreath' from
> this opera? No? Lucky man![126]

It was the 'song of songs', which Heine heard from the Oranienburger Tor to the Brandenburger to the Königstor. In case his readers didn't know the words, Heine copied them out. His good mood that morning, however, had been dispelled by schoolboys passing his windows, twittering 'Jungfernkranz'; the daughter of his landlady coming to life with a chorus; the barber singing it on the stairs; the little washerwoman trilling a similar melody. In fury he threw himself into a *Droschke*, in which the noise of the wheels effectively drowned all other sound, and paid a call on his beloved:

The door flew open. The sweet thing sat at the piano
and greeted me with a charming:
'Wo bleibt der schmucke Freiersmann?
Ich kann ihn kaum erwarten.'*

Heine uttered an involuntary 'Hilf Samiel!' and, on the
woman's advice, sought solace in the Tiergarten.[127]

Mozart had also contributed to the process of transferring
opera to a new home north of the Alps. In April 1815 his
Requiem was performed in Berlin. Later that spring it was
the turn of *Zauberflöte* in a new production with twelve new
sets, presumably the famous ones by Schinkel.[128] Zelter not
only records the 'staggering success' of *Freischütz*, but also
the tumultuous applause meted out to Hummel on his first
appearance in the capital in April 1821. Eight years later he
heard Paganini for the first time. He was as impressed as
everyone else. The virtuoso was a 'rather small man who
must possess great suppleness, strength and elasticity, for he
shows no signs of tiredness when he plays the most exhaus-
ting crescendo with clockwork precision'.[129]

Flashy, sub-standard Italian opera was not dead. Berlin still
had Spontini, although his reputation was rocked by the
success of Weber in 1821.[130] If Heine is to be believed,
the principal merit of Spontini's music was the amount of
noise it made. Commenting on *Olympia*, he said there was
'no lack of trumpets and drums', so that a wag suggested
that they should test the thickness of the walls at Schinkel's
new Schauspielhaus by playing it there. Another joker had
emerged from the opera to hear the stentorian tattoo on the
Linden. 'Ah, at last I hear some quiet music!' he said.[131]
Spontini's supporters, however, were forming a powerful
party against the Weberites. Among the nobility it was Spon-

---

* Actually 'Wie lang bleibt doch der Freiersmann? / Ich kann es
kaum erwarten.' ('When will a suitor come for me? / Oh, I am
tired of waiting.')

tini who was the current 'god'; the middle classes, more imbued with nationalism, preferred the newfangled German melodies of Weber.[132]

Zelter enjoyed an uneven relationship with the Italian composer. In February 1829 he noted with evident pleasure 'a carnival without an opera by Spontini'. Spontini had been told that Zelter was plotting against him in Paris. Whatever the truth of the matter Zelter had no time for the music. Later that winter he, too, went to *Olympia* and dismissed it as 'wretched'.[133]

Zelter is chiefly remembered these days for the encouragement he gave the young Mendelssohn. Mendelssohn now takes the credit for the rediscovery of Bach, particularly the Passions. In May 1820, when Mendelssohn was a (highly voluble) eleven-year-old, Zelter was praising the works of Handel and Bach to Goethe. Four years later he was singing the praises of Mendelssohn's *fourth* opera: 'From my – feeble – side, I can hardly master my amazement at the astonishing progress of the boy, who is just fifteen.'[134] In December 1824 Zelter told Goethe about the work he did to foster singing in the city:

> Apart from the two days at the Singing Academy I
> have had a session in my lodgings these past twenty
> years. Here I am both master and servant and the most
> talented of my boys, apart from practising their own
> works, perform proper works of music from the past;
> at the same time I learn them, practise them and gain
> insights into them myself. Every now and then we
> talk about them and examine them more than we play
> or sing them.[135]

Zelter was both encouraging Mendelssohn in his own compositions and pushing him towards Bach. In December 1824, Zelter reported: 'My Felix had his latest double concerto performed today. The boy has put down roots which promise a healthy tree.'[136] At the same time Zelter's other project, the Singakademie, was assuming a physical shape. On 1 July 1825 it had reached street level and Zelter was able to lay the foundation stone.[137] It was finished in January 1827, when Zelter wrote to Goethe to say how pleased he was with the acoustics.[138] In the meantime 'his' Felix had gone from strength to strength. His famous octet was completed in November 1825, and just after the consecration of the Singakademie he was off to Stettin, 'in order to perform his latest works himself . . . On the 3rd [February] the fellow reached the age of nineteen and his works are ever riper and more full of character. His latest opera has been with the Königliche Theater for over a year and has still not been produced. It lasts a whole evening. It will never see the light of day.'[139]

That was not true of Zelter's project to see a performance of the Matthew Passion in Berlin conducted by his young protégé.* On 12 March 1829 he wrote to his friend Goethe, 'We had our Bach music last night, and everything went according to plan. Felix proved a calm and erect conductor. The king and the whole court looked out on a completely full house . . . I wouldn't know how to comment on the work itself.'[140] Zelter's Singakademie had enjoyed its greatest moment.

Zelter composed rather old-fashioned *Lieder*, often dashing off a melody for one of the poems his friend Goethe sent him. On 10 April 1810 he was in a glum mood:

> I drank no wine at midday yesterday, because it gave
> me no pleasure; after the meal I went to sleep on the
> sofa. While I slept my sympathetic postman placed
> your blue envelope on my chest, which I happily
> recognised when I woke up. Before I opened it I called
> for wine to cheer myself up properly. While my
> daughter filled my glass, I broke the seal and cried out
> loud 'Ergo bibamus!' In fright the child dropped the

---

* Mendelssohn had actually memorised the score.

bottle, which I caught. Then I was cheerful and merry, and the wine, probably out of gratitude for its rescue, did its stuff.[141]

The poem was, of course, Goethe's delightful bacchanal *Ergo bibamus*. Zelter promptly sat down and set it to music.[142]

In the middle years of the century Berlin lost its musical pre-eminence. Meyerbeer was in charge between 1842 and 1849. When his (originally French) opera *Les Huguenots* was performed in Berlin, Frederick William IV was amused to see a Jew mediating between warring Protestants and Catholics.[143] Otto Nicolai, the composer of a *Die lustigen Weiber von Windsor* (of which the overture is occasionally played), trained at the Singakademie and is buried in Berlin, but he made his name as one of the founders of the Vienna Philharmonic. Meyerbeer's vicious adversary, Richard Wagner, paid Berlin a few visits in the thirties, to see his radical friends. He had hoped to make his career at the Königstadt Theatre, but was disappointed.[144] His future father-in-law, Franz Liszt, achieved cult status, with women throwing themselves at him when he came on a concert tour in 1842. In 1847 Glaßbrenner sent the whole tour up in a burlesque, *Franz Liszt in Berlin*, with a cast complete with swooning fans and rival groups of 'Hegelianer' and 'Schellingianer'.[145]

Wagner was bringing together his own group of *Schwärmer* in Berlin but he had trouble overcoming the prejudice of the Intendant Graf Hülsen, who remembered the composer's revolutionary posturing. Even Frederick William IV had difficulty swaying his courtier, enquiring 'whether it would not be possible to have one of the latest Wagner operas, which, I believe, form a cycle, performed here in Berlin'.[146] Wagner none the less had to wait until 1862. There were soon to be more places available for operatic productions. The Theater des Westens opened in 1896 and put on a *Ring* in 1914, despite their policy of playing only 'lighter opera'.

In 1905 the Comic Opera opened with Offenbach's *Contes d'Hoffmann*. In 1912 the Charlottenburgers decided that they should have an opera house too. In its heyday in the twenties they entrusted it to Bruno Walter.[147]

Choral works were served not only by the Singakademie, but also the Stern Choir and the Siegfried Ochs Choir. From 1888 the Philharmonic Choir sang works by Bach and Handel. Mendelssohn had mooted the subject of a Musical Academy in Berlin in 1843, but had chosen to found it in Leipzig instead. In 1868 the great violinist and friend of Brahms, Joachim, created a music academy in the Palais Raczynski. He planned to have Clara Schumann teach at the school and there is an evocative painting by Menzel of the two playing together. When the palace was demolished to make way for the new Reichstag building, the music school was transferred to its present site in Charlottenburg.[148]

The most important creation was the Berlin Philharmonic, founded in 1882. Its chief conductors were a dazzling series from Hans von Bülow to Artur Nikisch, Richard Strauss and Wilhelm Furtwängler. Furtwängler has remained a controversial figure since the late thirties because he continued to conduct during the Third Reich, even performing before Hitler at Bayreuth and once on the Führer's birthday. His conduct has been the subject of a recent play, *Taking Sides*, by the South African playwright Ronald Harwood,[149] which sensitively, but inconclusively, presented the arguments for and against.

Indeed, had Furtwängler left Germany in 1934 he would now be venerated as one of the great cultural opponents of Nazism along with the Manns and his fellow conductor Erich Kleiber. Like many Germans from the cultured bourgeoisie, Furtwängler liked to see himself above the sordid world of party politics. The Nazi *Machtergreifung* was passed over in silence. He was to the right, and would have had little time for what he saw as the chaotic Weimar Republic. When Hitler and his men decided that the Jews could no longer perform in German state orchestras, however, the conductor descended from his ivory tower and wrote a full-length article in the *Deutsche allgemeine Zeitung* stating: 'I acknowledge only one ultimate difference – between good and bad art.' In October 1934, Furtwängler once again took up the cudgels for art when he conducted the symphony from Hindemith's opera *Mathis der Maler*. His defence of Hindemith was to lead to a show-down with Goebbels. At first the old rivalry protected Furtwängler from the Minister for Propaganda. Göring had assumed the Linden Opera as part of his own booty, and was willing to lend the conductor an ear if it meant annoying his enemy Goebbels. After Furtwängler's defence of Hindemith, however, Göring witnessed scenes of adulation when the conductor appeared on the rostrum to perform *Tristan*. Later they even hissed the fat Minister President. After that Göring threw Furtwängler to the wolves.[150]

Furtwängler was progressively isolated from his contacts in the West and compromised by the superior cunning of the Nazis, who used one of their own party members, Herbert von Karajan, as a stick to beat the vain conductor with. Although he resigned from his official posts in the Third Reich, he was lured back on to the rostrum and played several times before Hitler, who treasured him above all others. Furtwängler still believed he was holding out against the moral cesspit of the Nazi state; he believed – possibly Hoffmann would have agreed – that great music had the power to lift his audiences to a better world: 'I knew that a single performance of a great German masterpiece was a stronger and more vital negation of the spirit of Buchenwald and Auschwitz than words.' When Thomas Mann attacked him for conducting *Fidelio* in Berlin, Furtwängler remarked: 'Does Thomas Mann think that *Fidelio* should not be heard in Himmler's Germany?'[151]

That opera *Fidelio* meant a lot to certain Berliners. A regime which banned *Wilhelm Tell* had slipped up when they

permitted Beethoven's one opera to be publicly performed.★
In October 1943 Ulrich von Hassell took his family to see
the opera: 'For me this is one of the most divine creations
of mankind – the prisoners in the courtyard of the castle –
very moving at the present time.'[152] He was in the thick of
plans to overthrow the regime. Less than a year later he
perished at the end of a piece of thin cord in Plötzensee.

The programmes of the BPO over the period show that the
Nazis were slow to effect the changes in the orchestra's
repertory. Even in the first concert following the *Machtergrei-*
fung when a performance was given of Gottfried Müller's
Variations and fugue on a German folksong, the soloist in the
Beethoven and Tchaikovsky pieces was Szymon Goldberg.
In January 1934 there was an aria from Méhul's opera *Joseph*,
from which the *Horst Wessel Lied* had been lifted, but this
didn't prevent the orchestra from playing the music from
Mendelssohn's *A Midsummer Night's Dream* the following
month. After May 1934, the programmes fell into line. A
political element creeps in: Russian music was heard while
Germany was allied to Stalin's Soviet Union. Once the
alliance had been broken by the Germans, there was a lot of
Sibelius on the programmes.[153]

The first post-war conductor of the Berlin Philharmonic
was the Russian-born Leo Borchard, who had played a small
role in the Opposition during the war and when the Red
Army entered Berlin had saved himself and his friends by
singing the Russian national anthem. Borchard was shot,
like the composer Anton von Webern, by an overzealous
American sentry.[154] He was succeeded by Sergiu Celibidache,
who had been Furtwängler's *répétiteur* during the war,[155]
and who now took hold of the reins of the orchestra while
Furtwängler went through the intentionally humiliating

★ The late Anthony Burgess once maintained in a radio talk that
Fidelio had indeed been banned in the Third Reich.

process of deNazification. Ultimately the orchestra fell into
the hands of Karajan, who, despite his faults (he was the
Albert Speer of Nazi music), was the natural successor. Furtwängler died in Switzerland in November 1954, broken by
the experiences of the past twenty years. As the doctor told
his wife: 'How can one save him if he has himself lost the
will to live?'[156]

V

Berlin had its popular arts. If there were no operetta com-
posers of the calibre of the Strausses in Vienna, there were
men such as Paul Lincke, who composed the ever popular
'Berliner Luft' in 1904, and Walter Kollo. There were comedians like Wilhelm Bendow and Martin Bendix, and of
course singers. The most popular of these was Claire Waldoff,
who came from Gelsenkirchen in Westphalia, but who was
wise enough to transform herself into a complete Berliner,
singing in *Berlinisch* in an invariable march time. The songs
were saucy and bawdy and politically irreverent. One even
suggested removing all men from politics and replacing them
with women. She was shifted into retirement when the Nazis
came to power.[157]

After so much nannying and censorship, Berlin achieved
a free press only when Bismarck realised that his repressive
policies had failed in the 1870s. After that time there grew
up in Kreuzberg the equivalent of London's Fleet Street.
Before 1874 real news had to be gleaned from imported
foreign papers. This was also to be the case after 1933.[158]
The creators of what was to be the 'world's great newspaper
city' were three men, Rudolf Mosse, Leopold Ullstein and
August Scherl. They added their titles to the emasculated
press as it had previously existed: the *Voßische Zeitung* (known
as 'Tante Voß', or 'Auntie'), the *Berlinische Zeitung*, the
Junkers' *Kreuzzeitung* and the *Sozial Demokrat* (the original

Vorwärts). All the Press barons had their serious titles, and the so-called 'boulevard' sheets, which became increasingly heavily illustrated as time went on, and concentrated more and more on scandal and less and less on news.[159]

They enjoyed a remarkable liberty while the going was good. In 1878 the *Berliner Zeitung* was able to demand a constitutional regime, and reproach the Bismarckian state for 'chancellor absolutism'. Another of the Ullstein papers, the *Berliner Morgenpost*, had achieved a circulation of 400,000 by 1930, a remarkable feat given the number of different titles available both from Berlin and the bigger provincial towns. The first of the wholly mindless 'boulevard' papers was the *BZ am Mittag*, which put the short-lived Maxwell *London Daily News* to shame by printing up to four times a day in 1904.

Some of the more banal titles attracted prestigious lists of contributors. *Die Dame* could boast Vicki Baum, Stefan Zweig and Bertolt Brecht as writers and Emil Orlik and Tamara de Lempicka as illustrators. Editors, too, were figures of legend: the great Theodor Wolff, the rabid nationalist who was later to die in Theresienstadt; Kurt Korff of the *Berliner illustrierte Zeitung*, who started *Life* in exile in the United States. In 1927 *Der Angriff*, Goebbels' scandal sheet, joined the club. In 1933 the Nazis also transferred production of the party organ, the *Völkische Beobachter*, to Berlin. More titles were to come. They had their own boulevard paper in the *Illustrierte Beobachter*, *NS Funk* was their '*Radio Times*', *Der SA Mann* was for the SA and *Das schwarze Korps* provided suitable reading for the SS. *Die Brennessel* (The Stinging Nettle) was their attempt at reproducing the popular political satire of the Weimar days. A writer such as Heinrich Mann was lampooned as his own creation Rosa Fröhlich in *Der blaue Engel*, complete with stockings and suspender belts.[160]

One of the bravest of the Weimar papers had been *Die Weltbühne* edited by Carl von Ossietzky, a pacifist who had used his columns to badger the Reichswehr and expose their secret attempts to rearm in contravention of the Treaty of Versailles. Ossietzky's trials before the courts are one more instance of the other face of Weimar Germany. In February 1927, for example, he was fined 500 marks for libelling the German navy. At the trial the judge dwelled at length on his connections with the navy, how many relatives he had in it, and how he sang in a naval choir.[161]

Neither he nor Tucholsky had adequately recognised the devil in their midst. They continued to believe that 'Prussian militarism' was the real target for their attacks, and not the Nazi party. The police, too, got their share: in 'Bloody May' 1929 there were violent clashes between the police and workers. Ossietzky described the trigger-happy 'Schupos' (armed policemen): 'I had the clear feeling that they absolutely had to have a corpse.'[162] In December 1930 the *Weltbühne* turned its attention to the Nazis who had run wild among the crowds waiting to see the film of Remarque's *Im Westen nichts Neues* (*All Quiet on the Western Front*): 'Fascism has won another battle. Today they have stifled a film, tomorrow it will be something else . . . You can only defeat Fascism on the streets. Against the National Socialist scum there is only the logic of the thicker cosh.'[163]

In 1932 Ossietzky was up before the courts once more for exposing the build-up of the Air Force, again in contravention of the Treaty of Versailles. This time he received an eighteen-month prison sentence. He was philosophic about the idea of being in gaol. To Tucholsky he wrote, 'Sadly, I have been refused permission to smoke, which I find barbaric.' He arrived at the prison gates with his supporters – Ernst Toller, Stefan Zweig, Erich Mühsam and Herwarth Walden – to turn himself in. The cases piled up. In July he was before the courts again for suggesting (with Tucholsky) that 'Soldiers are murderers'. He was none the less released in December.[164]

There was no hope for Ossietzky once the Nazis came to power. He was arrested like so many others on the night of the Reichstag blaze. For the next five years he was beaten and brainwashed while Tucholsky made furious efforts to gain international support for his release. He succeeded in having Ossietzky awarded the Nobel Peace Prize, and perhaps prolonging his life for a while. As for the great satirist and Berliner Tucholsky, he took his own life in lonely exile in Sweden.

7
Belial

I

It has *nearly* always been possible to lead a humdrum life in Berlin. Routines have a tendency to reassert themselves; whatever the circumstances, people get on with their lives. Even in November 1943, when Harris's bombing campaign began in earnest and bombs rained down on the city on virtually every cloudless day and night, Berliners were able to accommodate the destruction within the framework of their everyday existence. Indeed, even when the Russians took the shattered city in 1945, and rape and murder became an hourly commonplace, Berliners somehow maintained a certain rhythm to their lives.[1] They endeavoured to stay out of the paths of danger and worried about getting enough to eat. Man adapts, and the Berliner is a particularly hardy man, moulded perhaps by the climatic extremes of the Mark, as much as by historical experience.

The picture was always more sinister from without than from within. We hear the bad news from Berlin, rarely the good. Berlin is a city of pestilence, murder, revolution, destruction and division. It is not a city of beauty and devotion, like Rome; or a city of suave elegance and illumination, like Paris. Even during those periods when people appeared to enjoy themselves, as at times during the twenties, or in West Berlin before 1989, everything was done in a tense, neurasthenic way, so unlike the lazy, insouciant, fun-loving manner of the Viennese, for whom such things are seemingly effortless. Most tourists visit Berlin from motives of purest

Schadenfreude: they want to see how and where the great monster died.

Rioting is an established Berlin tradition, dating back to the time of the Berlin *Unruhe* of 1442, when the citizens rebelled against the Elector Frederick II, 'Irontooth', who appeared to ride roughshod over their liberties. Irontooth's reaction was to descend on Berlin with 600 knights. The news of his arrival threw the people into such a panic that they flung open the gates of the city and let him in. The Elector imposed new conditions on the town which had refused his right to build a proper fortress. Now work began. The town hall the Berliners shared with the Cöllners was confiscated. Here the Elector lodged his own *Hofrichter* to make sure nothing of the sort occurred again.[2]

But it did. The Berliners watched the progress of the new Schloss with concern. Six years later they saw the foundations of a fortress being laid in the area between the Dominican church and the city wall. To facilitate the work a breach had been made in the walls, leaving the city open. In the *Berliner Unwillen* (The Berlin Indignation), the citizens took their new *Hofrichter* prisoner and banished his servants, after which they got into the *Hohe Haus*, the seat of electoral authority in the town, and wrecked it. They then sat back and waited for help from the powerful Hanseatic League (of which they were a junior member until 1516–1518).[3]

It was not forthcoming. Instead the Elector returned and bided his time in Spandau until the insurgents gave in, whereupon he took away what remained of their municipal privileges and banished the ringleaders. He then speeded up the work on his *Burg*, where the rebels had contrived to flood the foundations.[4]

Berlin didn't see another disturbance on this scale until Elector John Sigismund took the decision to change his religion. It was thought that his conversion had something to do with his claims to the province of Cleves in the west, but it is more likely that he had been properly won over to

Calvinism. In the Petrikirche the preacher Peter Stüler banged his fist: 'If you* want to join the Reformed Church, go to Jülich – there are plenty of Calvinists there!' The Margrave, his brother, issued orders to have Stüler arrested, but that led to rioting. When the Margrave rode up to the crowd to remonstrate with them he was struck in the upper thigh by a stone. The rebels then turned their attention to ransacking the court preacher's house.[5]

The next few days were tense. The citizens were worried that the Margrave would proceed against the city. When the Elector returned, Deacon Stüler was banished, and free religion took the place of the formula *cuius regio, eius religio.* A new order was also promulgated to make Berlin easier to police. At the first signs of unrest, the good citizens were to gather in the Schloßplatz; that would allow the Elector to move against the insurgents with an appropriate degree of ruthlessness.[6]

The politically acquiescent Prussians ignored news of the French Revolution of 1789. By the 1830s things were different. The promised constitution was now fifteen years late. The news from Paris seems to have affected the tailors' assistants the most. On 17 September there was a demonstration on the Schloßplatz. A reversal of the system laid down in John Sigismund's day. Mounted soldiers with drawn swords moved against the rioters, lashing out at them. There were seventy-three arrests. The next day there was a second demonstration and a further sixty arrests.[7]

It was all very different in 1848, when Berlin had its first real revolution, as opposed to a bloody riot. Once more it was the news from Paris that brought the men and women out on to the streets, but it had been compounded by the recent political disappointments at home. The king had finally summoned a united *Landtag* in 1847, which looked, to all historically minded optimists, decidedly similar to the

* 'Du' in the original.

summoning of the Estates General by Louis XVI. In January a permanent committee was formed. Then on 25 February 1848 the news of Louis Philippe's departure came. Three days later Berliners learned that France had become a republic for the second time.[8]

Everyone wanted to jump on the reform bandwagon. The students at Schinkel's *Bauakademie* drew up an address for the king.[9] The workers called for a ministry of labour to protect them from the bosses.[10] The middle classes gathered in the cafés and *Lesecabinette*, where the uncensored non-Prussian press could be consulted. This seemed the natural place for a little restrained tub-thumping, with a call for a mass assembly to decide on reforms. This was duly despatched to one of the non-Prussian papers to be printed[11] and the crowds made for the Zelte in the Tiergarten on 6 March. Another meeting in the Zelte the next day drew even bigger crowds: artisans, men from the 'professions', shopkeepers, artists and students all turned up to speak and listen.[12]

The government was unprepared. Prussia had been too busy watching for signs of insurrection in the rest of Germany to pay adequate attention to itself. Orders were sent to bring in regiments from the Rheinland, Koblenz and Halle.[13] The crowd was still looking for a suitable place to hold their meetings. They sent a delegation to Kroll, who refused them (he died in the middle of April), and asked for police protection from the 3,000- to 4,000-strong crowd. This is possibly when the wily Stieber assumed control (see p. 128).[14] In the Zelte, the windows were kept open so that *hoi polloi* could glean a little of what was going on while the middle-class gentlemen inside adopted the black, red and gold colours of Germany. The guard was reinforced before the royal palace. On the 10th, Berlin's students gathered to renounce their privileges. The government was alarmed. On the same day they abolished censorship, but the measure proved an empty one as a newspaper was promptly denied permission to print an article critical of the Prussian government.[15]

Generalleutnant Karl Ludwig von Prittwitz none the less noted with distaste that 'all possible *odiosa*' was being served up by the papers coming from non-Prussian Germany.[16] Serious trouble started on the 13th. Prittwitz thought the crowd of men, women and children had been drinking. They had discovered a policeman in the crowd and that evening flooded into the Pariserplatz from the Tiergarten in fury. They retreated as a detachment of Gardes du Corps headed for the square. There was a fight in the Tiergarten, in which an officer was wounded. After that the battles spread to the Wilhelmstraße.[17] By the 14th the revolution had broken out properly. Prittwitz noted the mocking of soldiers on the Schloßplatz. When the soldiers drew their swords at a barricade in the Brüderstraße, they were pelted with stones and glass from the upstairs windows. Another barricade was found in the Spittelmarkt: six feet high and made up of two layers of fish barrels.[18]

In the rest of Germany all eyes were on Berlin. The *Frankfurter Journal* reported that the military had been wholly unprovoked. The *Deutsche allgemeine Zeitung* told its readers of the 'day of horror' in Berlin, and that the military had fired on the citizens.[19] The Berlin press was still effectively muzzled. The suggestion in the *Voßische Zeitung* that unemployment was 'sent by God' did not go down well with the workers, who broke the paper's windows the next day. Although workers had mingled with the middle-class Berliners in the Zelte, the latter tended to look down on them, attributing their unrest to the failure of the harvests in 1846 and 1847. One cartoon showed a group of workers puffing their pipes while the middle-class gentlemen offer them sausages: 'Dig in, noble friends: of all tyrants hunger is the grimmest! Destroy him. Here are the weapons!' The workers reply, 'Hunger hawwe hier keen, edler Volksfreund, awwer

Dorscht! Viel Dorscht!' ('No one here is hungry, noble friend of the people, but we're thirsty! Terribly thirsty!')[20]

On 16 March the liberal *Mannheim Abendzeitung* printed the latest news from Berlin. 'For a third day the streets have been daubed with the people's blood.' Communist rhetoric had been heard on the Schloßplatz. There was talk of 'surplus value' and the need to distribute the treasures housed in the palace cellars to create work. 'You have beaten our brothers to death,' shouted one energumen. 'Wait till we have arms!' It was the signal to disarm the guards. One was killed trying to resist.[21] A hail of stones drove back the soldiers who tried to intervene, until a bayonet charge was organised to drive the mob from the Schloßplatz. Prittwitz made an interesting social observation at this point: *Droschke* drivers were on the side of the military, for the simple reason that the barricades hindered them from working. 'You dogs, now you are really going to get your reward!' They cheered as the soldiers stormed the obstructions blocking the streets.[22]

Saturday 18 March saw the heaviest fighting. The attacks on the barricades by Lieutenant von Trützschler and Captain von Cosel had enraged the mob. Now the Berliners began to return the soldiers' rifle fire from the upper windows of the narrow streets in the old town. Increasing numbers were wounded clearing the barricades. At one point a howitzer was brought up. A cache of ammunition was found in the restaurant Rosch in the Heiligengeiststraße. When the soldiers entered, there was a cry of 'Beat the officer to death!' from a figure with an axe. He was shot down by a fusilier. Further examination of the restaurant revealed two corpses behind firing loopholes on the upper floor. Lieutenant von Schlegell was then attacked by a Badenese merchant with a sword. Prittwitz tells that some of the dead were Hessians.[23]

The bloodiest battle of the day was the siege of the *Rathaus* in Cölln. In the fighting seventy insurgents were killed, wounded or taken prisoner. The army, too, sustained losses: four NCOs and three grenadiers were killed; two officers, two NCOs and sixty-four grenadiers were wounded. Elsewhere the crowd tried to storm a barracks in order to grab guns from the arsenal, resulting in more deaths. Prittwitz was once again anxious to place the blame on non-Prussians. 'Among the prisoners there were a lot of Jews as well as a few foreigners, including a Frenchman. The rest were real proletarians who had been amply paid for their role.' The General was, of course, wrong. On the mood of the soldiers he was more accurate. The Prussian army had seen no fighting since the Wars of Liberation, a point to which Glaßbrenner frequently alludes in *Berlin wie esist – und trinkt*. They were 'excited and embittered . . . They knew of fighting and war only from the story-books.'[24] Their abuse at the hands of the Berliners came as a shock, and it sank deep into their collective consciousness. They took it out on anyone they found with arms in their hands, and shot them down.[25]

The next day soldiers were not only pelted with stones but doused in boiling oil and sulphuric acid. At midday Frederick William prevented the situation from worsening further when he made his proclamation to his 'dear Berliners'.

> Inhabitants of my loyal and beautiful Berlin, listen to
> the paternal voice of your king. Forget what has
> happened and I will forget it too in my heart for the
> sake of the great future which, with the peaceful
> blessings of God, will dawn for Prussia and through
> Prussia for Germany.

The troops were then withdrawn from the streets and censorship scrapped. Outside the houses of the victims collections were made for the dead.[26]

The fighting had claimed the lives of 230 civilians – men, women and children. Seven hundred prisoners had been taken, including three Swiss, two Dutchmen, two Danes, and

Prittwitz's Frenchman. Non-Berliners outnumbered citizens two to one.[27] In storming the 921 barricades around the city, twenty-four officers and men had been killed. They were buried in the Invalidenfriedhof.[28] On the 22nd there was a day of mourning and reconciliation. Black flags flew alongside the German flags and men wore crepe arm- or hatbands, the women black dresses. An enormous crowd of mourners filled the Schloßplatz. A service was held for the dead with Bishop Neander officiating. The mourners left to the chorale *Jesu meine Zuversicht* (Jesus my trust) and 'approached the coffins. The Court Marshal had despatched the chief gardener with some workers to arrange the flowers . . . The bereaved received fresh bouquets.'[29]

What the March days had highlighted was the rift between the demands of the politically impotent middle classes and the workers. Middle-class men and women like Theodor Fontane had supported the revolt, but Bernstein states that 90 per cent of the deaths occurred among the working-class insurgents. His figures are a little contradictory: he maintains that only seventy-five of those buried in Friedrichshain were actually involved in the fighting. The rest were either onlookers or workers 'pitilessly murdered' later by vengeful soldiers. Some areas were considered too dangerous for the army: there was no attempt to subdue the unrest in Voigtland or the Frankfurter Viertel.[30]

After the March days, the bourgeois insurgents and the workers formed political clubs. The middle-class organisations gathered in the newspaper libraries. Under the influence of the Communist Stephan Born, the Komitee für Arbeiter was formed. For once the workers (or, rather, artisans) outnumbered the Herr Doktors on the seven-man committee. The middle classes and the *petite bourgeoisie* formed their own *Bürgerwehr*, or civil guard, which carried on its work until Frederick William felt powerful enough to suppress it once again.[31] That was only after renewed clashes in May and the attempt to storm the Arsenal.

Of course the old *Kietz* still seethed with discontent. In October the Michaelskirchplatz on the Köpenicker Field was the scene of the last hiccups of the revolution. Berlin's building workers have always had to contend with the city's high water table and sandy soil. In this instance a steam pump had been installed to extract the water from the ground. The workers smelled a rat, and during the night some Luddite got it into his head to destroy the machine. A drunken celebration ensued, which led to a clash with the middle-class Civil Guard. A bayonet charge failed to disperse the mob. The master-baker Schulz then gave orders to fire a salvo into the crowd, thereby killing three workers.[32]

The crowd ran amok, pillaging the gunsmiths. Eventually they threw up a number of barricades in the Köpenicker, Dresdener, Roß and Alte Jakobstraße and dug in. The barricades, however, were poorly built and easily taken. In the battle another eleven workers and a number of Civil Guards were killed. Another battle took place the next day before order was re-established for a one-and-a-half-hour funeral march with speeches by the orators Bisty, Berends and Voß-winkel. Only the machine-workers had stayed out of the battle, for the obvious reason that they had seen nothing suspicious about the pump in the first place. Their attempts to reconcile the different factions, however, were only partly successful. They decided to place their own men between the two warring parties. One of their number then had to die before the riot came to an end.[33] On 12 November the army marched back into Berlin and in the course of the next three days the Civil Guard was disarmed. 'Reaction was Lord of Berlin.'[34]

II

By 1918 the middle classes had achieved their political aims, but the workers had not. Theirs was the revolution which followed defeat in the First World War. The ninth of November was a beautiful, sunny day. Already in the morning crowds were gathering on the streets and soldiers were to be seen speeding around in lorries. Writing that evening, Evelyn Blücher reported 'sinister-looking' red flags among the black, white and red. The Kaiser had abdicated, and the revolutionaries had come forward to fill the political void.[35] Fürstin Blücher would have agreed with Lenin that the Germans were unconvincing revolutionaries:

> I noticed the pale gold of young girls' uncovered
> heads, as they passed by with only a shawl over their
> shoulders. It seemed so feminine and incongruous,
> under the folds of those gruesome red banners flying
> over them. One can never imagine these pale northern
> women helping to build up barricades and screaming
> and raging for blood.[36]

The Brandenburg Gate had been draped with another red flag, and two machine-gun pickets stationed outside the Adlon. Groups of soldiers and civilians carrying guns spiked with small red flags forced soldiers and officers to tear off insignia of rank. They looked 'like schoolboys out on an escapade'.[37] Graf Kessler faced the day with his usual blend of political astuteness and *mondanité*. He watched a soldier harangue the crowd in front of the Potsdamer Bahnhof, managed to get into the bank opposite the state library and ended up having dinner with the future minister Hugo Simon. Their conversation was punctuated by rifle fire coming from the direction of the palace.[38]

After the meal he went up to the Reichstag and made his way to the chamber.

> A multitude swarmed among the seats, a sort of
> popular assembly, soldiers without badges, sailors
> with slung rifles, women, all of them with red arm-
> bands, and a number of Reichstag members.[39]

The next day the painter Lovis Corinth noted, 'Yesterday, Saturday, the revolution broke out. On the whole it was quite peaceful and, apart from a few unfortunate incidents, bloodless. Red flags fly over all the Imperial buildings. Liebknecht gave a speech from the window of the Schloss. Whatever happens we are standing before a new era.'[40]

Fürstin Blücher witnessed the first bloodshed the next day, but Kessler continued in the same vein. He had dinner with the Trieste-born poet Theodor Däubler, a pre-war denizen of the Café des Westens. After dinner Kessler attempted to check the poc: into the hotel for the night, where it was thought he would be safer. The manager decided that, as an Austrian, Däubler lacked the proper papers. The liberal Count Kessler flashed some papers at him to prove that he was a representative of the Soldiers and Workers Council. 'The manager bowed in the good old Prussian way to discipline, even though of revolutionary origin, and allotted him a room. No more sound and fury, servility alone remains.'[41]

The Alsatian Yvan Goll also thought the idea of a German revolution something of an oxymoron: 'The city affected to ignore [it]. For days and days there were occasional brawls on the street corners, the odd noisy explosion and cries from wounded men. The crowd rushed this way and that, through the passages, then suddenly order returned and the trams made their slow progress once again like snails after a sudden downpour, blazing a trail between broken canes and corpses.'[42]

The revolution flared and fizzled until March the following year. Regular forces were backed up by *Freikorps* units of doubtful political reliability. In the January fighting to wrest the city from the soldiers' and workers' councils, Colonel Reinhard's troops gave the least mercy. Their first stop was at the town hall in Spandau, where they swiftly dislodged a garrison of revolutionary Spartacists and promptly shot them before they had reached their allotted prison. A Major von Stephani led the attack on the offices of the newspaper

Vorwärts, bringing in cannon and heavy machine-guns to breach the walls of the building. Those who gave themselves up were despatched with grenades in the courtyard of the ruined newspaper offices. On the night of 11–12 January 1919, the forces under the ultimate control (if one can call it that) of Minister Noske retook police headquarters in the Alexanderplatz. Once again cannon was used to pierce the solid walls of the building. Once again numerous revolutionaries were put to death in the process.[43]

Within a few days order had been re-established. Now it was the moment for the army and the *Freikorps* to extract their revenge. 'The Spartacists were hunted like game from *quartier* to *quartier*.' The particular prizes the soldiers were looking for were Spartacist leaders Karl Liebknecht and Rosa Luxemburg.[44] On 15 January an article by Liebknecht appeared in the *Rote Fahne*. 'Those beaten today will be the victors of tomorrow.' That same day both of them were caught by Noske's men. Liebknecht was apprehended at the flat of some friends in the Mannheimerstraße in Wilmersdorf and taken to the headquarters of the Garde Kavallerie in the Eden Hotel. He tried to deny that he was Liebknecht, but the monograms on his linen gave him away.[45] On the 16th, 'Tante Voß' reported that Liebknecht had been shot trying to escape. In the same issue they reported the final hours of Rosa Luxemburg, who had been beaten up by the crowd outside the hotel, abducted in a car, and then shot. The mob had finally tossed her body into the Landwehrkanal.

The *Voßische* concluded its report in classically Prussian style. Complaining about this lynch justice, it stated that the punishment meted out to Rosa Luxemburg and Liebknecht 'should have been decided by a proper court of law'. That night Philipp Scheidemann made a speech in Kassel where he expressed the new government's frustration at the duo's repeated attempts to overthrow the state since 9 November 1918: 'Day after day they called the people to arms and for the violent overthrow of the government. Now they have themselves fallen victim to their own bloody terror tactics.' 'Tante Voß' was right. When the truth of the story came out, it marked an indelible stain on the moral credentials of the new republic.[46]

The next day, the 17th, *Die Freiheit* printed the most accurate version of the story to date. It put paid to the idea that the crowd had played a role in the death of the two revolutionaries. There hadn't been a crowd, for the simple reason that the Eden Hotel had been cordoned off. The fullest account of the assassinations came up at the trial of the murderous sailors before the Landgericht in Moabit. Rosa Luxemburg was probably dead after the soldier Runge beat her with his rifle butt. They were none the less taking no chances. She was shot through the temple in the car and her lifeless body hit with a revolver before she was jettisoned into the canal. She was not fished out again for another six months.[47]

Liebknecht had managed to bite the hand of one of his torturers. Once inside the car he had been struck with a heavy object from behind, and was bleeding heavily by the time they got to the Neue See. The man who fired the first shot was Kapitänleutnant Horst von Pflugk-Hartung, the son of a university professor and archivist. He was later cleared of the charges against him.[48]

The revolution, or uprising, of 17 June 1953 was the first of the failed attempts by Eastern Bloc states to alleviate the burden of Soviet-inspired socialism. The East German SED had decided to move against the surviving middle classes. In the countryside more and more land was taken away from the farmers to create co-operative farms. In the seaside resorts of the Baltic, the hotels and restaurants that were still in private hands were impounded and taken over by the state. The SED attacked the churches imprisoning some seventy pastors. East Germany was still over 90 per cent Christian, and similar moves against the intelligentsia led to a massive rise in emigration to the Bundesrepublik. The monthly tallies rose from 22,000 to 58,000 between December 1952 and March 1953. Between January 1951 and April 1953 447,000 East Germans left. They included not only middle-class East Germans, but also elements reputed to be loyal to the regime: soldiers and members of the FDJ, the socialists' version of the Hitler Jugend.[49]

Everywhere the SED promoted a new austerity. Wages were low, and prices rose. The price of schnapps went up, which was always a provocation to Berliners. Then Stalin died on 5 March, and the new regime in Moscow encouraged the SED to adopt a 'new course' and to breathe a little liberalism into the state by leaving the middle classes alone and abandoning their *Kirchenkampf*. The Russian policy split the SED and sowed confusion throughout the east.

Strikes proliferated. It was the workers who led the movement, often the youngest, who had grown up since Nazi days. In the countryside there were protests against the LPG co-operatives, but the middle classes kept out of the unrest, partly because they lacked any effective organs to represent their views. Berlin was not the city most affected by the revolt; more dramatic scenes were experienced in Halle and Magdeburg, even in little Görlitz. Still, on 17 June 100,000 East Berliners (and a few West Berliners) took to the streets, tearing down red flags and showering the Soviet tanks with stones on the Leipziger Platz. In general the Russians behaved with restraint. A total of fifty-one died, which included ten executions and six members of the security forces. There were about 7,000 arrests; of these, two-thirds were workers. In the West the radio station RIAS was obliged to cool its enthusiasm. West Berlin's greatest post-war mayor, Ernst Reuter, was stranded in Vienna at the beginning of the revolt, unable to find a means of getting to Berlin. His impotence on the day affected him gravely.[50]

Berlin's 'last revolution' occurred in the West in 1968 and led to a complete transformation of society within the island city. It began with a movement to reform the universities, which had come through German defeat virtually unscathed. Students wanted a freer, more American system. By 1960 a new generation had grown up. The older Berliners had turned their back on the past; they wanted to rebuild and forget. The threat from the East was such that the richer bourgeoisie had disappeared: Berlin was a *petit-bourgeois* city. According to one former student leader, the atmosphere was 'suffocating';[51] it was very traditional, and very provincial. From 1957 Willy Brandt had proved a popular Mayor but in 1961 the Wall had gone up and many students had lost friends and lovers who, by some unfortunate accident, had been domiciled in the Russian sector. Many East Berliners had studied at the Free University.

With the sixties came the 'causes': the Vietnam War, apartheid, Algeria, which excited the students' indignation. Further offence was caused by the lack of an effective opposition in Germany: the Communist Party was banned, the Nazi past was being swept under the carpet. The trials had ceased and many guilty men had got off scot-free.

All these things were felt more acutely in Berlin because of the large number of students who had been drawn to the old capital by the absence of national service, and because of the political tension caused by the Wall. In 1966 Brandt went to Bonn as Foreign Minister and was replaced by Pastor Heinrich Albertz. On 2 June 1967 Benno Ohnesorg was killed by the police in the course of a demonstration against a visit to West Germany by the Shah of Iran. Albertz unwisely congratulated the police for their handling of the demonstration, something which cost him his job.

The demonstrations continued into the following year with groups affirming their support for the West while others protested against imperialism. After a pro-Western march attracted 150,000 people, Rudi Dutschke led an anti-American demonstration of 12,000 students, in the course of which he was shot by a right-wing worker. Two days of rioting followed.[52] The left became increasingly radical with the creation of the Baader–Meinhof group, which in 1974 murdered the President of Berlin's Appeal Court, Günter von Drenkmann.

Former student revolutionaries still see 1968 as a success. It not only rid Berlin of Albertz, it won the students representation on the Senate. A new *Hochschulgesetz* was rushed through the Bundestag, opening a liberal era in the universities. Some would argue that it brought about the informality which marks the city, where no one is obliged to wear ties and most people readily address one another with the familiar 'Du'. In political terms, however, the gains lasted only until 1980, when Richard von Weizsäcker became mayor for the right-wing CDU. From then onwards the men and women of 1968 formed themselves into a loose political bond of 'Alternative', which became increasingly 'green' as the decade wore on.

III

Berlin's political assassins had not been nearly so successful in the nineteenth century. There were several attempts to kill Frederick William IV which simply resulted in Hinckeldey assuming greater and greater powers for his police force. According to Stieber the attack on Bismarck made by Ferdinand Cohen-Blind failed because the Chancellor wore a bullet-proof vest. Five shots were fired, three of which hit their target but bounced harmlessly off. Cohen-Blind committed suicide in prison the next night.[53]

The double murder of Rosa Luxemburg and Karl Liebknecht was to institute a new era of political *rendements de compte*: the pacifist Paasche and the politicians Erzberger and Rathenau were the most prominent. Murder was the speciality of the right's lunatic fringe, and with time almost all these forces would gravitate towards the new Nazi move-

ment, which promised plenty of opportunities for punch-
ups and street violence as well as the occasional killing,
especially when there was an equal and opposite provocation
from communist street gangs. The problems were blown out
of all proportion by the spiral of unemployment after 1929.
In April 1932 there were already 603,000 out of work in
Berlin. In 1928 one in four Berlin votes had been for the
KPD, which controlled the working-class districts of
Wedding, Friedrichshain, Neukölln, Weißensee and Lichtenberg. That neither the Kozis nor the Nazis nor the
Conservatives had any time for the Weimar Republic was
bad enough, but there was also considerable resistance to it
within the police, especially among the *Sipos* or *Sicherheitspolizei* (paramilitary security police). The KPD was also
riddled with police spies.[54]

Goebbels was an excellent choice as Gauleiter for Berlin.
He had been on the left of the Nazi Party and had always
loathed capitalism, a resentment he fed during his years as a
student and a journalist. He could speak to the Berlin
workers in their own socialistic language. In February 1927
Goebbels went over to the attack, deciding to fight the
Communists on their own ground. The venue he selected
was the Pharussäle in Wedding's Müllerstraße.* This led to
the 'heroic' *Pharusschlacht*, or Battle of Pharus, which went
down in the annals of the movement in Berlin. Although
Goebbels didn't control the SA, he couldn't do without their
help in battles of this sort.[55]

The SA remained a thorn in his side. An attempt to
impose some sort of order on them proved a nightmare. The
Berlin leader, Walter Stennes, was not going to have his
authority undermined. When Hitler appointed a new leader
in the murderer Edmund Heines, Stennes denounced the

---

* The building still exists. It is now a snack-bar serving 'German
food'. The author has been unable to determine whether this has
any sinister significance in what is now a chiefly Turkish area.

Nazi chief and declared for Hitler's rival Otto Strasser. Stennes was one of the strange, maverick figures who found their way into the movement in the early years: a former police captain whose uncle was Archbishop of the Metropolitan See of Cologne. He later left Germany to become an advisor to Chang Kai Shek, and preserved his life during the Röhm *Putsch* as a result.[56]

Despite attempts to contain them within the movement itself, Nazi thugs launched some spectacularly nasty *coups* in the declining Weimar years, such as beating up the cinema crowd in December 1930; or rioting in the lecture halls of Berlin University in June 1931; or attacking groups of Jews leaving the Fasanenstraße Synagogue on 12 September 1931.[57] A substantial part of their activities still involved baiting communists, who responded. Things came to a head at 9 p.m. on 14 January 1930, when a Frau Salm walked into Der Bär, a communist bar in the Dragonerstraße by the Alexanderplatz. She lived at Große Frankfurterstraße 62, where she rented a room to a young Nazi called Horst Wessel. Frau Salm was cross that Wessel had moved in his lover, a former prostitute 'aus dem Milljöh'. Wessel had refused to double the rent he paid her. In the meantime the woman's presence clogged up her kitchen.[58]

The truth about Horst Wessel is hard to determine. During the Third Reich there were *nineteen* biographies of the Nazi 'martyr'. Streets, squares and whole districts were named after him. His 'song' (with music cribbed from Méhul's *Joseph*) became the official Nazi anthem. There has only been one biography since the war: *histoire romancée*, complete with recreated dialogues. What emerges, however, is a long way from the vindictive portrait left by Hans Bernd Gisevius, who said that Wessel and Höhler were two pimps fighting over the same whore. Wessel was a pastor's son from Westphalia who had attended the Graue Kloster before matriculating in the law faculty of the University. He joined the Normannia student corps and, in December 1926, the

NSDAP. He now threw himself into the 'struggle' heart and soul. He spent a semester at the University of Vienna, where he doubtless found many willing to hear the new gospel but Wessel none the less discovered that his creed struck the Viennese as being dangerously far to the left.[59]

Although he was a member of the SA, Wessel's talent lay more in public speaking than rioting. In 1929 he spoke fifty-six times, chiefly in Friedrichshain, the area that was to bear his name after 1933. He had dropped his studies to make a little money by working as a chauffeur, with the BVG or on building sites. When his brother met an accidental death the shock made him reconsider his life: he decided to leave the SA and rematriculate in a provincial university where there would be fewer distractions. In the course of his missionary activities he came across Erna Jänicke, who walked the streets around the 'Alex' and in the Münzstraße, as well as working the *Alexanderquelle* and the *Mexiko* in the Prenzlauerstraße. He reclaimed Erna, and made her his fiancée. In return she did a little spying on the district's communists for him.[60]

Frau Salm managed to convince Ali Höhler and the other communists in the bar that Wessel was a dangerous Nazi. Höhler was more of an underworld figure than an idealist. He had been a member of the *Ringverein* 'Immertreu', and had already done time for aggravated 'offences against property', pimping and perjury. He had served sixteen sentences in all, with one of two and a half years for living off immoral earnings. He and two friends repaired to the Große Hamburgerstraße, where they found Wessel closeted with Erna and another woman. They shot him in the mouth, snapping out the left artery and ripping out most of his tongue, and left him for dead.[61]

But Wessel didn't die immediately. The Nazis were not able to make much capital of it at first. The *Völkische Beobachter* failed to come up with a motive for the attack (given its banality, this isn't surprising). Goebbels, however, had a better idea. He wanted to turn Wessel into the movement's first fully-fledged martyr since those killed in the Beer Hall *Putsch*. And this one would be a Berliner with a special relevance to the capital. Wessel was still alive: 'There he lies, sitting up on his cushions,' wrote Goebbels, 'his face ripped apart. But you still recognise him immediately. Those eyes are the same: big, fixed, grey-blue. With difficulty he lifts his hand and gives it to me, saying, "We must keep going!"' A rare feat for a man with only a quarter of a tongue.[62]

In the meantime the police had located and arrested Höhler. Wessel gave up the struggle and Goebbels prepared for a show funeral, even inviting President Hindenburg, who made his excuses. The communists enlivened the funeral march by shying stones at the cortège and turning over a few escort cars. On the Nazi side it was a good turnout: the pastor's son from the Jüdengasse was seen off by Göring, Goebbels and Auwi von Preußen. His student caps from the Normannia in Berlin and the Alemannen in Vienna were tossed into the grave. Höhler got six years from a Weimar court.

Soon after they came to power, the Nazis tracked Höhler down to Wohlau Prison. They had him released. His body was later found in woods to the east of Berlin.[63] According to the former *Kripo*, or CID-man, Gisevius, one night in his cups Diels confessed that he had shot Höhler. When the car had stopped in the secluded woodland lane, Diels had asked Höhler if he knew what was going to happen to him: 'One of you is going to bump me off' was his reply.[64]

IV

As far as the Nazis were concerned the real fun had started eight months earlier. On 30 January Goebbels had written: 'It is almost like a dream. The Wilhelmstraße belongs to us. The Führer is already working in the Reich's Chancellery.'[65]

Now was the time for those little vendettas. After the torchlit procession, Hans Maikowski and SA-Sturm 33 paid a call on the Wallstraße (now the Zillestraße) in Charlottenburg. They wanted to show the local *Kozis* who was boss. The result was the first street battle of the Third Reich. In the fight both Maikowski and a policeman called Josef Zauritz were killed. The communists maintained that both had been killed by the SA, but that got them nowhere. There was a massive *razzia*. On 5 February both the dead men received a state funeral and two streets were renamed in their honour. The Zauritzweg is still there.[66]

The clamp-down was to be a foretaste of what was to happen after the Reichstag blaze. Up to 10,000 Communists and left-wingers were rounded up and taken to *ad hoc* torture chambers and prisons, the so-called 'wild' concentration camps.* Rudolf Diels described the treatment meted out to anyone unfortunate enough to find himself in a 'wild' KZ. The men were beaten with iron bars, rubber truncheons and whips. Most had broken bones and teeth: 'When we came in, these living skeletons lay in rows with festering wounds on soiled straw. There was not one of them whose body did not betray from head to foot the blue, yellow and green signs of inhuman beatings . . . The sight of this hell reduced the police to silence. Neither Hieronymus Bosch nor Peter Brueghel [the elder] ever glimpsed such horror.'[67]

In June 1933 there was another battle in communist Köpenick. In the course of a week-long *razzia* the Nazis killed ninety-one people and dropped their bodies into the Dahme.[68] Of course, the most famous persecution was that of the Jews. There was nothing new here. As early as 1405, Berlin had gone through its first murderous bout of anti-Semitism when Jews were accused of buying and selling Christian boys. In 1466 they were banished, but the order

---

* The first large-scale camp in the Berlin area was opened in Oranienburg on the *Tag von Potsdam*, 21 March 1933.

doesn't seem to have been enforced. In 1510, there was a curious occurrence in Ketzin in the Havelland. A monstrance was stolen from the church together with a container with two consecrated hosts. The evidence pointed to Paul Fromm from Bernau, who confessed to the crime, saying at first that he had swallowed both hosts. Later he changed his tune and said he had swallowed only one, and sold the other to the Jew Salomo in Spandau. Under torture (which was still legal then in Brandenburg), Salomo admitted to having stabbed the host repeatedly with a knife, and that it had broken into *three* pieces, but that he was not able to swallow, destroy or wash away any of them. Further pressure was brought to bear on Salomo, who then admitted baking one of the bits into a matzo and leaving it in the synagogue in Spandau. The other bits he packed up and sent to his coreligionaries Jakob in Brandenburg and Markus in Stendal.[69]

Jakob thought he was cleverer than Salomo. He quickly claimed to have had a vision of the BVM and asked to be baptised immediately. His pleas fell on deaf ears. He too was tortured. He then admitted that he had attacked his fragment of the host together with the rabbi Slomann and his two sons. The rabbi and his sons then confirmed Jakob's story, adding that their fragment of the host had been produced at a Jewish wedding feast, where it had started to bleed. Another twenty-four Jews were found to be involved in this bizarre case.[70] The Stendal piece had been despatched to Brunswick. Later the number of those arrested rose to fifty-one. Thirty-eight of these, and Paul Fromm, were burned at the stake. Ten are presumed to have died under torture. Three saved their lives by converting to Christianity.[71]

In 1573 the 'court Jew' Lippold also went through a grisly execution. The Jews were promptly banished from the Mark. The ban lasted for the best part of a century. These were the last scenes of barbaric anti-Semitism in Berlin until the end of the nineteenth century. Before the Enlightenment altered perspectives on the Jews, they were treated as something of a joke, no more. On 24 November 1752 the Prince of Prussia attended a fancy-dress party in Grunewald disguised as a Jew. It must have been a successful costume, for little more than a year later, in January 1754, Lehndorff and various members of the court dressed up as Jews to amuse the Prince, even transforming one of the rooms in Prince Henry's palace into a synagogue for the occasion.[72]

Modern anti-Semitism was connected with two things: the shady financiers of the 'Gründerkrach' – the collapse of the market which followed on from the boom created by French millions after 1871 – and the increasing number of so-called *Ostjuden*: Polish and Russian Jews who converged on the capital after the eastern pogroms. The first Berliner in modern times to make anti-Semitism into an issue was Adolf Stöcker. Stöcker came from a poor family from the Harz Mountains and studied for the Church. In 1874 he had the luck to meet Kaiser William in Metz, who appointed him Court Preacher in Berlin. Stöcker's original objectives did not look so bad: he wanted to relieve the widespread poverty he saw around him and bring Berliners back into the churches. Only about a third were still practising Christians and more than half their children were not even baptised. In 1878 Stöcker created the Christlich-soziale Arbeiterpartei. It was not a great success. In 1878 it received 1,421 votes to the Socialists' 56,000.[73]

Three years later he dropped the word 'worker' from his party's name and introduced anti-Semitism to the programme. He was elected to the Reichstag for the first time in 1880, and, with a five-year interruption, sat until 1908. By 1880 he was the 'uncrowned King of Berlin'. Government circles eyed him with suspicion. They were keen to keep the patriotic Jews on their side. In 1885, William I tried to remove him from office, but his grandson came to his defence. William II changed his mind in 1890 and dropped him, allowing him only to continue with his 'Berlin Mission'. His influence remained a flash in the pan. In academic circles Treitschke was a powerful force. The Jews were Germany's misfortune, he argued. They arrived from over the border 'from their inexhaustible Polish cradle', 'a troupe of pushy, trouser-peddling youths whose children and grand-children will one day rule Germany's stock exchanges and newspapers'. It was something of the tenor of Gustav Frey-tag's best-selling novel *Soll und Haben* of 1855 (although that novel contains *good* Jews and *bad* Christians). Treitschke's arguments were not meant 'racially'. He felt Jews formed a foreign community within the new Germany and should convert, and become German. Walter Rathenau, a Jew, thought much the same.[74]

It was the same phenomenon throughout central and western Europe in the late nineteenth and early twentieth centuries. The arrival of armies of *Ostjuden* led to an upsurge of anti-Semitism at popular level. In French North Africa there were pogroms, not to mention the social upheaval caused by the Panama scandal and the Dreyfus case. In Austria the politicians Karl Lueger and Georg von Schönerer made it an election issue and fed the mind of the young Adolf Hitler. Even Alfred Döblin, himself a Jew from Stettin, was uneasy about the *Ostjuden*. In 1923 he witnessed ugly scenes developing in the Dragonerstraße. The police had cordoned off the street, 'the headquarters of the *Ostjuden*. A crowd was gathering. Most of them couldn't care less about anti-Semitism. They just want plunder.'[75]

It was a far cry from the deeply civilised world of the assimilated Berlin Jews, like the Rathenaus, whose culture was one hundred per cent German. The shock of 1933 must have been felt most keenly in these circles, where religious observance had dwindled away to a few feast days a year at the very most, and where there were those who had bled on the battlefields for Kaiser and country.[76] Some of these became 'Naumann Juden': members of Max Naumann's Verband national deutsches Juden which advocated the expulsion of the *Ostjuden*. Naumann went so far as to say they were racially inferior to German Jews and lent his support to the Nazis after 1929.[77] The cries of 'Deutschland erwache! Juda verrecke!' ('Germany awake! Death to the Jews!'), however, had been heard by every Berlin Jew who understood German. For the richer and more prominent Jews, the answer was emigration. By 1939 about two-thirds had left. Not so the poor Jews. It was they who bore the brunt of the Final Solution.[78]

The first Jewish martyr of the Third Reich in Berlin was Siegbert Kindermann, an apprentice baker who was beaten to death in the Hedemannstraße because he complained to the police that the Nazis had attacked him.[79] A certain number died in the 'wild' KZs, such as the lawyer Günther Joachim; the notary Kurt Lange, whose body was found floating in the Wannsee; the trader Moritz Anfang; the nephew of the owner of the *Berliner Tageblatt*, Hans Lachmann-Mosse; and the writer Arthur Landsberger. As soon as Oranienburg was opened, there was a 'Judenkompagnie'. On 1 April 1933 came the 'universal Jewish boycott', which most Berliners boycotted. It took Goebbels five years before he felt strong enough to try it again.[80] The day before, the SA had appeared before the dock in Moabit to have all Jewish members of the legal profession thrown out,[81] a measure which could only cause rejoicing among the small minority of non-Jews pleading at the courts.

On 7 April the ban was made official when all Jews were sacked from the civil service and the judiciary. Now a special pass was necessary. The medical profession had already been 'cleaned up' at the end of March. On 4 April 1933 the *Völkische Beobachter* chose to highlight the unworthiness of Jewish doctors by accusing them of having perpetual lusty thoughts about Aryan women. Jews were linked to 'the filthiest erotic literature', by the 'stifling air of big city nightclubs, from the repulsive randiness of modern nigger music . . . the inflammatory productions of Jewish film concerns, public and private scandals . . .' Finally the Jews were accused of using beauty competitions in order to grope Aryan women. If the Jewish doctors were in any doubt how the regime felt about them, on 7 July they were rounded up by their SA colleagues and invited to 'a little breakfast at Police Headquarters'.[82]

On 9 November 1938 came the 'Reichskristallnacht', when party members whipped up by Goebbels pretended to give a spontaneous demonstration against the Jews for the murder in Paris of the German diplomat vom Rath. The synagogues were put to the flame and Jewish businesses wrecked. Erich Kästner was travelling in a taxi along the Tauentzienstraße and the Kurfürstendamm. On both sides of the road men were breaking-in shop fronts with iron bars. 'They were SS men with black breeches and jackboots, but wearing civilian jackets and hats.' They went about their work calmly and systematically, each seeming to have been allotted about five shops. There appeared to be no one on the streets; only the next day did he hear that barmaids, night waiters and prostitutes had looted the shops.[83]

'I had the driver stop three times. Three times I tried to get out. Three times a policeman came out from behind a tree and delivered a peremptory "Criminal Police!" Three times the car door was slammed. Three times we drove on. When I wanted to get out a fourth time, the cabbie refused. "What's the point," he said, "and apart from everything else it constitutes resistance against the power of the state!" He didn't stop until we had reached the door to my block of flats.'[84]

Once the war started, the screws were tightened on the Jews. Their goods were confiscated and they were obliged to wear yellow Stars of David. The first transports to the assembly camp at Theresienstadt took place before the Wannsee Conference, when 70,000 Jews were shipped out in the autumn of 1941.[85] The maximum financial advantage was taken of them. They were given fifteen minutes to pack. Then the remaining contents were auctioned off in the flat.

Often bargain-hunters saw abandoned cups still filled with coffee.[86]

The Jewish *Kultusgemeinde* or welfare organisation played a tragic role in it all, selecting which Jews were to go. Even so it was thought that both they and the Berlin police were not moving fast enough. A year after the first deportations Alois Brunner was summoned from Vienna to show them how to do things.[87] He brought with him a special force of deportation police, the so-called *Jupos*. The *Kultusgemeinde* had no choice but to obey. If a transport was short, the *Jupos* shot the same number of officials. In January the 29,000 Jews working in Berlin industry were replaced by Poles, and they too were shipped out.[88]

By 1943 just 27,000 Jews remained in Berlin. Goebbels redoubled his efforts: he wanted to offer Hitler a birthday present of a Berlin completely *free of Jews*. Among those rounded up were 7,000 Jews who had married Gentiles before the ban on mixed marriages was imposed in 1935. The two thousand men married to Gentile women were used as forced labour until they were arrested *en masse* on 27 February and taken to an assembly point in the city centre. When their husbands failed to return from work, the wives descended on the Rosenstraße. They were mostly middle-class women and knew that the police were acting illegally. The women staged a sit-in outside the building where the men were interned, shouting: 'Gebt uns unsere Männer wieder!' ('Give us back our husbands!') They stayed in spite of the air raid which hit Berlin on 1 March, and despite the bitter weather. In desperation, machine-guns were mounted on the roof of the building. The women chimed 'Murderers!' Wehrmacht soldiers joined in the protest, as did Party members.

Goebbels was alarmed. Morale was low. The shouting was so loud that he was obliged to close Börse *U-Bahn* station nearby. Up to now the deportations had been carried out quietly, early in the morning. Goebbels feared that his entire policy might be disrupted. Shooting 2,000 Aryan women was not calculated to make administering the city easier and he ordered the men's release. It was discovered, however, that twenty-five of the men had already been shipped off to the east. The women continued their protest outside the Gestapo building in the Burgstraße. The unthinkable happened: they were brought back from the jaws of death. The men were sent to a labour camp at Großbeeren, where their wives could visit them. With the other 2,000 they survived the war.[89]

About another 1,500 Jews also survived through Gentile help. These were the so-called *U-Boote*, or submarines. They wandered permanently from place to place looking for hideouts. One recalls envying the crocodiles at the Zoo (he would have changed his mind after November 1943). Another said that it was comparatively easy to disappear once the city was wrecked, providing you had friends to provide you with food.[90]

The most famous monument to the deportation of not just Berlin's but all the European Jews is the Villa Minoux in Wannsee, a neo-classical mansion built for Geheimrat Ernst Marlier in 1914 by Paul Baumgarten, a student of Messel's. Minoux was a crooked businessman with political connections, who came close to achieving office under Chancellors Marx and Stresemann. The Nazis fined him 600,000 marks and put him in prison for fraud. His house was acquired for the SD. The idea of holding the Wannsee Conference there was that it would prove an attractive venue for the various civil servants involved. The meeting was chaired by Göring to find out what progress had been made in the 'Final Solution' – not to plan it: it was already in motion. The conference took place for two hours, then there was lunch. Eichmann took the minutes.[91]

V

The First World War not only precipitated the 1918 Revolution, it plunged Germany into the soul-destroying experience of inflation which rotted away the moral core of the middle classes. Much is familiar now. A *U-Bahn* ticket on 16 July 1923 cost 3,000 RMs. By the 30th it had risen to 6,000. On 6 August it was 10,000; two weeks later, 50,000. On 20 August, 100,000. On 21 September the milliard note was introduced. By then there were 360,000 unemployed, and 150,000 income-supported short-term workers.[92] There were always people who could pay the prices, particularly foreigners, who found Berlin rather fun. In one of the city's many dens of vice, a bottle of *Sekt* cost three-quarters of a milliard on 4 October – the equivalent of 15 pounds of butter, and butter was a luxury item. A pound of beef for roasting was 24m. RMs. On 14 October the bread ration was stopped because the cost of printing the cards had become too inflated. The people took to robbing bakers – always the most hated members of society when the chips are down. The cost of a 2,000-gram loaf had reached a milliard on 20 October. Two days later it was 2.5; on the 23rd, 5.5; the next, 7.5. AEG responded by paying a percentage of workers' salaries in bread.[93]

Inflation transformed Berlin society even more radically than the war had done. Savings were for nought. Unless you had land and could hang on to it there was little you could do. Everyone was on the fiddle. Crime was everywhere. Gambling was endemic. The best clubs were very well equipped, with their own hairdressing salon, bath and sitting-out rooms. Visitors to illegal clubs were treated to a three-course, candle-lit meal before being ushered to the gaming tables. The most notorious of these were the Harmonie in the Kantstraße in Charlottenburg and the Eintracht in the Joachimsthalerstraße nearby, the Berliner Rennsport in the

Augsburgerstraße and the Klub Neuberlin in the Bülow-straße.[94]

When inflation hit its highest point it was discovered that Post Office employees were robbing packages in the central post office. Butter was a useful commodity if you had relations who were farming folk. A pound bought you a month of music or elocution lessons, a pair of trousers, a small library of books, a painting, or a course of treatment for the flu. Bodies were occasionally sold for butter. *Hamstern*, or scrumping, came closer to pillaging. Parties of Berliners went out to the country to steal potatoes from the fields, but they didn't stop there. Often they literally went the whole hog, and took a pig, wrapping it up in old clothes. A *Gendarm* asking what such a package might be was told, '*Ach*, my grandmother is ill. We wanted to take her to the hospital.' On 30 October Döblin told his readers of a tragedy that had occurred on one of these scrumping expeditions, when a child was killed and another badly injured. The scavengers were hard to police because ostensibly they came only to glean what they could *after* the farmer had brought in his harvest.[95]

Heirlooms changed hands. The story ran that 'Raffke the Crook' wanted to possess a Rubens. The price was quoted at a 100m. RMs. 'You must be joking! For a second-hand painting!' Profiteering went on everywhere. Even the Kaiser's homosexual son Eitel Fritz was arrested for it. After complaints, the health authorities stepped in to examine the contents of Berlin sausages. There was a persistent rumour that they contained human flesh. This turned out to be unfounded. There was a small amount of dog or cat in some. Goat sausages were generally made of venison, mutton or pork. Horse sausages actually turned out to be beef, with some venison and rabbit. Sausage-makers were obviously scouring the country with rifles.[96]

It was a paradise for foreigners, especially foreign homosexuals. Men who had trouble paying the rent at home lived

like millionaires in Berlin. On a minor diplomatic salary one
lived like a king. Unter den Linden looked like 'Babel during
the time they were building the tower'. Cocaine was one
of the little extras; the women came virtually free. A foreigner visited a *Kaschemme* or criminal dive near the Alex.
He scattered money on the floor and then shouted that only
naked women were allowed to pick it up. 'Some of the girls
looked coy, but a fat, older woman quickly decided to drop
her blouse, skirt and petticoat and fall on her knees to grab
up the coins; then plenty of the other girls stripped off
quickly and, in a state of nature, rummaged around for the
gold.' The landlord was philosophic: 'Yes, what do you want?
The girls must work all day long to earn a cent – *Jeld schmeckt
süß* [money tastes sweet] – dollars above all.'[97]

In 1919 a reserve lieutenant and his wife had been caught
performing live sex in the Motzstraße. Among the members
of the audience they found a pastor. The most famous naked
dancer of her time was Josephine Baker. Kessler met her late
in February 1926, when Max Reinhardt rang him after
dinner one day and told him to come round 'because the
fun was starting . . . Reinhardt and Huldschinsky were surrounded by half a dozen naked girls. Miss Baker was also
naked except for a pink muslin apron, and the little Landshof
girl (a niece of Sammy Fischer) was dressed up like a boy
in a dinner-jacket.' Kessler described Josephine Baker as 'a
bewitching creature, but almost quite unerotic. Watching her
inspires as little sexual excitement as does the sight of a
beautiful beast of prey. The naked girls lay or skipped about
among the four or five men in dinner-jackets.' Later Kessler
got the dancer round to his flat, where he explained his ideas
for a ballet for her. She seemed more interested in doing a
double act with one of the collector's Maillols.[98]

Kessler's interest was possibly aesthetic, but that was not
always the case. The fashion for 'naked dancing' had been
started by Olga Desmond before the war. Nudity came into
its own after the conflict. Dancing and gymnastics were

considered healthier performed in the nude.* Naked soirées were organised on flimsy pretexts.[99]

With so many men dead in the war, women adopted a new approach to life. Children were left to their own devices, and grew up quickly. One complained there were no more 'Gretchens, Trudchens and Lenchens . . . Now they are all Margaretes, Gertrudes and Helenes. At fifteen they are ladies.' Peter Panter (Tucholsky) deconstructed the title of a contemporary song, *Wir versaufen unserer Oma ihr klein Häuschen*: 'We, the singers, are firmly convinced that we want to turn our esteemed grandmother's property, in particular, her house, into money, and the accruing sum we should like to invest in alcoholic beverages.'[100]

VI

There were times when the Berliner was overjoyed by the news of victory on the battlefield. When the news arrived from Prague on 9 May 1757 Lehndorff reported the people 'full of joy, but also worried about the losses'. On the 15th, 6,000 people made their way to the church to sing a *Te Deum*.[101] The Wars of Liberation gave rise to tremendous enthusiasm with the higher classes of the schools emptying as the boys rushed off to Breslau to join up.

Similar scenes not only greeted news of war in the 1860s, but also 1914. Hitler's war, however, was different. The prospect of empty bellies once again did not please the materialistic Berliner. There were tears, some of them of joy too, when the soldiers returned from the French campaign in 1940.[102] When the Scandinavian campaign had started a few weeks before, however, the American Howard Smith

---

* The argument has been used elsewhere. At the author's school, boys were obliged to swim in the nude for 'health reasons'. It was not, however, considered erotic, except possibly by the masters.

had overheard one Berliner tell another that German troops had marched into Norway. '*Ja*, Denmark too,' said the other, taking the cigarette out of his mouth. After Stalingrad the mood changed to resignation: 'If Germany loses they will murder all Germans.'[103]

The war encroached gradually on the lives of ordinary Berliners. The ban on dancing was lifted on 30 September 1939. After that, the city was as wild as it had been in the time of the 'System', as the Nazis called Weimar, with plenty of nudity on stage, *Negermusik* and American films to watch.[104] While the going was good, there was even a certain jealousy of the soldiers, who ate better than the civilians and always seemed to be packing their rucksacks with fine things.[105] After the beginning of Barbarossa, the Russian campaign, that all changed and there was a sharp drop in volunteers. The Nazis were aware of the Berliner's obsession with material comforts and devised a system of treats while they could still manage it: *Führerpakete* contained schnapps and cigarettes.[106]

Barbarossa changed the atmosphere in the city. There was no more fuel for unofficial cars. Café life on the Kurfürstendamm dried up. There were long queues for potatoes, turnips and cabbages. *Ersatzersatz* was back. The butchers were given permission to mix sausage meat with vegetables and rye.[107]

If shortages and losses in the field didn't do it, air raids brought the war home to the Berliner. The first raid happened before the war started; on 26 July 1939 there was a simulated air attack on Berlin. The press reported: 'Berlin is armed.' The first enemy aircraft to reach Berlin were Polish. No one noticed them, but they managed to set off the sirens.[108] On 25 August 1940 the British dropped 22 tons of explosive on Reinickendorf, Pankow and Lichtenberg. The flak was successful at keeping them out of the centre. There were seven more *Störangriffe* ('disturbance raids') that year. One of these managed to kill twelve people in the Kotbusser-straße. It proved an excuse for a dramatic funeral procession.[109]

On 29 September came 'Bomber' Harris's famous directive to bomb thickly populated areas and cause as much material damage as possible. By the end of the year there had been twenty-seven raids, bombs had hit the Schloss, the Cathedral, the Arsenal and the Altes Museum. On 8 October they hit the Charité. The tally for 1940 was 515 killed, 1,617 severely damaged buildings and 11,142 badly damaged ones. The population was so far more irritated than alarmed, especially as there was a great deal of pillage after the raids. One man reported a strange corpse at a friend's house after an attack. They concluded it was a thief who had been surprised by a second wave of bombers. Another friend, whose house had been only partially destroyed, lost all his clothes, wine, schnapps and cigarettes.[110]

Harris's attacks were getting more accurate. There were only thirty-one alarms in 1941, but he managed to wipe out the Potsdamer Platz, killing 100 people in one house alone. In 1942 that number declined to nine; British losses had been too great and there was a shortage of Lancaster bombers to carry out the task.[111] In 1943 the Americans joined in with 'area bombing'. On the night of 1–2 March aerial mines killed 700, not including the first victims among the animal inmates of the Zoo. Berliners took a sidelong glance at Hamburg that summer where Harris's bombs had levelled 25 square kilometres and left 30,000 dead. They had an inkling what was coming to them.

Berlin had an advantage over the older towns and cities of Germany in that it was not made of wood and had wide streets. It was hard for Harris and his staff to create the firestorms which had been so effective in the mediaeval centres of Hamburg, Cologne, Lübeck and Rostock (to name but four). Still, in September he took out 1.5 square kilometres of Berlin, with bombs falling on the centre, Marienfelde, Lichterfelde and Siemensstadt.[112] Harris's planes used the eastern lake of Müggelsee to guide them, which often meant they dropped their bombs on the suburbs.[113] The Anglo-Americans (as they were called) were getting the hang of things. This was the beginning of the 'Battle of Berlin' which lasted from 18–19 November 1943 to mid-March 1944. In the big raids which rocked Berlin at the end of November and the beginning of December 1943 they killed 8,000, and totally destroyed nearly 70,000 buildings, leaving 250,000 Berliners homeless.[114]

The next year saw innovations in the bombing campaign. The American Flying Fortresses were seen over Berlin, as well as British Mosquitoes. The name was the *mot juste*: the aircraft caused more disturbance than damage, especially at night. In the first three months of the year attacks killed another 6,166 and reduced a further 9.5 square kilometres to rubble. After the summer, when the Allies were concentrating on their efforts in France, the big raids returned in October. From February 1945 it 'continued almost without a break'. Those who lived through those February days will never forget the sight of refugees burning like human torches on the tarmac of the Wilhelmstraße. What was left by the Anglo-Americans was generally destroyed by the Russian advance. The total dead from bombing in Berlin is estimated at 50,000. Twenty-eight square kilometres of the city were destroyed, including 39 per cent of all buildings and 612,000 flats. Bombs tore out 70 per cent of the centre, wiped out 58 per cent of Tiergarten, Schöneberg and Friedenau and 25 per cent of Spandau. In his aptly named post-war *apologia*, *Bomber Offensive*, Arthur Harris gives the slightly lower figure of 6,427 acres, with the American daylight raids accounting for 1,000 of these. In the course of the battle he lost 300 planes: 6.4 per cent of the total.

The Nazis built huge concrete bunkers which proved impregnable to the bombs. They were well-appointed. In the Zoo bunker you could even have your hair done while you waited for the end of the raid. The walls were so thick that little could be heard from outside. The shock came when the Berliners emerged to see everything around them in flames: even the trees in the Tiergarten. Teams were on hand to help those who had been bombed out. Free coffee and bread and *Leberwurst* rolls were handed out to victims. Naturally such events couldn't help but sap morale. Pictures of mutilated corpses, children in particular, accompanied German visitors to neutral cities, and clearly had an effect on public opinion there.[115] In Berlin, at least, there was little talk of lynching pilots, although there was evidence of this elsewhere.[116]

The same men who took pictures of Harris's victims made their own attempt to end the war in July 1944. At 7 a.m. on the 20th Claus Stauffenberg and Werner von Haeften left Stauffenberg's Wannsee flat for Rangsdorf, whence they flew to Rastenburg in East Prussia. The story of that heroic failure has been told elsewhere: Stauffenberg's bomb proved too small to do the job. The colonel none the less left the scene of the explosion convinced that Hitler was dead, and launched the *coup* in Berlin. It is not known where he landed (Rangsdorf or Gatow), but he didn't arrive back at military headquarters in the Bendlerstraße until 4.30 p.m.; some of his fellow plotters had dithered and doubted and precious time had been lost. While the Bendlerstraße seethed with indecision, conspirators in the Foreign Office building in the Wilhelmstraße watched the street for signs that the necessary orders had been issued. When the streets were cordoned off, they believed that all had gone according to plan. Then the pickets were relieved. A siege of the Bendlerstraße was carried out after Goebbels talked round the officer commanding the Guards battalion, Major Remer. The main conspirators, including Stauffenberg and Haeften, were shot that night in the arclights of a lorry in the Bendlerstraße quadrangle. Around two hundred others were executed over the next few months.[117]

VII

Berlin had been invaded before. The Swedes had scorched it in the Thirty Years' War. Perhaps the most shaming conquest of all was the arrival of the Austrians in the city in 1757 while Frederick the Great's back was turned in Bohemia. Following on from the news of Prussian victory in Prague, the governor, General von Rochow, failed to take reports of the approaching army seriously. When news came that the Austrian soldiers under General Hadik were before the Kotbusser Tor, the court fled to Spandau. Hadik had only a tiny force with him and was easily paid off with 250,000 thalers. In the meantime Spandau proved an uncomfortable refuge for the court. Lehndorff reported scenes 'worthy of an inn'. Frederick the Great's 'Mütterchen', Gräfin Camas, sat on her *chaise percée* before the whole court. 'Little children,' she shouted, 'louder. I'm trying to rid myself of this wind, which is making me feel uncomfortable.'[118]

The Austrians had ransacked Charlottenburg, smashing the antique marbles, and plundered the Linden. Various Berliners took advantage of the vacuum and joined in. They beat a Herr von Bredow black-and-blue, robbed the Dutch consul, Graf Schwerin, and killed a Herr von Stosch by kicking him down the stairs. When order was restored it proved hard to protect Rochow from the mob. It had been discovered that there were almost four times as many troops in the garrison as Austrian invaders. Lehndorff visited the Köpernicker Tor, where the walls were still stained with soldiers' blood. The towns of Köpenick and Potsdam had resisted Hadik manfully, but not Berlin.

Three years later Berlin was briefly occupied for a second time. Russians under General von Tottleben shelled the city from the Hasenheide. Austrians were garrisoned in the Friedrichstadt, where they wrecked as much as they could during their short stay, defenestrating every portrait of the king they could find.[119]

The French came next. In October 1806 Davout had the honour of being the first to enter Berlin. Fürst Hatzfeld and Police Director Busching waited for him at the Halleschen Tor with the keys to the city. Napoleon had gone to Potsdam to look at the tomb of Frederick the Great. The city was actually occupied by General Augereau, who had served as an NCO in Frederick's armies, although he managed to pick up no German in the process. The Berliners were not impressed by their wig-less conquerors with their ragged uniforms, who smoked in the streets, and who exacted plenty of food and drink for their victory celebrations.[120]

A citizens' committee was formed to administer the city under the Intendant Bignon. General Clarke was made governor of the Electoral Mark. On that fateful day, 9 November, all Berlin's public servants had to swear an oath of loyalty to the French invader. His soldiers camped in the Tiergarten until a more solid 'Napoleonburg' was built above Köpenick. As in 1757, the Berliners put up a poor show of resistance. Only one minister, Graf von Redern, made a fuss about the oath; the others were happy to assent. That they wrote their names illegibly, and that someone negligently tipped a pot of ink over the document later, did not prevent Frederick William from sacking the lot of them once he was back in the saddle.[121]

Zelter complained of needing to feed so many hungry mouths garrisoned in his house, and of incessant theft. Others, like the prostitutes, found the French a useful source of income. Many Berliners collaborated. A pro-French press was established to report the Corsican's victories. There was a little display of patriotism from Iffland, who was sent to prison for praising Queen Louise on stage. The malcontents gathered in the salon of Henriette Herz, where the romantic movement forged their resentment of the French invasion into the first lance of German nationalism. The French took over Spandau when a Major von Beneckendorff (Hindenburg's family) yielded up the citadel without a fight. In 1813 they had to be literally blown out of it.[122] Everywhere the poor turn-out of Napoleon's troops appalled the Berliners; most seemed to have lost half their equipment and what they retained was in a shocking state of repair.[123]

This time the Russians came as liberators (they called themselves that in 1945, but few believed them then). On 21 February 1813 about 300 Cossacks closed in on Berlin, threw open the gates and shot down a number of French soldiers. The French restored control, camping in the streets that night. There were 12,000 French soldiers in the city; the Cossacks were camped on the hills outside. Yet it was peaceful: 'In the evenings you can hear the dogs barking.'

On 11 March the French withdrew and the main Russian army arrived, led by Graf (later Fürst) Ludwig Adolf Peter zu Sayn-Wittgenstein. The populace cheered the Russian troops for five and a quarter hours while they made their slow progress from the Alex to the Schloss.[124] Berlin had a new governor, Major von Juny, a Muscovite who 'spoke really good German'.[125] The city was not free from risk until General von Bülow secured the victory at Großbeeren. It proved the greatest moment for seven long years. No one went to the Stralauer Fischzug that year, but picnicked among the shattered, naked corpses at Großbeeren. An attempt by Ney to retake Berlin was easily beaten back at Dennewitz: 'I am soundly thrashed,' he said. On 21 September came the news from Leipzig. It was all over.[126]

It was not the same in 1945. The Soviet armies descended on a city of corpses. The Germans are rightly reproached for their barbarity in the last war, but it should be borne in mind how inured they had become to death. A traveller changing trains in Königs Wusterhausen, on the south-eastern limits of the city, found a train filled with frozen bodies. The refugees had died of the cold on their way from Silesia. Once the Russians arrived there were bodies everywhere, and no coffins to be had to bury them.[127] A British officer arriving in Berlin that summer remembers the large number of corpses floating in one of the fashionable lakes in the west. He had been told they were all women who had committed suicide after being raped by the Russians.

The Russians had been stirred up by the likes of Ilya Ehrenburg (a former denizen of 'Charlottengrad') to commit whatever bestial acts they pleased. There is no doubt that the violence was officially sanctioned. When the fighting ceased, there was an orgy of robbery: watches ripped from Berliners' wrists, drink and bicycles, which most of them couldn't ride – something that gave rise to comic scenes on the Berlin streets as the Russians took tumble after tumble.[128]

It is said that the soldiers behaved better in the working-class parts of Berlin than they did in the more affluent west. Also a knowledge of Russian saved some Berliners from rape, butchery or both. The journalist Margret Boveri discovered a sadly common scene when she went to see her friends the Manholts in Dahlem. The wife, Elsbeth, had been raped three times and fled across the street to a neighbour. There, in a dark passage, three more men fell on her. One smashed in her teeth, while another hit her with an iron bar, opening a hole in her skull. In her own house her husband Bob had been beaten black-and-blue and her daughter raped.

> When they went back to the Giese house at three in
> the morning they heard whimpering coming from
> the cellar: Frau Giese and her four lovely daughters, a
> Frau von Sydow and her daughter were hanging in
> the cellar. In the middle of the scene a Russian lay
> snoring.

The women had naturally been raped before they were killed. The four girls were aged between eight and fourteen.[129]★

Rape became such a commonplace that the women began

★ Margret Boveri records one instance of American soldiers also brutally raping a woman.[130]

to joke about it. A neighbour, Frau Holsten, recounted her experiences to Margret Boveri, laughing at the inexperience of the young soldier and the speed with which it was all over. Later another came: 'I Russian officer, not fucky-fucky.' He was kind to her, taught her some Russian, ate with them and slept in her bed, comforting the woman by pressing her hand when she took fright at the shooting outside. Then in the middle of the night, came the 'fucky-fucky'.[131]

There was a good deal of gallows humour:

> Our language is peppered with expressions gleaned
> from our darlings [sic]: 'Urr, Urr' when anyone is
> foolish enough to let his watch be seen in public. 'Frau
> komm' or 'Frau komm mit' ('Woman come' or
> 'Woman, come with') in a coarse tone with rolling
> 'r's. 'Du lügst' ('You're lying') caps every answer during
> interrogations. 'Du gesund?' ('You healthy?'), and for
> every affirmative response: 'Ich syphilis' ('I
> syphilis').[132]

Venereal disease added to the unpleasantness of life in immediate post-war Berlin, especially as the medicines needed to cure it were not forthcoming. There was an epidemic of abortion as women shed their 'Russenbabys'. It was said that Stalin had forbidden it, because he wanted to ensure the 'Slavification' of the population in this way.[133]

A few months earlier, the last reserves of Hitler's armies had perished in a futile last stand on the heights to the east of the city. On the streets the SS indulged their blood-lust in senseless acts of savagery. A professor who tried to throw his Nazi uniform into the Lietzensee had his throat cut; beside his body they daubed 'Traitor'.[134] Men hung from the street lamps as a result of summary executions. The political prisoners, some of the last survivors from 20 July 1944 among them, were released from their cells and torture chambers and taken out into the ruins of the city, where they were despatched with a single shot in the back of the head. One of the last to go was the intellectual Albrecht Haushofer. He thought he was being released and gathered up the sonnets he had written in captivity. The poems lay beside his mangled corpse.

> Wir alle wissen wohl daß unsre Leben
> so billig sind wie Stroh – der deutsche Strick
> die Russen Kugel jählings in Genick,
> die Briten Bomben sind als Los gegeben . . .[135]

> (We all know far too well that our little lives
> Are as cheap as dirt – the German gibbet,
> Sudden impact of a Russian bullet,
> British bombs are our fate, none of us survives.)

Not far away in his bunker in the Voßstraße stood the man who had brought it all about, surrounded by the last remnants of his gang, those 'flatulent clowns' who worshipped him to the end, while he fulminated in impotent fury against the German people and prepared to take his own life. The city he had stolen for a capital lay in its shattered remains all around.

> Was in Jahrhunderten gewachsen war,
> vernichtet nun in Stunden jäh die Kraft
> gewissenlos mißbrauchter Wissenschaft.[136]

> (What required whole centuries to construct,
> Now in a bare instant is destroyed.
> Misused, evil science creates a void.)

Epilogue

I had only three skirmishes with the old capital of the DDR, and then only when the regime was on its last legs. I had come to Berlin to research an earlier book, and the work took me to Dahlem in the bottom left-hand corner of West Berlin. With its leafy gardens and solid villas it was as normal and prosperous-looking a place as you could hope to see. I learned how to make the journey day after day from my crummy *pension* on the Lietzenburgerstraße. Time was too short for much exploration, but one day I managed to escape. After watching a lunatic haranguing the border guards from an observation platform by the Brandenburg Gate, I walked down to Checkpoint Charlie. The crossing was manned by British soldiers that day. I asked if I could just walk across. 'Are you in any way connected with the Services, sir?' I was not. The Russian on the other side was not so polite. I changed my 25 DMs for 25 useless *Ostmarks* and I arrived in Berlin-Mitte.

It is hard now to rid my memory of the gloss acquired from subsequent visits. Much has changed in such a short time. The city was empty and gloomy. I was most impressed by the tracts of ruined buildings north of the Linden, and the crumbling Biedermeier houses of the Scheunenviertel. I found no use for my *Ostmarks*. When I came again in the summer of 1989 I was more adventurous. I even sat down to lunch in a dull little place by the Marienkirche and ate a dish of *Teufelsfleisch* (literally 'devil's meat'). I was denied coffee.

After my unlovely lunch I went back to the Scheunen-

viertel. I noticed that restoration had begun on the Sophienstraße, and in a small pocket around the old Schillertheater
in the Friedrich-Wilhelmstadt. I struck up a conversation
with a man in a bar. He was aware that there were changes
taking place. Some businesses were being privatised. He took
me on a little walk and showed me a few sights. We even
went to look at the tomb of his hero, Bert Brecht.

The 'change' took me by surprise in Bourg-en-Bresse,
where I had gone to work on quite another project. I sat
impotently in my room at the Hôtel de France and watched
the queues of *Trabis* at the frontier on the television; the
revelling Berliners were popping *Sekt* corks on the Wall and
I wished I'd been there too. I didn't get to Berlin until New
Year's Eve. I had travelled up from Vienna on the train,
stopping in Prague, Dresden and Leipzig along the way to
observe the course of the 'Velvet' Revolutions. In Leipzig I
heard Hans Modrow make a speech on the radio telling
citizens of the DDR that the state would not succumb to
pressure from the west. In the *Ratskeller* I was quizzed about
my reasons for being there by a group of clean-cut young
men who seemed to have problems accepting the close proximity of an ebullient Ethiopian student.

Berlin was filled with the curious. There was not a hotel
room to be had; not even a free locker in which to lodge
an overnight bag. I ate a bad, overpriced meal in a Turkish
restaurant in the Uhlandstraße, then went to the Wall. In the
Western part of the Friedrichstraße, inhabitants of the flats
on either side were pelting the street with fireworks. As I
reached the Wall I could see huge crowds converging on the
Brandenburg Gate from the Tiergarten. Everywhere men
were chipping away at the Wall with chisels. Someone had
even set fire to a short stretch and continued to fan the
flames until a police car arrived to spoil his fun.

The East German police had opened the checkpoint at
the Brandenburg Gate. The officers were demanding papers
or passports, but the crowd was not buying: they simply

shook the policemen's hands and went through. The atmosphere was electric: an enormous street party. A television
crew filmed a group of men singing the *Ode to Joy*. One
man died climbing the Gate. Finally the *Vopos* found an
excuse to push the foreigners through the checkpoint again.
I slept, if that is the word, a few hours on the floor of the
Zoo Station. The next day I flew back to Vienna.

It was the spring of 1991 before I was in Berlin again and
much had already changed. After the party which I had
witnessed seventeen months before, the Quadriga had been
taken down from the Brandenburg Gate and placed in safe-
keeping awaiting repairs. The Friedrichstraße station seemed
quite empty without its little booths where foreigners were
lightened of 25 DMs for the privilege of crossing to the east.
There were no more gift and duty-free shops. *Ossis* weighed
up the pros and cons of the new deal in hushed tones. They
were pleased to see more food in the shops; oranges in
particular excited their imagination. During the war it had
been bananas.

So far little private enterprise had come to the east apart
from the profusion of sausage stalls and about ten times as
many taxi-cabs as could ever be needed. The property agency
Treuhand was slowly sifting through the dossiers to find out
who really owned what. Like so much else it was *Wessi*-
heavy: the top jobs all seemed have been taken by westerners,
including a few survivors from the old Prussian service
nobility. One of them told me that the *Ossis* did no work:
that East Berlin had been imbued with a 'Mediterranean'
spirit: they came late and left early, and did as little as they
humanly could while they were there.

Despite a huge upsurge in crime, especially in the more
prosperous quarters south of the Grunewald, the 'change'
was naturally most keenly felt in East Berlin. The old
security was gone. Jobs were lost and so was the self-assurance
which had come with being top dogs in the old Eastern
Bloc. Petty crime appeared on the streets for the first time

since 1933 and the feeling of disappointment was compounded by the attitude of the *Wessis*, who felt a natural
desire to stress the fact that the DDR had failed and had had
to be rescued by the West. Relieved of the authoritarian
system which had reined them in uninterrupted in two
successive regimes for nearly sixty years, young East Berliners
took to political violence and neo-Nazism, as much, I
thought, from spite as from conviction.

In June 1991 a friend came to visit me in Berlin and I
took him across to the east to show him the Linden and the
Museumsinsel. As we left the Friedrichstraße station we saw
a group of Berliners seated at a table beside a sausage stall.
It was late morning but they were already drunk from the
beer they had been tippling from their tins. Every now and
again one of them would stagger uneasily to his feet and offer
a *Deutsche Gruß*. We watched them for some minutes.
'What a lucky man you are!' I told the friend. 'Some journalists wait for weeks for such a sighting, and you witness it on
your second day in town!' At that point one of the older
members of the circle got up. He was old enough to have
lived under the Third Reich. He began to belch his way
through the old nationalist song *Die Wacht am Rhein*, but
half-way through it he forgot the words and had to sit down.
His fellows appreciated the gesture and got to their feet to
present a phalanx of Hitlerite salutes. 'Do you think they are
a risk to society?' I asked. 'I think they are more of a danger
to themselves,' concluded the friend.

They were not to be so easily dismissed. In 1993 they
vented their fury on the Jewish hut in Sachsenhausen, the
old concentration camp in Oranienburg a few miles north
of Berlin, and burned it to the ground. The authorities in
Brandenburg found the funds to rebuild the hut and the
culprits were caught and tried. It was, incidentally, the second
time the hut had been reconstructed. Sachsenhausen had
continued to exercise its murderous functions well into the
fifties, when the Russians used it as a prison camp for Nazis,

conservatives, monarchists, and anyone else they felt threatened their puppet state. About 14,000 are thought to have died there after 1945. When they closed the camp it was revamped to fit in with the SED's interpretation of the history of the Third Reich. A permanent exhibition featured the biographies of communists who had died there, but no mention was made of middle-class opponents of the regime.

Of course neo-Nazism and acute xenophobia were not confined to the eastern districts of the city. Hard by Checkpoint Charlie was and is the Deutschlandhaus, a natural pole of attraction for the *Ewig-Gestrigen* (yesterday's men) who refused to accept the new frontiers on the Oder and Neiße rivers. Each floor deals with the interests of the different groups of dispossessed: East and West Prussians, Grenzmärker, Pomeranians, Silesians, Sudeteners, and Germans from Russia, Hungary, Yugoslavia and the Siebenbürgen in Romania. The library of the Deutschlandhaus must be the ideal setting for a political thriller about Cold War Berlin.

One thing which imposed a highly individual character on both East and West Berlin after the war was the presence of hundreds of thousands of foreign soldiers in their various garrisons. They pulled out in the summer of 1994, leaving behind them great tracts of barracks buildings which, while the soldiers had been there, had obscured a few unpleasant memories of the Nazi past. The Andrews Barracks in Lichterfelde, for example, had been the old Prussian Kadettenanstalt, where middle- and upper-class Germans, including Hermann Göring, had trained as army officers. Göring put his *alma mater* to a new use in June 1934, when he led the purge known as 'The Night of the Long Knives' and had up to a hundred SA men and opponents of the regime murdered, many of them in the buildings of his old school.

In June 1991 I was invited to a drinks party in the Smuts Barracks in Spandau. I took a taxi from the Altstadt with an *Ossi* taxi driver who was perplexed to learn that the British army controlled such large amounts of Spandau. He knew only Russian barracks. When we got to the gate it was raining hard. The sentry told me I could come in, but not my driver. I arrived at the officers' mess and was offered a choice of coloured cocktails of varying strengths. One of the officers I met was an engineer. He explained that this was where Heß had lived all those years. His prison had been dismantled and the bricks scattered so that no German might develop a sentimental obsession with the site, which was now occupied by the NAAFI.

British officers lived well in Berlin and the posting was a popular one. Not only did they receive free petrol and more pay, they were garrisoned in neat, detached houses with gardens behind the Heerstraße in Charlottenburg. Just off the Theodor-Heuß-Platz they had their club in Marlborough House. After the war the club could boast a full palm-court orchestra. One officer explained to me that the members of the band had died off steadily since, so that by 1992 there remained only the pianist. In those twilight years of the British army of occupation the club continued to function as of old. I attended a polo-club ball there in black tie and was introduced to tequila by a friendly subaltern who explained: 'The trick is not to taste it.'

For the soldiers one of the pleasures of Berlin was being able to go to the barracks and messes of the other occupying powers. Once a year a coach left for Potsdam, where officers were entertained to vodka and Crimean wine by their Russian counterparts. The Americans in the south-west offered brunch with waffles, but the real treat was to cash in on the gastronomic possibilities offered by the French in the north. They had their *pavillon du lac* and on Sundays a Vietnamese lunch (the equivalent of the British army's Sunday curry) in their barracks in Tegel. I went along once with some friends from the British garrison and was treated to a moment of ordinary French chaos when an NCO decided that none of the British soldiers enjoyed the right to enter the French compound. An embarrassing scene ensued with a number of high-ranking British officers standing outside the gates with their families, not knowing quite what to do.

The NCO in his *képi* began to get worried. He must have reflected that his obduracy might have led, if not to an international incident, at least to some unpleasantness among the Allies. He turned to a soldier with a gun and told him to deal with 'ces gens anglais'. The soldier protested that he didn't speak English. I wound down the window of the car and asked him in French what was going on. He told me that the duty officer would be along in a moment and would deal with the situation. The crowd had grown; the British officers were clearly seething with fury. Finally a French lieutenant-colonel appeared and told the sentry that we were *all* his guests. He wrote down our names on a sheet of paper and handed it to the soldier and in we went.

The French may well have felt a slight inferiority complex about their status in Berlin. Another French colonel I met at a polo tournament on the Maifeld told me that the garrison numbered only 3,000 men, who had to lend their weight to defending the city against the estimated 270,000 Russians stationed in the East. He explained that the French had never been accorded the same privileges in Berlin as the British or the Americans. By that time there was little to fear from the Russians, who were already defecting in droves rather than returning to a politically unstable Russia. At the time of the Moscow *coup* in August 1991 I had the chance to study them at close quarters in Frankfurt an der Oder. Those who weren't fleeing were flogging their kit by the Brandenburg Gate. I recall a strange scene at Sanssouci: two Russian squaddies in uniform licking ice-creams while they watched another busily selling the selfsame hats and insignia they were wearing.

The Russians had been responsible for part of the chaos that affected transport in Berlin after the 'change'. During the *démontage* following the war, they had removed half the railway lines – which until very recently explained the pitiful slowness of trains travelling to the satellite towns of the Mark. After 1990 the old transport system had to be reconnected between east and west. It was not hard to recognise the greater inhumanity on the eastern side: pedestrian crossings were few and far between and most of the time you were forced to make an illegal dash for it, risking not only a police fine but also an ignominious death at the hands of a *Trabi*. The reopening of the U2 line greatly alleviated the problems. It allowed Berliners to rediscover the pretty station in the Potsdamer Platz which had ceased to function in the fifties. At the time of writing, the overhead line is being made ready to carry trains the full distance to the Warschauerstraße.

The *S-Bahn* now operates once again on a wide ring-rail round the city, but prices have soared and trains appear to be less frequent than they were. The east has a complexity all of its own and I have found it virtually impossible in the past *not* to miss any train I have tried to take from the old Schlesischer-Bahnhof in Lichtenberg: if you are not careful the *S-Bahn* train veers off towards Köpenick at Ostkreuz: a *Kreuzweg* indeed. Another calvary is called *Pendelverkehr*, or shuttle-traffic. This is possibly the nastiest form of torture conceived since the fall of the Third Reich. While the BVG works to improve the reunified lines, travellers are forced to descend at each station and take the train on the opposite platform. If you are caught unaware by *Pendelverkehr* you are very unlikely to reach an appointment on time.

There are many depressing sides to the reunited city. One has been the wanton destruction of pre-war buildings. It seems extraordinary that a place like Berlin, which has pre-served so little of its past, should be so gung-ho about tearing down its architectural heritage. The rarity value of nineteenth-century and early twentieth-century buildings is such that you find yourself boggling with delight at the sight of a stretch of neo-baroque *Mietshäuser* in Charlottenburg or

Kreuzberg. Fortunately the best bits of Kreuzberg, Prenzlauerberg, the Scheunenviertel and the pockets of
Biedermeier Berlin by the Rosenthaler Tor will probably
survive this new *Abrißwut*, or destructive fury. The windy
city of grey, stained concrete blocks which replaced the
blitzed alte Westen in the sixties has now spread to the historic hub with the extraordinary banality of the designs
for the new Friedrichstraße. These schemes inspire little
confidence in the massive works going on on the Potsdamer-,
Leipziger- and Pariser Plätze. The east is still painfully empty
and unfriendly. Finding an open café is a considerable
challenge.

The worst modern architecture in Berlin is the
Wilhelmstraße, where the blocks were actually designed and
constructed in the last months of the *ancien régime*. They are
quite breathtakingly awful. On the eastern side of the street
just two pre-war buildings survive as a memory of what was
once the seat of Prussian and German power and Frederick
the Great's noble boulevard. Incongruously, planners built a
kindergarten on the site of Hitler's chancellery in the
Voßstraße. On a boiling hot day during one of the city's
recent heatwaves when a good percentage of the population
was roasting its flesh in their allotment houses in the west, I
witnessed a gaggle of happy, naked children splashing about
in a giant tub on the same soil where Adolf Hitler had issued
his murderous commands.

Such evidence of humanity can be sadly rare. In the east
the spacious width of the streets constructed after 1945
inhibits pedestrian mobility. On the western side the car was
clearly originally intended to be king and traffic lights are
loaded in its favour. Getting down the Potsdamerstraße
quickly can prove frustrating. I have tried; it is impossible to
cross the Potsdamer Brücke without a pause for traffic unless
you make an undignified sprint. Berlin is at its worst around
the Kulturforum, probably because until very recently this
was just a wasteland up against the Wall, and, as such, con-

sidered ideal for planting urban motorways. Now the car is challenged by the bicycle. Whoever wins the contest, it is clear that two wheels are considered superior to two feet. Some Berlin pavements (not roads) have cycle tracks, but cyclists seem little disposed to use them and pedal at full pelt, scattering pedestrians as they go. Some people have been badly hurt in this way, but Berlin's politicians clearly see the vast city as a second Oxford or Amsterdam and won't allow anyone to dispute the green supremacy of the bicycle, or even put it where it belongs: on the roads.

It is all part of a West Berlin loopiness which stems from the time when it was a privileged island partly inhabited by political marginals. In the sixties it was the home of student protest. The radicals of the sixties became the greens of the eighties. These radicals are still there and still influential, running to fat and greying in their Kreuzberg flats. The sixties meant a lot to Berlin; sometimes you feel you are in a time warp in a Charlottenburg pub. The barmen have long hair and beards and play pop music long since forgotten in its country of origin. Until the authorities took poisonous measures around the Potsdamer Platz, much of Berlin was overrun by rabbits. Once I saw one lolloping along contentedly a hundred metres from the Kurfürstendamm. A woman on a bicycle smiled at me as if to say, 'This can happen in our city!' Being open-minded about wildlife can have its drawbacks for some, however; visiting the mother of a friend in Heiligensee, I was taken to inspect a suburban garden which had been recently ravaged by a pack of seventeen wild boars.

Loopiness infects many sides of modern Berlin life. The Bendler block in the Tiergarten, where Stauffenberg and his friends got so far in their attempt to unseat the tyrant Hitler, houses not only an interesting museum but also the government body which deals with Aids. It was here that the first official reference was made to the plot after the war, when Ernst Reuter made a speech to welcome those who had fled

the Russian sector after 17 June 1953. Widespread homosexuality is, of course, no innovation in the city: Berlin was
ever famous for this, only now there is official backing for
sexual diversity such as the museum dedicated to homosexuality in Kreuzberg and the women-only *Treff* on the
Pariserstraße in Wilmersdorf, where at night I have often
seen strangely assorted couples dancing a tender 'slow'.

Sometimes such extreme tolerance ends up by defeating
the purpose of the institution in question. The Staatsbibliothek is the Berlin branch of the national library. It is popular
with students, who challenge accepted norms by bringing
food into the library, reserving places for their fellows and
noisily greeting one another on the steps up from the
canteen. It is an article of faith that students with children
should not be inhibited from using the premises and infants
therefore come in to test the building's fine acoustics.
Libraries attract lunatics and the 'Stabi' is no exception. I
was once driven to despair by a Japanese who had cracked
up under the strain of work and carried on loud and furious
arguments with himself from his favourite seat on the top
floor. Another who never made it into the library proper
was always first in the queue outside the building at 8.45
a.m., dressed in see-through pedal-pants and carrying a collection of plastic bags containing food: cold spaghetti, which
he ate with his hands, and pots of *Quark*, which he spooned
up on the end of his finger. When he finished his snack he
smeared his dirty face on the grass. No one ever disputed
his right to be first into the building.

There were some who were ready to admit that Berliners
had been living in cloud-cuckoo-land since the beginning
of the sixties and that the situation could not last. In August
1994 I noted down a conversation I had had with one citizen
who had known the city from the thirties:

> Berlin was false, she said; the city was living in an
> unreal world of subsidies. It was a situation which

couldn't continue. There was also great uncertainty.
Whenever she heard a sonic boom outside she
thought that something was about to happen. In 1957
she had thought the Russians were going to invade.
She had made plans to send her children out of
Germany.

For all its nuttiness West Berlin had at least been a friendly place with little or no crime to speak of. Berliners have always been famous drunks, and drinking leads to punch-ups, but these were rarely serious affairs. There were those who fell outside the extremely broad margins of Berlin society and lived on the streets. One of these was the woman in the motorcycle helmet who presided over a huge heap of plastic bags at the junction of the Uhlandstraße and the Kurfürstendamm. She was still around in the summer of 1996. Shorn of much of her kit, she had taken up residence in the bus shelter outside the Café Kranzler.

The *maisons closes* had reopened after the war. They were relatively safe places where the prostitutes had regular inspections by doctors. After the 'change' Polish freebooters undercut their business from their pitches on the Kurfürsten-damm, between the Uhland- and the Meineckestraßen. For a while the Russians revived a sort of black market behind the Staatsbibliothek where they sold, among other trifles, fob-watches. It seemed ironic that the watches should finally have come home. One I saw had a double-headed Habsburg eagle. It had come up from Vienna, via Moscow.

The most noticeable thing about West Berlin (and East Berlin too, for that matter) was the almost total absence of 'chic'. Smart Berlin disappeared in 1929, or 1933 at the very latest. There have been moments when Berlin throbbed, a bit, but it has never regained an air of social smartness. There is no obvious high society in Berlin. Khrushchev's sabre-rattling in 1957 sent the last of the old families scuttling for safety to the west. There were no salons until Nicolaus

Sombart revived the *jour fixe* a couple of years ago. The art and fashion scene seems deeply provincial. It is hard to avoid the conclusion that Berlin is a small town under the skin of a big city.

One of the places where this lack of chic is most noticeable is in the restaurant world. West Berlin used to have, table for table, a greater concentration of restaurants than any other city in Europe, but they were no great shakes: Greek, Turkish and Yugoslavian places where the food was virtually inter-changeable. The only ray of light came from the odd Italian restaurant that was not Greek- or Turkish-owned and which offered wholesome food at modest prices. Berlin cafés could not be compared to Viennese, and the only food available from them seemed to be an all-day breakfast (which, with its similarity to the humble evening *Brot*, forms a large part of the Berliner's diet). Anyone with a craving for sausages, for example, had to go to an *Imbiß*, or stand and eat them at a roadside stall. The East had its own street-food specialities to match the *Currywurst* of the West: various little pieces of toast *mit Käse überbacken* (topped with melted cheese). The favourite was clearly the 'Hawaiian Toast', which included a piece of tinned pineapple.

The real speciality of the east was *Soljankasuppe*, a spicy, Ukrainian soup which is the one true monument to the long years of Russian occupation. In the west they treat *Soljankasuppe* with some scepticism, as if they were somehow allowing an advance guard to create a bridgehead outside the Russian sector. I was surprised to see it offered in the butcher's shop in the Potsdamerstraße where I frequently have my lunchtime soup. Generally this is a museum for Berlin culinary staples: *Mohreneintopf* (turnip stew), *Linsenein-topf* (lentil stew), and *Erbsensuppe mit Wurst* (pea soup with sausage). I was not astonished to hear my neighbour complain about the innovation to the shopkeeper. She thought it the beginning of the end.

Hotels had their own style in West Berlin: numerous small

Pensionen filled the floors of the larger *Mietshäuser.* When I first visited Berlin I used to stay in one called the Atlas. After 1989 it began to fill up with immigrants from Eastern Europe and I went to the Insel Rügen instead. It was not always easy to find a room in Berlin. Some of the *Pensionen* by the Kurfürstendamm seemed to be permanently full, and I always wondered who stayed in them. At the opposite end of the scale very few of the so-called top hotels had anything to recommend them. Since the 'change' the Brandenburger Hof and Karl Lagerfeld's new place in Grunewald have offered visitors a style of luxury not generally available before.

The old Interhotels in the East were both expensive and crummy and served only to wrest as much foreign currency out of travellers as they indecently could. The exception was the Grand in the Friedrichstraße, which opened in 1987 as a five-star hotel. My suspicion that the rooms had been bugged and that the entire staff were employed by the Stasi was not 100 per cent confirmed when I had a drink with the manager of the hotel in 1991. As she put it, 'We have had to change a lot of the staff since we took over.' The person in charge of guest relations had survived this purge, but she retained her loyalty to the old regime and told me proudly that she had never been to the West, and had no desire to go.

At first the Grand had a rather dated feel to it, with its themed bars and unconvincing attempt to recreate the old Café Bauer. It was never wholly able to rid itself of the vulgar touches of DDR baroque that had been with it from its conception. It managed, however, to turn its restaurant into one of the best in Berlin, but, typically for modern Germany, the crooners who serenaded you at dinner were not allowed to use the classics introduced by Tauber at the old Adlon, but limited their repertoire to the stale songs of Frank Sinatra.

After the 'change' the best bars quit Kreuzberg for Charlottenburg. In the east the Prenzlauerberg had already loosened up before the events of November 1989. Since 1992 the Scheunenviertel has been the hottest part of the old east. Some real Berlin character remains but it is often off the beaten track. Leydecke in Schöneberg, for example, is an old *Destillat* which survived the Blitz and continues to make flavoured schnapps in the old style. The atmosphere is bred by a crowd of arty Berlin regulars and the rough *Schnauze* of the staff. Visiting the bar for the first time in June 1991, I watched a little scene:

> Two men in the corner had obviously been drinking
> for some time; possibly all day and all night. One
> had got it into his head that he was a wild animal;
> possibly a Berlin bear. He started to growl. The growl
> got louder and, raising his paws in an ursine manner,
> he advanced on the other, locking his friend in a
> bear-hug and biting him on the neck. This caused
> great merriment in the bar and yielded a few fierce
> snaps from the strict woman behind it.
>
> The Bear went back to his drink but soon began
> to growl again. He fixed his eyes on a fat blonde woman
> who looked like an artist's model. Again his hackles
> went up, again he advanced on his prey, again he bit.
>
> The woman was not amused. She brought it to the
> attention of the strict woman. She told the Bear to
> go away and stop bothering the customers. He didn't
> look in the least disposed to take her advice.

Much of the atmosphere has been lost, not just of pre-1933 Berlin but also of the period between 1945 and 1989. Almost everywhere in the east the smell has gone: no more brown coal and Russian black tobacco. In the west they smoked Lucky Strikes. Since 1989 there has been no book-burning as such, but there is something which stirs the sensitive heart at the sight of the stalls outside the Humboldt University that sell badly bound DDR editions of Marx and Engels, Wilhelm Pieck, Anton Ackermann, Johannes R. Becher and the other stalwarts of Eastern Bloc ideology.

The Aufbau Verlag has been forced out of its home in the Jägerstraße by a Jewish bank which owned the property before 1933. It was the leading DDR literary institution, with its monopoly on the works of Brecht, Heinrich Mann and Arnold Zweig. The lift still smelled of brown coal and cheap leather in 1995, and at the back of the building was the dining-room or club where Walter Janka and his fellow editors were waited on, hand and foot, as they entertained their authors.

The rebuilding has occasioned other losses. It is hard not to lament the decision to erect a modern building on the site of the Akademie der Künste in the Pariser Platz. At one time a replica of the Schinkel façade was touted. The destruction of the remains of the Esplanade, after all these years, seems to be a metaphor for the way Berlin thinks about its past. Others would prefer to see it as the poisoning of the rabbits on the Potsdamerplatz. A dose which was not enough to kill them, they say, just enough to kill you if you tried to eat one.

On 8 March 1995 the *Süddeutsche Zeitung* drew up a list of Berlin's losses, most of which related to the time of the autonomous West Berlin of 1949–1989. There were no more: Allies; alternative or green politics; bonuses for working there; exemptions from military service; bicycle rides along the Wall; and football matches in front of the Reichstag. Theatres had disappeared; so had: the ghost stations on the *U-Bahn* in the east; the sparkle of the 'Kudamm'; free parking; long Kreuzberg nights; artists' studios; Rathaus Schöneberg; the radio stations RIAS and SFB; the 'socialist utopia'; tourists; and tax-free cigarettes.

Some unlikely things have survived, though, such as the odd eat-on-your-feet butcher's shop selling bowls of *Erbsensuppe*, or doughty restaurants such as Zum Nußbaum in Friedenau serving huge plates of *Kartoffelpuffer* and Prussian specialities from the severed regions: *Königsberger Klopse* and *Schlesisches Himmelreich*. Berlin *Schnauze* has survived, and is reinfiltrating the west. It gives me pleasure to hear now, on the western side of the Wall, a bank teller soften her 'g's in the old Berlin style. The Bärenschenke is still in the Friedrichinstraße, or it was last time I looked, an island of tradition in a sea of trendy bars; the Kurpfalz Weinstube celebrated its sixty years in 1995, still little changed; you can find homely, flea-pit cinemas in the west; there are still the local *Volksfeste* (street parties) in the dowdier parts of the city which I want to call 'Zillefeste' because everyone looks like characters from Zille's drawings.

There is a gradual (very gradual) homogenisation process: the two halves of the city are coming together. I once attended a breakfast party at the Kronprinzenpalais, where I was able to study at first hand the ghastly neo-baroque of the DDR time. It was thrilling to see this old East German government guesthouse used for such *mondanités*, and a Canadian with duelling scars kept the party amused by his convincing imitations of the Führer, with his lilting Austrian accent. After fifty years as a gutless ruin the Synagogue in the Oranienburgerstraße has risen proud and gilded from the ashes, while Berlin youth flocks to the bars at its feet, bringing life back to the Scheunenviertel for the first time since 1933.

There is an undeniable spirit of revival too. In 1993 a huge mock-up of the Schloss was parked in its rightful position to show what the building had meant to the Linden, and encourage planners to consider it as an alternative to modern buildings for the expected parliamentarians. In 1995 the Schloss was in the news once again when archaeologists uncovered the mediaeval foundations of the building which Wilhelm Pieck had been at such pains to destroy. In the Scheunenviertel small traders and artisans have moved into the little shops and galleries, imitating the Jewish craftsmen who were rounded up from these streets fifty years before. Indeed, there are signs that even the Jews are coming back.

Of course, the most obvious sign of revival is the massive

building site that encompasses the Pariser, Leipziger and Potsdamer Plätze. Good or bad, this will completely alter the picture of the city. Work is in progress; complete transformation will not be visible until the arrival of the Bundestag with 12,000 civil servants in 1999. Today Berlin lacks the institutions and salons that lend a city class, but this huge migration must surely tip the balance and bring back that more cosmopolitan feeling which once imbued the short-lived Berlin *Weltstadt*. Berlin is recovering from its wounds. It is hard to think of a city which has suffered so much. Harder still to think of another which has proved so clearly that it is inextinguishable.

Notes

Introduction

1 Conversation with Professor Dr Werner Knopp, Berlin,
23 May 1991.
2 Display cabinets in the Märkisches Museum, Berlin.
Martin Hürlimann, *Berlin, Königsresidenz, Reichshauptstadt,
Neubeginn*, Zurich and Freiburg im Breisgau 1981, 9.
Tacitus, *The Annals of Imperial Rome*, trans. Michael Grant,
Harmondsworth 1956, 57 (I. 40–44), 64 (I. 64).
Wolfgang Ribbe et al., *Geschichte Berlins*, 2 vols, Munich
1987, I, 21–23. Hereafter *Geschichte*.
3 Idem, 10. Gottfried Korff and Reinhard Rürup eds.,
Berlin, Berlin: Die Ausstellung zur Geschichte der Stadt,
exhibition catalogue 1987, 30. Hereafter *Berlin, Berlin*.
4 Ad. Brennglas [Adolf Glaßbrenner], 'Herr Buffey auf der
Berlin-Leipziger Eisenbahn', in *Berlin wie es ist – und
trinkt*, II, Leipzig 1844, 16–17.
5 Ribbe, *Geschichte*, I, 87. Cyril Buffet, *Berlin*, Paris 1993.
6 Theodor Fontane, *Wanderungen durch die Mark Brandenburg*,
3 vols, Munich and Vienna 1991, II, 18–19. Hereafter
Wanderungen.
7 Buffet, *Berlin*, 19. Georg Dehio, *Handbuch der deutschen
Kunstdenkmäler*, Berlin and Munich 1994, 453, 455.
8 Ribbe, *Geschichte* I, 139–140.
9 Idem, 155.
10 See the useful map of Berlin c. 1400 in Buffet, *Berlin*, 47.
11 Dehio, *Berlin*, 44.
12 Ribbe, *Geschichte*, 173.
13 Buffet, *Berlin*, 23.
14 Ribbe, *Geschichte*, I, 197.
15 Giles MacDonogh, *Prussia: The Perversion of an Idea*,
paperback edn., London 1995, 17. Gerd Heinrich,

Geschichte Preußens: Staat und Dynastie, Frankfurt am Main, Berlin and Vienna 1984, 49–50.
16 Ribbe, *Geschichte*, I, 251–252.

1 Ich bin ein Berliner

1 Theodor Fontane, 'Die Märker und die Berliner und wie sich das Berlinertum entwickelte', in *Wanderungen*, III, 649–662.
2 Marie-Louise von Plessen in *Berlin, Berlin*, 57.
3 Karl Nase, *Icke, dette, kiecke mal: Wesen und Werden der Mundart Berlins*, Leipzig 1937, 8.
4 Idem, 28.
5 Hürlimann, *Berlin*, 10.
6 Visit to the Französische Friedhof, 9 April 1995.
7 Buffet, *Berlin*, 69.
8 Etienne François, 'Berlin au XVIIIe siècle: naissance d'une capitale', in Etienne François and Egon Graf Westerholt eds., *Berlin: Capitale, Mythe, Enjeu*, Nancy 1988, 33.
9 Frédéric Hartweg, 'De Metz à Berlin: les réfugiés huguenots du pays messin dans la capitale de Brandebourg', in idem, 20.
10 Idem, 19.
11 MacDonogh, *Prussia*, 338.
12 Hartweg (op. cit.) gives a fifth, most authorities say the French represented a third of the inhabitants. See Plessen in *Berlin, Berlin*, 102. Pierre-Paul Sagave, *Berlin und Frankreich*, Berlin 1980, 13.
13 Hürlimann, *Berlin*, 46–48.
14 Plessen in *Berlin, Berlin*, 111.
15 Sagave, *Berlin und Frankreich*, 24.
16 Idem, 26. Dehio, *Berlin*, 57–58.
17 Sagave, *Berlin und Frankreich*, 21. Sagave quotes Luther's translation of Isaiah XV, 5: 'Lasse meine verjagten bei Dir herbergen, sei Du für Moab ein Schirm vor dem Verstörer'. Which is more appropriate. My text is from the King James version.
18 Helmut Engel, Stefi Jersch-Wenzel and Wilhelm Treue

eds., *Geschichtslandschaft Berlin: Orte und Ereignisse*, II, *Tiergarten*, Part 2, *Moabit*, Berlin 1987, XI.

19 Idem, 149–150.

20 Idem, XI.

21 Idem, 151–155.

22 Hans Ostwald, *Berlin und die Berlinerin: Eine Kultur- und Sittengeschichte*, Berlin 1911, 6.

23 Hürlimann, *Berlin*, 50.

24 Idem. Peter Schlobinski, *Berliner Wörterbuch*, Berlin 1993, 17.

25 Idem, 16.

26 Kurt Schleicher, *Adelbert von Chamisso*, Berlin 1988, 19.

27 Idem, 35.

28 Hürlimann, *Berlin*, 50.

29 Ribbe, *Geschichte*, I, 427.

30 Sagave, *Berlin und Frankreich*, 147.

31 Idem, 148.

32 Hartweg in *Berlin*, 27–28.

33 Dehio, *Berlin*, 157, 365–366, 537–538. Rürup in *Berlin, Berlin*, 30.

34 Volker Hassemer and Ulrich Eckhart in *Berlin, Berlin*, Geleitwort.

35 Ribbe, *Geschichte*, I, 239–240.

36 Idem, I, 357.

37 Rürup in *Berlin, Berlin*, 34.
   Ribbe, *Geschichte*, I, 357.

38 Walther Hubatsch, *Frederick the Great: Absolution and Administration*, trans. Patrick Doran, London 1973, 202.

39 Leonore Koschnick in *Berlin, Berlin*, 102. Heinrich, *Geschichte Preußens*, 182–183; Hürlimann, *Berlin*, 33.

40 Heinrich, *Geschichte Preußens*, 182–183.

41 Hubatsch, *Frederick the Great*, 37.

42 Idem, 65.

43 Idem, 139.

44 Franz Lederer, *Uns kann keener: Berliner Humor: Sprache, Wesen und Humor des Berliners*, Berlin 1927, 148.

45 Dehio, *Berlin*, 80.

46 Dominique Bourel, 'Berlin et les juifs: une histoire d'amour et de tragédie', in *Berlin: Capitale*, 88–89.

47 Idem, 90–91.

48 Idem, 91. Dehio, *Berlin*, 73.

49 Engel, Jersch-Wenzel and Treue eds., *Moabit*, 134.
50 Helmut Engel, Stefi Jersch-Wenzel and Wilhelm Treue, *Kreuzberg*, Berlin 1994, XXIV.
51 Alfred Döblin, *Ein Kerl muß eine Meinung haben: Berichte und Kritiken 1921–1924*, Freiburg im Breisgau 1976, 115.
52 Idem, 37.
53 Hans-Norbert Burkerl, Klaus Matußek and Wolfgang Wippermann, *'Machtergreifung' Berlin 1933*, Berlin 1982, 114.
54 Alfred Döblin, *Berlin-Alexanderplatz*, DTV edn., Munich 1979, 10–11.
55 Ribbe, *Geschichte*, II, 950.
56 Idem.
57 Idem, 1005. Hans-Dieter Schäfer, *Berlin im zweiten Weltkrieg*, Munich 1985, 27.
58 Wolfgang Ribbe, *Spandau*, Berlin 1991, 117.
59 Ribbe, *Geschichte*, I, 382.
60 Rürup in *Berlin, Berlin*, 32.
61 Engel, Jersch-Wenzel and Treue, *Kreuzberg*, XIV.
62 Koschnick in *Berlin, Berlin*, 102, 112.
63 Heinrich Kaak, *Kreuzberg*, Berlin 1988, 31–32. Dehio, *Berlin*, 311.
64 Kaak, *Kreuzberg*, 32.
65 Döblin, *Berlin-Alexanderplatz*, 53.
66 Gerhard Wolf ed., *Und grüß mich nicht Unter den Linden: Heine in Berlin, Gedichte und Prosa*, Frankfurt am Maine 1981, 130.
67 Fritz Mierau ed., *Russen in Berlin 1918–1933: Eine kulturelle Begegnung*, Leipzig 1987, viii, xii.
68 Bénédicte Dumouchel-Odièvre, 'Les russes à Berlin dans les années vingt', in Gilbert Krebs ed., *Berlin, carrefour des années vingt et trente*, Paris 1992, 77.
69 Idem, 80–81.
70 Döblin, *Ein Kerl*, 31.
71 Christine Gascuel, 'Le Berlin fictif de Vladimir Nabokov', in Krebs ed., *Berlin, carrefour*, 91.
72 Dumouchel-Odièvre in Krebs ed., *Berlin, carrefour*, 78–79.
73 Nicolaus Sombart, *Jugend in Berlin*, Munich and Vienna 1984, 118.
74 Idem, 125.
75 Idem, 126.

76 Engel, Jersch-Wenzel and Treue, *Kreuzberg*, XXVI.

77 Helmut Engel, Stefi Jersch-Wenzel and Wilhelm Treue, *Charlottenburg*, I, *Die historische Stadt*, Berlin 1986, 200–202.

78 Friedrich Nicolai, *Beschreibung der königlichen Residenzstädte Berlin und Potsdam, 1769*, facsimile edn., Hildesheim, Zurich and New York 1988, 116.

79 [Wilhelm Stieber], *Die Prostitution in Berlin und ihre Opfer, in historischer, sittlicher, medizischer und polizeilicher Beziehung beleuchtet*, 2nd edn., Berlin 1846, 129.

80 Hürlimann, *Berlin*, 50–51.

81 Rürup in *Berlin, Berlin*, 32. Ribbe, *Geschichte*, I, 382–383.

82 Zivier in 'Das romanische Café', in Volker Spieß, ed., *Gauner, Künstler, Originale: die 20ᵉʳ Jahre in Berlin*, Berlin 1988, 69.

83 James Gerard, *My Four Years in Germany*, London 1917, 120–121.

84 Idem, 124–127.
Christabel Bielenberg, *The Past is Myself*, London 1984, 77–78.

85 Gerard, *Four Years*, 223, 224.

86 Ursula von Kardorff, *Berliner Aufzeichnungen 1942 bis 1945*, DTV edn., Munich 1994, 264.

87 Schäfer, *Berlin im zweitem Weltkrieg*, 66.

88 Ribbe, *Geschichte*, I, 349.

89 Idem, 376–377.

90 Idem, 382.

91 Hubatsch, *Frederick the Great*, 137.

92 Nicolai, *Beschreibung*, 18.

93 Rürup in *Berlin, Berlin*, 32.

94 Gunther Jahn, *Die Bauwerke und Kunstdenkmäler von Berlin: Stadt und Bezirk Spandau*, Berlin 1971, 14.

95 Ribbe, *Geschichte*, I, 410–411.

96 Dr Clauswitz ed., *Die Städteordnung von 1808 und die Stadt Berlin: Festschrift zur hundertjährigen Gedenkfeier der Einführung der Städteordnung*, Berlin 1908, 3.

97 Ribbe, *Geschichte*, I, 428.

98 Eva Brücker in Engel, Jersch-Wenzel and Treue, *Kreuzberg*, 434; MacDonogh, *Prussia*, 39; Dehio, *Berlin*, 282.

99 Manfred Nöbel, 'Damals war's . . . David Kalisch und die

Berliner Revolutionsposse', in David Kalisch,
Einmalhunderttausend Taler: Altberliner Possen 1846–1848,
Berlin 1988, I, 5–72.

100 Idem, I, 192; II, 81.

101 Kurt Tucholsky ed., *Ich kann nicht schreiben ohne zu lügen*,
Briefe 1913 bis 1935. Hsg Fritz Rattalz, Hamburg 1989,
211.

102 Margrit Bröhan, *Hans Baluschek, 1870–1935*, Berlin 1985,
14.

103 Ostwald, *Berlin und die Berlinerin*, 52.

104 Nase, *Icke, dette, kieke mal*, 31.

105 Lederer, *Uns kann keener*, 5.

106 Max Hecker ed., *Der Briefwechsel zwischen Goethe und
Zelter, II (1819–1827)*, Leipzig 1915, 12.

107 Hans von Müller ed., *E. T. A. Hoffmann: Zwölf Berlinische
Geschichten aus den Jahren 1551–1816*, Munich 1921, XI.

108 Annemarie Lange, *Berlin zur Zeit Bebels und Bismarcks:
Zwischen Reichsgründung und Jahrhundertwende*, Berlin
(East) 1972, 85.

109 Rürup in *Berlin, Berlin*, 41.

110 Idem.

111 Heinrich Mann, *Werk und Leben in Dokumente und
Bildern*, Berlin and Weimar, 1971, 125.

112 Wolf Thieme, *Das letzte Haus am Potsdamer Platz: Eine
Berliner Chronik*, Hamburg 1988, 26.

113 Peter Moses-Krause, 'Nachbemerkung zur Neuausgabe',
in Arthur Eloesser, *Die Straße meiner Jugend: Berliner
Skizzen*, Berlin 1987, 119.

114 Eloesser, *Straße meiner Jugend*, 17.

115 Idem, 67.

116 Idem, 98.

117 Evelyn, Princess Blücher, *An English Wife in Berlin*,
London 1920, 230.

118 Vladimir Nabokov, *Laughter in the Dark*, Harmondsworth
1963, 32.

119 Döblin, *Ein Kerl*, 23.

120 Idem, 182.

2 Berlin Itineraries

1 Friedrich F. A. Kuntze, *Das alte Berlin*, Berlin and Leipzig 1937, 33; Plessen in *Berlin, Berlin,* 58; Ribbe, *Geschichte,* I, 275–278.

2 Idem. Regina Hanemann, *Das Berliner Schloß: Ein Führer zu einem verlorenen Bau,* Berlin 1992, 9.

3 A contemporary print from the picture is reproduced in Buffet, *Berlin,* 63; Hanemann, *Das Berliner Schloß,* 32 shows A. Geyer's reconstruction of the Kleiner Schloßhof. Professor Banister Fletcher and Banister F. Fletcher, *A History of Architecture,* 5th edn., London 1905, 219. Ribbe, *Geschichte,* I, 278.

4 Idem. Hanemann, *Das Berliner Schloß,* 14–16.

5 Idem, 13–14, 34–35; Ribbe, *Geschichte,* I, 327.

6 Koschnick in *Berlin, Berlin,* 83.

7 Idem.

8 Hanemann, *Das Berliner Schloß,* 34–35.

9 Ribbe, *Geschichte,* I, 352.

10 Koschnick in *Berlin, Berlin,* 88; Konstantin Akinscha and Gregori Koslow, *Beutekunst: Auf Schatzsuche in russischen Geheimdepot,* Munich 1995, 25.

11 Ribbe, *Geschichte,* I, 353, 371.

12 Idem, I, 358.

13 Hanemann, *Das Berliner Schloß,* 20–22, 29–34, 42–45.

14 Ribbe, *Geschichte,* I, 372.

15 Frederick the Great, *Mémoires pour servir à l'histoire de la maison de Brandebourg,* 110. Quoted in MacDonogh, *Prussia,* 29.

16 Ribbe, *Geschichte,* I, 373.

17 Idem, I, 376–377. Kuntze, *Das alte Berlin,* 45.

18 Hanemann, *Das Berliner Schloß,* 18–19.

19 Karl Eduard Schmidt-Lötzen ed., *Dreißig Jahre am Hofe Friedrichs des Großen. Aus den Tagebüchern des Reichsgrafen Ernst Ahasverus Heinrich von Lehndorff, Kammerherrn der Königin Elisabeth Christine von Preußen,* Gotha 1907, 456–457.

20 Hanemann, *Das Berliner Schloß,* 24–25, 50–51.

21 Idem, 26. Förderverein Berliner Stadtschloß, *Das Schloß? Eine Ausstellung über die Mitte Berlins,* Berlin 1993, 48–50.

22 There is a large canvas by Franz Krüger of the scene (*Potsdam Schlösser und Gärten*).

23 Bettina von Arnim, *Dies Buch gehört dem König*, in Bettina von Arnim, *Sämtliche Werke*, VI, 5, Frechen 1959–1963

24 Dehio, *Berlin*, 75.

25 Theodor Fontane, *L'Adultera*, in *Fontanes Werke in fünf Bänden*, Berlin and Weimar 1986, II, 200.

26 Hanemann, *Das Berliner Schloß*, 10, 40–41.

27 Dehio, *Berlin*, 81.

28 See MacDonogh, *Prussia*, 64.

29 Margrit Bröhan, *Franz Skarbina*, Berlin 1995, 83.

30 Hanemann, *Das Berliner Schloß*, 10; Förderverein Berliner Stadtschloß, *Das Schloß*, 40.

31 Idem, 52.

32 Ribbe, *Geschichte*, II, 791.

33 Gerard, *Four Years*, 139.

34 Blücher, *An English Wife*, 294.

35 Charles Kessler ed., *The Diaries of a Cosmopolitan: Count Harry Kessler 1918–1937*, London 1971, 8–9.

36 Idem, 44–45.

37 A. L. Rowse, *All Souls and Appeasement*. Quoted in Giles MacDonogh, *A Good German*, expanded edn., London 1994, 26.

38 Förderverein Berliner Stadtschloß, *Das Schloß*, 71.

39 Idem.

40 Idem, 75.

41 Idem.

42 Idem.

43 Idem.

44 Janos Frecot and Helmut Geisert, *Berlin, frühe Photographien Berlin 1857–1913*, Munich 1984, Plates 15–17.

45 Lederer, *Uns kann keener*, 121.

46 Dehio, *Berlin*, 63–68.

47 Gerhard Wolf ed., *Und grüß nich nicht Unter den Linden: Heine in Berlin*, Gedichte und Prosa, Frankfurt am Main 1981.

48 MacDonogh, *Prussia*, 126–127.

49 Alfred Schinz, *Akademie der Künste: Bauen in Berlin 1900–1964*, Berlin n.d., 13.

50 Wilhelm Raabe, *Die Chronik der Sperlingsgasse*, 2nd edn., Berlin 1878, 17–19.

51 Ribbe, *Geschichte*, II, 881.

52 Idem, I, 366. Kuntze, *Das alte Berlin*, 25. Dehio, *Berlin*, 44–49.

53 Ribbe, *Geschichte*, I, 366. Imre Lazar, *Der Fall Horst Wessel*, Stuttgart and Zurich 1980, 40.

54 Nicolai, *Beschreibung*, 88.

55 Kuntze, *Das alte Berlin*, 26. Dehio, *Berlin*, 48–55. Fontane, *Wanderungen*, I, 992–993.

56 Kuntze, *Das alte Berlin*, 26; Wolfgang Schulz, *Stadtführer durch das historische Berlin*, 5th edn., Berlin 1988, 17.

57 Edit. Trost, *Eduard Gaertner*, Berlin 1991, Plates 5–7.

58 Rudolf Herz, *Berliner Barock: Bauten und Baumeister aus der ersten Hälfte des 18. Jahrhunderts*, Berlin 1928, 4. Dehio, *Berlin*, 61–63.

59 Trost, *Gaertner Eduard*, Plate 7.

60 Herz, *Barock*, 4.

61 Idem, 8; Kuntze, *Das alte Berlin*, 61; Herz, *Barock*, 15.

62 Idem, 15.

63 Idem, 20. Dehio, *Berlin*, 62–63. There are some lovely early colour photographs of the Heiliggeistkirche by Alfred von Loebenstein, *Spaziergang durch das alte Potsdam*, Potsdam 1990, Plates 4 and 11.

64 Kuntze, *Das alte Berlin*, 71.

65 Frederick the Great, 'Testament politique'. Quoted in MacDonogh, *Prussia*, 337.

66 Hans-Joachim Giersberg, 'Die Bauten Friedrichs des Großen', in Johann Georg Prinz von Hohenzollern ed., *Friedrich der Große, Sammler und Mäzen*, Munich 1992, 52–53.

67 J. D. E. Preuß ed., *Oeuvres de Frédéric le Grand*, XVII, Berlin 1851, correspondence with Algarotti, 84–85, 85 n.a.

68 Blücher, *An English Wife*, 11–12.

69 Helmuth James von Moltke, *Letters to Freya: A Witness against Hitler*, London 1991; see, for example, 217 and n3 and 218 and n1.

70 Hans Rothfels, *The German Opposition to Hitler*, London 1970, 32.

71 Kuntze, *Das alte Berlin*, 72.

72 Schulz, *Stadtführer*, 66.
73 Idem. Dehio, *Berlin*, 107–109.
74 Klaus Mann, *Mephisto*. Reinbek 1981, 11.
75 Roger Manvell and Heinrich Fraenkel, *Doctor Goebbels: His Life and Death*, London 1960, 130–131; André François-Poncet, *Souvenirs d'une ambassade à Berlin septembre 1931–octobre 1938*, Paris 1946, 136.
76 *Tagesspiegel*, August 1995.
77 Kuntze, *Das alte Berlin*, 57.
78 Wolf ed., *Und grüß mich nicht*, 131–132.
79 Eloesser, *Straße meiner Jugend*, 51.
80 Idem, 52.
81 Müller ed., *Berlinische Geschichten*, 274.
82 Idem, 273.
83 Idem, 274.
84 Frederick Pottle ed., *Boswell on the Grand Tour: Germany and Switzerland 1764*, London 1953, 19, 32.
85 Bert Becker, 'Das Niederländische Palais: Ein Beitrag zur Geschichte der Oranien in Berlin', *Mitteilungen des Vereins für die Geschichte Berlins*, Heft 3, July 1993.
86 Dehio, *Berlin*, 81–82. Author's visit, 25 August 1991.
87 Rothfels, *Opposition*, 89–91.
88 Dehio, *Berlin*, 77–79.
89 Herz, *Barock*, 12–13.
90 Detlef Graf von Schwerin, *Dann sind's die besten Köpfe die man henkt: Die junge Generation im deutschen Widerstand*, Munich 1994, 289–290.
91 Schulz, *Stadtführer*, 6–9.
92 Schinz, *Bauen in Berlin*, 13.
93 Idem, 27.
94 Idem, 16.
95 Walter Zille, *Heinrich Zille und sein Berlin: Persönliche Erinnerungen an den Meister*, Berlin 1949, 9.
96 Newspaper extracts exhibited in the cabinets of the Märkisches Museum.
97 Julius Rodenberg, *Bilder aus dem Berliner Leben in einem Auswahl*, Halle an der Saale n.d. [possibly 1892], 49–50. Idem, 50. Frecot and Geisert, *Berlin*, Plate 50. Trost, *Gaertner*, Plates 22–24.
98 Erich Kästner, *Fabian: Die Geschichte eines Moralisten*, 1931, DTV edn., Munich 1989, 60.

99 Ribbe, *Geschichte*, I, 408. Dronke, *Aus dem Volk*, Frankfurt am Main 1846, 14.
Zille's photographs in particular show the charm of the Fischer-Kietz. See Frecot and Geisert, *Berlin*, Plates 57 and 58.

100 Preuß ed., *Oeuvres de Frédéric le Grand*, XXII, 307.

101 Karl von Holtei, *Vierzig Jahre: Lorbeerkranz und Wanderstab. Lebenserinnerungen des Schauspielers und Poeten*, Berlin 1932, 312–313.

102 Döblin, *Berlin-Alexanderplatz*, 105.

103 Susanne Everett, *C'était Berlin*, Paris 1980, 114–115. Thomas Friedrich, *Berlin: A Photographic Portrait of the Weimar Years 1918–1933*, London 1991, 98–99.

104 In Zille, *Zille und sein Berlin*.

105 Schäfer, *Berlin im zweitem Weltkrieg*, 57.

106 Lazar, *Horst Wessel*, 40.

107 Schulz, *Stadtführer*, 10.

108 Eloesser, *Straße meiner Jugend*, 22.

109 Dörte and Peter Wolfgang Ruff, 'Die Charité – das älteste fortbestehende Krankenhaus in Berlin', in *Die Charité in der Geschichte der Berliner Medizin (1710–1987)*, *Wissenschaftliche Zeitschrift der Humboldt-Universität zu Berlin*, 36 Jg. 1987, Heft 1/2, 10.

110 Idem, 11; Georg Harig and Hans-Uwe Lammel, 'Zur Geschichte der Beziehungen zwischen der Charité und Berlin (1710–1945)', in idem, 14, 15, 18.

111 Idem, 18.

112 Dehio, *Berlin*, 91–93.

113 Ernst Dronke, *Berlin*, Frankfurt am Main 1846, 237.

114 Idem.

115 Theodor Fontane, *Stine*, in *Fontanes Werke in fünf Bänden*, II, 291.

116 Dehio, *Berlin*, 161; Schulz, *Stadtführer*, 56. Author's visit to the cemetery, 9 April 1995.

117 Dehio, *Berlin*, 22.

118 Idem, 69–70.

119 Trost, *Gaertner*, Plates 25–32.

120 The panoramas are now in the Schinkel-Pavillon in Charlottenburg.

121 Dehio, *Berlin*, 112–113.

122 Frecot and Geisert, *Berlin*, Plate 48.

123 Fontane, *Wanderungen*, I, 306.
124 Kuntze, *Das alte Berlin*, Berlin and Leipzig, 1937, 66–67. Michael Bloch, *Ribbentrop*, London 1992, 158. Joseph Goebbels, *Tagebücher 1945: Die letzten Aufzeichnungen*, Hamburg 1977, 315.
125 Manvell and Fraenkel, *Doctor Goebbels*, 123.
126 Reinhard Rürup ed., *Topography of Terror: Gestapo, SS and Reichssicherheitshauptamt on the 'Prinz-Albrecht-Terrain': A Documentation*, trans. Werner Angress, Berlin 1989, 19–22.
127 Engel, Jersch-Wenzel and Treue, *Kreuzberg*, 18.
128 Photographs by Hermann Rückwardt, 1871–1916. Exhibited in the Märkisches Museum, summer 1995.
129 Adolf Brennglas, 'Hökerinnen', in *Berlin wie es ist – und trinkt*, I, Leipzig 1943, 14.
130 Idem, 21.
131 E. T. A Hoffmann, 'Des Vetters Eckfenster', in *Hoffmanns Werke in drei Bände*, Berlin and Weimar 1990, II, 303.
132 Idem, 304.
133 Idem, 305, 307.
134 Idem, 309.
135 Idem, 314.
136 Bröhan, *Skarbina*, 145–148.
137 Carl Zuckmayer, *Der Hauptmann von Köpenick*, Frankfurt am Main 1990, 18.
138 Heinrich Mann, *Der Untertan*, Berlin and Weimar 1993, 12–13.
139 Schinz, *Bauten in Berlin*, 22. Boda Rollka, Volker Spieß and 'Bernhard Thieme' eds., *Berliner Biographisches Lexikon*, Berlin 1993, 422.
140 Engel, Jersch-Wenzel and Treue, *Kreuzberg*, 267.
141 Idem, 269.
142 Fontane, *Irrungen, Wirrungen*, in *Werke*, III, 12.
143 Rollka, Spieß and Thieme eds., *Lexikon*, 422.
144 Ribbe, *Geschichte*, I, 350.
145 Kuntze, *Das alte Berlin*, 54. Frecot and Geisert, *Berlin*, Plates 41–42.
146 Dehio, *Berlin*, 140–141.
147 Hecker ed., *Briefwechsel*, II, 101.
148 Ribbe, *Geschichte*, I, 370. Hürlimann, *Berlin*, 51.
149 Dehio, *Berlin*, 145.

150 Adolf Wermuth, *Ein Beamtenleben: Erinnerungen*, Berlin 1922, 142–143.
151 Engel, Jersch-Wenzel and Treue, *Tiergarten*, I, 24. John Wheeler-Bennett, *Knaves, Fools and Heroes*, London 1974, 70.
152 Lovis Corinth, *Selbstbiographie*, Leipzig 1993, 164.
153 Nicolai, *Beschreibung*, 110. Schulz, *Stadtführer*, 58. Kardorff, *Aufzeichnungen*.
154 Nicolai, *Beschreibung*, 110.
155 Author's visit to the exhibition tent, building site, etc., 22 August 1995.
156 Fontane, *Wanderungen*, II, 11. Quoted in Ribbe, *Geschichte*, I, 6.
157 John Lukacs, *Budapest 1900: A Historical Portrait of a City and Its Culture*, London 1993, 69, 72.
158 Vladimir Nabokov, *A Russian Beauty and Other Stories*, Harmondsworth 1975, 29.
159 Quoted in Ribbe, *Geschichte*, I, 410.
160 Dronke, *Berlin*, 11.
161 Rollka, Spieß and Thieme eds., *Lexikon*, 99–100. Dronke, *Berlin*, 11.
162 Rürup in *Berlin, Berlin*, 36.
163 Idem, 34.
164 Hürlimann, *Berlin*, 40.
165 Rürup in *Berlin, Berlin*, 39.
166 Idem, 40–41.
167 Idem.
168 Rodenberg, *Bilder*, 109.
169 Ribbe, *Geschichte*, II, 694.
170 Helga Pilz, Wolfgang Hofmann and Jürgen Thomisch, *Berlin-W: Geschichte und Schicksal einer Stadtmitte*, Berlin 1984, I, 66.
171 Idem, 77.
172 Ribbe, *Geschichte*, II, 663.
173 Idem.
174 Idem.
175 Engel, Jersch-Wenzel and Treue, *Kreuzberg*, XVII.
176 Idem.
177 Idem.
178 Idem.
179 Ribbe, *Geschichte*, II, 665.

180 Idem.
181 Engel, Jersch-Wenzel and Treue, *Kreuzberg*, XVII–XVIII. Visit to the flat of Gottfried von Bismarck, 27 August 1992.
182 Engel, Jersch-Wenzel and Treue, *Kreuzberg*, XVIII. Conversation with Will Dambisch, 7 April 1995. Dambisch's father, a judge, lived in a ten-room flat on the street front in Schöneberg.
183 Ribbe, *Geschichte*, I, 170–172.
184 Wolfgang Menge, *Alltag in Preußen, ein Bericht aus dem 18. Jahrhundert*, Weinheim and Basel 1991, 64.
185 Ribbe, *Geschichte*, I, 326.
186 Idem.
187 Hans Jessen ed., *Der Dreißigjährige Krieg in Augenzeugen-berichten*, 2nd edn., Düsseldorf 1963, 241, 264–265.
188 Buffet, *Berlin*, 69–70.
189 Idem. Ribbe, *Geschichte*, I, 344. Reinhard Rürup, 'Berlin – Umrisse der Stadtgeschichte' in *Berlin, Berlin*, 28.
190 Dehio, *Berlin*, 148–149; idem, 9; *Berlin in Kartenbild: Zur Entwicklung der Stadt 1650–1950*, Ausstellung der Staatsbibliothek preussischer Kulturbesitz 1981, catalogue 6.
191 Menge, *Alltag*, 30–31.
192 Nicolai, *Beschreibung*, 11.
193 *Berlin in Kartenbild*, catalogue 14. Kuntze, *Das alte Berlin*, 7; Rürup in *Berlin, Berlin*, 32.
194 Kuntze, *Das alte Berlin*, 10–11; Ribbe, *Geschichte*, I, 407–408; *Berlin in Kartenbild*, catalogue 20.
195 Ribbe, *Geschichte*, I, 408.
196 Idem, 410–411. Johannes C. Prittwitz, *Mark Brandenburg, Wanderbuch*, I, Berlin 1990, 39–43.
197 Idem.
198 David Marsh, *The New Germany: At the Crossroads*, London 1990, 118–120; Marion Gräfin Dönhoff, *Weit ist der Weg nach Osten: Berichte und Betrachtungen ans fünf Jahrzehnten*, Munich 1988, 86–89.
199 E. T. A. Hoffmann, *Ritter Gluck: Eine Erinnerung aus dem Jahre 1809*, in *Werke*, I, 3.
200 Karl Edouard Schmidt-Lötzen ed., *Dreißig Jahre am Hofe Friedrichs des Großer. Aus den Tagebüchern des Reichsgrafen*

Ernst Ahasverns von Lehndorff, Kammerherrn der Königin Elisabeth Christine von Preußen. Gotha, 1907.

201 Engel, Jersch-Wenzel and Treue, *Tiergarten*, I, XII.
202 Idem.
203 Hans-Rainer Sandvoß, *Stätten des Widerstandes in Berlin*, Berlin n.d., 22. Rodenberg, *Bilder*, 70.
204 Dehio, *Berlin*, 488. Schulz, *Stadtführer*, 22.
205 Hürlimann, *Berlin*, 131.
206 Engel, Jersch-Wenzel and Treue, *Tiergarten*, I, 39.
207 Idem. Sybille Einholz, 'Reinhold Begas und sein Kreis', *Mitteilungen des Vereins für die Geschichte Berlins*, Heft 3, July 1994, 274–283.
208 Walter Benjamin, *Berliner Kindheit um Neunzehnhundert*, Frankfurt am Main 1950, 19.
209 Corinth, *Selbstbiographie*, 167.
210 Illustrated in Marion Gräfin Dönhoff, *Preußen: Maß und Maßlosigkeit*, Berlin 1987, 72–73. Pages 70–71 show some of the *Ahnen*.
211 Mann, *Der Untertan*, 419.
212 Engel, Jersch-Wenzel and Treue, *Tiergarten*, I, 17.
213 Rodenberg, *Bilder*, 73–74; Engel, Jersch-Wenzel and Treue, *Tiergarten*, I, 58–60.
214 Giles MacDonogh, *Brillat-Savarin: The Judge and His Stomach*, London 1992, 170.
215 Idem. Rodenberg, *Bilder*, 75.
216 Idem, 76; Engel, Jersch-Wenzel and Treue, *Tiergarten*, I, 58; Miss (Anne) Topham, *Souvenir de la cour du Kaiser*, Paris n.d., 110, 119.
217 Engel, Jersch-Wenzel and Treue, *Tiergarten*, I, 60.
218 Idem. Letter to the author from Professor Shlomo Avineri, 2 May 1993.
219 Dehio, *Berlin*, 463–465.
220 Michael Cullen, *Der Reichstag: Die Geschichte eines Monumentes*, Stuttgart 1990, 190–191.
221 Idem, 33.
222 Idem, 32, 37.
223 Idem, 32, 39–40.
224 Schinz, *Bauten in Berlin*, 15.
225 Kessler, *Diaries*, 117.
226 Idem, 185–186.
227 François-Poncet, *Souvenirs*, 92

228 The debate is presented in Fritz Tobias, *The Reichstag Fire: Legend and Truth*, London 1963.
229 Cullen, *Reichstag*, 385.
230 Alexander von Falkenhausen, *Mémoires d'outre guerre*, Brussels 1974.
231 Engel, Jersch-Wenzel and Treue, *Tiergarten*, I, 24–25.
232 Wilhelm J. C. E. Stieber, *Spion des Kanzlers: Die Enthüllungen von Bismarcks Geheimdienstchef*, Stuttgart 1978, 60.
233 Engel, Jersch-Wenzel and Treue, *Tiergarten*, I, 14.
234 Idem, 126; Thomas Wieke, *Vom Etablissement zur Oper: Die Geschichte der Kroll-Oper*, Berlin 1993, 56.
235 Engel, Jersch-Wenzel and Treue, *Tiergarten*, I, 131.
236 Viktor Klemperer, *Ich will Zeugnis ablegen bis zum letzten: Tagebücher 1933–1945*, Berlin and Weimar 1995, I, 251.
237 Engel, Jersch-Wenzel and Treue, *Tiergarten*, I, 131.
238 Idem, 135.
239 Giles MacDonogh, *A Palate in Revolution*, London 1987, 61.
240 Archives départementales de la Gironde, 13 L 26, Wittfooth.
241 Engel, Jersch-Wenzel and Treue, *Tiergarten*, I, 135.
242 MacDonogh, *Prussia*, 177.
243 Engel, Jersch-Wenzel and Treue, *Tiergarten*, I, XIV.
244 Conversation with Karl Henssel, Clarita von Trott and Will Dambisch, Berlin-Dahlem, 7 April 1995.
245 Pottle ed., *Grand Tour*, 39 and 41, n1.
246 Ribbe, *Geschichte*.
247 See Fontane, *Schach von Wuthenow*, in *Werke*, II, 20.
248 Ribbe, *Geschichte*, II, 409.
249 Engel, Jersch-Wenzel and Treue, *Tiergarten*, I, XIII.
250 Lederer, *Uns kann keener*, 15; Benjamin, *Kindheit*, 13, 18.
251 Kessler, *Diaries*, 278.
252 Bella Fromm, *Blood and Banquets: A Berlin Diary 1930–38*, New York 1990, 134–135. Bella Fromm's book was put down during the war. There are signs that it was influenced in places by the war-effort.
253 Idem.
254 Engel, Jersch-Wenzel and Treue, *Tiergarten*, I, XIV; idem, 299; Schulz, *Stadtführer*, 30.
255 Engel, Jersch-Wenzel and Treue, *Tiergarten*, II, 299.

SOURCE NOTES TO PAGES 134-142

256 Marie 'Missie' Vassiltchikov, *The Berlin Diaries, 1940–1945*, London 1985, 303.
257 Pilz, Hofmann and Thomisch, *Berlin-W,* Einführung. Fromm, *Blood and Banquets*, 263.
258 Ostwald, *Berlin und die Berlinerin*, 186.
259 Dehio, *Berlin*, 476.
260 Giles MacDonogh, 'Letter from Germany', *Financial Times*, 30 September 1995.
261 Idem.
262 Idem.
263 Jutta Rosenkranz, *Berlin im Gedicht*, Husum 1987, 39–40.
264 Eloesser, *Straße meiner Jugend*, 57.
265 Idem, 59–60.
266 Peter Klaus Schuster, *George Grosz, Berlin – New York*, Berlin 1995, 388.
267 Thieme, *Das letzte Haus*, 27.
268 Idem, 15.
269 Idem, 11.
270 Benjamin, *Kindheit*, 127.
271 Harro Strehlow, 'Einige Dokumente aus der Frühgeschichte des Zoologischen Gartens', *Mitteilungen des Vereins für die Geschichte Berlins*, Heft 1, January 1994.
272 Dronke, *Berlin*, 59.
273 Fontane, *Irrungen, Wirrungen*, in *Werke*, III, 33.
274 Adlon, *Hotel Adlon*, 21, 24.
275 Mann, *Der Untertan*, 22.
276 Benjamin, *Kindheit*, 56, 98.
277 Herta Ramthun ed., Bertolt Brecht, *Tagebücher 1920–1922, autobiographische Aufzeichnungen 1920–1954*, Frankfurt am Main 1975, 176.
278 Wolfdietrich Schnurre, *Als Vaters Bart noch rot war*, Berlin 1996, 30.
279 Idem, 33.
280 Engel, Jersch-Wenzel and Treue, *Tiergarten*, I, 307.
281 Schäfer, *Berlin im zweitem Weltkrieg*, 160–162.
282 Idem, 164.
283 Vassiltchikov, *Berlin Diaries*, 111.
284 Kardorff, *Aufzeichnungen*, 130.
285 Hans-Georg von Studnitz, *While Berlin Burns*. Quoted in MacDonogh, *A Good German*, 253.
286 Akinscha and Koslow, *Beutekunst*, 83.

287 Schinz, *Bauen in Berlin*. Helmut Engel, Stefi Jersch-Wenzel and Wilhelm Treue, *Charlottenburg*, II, *Der neue Westen*, Berlin 1985, 325.

288 Kardorff, *Aufzeichnungen*, 130.

289 Edward Crankshaw, *Bismarck*, London 1981, 120–121.

290 Engel, Jersch-Wenzel and Treue, *Charlottenburg*, II, 172–173.

291 Idem, 185.

292 Idem, 189.

293 Quoted in MacDonogh, *A Good German*, 284.

294 Erich Kästner, *Notabene 45*, Zurich 1961, 26.

295 Canvases in the Ephraims Palais.

296 Bröhan, *Skarbina*, 56–57.

297 Kelly Morris and Amanda Woods eds., *Art in Berlin*, Atlanta 1989, 136.

298 Ribbe, *Geschichte*, II, 705.

299 Idem, 707.

300 Fontane, *Irrungen, Wirrungen*, 106.

301 Paul Ortwin Rave and Irmgard Wirth, *Die Bauwerke und Kunstdenkmäler von Berlin: Stadt und Bezirk Charlottenburg*, Berlin 1961, 11.

302 Idem.

303 Margarete Kühn, *Schloß Charlottenburg: Die Bauwerke und Kunstdenkmäler von Berlin*, Berlin 1970, 1. Dehio, *Handbuch der deutschen Kunstdenkmäler*, Berlin/DDR and Potsdam, Berlin (East) 1983, 246–247.

304 Rave and Wirth, *Charlottenburg*, 15.

305 Kühn, *Charlottenburg*, 11.

306 Idem, 117–129, 139–141.

307 Rave and Wirth, *Charlottenburg*, 18.

308 Schmidt-Lötzen ed., *Dreißig Jahre*, 24.

309 Rave and Wirth, *Charlottenburg*, 20. See also: Eckhart Kleßmann, *E. T. A. Hoffmann Oder die Fiefe Zwischen Stern und Erde*, Stuttgart 1988.

310 Rave and Wirth, *Charlottenburg*, 25.

311 Idem, 108.

312 Brennglas, 'Berliner Fuhrleute', in *Berlin wie es ist – und trinkt*, 3–4.

313 Rave and Wirth, *Charlottenburg*, 27; Engel, Jersch-Wenzel and Treue, *Charlottenburg*, I, XVI. Frecot and Geisert, *Berlin*, Plate 173.

314 Rave and Wirth, *Charlottenburg*, 28.
315 Dieter Schütte, *Charlottenburg*, Berlin 1988, 36.
316 Rave and Wirth, *Charlottenburg*, 28.
317 Ernst Wiechert, *Jahre und Zeiten: Erinnerungen*, Frankfurt am Main and Berlin 1989, 285.
318 Schütte, *Charlottenburg*, 89; Engel, Jersch-Wenzel and Treue, *Charlottenburg*, I, XV–XVI.
319 Idem.
320 Idem. Schütte, *Charlottenburg*, 87.
321 Engel, Jersch-Wenzel and Treue, *Charlottenburg*, II, XII.
322 Schinz, *Bauten in Berlin*, 92; Dehio, *Berlin*, 198–199.
323 Kessler, *Diaries*, 274–275.
324 Engel, Jersch-Wenzel and Treue, *Charlottenburg*, II, 38–40.
325 Author's visits to members of the British garrison, 1991–1992.
326 Helmut Engel, Stefi Jersch-Wenzel and Wilhelm Treue, *Zehlendorf*, Berlin 1992, XV.
327 Sombart, *Jugend*, 10.
328 Idem; MacDonogh, *Prussia*, n222.
329 Spieß ed., *Gauner*, 57; Walter Huder and Thomas Koehner eds., Alfred Kerr, *Ich kam nach England: Ein Tagebuch aus dem Nachlaß*, Bonn 1979, 23.
330 Sombart, *Jugend*, 17.
332 Klaus Mann, *Mephisto*, Reinbek 1981, 296
333 Kästner, *Fabian*, 77, 78.
335 Conversation with Werner Knopp, Berlin-Tiergarten, June 1991.
334 Heinrich Haak in Engel, Jersch-Wenzel and Treue, *Zehlendorf*, XV.
335 Idem, 160.
336 Idem, 162.
337 Idem, 165–166; Dehio, *Berlin*, 586, 588.
338 Sombart, *Jugend*, 214.
339 See Leistikow's *Grunewaldsee*, for example, in the Neue Nationalgallerie. Liebermann's villa, Am Großen Wannsee 42, still exists. Until recently it was used by a sporting club. There are plans to restore the gardens. Engel, Jersch-Wenzel and Treue, *Zehlendorf*, 429.
340 Engel, Jersch-Wenzel and Treue, *Zehlendorf*, 432–4.
341 Idem, 435–441.

342 Giles MacDonogh, 'Easily Forgotten', *Literary Review,* October 1994; Naomi Shepherd, *Wilfrid Israel,* London 1984, quoted in MacDonogh, *A Good German,* 73.

343 Engel, Jersch-Wenzel and Treue, *Zehlendorf,* 412–413.

344 See Ralf Georg Reuth, *Goebbels: The Life of Joseph Goebbels, the Mephistophelean Genius of Nazi Propaganda,* London 1993, 236–237.

345 Idem, 218

346 Engel, Jersch-Wenzel and Treue, *Zehlendorf,* 478–479.

347 Michael Seiler, 'Die russische Rutschbahn auf der Pfaueninsel', *Mitteilungen des Vereins für die Geschichte Berlins,* Heft 2, April 1993; Engel, Jersch-Wenzel and Treue, *Zehlendorf,* 492; François-Poncet, *Souvenirs,* 265.

348 For Auwi's career in the Nazi Party, see MacDonogh, *Prussia,* 102–107.

349 Engel, Jersch-Wenzel and Treue, *Zehlendorf,* 60.

350 Fontane, *Wanderungen,* III, 340.

351 Idem.

352 Idem, 340, 344.

353 Dronke, *Berlin,* 240.

354 Engel, Jersch-Wenzel and Treue, *Zehlendorf,* 447–456.

355 Idem.

356 Gräfin Malve Rothkirch, *Prinz Carl von Preußen, Kenner und Beschützer des Schönen, 1801–1883,* Osnabrück 1981, 116–117.

357 Helmut Engel, 'Friedrich Wilhelm IV und die Baukunst', in Otto Busch ed., *Friedrich Wilhelm IV in seiner Zeit: Beitrag eines Colloquiums, Historische Kommission zu Berlin,* Berlin 1987, Plates 111–114.

358 Döblin, *Ein Kerl,* 88.

359 Döblin, Idem.

360 Engel, Jersch-Wenzel and Treue, *Zehlendorf,* 42.

361 Idem, XVIII, 132.

362 MacDonogh, *A Good German,* 47.

363 Engel, Jersch-Wenzel and Treue, *Zehlendorf,* 136.

364 Idem 395–407.

365 Heinrich Assel ed., *Der du die Zeit in Händen hast, Rudolf Hermann und Jochen Klepper 1925–1942,* unter Mitarbeit von Arnold Wiebel, Munich 1992, 9.

366 Brennglas, *Berlin wie es ist – und trinkt,* 4.

367 Idem, 5.

368 Idem, 34.
369 Engel, Jersch-Wenzel and Treue, *Moabit*, II, XII–XVI.
370 See, for example, Dr Neuse, *Spandau, ein Märkisches Stadtbild*, Spandau-bei-Berlin 1913, 8; Neuse argues against the existence of a Wendish town.
371 Jahn, *Spandau*, 5–6.
372 Idem, 8.
373 Neuse, *Spandau*, 18.
374 Jahn, *Spandau*, 12–13.
375 Neuse, *Spandau*, 18.
376 Ribbe, *Spandau*, 55.
377 Neuse, *Spandau*, 51.
378 Jahn, *Spandau*, 269–272; Vita Sackville-West's, *Pepita*, 2nd edn., London 1961, is silent on the subject.
379 Nicolai, *Beschreibung*, 46.
380 Mann, *Der Untertan*, 25.
381 Carl Schulz, *3,000 Berliner Kolonisten und Kolonistensöhne 1686–1812*, Neustadt-an-der-Aisch 1972, 13.
382 Fontane, *Wanderungen*, II, 157.
383 Idem.
384 Kästner, *Fabian*, 165.
385 Eduard Bernstein, *Die Geschichte der Berliner Arbeiterbewegung 1907*. (Reprint Grashutten im Taurus), 38
386 Lederer, *Uns kann keener*, 30; Schlobinski, *Berliner Wörterbuch*, 52; Dehio, *Berlin*, 384.
387 Ribbe, *Geschichte*, I, 453; Schäfer, *Berlin im zweitem Weltkrieg*, 69.
388 Engel, Jersch-Wenzel and Treue, *Kreuzberg*, XII.
389 Ribbe, *Geschichte*, I, 408.
390 Engel, Jersch-Wenzel and Treue, *Kreuzberg*, X.
391 Idem, 440–441.
392 Idem, 443.
393 Idem.
394 Agnes Lanwer in idem, 449–452.
395 Dehio, *Berlin*, 295.
396 Kästner, *Fabian*, 109–110.
397 Rosenkranz, *Berlin im Gedicht*, 21.
398 Rodenberg, *Bilder*, 82. Baudelaire, *Du vin et du hachisch*, in Baudelaire, *Oeuvres complètes*, preface de Claude Roy, Paris 1980, 216.

399 Nicolai, *Beschreibung*, 6; Escher, *Neukölln*, Berlin 1988, 26.

400 Idem, 56.

401 Adolf Brennglas, 'Der Stralower Fischzug', in *Berlin wie es ist – und trinkt*, III, Leipzig 1845, 32.

402 Idem. 38.

403 Kalisch, *Einmalhundertausend Taler*, 204–205.

404 Erika von Hornstein, *Adieu Potsdam*, 2nd edn., Munich 1986, 171–179.

3 Berlin Life

1 Schmidt-Lötzen ed., *Dreißig Jahre*, 137, 185.

2 Max Hecker ed., *Der Briefwechser zwischen Goethe und Zetter*, 3 vols, Leipzig 1915. Hereafter, *Briefwechsel*, II, 48.

3 Idem, 115; Nicolai, *Beschreibung*, 396.

4 MacDonogh, *Prussia*, 251.

5 Princess Marie Radziwill, *This was Germany: An Observer at the Court of Berlin*, edited by Cyril Spencer Fox, London 1937, 111.

6 Schmidt-Lötzen ed., *Dreißig Jahre*, 41.

7 Idem, 23.

8 Dronke, *Berlin*, 31.

9 Idem, 35.

10 Fontane, *Der Stechlin*, in *Werke*, V, 315.

11 Dronke, *Berlin*, 33–34; Bodo Rollka, Volker Spieß, Bernhard Thieme, *Berliner biographisches Lexicon*, Berlin 1993, 374; Michael Kennedy, *Dictionary of Music*, Oxford 1980, 610.

12 Sombart, *Jugend*, 10.

13 Blücher, *An English Wife*, 208.

14 Sombart, *Jugend*, 90.

15 Idem, 94.

16 Idem, 101.

17 Fromm, *Diary*, 21–22.

18 Idem, 23–24.

19 Idem, 59.

20 MacDonogh, *A Good German*, 43.

21 Fromm, *Diary*, 85.

22 Idem, 87.

23 Sombart, *Jugend*, 107.

24 Ribbe, *Geschichte*, I, 381.

25 Stieber, *Spion des Kanzlers*, 47–48.

26 Ribbe, *Geschichte*, II, 656.

27 MacDonogh, *Prussia*, 327.

28 Clauswitz, *Städteordnung*, 6.

29 Alfred Döblin, *Autobiographische Schriften und letzte Aufzeichnungen*, Freiburg im Breisgau 1980, 17.

30 Clauswitz, *Städteordnung*, 4.

31 Idem, III; Buffet, *Berlin*, 423–424.

32 Hecker ed., *Briefwechsel*, I, 15.

33 Quoted in Gordon A. Craig, 'The Way to the Wall', *New York Review of Books*, 28 June 1990.

34 Dronke, *Berlin*, 20.

35 Zille, *Zille und sein Berlin*, n.p.

36 Schleicher, *Chamisso*, 41–42.

37 Idem, 44.

38 Hannah Arendt, *Rahel Varnhagen, Lebensgeschichte einer deutschen Jüdin aus der Romantik*, Munich 1981, 62.

39 Ostwald, *Berlin und die Berlinerin*, 226.

40 See Isobel Hull, *The Entourage of Kaiser Wilhelm II 1888–1918*, Cambridge 1982 45–75.

41 'Comte Paul Vasili', *La Société de Berlin*, Paris 1884, 164.

42 Idem, 163.

43 Idem, 166.

44 Idem.

45 Stewart Spencer and Barry Millington, *Selected Letters of Richard Wagner*, London 1987, 820, 836.

46 'Vasili', *La Société de Berlin*, 172.

47 Idem, 175.

48 Sombart, *Jugend*, 12–13.

49 Idem, 68, 107.

50 Vassiltchikov, *Berlin Diaries*, 162.

51 Idem, 197.

52 Sombart, *Jugend*, 10, 81.

53 Zille, *Zille und sein Berlin*, 11.

54 Idem. Claire Waldoff, *Es gibt nur ein Berlin*, Edition Berliner Musenkinder n.d.; Otto Schneidereit, *Berlin wie es weint und lacht*, Berlin (East) 1976, 205.

55 Bernstein, *Arbeiter-bewegung*, III.

56 Idem, 1; Morris and Woods, *Art in Berlin*, 115, 53.

57 Trost, *Gaertner*, Plate 70.

58 Bernstein, *Arbeiter-bewegung*, 2.

59 Idem.

60 Idem, 4.

61 Idem, 8.

62 Idem, 85.

63 Idem, 94.

64 Idem, 116.

65 Dronke, *Berlin*, 229–232.

66 Dronke, *Aus dem Volk*, 14–15.

67 Idem, 21.

68 Arnim, *Dies Buch*, 453; see also Johann Friedrich Geist and Klaus Kürvers, *Das Berliner Mietshaus 1740–1862*, Munich 1980, 26–27.

69 Idem, 454.

70 Idem, 459.

71 Idem, 456.

72 See MacDonogh, *Prussia*, 288–291.

73 Arnim, *Dies Buch*, 454.

74 Ribbe, *Geschichte*, II, 658.

75 Engel, Jersch-Wenzel and Treue, *Tiergarten* and, II, *Moabit*, 157–159.

76 Idem, 160–166.

77 Idem, 168.

78 MacDonogh, *A Good German*, 215.

79 Engel, Jersch-Wenzel and Treue, *Tiergarten*, II, *Moabit*, 173.

80 Hürlimann, *Berlin*, 38–39.

81 Engel, Jersch-Wenzel and Treue, *Kreuzberg*, XV.

82 Engel, Jersch-Wenzel and Treue, *Tiergarten*, II, *Moabit*, XVI.

83 Idem, 16.

84 Idem, 34.

85 Idem, 36, 40–41.

86 Döblin, *Ein Kerl*, 49–51.

87 Nase, *Icke, dette, kieke mal*, 15.

88 Idem, 30–31.

89 Idem, 18. Eloesser, *Straße meiner Jugend*, 54.

90 See Rétif de La Bretonne, *Les Contemporains* and *Le Drame d'une vie*. Paul Thiel, introduction to Adolf

Glaßbrenner, *Berlin wie es ist – und trinkt*, Berlin (East) 1987, 1, XX.

91 Detlef Kruse, *Glaßbrenner und der Berliner Dialekt*, Berlin 1987, 86.

92 Idem, 67.

93 Brennglas, 'Herr Buffey auf der Berlin–Leipziger Eisenbahn', in *Berlin wie es ist – und trinkt*, II 30.

94 Brennglas, 'Nante Nantin', in *Berlin wie es ist – und trinkt*, II, 30–31.

95 Brennglas, 'Herr Buffey in der Zaruoek Gesellschaft', in *Berlin wie es ist – und trinkt*, II, 6.

96 Dronke, *Berlin*, 18.

97 Idem, 18–19.

98 Lederer, *Uns kann keener*, 8–9.

99 Idem, 13, 36.

100 Idem, 40.

101 Idem, 41–42.

102 Idem, 43.

103 Fontane, *Wanderungen*, II, 779.

104 Schadow exhibition, Berlin Alte National Gallerie, 1995. *Déjeuner à la fourchette* is no. 119 in the catalogue. Rudolf Pfefferkorn in *Berliner Zeichner von Schadow bis Krüger: Aus dem Besitz des Vereins Berliner Künstler* (exhibition catalogue), 1970–1971 (no page nos.).

105 Lederer, *Uns kann keener*, 52.

106 Engel, Jersch-Wenzel and Treue, *Tiergarten*, I, 40–41. Spieß ed., *Gauner*, 167.

107 Egon Jameson in idem, 87.

108 Idem, 166. Zille, *Zille und sein Berlin*, 8–9.

109 Idem, 11.

110 Idem,

111 Engel, Jersch-Wenzel and Treue, *Tiergarten*, I, 133.

112 Konrad Warner in Schäfer, *Berlin im zweiten Weltkrieg*, 203.

113 Conversation with Clarita von Trott zu Solz, Will Dambisch and Karl Henssel, Berlin-Dahlem, April 1995.

114 Information from members of the British garrison, Berlin, 1991–1992.

115 Ribbe, *Geschichte*, I, 305.

116 Idem, 306.

117 Dronke, *Berlin*, 80.
118 MacDonogh, *Prussia*, 137–139.
119 Spieß ed., *Gauner*, 171.
120 Stieber, *Spion des Kanzlers*, 55–57.
121 Spieß ed., *Gauner*, 208–221.
122 Idem, 174–176.
123 Idem, 230.
124 Ribbe, *Geschichte*, II, 868; Christian Engeli, *Gustav Böß, Oberbürgermeister von Berlin 1921–1930*, Stuttgart, Cologne and Mainz 1971, 230.
125 Ribbe, *Geschichte*, II, 869.
126 Idem, 870.
127 Spieß ed., *Gauner*, 193.
128 Ribbe, *Geschichte*, II, 871; Engeli, *Böß*, 238.
129 Thieme, *Das letzte Haus*, 84.
130 Engeli, *Böß*, 243–244; Ribbe, *Geschichte*, II, 872.
131 Ribbe, *Geschichte*, I, 427–428.
132 Akinscha and Koslow, *Beutekunst*, 7, 123.
133 Idem, 51.
134 Lynn Nicholas, *The Rape of Europa*, London 1994, 405.
135 Akinscha and Koslow, *Beutekunst*, 72.
136 Idem, 74–76.
137 Idem, 114–115.
138 Lynn Nicholas, *Rape*, 441.
139 Akinscha and Koslow, *Beutekunst*, 99.
140 Inge Marßolek, *Die Denunzianin: Helene Schwärzel 1944–1947*, Bremen 1992, 53–56.
141 Idem, 62, 72.
142 Ostwald, *Berlin und die Berlinerin*, 10; Friedrich von Oppeln-Bronikowski, *Abenteurer am Preußischen Hofe 1700–1800*, Berlin and Leipzig 1927, 105, 117.
143 Hürlimann, *Berlin*, 41; Pottle, *Grand Tour*, 88, 89.
144 Dronke, *Berlin*, 29.
145 Idem, 31.
146 Fontane, *Stine*, in *Werke*, II.
147 Dronke, *Aus dem Volk*, 34.
148 Idem, 46.
149 Dronke, *Berlin*, 40.
150 Idem, 41.
151 Stieber, *Spion des Kanzlers*, 61.
152 Idem, 62–63.

153 Idem, 68.

154 [Stieber], *Prostitution.*

155 Idem.

156 Idem.

157 Idem, 18–26.

158 Idem, 29–33.

159 Idem, 35.

160 Idem, 36–37.

161 Idem, 48–49.

162 Idem, 49–53.

163 Quoted in idem, 59.

164 Idem, 60; See also Röhrmann [C. W. Zimmermann], *Der sittliche Zustand von Berlin nach Aufhebung der geduldeten Prostitution des weiblichen Geschlechts: Ein Beitrag zur Geschichte der Gegenwand*, Leipzig 1846 reprinted 1981, 8, 60–62.

165 [Stieber], *Prostitution*, 63–66 [Zimmermann], *Sittliche Zustand*, 40.

166 [Stieber], *Prostitution*, 76.

167 Dronke, *Berlin*, 76–77.

168 [Stieber], *Prostitution*, 84–86; [Zimmermann], *Sittliche Zustand*, 24–25.

169 Idem, 96–100, 171; [Stieber], *Prostitution*, 92–98.

170 Idem, 102.

171 Idem, 113.

172 Idem, 153.

173 Idem,

174 Idem, 155.

175 Idem, 158.

176 Idem, 160.

177 Klaus Ullmann, *Schlesien Lexicon*, 4th edn., Mannheim 1985, 116.

178 Idem, 170–171.

179 Kästner, *Fabian*, 99.

180 Schäfer, *Berlin im zweitem Weltkrieg*, 211.

181 MacDonogh, *A Good German*, 193.

182 A. A. Löwenthal, 'Die Lietzenburgerstraße, ein Versuch der historischen Kontinuität', in *Gesammelte Schriften*, Tübingen and Stuttgart 1956, III, 124–137.

183 *Tagesspiegel*, 5 April 1995.

184 Engel, Jersch-Wenzel and Treue, *Kreuzberg*, 358.

185 Schäfer, *Berlin im zweitem Weltkrieg*, 212.
186 Hecker ed., *Briefwechsel*, I, 448.
187 [Stieber], *Prostitution*, 208.
188 Idem, 209–210.
189 MacDonogh, *Prussia*, 204–230 passim.
190 Engel, Jersch-Wenzel and Treue, *Charlottenburg*, I, 129–132.
191 Idem, 132.
192 Idem, 134.
193 Idem, 135–137.
194 Goll, *Sodome et Berlin*, 62.
195 Lange, *Berlin zur Zeit Bebels und Bismarcks*, 25.
196 Idem, 257.
197 Stieber, *Spion des Kanzlers*, 95.
198 Idem, 99–100.
199 Idem, 107–110.
200 Engel, Jersch-Wenzel and Treue, *Charlottenburg*, I, 7.
201 Ribbe, *Geschichte*, II, 649.
202 Engel, Jersch-Wenzel and Treue, *Charlottenburg*, I, 7.
203 Ribbe, *Geschichte*, II, 643, 649.
204 Idem, 649.
205 Engel, Jersch-Wenzel and Treue, *Charlottenburg*, I, 11.
206 Stieber, *Spion des Kanzlers*, 90.
207 Heinrich, *Geschichte Preußens*, 388.
208 Engel, Jersch-Wenzel and Treue, *Charlottenburg*, I, 11; Stieber, *Spion des Kanzlers*, 90.
209 Ribbe, *Geschichte*, II, 650.
210 Stieber, *Spion des Kanzlers*, 91.
211 Robert Hellman, *Berlin: The Red Room and White Beer: The 'Free' Hegelian Radicals in the 1840s*, Washington DC 1990, 33–34.
212 Ernst Dronke, *Polizei Geschichten*, Leipzig 1846, 1; Edward Crankshaw, *Gestapo, Instrument of Tyranny*, London 1990, 74–75;
213 H. B. Gisevius, *Bis zum bittern Ende*, Darmstadt 1947, I, 50.
214 Crankshaw, *Gestapo*, 45.
215 Engel, Jersch-Wenzel and Treue, *Kreuzberg*, 40.
216 Idem, 41–42, 44.
217 Idem, 46.

218 Friedrich Holtze, *Lokalgeschichte des königlichen Kammergerichts*, Berlin 1896, 1–4.

219 Idem, 65–69.

220 Engel, Jersch-Wenzel and Treue, *Kreuzberg*, 238.

221 Idem, 235; Hubatsch, *Frederick the Great*, 216–217.

222 Friedrich Holtze, *Geschichte des Kammergerichts in Brandenburg-Preußen*, IV *Das Kammergericht im 19. Jahrhundert*, Berlin 1904, 80–82.

223 Idem, 82; see also Ernst Wichert, *Richter und Dichter: Ein Lebensausweis*, Berlin and Leipzig 1899, 235, 262.

224 Holtze, *Geschichte des Kammergerichts*, 82.

225 Alfred Hoffmann, *E. T. A. Hoffmann: Leben und Arbeit eines Preußischen Richters*, Baden-Baden 1990, 62.

226 Idem

227 Idem, 61.

228 Idem, 114–115.

229 Idem, 112.

230 Idem, 188–189; E. T. A. Hoffmann, *Lebensansichten des Katers Murr*, in *Werke*, III, 242.

231 Wolf. ed., *Und grüß mich nicht*, 140.

232 Hoffmann, *Hoffmann*, 190.

233 Wolf ed., *Und grüß mich nicht*, 162–163.

234 Idem, 197.

235 Hoffmann, *Hoffmann*, 202–203, 216.

236 Holtze, *Geschichte des Kammergerichts*, 84–85.

237 Engel, Jersch-Wenzel and Treue, *Kreuzberg*, 235.

238 Engel, Jersch-Wenzel and Treue, *Charlottenburg*, II, 151–165.

239 Moltke, *Letters to Freya*, 401–402.

240 Engel, Jersch-Wenzel and Treue, *Tiergarten*, I, 224.

241 Idem, 225–228; information from Clarita von Trott and Angela Bielenberg.

242 Engel, Jersch-Wenzel and Treue, *Tiergarten*, II, 221; Lange, *Berlin zur Zeit Bebels und Bismarcks*, 670.

243 See MacDonogh, *Prussia*, 204–230.

244 Engel, Jersch-Wenzel and Treue, *Tiergarten*, II, 225–226.

245 Rosamunde Neugebauer, 'Der Satire wird der Prozeß gemacht – der Fall Grosz', in *George Grosz Berlin – New York*, Berlin 1994, 169, 170.

246 Elias Canetti, *Die Fackel im Ohr: Lebensgeschichte*

1921–1931, Munich and Vienna 1980, 312. I am grateful to Stuart Pigott for directing me to this book.

247 Neugebauer in *George Grosz, Berlin – New York*, 171.

248 Idem, 172.

249 Engel, Jersch-Wenzel and Treue, *Tiergarten*, II, 228–229.

250 Idem, 230.

251 Schmidt-Lötzen ed. *Dreißig Jahre*, 101; Preuss ed., *Oeuvres de Frédéric le Grand*, XVIII, 91–92, 92 n.a.

252 Menge, *Alltag*, 181.

253 Idem, 182–183.

254 Idem, 184, 187.

255 Lehndorff, *Tagebücher*, 17.

256 Werner Notz, 'Richard Wagner und Berlin, III', in *Mitteilungen des Vereins für die Geschichte Berlins*, Heft 3, July 1992, 60ff. Spencer and Millington, *Selected Letters of Richard Wagner*, 38.

257 Dronke, *Berlin*, 308–310.

258 Engel, Jersch-Wenzel and Treue, *Tiergarten*, II, 187.

259 Idem, 188.

260 Ribbe, *Spandau*, 113.

261 Albert Speer, *Spandau, the Secret Diaries*, trans. Richard and Clara Winton, London 1976, 66–67.

262 Idem, 5, 67.

263 Peter Padfield, *Hess, the Führer's Disciple*, London 1995, 339, 364.

264 Ribbe, *Spandau*, 74–75.

265 Information gleaned at a cocktail party given near the site of the prison, 19 June 1991.

266 Engel, Jersch-Wenzel and Treue, *Charlottenburg*, I, 215.

267 Harald Poelchau, *Die letzten Stunden: Erinnerungen eines Gefängnispfarrers*, aufgezeichnet von Graf Alexander Steinbock-Fermor, Cologne 1987, 8–12.

268 Idem, 16.

269 Idem, 18.

270 Idem, 25.

271 Idem, 26.

272 Idem, 28.

273 Idem, 29.

274 Idem, 31–33.

275 Idem, 41–42.

276 Idem, 48.

277 Idem, 49.
280 Idem, 99.

4 Berlin Bacchanalia

1 Kästner, *Notabene 45*, 17.
2 Conversation with Inga Haag, 8 September 1995.
3 Nicolai, *Beschreibung*, 414.
4 Hürlimann, *Berlin*, 33.
5 Nicolai, *Beschreibung*, 417, 419.
6 Idem, 428–431. Ribbe, *Geschichte*, I, 409.
7 Engel, Jersch-Wenzel and Treue, *Charlottenburg*, I, XIV, 319.
8 Engel, Jersch-Wenzel and Treue, *Moabit*, 33.
9 Engel, Jersch-Wenzel and Treue, *Kreuzberg*, XIX.
10 Bröhan, *Baluschek*, 45.
11 Rodenberg, *Bilder*, 63.
12 See Giles MacDonogh, 'E. T. A. Hoffmann, Dionysos, vin, ivresse', in Gilbert Garrier ed., *Actes du symposium: Les Rencontres de Dionysos 93*, Nîmes 3–6 novembre 1993, 109–118.
13 Müller ed., *Berlinische Geschichten*, 117, 142.
14 Idem, 197.
15 See MacDonogh, 'E. T. A. Hoffmann, Dionysos, vin, ivresse', 110.
16 J. W. Goethe, *West-Östlicher Divan*, Vorwort und Erläuterungen von Max Rychner, Zurich 1952, 105 and note, 535.
17 Idem, 198.
18 Idem, 199–205.
19 Ribbe, *Geschichte*, I, 325.
20 Lederer, *Uns kann keener*, 156.
21 Ribbe, *Geschichte*, I, 325.
22 Fontane, *Wanderungen*, II, 437.
23 Rodenberg, *Bilder*, 8.
   Michael Jackson, *Beer Companion*, London 1993, 53. This gives the recipe for modern *Weiße*.
24 Text in Lederer, *Uns kann keener*, 156–157; music: Hermann Prey, *Ich sing mein schönstes Lied*, Capriccio, Königsdorf, 1989.

25 Plessen in *Berlin, Berlin,* 212; Frecot and Geisert, *Berlin,* Plates 97 and 119 show the signs.
26 Fontane, *Der Stechlin,* in *Werke,* V, 321.
27 Plessen in *Berlin, Berlin,* 212.
28 Idem.
29 Canetti, *Fackel,* 322, 333.
30 Goll, *Sodome et Berlin,* 110; Döblin, *Berlin-Alexanderplatz,* 146.
31 Plessen in *Berlin, Berlin,* 213.
32 Dehio, *Berlin,* 138–139.
33 Idem, 215.
34 Jahn, *Spandau,* 412.
35 Author's visit to the Tivoli Brewery, August 1991. 'Still in the Dark Ages', *Financial Times,* 2 November 1991.
36 Hasso Spode in Engel, Jersch-Wenzel and Treue, *Kreuzberg,* 399–408.
37 Idem, 414.
38 Ribbe, *Geschichte,* I, 325.
39 Spode in Engel, Jersch-Wenzel and Treue, *Kreuzberg,* 399.
40 Rodenberg, *Bilder,* 53.
41 Lederer, *Uns kann keener,* 158.
42 Rodenberg, *Bilder,* 160.
43 Wolf ed., *Und grüß mich nicht,* 126.
44 Idem, 133
45 Idem, 134–135.
46 Hellman, *Red Room,* 15.
47 Dronke, *Berlin,* 50.
48 Hellman, *Red Room,* 18.
49 Reproduced, for example, in Morris and Woods eds., *Art in Berlin,* 44.
50 Dronke, *Berlin,* 51–54.
51 Engel, Jersch-Wenzel and Treue, *Charlottenburg,* II, 325.
52 Idem, 442. Peter Hielscher in *Berlin, Berlin,* 431.
53 Idem.
54 Erich Mühsam, *Unpolitische Erinnerungen,* Berlin 1961, 129.
55 Idem, 131–133.
56 Vicki Baum, *Es war alles ganz anders: Erinnerungen,* Cologne 1987, 291.
57 Gerard, *Four Years,* 299.

58 Spieß ed., *Gauner*, 14, 15.
59 Idem.
60 Idem, 15.
61 Kessler, *Diaries*, 114.
62 Spieß ed., *Gauner*, 25.
63 Idem, 38.
64 Engel, Jersch-Wenzel and Treue, *Charlottenburg*, II, 431.
65 Spieß ed., *Gauner*, 26.
66 Idem, 34; Engel, Jersch-Wenzel and Treue, *Charlottenburg*, II, 431.
67 Zivier in Spieß ed., *Gauner*, 61–62.
68 Brecht, *Tagebücher*, 177.
69 Canetti, *Fackel*, 334.
70 Engel, Jersch-Wenzel and Treue, *Charlottenburg*, II, 431.
71 Zivier in Spieß ed., *Gauner*, 79.
72 Idem, 28.
73 MacDonogh, *A Good German*, 304.
74 Zivier in Spieß ed., *Gauner*, 42.
75 Idem, 70, 79.
76 Idem,
77 Engel, Jersch-Wenzel and Treue, *Tiergarten*, I, 200.
78 Goll, *Sodome et Berlin*, 70–71.
79 Schäfer, *Berlin im zweitem Weltkrieg*, 211–213.
80 Discussion with Roland Mary at Borchardt, 30 August 1995 and documents copied for the author on that occasion; 'From Prussian Royalty to Kevin Costner', *Financial Times*, 21 October 1995; Ostwald, *Berlin und die Berlinerin*, 177.
81 Celebratory article published on Borchardt's 50th anniversary. Communicated by Herr Mary.
82 Norman Rich, *Friedrich von Holstein: Politics and Diplomacy in the Era of Bismarck and William II*, Cambridge 1965, I, 113.
83 Fontane, *Irrungen, Wirrungen*, in *Werke*, III, 37; *Stine*, in *Werke*, II, 307.
84 Daniel Keel ed., *Das Ringelnatz Lesebuch*, Zurich 1984, 85.
85 Roland Mary, who heard it from old Borchardt customers; Kardorff, *Aufzeichnungen*, 222.
86 Information from Inga Haag, autumn 1992; visit to Horchers in Madrid, autumn 1992; 'Grand Restaurant

with a Past', *Financial Times*, 30 January 1993;
conversations with Günter Farnleitner and Uwe Kohl,
Vienna 1996; Egon Fodermayer, *Mein Leben mit der 3
Husaren*, Tulln 1985, 11–16.

87 Information from Christopher Moorsom, autumn 1992.

88 'Berlin, where East is Best', *Financial Times*, 15 July 1995.

89 'A Taste of Two Cities', *Financial Times*, 6 November
1994.

90 Rollka, Spieß and Thieme eds., *Lexikon*, 91–92.

91 MacDonogh, in *Les Rencontres de Dionysos*, 118.

92 Dronke, *Berlin*, 63.

93 Rodenberg, *Bilder*, 91–93.

94 Theodor Fontane, *Die Poggenpuhls*, Munich 1986, 44.

95 Kuntze, *Das alte Berlin*, 80. Information from Roland
Mary who took the author over the site.

96 Conversation with Inga Haag.

97 Canetti, *Fackel*, 302.

98 Conversation with Will Dambisch, 7 April 1995;
Hürlimann, *Berlin*, 236.

99 Idem.

100 Information from Inga Haag; letter from Gerald Long,
18 August 1995.

101 Waltraud Schade in Engel, Jersch-Wenzel and Treue,
Kreuzberg, 79–80.

102 Hürlimann, *Berlin*, 236. Zivier in Spieß ed., *Gauner*, 71.

103 Canetti, *Fackel*, 319, 323.

104 Georg Zivier, 'Das romanische Café', in Volker Spieß,
ed., *Gauner, Künstler, Originale*: die 20er Jahre in *Berlin*,
Berlin 1988, 46.

105 Schäfer, *Berlin im zweitem Weltkrieg*, 90–91.

106 Idem, 113.

107 Idem, 231.

108 Kardorff, *Aufzeichnungen*, 150.

109 Letter from Gerald Long, 18 August 1995.

110 Conversation with Inga Haag.

111 Bodo-Michael Baumunk in *Berlin, Berlin*, 204.

112 Idem.

113 Idem, 205.

114 Visit to the Grand Hotel accompanied by the general
manager, August 1991; 'East Berlin's New Menu',
Financial Times, 28 September 1991.

115 C. E. Collins in the *Balliol College Annual Record*, 1987, 89; MacDonogh, *A Good German*, 41.

116 Baumunk in *Berlin, Berlin*, 205.

117 MacDonogh, *Prussia*, 224.

118 Adlon, *Hotel Adlon*, 347–348.

119 'Berlin 1926–1929: A Paradise Lost', BBC Vintage Collection 1990. A thief got the cassette, but she left me the box together with John Thornley's sleeve notes.

120 Goll, *Sodome et Berlin*, 36.

121 Adlon, *Hotel Adlon*, 355; conversation with Inga Haag.

122 Adlon, *Hotel Adlon*, 394.

123 Vassiltchikov, *Berlin Diaries*, 182.

124 MacDonogh, *A Good German*, 298.

125 'Bulldozers in Brutal Berlin', *Financial Times*, 30 September 1995.

126 Engel, Jersch-Wenzel and Treue, *Tiergarten*, I, 214–215.

127 Blücher, *An English Wife*, 98.

128 Idem, 102–103.

129 Idem, 105–107.

130 Idem, 135.

131 Idem, 163.

132 Engel, Jersch-Wenzel and Treue, *Tiergarten*, I, 217.

133 Ulrich Heinemann, *Ein konservativer Rebell: Fritz Dietlof Graf von der Schulenburg und der 20. Juli*, Berlin 1990, 161.

134 Schwerin, *Dann sind's die besten Köpfe die man henkt*, 383.

135 *Charlotte Gräfin von der Schulenburg zur Erinnerung*, zusammengestellt von Elisabeth Ruge, privately printed 1992, 33–34. I am grateful to Charlotte von der Schulenburg's daughter Angela Bielenberg for presenting me with a copy of this book.

136 Conversation with Tisa Gräfin von der Schulenburg, Wales, 20–21 June 1995; Tisa von der Schulenburg, *Ich hab's gewagt*, Freiburg im Breisgau 1981, 160–161.

137 Engel, Jersch-Wenzel and Treue, *Tiergarten*, I, 218.

138 'Bulldozers in Brutal Berlin', *Financial Times*, 30 September 1995.

139 Baumunk in *Berlin, Berlin*, 204.

140 Schade in Engel, Jersch-Wenzel and Treue, *Kreuzberg*, 70–71.

141 Idem, 72.

142 Wolfgang Müller, quoted in idem, 74.
143 Idem, 76.
144 Idem, 78.
145 MacDonogh, *A Good German*, 194.
146 Schade in Engel, Jersch-Wenzel and Treue, *Kreuzberg*, 71.
147 Baumunk in *Berlin, Berlin*, 204.
148 Engel, Jersch-Wenzel and Treue, *Tiergarten*, I, 353.
149 Heinrich Hannover and Elisabeth Hannover-Drück, *Der Mord an Rosa Luxemburg und Karl Liebknecht: Dokumentation eines politischen Verbrechens*, Göttingen 1989, 46–47.
150 Engel, Jersch-Wenzel and Treue, *Tiergarten*, I, 364.
151 Vassiltchikov, *Berlin Diaries*, 160.
152 E. T. A. Hoffmann, *Nachlese: Dichtungen, Schriften, Aufzeichnungen und Fragmente*, Munich 1981, 68.
153 Engel, Jersch-Wenzel and Treue, *Zehlendorf*, 431.
154 Nabokov, *Laughter in the Dark*, 62.
155 See Hans Ostwald ed., in collaboration with Heinrich Zille, *Das Zille Buch*, Berlin 1929, Plate 13, 'Zurück zur Natur'.
156 Engel, Jersch-Wenzel and Treue, *Zehlendorf*, 432.
157 Idem, 429; Dehio, *Berlin*, 592.
158 Engel, Jersch-Wenzel and Treue, *Zehlendorf*, 432.
159 Idem, 434–441.
160 Menge, *Alltag*, 44.
161 Idem.
162 Idem, 45.
163 Idem, 47.
164 Plessen in *Berlin, Berlin*, 213.
165 Döblin, *Berlin-Alexanderplatz*, 117–118.
166 Idem, 119.
167 I have never been to Berlin during the *Rübe* season, but in January 1996 Stuart Pigott and Ursula Heinzelmann brought me a kilo of them in the course of their visit to London. I cooked them according to Ursula's instructions.
168 Hecker ed., *Briefwechsel*, I, 105.
169 Idem, 106.
170 Maria von Treskow, *Berliner Kochbuch: Aus alten Familienrezepten*, Weingarten 1987, 17.
171 Hecker ed., *Briefwechsel*, I, 185.
172 Idem, 543.

173 Hecker ed., *Briefwechsel*, II, 3.

174 Idem, 6.

175 Sombart, *Jugend*, 72.

176 Hornstein, *Adieu Potsdam*, 197.

177 Kuntze, *Das alte Berlin*, 22.

178 Menge, *Alltag*, 32–35.

179 Blücher, *An English Wife*, 225.

180 Idem, 331.

181 The author has been told that *he* is to blame for the allegedly spindly legs of a Berlin woman, born in 1917; Buffet, *Berlin*, 252.

182 See *A Woman in Berlin*, Anon, trans. James Stern, London 1955.

183 Idem, 15, 18, 29.

184 Kardorff, *Aufzeichnungen*, 157.

185 Vassiltchikov, *Berlin Diaries*, 150.

186 Molke, *Letters to Freya*, 391.

187 Schäfer, *Berlin im zweitem Weltkrieg*, 113.

188 Idem, 119.

189 Idem, 120.

190 Margret Boveri, *Tage des Überlebens, Berlin 1945*, Frankfurt am Main 1996, 111–112.

191 Peter Gosztony ed., *Der Kampf um Berlin 1945 in Augenzeugen berichten*, Düsseldorf 1970, 30–31.

192 Thieme, *Das letze Haus*, 10.

5 City of Order

1 Schulz, *Stadtführer*, 81.

2 Hornstein, *Adieu Potsdam*, 111.

3 Mühsam, *Erinnerungen*, 103.

4 Dronke, *Aus dem Volk*, 16–17.

5 Kleßmann, *Hoffmann*, 344–345

6 Sombart, *Jugend*, 10.

7 Idem, 199.

8 Idem, 199–200.

9 Canetti, *Fackel*, 297.

10 Ranthun, ed. Brecht, *Tagebücher*, 215.

11 Gottfried Benn, *Autobiographische und vermischte Schriften*, Wiesbaden 1961, 173.

12 Ribbe, *Geschichte*, II, 683, 691; Rodenberg, *Bilder*, 147.
13 Information from Judy Dempsey, Berlin, August 1994.
14 Information from Markus Müller, Berlin, August 1995.
15 Ribbe, *Geschichte*, I, 378.
16 Menge, *Alltag*, 24.
17 Idem, 27.
18 Clauswitz, *Städteordnung*, 6.
19 Engel, Jersch-Wenzel and Treue, *Zehlendorf*, XVI. Engel, Jersch-Wenzel and Treue, *Tiergarten*, I, 185.
20 Schulz, *Stadtführer*, 35.
21 Idem, 58.
22 Benjamin, *Kindheit*, 31.
23 Quoted in Christine Roik-Bogner in Engel, Jersch-Wenzel and Treue, *Kreuzberg*, 59.
24 Idem, 65–67.
25 Ribbe, *Geschichte*, II, 707.
26 Idem, 734.
27 Idem, 737.
28 Eva Brücker in Engel, Jersch-Wenzel and Treue, *Kreuzberg*, 103–104.
29 Idem. 106–107. Kurt Pinthus ed., *Menschheitsdämmerung: Ein Dokument des Expressionismus*, Hamburg 1993, 39.
30 Ribbe, *Geschichte*, II, 739.
31 Döblin, *Ein Kerl*, 23.
32 Brücker in Engel, Jersch-Wenzel and Treue, *Kreuzberg*, 110.
33 Schäfer, *Berlin im zweitem Weltkrieg*, 122.
34 Idem, 123.
35 See the historical novel by '-ky' (Professor Dr Horst Bosetzky), *Wie ein Tier: Der S-Bahn Mörder: Dokumentarischer Roman*, Berlin 1995, which reconstructs the events. I am grateful to Ursula Heinzelmann for alerting me to the existence of this book.
36 Quoted in Brücker and in Engel, Jersch-Wenzel and Treue, *Kreuzberg*, 111.
37 Idem; Wolfgang Paul, *Kampf um Berlin*, Munich and Vienna 1962, 20.
38 Dehio, *Berlin*, 453.
39 Gisevius, *Bis zum bittern Ende*, I, 218.
40 Hugh Trevor-Roper, *The Last Days of Hitler*, 7th edn., London 1995, 153.

41 Dietrich Staritz, *Geschichte der DDR*, expanded edn., Frankfurt am Main 1996, 23.

42 Ribbe, *Geschichte*, II, 1061–1066; Gerhard Keiderling, *Berlin 1945–1986: Geschichte der Hauptstadt der DDR*, Berlin 1987, 284–294. This is an East German history, and turns aspects of the story on its head.

43 Plessen in *Berlin, Berlin*, 70.

44 Ribbe, *Geschichte*, I, 365.

45 Idem.

46 Schmidt-Lötzen ed., *Dreißig Jahre*, 56.

47 Dronke, *Berlin*, 15.

48 Idem, 271, 274.

49 Burkerl, Matußek and Wippermann, *Machtergreifung*, 132–133.

50 See J. P. Stern, *Hitler: The Führer and the People*, revised edn., London 1990, 70–75.

51 See MacDonogh, *Prussia*, 87–102.

52 Burkerl, Matußek Wippermann, *Machtergreifung*, 133.

53 Idem, 135.

54 Idem, 138.

55 Idem, 138–139.

56 Idem, 139–141; Engel, Jersch-Wenzel and Treue, *Zehlendorf*, 144–147.

57 Idem, 147–148.

58 Anton Gill, *An Honourable Defeat: A History of the German Resistance to Hitler*, London 1994, 50.

59 Idem; Engel, Jersch-Wenzel and Treue, *Zehlendorf*, 149.

60 Dronke, *Berlin*, 18.

61 Ribbe, *Geschichte*, I, 297.

62 Rürup in *Berlin, Berlin*, 32.

63 Ribbe, *Geschichte*, I, 365.

64 Conversations with Dr Urs Müller-Plantenberg, 1994, 1995.

65 Engel, Jersch-Wenzel and Treue, *Charlottenburg*, II, 22–24, 41–43, 57.

66 Idem, 24.

67 Kühn, *Charlottenburg*, 2.

68 Hecker ed., *Briefwechsel*, I, 178.

69 Schleicher, *Chamisso*, 98.

70 Hürlimann, *Berlin*, 73.

71 Dronke, *Berlin*, 43–44.

72 Idem, 323.
73 Idem, 324–329.
74 Idem, 331.
75 Ribbe, *Geschichte*, I, 673.
76 Idem, 779.
77 Engel, Jersch-Wenzel and Treue, *Zehlendorf*, 218–219.
78 Idem, 220–222.
79 Idem, 231.
80 Idem.
81 Idem, 235–238.
82 Idem, 272.
83 Idem, 274–275.
84 Idem.
85 Engel, Jersch-Wenzel and Treue, *Kreuzberg*, 301–313.
86 Benn, *Autobiographische Schriften*, 27.
87 Engel, Jersch-Wenzel and Treue, *Zehlendorf*, 198–200.
88 Ribbe, *Geschichte*, II, 742–745.
89 Idem, 745–746.
90 Idem, 746–750.
91 Wermuth, *Beamtenleben*, 322.
92 Idem, 324.
93 Idem, 327.
94 Idem, 347–348; Fontane, *Wanderungen*, II, 606–616.
95 Dehio, *Berlin*, 333–334.
96 Wermuth, *Beamtenleben*, 362–363.
97 Idem, 387.
98 Ribbe, *Geschichte*, 816
99 Rürup in *Berlin, Berlin*, 44.
100 Ribbe, *Geschichte*, II, 898.
101 Rürup in *Berlin, Berlin*, 47.
102 Engeli, *Böß*, 13.
103 Idem, 19.
104 Idem, 20.
105 Idem, 85.
106 Idem, 143–147.
107 Idem, 222.
108 Idem, 242.
109 Idem, 267–271.
110 Idem, Ribbe, *Geschichte*, II, 974, 976–977.
111 Henry Picker, *Hitlers Tischgespräche im Führerhauptquartier*, Stuttgart 1976.

112 Joseph Goebbels, *Kampf um Berlin: Der Anfang*, 5th edn., Munich 1934, 50.

113 Ribbe, *Geschichte*, II, 929.

114 Idem, 928.

115 Idem, 934.

116 Idem, 980–981.

117 Kuntze, *Das alte Berlin*, 10; Pilz, Hofmann and Thomisch *Berlin-W,* 217–218.

118 Schinz, *Bauten in Berlin*, 108.

119 Pilz, Hoffmann and Thomisch *Berlin-W,* 219–220.

120 Ribbe, *Geschichte*, II, 982.

121 Idem, 984; Schinz, *Bauen in Berlin*, 108.

122 Assel ed., *Rudolf Hermann und Jochen Klepper*, 62.

123 Pilz, Hofmann and Thomisch *Berlin-W,* 225; the continued presence of the old Siegesallee (now Straße des 17 Juni) was pointed out to me by Stuart Pigott.

124 Information from Major 'Garbo' Garbutt, Berlin, August 1991.

125 Ribbe, *Geschichte*, II, 992–993.

126 Idem, 996.

127 Idem, 993. Again I am grateful to Stuart Pigott for pointing out the marble in the Mohrenstraße station.

128 Ribbe, *Geschichte*, II, 1027.

129 Idem.

130 Schäfer, *Berlin im zweitem Weltkrieg*, 10.

131 Pilz, Hofmann and Thomisch *Berlin-W,* 118, 158, 171, 195, 221, 371.

132 Schäfer, *Berlin im zweitem Weltkrieg*, 10.

133 Schinz, *Bauten in Berlin*, 111.

6 Bohemian Berlin

1 For the scattered nature of German literary life at the time see Herder, *Briefe in einem Band*, Berlin and Weimar 1983; Gerlinde Wappler, *Gleims Leben und seine Beziehungen zu berühmten Zeitgenossen*, Halberstadt 1988.

2 Plessen in *Berlin, Berlin*, 112.

3 Idem.

4 Lessing, *Nathan der Weise*, II, 5.

5 Idem.

6 Idem; Plessen in *Berlin, Berlin*, 114.
7 Rodenberg, *Bilder*, 108.
8 Schleicher, *Chamisso*, 80.
9 Plessen in *Berlin, Berlin*, 114.
10 Schleicher, *Chamisso*, 44.
11 Hürlimann, *Berlin*, 62.
12 Horst Häker, *Kleists Berliner Aufenthalte*, Berlin 1989, 79–86.
13 Engel, Jersch-Wenzel and Treue, *Kreuzberg*, 89.
14 Schleicher, *Chamisso*, 118.
15 Müller ed., *Berlinische Geschichten*, 25.
16 E. T. A. Hoffmann, *Meister Floh*, in *Werke*, II, 183.
17 Müller ed., *Berlinische Geschichten*, 160.
18 Idem, 164.
19 Hellman, *Red Room*, 91.
20 Idem, 102.
21 Idem, 123.
22 Max Stirner, *Der Einzige und sein Eigenthum*, 3rd edn., Leipzig 1901, 7–8.
23 Idem, 16.
24 Idem, 76.
25 Idem, 81.
26 Idem, 179.
27 Idem, 189.
28 Idem, 219.
29 Idem, 300.
30 John Henry Mackay, *Max Stirner: Sein Leben und sein Werk*, Berlin 1898, 14–15.
31 Idem, 46.
32 Idem, 47.
33 Idem, 55.
34 Idem, 59.
35 Idem, 67.
36 Stirner, *Einzige*, 323.
37 Idem, 70; Hellman, *Red Room*, 91.
38 Mackay, *Stirner*, 72.
39 Idem, 84.
40 Idem, 91.
41 Idem, 122.
42 Idem, 124–125, 206.
43 Idem, 218.

44 Christiane Knop, ' "Im alten Eisen" – Ein Berlinische Roman', *Mitteilungen des Vereins für die Geschichte Berlins*, Heft 1, January 1994.

45 Fontane, *Die Poggenpuhls*, 44.

46 Herman Sudermann, *Die Ehre*, Stuttgart 1982, 32.

47 Idem, 65.

48 Hecker ed., *Briefwechsel*, III, 268.

49 Paul Ortwin Rave, *Karl Friedrich Schinkel*, bearbeitet von Eva Börsch-Supan, Munich 1981, 17.

50 There was an exhibition to celebrate the Academy's 300-year history from 9 June to 15 September 1996. See also Kerstin Diether et al., *Akademie der Künste*, Berlin 1991.

51 Both hang in the Ephraims Palais.

52 Peter Paret, *The Berlin Secession*, Cambridge, Mass, and London 1980, 17.

53 Idem, 27.

54 Idem, 29.

55 Corinth, *Selbstbiographie*, 175.

56 Mühsam, *Erinnerungen*, 49.

57 Engel, Jersch-Wenzel and Treue, *Zehlendorf*, 356.

58 Idem.

59 Mühsam, *Erinnerungen*, 50.

60 Idem, 51.

61 Idem, 62.

62 Idem, 77.

63 Idem, 80.

64 Idem, 81, 85, 86.

65 John Höxter, *Ich bin noch ein ungeübter Selbstmörder*, Hanover 1988, 15.

66 Idem, 25.

67 George Grosz, *Ein kleines Ja und ein grosses Nein*, Hamburg 1955, 134.

68 Kessler, *Diaries*, 187–188. Kay Flavell's *George Grosz: A Biography*, New Haven and London 1988, would take a different view.

69 Canetti, *Fackel*, 298.

70 Idem, 314.

71 Idem, 315.

72 Schuster ed., *Grosz*, 190–191. Canetti, *Fackel*, 337.

73 Idem.

74 Idem, 303.
75 Idem, 307.
76 Idem, 306, 334
77 Benn, *Autobiographische Schriften*, 90.
78 Idem, 91.
79 Idem, 106.
80 Kerr, *Ich kam nach England*, 23; Alfred Kerr, *Die Diktatur des Hausknechts und Melodien*, Hamburg 1981, 13.
81 Idem.
82 Papers communicated to the author by Tisa Gräfin von der Schulenburg and conversations with the same in Wales, 1995.
83 Kerr, *Diktatur*, 13
84 Ribbe, *Geschichte*, II, 949.
85 Paul Ortwin Rave, *Kunstdiktatur im Dritten Reich*, Berlin 1949, 22.
86 Idem, 23–24.
87 Idem, 56.
88 Idem, 56.
89 Idem, 66.
90 Idem, 75.
91 He was referring to *neue Sachlichkeit*.
92 Idem, 88.
93 Idem, 96. One of Willrich's folksy drawings of a German soldier is illustrated in Peter Adam, *The Arts of the Third Reich*, London 1992, 169.
94 Rave, *Kunstdiktatur*, 124.
95 Ernst Riemschneider, *Der Fall Klepper: Eine Dokumentation*, Stuttgart 1975, 37.
96 Idem, 116.
97 Nicolai, *Beschreibung*, 394.
98 Hecker ed., *Briefwechsel*, I, 75.
99 Schiller, *Wilhelm Tell*, II, 2. Information from the Schillerhaus in Weimar.
100 Hecker ed., *Briefwechsel*, I, 145; III, 337.
101 Idem, I, 152.
102 Idem, I, 244.
103 Idem, I, 457; II, 62, 68.
104 Idem, I, 456.
105 Holtei, *Vierzig Jahre*, 214.
106 Idem, 265.

107 Dronke, *Berlin*, 337–338.

108 Idem, 345.

109 Idem, 349.

110 Rürup in *Berlin, Berlin*, 42.

111 Ribbe, *Geschichte*, II, 783.

112 Idem, 888.

113 Döblin, *Ein Kerl*, 18–19.

114 Idem, 34.

115 Idem, 63.

116 Idem, 107.

117 Idem, 163.

118 Idem, 135.

119 See Ruth Andreas Friedrich, *Berlin Underground 1938–1945*, trans. Barrows Mussey, New York 1947. Conversation with Will Dambisch, 7 April 1995.

120 Kühn, *Charlottenburg*, 2.

121 Schmidt-Lötzen ed., *Dreißig Jahre*, 34.

122 Nicolai, *Beschreibung*, 394.

123 Hecker ed., *Briefwechsel*, I, 17, 57.

124 Idem, 328, 360.

125 Wolf ed., *Und grüß mich nicht*, 156.

126 Idem, 144.

127 Idem, 145.

128 Idem.

129 Hecker ed., *Briefwechsel*, I, 423, 453.

130 Idem, III, 146.

131 Wolf ed., *Und grüß mich nicht*, 149.

132 Idem, 149–152.

133 Hecker ed., *Briefwechsel*, III, 120, 267.

134 Idem, II, 264–265.

135 Idem, 310.

136 Idem, 313.

137 Idem, 351.

138 Idem, 478.

139 Idem, 373, 487.

140 Idem, III, 130.

141 Idem, I, 265.

142 There is a recording by Dietrich Fischer-Dieskau of Zelter's songs, *Carl Friedrich Zelter – Lieder*, Orfeo 1984, but sadly *Ergo Bibamus* is not included.

143 Roger Fulford ed., *Dearest Child, Private Correspondence*

of Queen Victoria and the Princess Royal, 1858–1861. London 1977, 91 n.1

144 Spencer and Millington, *Selected Letters*, 81.
145 See Adolf Brennglas, *Franz Liszt in Berlin*, Leipzig 1847.
146 Ribbe, *Geschichte*, II, 675.
147 Idem, 784.
148 Engel, Jersch-Wenzel and Treue, *Charlottenburg*, I, 591–592.
149 Performed at the Criterion Theatre in London in 1995.
150 Giles MacDonogh, 'Conduct Unbecoming', *Opera Now*, April 1991. Berta Geismar, *The Baton and the Jackboot*, London 1944.
151 Quoted in MacDonogh, *'Conduct Unbecoming'* Brian Hunt, 'Memories of the Maestro', *Daily Telegraph*, 25 October 1995.
152 Ulrich von Hassell, *Vom andern Deutschland*, Zurich and Freiburg 1946, 291.
153 Wilhelm Furtwängler, *Die Programme der Konzerte mit dem Berliner Philharmonischen Orchester*, Wiesbaden 1965.
154 Friedrich, *Schauplatz Berlin*, 97–99.
155 Sombart, *Jugend*, 245. See also Klaus Lang, *Lieber Herr Celibidache: Wilhelm Furtwängler und sein Statthalter*, Zurich 1988.
156 Wolfgang Stresemann, *Ein seltsamer Mann: Erinnerungen an Herbert von Karajan*, Berlin 1991, 30.
157 Claire Waldoff, *Es gibt nur ein Berlin* and *Raus mit den Männern*, in Ute Lemper, *Berlin Cabaret Songs*, Decca 1996.
158 Engel, Jersch-Wenzel and Treue, *Kreuzberg*, 185.
159 Idem, 192.
160 Idem, 195.
161 Richard von Soldenhoff ed., *Carl von Ossietzky 1889–1938: Ein Lebensbild*, Weinheim and Berlin 1988, 118.
162 Idem, 137.
163 Idem.
164 Idem, 181, 183.

7 Belial

1 See Anon., *A Woman in Berlin*; Friedrich, *Schauplatz Berlin*.
2 Ribbe, *Geschichte*, I, 263–264; Buffet, *Berlin*, 56.
3 Idem, 57.
4 Idem, 56.
5 Ribbe, *Geschichte*, I, 334–336.
6 Idem, 337.
7 Idem, 526.
8 Karl Ludwig von Prittwitz, *Berlin 1848*, bearbeitet und eingeleitet von Gerd Heinrich, Berlin and New York 1985, 13.
9 Idem, 18.
10 Bernstein, *Arbeiter-bewegung*, 9.
11 Adam Wolf, *Berliner Revolutions Chronik: Darstellung der Berliner Bewegung im Jahre 1848*, 1851, reprinted, Liechtenstein 1979, I, 14–16.
12 Idem.
13 Prittwitz, *1848*, 22.
14 Idem, 32.
15 Wolf, *Revolutions Chronik*, 30, 46.
16 Prittwitz, *1848*, 42.
17 Idem, 52.
18 Idem, 54. 62–63.
19 Wolf, *Revolutions Chronik*, 62, 80.
20 Bernstein, *Arbeiter-bewegung*, 11.
21 Wolf, *Revolutions Chronik*, 81.
22 Prittwitz, *1848*, 75.
23 Idem, 179–183.
24 Idem, 209–221.
25 Idem, 239–240; see also Theodor Fontane, *Der achtzehnte März*, in *Werke*, I, 280–281.
26 Prittwitz, *1848*, 239–240, 258–259, 358.
27 Wolf, *Revolutions Chronik*, 174–176.
28 Prittwitz, *1848*, 417–419.
29 Wolf, *Revolutions Chronik*, 319.
30 Bernstein, *Arbeiter-bewegung*, 11–12.
31 Idem, 39.
32 Idem, 65.
33 Idem, 67–68.

34 Idem, 68.

35 Blücher, *An English Wife*, 279.

36 Idem, 280.

37 Idem, 281.

38 Kessler, *Diaries*, 6–9.

39 Idem, 7–8.

40 Corinth, *Selbstbiographie*, 166.

41 Kessler, *Diaries*, 10.

42 Goll, *Sodome et Berlin*, 15.

43 Jacques Benoist-Méchin, *Histoire de l'armée allemande 1918–1937*, Paris 1964, I, 100–106.

44 Idem, 106.

45 Hannover and Hannover-Drück, *Rosa Luxemburg und Karl Liebknecht*, 36.

46 Idem, 42.

47 Idem, 127.

48 Idem, 116–117.

49 Staritz, *DDR*, 100–109.

50 Idem, 109–122.

51 Conversation with Urs Müller-Plantenberg, 28 August 1996.

52 Buffet, *Berlin*, 399.

53 Stieber, *Spion des Kanzlers*, 125; Hannah Pakula, *An Uncommon Woman*, New York 1995, 229.

54 Ribbe, *Geschichte*, II, 905, 910.

55 Idem, 913.

56 Idem, 915–917.

57 Idem, 918.

58 Lazar, *Horst Wessel*, 22.

59 Idem, 45, 63, 64.

60 Idem, 70.

61 Idem, 98.

62 Idem, 19.

63 Idem, 32.

64 Idem, 157; Gisevius, *Bis zum bittern Ende*, I, 73.

65 Burkerl, Matußek and Wippermann, *Machtergreifung*, 20.

66 Idem, 64.

67 Idem, 66.

68 Idem, 67.

69 Ribbe, *Geschichte*, I, 288–289.

70 Idem, 289.

71 Idem, 317.
72 Schmidt-Lötzen ed., *Dreißig Jahre*, 31, 131.
73 Ribbe, *Geschichte*, II, 767–768.
74 Idem, 768–769; Peter Berglar, *Walther Rathenau: Ein Leben zwischen Philosophie und Politik*, Graz, Vienna and Cologne 1987, 249.
75 On Austria see Gordon Brook-Shepherd, *The Austrians: A Thousand Year Odyssey*, London 1996, 101–104. Döblin, *Ein Kerl*, 220.
76 Rürup in *Berlin, Berlin*, 49.
77 Robert Wistrich, *Who's Who in Nazi Germany*, London 1982, 177.
78 Burkerl, Matußek and Wippermann, *Machtergreifung*, 113.
79 Idem.
80 Idem, 116.
81 Idem, 118.
82 Kästner, *Notabene 45*, 181.
83 Idem, 182.
84 Schäfer, *Berlin im zweitem Weltkrieg*, 25.
85 Idem, 129.
86 Engel, Jersch-Wenzel and Treue, *Moabit*, 142.
87 Ribbe, *Geschichte*, II, 1004.
88 Peter Prager, 'Love Prevailed on the Street of Roses', *The European Magazine*, 7–13 March 1996.
89 Schäfer, *Berlin im zweitem Weltkrieg*, 140; conversation with Will Dambisch, 7 April 1995.
90 Ribbe, *Geschichte*, II, 1007. Engel, Jersch-Wenzel and Treue, *Zehlendorf*, 499.
91 Ribbe, *Geschichte*, II, 839–840.
92 Idem, 841–842.
93 Hans Ostwald, *Sittengeschichte der Inflation: Ein Kultur-dokument aus den Jahren des Marksturzes*, Berlin 1931, 33–34.
94 Idem, 50, 61.
95 Idem, 62, 78.
96 Idem, 82–83, 99, 128.
97 Idem, 130–131; Kessler, *Diaries*, 279, 283–284.
98 Ostwald, *Sittengeschichte*, 135–136, 145–146.
99 Idem, 197, 219.
100 Schmidt-Lötzen ed., *Dreißig Jahre*, 320.
101 Schäfer, *Berlin im zweitem Weltkrieg*, 96.

102 Idem, 94, 109.

103 Idem, 14.

104 Idem, 18.

105 Idem, 20.

106 Idem, 23.

107 Ribbe, *Geschichte*, II, 996.

108 Idem.

109 Idem, 1010; Schäfer, *Berlin im zweitem Weltkrieg*, 192.

110 Ribbe, *Geschichte*, II, 1011–1012; Arthur Harris, *Bomber Offensive*, London 1947, 135.

111 Idem, 181; Ribbe, *Geschichte*, II, 1012–1014; conversation with Inga Haag.

112 Ribbe, *Geschichte*, II, 1014.

113 Harris, *Bomber Offensive*, 187, 188, 261

114 Schäfer, *Berlin im zweitem Weltkrieg*, 145–152; MacDonogh, *A Good German*, 273.

115 Ribbe, *Geschichte*, II, 1010; Tisa von der Schulenburg reports the murder of some American airmen in Mecklenburg in her book *Ich hab's gewagt*.

116 See Peter Hoffmann, *The German Resistance to Hitler*, Harvard 1988.

117 Schmidt-Lötzen ed. *Dreißig Jahre*, 350.

118 Idem, 354; Holtze, *Lokalgeschichte*, 77.

119 Ribbe, *Geschichte*, I, 424.

120 Idem, 425–426.

121 Idem, 440.

122 Ribbe, *Spandau*, 63.

123 Ribbe, *Geschichte*, I, 458.

124 Franz Prinz zu Sayn-Wittgenstein, *Die Wittgenstein: Geschichten aus einer alten Familie*, Munich 1979, 146.

125 Idem, 463; Hecker ed., *Briefwechsel*, 358–359, 361.

126 Ribbe, *Geschichte*, I, 471.

127 Boveri, *Tage des überlebens*, 28, 91.

128 Idem, 127.

129 Idem, 114.

130 Idem, 234–235.

131 Idem, 120.

132 Idem, 169.

133 Idem, 263.

134 Idem, 78.
135 Rosenkranz, *Berlin im Gedicht*, 59.
136 Idem, 61.

Index

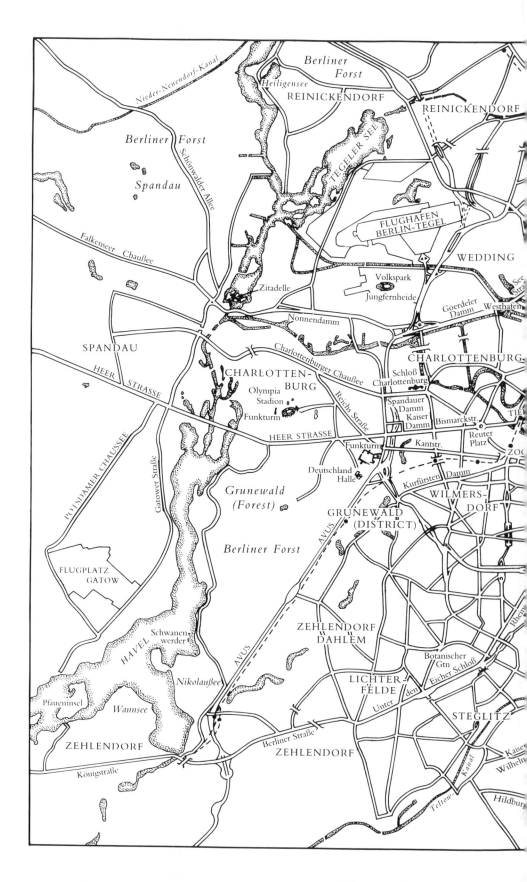